FRIENDS
OF ACPL

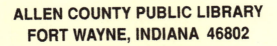

Concord and Conflict

Concord and Conflict

The United States and Russia, 1867–1914

Norman E. Saul

 University Press of Kansas

In memory of my father and mother—
Ralph Odis Saul and Jessie Neff Saul

© 1996 by the University Press of Kansas
All rights reserved

Published by the University Press of Kansas (Lawrence,
Kansas 66049), which was organized by the Kansas Board of
Regents and is operated and funded by Emporia State
University, Fort Hays State University, Kansas State
University, Pittsburg State University, the University of
Kansas, and Wichita State University

Library of Congress Cataloging-in-Publication Data

Saul, Norman E.
    Concord and conflict : the United States and Russia,
1867–1914 / Norman E. Saul.
        p.   cm.
    "Continues the history of the Russian-American
experience begun in Distant friends"—xi.
    Includes bibliographical references and index.
    ISBN 0-7006-0754-4 (hardback)
    1. United States—Relations—Russia. 2. Russia—
Relations—United States. 3. United States—Foreign
relations—1865–1921. 4. Russia—Foreign relations—1855–
1881. 5. Russia—Foreign relations—1881–
1894. 6. Russia—Foreign relations—1894–1917.
I. Saul, Norman E. Distant friends. II. Title.
E183.8.R9S383   1996
303.48′273047—dc20   95-25606

British Library Cataloguing in Publication Data is available.

Printed in the United States of America

10 9 8 7 6 5 4 3 2 1

The paper used in this publication meets the minimum requirements of the American National Standard for Permanence of Paper for Printed Library Materials Z39.48–1984.

In the course of his lectures the Prince
[Sergei Volkonskii] gave us a glimpse of
Russia as it is and America as it is, and
emphasized the fact that while each is great
in its way, the greatest of all is Humanity.

—Jacob Gould Schurman (president of
Cornell University) to Andrew Dickson White
(minister to Russia), 6 December 1893, White
Papers, Cornell.

Contents

Illustrations

Preface

This volume continues the history of the Russian-American experience begun in *Distant Friends: The United States and Russia, 1763–1867,* from the purchase of Alaska to the beginning of World War I. As in the case of its predecessor, this work falls between the traditional scholarly monograph and the general survey. The goal is to demonstrate the extent and nature of relations over a time frame that allows analysis of change and continuity and of nuances in political, economic, social, and cultural affairs. Above all, the intention has been to show how perceptions that each people had of the other developed and changed over time. A third volume covering the tumultuous period of war, revolution, and civil war, 1914–1924, is in process.

Unlike *Distant Friends,* which had as a guide the work of the eminent Russian scholar, Nikolai Bolkhovitinov and of several others, much of *Conflict and Concord* sails through comparatively uncharted waters. Although islands of excellent scholarship exist, the task of connecting them loomed large. On the other hand, a very rich quantity of documentation exists for this period, much of it unmined, in both American and Russian archives. This fact introduced the problem of weaving in and making sense of a mass of detail. With the rise of American and Russian contacts came an abundance of contemporary memoir and travel literature, providing insights and descriptions of varying quality. Much information is also available in the voluminous pages of newspapers and periodicals that flourished during this period. It seemed as though I was panning for gold as I hunted for slivers of Russian America in tons of sand.

The complete unveiling of many of the episodes, themes, individuals, and events will remain for others. Given financial limitations, it simply has not been possible to investigate all possible sources. For example, additional material no doubt exists in government records in the St. Petersburg Central State Historical Archive. Similarly, no effort was made to explore the Russian military archives. Even in the United States almost every state has material on the subject, and new, pertinent documents are added annually. For a work of this scope, there had to be limits. Naturally, therefore, the documentation is stronger on the American side, but even there not all leads could be pursued. Some were simply lost in a mountain of files, as for example in the extensive records of the International Harvester Company.

Then, too, gaps exist that may later be filled. The war, revolution, and civil war in Russia caused the destruction or displacement of many records, including official American diplomatic papers. Some of these, such as the Odessa consulate post records, may still be found. Many family papers on the Russian side have apparently disappeared; though such materials abound in the United States, they are not always easy to retrieve or are incomplete, especially the business records. Some files had been only recently accessioned or declassified, but others were closed for recataloging or microfilming.

The most significant new material for this work came from the Diplomatic Post Records in the National Archives, containing the incoming and outgoing communications of the diplomatic and consular offices in Russia; the Russian diplomatic correspondence housed in the "old" ministry archive; a number of collections of personal and business papers, which are unfortunately weak on the Russian side; and American and Russian newspapers and periodicals. Although the search was both extensive and intensive, some information was discovered quite by accident. Of course, a large variety of published secondary sources and memoir literature has been reviewed.

Much physical and mental ground has been covered, and for the support of this effort I owe an enormous debt to the Kennan Institute for short-term grants for work in Washington, D.C.; to IREX for research in Moscow; to the American Philosophical Society for travel to collections in the Midwest; to the University of Illinois Russian Summer Research Laboratory for access to rare periodicals; and especially to the University of Kansas for sabbatical leave, summer research grants, and a Hall Center for the Humanities fellowship.

The Russian-American scholarly community contributed more than can be adequately acknowledged to the total work. Those who have been especially encouraging in my long-term endeavors and at more specific stages include John T. Alexander, Levon Arustamyan, Daniel Bays, Allison Blakely, Nikolai Bolkhovitinov, Jack Bricke, Margaret Bricke, Maria Carlson, Anna Cienciala, Alexander Dallin, John Dardess, Basil Dmytryshyn, David Fogelsong, John Gaddis, Ilya Gaidar, Rose Greaves, Dane Hartgrove, Helen Hundley, Robert Ivanov, Gennady Kuropiatnik, Walter LaFeber, Roy Laird, Ivo Lambi, Thomas Lewin, Donald McCoy, Richard McKenzie, Rex Martin, Bruce Menning, Rita Napier, Aleksandr Nikoliukin, Vladimir Pozniakov, Hans Rogger, Grigory Sevost'ianov, Frederick Travis, Donald Treadgold, Betty Unterberger, and Theodore Wilson.

More than they realize, students were foils for ideas or volunteered their own, particularly during the course of this work: Michael Cassella-Blackburn, Wayne Chinander, Elizabeth Morrow Clark, Carl DauBach, William Drummond, Arthur Frame, Rachel Goossen, Georgianna Kelly, Oleg Khripkov, Jill Lally, Raymond Leonard, Carlyse Marshall, Ellen Paul, Shannon Peters, Kelvin Richardson, George Steger, John Steinberg, Laurie Stoff, and Sandra Van Hoosen. Much work remains for them.

Above all, for such a large and long-term project, the support of my family—Alyssa and Jim Lyon, Kevin and Julia Saul, and especially Mary Ann—was crucial.

Although libraries and archives varied widely in their working conditions, they steadily improved over the years in facilities and efficiency. The professional staffs, moreover, have been truly helpful and supportive. This is their book as much as mine. Even more directly involved in its production were the professional staffs of the Department of History, the Hall Center for the Humanities, the College of Liberal Arts and Sciences Word Processing Center, and the University Press of Kansas, especially Cindy Ingham and Megan Schoeck.

Scholars of the subject should also be warned that some citations are to collections for which volume or box numbers were uncertain or were in the process of reorganization, such as the Diplomatic Post Records, which are likely to be rearranged in the move to a new facility. Also, as the typewriter and carbon paper age dawned in the middle of the period, copies of documents can be found in various files. For the years after 1906, when American diplomatic filing changed to numerical and decimal subject indexing, I have relied more on the Diplomatic Post Records, which preserve the sense of place and chronology. Nor has it been possible to indicate in every instance whether a document has been published and to indicate that source or sources.

My hope is that both the academic scholar and the general reader may enjoy and learn from what follows.

Note on Transliteration and Spelling

For Russian names and titles I have used the simplified Library of Congress transliteration in Notes and Bibliography. In the text the more familier Russian names are usually Anglicized: Nicholas II for Nikolai II, Grand Duke Alexis, Nicholas Chernyshevsky, Peter Tchaikovsky (but Nikolai Chaikovskii for the unrelated socialist revolutionary). Some compromises and inconsistencies will be found; for example, Grand Duke Constantine and Konstantin Nikolaevich might be used for the same person. The original spelling has been preserved in quotations with some exceptions. The same is true of place-names: for the more familiar such as Moscow, Warsaw, and Yalta the standard English version is natural. Some appear as they did at the time: Tiflis for Tbilisi. Fortunately, the renaming of cities in the Soviet period no longer creates as much confusion as most of them have reverted to their nineteenth-century form: St. Petersburg, Nizhni-Novgorod, Tver.

Foreign names in Russian pose several problems. On one hand, it was not always easy to decipher American names from their Russian phonetic renderings, but it seemed logical to indicate a process of russianization by leaving a name in its Russian form: Vil'iams for Williams for a second-generation Russian American. Smith is, of course, a common English name, and there were many of them in Russia, and it is not always easy to distinguish among them. Choices had to be made in the spelling of Russian officials of non-Russian origin, and the judgment calls will reveal more feel than consistency; for example, Cassini for Kassini but Kantakuzen for Cantacuzene.

The Russian calandar was twelve days behind that used in the West in the nineteenth century, thirteen days in the twentieth century until official Russia converted to the Western calendar in 1918. Most Russian sources and newspapers for the period have both dates and are included that way in the notes (13/26 July 1909); the dates in the text are consistent according to the Western calendar. For a few sources the date used in not clear or is left as indicated, "o.s." or old (Russian) style. Fortunately, documents with no or erroneous dating are rare. Diplomats, businessmen, and scholarly observers have one thing in common—a sense of time and place.

Abbreviations Used in Notes

AVPR	Arkhiv Vneshnoi Politiki Rossii (Archive of the Foreign Policy of Russia)
BA	Bakhmetev Archive, Columbia University
BPI	Bureau of Plant Industry
BPL	Boston Public Library
(c)	copy
cf.	case file
ChicagoHS	Chicago Historical Society
CHS	California Historical Society
CR	*Consular Reports*
d.	delo (box or package of documents)
DI	Diplomatic Instructions
DPR	Diplomatic Post Records
DUSC	Despatches from United States Consuls
DUSM	Despatches from United States Ministers
f.	fond
HSP	Historical Society of Pennsylvania
IH	International Harvester
ISHS	Iowa State Historical Society
KSHS	Kansas State Historical Society
LC	Library of Congress
MassHS	Massachusetts Historical Society
MCHC	Milwaukee County Historical Center Library
MinnHS	Minnesota Historical Society
NA	National Archives
NLR	National Library of Russia (former Lenin Library)
NMF	Numerical and Minor Files, Department of State
NRL	Notes from Foreign Legations, Russia
NYHS	New-York Historical Society
NYPL	New York Public Library

op.	opis (inventory, part of collection)
OZ	*Otechestvennyia Zapiski*
PRFRUS	*Papers Relating to the Foreign Relations of the United States*
RG	Record Group
RNL	Russian National Library
SA	Smithsonian Archives
SHSM	State Historical Society of Missouri
SHSW	State Historical Society of Wisconsin
(t)	telegram, cable
TsGAOR	Central State Archive of the October Revolution
UNC	University of North Carolina
USC	University of South Carolina

1

Innocents Abroad: 1867–1874

The appearance of a large American tourist ship, the *Quaker City*, in the Black Sea in late summer 1867 heralded a more intensive stage in Russian-American relations. Not only did a shipload of American sightseers disembark on Russian territory for the first time, but news about their experiences was widely disseminated by one of the passengers, a Missouri-born California newspaper reporter who had already achieved a national reputation as a homespun satirist. More revealing than Mark Twain's tongue-in-cheek description of the tourists' reception in Livadia Palace by the "tinsel king," Alexander II, was the fact that the whole event was arranged through the special efforts of two Americans who themselves represented a significant change in the Russian-American relationship. They were among a select few who were now fluent in Russian and familiar with the country: Timothy Smith, consul in Odessa, and Jeremiah Curtin, the secretary of the American legation in St. Petersburg, who happened to be traveling in the area.[1]

The *Quaker City* with about sixty-five passengers aboard first stopped at Sevastopol for a tour of the Crimean War battlegrounds, where, according to Twain, some Russians suggested that they try to see the emperor, who was vacationing at his Livadia Palace near Yalta. The ship then sailed on to Odessa, which impressed Twain as very American: "Look up the street or down the street, this way or that way, we saw only America! There was not

1. Mark Twain, *The Innocents Abroad, or The New Pilgrims' Progress* (Hartford, Conn.: American Publishing Company, 1869); see also Dewey Ganzel, *Mark Twain Abroad: The Cruise of the "Quaker City"* (Chicago and London: University of Chicago Press, 1968). The visit made headlines independently of its famous author-witness; for example, "The Quaker City in Russian Waters," Charleston *Daily Courier*, 28 September 1867.

one thing to remind us that we were in Russia."[2] Acting upon the group's request, Smith and Curtin succeeded in obtaining permission for an imperial audience at Yalta. Twain, traveling under his real name, Samuel Clemens, headed a committee of the tourists that on the voyage back to the Crimea drafted a formal speech to be read to the tsar by Smith.

The consul, Twain, and the tourists were obviously quite impressed by the subsequent reception at Yalta, for it was attended by not only the tsar but also his immediate family, his brother Grand Duke Michael, Prince Nikolai Dolgorukov, Baron Ernst Ungern-Sternberg (who had recently visited the United States), Admiral Gottlieb Glazenap (military governor of the region), Baron Alexander Wrangell, and General Eduard Totleben of Crimean War engineering fame. They spent about an hour in conversation with the Americans. The tsar "expressed the hope that good friendship between our two countries would forever remain unbroken" and proceeded to take the tourists on a guided tour of his summer retreat.[3]

While these Americans were cruising into the Black Sea to be entertained in imperial splendor at Yalta, a number of Russian subjects found themselves on American soil without even moving—by virtue of the sale of Alaska by Russia to the United States. Whether that topic came up at Yalta is not clear, but it must have been on the minds of many given the discussion and debate it had already generated in both countries.

Walrussia

Rumors had circulated in Washington circles for several years about the cession of the Russian territories administered by the Russian America Company to the United States, but the actual signing of the treaty by Secretary of State William H. Seward and Russian minister Eduard Stoeckl in the wee hours of 30 March 1867 came as a surprise to most politicians and diplomats

2. *Innocents Abroad*, p. 387.

3. Timothy Smith to Seward, 3 September 1867, DUSC, Odessa, vol. 4 (roll 2, M 459), RG 59, NA. See also Frederick Anderson et al., eds., *Mark Twain's Notebooks and Journals, 1855–1873*, vol. 1 (Berkeley and Los Angeles: University of California Press, 1975), pp. 375–76, 403–11. Twain was especially impressed by Ungern-Sternberg, "a boisterous, whole-souled, jolly old brick of a nobleman, . . . a man of progress and enterprise—and representative man of the age—what is called a 'rustler' in California." *Daily Alta California*, 10 November 1867. Curtin regretted that the ladies on board the *Quaker City* "were only ordinarily good-looking women, for at that time much was being said in Russia about the beauty of American women." Joseph Schafer, ed., *Memoirs of Jeremiah Curtin*, Wisconsin Biography Series no. 2 (Madison: State Historical Society of Wisconsin, 1940), pp. 135–36.

and to the general public. Partly for that reason and partly for the secrecy surrounding the two-week intensive negotiations that preceded the signing, initial public reaction was very negative. Another factor was the political climate in the capital, where powerful voices in Congress were already raised against the Johnson administration and its potentatish secretary of state.[4] The Radical Republicans were especially annoyed with Seward for his "betrayal" of their Reconstruction program.

Horace Greeley's New York *Tribune* led the press attack, coining the term "Walrussia" to emphasize the worthlessness of the proposed annexation. Its rival, the *Herald*, while acknowledging that Alaska's chief products were snow, ice, and icebergs, backed the purchase for political reasons, mainly because it would put pressure on the British presence in North America and cement the accord with Russia.[5] The New York *Times* was more direct in its support of Seward and accused the *Tribune* of lacking a sense of national destiny: "While narrow-minded political bigots have been exhausting all their resources in branding him a traitor to his party, he has been quietly pursuing great objects of permanent and paramount interest to his country."[6] But *Harper's Weekly* objected to the timing: "A more inopportune moment than this for the territorial expansion of the United States could not be found . . . [the territory] would be practically a remote colony, with a foreign population. . . . The practical question is, whether it is wise at this time to enlarge our territory in any direction at such an expense."[7]

To no one's surprise, sentiment on the West Coast was more positive, with

4. The purchase has been the subject of a number of excellent studies. See especially Ronald J. Jensen, *The Alaska Purchase and Russian-American Relations* (Seattle and London: University of Washington Press, 1975), and Paul S. Holbo, *Tarnished Expansion: The Alaska Scandal, the Press, and Congress, 1867–1871* (Knoxville: University of Tennessee Press, 1983). The best and most recent of these studies is N. N. Bolkhovitinov, *Russko-Amerikanskie otnosheniia i prodazha Aliaski, 1834–1867* (Moscow: Nauka, 1990).

5. New York *Herald*, 1 April 1867.

6. "The Treaty with Russia—Acquisition of Territory on the Pacific," New York *Times*, 1 April 1867.

7. "The Russian Treaty," *Harper's Weekly*, 13 April 1867, but *Harper's* supported the principle of expansion: "Undoubtedly, also, it is our 'manifest destiny' ultimately to rule the continent; but that is no reason why we should immediately annex Mexico, or make war upon Canada, or buy Russian America. Before we extend our borders let us thoroughly organize our present possessions."

For a study that stresses the positive press response, see N. Bolkhovitinov, "Obshchestvennost' SShA i ratifikatsiia dogovora 1867 g.," in *Amerikanskii Ezhegodnik 1987* (Moscow: Nauka, 1987), pp. 157–74, though the author did not include the popular weeklies.

William H. Seward, secretary of state. Harper's Weekly, 26 October 1872, courtesy of the Kansas Collection, University of Kansas Libraries

San Francisco's *Daily Alta California*, for example, emphasizing the wealth of Alaska in minerals and fish and the future strategic and commercial importance of the North Pacific.[8] Other northern sources claimed that we at least owed a favor to Russia for assistance to the Union during the Civil War, prompting congressman and Civil War general Benjamin Butler to remark that true reciprocity would be to just pay the money and let Russia keep the territory.[9] In the South enthusiasm for the "northern" acquisition was muted, to say the least, and the tendency was simply to quote the *Tribune*. The Mobile *Daily Register* added its own comment: "Owing to the rapid

8. *Daily Alta California*, 13 April 1867.
9. Robert S. Holzman, *Stormy Ben Butler* (New York: Octagon Books, 1878), p. 190.

decrease of the animals of that region and the decline of the fur trade, the country will hardly pay expenses. It is probable that the purchase was made for some political purpose not yet made public."[10]

Private reactions also followed the *Tribune*'s lead. John Bigelow, a friend of Seward's and a former minister to France, wrote in a letter dated 1 April: "Henceforth we need apprehend no failure of our ice crop. . . . What good the Alaskan territory can ever do us, God only knows, unless the peaceful mode of its acquisition discourages any future attempts of European powers to Caesarize on the continent."[11] And eminent diarist George Templeton Strong reflected on 2 April: "It would seem that the Administration is buying Russian America for seven million! What can the country gain by ownership of that desolate, dreary, starved region? It produces a few furs steadily diminishing in quantity, . . . and it produces nothing else I know of. But the acquisition of territory is an achievement on which any administration can rely as endearing it to the people."[12] A few days later, he boasted, "I would make a good superintendent of walruses—a very efficient and disinterested head of a Polar Bear Bureau—an admirable military governor of Oonalaska."[13]

As several studies have shown,[14] the majority of press sentiment, even on the East Coast, eventually supported the purchase, but enthusiasm was definitely lukewarm, and some of the most influential organs, such as Greeley's *Tribune* and the popular weeklies, remained adamantly opposed. Perhaps the most widely distributed of the weeklies, *Frank Leslie's Illustrated Newspaper*, was sarcastic in its criticism:

It is a pleasant thing to know that our country is growing . . . in spite of the recent paralysis at its heart. . . . What if it lie chiefly within the

10. 10 April 1867; see also Charleston *Daily Courier*, 6 April 1867, and New Orleans *Daily Picayune*, 8 April 1867.

11. To William Hargreaves, in John Bigelow, *Reflections of an Active Life*, 5 vols (New York: Baker and Taylor, 1909–1913), 4:59. Bigelow was a friend of Seward's and dined with him the night Stoeckl brought the news that the treaty was ready to sign; ibid., p. 53. Bigelow later reflected, "I doubt if there was any member of either house of Congress who supposed the Government then had any other motive in the purchase of Alaska than to recognize its obligations to the Czar, or that as Territory it had any value except as ridding us of an alien neighbor." Ibid., 1:499n.

12. George Templeton Strong, *Diary of George Templeton Strong*, 4 vols. (New York: Macmillan, 1952), 2 April 1867, 4:129.

13. Ibid., 12 April 1867, p. 130.

14. For an excellent review, see Bolkhovitinov, *Russko-Amerikanskie otnosheniia i prodazha Aliaski*, pp. 221–39, and the unpublished dissertation by Richard Emerson Neunherz, "The Purchase of Russian America: Reasons and Reactions" (Ph.D. diss., University of Washington, 1975).

Arctic zone—that no agriculture be possible within its borders—that terrible snow and ice are the features that most impress themselves on the traveler who tries to pierce its vast and untrodden solitudes—shall such conditions weigh for a moment against the opportunity now given of rounding off our national domain?[15]

And *Leslie's* was one of the few to express concern about the local population.

The idea of an Esquimaux Indian having any choice as to what Government he will live under may seem very droll to the Tartar mind; and still more absurd would be the idea of submitting to the vote of the inhabitants whether they prefer to live under our laws, of which they know nothing, or those with which their fathers have been familiar. . . .

We have done all we can for Russia, but really to ask us to pay $7,000,000 for exhausted hunting-grounds and an Arctic climate, no matter how extensive, with the seignorial rights over 80,000 semi-savages who must be made American citizens, is imposing too much on our good nature.[16]

Both Stoeckl and Seward were surprised by the extent of the opposition, but expansionism prevailed with the help of several ploys: a carefully drafted letter to newspapers by Perry Collins, pioneer of the well-publicized but recently canceled telegraph expedition ito the area; a speaking tour through New England by Gustavus Fox, leader of an official mission to Russia the previous year; and a series of dinners given by Seward in early April for recalcitrant senators. Even the *Tribune* came around.[17] The Senate's approaching date for adjournment had speeded the treaty making, and it quickly referred the matter to its Foreign Relations Committee for formal review—where one member argued that the committee's approval should stipulate that Seward be forced to live in Alaska. With the support especially of Charles Sumner, who chaired the committee, and other influential friends of expansion in the Senate, the treaty was finally ratified, but only af-

15. "Our New Arctic Possessions," *Frank Leslie's Illustrated Newspaper*, 20 April 1867, p. 65.

16. Ibid.

17. The most thorough treatment is that by Bolkhovitinov, *Russko-Amerikanskie otnosheniia i prodazha Aliaski*, pp. 221–46.

ter a move to postpone action was narrowly defeated.[18] The document was then on its way to St. Petersburg with Vladimir Bodisko, Russian legation secretary, to complete the process.

The fate of the purchase agreement was far from settled, however, chiefly because of the mounting antipathy to the Johnson administration in Congress, especially in the House of Representatives, which had to approve the funding. Some members also saw an opportunity to enlarge that body's role in foreign affairs. Realizing that this could be a problem, Seward had managed to secure possession of the area before payment by a special clause in the treaty. The obligation was due in nine months, or 1 January 1868, and the delay was justified to Stoeckl by the facts that Congress would not be back in session until late fall and that the Russian America Company's contract for selling ice to the San Francisco concern extended to that date. For these concessions Seward added an extra $200,000 to the agreed-upon price of $7 million. This also gave the secretary of state more time to marshal crucial support.

Seward's publicity campaign continued, initially spearheaded by letters printed in newspapers and journals across the country from "knowledgeable" people, such as Collins, Fox, and Spencer Baird, assistant secretary of the Smithsonian Institution.[19] They all stressed the value of the new territory. Particularly important allies of the acquisition were Thurlow Weed, an influential New York editor and publicist, and Thaddeus Stevens, a representative from Pennsylvania who was also a leader of the movement to impeach President Johnson.[20] Through Stevens, a significant part of the opposition bloc in Congress became advocates of the purchase.

Through the rest of 1867 American press reports on Alaska remained partisan in their coverage of various questions—for example, the supplanting of Russian administration of the area. Alaskan explorer William H. Dall pointed out the Russian America Company's long neglect of administrative affairs and the impoverished condition of the natives as he developed a social and humanitarian as well as a scientific reason for the purchase; others emphasized that the responsibility for the local institutions, such as schools

18. Jensen, *Alaska Purchase*, pp. 83–91. There are absolutely no grounds for claims that surfaced in Russia in the 1990s that this was a fictional sale or only a lease and that the territory rightfully still belonged to Russia.

19. For the enthusiastic responses of Collins and Fox to Seward's requests, see Collins to Seward, telegram 8 April 1867, and Fox to Seward, 8 April 1867, Seward Papers, Rush-Rhees Library, University of Rochester. A key letter by Collins was printed in the New York *Times*, 9 April 1867.

20. Jensen, *Alaska Purchase*, pp. 86–89.

established under the paternal care of the Russian America Company, would now need to be assumed by the United States government at considerable annual expense.[21] On the positive side there was at least some genuine effort to educate Americans about their new acquisition. Scribner's *Hours at Home* concluded a long, detailed description of the new territory with a backhanded compliment: "It is doubtful if there be a spot on the globe that can truly be called useless."[22]

During the debate anyone familiar with the area was called on to furnish information. For example, a former agent of the San Francisco–based American Russian Commercial Company at Sitka offered a favorable assessment of the fur, fish, mineral, ice, and timber resources of the land but added stoically, "It is, without any doubt, an isolated, God-forsaken country."[23] Many people, however, could not wait for a definitive American judgment and, encouraged by West Coast articles extolling the riches of the area, descended in large numbers on the hapless region. Already in May Californians and Canadians were scrambling aboard ships for the new "El Dorado," producing a short-lived economic boom.[24] By October Sitka was a captured city:

> As might be expected, some of our fast people have squatted over the whole vicinity of Sitka—preempted the Governor's house, and one godless individual has even recorded a claim for the Church and Church lands! Much displeasure has been expressed at such unseemly proceedings, but it is some little satisfaction to know that many of the preemptors are not American citizens. Some of the Hudson Bay employees have preempted and recorded claims, and having now reasonable doubts about their rights in such matters, are quietly going halves with Americans and letting the claims go into their hands.[25]

The situation was aggravated by one of the stipulations of the treaty that all immobile property belonging to the Russian America Company be transferred to the United States government (raising the negotiated price from $6 million to $7 million). Unforeseen was that Sitka and other posts were essentially company towns where most employees and their families lived in homes provided for them. When American military authorities reached the

21. *Daily Alta California*, 27 June 1867.
22. "Russian America: Its Physical Characteristics and Native Tribes," *Hours at Home* 5, 3 (July 1867): 255–57.
23. "Walrussia," *Leslie's Illustrated*, 26 October 1867.
24. "Our New Russian Possessions," *Daily Alta California*, 25 May 1867.
25. "Scientific Expedition to Alaska," *Daily Alta California*, 1 October 1867.

scene, they enforced this property transfer, thus depriving many permanent residents of homes they considered their own, and then they favored the new claims of arriving American adventurers. The Russian America Company payroll ceased at the same time that the new influx caused prices to rise. As a result, many Russian and creole residents, who were at first inclined to stay and become American citizens, took advantage of the redress offered by the treaty of free transportation to Russia or San Francisco; there they would subsequently bemoan their treatment and reminisce about the "good old days" in *Russian* America.[26]

On 18 October, at 3:30 in the afternoon, the official transfer took place before a small, rather solemn crowd in front of the "Baranov" (Governor's) Palace. A fitting mishap occurred; as the large Russian flag was being lowered, it became entangled and wrapped tightly around the pole. After several efforts, it was successfully dislodged, only to float down onto the bayonets of the small Russian honor guard.[27] A few days later there was another bad omen when a rare hurricane hit the town, causing serious damage to buildings and to ships in the harbor. The *Konstantin*, whose ducal namesake was largely responsible for the sale, was totally destroyed, as was one of the large, American-built ice houses.[28] Seward's "ice box" was thus delivered in rather dented condition.

Although in "possession," the United States had not yet paid for Alaska, not even a down payment, and, embarrassingly, opposition continued. In November the House of Representatives passed a resolution offered by Cadwalader Washburn of Wisconsin repudiating the obligation to pay for

26. For interviews with expatriate Alaskans in San Francisco, see Pavel Ogorodnikov, *V Strane svobody*, 2 vols., 2d ed. (St. Petersburg: Rossiiskoi bib., 1882), 1:288–308. A document enclosed in one of Katakazi's dispatches recorded that only 15 Russians remained of 300 inhabitants of Sitka by the end of 1870; the officer complained of the lowering of morale among the army garrison, because "women almost without exception are prostitutes and even girls of 12 or 13 years must be included in the number." D. A. Lyle's report, countersigned by W. T. Sherman, 30 December 1871 (c), f. 133, op. 470, d. 43, AVPR.

27. Jensen, *Alaska Purchase*, p. 101; Richard A. Pierce, "Prince D. P. Maksutov: Last Governor of Russian America," *Journal of the West* 6, 3 (1967): 404–5. The Boston *Daily Evening Transcript* (14 November) put as good a face as possible on the proceedings: "The transfer was conducted in a purely diplomatic and businesslike manner, neither banquets nor speech-making following."

28. "Acquisition of Alaska," *Daily Alta California*, 14 and 23 November 1867. The author of this series, Angus McPherson, was an agent of the San Francisco ice company and was naturally biased in favor of the sale; he stressed agriculture potential, availability of coal, and Kodiak's untapped fishing wealth, including salmon, halibut, and "mammoth crab." Ibid., 25 and 29 November 1867.

any territorial acquisition. Naturally alarmed by this, Seward and Stoeckl began a desperate underhanded effort to purchase crucial political and press support through Robert J. Walker, an ardent expansionist who was in need of money.[29] In what was the most unsavory aspect of the Alaska transaction, cash payments were doled out to politicians, correspondents, and agents. Although some of these bribes may have been part of the extended lobbying effort of Seward and his friends, most came from the Russian minister. Overly alarmed by the talk of delays, and even refusal, by the House to appropriate the purchase sum, and anxious to have settled the crowning achievement of his diplomatic career, Stoeckl distributed some of the "extra" $200,000 through Walker and Thomas Cottman, who had been associated with the first public consideration of the purchase of Alaska in 1854.[30]

The whole affair was badly mishandled by all concerned and was soon exposed in inaccurate and exaggerated press reports, which prompted a formal investigation and various charges, denials, and countercharges.[31] Stoeckl's long term (since 1854) as minister to the United States thus ended rather ignominiously. Rewarded with a sizable bonus from his government, though not as large as he had expected, Stoeckl failed to receive promotion to another post and retired from public service, spending much of his time in Paris, where he was more a part of the displaced American society, through his American wife, than the Russian.[32]

Finally, on 14 July 1868 the House of Representatives, shepherded by Nathaniel Banks and Stevens and greased by Stoeckl's bribes, passed the Alaska appropriation by a vote of 113 to 43, with 44 abstaining. The press virtually ignored this final act of the purchase in the heat of presidential nominating conventions. Public resentment about "Seward's Folly," however, continued to grow, nurtured by critical accounts, such as one that appeared in *Leslie's Illustrated* early in 1869.

> The folly of the Alaska purchase is every day becoming more and more apparent. The attempt to erect a Territorial Government there, with an army of office-holders, at the cost of a quarter of a million a year, was promptly squelched in the House of Representatives. We now hear that

29. For details, see Robert H. Luthin, "The Sale of Alaska," *Slavonic and East European Review* 16 (July 1937): 168–82.

30. Cottman to Katakazi, 9 October 1871, f. 133, op. 470, d. 123 (1871), AVPR. It is interesting to discover—and it is only known from this source—that Cottman played a role again in the final settlement of Alaska.

31. See Holbo, *Tarnished Expansion*, for details.

32. "Latest News from Alaska," *Leslie's Illustrated*, 30 April 1870.

"the Russians have mostly left, and that Sitka is almost depopulated."
. . . We believe the orange and fig crops were failures, and the vineyards
not productive. . . . Mr. Seward's villa, in this new Vale of Cashmere,
will not be commenced until after he leaves the Cabinet.[33]

This picture was partially mitigated by the saner and more erudite efforts of
Smithsonian agents Dall and Frederick Whymper to explain the real value
of the territory.[34]

Comparatively little open publicity or debate about the sale transpired in
Russia because of autocratic influence and censorship. The liberal newspaper *Golos* (Voice) did issue a strong initial criticism, however. It first treated
the news of the sale as a joke, arguing that the many serious and sacrificial
endeavors of the Russian America Company surely would not be destroyed
for so little gain, that new riches including gold had been found there, that
the Hudson's Bay Company would have paid three or four times as much,
that the income would be only "a drop in the sea" for the Russian budget,
and that perhaps the next day would bring news of the selling of the Crimea
or the Caucasus. It also noted that the earlier sale of Fort Ross (California)
had long been recognized as foolish. "Why repeat such a mistake and sell
out the work of the great heroes Shelekhov [sic], Baranov, and Khlebni-
kov?"[35]

This negative reaction was especially pronounced because of the newspaper's opposition to the simultaneously proposed sale of the Nikolaevskii (St.
Petersburg–Moscow) railroad, which gave the appearance that the Russian
government was having a gigantic garage sale. A response from an official
newspaper even supported that image. "Neznakomets" (Stranger) wrote that
it was best to sell things that have little value and that the sale would support the development of the Amur region (Grand Duke Constantine's goal).
Stressing the cost of upkeep, he noted that Russia could create a whole ministry just for the area but that its tasks would be light because so much of its

---

33. "Alaska," *Leslie's Illustrated*, 6 February 1869. This accompanied a series of long,
critical articles by former resident, Captain Edward G. Fast; see issues of 30 January and
6, 13, 20, and 27 February. Seward did in fact make a triumphal and much ballyhooed
visit to Alaska in 1869.

34. William H. Dall, *Alaska and Its Resources* (Boston: Lee and Shepard, 1870); Frederick Whymper, *Travel and Adventures in the Territory of Alaska* (New York: Harper and
Bros., 1869). In a subsequent article, Dall tried to prove that Alaska was a bargain compared to Florida, New Mexico, and even Texas, but he added in the costs of the wars involved in those acquisitions. "Is Alaska a Paying Investment?" *Harper's Monthly* 44, 260
(January 1872): 252–57.

35. *Golos*, 25 March/6 April 1867.

jurisdiction was empty. "We do not have money for such luxury and America does. This is like selling old furniture that is worn out and realizing something for it. We have enough ministries and officials but little money."[36]

Golos soon took solace in the deal as a means to strengthen Russian-American relations but then railed at the Americans for their ingratitude in opposing the purchase and delaying payment.[37] The Russian America Company stockholders were evidently quite opposed to the sale, though the company eventually received some of the money and its stock rose considerably at the news that it had been rescued from a losing situation. Although more muted for fear of the censor, other Russian press reports fussed about the price being so low but acknowledged that it would strengthen the bond with the United States. Another tactic to evade the censor was to quote from the European newspapers, in which somewhat alarmist views of a Russian-American conspiracy or alliance were expressed. A French paper even cited as evidence Alexis de Tocqueville's prediction of the 1830s about the mutual ascendancy of Russia and the United States to world power.[38]

Behind the scenes, much of conservative Russian society, as surprised as everyone else, was obviously disturbed by the loss of any territory of the empire. Moreover, the delay in payment prompted a decidedly negative reaction by the summer of 1868. Consul Eugene Schuyler, beginning a distinguished career as a Russian expert, warned Seward from Moscow of this changed climate of opinion:

> To voluntarily cede a portion of their territory was contrary to all Russian feeling and the mass of the Russians were not content with the action of the Government in disposing of Alaska. The only softening circumstance was that it was acquired by the United States, to whom a genuine friendly feeling was then existing. Even six months ago there was a disposition to extend unusual favors and facilities to Americans engaged in business or travelling here. Since the delays in Congress with regard to the appropriation this has changed.[39]

Although heralded in some quarters as a sign of friendship between the two nations and even the prelude to a political alliance, the sale of Alaska was more of a test of the relationship that fostered resentment on both sides.

36. *St. Peterburgskiia Vedomosti*, 4/16 April 1867.
37. *Golos*, 12/24 and 14/26 April 1867.
38. Bolkhovitinov, *Russko-Amerikanskie otnosheniia i prodazha Aliaski*, pp. 252–55.
39. 7 July 1868, DUSC, Moscow, vol. 1 (roll 1, M 456), RG 59, NA.

While many Americans felt they were paying for a worthless burden and assuming an untimely obligation out of appreciation for past favors, Russians sensed a wound to their grand empire that had become infected with American ingratitude. Russia did in fact lose the American part of its national psyche, an important but incalculable feature of its imperial outreach. The United States could not yet appreciate the value of such distant and unknown lands except in a vague sense of fulfilling a destiny, and indeed it seemed to many at the time as an embarrassing caricature of true "manifest destiny." The real losers were the people of the region—Russian, creole, and native—who were not consulted and then forced to suffer neglect and administrative bungling. The only immediate "winners" were the few individuals in Washington, New York, and Sitka who realized a direct monetary gain, thanks to Stoeckl's clumsy payoffs and speculations in the property of the Russian America Company. Many of them would face public scandal.[40]

Dancing Diplomats

The American minister in St. Petersburg, Cassius Clay, must have felt a little miffed at not playing a part in this grand affair; he could only stand on the sidelines and begrudge the success of his old nemesis, Seward. The eccentric Kentuckian was by this time well-known in St. Petersburg for his striking and irregular appearances in and out of the court, especially his strange moves on the dance floor. He nevertheless kept busy with both public and private affairs. Jeremiah Curtin, who was to be the next victim of the minister's vanity, seemed to be more on Clay's mind than Alaska in 1867. Curtin possessed a special talent for languages, learned Russian during the fleet visit to New York in 1863–1864, and obtained from Clay the post of secretary in the St. Petersburg legation.[41] He used his facility in Russian extensively during the festivities attending the Gustavus Fox mission in 1866, to the annoyance and chagrin of the upstaged Clay.

Clay complained publicly that Curtin was Seward's spy, but he told Seward privately that he regarded the secretary not only as his "secret enemy"

40. See Holbo, *Tarnished Expansion*, and Bolkhovitinov, *Russko-Amerikanskie otnosheniia i prodazha Aliaski*, pp. 283–314.
41. Among those recommending Curtin for the post in lavish terms were James Russell Lowell, William M. Evarts, Charles Sumner, George William Curtis, and the Russian consul general Robert Osten-Saken. Recommendation letters, file 1864, Curtin Papers, SHSW.

but as "the protégé" of Mr. Sumner, Seward's rival.[42] Curtin tried to escape Clay's growing resentment in 1867 by touring the Caucasus and southern Russia (where he met Mark Twain), though he was apparently not aware of the seriousness of the rift until he returned to St. Petersburg late in the year.[43] And it was not until November that Clay formally asked for Curtin's recall, citing his long absence without permission, his inebriation at a theater in Moscow during the Fox visit, his indebtedness in St. Petersburg, and his direction of a conspiracy against Clay.[44] Curtin fled to Washington to defend himself.

With the secretarial post apparently vacant, Clay hoped to secure the services of Mell Landon, who had come to Russia in 1857 to visit his cousin, Robert O. Williams, a prominent Moscow manufacturer.[45] However, Seward perversely reassigned Curtin as secretary to Clay. When Curtin returned to Russia in 1868, Clay would have nothing to do with him—and even forwarded all his mail back to Washington.[46] But as one pioneering American Russian-language expert was forced to abandon the country, another entered through Moscow.

The American consulate had only been established in Russia's second city in 1857 but had already caused Clay problems. In 1861 John Hatterscheidt of Kansas was appointed to the post in recognition of his work for the Lincoln campaign in that state. Originally from Cologne, Hatterscheidt still spoke with a heavy German accent; from Moscow he sent long, semiliterate but nevertheless insightful reports on Russian economic life. He also emulated Clay, without the same adroitness, by wearing fancy uniforms and dabbling in nefarious business operations. He soon wore out everyone's patience, and Clay requested his replacement in 1865. Riker Fitzgerald of Philadelphia was duly designated for the post and arrived in Moscow early in

42. Clay to Seward, 23 April 1867, Seward Papers, indexed correspondence, reel 100, Rush-Rhees Library, University of Rochester.

43. *Memoirs of Jeremiah Curtin*, pp. 16–17.

44. Clay to Seward, 18 November 1867, DUSM, Russia, vol. 21 (roll 21, M 35), RG 59, NA. Curtin, of course, denied the charges; Curtin to Seward, 25 January 1868 (two unnumbered letters of the same date), ibid. Clay repeated and expanded his accusations to Seward's successor, Hamilton Fish, 6 and 11 May 1869, ibid.

45. Landon to Eliza Meacham, 17/29 August 1867 (Moscow) and 20 February 1868 (Washington), Hoyt and Meacham Papers, NYHS. Landon also assisted Clay by obtaining evidence against Curtin in Moscow; Landon (Washington) to Frederick Seward, 1 July 1868, DUSM, Russia, vol. 21 (roll 21, M 35), RG 59, NA.

46. Curtin (St. Petersburg) to Seward, 12 and 29 May 1868, and Clay to Seward, 11 May and 30 June 1868, DUSM, Russia, vol. 21 (roll 21, M 35), RG 59, NA.

January 1866, only to depart within a few days—but not before sizing up Hatterscheidt:

> I regret to say that he is totally unfit for the position. Besides wearing an absurd, gaudy uniform, not allowed by the Consular Regulations, he has, by improper actions, rendered himself unpopular; and I believe him to be entirely untrustworthy. I have it from high authority that he has behaved badly towards Americans. . . . I have seen but little of him—but he did not impress me favorably.[47]

Fitzgerald's hasty retreat left Hatterscheidt at his post while Seward and Clay tried to replace him. Phillip Schuyler, also from Kansas, was confirmed by the Senate but then withdrew.[48] James Wentworth of Missouri actually reached Moscow on 21 November 1866, only to be driven away by Hatterscheidt and the Russian winter.[49] To Seward he complained, "It was no slight embarrassment to have been necessarily brought . . . in contact with so rude a person as my predecessor."[50] Wentworth left Moscow in April 1867, delegating Samuel Young, who had a local hardware business, to wrestle the consulate from Hatterscheidt.[51] Finally, Phillip Schuyler's nephew Eugene accepted the post.[52]

A Yale and Columbia Law School graduate, Eugene Schuyler—like Curtin—had picked up some knowledge of Russian from the officers of the Russian fleet that visited New York in 1863. Upon arrival in Moscow in October 1867, he immediately set about putting the consulate back in order,

47. Fitzgerald to Seward, 9 January 1866, DUSC, Moscow, vol. 1 (roll 1, M 456), RG 59, NA. Fitzgerald could not stand the Russian climate.

48. Seward to Clay, 29 May 1866, DI, Russia, vol. 15 (roll 137, M 77), RG 59, NA.

49. Wentworth to Seward, 4 December 1866, DUSC, Moscow, vol. 1 (roll 1, M 456), RG 59, NA.

50. Wentworth to Seward, 26 December 1866, ibid. Clay complained to Seward, "I am rejoiced at the removal of Hatterschied [sic], as he has become the nucleus of an abandoned set of men who infest this remote empire, [and] who make it a point to traduce this legation." 5 December 1866, DUSM, Russia, vol. 21 (roll 21, M 35), RG 59, NA. Hatterscheidt, who had married a Russian, moved his lumber business to Kazan, where he died virtually penniless in 1874. Jomini to Schuyler, 21 August 1875, DPR, Russia, vol. 4505 (notes received), RG 84, NA; Billhardt to Uhl, 14 November 1895, DUSC, Moscow, vol. 2 (roll 2, M456), RG 59, NA, answering an inquiry about Hatterscheidt's estate.

51. Young to Seward, 17 April 1867, DUSC, Moscow, vol. 2 (roll 2, M 456), RG 59, NA.

52. Schuyler (New York) to Seward, 18 July 1867, ibid. The relationship is established by a report that Eugene visited Phillip's Kansas home in 1871; *Osage Chronicle* (Burlingame, Kansas), 20 July 1871.

perfecting his Russian and collecting a variety of information about Russia—until his transfer to the consulate at Reval two years later. In a game of diplomatic musical chairs, Schuyler was then called to St. Petersburg after only a few months to become secretary of legation, a post he held for almost five years. He put this time to good use, translating and writing articles and books.

In Odessa, another important consulate, the veteran Timothy Smith performed ably, entrenched in local society with his wife and seven children in residence. Business, however, other than the occasional tourist group, was slack. Although Smith had gained considerable expertise he too was removed rather abruptly in 1875 when an altercation with the local postmaster ruffled the Russian bureaucracy and forced a response from Schuyler, who was temporarily in charge of legation affairs. The chief consulate in St. Petersburg, meanwhile, was under the minimal superintendency of George Pomutz, a naturalized Hungarian from Iowa, who apparently successfully stayed out of Clay's path by being ill most of the summer of 1867 and absent for long stretches of time thereafter.[53]

Clay thus performed his duties in 1867 and 1868 without a secretary and essentially without a consul. His biggest problem, however, was the Chautems affair. Because of its nature and the recriminations and accusations arising from it, the details remain unclear. According to Clay, his admitted frequenting of "a secret house of assignations" managed by a Swiss-Irish couple, Jean and Elisa Chautems, was purely innocent, but Mrs. Chautems charged Clay with molesting her fourteen-year-old daughter (reminiscent of an experience John Paul Jones had in St. Petersburg many years before).[54] Clay typically dispersed the blame around the city—for example, accusing the British ambassador and the French and British clergy of using this allegation to remove him from his post. "The French and English would give millions to drive me from Russia because of the friendly relations which I keep up between the nations," declared the paranoid-inclined minister. "To these are added Prince of the house of Ropes & Co. of Boston, Hatterscheidt, and Caleb Croswell, all of whom are infamous men and very ma-

---

53. Pomutz to Seward, 12/24 October 1867, DUSC, St. Petersburg, vol. 12 (roll 7, M 81), RG 59, NA. Pomutz averaged four dispatches a year, mostly brief quarterly reports.
54. Clay to Seward, 21 April 1867, DUSM, Russia, vol. 21 (roll 21, M 35), RG 59, NA. Clay did not divulge all details in his letter, though he must have suspected that Seward knew them. He was more revealing in his later memoirs: *The Life of Cassius Marcellus Clay: Memoirs, Writings, and Speeches* (Cincinnati: J. Fletcher Brennan, 1886), pp. 464–67.

lignant."[55] Behind everything was Laslo Chandor, an old business associate and the author of a scurrilous pamphlet, "A Synopsis of Forty Chapters on Clay," dated 1 May 1867.

Separated from his wife since his return to Russia in 1863, Clay had quickly earned a reputation in St. Petersburg for his liaisons; besides affairs with Madame Chautems and possibly her daughter, stories circulated about a Princess Kochubei and especially Anna Petrova, a ballerina who danced under the name of Maria Petipa. Clay had a son by Maria in 1866 and later took him back to Kentucky, where he was raised as Launay Clay.[56] As far as the Chautems were concerned, Clay dismissed them as a former Swiss cook for the emperor and "a drunken Irish woman" whom he had met through Chandor.[57] And he maintained they had swindled (or perhaps blackmailed) him out of several thousand dollars.

With these scandals occupying a sizeable portion of his diplomatic correspondence, it would seem likely that Clay would have little time for more regular business. This was obviously not the case, since Clay also had the reputation of vying with everyone in the Russian capital in hospitality (of a proper diplomatic kind). He assured Seward that the adverse publicity from the Chandor charges had not affected attendance at his entertainments at all. In his memoirs, Clay offered a clue to his enduring social success: "The aristocracy of Russia, men and women, are models of form and refinement; and . . . I was in the prime of life, not a bad-looking fellow, who had seen much of the world, and who determined to please. I broke through all etiquette so far as to be affable to all classes alike; and when I made a *gaucherie*, I was the first to laugh at it."[58]

Moreover, Clay was always responsive to the increasing number of visiting Americans. One must applaud, for example, his assistance to Captain T. Morris Chester, an African-American Civil War veteran who came to Russia in January 1868 to escape an unhappy experience in Liberia. Clay arranged an interview with Chancellor Alexander Gorchakov, who directed Russia's foreign affairs, and even a private lunch with the imperial family. In Clay's view, "it is the duty of all good citizens to try and elevate the African

55. Clay to Seward, 21 April 1867, DUSM, Russia, vol. 21 (roll 21, M 35), RG 59, NA.

56. H. Edward Richardson, *Cassius Marcellus Clay: Firebrand of Freedom* (Lexington: University of Kentucky Press, 1976), pp. 116–17. Understandably, this strained relations with his wife even more, and they were divorced in 1878.

57. Clay to Seward (private), 19 May 1867, DUSM, Russia, vol. 21 (roll 21, M 35), RG 59, NA.

58. *Life of Cassius Clay*, p. 295.

race in America, and inspire them with all possible self-respect—and prepare them for that ultimate influence which they must sooner or later have upon the political and economical interests of the United States."[59] A scoundrel of the old school he may have been, but Clay was well ahead of most of his fellow citizens in certain respects. Chester was actually offered an appointment in the Russian army, but as his main priority had become funding for Negro colleges in America, he passed up the Russian post.

The major American visit of this period was that of a naval squadron of four ships under the command of Admiral David Farragut, which spent over three weeks anchored at Kronstadt in August 1867. Farragut and his officers were lavishly entertained by Naval Minister Grand Duke Constantine, by Admiral Stepan Lesovskii, who had commanded the Russian squadron to New York in 1863, and by Clay himself. Commented Clay, "The impressions produced here, by the American fleet and its gentlemanly officers, has been most favorable; and has relieved us from the unfavorable effects of the misconduct and excesses of some of the officers of Asst. Secretary Fox's expedition in 1866."[60] True to form, Clay sidestepped any mention of his own indiscretions.

Somewhat tainted by scandals, Stoeckl and Clay, veterans of one of the most active periods of Russian-American relations, retired from political life at about the same time, though they had had very little direct contact. Upon learning that Stoeckl's successor was to be Konstantin Katakazi, Clay observed, "Mr. Catacasy speaks American well. . . . I regard him as a very good appointment for us: as he is a gentleman of fine sense and address: and without the prejudices against a Republic, which too often exist in European court circles." He then gave Stoeckl a slap by noting that Katakazi had always supported the Union, sentiments "which I regret to say, were quite wanting in some others of those who unhappily represent Russia at this time in Washington."[61]

Clay at last tendered his own resignation in late 1868 to take effect on 1

59. Clay to Seward, 9 February 1867, DUSM, Russia, vol. 21 (roll 21, M 35), RG 59, NA. See also Allison Blakely, *Russia and the Negro: Blacks in Russian History and Thought* (Washington, D.C.: Howard University Press, 1986), pp. 42–43. Chester credited Clay with his subsequent grand reception in Denmark; Chester (London) to Clay, 2 April 1868, Clay Papers, Lincoln Memorial University.

60. Clay to Seward, 28 August 1867, DUSM, Russia, vol. 21 (roll 21, M 35), RG 59, NA; M. D. Landon, who attended Clay's banquet for Farragut and his wife, to Eliza Meacham, 17/29 August 1867, Hoyt and Meacham Papers, NYHS; Alfred T. Mahan, *Admiral Farragut* (reprint: New York: Haskell House, 1968), pp. 298–99.

61. Clay to Fish, 24 June 1869, DUSM, Russia, vol. 21 (roll 21, M 35), RG 59, NA.

April of the next year. His successor, Andrew G. Curtin, (no relation to Jeremiah), was selected by the new Grant administration and made the usual slow journey to St. Petersburg, spending several weeks at a European spa.[62] Awaiting Curtin's arrival, Clay remained at his post until 15 October; he was given a fitting send-off, with dinners hosted by the diplomatic community and by businessman William L. Winans, who was still in charge of the large locomotive works in the suburbs. From visiting senator Thomas Osborn of Florida, Clay learned the reason why Seward had not replaced him earlier: the Senate in a special caucus had insisted on Clay's remaining. He took satisfaction in surviving Seward in office: "Thus perished the political aspiration of my ablest, meanest, and most cowardly enemy, W. H. Seward."[63]

Before leaving Russia, however, Clay fired more diatribes against Seward and Jeremiah Curtin for the benefit of the new secretary of state, Hamilton Fish. He in turn felt obliged to admonish Clay: "Permit me to express my regret that you have thought proper to write, and to forward to this department, a consecutively numbered despatch [rather than private], containing such personal aspersions upon a gentleman who has occupied so conspicuous a position in the history of this country, and who has held the office of Secretary of State during the most trying period in its existence."[64]

Andrew Curtin's appointment reflected the esteem with which the Grant-Fish administration initially regarded Russia. His popularity and service as governor of Pennsylvania during the Civil War won him serious consideration as Grant's running mate in 1868, but he withdrew from contention and was awarded the consolation prize of a diplomatic mission. Philadelphia gave Curtin a grand farewell dinner at the Academy of Music attended by over 500 guests, including William D. Lewis (who had been resident in Russia in 1813–1817) and Russian consul general Vladimir Bodisko.[65] At the gala, the minister-designate responded to toasts with a short speech:

62. Curtin (Hamburg) to Clay, 11 July 1869, Clay Papers, Lincoln Memorial University.

63. *Life of Cassius Clay*, p. 409.

64. Fish to Clay, 8 May 1869, DI, Russia, vol. 15 (roll 137, M 77), RG 59, NA. Fish was even more upset when he learned that Clay had formally asked for Gorchakov's intervention on his behalf; Clay to Gorchakov, 9 May 1869, and "Forty Chapters upon Clay," copies enclosed in Clay to Fish, 11 May 1869, DUSM, Russia, vol. 21 (roll 21, M 35), RG 59, NA. Fish responded by saying that the president wished Clay to be more prudent about topics discussed in Russia; Fish to Clay, 7 June 1869, DI, Russia, vol. 15 (roll 137, M 77), RG 59, NA.

65. Philadelphia *Inquirer*, 14 and 18 June 1869.

It is somewhat anomalous that the freest and strongest government in the New World should have maintained the most amicable relations with the most absolute monarchy and the strongest government of the Old World. America and Russia have never had an interruption of their friendly relation. It is my earnest prayer that, during my residence at the Court of the Autocrat of all the Russias, nothing will occur to break these relations.[66]

He would be sadly disappointed.

The Perkins Claim

Clay and Stoeckl and their successors had at least one thing in common—opposition to the Perkins claim against Russia. Clay's response to the problem was to ignore it, which was also the preferred stance of the Russian government. Stoeckl, however, was faced with American administrations that sympathized with the case or at least felt politically obligated to lend it support. After lying dormant for a few years, the claim was resubmitted just before the negotiation for the Alaska treaty, but Clay simply refused to carry any appeal to the Russian government.[67] The issue quickly slid to the back burner in Washington during the Seward-Stoeckl bargaining over the price of Alaska, and it does not appear that the claim was on Andrew Curtin's list of foreign affairs broached during initial conversations with Gorchakov in July or October 1869.[68]

Benjamin Perkins, a respected Worcester, Massachusetts, sea captain, had been enticed in 1855 by Stoeckl and military agent Otto Lilienfeldt into arranging shipments of 150 tons of gunpowder and 35,000 modified rifles for Russia. These orders were abruptly canceled when the Crimean War came to a close. Perkins lost money already committed to producers, such as the Whipple Powder Company of Boston, and was financially ruined. He argued that the agreements, though only verbal, were legal contracts and that the Russian government was liable for the losses. After the death of Perkins

66. *Harper's Weekly*, 3 July 1869, p. 422.
67. Seward to Clay, 31 December 1866, DI, Russia, vol. 15 (roll 137, M 77), RG 59, NA; Clay to Seward, 17 January 1867, DUSM, Russia, vol. 21 (roll 21, M 35), RG 59, NA.
68. Curtin to Fish, 1 November 1869, DUSM, Russia, vol. 22 (roll 22, M 35), RG 59, NA. Before reaching St. Petersburg Curtin met with Gorchakov informally at Baden-Baden in a "most pleasant interview," but he did not disclose the topics of their conversation; Curtin to Fish, 23 July 1869, ibid.

in 1858, interested parties took up the case on behalf of his widow and daughter. The main factor that kept it alive for so long was the increasing amity between Russia and the United States, which fostered the belief among the claimants that Russia, out of friendship, would eventually honor the contracts. The Republican, northern ascendancy in American foreign relations after 1860 also raised hopes. The allocation of a sizable sum from the United States Treasury for Alaska naturally provoked notions of getting some of the payment earmarked to satisfy the debt to Perkins.

The prime mover of the claim, which had risen in 1868 to over $500,000, was Joseph B. Stewart, an influential New York attorney and Washington lobbyist.[69] He first pressed the case in 1861 but dropped it for the duration of the war; then he renewed it late in 1866 only to relent to Seward's wish that it not interfere with the Alaska negotiations.[70] The next summer, however, he was back on the attack, as he wrote, "to force the Russian minister to feel the necessity of making a settlement or refer the case to some responsible tribunal for a proper adjustment which up to this time has been successfully evaded."[71] In reviewing the case for the stubbornly unheeding Clay, Stewart made his strongest point a plea of simple humanity: "Take notice of one fact, and don't forget, Perkins was no mere adventurer, he was an honest old ship Captain, and was respected most by those who knew him best, and for whom he had sailed longest."[72]

Quite a battle of words then ensued in Washington between Stewart and Stoeckl, with Congress caught in the middle and the press obviously relishing the whole business. Nathaniel Banks, the influential congressman from Massachusetts who chaired the House Committee on Foreign Affairs, at first actively supported the claim, but he had no intention of letting it inter-

---

69. Allan Nevins described Stewart as "able, unscrupulous, a reckless gambler in gold and stocks, [who] was for years 'the big boss of the lobby!'" He considered the Perkins case, "perhaps the most malodorous of the many claims upon which lobbyists, shysters, and political harpies fed during the Gilded Age." *Hamilton Fish: The Inner History of the Grant Administration*, 2 vols. (New York: Dodd, Mead, 1936), 1:503–4. Nevins's synopsis of the affair is not very reliable, however.

Clay reported that by early 1869 the claim had reached $685,711.70; Clay to Fish, 15 June 1869, DUSM, Russia, vol. 21 (roll 21, M 35), RG 59, NA.

70. Seward to Clay, 31 December 1866, DI, Russia, vol. 15 (roll 137, M 77), RG 59, NA.

71. Stewart to Seward, 27 July 1867, DPR, Russia, vol. 4502 (notes received), RG 84, NA.

72. Stewart to Clay, 25 December 1867, ibid. He also indicated that he was involved, as one of the contracting parties for the clearing of Sevastopol harbor, in another dispute with the Russian government.

fere with his drive to have the Alaska appropriation passed with no strings attached. In the midst of mounting exasperation, the exchanges became increasingly political and vitriolic during the waning months of the Johnson administration, especially when a former State Department clerk named Louis Tasistro accused Banks of taking money from Stoeckl.[73] The two major issues in Russian-American relations were thus becoming intertwined in 1868, and Stoeckl may have resorted to bribery as much to ward off Stewart and his allies as to protect the Alaska treaty.

With the coming of a new administration and Stoeckl's replacement by Katakazi, the Perkins case became even more pernicious. Like his predecessor, Hamilton Fish supported the claim in deference to the Republican political powers of New England and New York, namely Stewart, Banks, Senator William Evarts, Congressman Benjamin Butler, and especially Caleb Cushing, former attorney general and diplomatic troubleshooter.[74] President Grant's brothers-in-law, Frederick and Louis Dent, also became involved and helped gain the backing of the president.[75] Banks failed to obtain an appointment as minister to Russia, which he sought primarily in order to press the claim, but he attempted to win over Andrew Curtin and followed him to Russia in September 1869. Although the congressman received a friendly reception from Gorchakov and attended a formal military review, he was sidetracked into other schemes—such as one proposed jointly with Nathan Appleton to erect grain elevators in Odessa—and apparently did not discuss the Perkins claim, at least with Gorchakov.[76]

Katakazi, who received rather specific but contradictory written instructions to resolve the matter once and for all,[77] reported back to Gorchakov

73. Fred Harvey Harrington, *Fighting Politician: Major General N. P. Banks* (Philadelphia: University of Pennsylvania Press, 1948), pp. 182–85.

74. Stewart to Louis Dent, 2 March 1870, vol. 68, Fish Papers, LC.

75. Nevins, *Hamilton Fish*, 1:505.

76. Harrington, *Fighting Politician*, pp. 183, 195; Curtin to Fish, 1 November 1869, DUSM, Russia, vol. 22 (roll 22, M 35), RG 59, NA; Timothy Smith to Fish, 20 November 1869, DUSC, Odessa, vol. 4 (roll 2, M 459), RG 59, NA.

77. The tattered and lengthy original instructions, filed under the year 1877, read in part: "Between the two powerful states there is a good durable understanding on the basis of a respected reciprocity which contains in part a tolerance of the foibles of the other. . . . By this mutual respect, we remain good friends. . . . Various European powers have adopted in regard to the United States a system of concessions that do not stop even at considerable sacrifices of interests and dignity. We have adopted this same system and it is this that the representative of His Majesty at Washington must not lose sight of in a single instance. . . . [But] in the Perkins' Affair we cannot cede anything on principle. . . . We cannot admit a pretention so arbitrary, and the representative of His Majesty is authorized to declare this categorically." Gorchakov to Katakazi, 9 June 1869, f. 170, op. 512/3, d. 128 (1877), AVPR.

Prince Alexander Gorchakov, chancellor and foreign minister, 1856–1882. From Gustavus Fox, Mission to Russia *(1866)*

privately that he thought Stoeckl had indeed misled Perkins in 1855 and compromised the Russian government by not informing it of all the particulars. Regardless, he contended that the case had no legal grounds; "it is certain that this whole affair is a fraudulent machination."[78] Katakazi, who was familiar with backdoor tactics, then used Tasistro and Frank Turk, a local attorney, as intermediaries in dealing with Stewart. After the president initiated a cabinet discussion of the affair in early 1870, Fish sensibly proposed neutral arbitration of the claim. This solution was fractured in March and April 1870 when Stewart revealed to an associate extracts from Katakazi's official correspondence with St. Petersburg that had been passed to him by Tasistro; the clerk later stated that he had received them from an inside source at the Russian legation—"Bodisko."[79] One draft purported to be a dis-

78. Katakazi to Gorchakov, 10/22 November 1869, f. 138, op. 467, d. 71/76/77 (1867–1881), AVPR. He added in another letter of the same date, "It is only to Your Excellency that I tell this."

79. Perry Collins to Fish, 27 April 1870, vol. 69, Fish Papers, LC. The name of the source was passed verbally.

patch to the "Russian foreign minister," in which Katakazi made undiplomatic and unflattering references to Hamilton Fish ("a very weak and vacil-
lating man") and mentioned an instruction that professed the Russian
government's desire to settle the claim. Stewart prevailed on Louis Dent to
take these documents, which would strongly prejudice Katakazi's position,
directly to the president, who quickly summoned his secretary of state. Fish
then conferred with Stewart on 10 March to confirm the circumstances of
the leak.[80]

Unfortunately for Stewart and the Perkins claim, the authenticity of this
correspondence had not been thoroughly checked. The report, allegedly
written by Katakazi, referred to an instruction from the foreign minister's
"recent predecessor," but Gorchakov had held that position continually
since 1856. When Fish summoned Katakazi to explain his insulting language, the Russian envoy easily convinced the secretary that the documents
were forgeries on the basis of this rather obvious error.[81] Fish was also
annoyed by two other aspects of the affair. The letter asserted that Fish had
not supported the Perkins claim and had even recommended his son-in-law
to Katakazi as a New York attorney who could assist him in combating
Stewart. Fish and Katakazi knew that these insinuations were far from the
truth; the documents thus gave the appearance that the author was trying
to damage both men. The secretary of state was also unhappy that Stewart
and Dent had gone to the president first, thus needlessly agitating him, before the documents had been throughly examined by the State Department.[82]

In a follow-up investigation, Tasistro failed to identify Konstantin Bodisko, the secretary of legation, as the "Bodisko" who brought him the documents, while Vladimir Bodisko, the acting consul general in New York,

80. Stewart to Dent, 2 March 1870, and Stewart to Fish, 8 March 1870, vol. 68, and
Stewart to Fish, 24 April 1870, vol. 69, Fish Papers, LC; Fish diary, 3, 13, and 14
March, reel 2, ibid. The undated documents in question are contained in vol. 74 of the
Fish Papers. Fish conducted much of the business of the State Department during his
tenure under the cover of "private and confidential"—and kept the documents for his
own personal files. The official diplomatic papers in the National Archives, consequently, reveal only a part of American foreign relations for this period.

81. Katakazi to Fish and Fish to Katakazi, 13 March 1870, vol. 68, Fish Papers, LC.

82. Fish gave Dent a lecture about this: "The ordinary course of such things is
through the State Department and not through the President. . . . I think that your
personal relations to the President ought to have prevented you from going there in a
matter of advice." Dent's meek response was, "I shall learn something of diplomacy."
Fish, memorandum of interview with Stewart and Dent, 4 May 1870, vol. 69, Fish Papers, LC.

flatly denied having had anything to do with it.[83] Forced to admit that the
papers were forgeries and that his handling of the business had been imprudent, Stewart felt he had somehow been a victim of Katakazi's manipula-
tions.[84] As evidence he cited the remarkable similarity between the wording
in the "forgery" and that in an indisputably genuine letter, which Katakazi
had unwisely published on 11 March, along with one Cassius Clay had
written to him; both pieces were sharply critical of the Perkins claim.[85] It is
unlikely that Katakazi would have risked the serious backlash from planting
such a document with Tasistro, but he already had a reputation for being
careless with both pen and tongue and for being something of a schemer.
The Russian minister, of course, claimed that Stewart and his henchmen
were responsible. The real author remains unknown, but it was probably
someone outside the diplomatic corps who was opposed to both Katakazi
and Fish, who supported the Perkins claim, and who may have lifted draft
dispatches from the premises of the Russian legation.

The outcome was better than Katakazi could have expected—a significant
setback for the Perkins claimants and for Stewart personally. But Katakazi
also saw his relations with the Grant administration deteriorate over the
published letter to Clay and because of questions raised about him by the
Perkins claimants.[86] Most important, the brouhaha in Washington forced
Gorchakov to restate his opposition to the claim while strongly denying the

83. Bodisko to Fish on 26 April, Fish memorandum, 4 May 1870, ibid. Perry Collins, an old friend of the Bodiskos, witnessed the confrontation with Tasistro; Collins to
Fish, 27 April 1870, ibid. Tasistro, who was aged and ill and desperate for financial support, would later cite additional evidence of Katakazi's alleged disrespect toward Grant
and Fish, giving "Kuastoff" as his source in the Russian legation, but there was no one
by or close to that name on the staff; Tasistro to Fish, 17 January 1872, vol. 85, Fish Papers, LC; *Annuaire diplomatique de l'Empire de Russie pour l'année 1870*, vol. 10 (St. Petersburg: Journal de St.-Petersbourg, 1870), p. 43.

84. Katakazi reported that Stewart boasted in a tavern "of having succeeded 'to
break the neck of that infernal Russian Minister.' " Katakazi, who usually wrote in English to Americans, to Fish, 26 April 1870, vol. 69, Fish Papers, LC.

85. "Russia and America," Washington *Chronicle*, 11 March 1870, containing Clay
to Katakazi, 1 March 1870, and Katakazi to Clay, 8 March 1870. Clay authorized Katakazi to publish his letter if he wished, no doubt tempting the minister to act rashly.
Stewart then noted the similarities to the forgery and had them printed for circulation;
Stewart to Fish, 24 April 1870, vol. 69, Fish Papers, LC.

86. See, for example, Washington *National Republican*, 22 April 1870. Katakazi per-
sistently argued with Fish about the charges but kept his sense of humor. When he
asked for one more interview before the matter rested for the summer, he added, "I
hope that for the last time you will submit to that annoyance without saying to me,
'Shoo, Russian fly don't bother me.' " Katakazi to Fish, 7 June 1870, vol. 70, Fish Papers, LC.

authenticity of the documents. When Fish asked Curtin to discuss the possibility of an unbinding arbitration, "leaving the Imperial Government free to accept or reject a report in favor of the claim at its pleasure," Gorchakov's response was recorded by Curtin for Fish's private consumption:

> "But," said the Prince, "the claim has been repeatedly presented and examined and rejected, and I cannot find the least shadow of foundation for it. . . . Do not let us have this Perkins claim disturb and annoy us. It should not be considered by the Government of the United States and the Government of My August Master. It has no foundation but is an attempt to perpetuate a fraud and to extort money. I do so love and admire your country and I have shown my friendship." I expressed my satisfaction at such words, and he said: "Say it to the President and to Mr. Fish; let us not weaken a sincere friendship by meddling with this baseless claim." As I left his room, he repeated, "Do say that to Mr. Fish."[87]

Curtin reflected on the conversation: "Mr. Catacazy has developed in Washington the traits of character which made him in a large measure unpopular here, and I am quite sure he is the cause of the irritation which Prince Gortchacoff exhibits when the Perkins claim is mentioned."[88] Though asserting that it had nothing to do with the Perkins wrangle, Gorchakov had his own card to play: a charge for interest owed for the delay in the payment for Alaska.[89]

Meanwhile, the Russian envoy inexplicably agreed to Fish's suggestion to have an impartial government official judge the merits of the case on the understanding that the results were not binding. In May 1871, E. Pestrine Smith, a solicitor for the State Department, disallowed the claim on the powder contract (for the curious reason that Russia had no authority to make such an arrangement in the United States) but upheld the second claim on the rifles for a grand total of $550,000, including interest.[90] Not only was this an unsatisfactory decision for Russia, but Gorchakov had already firmly ruled out any such settlement; the whole business was soon awash with diplomatic bodies.

87. Curtin to Fish, 11 May 1870, vol. 69, Fish Papers, LC.
88. Curtin to Fish, 20 May 1870, DUSM, Russia, vol. 22 (roll 22, M 35), RG 59, NA.
89. Curtin to Fish (private and confidential), 13/25 May 1870, ibid.
90. Stewart to Fish, 27 September 1873, vol. 97, Fish Papers, LC.

The Katakazi Affair

Stoeckl's successor as Russian minister to the United States was a flamboyant, egotistical diplomat of Greek nationality with several years' previous experience in the United States as a secretary to Alexander Bodisko in the 1850s. More recently, Katakazi had held a position in Gorchakov's ministry in St. Petersburg that involved censoring or at least managing information printed in Russia about foreign relations. In his efforts to shape public opinion to support the government's goals, he corresponded with publicists such as Mikhail Katkov, the influential editor of *Moskovskiia Vedomosti* (Moscow record). He was thus familiar with and accustomed to press manipulation, and he would put this skill to use in the United States, with unhappy results. Katakazi owed his status as Gorchakov's protégé to the fact that his father was an old service friend of the chancellor's.[91]

After he was named as Stoeckl's replacement, Katakazi confided to Katkov that close relations between Russia and the United States were especially important for Russia's objectives "on Eastern soil," by which he meant the Balkans and the eastern Mediterranean. Because of his familiarity with those goals, Katakazi declared, Gorchakov had personally selected him. He hoped that Katkov would support him in his new endeavors and against the efforts of his Petersburg enemies, such as Karl Osten-Saken—thus hinting of another reason for his departure for Washington.[92]

Besides his opponents in St. Petersburg and his fondness for publicity, Katakazi had one other possible liability for his new diplomatic assignment—his spouse. Before his first American tour Katakazi served as a secretary to the legation in Rio de Janeiro, where he reportedly stole the young and pretty wife of the elderly Neapolitan minister. He then brought her, as his mistress, to Washington, where she was duly ostracized by the diplomatic community. Now she returned as wife of the minister of a vital and friendly country, and she had access to a practically unlimited expense account, which put Washington society in a quandary.[93] Moreover, she was still beautiful—and flaunted it. According to *Harper's Weekly*, "Madame De Catacazy, wife of the Russian ambassador, is reported to be a woman of remarkable beauty. Her complexion is wonderfully clear, her form 'perfect,' and her manners courtly and elegant. But her crowning beauty is her wealth of

91. For several letters from the elder Katakazi, see f. 828, op. 1, d. 455 (chefs et collègues de service, 1823–1834), TsGAOR.
92. Katakazi to Katkov, 9/21 June 1869, Katkov Papers, f. 39, RNL.
93. Alexandre Tarsaidze, *Czars and Presidents: The Story of a Forgotten Friendship* (New York: McDowell, Obolensky, 1958), p. 261.

golden hair, which all admit to be natural in color and quantity, and which is of that rare shade about which poets and painters rave."[94] She thus managed to attract considerable crowds to her lavish Monday evening soirees, while district tongues wagged.

In weathering the Perkins storms, Katakazi had clearly demonstrated his arrogance and lack of tact when he published his correspondence with Cassius Clay. Moreover, at a gala 1870 Fourth of July celebration in Woodstock, Connecticut, attended by President Grant and other political dignitaries, he had managed what was interpreted as an incautious insult:

It was eminently proper that the Russian Minister should make a speech; not that the Muscovites have achieved fame as orators, but because, as a representative of a friendly nation, the honorable gentleman from St. Petersburg had a right to be heard. He was in no wise abashed by the artillery, flags and enthusiasm—this envoy of the Czar's. But rising superior to the indigenous self-glorification of the happy occasion, he coolly took us down a peg or two by the information that "he expressed the feelings of 82,000,000 Russians, and he hoped that feeling was reciprocated by 40,000,000 of Americans." The feeling alluded to was one of the warmest friendship, but it came from 82,000,000 to 40,000,000. In other words, the Russian orator represented double the number of people than the President of the United States. . . . But the race is not always to the swift, nor the battle to the strong; and, notwithstanding the immense majority, we still think that our people can celebrate their National anniversary with more vim and sincerity than three times the number of Russians.[95]

Regarding the Perkins claim, the new minister was obviously annoyed that Americans could not take "no" for an answer and that each new administration stubbornly renewed the case. He decided, since the Alaska business was settled and the check safely in the bank, that he would launch

94. *Harper's Weekly*, 12 March 1870, p. 171. Apparently, Katakazi was not unappreciative of his wife. The Boston *Daily Advertiser*, 31 January 1871, reported: "Mr. De Catacazy . . . devised a very pretty method of celebrating his wife's birthday. . . . Her husband's monogram, wrought in flowers, was sent her on a silver platter. In every flower forming the monogram was placed a gold dollar. At the dinner that day concealed music again lent its charms to the happy anniversary."

95. Philadelphia *Inquirer*, 6 July 1870.

a counterattack and get rid of this business once and for all. He seized upon the opportunity of the Clay letter and accomplished his goal, but at the cost of his career, his mental health, and considerable strain to Russian-American relations.

As noted previously, Fish formally unloaded the claim once more on the Russian legation, along with a proposal for arbitration after President Grant indicated an interest in the problem at a cabinet meeting at the end of January 1870.[96] After the forged documents episode and the arbitration outcome, a succession of unsatisfactory conversations and exchanges of notes followed. In one, Katakazi overloaded Fish with a 120-page refutation, arguing in no uncertain terms that the entire claim rested on "absolutely fictitious foundations."[97] Katakazi went on to declare that it was devised as a plot against Stoeckl and the Russian government, that it was impossible that Stoeckl had concluded any agreement with Perkins without authorization from St. Petersburg, and that the "contract" in question was the work of an unscrupulous "Jewish" spy from Poland named Charles Rackelwicz. According to Katakazi, "it is evident that Perkins and Rakielevitch formed a partnership in order to set a trap for Mr. Stoeckl." He thought it was absurd to suppose that the Russian government would deal with a man like Benjamin Perkins. "It is then to a captain in the merchant marine, who caused the wreck of several vessels; to a man entirely without means, and addicted to drunkenness, that Mr. Stoeckl applied to furnish an immense quantity of powder and arms to his Government?" He charged Stewart with forging documents and "propagating the most calumnious assertions against the Imperial Government and its Representative in the United States."[98]

Katakazi had clearly overstepped diplomatic decorum, but his real troubles began with a series of newspaper articles. The opening salvo was an anonymous letter to the editor of the New York *World*, published on 29 November 1870, that accused President Grant himself with personal involvement in the Perkins case and described in detail Katakazi's grievances against the United States government. The minister denied authorship, writing Fish privately that these "absurdities . . . created an uncomfortable feeling against me in the mind of the President as well as in yours."[99] The sec-

96. Nevins, *Hamilton Fish*, 1:505.
97. Katakazi to Fish, 12/24 August 1870, NRL, vol. 7 (roll 5, M 39), RG 59, NA.
98. Ibid. For more on the case, see Norman E. Saul, *Distant Friends: The United States and Russia, 1763–1867* (Lawrence: University Press of Kansas, 1991), pp. 213, 232, 254–56.
99. Katakazi to Fish, 1 December 1870, vol. 74, Fish Papers, LC.

retary of state and many others, however, believed Katakazi was trying to sway American public opinion in his favor and against the Grant administration. George Adams, the *World's* chief Washington reporter, assumed responsibility but would not at first reveal his source. Further investigation indicated that the "letter" was actually written by E. J. Harrington, who said he had received the material directly from Katakazi and had left the text for him to check before it was approved by Adams and sent to New York. Katakazi denied this, while Harrington inconveniently disappeared.[100]

A detective, hired by Fish to investigate, uncovered three other press connections with Katakazi: a "messenger" for the New York *Herald*, a Miss Snead who wrote under the name of Mrs. Grundy for the *World*, and free-lance attorney Turk were all habitués at the Russian legation. He also brought to light that the Russian minister was "a frequenter of common saloons and tippling shops" and used extremely profane language in public.[101] By this time, Katakazi had additional complaints, such as exclusion from Fish's diplomatic dinners and receptions, which he had mentioned in the *World* letter.[102] The aggrieved Russian minister now openly took his case to the public with the help of the New York *Herald*, but he only exacerbated the situation.

Relations between the Russian legation and the Grant administration seemed to improve briefly in the early months of 1871, as Fish was immersed in other issues, notably the negotiations with Britain over the *Alabama* claims (Treaty of Washington) and the Canadian fisheries dispute. In March, however, reports surfaced in both Washington and St. Petersburg that Katakazi was intermeddling in these affairs in an effort to prevent an Anglo-American rapprochement. To Fish the minister flatly denied it, but in recommending to Gorchakov the promotion of Boris Danzas to the position of first secretary, Katakazi praised his role in "suppressing the English cause."[103] Meanwhile, Curtin learned from the British embassy in St. Petersburg that the foreign minister was preparing a formal protest of Katakazi's actions, and

100. Katakazi to Fish, 24 December 1870, ibid. Harrington was the son of a former minister to Sweden and had visited Russia. In 1872, Stewart ran into Harrington in a Topeka, Kansas, hotel. In an interview with Stewart, Harrington confirmed that the letter was based on material furnished by Katakazi and was approved by him. Stewart (Topeka) to Fish, 30 November 1872, vol. 91, Fish Papers, LC; "The Catacazy Imbroglio," Topeka *Daily Commonwealth*, 30 November 1872.

101. H. C. Whitley to Fish, 1 February 1870 [1871], vol. 76, Fish Papers, LC.

102. Katakazi to Fish, 3 December 1870, vol. 74, Fish Papers, LC.

103. Katakazi to Fish, 12 March 1871, vol. 77, Fish Papers, LC; Katakazi to Gorchakov, 2/14 April 1871, f. 133, op. 470, d. 124 (1871), AVPR.

he led Fish to believe that Russia was about to make a change in its Washington mission.[104]

The last straw, as far as Fish was concerned, was a newspaper piece that appeared in the Cincinnati *Inquirer* over the name of a "Washington correspondent," Don Piatt, who could not be identified; the article focused on President Grant's bias toward Britain, a sensitive political matter. The secretary of state once more confronted the Russian minister, who again protested his innocence and blamed a conspiracy led by the claimants to obtain his recall.[105] Tension mounted as the "forgeries" of a year earlier now appeared in the press.[106] Fish and his assistant Bancroft Davis believed that Katakazi was deliberately trying to undermine the negotiations with Britain. Seeking proof, they applied pressure to Frank Turk, who then confessed: "I am compelled to say in justice to myself that while I do not now and never have charged Mr. Catacazy with the authorship of the article in question [Cincinnati *Inquirer*], he most certainly and positively asserted to me on my calling his attention to the same, that he knew all about it for he himself had written it."[107] Katakazi hotly denied it, accusing Fish and his department of fabricating the story in a sharply worded, undiplomatic letter.[108]

Fish took the letter as a personal insult and formally demanded through Curtin on 16 June 1871 that Russia recall Katakazi; he then dropped the subject for a while as Washington began its usual summer recess, leading Katakazi to believe that the quarrel was dissipating.[109] While at a retreat on Staten Island, the Russian envoy met with Fish in mid-August as the secretary passed through New York, and he asked that one of his harshly worded notes be returned for amendment. Fish refused and informed him of the request for his dismissal. The next day the shocked Katakazi called unan-

104. Curtin to Fish, 8/20 March 1871, vol. 77, Fish Papers, LC.

105. Katakazi to Fish, 16/28 April [16/28 May] 1871, vol. 79, and Fish to Katakazi (draft), 31 May 1871, vol. 80, Fish Papers, LC.

106. Washington *Evening Post*, 10 June 1871.

107. Turk to Fish, 12 June 1871, vol. 80, Fish Papers, LC.

108. Katakazi to Fish, 31 May/12 June 1871, ibid. As a curious sidelight, General Nikolai Ignat'ev, Russian ambassador to the Ottoman Empire, later claimed that Blacque Bey, the Turkish minister in Washington, was at the bottom of Katakazi's troubles, that he had "set him up" with reporters and encouraged his publications. The suggested motive was Turkish anxiety about growing Russian-American friendship. "Ignatieff really believes that in the Catacazy affair Blacque, by his cunningly contrived and bad advice, sought to embroil the enemy of his country with the U.S., and thus weaken the ancient friendship existing between us and Russia." George Henry Boker (Constantinople) to Fish, 2 June 1873, vol. 94, Fish Papers, LC.

109. To Curtin, 26 June 1871, DI, Russia, vol. 15, (roll 137, M 77), RG 59, NA.

nounced on President Grant at Long Branch to plead his case, much to the president's annoyance.[110]

In St. Petersburg the request for recall also came as a surprise and reached Russia at an awkward time in the summer of 1871 when Gorchakov was on an extended leave at a spa in Germany. Vladimir Westmann, in charge of the ministry, insisted that he lacked authority to act on it himself and desperately wanted to keep the news from the emperor for fear of his reaction.[111] According to George Pomutz, who had accompanied Curtin for an interview on the subject and kept a memorandum of the conversation,

> he [Westmann] continued to say: that in regard to America and the ministers accredited there, the difficulty is much greater, on account of the free press and speech ruling there, and of everybody being permitted to write or say what he pleased, and what he thinks most necessary for the purpose of advancing—openly or underhand—his private interests. . . . There is another class of men that may have an interest in fostering disharmony between Mr. Fish and Mr. Catacazy—namely: such of other nationalities as were always jealous of the good relations and friendship between this and the American people; America and Great Britain are now approaching each other with friendly feelings soon to be restored between them fully.[112]

Westmann also remarked, pointedly but not in excuse, that the Russian government had tolerated all sorts of bad behavior on the part of Cassius Clay.

One of the chief concerns on both sides was the impending visit to the United States of Grand Duke Alexis, the third son of the emperor. Westmann thought that the demand for the minister's recall might force a cancellation of the visit, but Fish hoped to avoid having to deal with Katakazi in connection with any formal reception of the grand duke in Washington. He was therefore disappointed that Russia did not immediately respond to

110. Fish to Katakazi (draft), 25 August 1871, vol. 82, Fish Papers, LC; Katakazi (New York) to Westmann, 10/22 August and 20 August/1 September 1871, f. 170, op. 512/3, d. 107, AVPR. Obviously surprised and agitated, Katakazi claimed in his note of 10/22 August that "his recall [was] without precedent in the annals of diplomacy" and referred to the whole business as "a triple intrigue."

111. Curtin to Fish, 7/19 July 1871, DUSM, Russia, vol. 22 (roll 22, M 35), RG 59, NA. Westmann also admitted another element of the reluctance to act: the emperor had not wanted to appoint Katakazi but had been convinced by the Foreign Ministry, so a recall would damage the reputation of the ministry and Gorchakov personally.

112. Pomutz to Fish, 9/21 July 1871, ibid.

his request, believing that Westmann and Gorchakov could have resolved the matter by telegraph.[113] Fish then cabled Curtin that he must not have pressed the recall energetically enough and in strong language demanded action: "*Catacazy has* through the press and in conversation endeavored to give it [the Perkins claim] undue importance and *to make it the cause of trouble between the governments and of annoyance.* He has made himself *personally offensive* in conversation and by publications *abusive of the President* and it is for this cause, that *his recall is asked.*"[114]To compound the tragicomedy, this telegram was garbled in transmission, leaving Curtin quite confused until clarifications reached him. He immediately sought another meeting with Westmann and at last obtained Russia's agreement to a recall on the condition that it be delayed until after the grand duke's visit. In a long telegram Curtin reflected on the ironic context of the recent events:

The Grand Duke has sailed—his visit is looked upon in Europe as having great political significance—it has been magnified into ridiculous and absurd extravagance by the press of our country and has excited expectation in our people that to disappoint would require explanation. Besides there is in the United States an impression that there is great sympathy between the peoples of the two countries which is a delusion a residence here soon dispels. There are not nations in Christendom more dissimilar and there are in fact no privileged classes no legitimate rulers in Europe who have a more decided disrelish of free institutions than those who rule this Empire.[115]

This cable arrived at the State Department at 8:00 P.M. on 14 September, and a clerk spent the night decoding it.[116] The next day Fish showed it to the president, who thought Katakazi "should be presented with his *walking papers*" at once.[117] Emulating Curtin's language, Fish wrote:

Our people have an exaggerated idea of the friendship of Russia for this Government—like all international friendships this one is of interest rather than sentiment or sympathy, but the popular belief that it is real

113. Fish to Curtin, 18 August 1871 (t), DI, Russia, vol. 15 (roll 137, M 77), RG 59, NA.
114. Fish to Curtin, 5 September 1871 (t), ibid.
115. Curtin to Fish, 10 September 1871, vol. 82, Fish Papers, LC.
116. The clerk commented about the task: "Yes our Cipher is a grand one, if its only mission is to make a man crazy." Chew to Fish, 18 September 1871, ibid.
117. Grant (Long Branch) to Fish, 10 September 1871, ibid.

cannot be mistaken. Russia has used it (as we have also done) as an element to operate upon other Powers, in negotiating with them. It may still be of some avail to us, while the arbitration of the Alabama question and of the San Juan boundary are pending—and although the peremptory dismissal of a minister would not afford any just grounds of complaint, it might produce some irritation, which would exhibit itself by arresting the visit of the Prince, of which an effort will be made to take advantage in connection with pending arbitrations.[118]

Fish did seek a compromise solution—to allow Katakazi to remain until the grand duke's arrival—and Grant reluctantly agreed: "The course you recommend is no doubt right, but I feel very much like sending Mr. C. out of the country very summarily. . . . No Minister of any pride of character would consent to remain at a Capital after just such an interview as Mr. C. had with me [at Long Branch]. How he is to be received now at any entertainment given to the Prince I do not exactly see."[119]

By nature, Katakazi could not remain inactive, and behind the scenes in New York he carried on contradictory campaigns to both pacify and undercut Fish. He asserted that he had support from a number of influential Americans—senators Charles Sumner and Simon Cameron, Thomas Cottman, General Benjamin Butler, Judge Charles Daly, Admiral David Porter, Gustavus Fox—who either had little use for the secretary of state or were willing to lend a sympathetic ear to the Russian minister.[120] With their help he also doubled his efforts to organize a colossal reception for the grand duke, which would also serve as a demonstration against Grant and Fish.

Meanwhile, Katakazi received reports in September of a plot formed by

118. Fish to Grant, 15 September 1871, ibid.

119. Grant (Long Branch) to Fish, 19 September 1871, ibid. Another reason for Gorchakov's hesitation about changing ministers that apparently eluded Fish and Grant was his desire to maintain stability in the Russian diplomatic corps. The leading Russian diplomats at the time and total tenures at their assignments were: Philipp Brunnow (London)—30 years; Iakov Dashkov (Stockholm)—20 years; Paul Oubril (Berlin)—17 years; Artur Mohrenheim (Copenhagen)—15 years; Nikolai Orlov (Paris)—13 years; Ignat'ev (Constantinople)—13 years; Nikolai Stolypin (The Hague)—13 years; Evgenyi Novikov (Vienna)—9 years. Erik Amburger, *Geschichte der Behördenorganisation Russlands von Peter dem Grossen bis 1917* (Leiden: E. J. Brill, 1966), pp. 443–51.

120. Katakazi (New York) to Westmann, 1/13 September 1871, f. 170, op. 512/3, d. 108, AVPR. Thomas Cottman, fearing damage to Russian-American relations, wrote to Katakazi with "expression of my sentiments touching on the unjust persecution you have experienced." Cottman to Katakazi, 9 October 1871, f. 133, op. 470, d. 123 (1871), AVPR.

dissident emigré Poles against the life of the grand duke. He hired the Pin-kerton Detective Agency, and they found some substance to the rumor that a New York Polish secret committee was seeking a hit man from Switz-erland. So alarmed was the minister that he even stooped to an interview on 27 September with the secretary of state on the subject, and the New York police were duly alerted.[121]

By the beginning of October, when the news that he would only "be tol-erated" became public, Katakazi gave up on Fish. He wrote to Senator Cameron, former minister to Russia, that he was putting an end to all ef-forts at reconciliation.

> There are limits that cannot be passed without loss of dignity and self respect. . . . I said and repeated to Mr. Fish [apparently on 27 Septem-ber] that I asked . . . to be relieved from the irksome duty of remaining in Washington. . . . The renewed outrage was consequently as gratui-tous as it was unprovoked and it must be difficult to find a precedent for it in the annals of international history of civilized nations.

The same day Katakazi facetiously wrote to Westmann that he was "happy to be sacrificed to the interests of the Emperor."[122]

Gorchakov, returning from his rest to find relations with the United States in upheaval, notified Katakazi that he should cease his functions as minister as soon as the grand duke completed his tour.[123] Fish, however, in-formed Katakazi that he would suffer his presence only through the official reception in Washington, leaving an awkward gap.[124] To his diplomatic

121. Katakazi to Fish, 16/28 September 1871 (draft) and Katakazi to Westmann, 30 September/12 October 1871, f. 170, op. 512/3, d. 108, AVPR. Aleksandr Gorlov later sent a check to Pinkerton's for $1,080.80; Gorlov to H. W. Davies, Pinkerton's (c), 16/28 December 1871, ibid.

122. Katakazi to Cameron, 3 October 1871 (c) and 21 September/3 October 1871, ibid.

123. Gorchakov to Katakazi, 30 October and 25 November 1871 (t), f. 133, op. 470, d. 124, AVPR; Gorchakov to Curtin, 21 December 1871, DPR, Russia, vol. 4503 (notes received), RG 84, NA. On 26 December, Gorchakov cabled his surprise that the minis-ter was not back in St. Petersburg; Gorchakov to Katakazi, 14 December 1871, f. 133, op. 470, d. 124, AVPR.

124. Katakazi to Gorchakov, 2/14 and 6/18 November 1871 (nos. 99 and 100), f. 133, op. 470, d. 123, AVPR. In agreeing to Gorchakov's insistence that Katakazi stay for Alexis's arrival, Fish had already cabled Curtin: "The President, however, will not for-mally *receive Mr. Catacazy* except when he *accompanies* the *Prince*, and can *hold no con-versation* with him." Draft, 20 September 1871, vol. 82, Fish Papers, LC; without em-phases, see DI, Russia, vol. 15 (roll 137, M 77), RG 59, NA.

corps, Fish exaggerated the extent of Katakazi's meddling, making it appear that the Russian minister had published many slanderous letters rather than two or three, and implied that he had absolute proof of Katakazi's authorship of the *Inquirer* letter.[125]

But the Russian foreign minister issued his last words on the matter and won the day. In a note, dated 16 December, Gorchakov declared a final and firm rejection of the Perkins claim, decried the "want of courtesy" on the part of the United States, and lamented "that such things might have the effect of injuring the friendly relations which had hitherto existed."[126] He also defended Katakazi against Fish's charge that he had attempted to hinder an Anglo-American rapprochement in the *Alabama* settlement. And a more explicit article in *Moskovskiia Vedomosti*, which Gorchakov no doubt had published, accused the president of being childish and undignified and charged Bancroft Davis of the State Department with pro-British and anti-Russian prejudices. Yet, the article concluded: "These people come and go, but the state remains, the nation remains, its real interests remain, and Americans understand their own interests very well, and we can be assured of the maintenance of our good relations with them."[127]

One serious complication was that Katakazi at this time did not have an able secretary present in Washington, since the Bodiskos were on leave in St. Petersburg. Boris Danzas, the second secretary, was suffering an acute mental disorder, caused by being nearly trampled by the crowd greeting Alexis and perhaps by the stress of the diplomatic squabbling. In any event Katakazi thought that he had been too intimately involved in the Perkins communications to be acceptable to Fish.[128] So, Major General Aleksandr Gorlov, a quasi-secret military agent who spent most of his time at the Colt factory in Hartford, Connecticut, was independently named by Katakazi as

125. For example, Fish to J. P. Brown (Constantinople), 10 October 1871, DI, Turkey, vol. 2 (roll 163, M 77), RG 59, NA. Fish concluded this long explanation: "The object of sending you this statement, is not that you give publicity to what is stated, but that you may correct any erroneous representations of the circumstances, and may, if necessary, explain the action of this Government."

126. Enclosure (translation by Schuyler) in Curtin to Fish, 18 December 1871, DUSM, Russia, vol. 23 (roll 23, M 35), RG 59, NA.

127. Gorchakov note, 21 December 1871/2 January 1872, and article dated 23 December, enclosures translated by Schuyler, in Curtin to Fish, 6 January 1872, DUSM, Russia, vol. 23 (roll 23, M 35), RG 59, NA.

128. Katakazi to Gorchakov, 16/28 November 1871 (no. 102), f. 133, op. 470, d. 123 (1871); and 22 December/3 January 1872, f. 133, op. 470, d. 112 (1872), AVPR.

"temporary liaison" to the State Department for the Russian mission.[129] Katakazi later obeyed Gorchakov's explicit instructions, transferred his authority in early January 1872 to third secretary Vladimir Shirkov, and departed for St. Petersburg.[130]

In the interim, Fish summed up all the charges directly to Katakazi on 24 November, underscoring his slander of the president. The minister answered with bitterness: "I am under the necessity . . . of protesting at once in the most formal manner against all the charges made against me in that note. . . . I have on no occasion and in no manner been wanting in the profound respect due to the chief magistrate of the American people, and to the regard of the Federal Government."[131] Katakazi concluded by wisely asking for continued diplomatic immunity until his departure from the United States. This was granted provided that he not take legal action against any American.[132]

Heinrich Offenberg, who had held only a minor diplomatic appointment (minister to Rumania), was named Katakazi's successor and arrived in Washington in late April 1872, thus finally putting official relations on a regular basis again.[133] He was explicitly told to forward anything relating to the Perkins affair directly to St. Petersburg "without any discussion whatsoever."[134] But the claim was definitely and finally dead. Offenberg, however, following the lead of

---

129. Curtin to Fish, 22 December 1871, DUSM, Russia, vol. 23 (roll 23, M 35), RG 59, NA. Katakazi also distrusted Gorlov who, he claimed, mismanaged correspondence and nearly got into a duel with Shirkov over an insult to a woman; Katakazi (Montreal) to Gorchakov, 5/17 December 1871, f. 133, op. 470, d. 124 (1871), AVPR.

130. Katakazi to Gorchakov, 22 December 1871/3 January 1872, f. 133, op. 470, d. 112, AVPR. Within six weeks Katakazi was in Paris, complaining of ill health; Katakazi to Gorchakov, 28 January/9 February 1872, ibid.

131. Katakazi to Fish, 15/27 November 1871, NRL, vol. 7 (roll 5, M 39), RG 59, NA.

132. Shirkov to Gorchakov, 28 December 1871/9 January 1872, f. 133, op. 470, d. 112, AVPR. Stewart, dismayed by the downfall of the Perkins case and his own reputation, begged Katakazi to waive immunity for a judicial investigation and promised to claim no damages, "my only object being to vindicate myself from the false position in which you have placed me." J. B. Stewart to Katakazi, 3 January 1872, f. 170, op. 512/3, d. 107 (1871), AVPR.

133. Offenberg to Gorchakov, 18/30 April 1872, f. 133, op. 470, d. 112 (1872), AVPR. It is not clear from the records whether the appointment of this minister was a sign of Gorchakov's disfavor toward the United States or whether Offenberg was the only reliable person available on short notice. He was, nonetheless, preceded by favorable impressions from Schuyler and George Bancroft, the American minister in Berlin—for example, Bancroft to Fish, 24 March 1872, vol. 86, Fish Papers, LC.

134. Gorchakov to Offenberg, 20 January 1872, f. 133, op. 470, d. 112 (1872), AVPR.

some of his American counterparts, could not tolerate the Washington climate and retired in May 1874 to his home in Kurland.[135]

Gorchakov and Fish were both happy to have the affair settled, but a black cloud seemed to hang over the grand duke's arrival. Certain voices in the press also declared that Russian-American relations had reached a definite turning point: "The Catacazy affair has plainly ended in the rupture of the *entente cordiale* between this country and Russia."[136] More typical, however, was an editorial comment in the Washington *Evening Star*: "The affair is not unlike getting rid of a rotten tooth—an unpleasant proceeding, in every way, but all the better for being done with and out of the way."[137]

The "rotten tooth" was at first sanguine about the outcome. In a speech he gave in Boston on the occasion of the grand duke's visit, Katakazi reflected candidly, "If the goddess of diplomacy were to be sculptured I would present her wrapped in a dark robe with a finger on her lips. More than anyone else I should adopt that attitude, and wrap as close as possible and hold my finger as tight as possible to chain my lips."[138] But after the publication of Fish's charges against him, as well as the unkind words in Gorchakov's letter of recall, he became very bitter. He pressed his case in St. Petersburg to no avail and left after a few weeks for permanent exile in Paris, where he would spend more time defending himself.[139]

Disgraced by his government, Katakazi seemed to become unhinged for a while. Prince Nikolai Orlov, the Russian ambassador to France, told the American minister that Katakazi looked very strange and that his wife thought he was crazy. "He is a very dangerous man, and I tell you this confidentially that I have orders to put him under surveillance—He says there must be war between Russia and the United States and he will do all the harm he can."[140] In fact, Katakazi regained some stature and more notoriety

135. Offenberg to Gorchakov, 23 April/5 May (Washington) and 16/28 June (Heidelberg) 1874, f. 133, op. 470, d. 144 (1874), AVPR.

136. *Nation* 14, 342 (18 January 1872): 33–34.

137. 24 November 1871. William Campbell put it more colorfully to Fish: "There is a little household instrument called an *extinquisher*; you have put it on his head and his fire has literally gone out." 19 December 1971, vol. 84, Fish Papers, LC.

138. New York *Times*, 11 December 1871.

139. According to Schuyler, in charge while Curtin vacationed in Nice, Katakazi left Russia at the end of March. Schuyler to Fish, 31 March 1872, vol. 86, Fish Papers, LC. For his continuing apologia, see M. de Catacazy, *Un incident diplomatique: Lettre au Chief Justice S. Chase* (Paris: Arnyot, 1872); Katakazi to Gorchakov, 15/27 December 1871, f. 133, op. 470, d. 112 (1872), AVPR.

140. As quoted in Elihu Washburne to Fish, 16 April 1872, vol. 87, Fish Papers, MD, LC.

as a Pan-Slavist foreign agent and opponent of a Franco-Russian alliance in the 1880s.[141]

Retired former minister Stoeckl, fearing permanent damage to Russian-American relations because of the Katakazi affair, wrote a rare letter of advice to the Foreign Ministry. Although he had been out of action, "like an old battle horse," he retained his interest in the United States. Stoeckl stressed the importance of good relations for Russia and observed that "there are among us Americaphobes who claim that it is dangerous to be friends with a nation whose interests are so mobile."[142] He emphasized the importance of the Washington post, because most diplomacy is conducted there. Meanwhile, both Russia and the United States (and most historians) tried to sweep Katakazi and the Perkins imbroglio into their diplomatic and historical dustbins.[143] Reverberations, however, would shake Russian-American relations for several more years.

Other Troubles

American creditors and ventures in Russia were not faring well at this time. Another New England sea captain, D. C. Pierce, pursued a claim for losses incurred when his ship, loaded with railroad ties, was seized by the authorities of a Black Sea port on a legal technicality. Distance and bureaucratic obstacles caused long delays, and Pierce never obtained redress. Fish was careful to stay out of this one on the logical grounds that it was an internal

141. Katakazi (Paris) to Alexander II, 13/25 September 1879, f. 678, op. 1, d. 668, TsGAOR; George F. Kennan, *The Decline of Bismarck's European Order: Franco-Russian Relations, 1875–1890* (Princeton, N.J.: Princeton University Press, 1979), pp. 214, 326. Ilia Tsion, a Russian agent in France who knew Katakazi, later accused him of being a venomous triple agent—a manipulator of the French press for Foreign Minister Giers, chief of the Russian secret police in Paris, and Bismarck's tool against Katkov's plan to engineer a Franco-Russian alliance. Elie de Cyon, *Histoire de l'entente Franco-Russe, 1886–1894: Documents et souvenirs* (Paris: A. Charles, 1895), pp. 322–24, 361–62. Tsion asserted that Katakazi was exposed by the Paris newspaper *Figaro,* 16 January 1888.

142. Stoeckl (Paris) to Westmann, 19 October 1874, f. 133, op. 470, d. 127, AVPR.

143. They are not found at all in G. P. Kuropiatnik, *Rossii i SShA: Ekonomicheskie, kul'turnye i diplomaticheskie sviazi, 1867–1881* (Moscow: Nauka, 1981), the most complete source on the period, or William S. McFeely, *Grant: A Biography* (New York and London: W. W. Norton, 1981). Gorchakov's final word was that "Catacazy was a shrewd man of good ability and a fine writer, who had been with him four or five years in the Foreign Office, who he thought would be of great service in America, but that he turned out a meddlesome fellow, greatly lacking in judgment." Orr to Fish, 18 March 1873, DUSM, Russia, vol. 25 (roll 25, M 35), RG 59, NA.

matter for the Russian courts.[144] Silas Burrows, an old ally of Russia's, also failed in a renewed attempt to receive payment for losses that extended back to 1830.[145] Another friend in need to Russia, John P. Gowen, restated in vain his case for money still owed for the clearing of Sevastopol harbor after the Crimean War.[146] Even Anna Whistler ("Whistler's Mother") resubmitted a claim for salary due to her husband at the time of his death in Russian service in 1849, but without success.[147]

The most serious setback to American business in Russia occurred when the Russian government rejected William L. Winans's bid to purchase the St. Petersburg–Moscow Railroad. Winans had been involved with the manufacture and repair of locomotives and cars for this line since construction began in the early 1840s. In more recent years he had also operated the state railroad for the Russian government under a lucrative contract. Almost concurrent with the decision to sell Alaska, the government decided to divest itself of railroads. Winans spent a year preparing his bid of 100 million rubles to be paid over a five-year period. Sensing its rejection, he offered an additional guarantee of 6 million rubles per annum in a split of the profits.[148]

Instead, the government accepted the offer of the "Grand Society of Russian Railroads," which already controlled the lines from Warsaw to St. Petersburg and from Moscow to Nizhni-Novgorod. Schuyler, observing the defeat from Moscow, thought it was connected with Russian discontent over the delay in payment for Alaska and a rise in nationalist sentiment: "One great obstacle to Mr. Winans' success was the fact that he was an American. There was a great prejudice against allowing such an important road and so much money to go into the hands of a foreigner."[149]

There may have been another reason the Winans bid was passed over.

144. Curtin to Fish, 10 July and 28 September 1870, DUSM, Russia, vol. 21 (roll 21, M 35), RG 59, NA; Fish to Clay, 5 October 1870, DI, Russia, vol. 15 (roll 137, M 77), RG 59, NA.

145. Fish to Curtin, 26 September 1870, DI, Russia, vol. 15 (roll 137, M 77), RG 59, NA.

146. Gowen (St. Petersburg) to Boker, 15 March 1876, and to minister of navy, 29 January/February 10 1876, DPR, Russia, vol. 4436 (misc. received), RG 84, NA.

147. Arthur Livermore (U.S. consul, Londonderry) to Boker, 22 November and 11 December 1876, and 4 March 1877; Anna Whistler to Livermore, 9 December 1876, ibid.

148. Winans to Clay, 12 June 1868, and enclosed petitions dated 30 May/11 June and 6/18 June 1868, DPR, Russia, vol. 4534 (notes received), RG 84, NA. See the Boston *Daily Evening Transcript*, 6 November 1867, for an earlier version of the Winans bid that notes the involvement of London partners.

149. Schuyler to Seward, 7 July 1868, DUSC, Moscow, vol. 1 (roll 1, M 456), RG 59, NA.

Samuel Prime, a Presbyterian minister from New York, traveled by train between Moscow and St. Petersburg in the summer of 1867. "It is said in its praise that this great road was constructed by Americans, and it jolts us so naturally that we felt *at home* as soon as we started. It is no credit to our country that its road is the roughest in Europe."[150] Winans soon brought his Russian operations to a close and retired to Britain with the fortune he had made.[151] His defeat also affected the fortunes of industrialist Robert Williams, who complained of a sudden break in expected government orders for his Moscow factory.[152] Williams remained, however, and his large Russianized family occupied a prominent place in Moscow society.

The Winans family legacy lived on for a number of years through many employees who worked and were trained in their shops. For example, John Lehrs, a senior mechanic for the company, helped build the rail line to Sevastopol and then in the 1870s superintended the expansion of the Struve Bridge Works in Kolomna. His specialty was pattern making and casting. An Englishman in his company later commented, "I am told the workmen except the old hands have deteriorated since the days of Winans Brothers and the Nicolay Railway, the workshops of which formed the nucleus of the mechanical race of Russia."[153]

The Blackford Affair

The relative calm that descended on the American legation in St. Petersburg after the departure of Cassius Clay and the "settlement" of Katakazi was suddenly disrupted in April 1874. Harriet C. Blackford, an American citizen also known as "Phoenix" and as "Fanny Leer," had become the mis-

150. Prime diary, 14 June 1867, Speer Library, Princeton Theological Seminary. See also Samuel Irenaeus Prime, *The Alhambra and the Kremlin: The South and the North of Europe* (New York: Anson D. F. Randolph, 1873), p. 322.

151. The Winans family estates in Baltimore, Newport, and Brighton (England) were among the most lavish and impressive of the period, as was that of former partner Joseph Harrison, Jr., whose Philadelphia Rittenhouse Square mansion was modeled after a St. Petersburg palace and contained probably the finest private art collection in the United States, all bought with profits from Russia. Harrison obituary and editorial, Philadelphia *Inquirer*, 28 March 1874; E. Digby Baltzell, *Philadelphia Gentlemen: The Making of a National Upper Class* (Glencoe, Ill.: Free Press, 1958), pp. 183–84.

152. Schuyler to Seward, 30 July 1868, DUSC, Moscow, vol. 1 (roll 1, M 456), RG 59, NA.

153. Alfred Edward Garwood, partial manuscript of book, p. 87, copy in Duke University library.

tress of Grand Duke Nikolai Konstantinovich, the unstable son of Grand Duke Constantine and nephew of the tsar. Their affair first came to the attention of Marshall Jewell, the American minister, in January, when he learned that the grand duke had beaten her for being overly friendly to the Prince of Wales during a state visit.[154] The pair then came under suspicion when jewels belonging to the grand duke's mother were found by the secret police in a local pawn shop. But before the case broke, Blackford deposited a sizable amount of jewelry and a number of papers at the American legation. She was arrested, strip searched, and jailed. Petr Shuvalov, director of the notorious Third Section (state police), demanded that the jewelry and papers in the legation be turned over to him at once; it was believed that one document was a will leaving the grand duke's entire estate to Blackford.

Eugene Schuyler, as secretary of legation, negotiated with Shuvalov and police chief Fedor Trepov to have Blackford transferred to "a comfortable apartment." Although Jewell considered the objects in the legation under American custody, he had little sympathy for a woman with such a soiled reputation. To complicate matters further, the Russian Foreign Ministry would have nothing to do with the business. Jewell then sought the advice and intervention of the British and French ambassadors, the latter considered the dean of the diplomatic corps. Under pressure from various quarters, Blackford agreed to turn over the jewelry and papers, leave the country within ten days, and not appear in public, in exchange for a 50,000-ruble settlement ($25,000) and the return of any papers of a purely personal nature.[155] The grand duke was assigned to permanent duty in Central Asia.

Jewell was obviously worried and perplexed by the legal implications of the affair: "I am told that this is the first instance—in recent times at least—in which a Foreign Government has ever been brought in conflict with the Secret Police of Russia. . . . Such arrest and detention is clearly a violation of our treaty stipulations." He reported that the French ambassador told him "that it was the most grave, most delicate, and complicated question that he had ever known to arise here. He warmly commended my whole action in the affair and especially that I had shown such great willingness to

154. Jewell to Fish, 4 May 1874 (private), vol. 101, Fish Papers, LC. Jewell noted, "I have seen her many times on the street for she is very notorious but have never spoken to her."

155. Jewell to General Fedor Trepov (police chief of St. Petersburg), 16/28 April 1874 (c), DPR, Russia, vol. 4535 (notes sent), RG 84, NA; Jewell to Fish, 4 May 1874, DUSM, Russia, vol. 26 (roll 26, M 35), RG 59, NA. The details of the affair in this latter dispatch required thirty-four pages of text plus various enclosures.

avoid wounding the feelings of the Imperial family by consenting to avoid publicity."[156] Despite the singularity of the episode, Jewell concluded his laborious report by asking the secretary of state for advice on what to do in future cases!

Scrambled Commerce

Russian-American trade was a disappointment. The direct shipment of cotton to Russia, which had seemed so promising in the years between the Crimean War and the American Civil War, continued to decline. The Civil War itself was the main factor, combined with the disruption of plantation production in the Reconstruction period. Direct cotton imports never recovered to their prewar levels, and the British regained a near-monopoly of transatlantic haulage. When the war cut off Russia's prime source, demand spurred the expansion of cotton cultivation in Central Asia and the discovery of new sources in Egypt.[157] As a result, less cotton was carried on the few American ships that frequented Russian ports after 1867, though some cargoes came direct on foreign ships.[158]

Russian products such as hemp, linen cloth, and iron were also no longer in great demand in the United States, because of competition from domestic supplies or from new sources. For example, Americans increasingly used jute and sisal from the Philippines and Yucatan for rope and twine. But traditional Russian items still accounted for most of the exports from Russia: superior sheet iron cast from Ekaterinburg ore, bristles invested with special strength by the hard winters, horse hair available cheap, hemp of higher

156. Jewell to Fish, 4 May 1874, DUSM, Russia, vol. 26 (roll 26, M 35), RG 59, NA. The minister was also disturbed by evidence that "the Secret Police were even above the Foreign Office and acted by the direct orders of his Imperial Majesty, a state of things which of course I do not recognise officially."

157. "Report on the Cotton Trade of Central Asia," enclosure in Schuyler to Seward, 27 June 1868, DUSC, Moscow, vol. 1 (roll 1, M 456), RG 59, NA. Schuyler emphasized the connection between cotton demand and the Russian conquest of Central Asia, the use of irrigation in the area around Khiva, and the transport by camel caravan to Orenburg and from there by wagon train to Nizhni-Novgorod. See also Saul, *Distant Friends*, p. 264.

158. Although records are incomplete, the number of American ships registered in St. Petersburg (Kronstadt) declined from thirteen in 1867 to seven in 1871. Twelve arrived in 1872, buth their total tonnage was a new low. Pomutz reports, DUSC, St. Petersburg, vol. 18 (roll 8, M 81), RG 59, NA.

quality than the typical American variety, and, of course, the much-fancied Russian leather.[159] None of these were exported in large volume.

One successful import in these years was petroleum from the Pennsylvania fields, sent directly from the United States to northern Russia. Most of this trade was handled by the Boston-based Ropes and Company, now well into its second generation of operation in St. Petersburg. In fact, this brief period before the explosive development of the rich Russian sources might be called the "oil era" of Russian-American trade, which reached a level of 150,000 barrels imported in 1873. Yet, that was still well below the value of cotton that was coming directly to Russia.[160] Ironically, Americans (such as St. John Constant and Laslo Chandor) were in the forefront of prospecting and refining in the Caucasus region while American oil was being imported into St. Petersburg and Odessa. American consuls predicted that "Baku oil" would soon price the American commodity out of the market.[161]

Other American business in the south of Russia remained undeveloped. Timothy Smith, the American consul in the major Black Sea port, remained optimistic about the future of American business in that area; he predicted that the opening of the Suez Canal would have beneficial effects. But, aside from an occasional tourist ship, American vessels generally avoided the Bosphorus and Dardenelles Straits. The primary check on an American commercial presence in the Black Sea was the growth of the Italian, Austrian, Greek, and even Russian merchant marines. Russian wool, much appreciated by the North during the Civil War, was still a key import from the area (from Rostov and Taganrog), but it was carried mostly on Italian ships.[162] Given this commercial picture, it is not surprising that there were periodic congressional threats to eliminate consulates in Russia.[163]

159. Pomutz to Fish, 1 December 1874, DUSC, St. Petersburg, vol. 13 (roll 8, M 81), RG 59, NA.

160. Ibid. According to the consul's figures, over a two-year, nine-month period (1872–1874), direct imports from Russia were valued as follows: cotton $9,929,161; petroleum $859,614; locomotives $197,628; total $14,870,381.

161. Smith to Fish, 31 December 1869, DUSC, Odessa, vol. 4 (roll 2, M 459); and Pomutz to Fish, 1 December 1874, DUSC, St. Petersburg, vol. 13 (roll 8, M 81), RG 59, NA. Pomutz listed American oil imports by Russia as follows: 1867—25,000 barrels, 1870—60,000, 1871—100,000, 1873—150,000.

162. Smith reports of 30 May 1868 and 1 October 1869, DUSC, Odessa, vol. 4 (roll 2, M 459), and 5 February 1870 and 28 March 1871, DUSC, Odessa, vol. 5 (roll 3, M 459), RG 59, NA.

163. See the defenses of Smith, 4 June 1870, DUSC, Odessa, vol. 5 (roll 3, M 459); and Marshall Jewell to Fish, 28 April 1874, DUSM, Russia, vol. 26 (roll 26, M 35), RG 59, NA.

The slackening of direct trade did not mean that the overall exchange of goods between the two countries had declined. To the consternation of veteran American consuls, much American cotton was still transshipped through Britain—and tobacco through Hamburg—and many other items, from sewing machines and scales to firearms and reapers, entered Russia through a variety of third parties. Smith, for example, reported at the end of 1869 that "the supply of American goods increases here perceptibly from year to year, but they are generally shipped to England and transshipped from there to Odessa."[164] Prospects of further developing an expanding Russian market suffered from European competition and the loss of important dealers. Gaun M. Hutton, the former California forty-niner and a successful salesman of American machines in Russia since 1856, died in 1870, leaving his large business to his widow and nephew.[165]

Filling some of the gap in Russian-American commerce left by the withdrawal of Winans were sales of locomotives, beginning with ten shipped from the Baldwin Works at Philadelphia to St. Petersburg in 1872, followed by twenty more in 1873. The next year fifty were ordered from the Grant factory in New York, in large part because of the intermediary boosting of Schuyler and Vladimir Bodisko. Interestingly, the import of these large American-made locomotives stimulated the development of anthracite coal fields in Russia, especially around Voronezh.[166] Americans had less success in marketing Pullman-type sleeping cars in 1874.[167] Other individual business ventures, such as ones to sell soda-cracker-making machines and a portable steam brick-making apparatus, evidently came to nothing.[168]

One very important product of both countries does not appear in the figures on Russian-American trade—grain. The big expansion of American grain production and exports following the Civil War was naturally cause for concern in Russia, heavily dependent on its grain exports. During his brief tenure in Reval in 1870, Schuyler translated a long article on this sub-

164. Smith to Fish, 31 December 1869, DUSC, Odessa, vol. 4 (roll 2, M 459), RG 59, NA.

165. According to a suit against Hutton's estate, he left over $60,000 in addition to the business; Patrick Mathews petition, 27 October 1871, DPR, Russia, vol. 4435 (misc. received), RG 84, NA.

166. Pomutz to Seward, 1 December 1874, DUSC, St. Petersburg, vol. 13 (roll 8, M 81), RG 59, NA; Schuyler to Jewell, 14 December 1874, Schuyler Letterbook, LC.

167. New York *Times,* 11 October 1874.

168. Henry D. Moore (Philadelphia) to Curtin, 27 January 1870, and C. A. Winn (Lock Haven, Pa.) to Curtin, 26 November 1869, DPR, Russia, vol. 4434 (misc. received), RG 84, NA.

ject from *Birzhevnaia Gazeta* (Exchange gazette), the leading Russian news-paper on economic matters.

> We must expect that the always faster developing culture of America will consolidate and strengthen itself from year to year. In the measure of this consolidation will grow the danger to our exports. America will not refuse, from love to us, from getting to itself the market, on the con-trary it uses every effort to keep it for itself in the future. Can we give up without a struggle the markets in which we thought we dominated? No one of course will say that: we do not wish to be suffocated with our own fat: extensive and regular exportation is just as necessary to us as a piece of daily bread. We therefore have no other choice left, than to enter into the competition and without wavering bring to the affair all the means that can give us the victory.[169]

Although high demand in Europe during the Franco-Prussian War (1870–1871) temporarily masked the rising competition, the long-term figures were not encouraging for Russia. According to the St. Petersburg consul's annual report for 1875, the United States in 1867 supplied 14 percent of the British market for grain while Russia provided 44 percent. In only six years the fig-ures were almost reversed: United States 44 percent, Russia 21 percent.[170] The great American westward movement, both in settlement and railroads, was, of course, the key factor. As with oil production, some Americans found opportunity in offering American experience and technology in the handling of grain, especially in erecting elevators. Nathan Appleton in 1871 was one of the first to pursue a plan to construct them at the port of Odessa.[171] Others soon followed with similar schemes, but none broke through Russia's bureaucratic conservatism and economic backwardness.

Another Coast

American business relations with Russia confronted changing times in the Pacific as well. The center of American attention—Nikolaevsk on the

169. From translated article dated 24 January/5 February 1870, enclosed in Schuyler to Fish, 9 February 1870, DUSC, Reval, vol. 1 (roll 1, M 484), RG 59, NA.

170. Pomutz to Fish, 10 January 1876, DUSC, St. Petersburg, vol. 13 (roll 8, M 81), RG 59, NA.

171. Charles B. Norton to Nathan Appleton, 15 September 1871, Appleton Papers, Duke University.

Amur—suffered from the shift of the Russian navy and government administration to Vladivostok in 1867 and from the collapse of the joint telegraph construction project.[172] Charles Gordon Chase, the American "commercial agent," was extremely pessimistic about the future there. Having served twelve years as representative for the leading American merchant house in the area, William Bordman of Boston, Chase was especially critical of the attitude of the local authorities and the many petty duties and annoyances that beset resident Americans.[173] In disgust he resigned his post and fled to St. Petersburg, where he complained bitterly to Cassius Clay that the Russians intended "to drive the Americans from their coasts."[174]

Chase left another long-time Bordman agent, Henry Winans Hiller, to face yet one more blow to Amerian business: a new tax imposed in December 1867 on liquor, the most lucrative item of trade. Hiller's main complaint was that it took effect immediately after that year's orders had been placed on the basis of the previous prices. Hiller journeyed all the way to Irkutsk during the winter to petition the governor general to restore Nikolaevsk's status as a free port or at least to delay the imposition, but this official only forwarded the petition to the Ministry of Finance in St. Petersburg, with no result.[175]

The Russian government also began to stiffen its previously tolerant policy toward American whaling along the coast of the Sea of Okhotsk, the richest hunting grounds. During the summer of 1867, three whalers were stopped and notified by the commander of a Russian gunboat that they would no longer be allowed to hunt in those waters. When one of the ships persisted, the officer ordered a gun loaded and fired—not without some difficulty, according to an eyewitness.[176] Protests of this action involved the troublesome and time-consuming collection of depositions, but the conflict over whaling remained open.[177]

---

172. The population of Nikolaevsk declined from 4,017 in 1864 to 3,300 in 1873; Aleksandr Kirillov, *Geografichesko-statisticheskii slovar' Amurskoi i primorskoi oblastei* (Blagoveshchensk: D. O. Moken, 1894), p. 275. For the fate of the telegraph project, see *Distant Friends*, pp. 360–70, and Western Union Telegraph Expedition Collection, SA.

173. Chase to Seward, 13 September 1867, DUSC, Amur, vol. 2 (roll 2, T 111), RG 59, NA.

174. Clay to Seward, 23 May 1868, DUSM, Russia, vol. 21 (roll 21, M 35), RG 59, NA.

175. Hiller to Seward, 5/13 May 1868, DUSC, Amur, vol. 2 (roll 2, T 111), RG 59, NA.

176. Hiller to Seward, 17/29 May and 12/24 August 1868, ibid.

177. Seward to Clay, 24 February 1868, DI, Russia, vol. 15 (roll 137, M 77), RG 59, NA.

Two other old Siberia hands made last efforts in hopeless causes. Perry Collins, thinking perhaps that Secretary of State Fish was indebted to him for supporting the Alaska purchase, sought his assistance in reviving the Bering Strait telegraph connection. He argued that with the United States now closer to Siberia by way of Alaska, an alternative to the Atlantic cable made even more sense. After visiting Seward at his home in August 1868, he formed a company for that purpose, but little else was heard about it.[178]

Otto Esche had been in the North Pacific spotlight before the Civil War for his colorful feat of importing camels from Nikolaevsk into San Francisco. Convinced that a rapid expansion of steamship lines to Siberia was inevitable, he now sought a franchise for coal on Sakhalin Island, recently claimed by Russia. Mining had actually begun several years earlier when the area was still up for grabs. In partnership with Elisha Rice, American consul in Yokohama, Esche solicited Clay's support, which was granted only in return for a share of the enterprise. Additional funding was required to expand the mines and reach a production level of 50,000 tons a year.[179] For that Esche needed a monopoly guarantee. As Clay informed Westmann, "I am assured that the proper capital can be procured, if the Russian government would grant a company the *exclusive privilege* of working all of the island mines, for twenty years, or more."[180] But Gorchakov replied sharply that this was an inopportune time to press a monopoly contract on the Russian government. Clay thought the Perkins affair had dampened the prospects for the venture. In any event, Esche's financial health "became deranged," and he withdrew from the enterprise.

Meanwhile, the American Amur "agency" struggled through difficult times. In June 1869 the Grant administration appointed New Yorker O. S. Smith, who had no experience in Russia, as commercial agent to replace Chase and Hiller. He took his time getting there, complaining from Hong Kong, "I hardly know what to do. It is such an out of the way place."[181] Winding through Shanghai and Yokohama to Nikolaevsk, he finally arrived on 10 August 1870. Although this was probably the best time of the year at the mouth of the Amur, Smith submitted his resignation ten days later:

178. Collins to Seward, 4 January 1869, DUSC, Amur, vol. 2 (roll 2, T 111), RG 59, NA.

179. Esche (Nikolaevsk) to Clay, 28 September/10 October 1868, enclosure in Clay to Fish, 17 April 1869, DUSM, Russia, vol. 21 (roll 21, M 35), RG 59, NA.

180. Clay to Westmann, 26 December 1868, enclosed in ibid.

181. Smith to Fish, 15 November 1869, DUSC, Amur, vol. 2 (roll 2, T 111), RG 59, NA.

"My short sojourn here has brought upon me rheumatism that threatens to be very serious were I to remain."[182] He added that Hiller was managing the meager commerce just fine.

But Hiller soon found himself adrift. When Bordman died in Boston in 1872, his company's operations ceased, and Hiller was forced to return home with his Russian wife and children, passing the agency baton to his friend Enoch Emery, an independent American merchant in the area.[183] Emery sent only a few reports before closing up the agency on 30 June 1874, abandoning the archives to "Col. M. D. Gouberoff, a citizen of Russia"— who also happened to be Hiller's father-in-law.[184]

Diplomatic Tragedies and Instability

As if there were not enough tedious problems in Russian-American relations in these years, death stalked the American community in Russia. The first victim was Henry Stacey from Vermont, who died at his consular post in Reval (Estonia) in June 1869.[185] Then a tragic fate befell Anson Burlingame, one of the foremost American diplomats of the era. A Harvard Law School graduate who served two terms in Congress in the 1850s, Burlingame in 1861 was appointed by President Lincoln as minister to China. He won the confidence of Chinese authorities so completely that he was asked to head an extraordinary Chinese embassy to the West in 1868 to regularize Chinese-Western relations through formal treaties. His special mission, first to the United States and then to Europe, was highly successful in gaining for China reciprocal treatment by the Western powers. The embassy, which included his wife and son, a British secretary, and a number of

182. Smith (Nikolaevsk) to Fish, 20 August 1870, ibid. This waste of the taxpayers' money apparently never came up in the scandals that plagued the Grant administration. Smith also took (and claimed pay for) 138 days to get home; Smith to Fish, 27 July 1871, ibid.

183. Hiller to Fish, 30 September 1872, ibid.; "Silverware and Lace," manuscript letters by Hiller, and his wife's diary for 1872, vols. 6 and 7, box 2, Hiller Papers, Mystic Seaport Library. After some difficulty, Hiller received a cash settlement of $3,000 from the Bordman estate; George S. Cushing (Boston) to Hiller, 8 December 1873, vol. 7, Hiller Papers.

184. Emery to Fish, 30 June 1874, DUSC, Amur, vol. 2 (roll 2, T 111), RG 59, NA.

185. S. D. Jones to Fish, 19 June 1869, DUSC, Reval, vol. 1 (M 484), RG 59, NA; Abby Maria Hemenway, ed., *The Vermont Historical Gazetteer: A Magazine Embracing a History of Each Town*, vol. 2 (Burlington: N.p., 1871), pp. 967–69.

Chinese functionaries, was received in St. Petersburg in early February 1870 with extreme cordiality by Alexander II and his ministers. Immediately after his audience with the emperor on 16 February, however, Burlingame fell ill. He died a week later of viral pneumonia.[186] Anxiety about his mission and the Russian climate had ended the life of one of America's most promising talents.[187]

Andrew Curtin had also established a good reputation for diplomacy during the Katakazi affair, but afterwards he seemed to lose interest in his post. He spent the spring of 1872 in Nice, submitted his resignation, and returned to Russia only for a short time in the summer. His secretary, Titian Coffey, remarked later, "The strictly diplomatic duties of the Minister were not very laborious or important."[188] In his farewell audience with Alexander II, Curtin was embarrassed that the tsar brought up the Katakazi affair and apologized for it.[189] Schuyler was again left in charge of the legation.

In December, James L. Orr accepted the ministerial appointment. Although he was former governor of South Carolina and a former congressman with a distinguished record, one veteran Russian diplomat considered the designation of an "ex-rebel" an affront to Russia.[190] With his wife and son, Orr made his way in winter through Washington and New York and across the Atlantic to arrive in St. Petersburg in mid-March. Already exhausted by a strenuous election campaign, he left the United States with a bad cold from which he never recovered, and, though dutifully making the

186. Curtin to Fish, 23 February 1870, DUSM, Russia, vol. 22 (roll 22, M 35), RG 59, NA; Edward L. Burlingame to his grandfather, 28 February 1870, box 1, Burlingame Papers, LC. M. Leavy Brown, the English secretary, now became the head of the mission, suddenly raising fears that its control was shifting from the United States to Britain.

187. *Commonwealth* (Boston), 19 March 1870. Jeremiah Curtin spent most of an evening reminiscing with Burlingame and vouched for his worried state. He remembered the illness lasting only two days; *Memoirs of Jeremiah Curtin*, p. 206.

188. Titian J. Coffey, "Curtin as Minister to Russia," in William H. Egle, *Life and Times of Andrew Gregg Curtin* (Philadelphia: Thompson Publishing Company, 1896), pp. 435–36.

189. Curtin to Fish, 1 July 1872, DUSM, Russia, vol. 24 (roll 24, M 35), RG 59, NA. Privately Curtin wrote, "He is certainly anxious to have the unhappy affair forgotten and to resume intimate and kind relations." To Fish, 2 July 1872, vol. 89, Fish Papers, LC.

190. Boker reported from Constantinople that Ignat'ev was especially critical: "He said openly that the sending of an ex-rebel to Russia was an insult to a Power that had stood by us so faithfully during the whole of the Rebellion." To Fish, 2 June 1873, vol. 94, Fish Papers, LC.

formal diplomatic rounds, Orr died on 6 May.[191] Schuyler had just left for Central Asia, so consul George Pomutz tended to the legation's business until his return the following November. Marshall Jewell, another former governor (Connecticut), was named minister in May but did not reach St. Petersburg until December. After six months, he resigned to serve as postmaster general in the second Grant administration.

Musical Interludes

Observant Americans might have noticed the influx of Russians into the country. Most of those arriving on the West Coast came because of the deterioration in Alaskan conditions after the purchase, while many others emigrated from Russia to escape increasing repression or minor criminal infractions at home. Some came just to satisfy their curiosity. Yet the appearance in New York of a choral group led by Dmitri Agrenev-Slavianskii in late 1869 still came as a surprise. Agrenev was a Crimean War veteran who became interested in Slavophilism (extolling the distinctive Slavic character) while attending the University of Moscow. He then launched his own career as a concert singer of Russian national songs, earning a respected reputation in Europe. By 1868 he had organized a choral group in Prague for Russian and European tours for the benefit of Pan-Slavic causes.[192] Along the way, he adopted the name Slavianskii to fit his cultural mission.

With little advance advertisement the chorus opened before a large crowd at Steinway Hall on 29 November. A review was very favorable:

> The tenor, Mr. Agreneff Slaviansky, has an excellent voice and gained much applause in the Russian sailor's song. The great feature of the performance, however, was the Russian national song, accompanied by

191. James Orr, Jr. (St. Petersburg), to sister (Weimar), 10 April 1873, Orr Papers, UNC; Orr to Fish, 18 March 1873, Schuyler to Fish, 22 March 1873, and Pomutz to Fish, 6 May 1873 (t), DUSM, Russia, vol. 25 (roll 25, M 35), RG 59, NA; Alma Curtin to her mother (Mrs. James Cardelle), 26 April/8 May 1873, box 19, Jeremiah Curtin Papers, MCHC.

192. A. Khitrovo, *Dmitrii Aleksandrovich Slavianskii i ego deiatel'nost'* (Tver: F. S. Murav'ev, 1887), pp. 18–23; Kuropiatnik, *Rossiia i SShA*, pp. 121–22. The series of concerts in 1868 was sponsored by the Moscow Slavic Benevolent Committee; Slavianskii to N. A. Popov, 13 April and 14 June 1868, 239 NP.18.29, RNL.

the clarinet and a dance, very similar in its features to our own clog dance. . . . Great credit is due to the selection both of the artists and the music, and Mr. Slaviansky's success is certainly based upon the merits of his entertainment.[193]

Despite artistic acclaim, Slavianskii was disappointed with his paltry profits, the result of the high price of reserving the hall on short notice and the hiring of managers and interpreters.

The small New York Russian community initially gave its support and responded to his call for additional singers to stage an opera series that featured Aleksei Verstovskii's "Askold's Tomb" at the French Theatre. It opened on 15 December to mixed reviews. The *Tribune* was disappointed in the lead singing by Slavianskii, his wife, and Nadezhda Levitskaia: "It was certainly a novelty, and proved to everybody a most pleasing one, though not quite up to the expectations of a good many. . . . It is a simple love story, with scarcely any justifiable reason for giving it such a gloomy name. . . . It is certainly a strong company, and the appointments and costumes all being Russian, as well as the music, give it a unique character."[194]

The stress of putting together the cast in haste, dependency on a local orchestra unfamiliar with the music, and the use of local amateurs contributed to considerable dissension within the troupe. Two leading female vocalists were literally wooed away by resident Russians. One was identified as "Rogasin," a former adjutant in the Russian army who had come to the United States a few months earlier to study cotton trading. He played opposite Levitskaia in a climactic scene in which he rescues her from a harem. In the ninth and last performance, they went right off the stage at this point and hopped a train to Philadelphia, where they were married by the mayor. She reportedly had most of the gate receipts ($1,300) with her, which led to their arrest—but subsequent exoneration—upon their return to New York.[195] The other case involved even more disruption in the Russian community because the woman was already married, though she had acquired several local

193. New York *Tribune*, 30 November 1869. A national paper noted more briefly: "The members appeared in Russian habit, which, with their vernacular, made them objects of curiosity. Their singing was carefully executed and frequently encored." *Leslie's Illustrated*, 18 December 1869.

194. New York *Tribune*, 16 December 1869.

195. Nikolai Slavinskii, *Pis'ma ob Amerike i Russkikh pereselentsakh* (St. Petersburg: P. P. Merkulev, 1873), pp. 208–16. Slavinskii was a Russian tourist who happened to be in town at the time and who observed the Russian community in New York. His detailed

suitors. A "Dr. M.," who had practiced medicine in St. Petersburg and served in Garibaldi's army before reaching New York, finally won the hand of "K" but at the cost of being ostracized by the New York circle.[196]

Slavianskii persisted in his quest to expose Americans to Russian music and set off on a tour of New England with the remaining company, staging impressive songfests in Hartford, Providence, Springfield, and finally Boston. These choral concerts were more successful than the opera, and Slavianskii himself was impressed by the large crowds, even on Sunday, by Americans standing for "God Save the Tsar," and by a lavish reception that Mrs. Samuel Colt hosted in Hartford.[197] An extended repertoire, performed from 22 January to 20 February 1870 in Boston, was even better received, as Slavianskii seemed to warm to the occasion. One newspaper commented: "They appear in national fancy costumes and are men of interesting look and bearing. Mr. Slaviansky himself, their leader and director, a man of noble and commanding presence, has one of the sweetest, purest, and most cultivated tenors we have heard since Mario; indeed his upper tones remind us of that singer."[198] But his troubles were not over. Immediately after the Saturday performance on 19 February, the whole choir defected and arranged its own tour of a number of other cities as far west as Chicago and St. Louis. The final scheduled performance in Boston was thus improvised: Slavianskii and two Americans drafted for the occasion each sang solos.[199] The Russian impresario then hurried home to form another ensemble.

The concert tour of another musician from Russia was less problematic, since the fame of Anton Rubinstein as a world-class pianist preceded his arrival in September 1872. He may also have benefited from the publicity attending Grand Duke Alexis's tour the previous year. Under the sponsorship of William Steinway himself, Rubinstein's itinerary was ably managed by

"letters" were first serialized in a major Russian journal, *Otechestvennyia Zapiski*, in 1872. Unfortunately, Slavinskii used only the first initial of last names in his narrative, though some can be identified by other sources—for example, the Philadelphia *Inquirer*, 17 January 1870. Russian names are difficult enough without this shorthand—consider the coincidental similarity of Slavianskii and Slavinskii.

196. Slavinskii, *Pis'ma ob Amerike*, pp. 220–22.

197. Khitrovo, *Slavianskii*, p. 32. This is based on several of Slavianskii's letters published that year in the newspaper *Slovo*.

198. "The Russian Singers," *Dwight's Journal of Music*, 29 January 1870. *Leslie's Illustrated*, 26 February 1870, confirmed this impression: "The Russian singers were better appreciated in Boston than in New York City."

199. *Commonwealth* (Boston), 26 February 1870; Slavinskii, *Pis'ma ob Amerike*, p. 218.

Maurice Grau. The nine-month American celebration of the virtuoso began with a "serenade" to him by the New York Philharmonic on 13 September. His sell-out opening concert at Steinway Hall ten days later featured selections from Handel, Mozart, Beethoven, Schumann, and, of course, Rubinstein and received a full column of praise from the New York *Times*.[200]

The ensuing tour took him to Boston, Buffalo, Toronto, Montreal, Detroit, Cleveland, Cincinnati, Memphis, Baltimore, and Philadelphia, then final concerts in New York and Boston. The "Rube" craze followed him everywhere, but he gave unstintingly of his talents, practicing almost constantly, shunning all receptions and social invitations, and ending up totally exhausted. At one of his last concerts he performed all six Beethoven sonatas. His own variations on "Yankee Doodle" headed the many encores. The one sour note was that he despised the talented Polish violinist Henri Wieniawski (Veniavskii), who had been contracted to provide variety (and relief) in the program and who captured a deserving share of American praise. They did not speak to each other during the entire tour! For his efforts, Rubinstein cleared $60,000, which facilitated his retirement from the concert stage and allowed him to devote the rest of his life to teaching, composing, and occasional conducting.[201]

Grand Duke Alexis

For several years rumors had fed expectations that a Russian grand duke would visit the United States. They first centered around Grand Duke Constantine, the brother of Alexander II, after the Crimean War. Then the heir apparent, Nicholas, became the focus, and, after he died, the tsar himself was reported to be planning a visit. Finally, as early as 1869, the word was that the third son of Alexander II and Empress Mariia Aleksandrovna, Alexis, would make an ap-

200. New York *Times*, 24 September 1872. In his memoirs, Rubinstein recalled how impressed he was with his American reception; cited in Kuropiatnik, *Rossiia i SShA*, p. 123.

201. Catherine Drinker Bowen, *"Free Artist": The Story of Anton and Nicholas Rubinstein* (New York: Random House, 1939), pp. 233–48.

A few American musicians penetrated Russia but with little fanfare. John Groves was employed as a conductor in Saratov, and a black American was said to be playing in an orchestra in Moscow; *Distant Friends*, p. 360; Bowen, *"Free Artist,"* p. 227. The Philadelphia *Inquirer* reported on 15 November 1869 that "Miss Minnie Hauck [a popular soprano] has had a great reception in Moscow. In 'Lucia' she was recalled twenty times, and in 'Faust' eight times at the close of the cathedral scene."

pearance any month. Still, there were delays, ostensibly because of the comparative youth and inexperience of the grand duke.[202]

Gorchakov officially informed Katakazi in February 1871 of the approaching world tour. The minister suggested an American itinerary that would include New York, a visit with the president at Long Branch (anticipating arrival in summer), West Point, Hartford (Colt works), Bridgeport (cartridge factory), Washington, Annapolis, Boston, Cambridge, Newport (for rest), Niagara Falls, Cleveland, Detroit, Chicago, Cincinnati, St. Louis, the Rocky Mountains, and San Francisco, where he would rejoin his squadron. He also advised Gorchakov that Americans especially valued malachite presents.[203] By July the proposed itinerary had expanded to include a buffalo hunt on the prairie and a swing through the South—New Orleans and Charleston—but would now extend west only as far as Salt Lake City and would conclude with a return visit to Washington.[204]

Although the State Department was duly informed of this impending Russian invasion, and although it was announced in the press in April, Fish was still dubious. As he cabled Curtin in June, "Is there reason to expect that the Grand Duke is coming to this country. We cannot believe, what the Minister says."[205] Further delays heightened suspense about the possibility of a cancellation. Finally, in mid-November a Russian squadron, consisting of the *Svetlana* (flagship), *Bogatyr*, and *Abrek*, under the command of Viceadmiral Konstantin Pos'et, arrived in New York harbor and was greeted with much fanfare despite a heavy downpour. Although the grand duke was technically only "officer of the watch" aboard the *Svetlana*, there was no pretense of anonymity or informality for the visit.

Preparations were considerable on both sides. For the tour the grand duke was accompanied by the admiral, who had long served as his chief tutor; se-

---

202. According to the Philadelphia *Inquirer* (19 December 1871), which did not give its source, Alexander II had wanted to send the heir apparent, Grand Duke Alexander, instead of Alexis, but Grand Duchess Maria Fedorovna had objected. "If this royal dame had known how dearly we love to do homage to first-class princes and inchoate monarchs she would have crossed the ocean with her royal husband rather than have sent us her young brother-in-law."

203. Katakazi to Gorchakov, 9/21 March 1871, f. 133, op. 470, d. 123 (1871), AVPR.

204. Katakazi to Gorchakov, 2/14 July 1871, ibid. An American in St. Petersburg described Alexis before his departure: "He speaks English well, sings well, is rather a nice young man, with side whiskers." He indicated a desire to see all the sights, especially Indians. Sarah Hagar to her sister, 1 May 1871, Hagar Papers, University of Vermont.

205. Fish to Curtin, 9 June 1871, DI, Russia, vol. 15 (roll 137, M 77), RG 59, NA.

lected English-speaking officers, such as Oskar Kremer; Vladimir Bodisko, an experienced diplomat and Americaphile; aides-de-camp Aleksandr Olsuf'ev and Pavel Shuvalov, both of whom would later serve in high military and diplomatic positions; William Machin, a British-born tutor of English; and Dr. Vladimir Kudrin, naval surgeon and the duke's personal physician. During the Atlantic passage the group had discussed Russian-American relations, studied American speech expressions, and listened to lectures given in English by Shuvalov on American history.[206] They were about as well-prepared as any official visitors to the United States would be.

Making the trip out to the *Svetlana* in the heavy rain was a distinguished reception committee that included generals John A. Dix, Henry Dodge, and Irwin McDowell; business promoters Cyrus Field, Samuel F. B. Morse, Sylvanus Macy, and William Aspinwall; Henry Bergh, former secretary of the legation in St. Petersburg and more recently the founder of the Society for the Prevention of Cruelty to Animals; and some of the most prominent names of New York aristocracy—Vanderbilt, Pierrepont, Harriman, Van Rensselaer, among others.[207] The landing and parade that was to follow had to be postponed, although a huge throng had already gathered at the Battery. "Never was there a more thoroughly rain-soaked and disappointed crowd, . . . a waving sea of dripping umbrellas." When three Russian officers finally did disembark, they were mobbed, jeered at, and forced to run a gauntlet of vile abuse. " 'He ain't no Duke,' exclaimed a rough, 'he's only a carpet-bagger.' "[208] Upset by the failure of Alexis to appear as scheduled, "urchins" tore down the reviewing grandstand in disgust.

When the skies cleared the next day, a more dignified reception was staged. Alexis rode in a carriage with Katakazi, escorted by Aspinwall and Macy and led by a battalion of police and several national guard units. Row-

206. Pos'et (New York) to Alexander II, 6/18 November 1871, f. 678, op. 1, d. 1011, TsGAOR. As tutor and guardian for a number of years, Pos'et had special responsibility for Alexis—and reported personally to the tsar. These communications were obviously affected by a busy schedule and are partly in direct letters and partly in diary form, submitted at the end of the journey.

207. "The Russian Prince: Safe Arrival of Grand Duke," New York *Times*, 20 November 1871; "The Russian Duke," Boston *Daily Advertiser*, 21 November 1871. See also William F. Zornow, "When the Tsar and Grant Were Friends," *Mid-America* 43, 3 (July 1961): 164–81.

208. New York *Times*, 21 November 1871. Colorful newspaper accounts of the grand duke's tour of America were collected for contemporaries by William W. Tucker, *His Imperial Highness the Grand Duke Alexis in the United States of America During the Winter of 1871–1872* (Cambridge, Mass.: Riverside Press, 1872; reprint, New York: Interland Publishing, 1972). Since he did not identify sources, originals are cited when possible.

The Grand Duke Alexis's visit: departure from the Svetlana. *Harper's Weekly, 9 December 1871, courtesy of the Kansas Collection, University of Kansas Libraries*

dies closed in behind, knocking aside women and children. The papers delighted in recording the popular mood. "Of all the motley gatherings which old New-York has known, none, perhaps, ever surpassed that which yesterday hurrahed till it was black in the face. . . . The candy-sellers, the chestnut roasters, and the boot blacks reaped such a splendid harvest; never perhaps were so many bags of pea-nuts consumed in New-York, in one day."[209] General Dix gave a fitting welcoming speech, to which the grand duke offered a response that may have had a double meaning: "The friendship between America and Russia is so strong and lasting, *nothing* can disturb it."[210]

The remainder of the first New York stay was a short and simple one. After a rest at the Clarendon House, the grand duke observed an English-language service at the Russian Orthodox Church and left the next day, November 22, for Washington. This was planned as a formal stopover to last no more than twenty-four hours, and the denizens of the city acted accordingly. Alexis was ushered into the Katakazi residence with the traditional bread and salt greeting and met with the local press corps. Hamilton Fish, no doubt to his immense discomfort, called at the minister's residence for an introduction and to escort the grand duke to the White House, where a stiff

209. "The Landing and the Parade," New York *Times,* 22 November 1871.
210. "Honors to Alexis," ibid. (emphasis added).

Reception of the Grand Duke Alexis in New York: (top) on board the Mary Powell *in New York harbor; (bottom) procession passing the grandstand (both from Harper's Weekly, 9 December 1871, courtesy of the Kansas Collection, University of Kansas Libraries)*

Ball for Grand Duke Alexis at Brooklyn Naval Yard. Harper's Weekly, *16 December 1871, courtesy of the Kansas Collection, University of Kansas Libraries*

ten-minute meeting was endured by both hosts and guests.[211] A more cordial diplomatic reception followed, though neither Fish nor Grant attended.[212]

Alexis departed Washington the next morning for a more congenial tour of the Naval Academy in Annapolis. Then he returned to New York for more festivities, highlighted by a grand affair at the Brooklyn Navy Yard. The sail loft of an old warehouse was converted into a gala ballroom; everything went well, except for the hour's wait for carriages to unload and some undecorous attempts to see the grand duke.[213] Other events were less taxing:

211. "Alexis in Washington," Washington *Evening Star,* 23 November 1871; Boston *Herald,* 23 November 1871. Katakazi instructed the grand duke regarding the precise timing of his conversation with the president. He was then to inquire about Mrs. Grant, shake hands with the members of the cabinet, and leave. Katakazi to Gorchakov, 16/28 November, f. 133, op. 470, d. 123 (1871), AVPR.

The press was bemused by the contrast between Katakazi and Alexis: "Mr. Catacazy is a short and rather spare gentleman, with blue eyes, square forehead, short hair, beard and mustache. . . . The Duke is six feet one inch in height, of youthful appearance, has clear blue eyes, wears blonde mustache and side whiskers, and is exceedingly winning and courteous in his manner." Philadelphia *Inquirer,* 27 November 1871.

212. Pos'et to Alexander II, 24 November/6 December 1871, f. 678, op. 1, d. 1011, TsGAOR.

213. "Honors to the Duke," *Army and Navy Journal* 9, 16 (2 December 1871): 248.

a cruise on the East River; a tasteful reception and ball at Governor's Island, where Alexis danced five and a half hours with the belles of New York;[214] operas at the Academy of Music ("Faust" and "Mignon"); requisite visits to Matthew Brady's photographic studio at Tenth and Broadway; a ride through Central Park with Edwin W. Stoughton, future minister to Russia; a Thanksgiving Day service at the Russian church; another grand ball and dinner at the Academy of Music; an excursion arranged by Aspinwall up the Hudson to West Point; and a concluding reception on the *Svetlana* on 2 December.[215] As he detailed all this to Alexander II, Pos'et also fretted about the duke's stamina and health, the decrepit boilers on the *Svetlana*, the duration and extent of the journey, the political strain created by Fish and Katakazi, and the expense of the tour (about $1,500 a day).[216]

The busy duke then made a one-day visit to Philadelphia for a dinner of caviar, stewed terrapin, roast pheasant, broiled grouse, and a hundred other delicacies. A reception followed at Independence Hall and then a lavish ball, which was described by a witness as "the greatest and grandest social event in the history of the city."[217] The party went from there back to New York on a special train, hired from the Pennsylvania Central Railroad and under the management of Frank Thompson.[218]

A tour of New England featured a visit to the Colt works in Hartford and a cartridge factory in Bridgeport. The next stop, Boston, was the climax of his East Coast travels. Alexis now seemed to be enjoying all the fuss made over him and appeared at ease amid the mob at a reception at Revere House. He danced for hours at a grand ball at the Boston Theater; toured the mills at Lowell, where he also lunched with Gustavus Fox; and was guided around Harvard Yard and campus by President Charles Eliot. One event in particular—dinner at the Music Hall—was the talk of the country for days. Included in the banquet party were Eliot, James Russell Lowell, Henry Wadsworth Longfellow, astronomer Asa Gray, Richard Dana, and Oliver

214. Pos'et to Alexander II, 24 November/6 December 1871, f. 678, op. 1, d. 1011, TsGAOR.

215. New York *Times*, 27–30 November and 1–3 December 1871.

216. In Pos'et's reports to the tsar and diary, f. 678, op. 1, d. 1011, TsGAOR.

217. Alexander K. McClure, *Recollections of Half a Century* (Salem, Mass.: Salem Press, 1902), p. 366.

218. The best source for the train, featuring luxurious Pullman sleeping, dining, and salon cars, is "Alexis," *Kansas State Record*, 24 January 1872; this reporter was guided through the train in Topeka by Thompson. For the long western trip, the train would usually pull onto a siding at night so Alexis could have a quiet sleep. From St. Louis to Topeka the army cars of General Sheridan were attached.

Wendell Holmes. The latter sang a poem to the tune of the Russian national anthem, which in part gushed:

> The flowers are fullblown in the garlanded hall,
> They bloom round his footsteps whereever they fall,
> For the splendor of youth and the sunshine they bring,
> Make the roses believe 'tis the summons of spring.[219]

Lowell followed with a few, more stylish remarks and a clever pun: "When referring to our purchase of Alaska, he said that our relations with Russia are now of the most cordial and intimate kind, for the Emperor has made us the keeper of his seals."[220]

As the nation warmed to their guest from Russia, some individuals and journalists began to poke fun at all the fawning over royalty. In New York, diarist George Templeton Strong had tickets for the main events but abstained from the ceremonies. Pledging that he would "not fash myself about this Muscovite," he observed archly, "We are all sovereign in America, and Alexis is a mere princeling."[221] *Harper's Weekly* was especially critical of the New York reception: "There was, of course, in itself something very comical in the eager interest of a great city and country in a youth of whom nothing whatever can be said but that he is an emperor's son; and it was very natural to say Yankees love a lord. . . . It is not because we love a lord, but because we enjoy ourselves, that we welcome the Russian with such enthusiasm."[222] The journal followed this with a little merriment of its own:

> There was a reception committee
> Which was rather more wealthy than witty
>   When the Prince came ashore
>   He remarked, "What a bore
> To be dogged by this self-made committee!"

> But after the Academy crusher
> When asked, "Do you think that in Russia
>   They'd give such a ball?"

219. "The Russian Prince," New York *Times*, 11 December 1871; and Katakazi to Gorchakov, 30 November/12 December 1871, f. 133, op. 470, d. 123 (1871), AVPR, attesting to the tune.

220. New York *Times*, 11 December 1871.

221. Strong, *Diary*, 4: 394, 401.

222. *Harper's Weekly*, 9 December 1871, p. 1145.

Thomas Nast cartoon of the reception of Grand Duke Alexis. Columbia:
"My long lost Alexis! I am so glad you have come!" Harper's Weekly, 9
December 1871, courtesy of the Kansas Collection, University of Kansas
Libraries

He replied, "Not at all!"
This courteous young man from Russia.[223]

Almost universally, however, the press and private individuals praised the
handsome grand duke, highlighting his manners, modesty, good humor,
and spoken English. This favorable reaction, the large crowds, and publicity
about the strictly formal and brief visit to Washington caused Hamilton
Fish to have second thoughts. After acting minister Gorlov threatened that
the tour would be shortened, thereby excluding the invitation from General
Philip Sheridan and Chief of Staff William T. Sherman to hunt buffalo on

223. *Harper's Weekly*, 16 December 1871, p. 1171.

the prairie, Fish pleaded with Gorlov to allow another visit to the capital. He expressed regret that Alexis's stay in Washington had been so short and hoped that he would have an opportunity to see more of him.[224] But the grand duke, on Katakazi's and Pos'et's advice, turned down Fish's special invitation on the excuse that he had to keep to a schedule.[225]

After a side trip to Montreal, the grand duke and his company reentered the United States at Niagara Falls, then proceeded through Buffalo, Cleveland (where they visited with former president Millard Fillmore), and Detroit to Chicago, arriving in time to celebrate a quiet (because it was a Sunday) New Year's Eve. General Sheridan called on the grand duke that day to convince him to go on the buffalo hunt, and he was persuaded, probably because Sheridan promised that a number of Native Americans would be participating.[226] Shepherded by Sheridan, George M. Pullman, and Cyrus McCormick, Alexis then viewed what remained and what had been rebuilt after the disastrous fire a few months earlier—the stockyards, the business district, and the temporary building for the McCormick implement plant—and took time out for pigeon shooting in Dexter Park.[227]

Jeremiah Curtin arranged a diversion to Milwaukee, where a fancy dinner was held in a hall decorated with banners in Russian.[228] Of the many speeches delivered, the press singled out Vladimir Bodisko's:

Although Russia has parted with her last foot of soil in this country you have still a Russian American among you. I have lived in this

---

224. Gorlov to Fish, 27 November/9 December and 6/18 December 1871, NRL, vol. 7 (roll 5, M 39), RG 59, NA; Fish to Gorlov, 19 December 1871, f. 133, op. 470, d. 112 (1872), AVPR. The proposed swing through the South had already been canceled because of reports about Ku Klux Klan activity in South Carolina; Katakazi to Gorchakov, 21 October/2 November 1871, f. 133, op. 470, d. 123 (1871), AVPR. The idea of a buffalo hunt apparently originated with Sherman and Secretary of War William Belknap in early November on the basis of a successful publicity hunt arranged for eastern reporters the previous September; Sheridan to Gen. Townsend, 22 November 1871 (c), reel 3, Sheridan Papers, LC.

225. Gorlov to Fish, 26 December 1871, NRL, vol. 7 (roll 5, M 39), RG 59, NA; Pos'et (St. Louis) to Alexander II, 30 December/11 January 1872, f. 678, op. 1, d. 1011, TsGAOR.

226. "Our Distinguished Visitors," Chicago *Tribune*, 1 January 1872; Pos'et diary, 18/30 December 1871, f. 678, op. 1, d. 1011, TsGAOR. "The Grand Duke is determined to have the buffalo hunt. I will be at North Platte on the 11th with him." Sheridan to Lt. Hays (t), 31 December 1871 (c), reel 3, Sheridan Papers, LC.

227. "Our Distinguished Visitors," Chicago *Tribune*, 3 January 1872. Sheridan was in Chicago, to the annoyance of the city government, to police the fire-devastated areas.

228. Curtin, *Memoirs of Jeremiah Curtin*, pp. 210–14.

country for some years. I have been to California by way of the isth-
mus, but now I am in the West for the first time. The saying is true—
"Westward the star of empire takes its way." . . . In Russia it is Eastward
that the Star of Empire takes its way, and the two nations will soon
shake hands across the Behring Strait.[229]

Senator James Doolittle, responding for the hosts, stressed the usual debts of
friendship and the "two young nations" theme, and Curtin impressed the
guests with flattering greetings in their language.[230]

Throughout the trip, the Russians paid their own expenses, which included gifts dispensed everywhere. This largesse placed a considerable additional drain on the budget. For the twenty-three rooms at the Plankinton
Hotel during the brief visit to Milwaukee, Pos'et wrote a check for $600, and
that was deemed quite a bargain, since there were reports that the party had
been bilked at several places.[231]

Back in Chicago, Alexis was forced to endure what was perhaps his most
painful American experience, a "pump-handle levee" in the dining room of
his hotel. By one estimate he shook hands with over 2,000 people, mostly
women, workers, and merchants. The *Tribune* commented that "the levee
. . . succeeded better than any Presidential levee ever held, in bringing out
all that is awkward and ungracious in American manners." Only one in
twenty-five men, it reported, had the courtesy to bow.[232] Alexis must have
felt relieved to escape Chicago the next day for the West by way of St. Louis
and Omaha. The grand ball in St. Louis was apparently in good taste, even
with the presence of Cassius Clay,[233] and more to the liking of Alexis, who

229. Clipping enclosed in Katakazi to Gorchakov, 22 December 1871/3 January
1872, f. 133, op. 470, d. 112 (1872), AVPR; Milwaukee *Daily News*, 3 January 1872.
230. "Alexis," Milwaukee *Daily Journal*, 4 January 1872. Among other things, Curtin observed, "This bond of mutual confidence and sympathy existing between the
people and its chief is the great striking characteristic of Russian history." Ibid., 10 January 1872; clipping file, box 15, Curtin Papers, MCHC.
231. "Alexis," Milwaukee *Daily Journal*, 9 January 1872; this was also reported as the
only place where the grand duke did not sleep in his own bed, which was carried along
as part of the baggage.
232. Chicago *Tribune*, 5 January 1872.
233. The former minister to Russia had hoped to attend the reception in New York
but was prevented by an attack of rheumatism. Clay to Rollins, 29 December 1871, box
4, file 109, Rollins Papers, SHSM.

reportedly became enamored with one of his dance partners, Sallie Shannon of Lawrence, Kansas.[234] He was also impressed by singer Lydia Thompson, who performed in a burlesque rendition of "Blue Beard," and presented her with an expensive bracelet. It was in St. Louis that the duke first met Native Americans—a group of "civilized" Creeks.[235]

Alexis and his entourage, which had by now grown to include a number of newspaper reporters and U.S. Army officers, reached North Platte in Western Nebraska on the morning of 13 January. They were met by General George Custer and William F. Cody, already better known as Buffalo Bill, who, along with Innis Palmer, were in charge of local arrangements for the buffalo hunt. After a rough, thirty-mile wagon trek across the open prairie, they arrived at "Camp Alexis" on Red Willow Creek, where the Second U.S. Cavalry band greeted them with "Hail to the Chief" and the Russian national anthem.[236] Besides Sheridan and Custer, the American hosts included six other generals, mostly brevet. As a later historian reflected, "At few times could the United States Army have produced a greater array of brass and gold braid to greet a distinguished visitor."[237] Even rarer, perhaps, was the peaceful assemblage of Sioux chiefs—Spotted Tail, War Bonnet, Red Leaf, Whistler, and Pawnee Killer—and at least 600 others of their tribe, drawn there by the promise of wagon loads of gifts.

On the first day of the hunt, Alexis had difficulty making a kill, until Cody loaned him his horse and his rifle and rode beside him to tell him where to aim and when to shoot. After the grand duke achieved success by bringing down a large bull, Buffalo Bill was ready to go home. But when Alexis dismounted, sat on the dead buffalo, cut off its tail, gave an Indian war whoop, and ordered his aides to break out champagne, Cody reconsidered. "I was in hopes," he later recalled, "that he would kill four or six more

234. Later, from Colorado, Miss Shannon received an invitation to join the grand ducal party on their return trip; if that was not possible, Alexis would call at her home. Chicago *Tribune*, 29 January 1872; Lawrence *Daily Kansas Tribune*, 23 January 1872.

235. "Our Imperial Guest," St Louis *Missouri Republican*, 7 January 1872; "The Grand Duke," 8 January 1872. The bracelet reportedly cost $1,500.

236. "The Buffalo Hunt," Chicago *Tribune*, 19 January 1872. The *Tribune* seems to have obtained the most complete coverage of the western events. Sheridan had futilely telegraphed ahead: "Do not let any newspaper reporters to get to the camp—or with the party." To Palmer, 9 January 1872, reel 3, Sheridan Papers, LC.

237. Don Russell, *The Lives and Legends of Buffalo Bill* (Norman: University of Oklahoma Press, 1960), p. 176.

buffaloes before we reached camp, especially if a basket of champagne was to be opened every time he dropped one."[238]

On the morning of the second day the herd was thinned some more, and the score was Alexis 2, Sheridan 2, Indians 8. Over fifty buffalo were killed that day but at least for good purpose, as the Sioux took the skins, tongues, and humps as reward for their cooperation. Some in the Russian party may not have enjoyed their enforced participation. Admiral Pos'et, out of his element on the prairie, was thrown from his horse, and Bodisko suffered minor injuries when his "ambulance" wagon capsized.[239]

That evening the hunters were treated to a Native American powwow and a demonstration of bowmanship by Sioux warrior Two Lance, who shot an arrow completely through a large buffalo that had been herded into the camp.[240] The peace was genuinely threatened, however, when Custer, probably having imbibed too much Russian champagne, made crude overtures to Spotted Tail's pretty sixteen-year-old daughter. Alexis helped calm the situation with gifts of red and green blankets, ivory-handled hunting knives, and a large bag of silver dollars. At a formal council in Sheridan's tent, a peace pipe was passed, and Alexis listened to Spotted Tail take advantage of the occasion to demand the right to hunt freely south of the Platte and to have more than one store in which to trade. The chief also thanked Sheridan for the opportunity to meet a representative of "the great white chief across the water."[241]

After a harrowing ride back to the train, the party journeyed westward

238. Ibid., pp. 178–79, citing a rare manuscript in Cody's handwriting. The story is corroborated by a separate eyewitness account: James Albert Hadley, "A Royal Buffalo Hunt," *Transactions of the Kansas State Historical Society, 1907–1908* 10 (1908): 569–70. For more details on the hunting expedition, see John I. White, "Red Carpet for a Romanoff: 1872 Hunting Party in Honor of the Grand Duke of Russia," *America West* 9, 1 (January 1972): 4–10.

The event was celebrated around the country in humorous sketches and poems. One credited to the Mobile *Register* and cited in the Memphis *Daily Appeal* (26 January 1872) went in part: Alexis shot a buffalo; and Europe questions—"How?" / Why, just like any man would shoot an inoffensive cow. / You gallop to the creature's side / And put a bullet in its hide; / And then away exulting ride / And cool your heated brow.

239. Chicago *Tribune*, 19 January 1871.

240. Roy Morris, Jr., *Sheridan: The Life and Wars of General Phil Sheridan* (New York: Crown, 1992), p. 340.

241. "The Grand Duke: The Imperial Shooting Party at Camp Alexis," Chicago *Tribune*, 21 January 1872. Custer appeared to enjoy the whole affair and competed with Buffalo Bill in attire, dressing colorfully in buckskins and sealskin cap; Chicago *Tribune*, 19 January 1872.

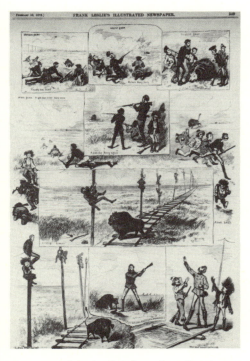

Cartoons of the buffalo hunt from Frank
Leslie's Illustrated Newspaper, *10 February
1872, courtesy of the Kansas State Historical
Society*

via Cheyenne to Denver and Golden.[242] The Russians toured local silver
mines, then, accompanied by Sheridan and Custer, they returned through
Kansas to St. Louis.[243] Along the way they learned about another buffalo
herd on their route near Kit Carson in eastern Colorado and stopped to
hunt. This time there was little advance preparation, Buffalo Bill was not
present to offer advice, Indians were unavailable to dignify the proceedings,

242. Chicago *Tribune,* 29 January 1872. Later accounts have Buffalo Bill driving
Alexis in a brakeless open carriage at record speed down a long incline; Nellie Snyder
Yost, *Buffalo Bill: His Family, Friends, Fame, Failures, and Fortunes* (Chicago: Swallow
Press, 1979), pp. 54–55. Perhaps for good reason, Cody separated from the group at
North Platte and headed east to New York.

243. From Topeka, Sheridan and his staff were called back to Chicago; Custer remained to accompany Alexis all the way to New Orleans; "The Grand Duke in Topeka," North Topeka *Times,* 25 January 1872.

and most of the horses used were cavalry horses and were unaccustomed to buffalo. Custer served as guide for Alexis and led an uncoordinated charge that turned into general confusion. The herd nearly triumphed over the hunters after many of them were unhorsed, thanks to an unseen prairie dog village. Horrified by the near-loss of a Russian duke, Sheridan dressed down the whole party, not sparing Alexis. A counterattack, however, produced a bloody slaughter of animals with Alexis credited with bagging as many as twenty-five.[244] And as the train chugged slowly across western Kansas, he shot a few more from the safety of a baggage car.

The visit to the capitol building in Topeka was more civilized though scarecely more sedate. A large crowd brought by special excursion trains from surrounding towns lined the streets from the Kansas Pacific depot. The whole party stopped first at J. Lee Knight's photographic gallery to have some memorable pictures taken of the buffalo hunting party, after which Sheridan made a quick escape on a fast train to Chicago.[245] At the capitol, following the usual unctuous speeches, the Topeka coronet band accompanied a special chorus and the entire legislature in serenading the duke to the tune of "Old John Brown":

> Mid the grandeur of the Prairies, how can youthful Kansas vie
> With her Russia-loving sisters, in a fitting welcome cry?
> With her heart give full expression, and the answer echo high
>   The Czar and Grant are Friends!
>   Ho! For Russia and the Union
>   Ho! For Russia and the Union
>   The Czar and Grant are Friends![246]

244. Hadley reported that the hunting party looked like a beaten army at the end of the day: "It was a miracle that nobody was killed or crippled that day." In fact, a wild shot by Bodisko went through Sheridan's coat; no wonder the general was upset. "A Royal Buffalo Hunt," pp. 572–73; to this is appended, pp. 575–80, "Chalkley M. Beeson's account."
Alexis should bear some of the blame for the near-extinction of the buffalo, since the publicity attending his western forays contributed to a veritable stampede to hunt these animals in subsequent years. One source (Hadley, "A Royal Buffalo Hunt," p. 573) estimated 3,698,780 slaughtered from 1872 to 1874, only about 500,000 by Indians. The great southern herd, which Alexis had hunted, was totally destroyed within three years.
245. "Alexis at Topeka," Abilene *Chronicle*, 25 January 1872. Sheridan, relieved to have the buffalo escapade behind him, reported to the secretary of war that the hunt "was very successful. . . . I think I may safely say it gave more pleasure to the Grand Duke than any other event which has occurred to him since he has been in our country." To Belknap, 27 January 1872 (c), reel 3, Sheridan Papers, LC.
246. Leavenworth *Times*, 24 January 1872.

General George Custer and Grand Duke
Alexis after the buffalo hunt in Topeka, Kan-
sas, 1872, courtesy of the Kansas State His-
torical Society

At the grand dinner at the Fifth Avenue Hotel, a reporter quipped that Alexis borrowed a leaf from the legislature and did not pass the bill of fare without a third reading.[247] After a brief pause in Lawrence and a quiet overnight stop in Kansas City, the Topeka scene was duplicated in Jefferson City.

St. Louis provided a welcome rest and an opportunity for the grand duke to catch up on correspondence and to record some of his impressions. To his mother he recounted having secretly observed his twenty-second birthday at the hunting camp. "American society," he wrote simply and honestly, "makes a very strange impression on me." The middle class in general were clever and energetic but lacking in manners and ordinary civility. Army and navy officers, however, were quite the opposite, well-educated and polished.

247. Ibid. This cynical reporter-editor covering the dinner was D. R. Anthony, the brother of Susan B. Anthony. Commenting earlier on the impending visit, he wrote: "But every duke will have his day, and Duke Alexis' day will be the day that he gazes on the Kansas Legislature in full dress parade, fawning at his imperial feet." Ibid., 13 January 1872.

"We have in general a false impression about them in Europe." Supposing that his mother might hear stories about his social life, Alexis assured her: "Regarding my success with American ladies about which so much is written in the newspapers, I can openly say, that this is completely nonsense. They looked on me from the beginning as they would look on a wild animal, as on a crocodile or other unusual beast."[248]

Dragged by Custer to Louisville, the grand duke was surprised by the lavish reception, since "we were for the North during the war and against the Southern States" He then observed, "I must say there is a remarkable difference between Americans of the North and those of the South. Here they are more like Europeans . . . and in general resemble our old nobility."[249] Alexis was also impressed—and exhausted—by a six-hour excursion into Mammoth Cave.

Passing up an invitation from Cincinnati, much to the chagrin of its citizens, the party turned southward, riding the rails through Nashville to Memphis. Not even an icy drizzle could dampen their entrance: "When the regular train arrived there was a hooting and yelling set up that would deafen the ears of a donkey. . . . Disorder reigned supreme until the arrival of a section of police . . . mounted on their well-fed and sleek horses. . . . The scenes that occurred during this process were more comic than grand."[250] The stay in Memphis was longer than planned; though they had intended to board a riverboat, an ice jam on the river blocked its approach. Quartered at the Peabody Hotel and regaled with the best southern hospitality (including chicken gumbo, hominy, and coconut custard pie), the party seemed relaxed and glad to be on the homestretch. Pos'et was perhaps the most relieved to be out of buffalo country and enjoyed a tour of the cotton processing industry and conversations with Jefferson Davis, the former leader of the Confederacy.[251] A Memphis paper observed approvingly:

> The admiral, who accompanies the Grand Duke, is the most attractive socially of the whole party . . . of a high order of natural endowments.

248. To Empress Mariia Aleksandrovna, January 1872 (St. Louis), f. 641, op. 1, d. 34, TsGAOR. Alexis, however, was impressed by the beauty of American women, and later (29 February 1872) from Havana he noted how much less pretty the Spanish women were. Libbie Custer also thought that the grand duke was more interested in "pretty girls and music" than the country he was passing through. See her diary, as quoted in Stephen E. Ambrose, *Crazy Horse and Custer: The Parallel Lives of Two American Warriors* (Garden City, N.Y.: Doubleday, 1975), p. 347.

249. To Mariia Aleksandrovna, 23 January 1872, f. 641, op. 1, d. 34, TsGAOR.

250. "Alexis," Memphis *Daily Appeal*, 3 February 1872.

251. Pos'et (Pensacola) to Alexander II, 11/23 February 1872, f. 678, op. 1, d. 1011, TsGAOR.

He loves to talk, and talks well. His English is more accurate than copious, but unlike many Americans he uses good English, . . . [and] watches keenly every incident indicative of American character, and how eagerly he gathers facts affecting the fortunes and resources of this country.[252]

Alexis was also presented in Memphis with a painting by local African-American artist Albert Thomas, depicting the dinner at Katakazi's house in Washington.[253]

Still accompanied by Custer (now joined by his wife and her attractive cousins), the grand ducal party finally boarded the steamboat for the journey down the Mississippi. Stopping off at Vicksburg to tour the battlefield, they reached New Orleans on 11 February, where the annual celebration was in full swing. A local paper, in recording the arrival, delighted in announcing that Alexis was outranked for the first time during his tour of America—by the king of the Mardi Gras. The festivities attending the carnival were reported to be the grandest and most crowded yet, owing to the presence of Alexis, who in turn seemed to be busier than ever with operas, the circus, dinners, and receptions. A ball that would have included all elements of the population was canceled, however, when a local merchant who also served as the Russian vice-consul refused to socialize with blacks.[254]

On 19 February the Russian party boarded a train for the last leg of their American tour. Passing through Mobile to Pensacola, they were met by the squadron that brought them to the United States and embarked without fanfare for Cuba.[255] Alexis's cruise home would take him around the world with extended stopovers in Japan and China, all dutifully covered by the American press. His visit had lasted over three months and had exposed Americans to Russia and Russians as never before. During that period every major newspaper and journal in the country had followed the tour in detail. At almost every stop photographs were taken and made available to the general public. And many from all ranks in American society had been able to see, meet, even speak with Russians directly. It was no doubt a profound ex-

252. Memphis *Daily Appeal*, 3 February 1872.

253. Philadelphia *Inquirer*, 7 February 1872. The painting colorfully depicted Alexis presenting Mrs. Katakazi his cigar to light her cigarette; "Art and Alexis," Memphis *Daily Appeal*, 5 February 1872. Its subsequent disposition is unknown.

254. New Orleans *Daily Picayune*, 14 February 1871.

255. "The Grand Duke—His Arrival and Departure," Mobile *Daily Register*, 21 February 1872.

perience for Alexis himself and his entourage. In Cuba a New York reporter asked the grand duke how he liked his trip through America.

> If I had anything unpleasant to say, I should remain silent, and not an-
> swer your question, but my stay was so pleasant, and the people were
> so kind, that I can only regret that I could not remain longer, and if I
> did not have my path in life laid out for me, I should like to live in
> America altogether, dividing my time from May to January between
> New York and the prairies, and spending the remainder in New Or-
> leans. I may go back there if I can.[256]

He would revisit the United States five years later, obviously retaining an affection for the country and some of the people he had met.[257]

Pos'et also reflected favorably in his official report of the visit on the varied richness of the American scene, contrasting the coal and oil of the East
with the agricultural potential of the West and the rise of a new, reformed
South. He stressed the friendliness of their receptions everywhere and the
heartfelt community of interests between the two countries. The detailed
journal he kept was reportedly read with considerable interest by Alexander
II and by Grand Duke Alexander, future tsar.[258] Sheridan apparently remembered fondly his association with the tour, since the following year he tendered his services to Russia.[259] In a number of ways the American experiences influenced the later careers of both Alexis and Pos'et during their long
tenures in important government positions, as minister of navy and minister
of transportation, respectively. They both took special care to receive visiting Americans and favor American business ideas and proposals.

Alexander II was naturally very pleased at the success of his son's tour
and at the universal welcome he received and made a point of commenting
on it when the occasion was presented. One story that circulated in the

256. New York *Times*, 11 March 1872.
257. Alexis recorded later how shocked he was to learn about the Battle of Little Big
Horn and that Custer had been "scalped by Indians." "He was a *sympaticheskii che-
lovek*" (a nice man). To his mother, 3 January 1877 (Norfolk), f. 641, op. 1, d. 34,
TsGAOR.
258. Report of Pos'et, 27 April/9 May 1872, and letter of Alexander to Alexis, 18/
30 March 1872, cited in Kuropiatnik, *Rossiia i SShA*, pp. 222–23; see also Pos'et (Rio de
Janiero) to Alexander II, 28 May/9 June 1872, in *Morskoi Sbornik* 122, 9 (September
1872).
259. P. H. Sheridan to Offenberg, 20 June 1873, f. 170, op. 512/3, d. 110 (correspondance non-officielle), AVPR.

United States quoted the tsar's request to the departing minister, Andrew Curtin, to carry back his thanks to the American people. Curtin, thinking he had accidentally failed to mention the government, said nothing. But when it was repeated by the empress, Curtin responded, "I shall be happy to carry your Majesty's thanks to my Government and people." To which the Empress retorted, "I sent my thanks, sir, to the people—and only to the people." Curtin later conferred with Gorchakov about this, and he showed Curtin a secret letter of 1863 to Admiral Lesovskii instructing him to place his squadron at the disposal of the Union in the event of war with Britain. Gorchakov then added, "We saved your country, and now your President insults our representative."[260] But, in general, the royal visit had removed most of the bad taste left by the Katakazi affair, broadened the friendly feelings of Americans toward Russia, and stimulated interest in Russia.

Sherman's March Through Russia

Not long after Alexis departed the United States, one of the most famous warriors of the time, General William Tecumseh Sherman, paid a visit to Russia as part of a sweeping European tour. The trip was attended by much less fanfare and publicity than that of the grand duke but was still a notable American military visit to Russia. Sherman was accompanied by his long-time aide, Colonel Joseph Audenreid, and by the president's son, Lieutenant Frederick T. Grant, a recent graduate of West Point. The group entered Russia from the south, through the Black Sea, landing at Sevastopol in the spring of 1872. The general was well known in Russia from the attention given there to the course of the Civil War, and the Russian government was amply forewarned of his coming.[261]

Friction, however, had already developed between young Grant and others in the party about his treatment as "Prince Fred." At a breakfast with the sultan in Constantinople, Lieutenant Grant was given the place of honor. In a letter to his brother, Sherman commented jealously, "The Rus-

---

260. "A Diplomatic Secret," Chicago *Tribune*, 27 August 1874. This might be easily dismissed as journalistic rumor-mongering, but Marshall Jewell attested to hearing essentially the same story directly from Curtin; Jewell to Fish, 3 September 1874, vol. 96, Fish Papers, LC.

261. Curtin (Nice) to Gorchakov, 7 April 1872 (c), and Schuyler (St. Petersburg) to Gorchakov, 31 March/12 April 1872, DPR, Russia, vol. 4534 (notes sent), RG 84, NA.

sian ambassador and English have entertained us, and they knew perfectly our relative ranks."[262] Fortunately, Sherman and Audenreid would enjoy an overcorrection in Russia and escape being the Pos'et and Bodisko of a "grand ducal" tour of Russia.

The American minister, Andrew Curtin, who had been on holiday with his family at Nice, joined the Sherman party in Constantinople. From there they sailed to Sevastopol on the sultan's private yacht in order to tour the battlefields and be entertained at Yalta. Of Russian hospitality Audenreid observed, "I found that Russians as well as Americans have one thing in common and that is to drink too much wine when a good excuse arises."[263] By accident they met the empress while riding near Yalta but passed up an invitation to dine with her.[264] Again by boat, they went to Batum for a rough ride over the Caucasian military highway to Tiflis, the capital of Georgia, where they were entertained by Grand Duke Michael.[265] There Sherman recorded a prescient and future-looking observation in his diary:

> I should not be surprised, after all, if the Russians reach for the Persian Gulf rather than for India, as is generally supposed from their reaching out for Bokhara. I much doubt if Russia gains actual strength by spreading herself over these Asiatic lands. Her expenditures of men and money must tax Russia proper, and in case of a European war she could not withdraw these forces, as the natives would surely rise.[266]

From Georgia the party made its way to Taganrog on the Sea of Azov and then by train northward, arriving in Moscow on 18 May. They were met by Eugene Schuyler, who had arranged through Governor-general Vladimir Dolgorukov an interview on the station platform with Alexander II, pausing on his way to join the empress at Yalta.[267] After pleasant greetings to Sherman, in which he expressed appreciation for the American people's recep-

262. 16 April 1872, vol. 32, reel 17, Sherman Papers, LC. This is also published in Rachel Sherman Thorndike, *The Sherman Letters: Correspondence Between General and Senator Sherman from 1837 to 1891* (New York: Charles Scribner's Sons, 1894), p. 337.

263. To Mrs. Sherman, 25 April 1872, vol. 32 reel 17, Sherman Papers, LC.

264. "Sherman in Russia," New York *Herald,* 8 June 1872; Curtin to Sherman, 21 June 1872, vol. 32, reel 17, Sherman Papers, LC.

265. "Sherman's March to the Caucasus," New York *Herald,* 26 June 1872.

266. Sherman, "Extracts from the Diary of General W. T. Sherman," 6 May 1872, *Century* 57, 6 (April 1899): 868.

267. Schuyler to Fish, 24 May 1872, vol. 88, Fish Papers, LC. The whole interview lasted about twenty minutes, according to Schuyler. Dolgorukov, incidentally, was no stranger to Americans during his long, thirty-five-year tenure as governor general.

tion of his son, the tsar was introduced to Fred Grant. According to an American eyewitness, he deliberately snubbed Grant by immediately turning away to resume his conversation with Sherman and Curtin, thus presumably demonstrating his continued animosity toward the president for his treatment of Katakazi and Alexis.[268] The visit to Moscow ended with a lovely evening spent overlooking the city from Sparrow Hills and a dinner hosted by Dolgorukov.

In St. Petersburg Sherman and Curtin had an extended meeting with an "old and ailing" Gorchakov on 24 May. The chancellor mentioned in passing that he wished that the Katakazi affair had been left for him and Curtin to settle. Soon after this interview, the young Grant, apparently not finding Russia to his taste, departed for Stockholm. Sherman and Audenreid were then left to enjoy a reception at Tsarskoe Selo, hosted by Grand Duke Alexander and his wife, Grand Duchess Maria Fedorovna. The latter had a long conversation with them. "We both agreed that she was, besides a princess, an accomplished lady. Her face does not entitle her to the compliment of being the handsomest princess of Europe, but surely her manners do."[269]

After a day at the Hermitage, Sherman, Audenreid, and Curtin dined with Grand Duke Nicholas and the next day joined Grand Duke Constantine, the tsar's brother, for a cruise on his yacht to the Kronstadt naval base. Most pleasant of all for Sherman, however, was an opportunity to reminisce about the Civil War siege of Memphis with Admiral Lesovskii, who had visited his camp then and "seems to retain a clear memory of what he saw there, and showed a most friendly interest in the persons he met." Afterwards, Sherman sat up all night talking with Curtin about their Russian experiences.[270]

The Great Mennonite Migration

During the late eighteenth century, as part of Catherine the Great's effort to develop the Russian economy along physiocratic lines, a number of Germanic-speaking families accepted invitations to settle in frontier areas of the

268. New York *Herald*, 13 June 1872. This version of the meeting was given wide circulation in the American press—for example, Philadelphia *Inquirer*, 14 June 1872—but the slight was not mentioned by Schuyler; see Schuyler to Fish (private), 24 May 1872, vol. 88, Fish Papers, LC. Sherman found the tsar "strong, healthy but care-worn, and on the whole a fine-looking man"; "Extracts from Diary," 872.

269. Sherman, "Extracts from Diary," 873; Curtin to Fish, 3 June 1872, DUSM, Russia, vol. 24 (roll 24, M 35), RG 59, NA.

270. Sherman, "Extracts from Diary," 875.

empire. Many of these were Dutch and Swiss Mennonites who were un-happy about the pressures of war and taxation, especially in Frederick the Great's Prussia. Catherine guaranteed them free lands in sizable self-administered colonies, exemption from recruitment, freedom from taxation for a period, and assistance in moving. Among the largest of these migrations at that time were those from the Danzig area of Prussia to Ukraine, mainly to the colonies of Chortitza (founded 1789) on the Dnieper River south of Kiev, and Molochna (1804), about fifty miles north of the port of Berdiansk on the Sea of Azov. This area had recently been acquired by the annexation of the Crimean khanate and was then known as "New Russia."[271] As early as the 1760s, many other German-speaking people had moved from the war-torn states of Germany to Russia, concentrating on both sides of the Volga, near Saratov and Samara, in Bessarabia, and elsewhere along the Black Sea. They also included a number of Swiss and Palatinate Mennonites, who chose the province of Volynia (southeast Poland or west Ukraine).

These and other smaller groups of foreign settlers—Bulgarians, Serbs, Greeks, Jews, and others—were left almost undisturbed for about a hundred years, prospered relative to native Ukrainians, Russians, and Tatars around them, and were a significant factor in Russia's growth as a grain-exporting country in the nineteenth century.[272] Ironically, their situation changed dramatically during the reform era of Alexander II. One basic principle of these changes was the elimination of special privileges, such as exemption from recruitment into the Russian army. By the military reform law of 1874 everyone would become liable to military service. An announcement in 1870 warning the population of this naturally alarmed the pacifist Mennonites. Volga German Lutherans and Catholics were also concerned that their young men would be converted to Russian Orthodoxy in the Russian army.[273]

271. For an excellent geo-historical study, see William Schroeder and Helmut T. Huebert, *Mennonite Historical Atlas* (Winnepeg: Springfield Publishers, 1990).

272. Russian authorities respected Mennonite agricultural accomplishments and publicized them in the journal of the Ministry of State Domains, and progressive Mennonites such as Johann Cornies of Chortitza wrote articles for Russian publication. The best sources on the Russian background are A. A. Klaus, *Nashi kolonii: Opyty i materialy po istorii i statistike inostrannoi kolonizatsii v Rossii* (St. Petersburg: Nusvalt, 1869), and Karl Stumpp, *The Emigration from Germany to Russia in the Years 1763 to 1862* (Tubingen: By author, 1972), which deals primarily with the non-Mennonite Germans.

273. C. Henry Smith, *The Coming of the Russian Mennonites: An Episode in the Settling of the Last Frontier, 1874–1884* (Berne, Ind.: Mennonite Book Concern, 1927), pp. 44–45. See also Adam Giesinger, *The Story of Russia's Germans from Catherine to Khrushchev* (Battleford, Saskatchewan: Marian Press, 1974).

Other factors were involved in the decision to emigrate from Russia. A number of the Mennonites had already moved outside their colonies, some because of religious controversy—such as a group that split off from the Molochna colony, settled in the Crimea, and became known as the Krimmer Mennonite Brethren. Others left to pursue business opportunities in milling and shipping in port cities such as Berdiansk, where news about the rest of the world was readily available. By this time the original colonies were overcrowded with little possibility of expansion. The Mennonites also had a tradition of subdividing to found new colonies, and they had already in the 1860s considered—and rejected—an opportunity to move to the distant Amur River basin. Moreover, by the beginning of the 1870s, migration was facilitated by railroads, bringing the telegraph, newspapers, and fast, cheap transportation as far as Sevastopol and Saratov. Perhaps as crucial, the new Russification movement was leading to more direct interference in their affairs as a whole by Russian authorities.

In the spring of 1871 a Mennonite delegation went to St. Petersburg to express their concerns about present conditions and the approaching changes. General Friedrich Heyden of the military reform committee informed them of a possible arrangement for noncombatant service in the hospitals or sanitary departments of the army. But the Mennonites objected to any labor that would in any way support military activity. Heyden, reluctant to start granting exceptions, thought their only other recourse might be to leave the country and gave them a ten-year grace period in which to decide. To avoid this ultimatum, other Mennonite delegations followed, and one even vainly sought an interview with the emperor at Yalta, but the wheels of the Russian bureaucracy moved as slowly as usual in resolving such matters.[274]

In 1871 a leading Mennonite merchant of Berdiansk began a correspondence with John Funk, an American Mennonite newspaper editor in Elkhart, Indiana. The next year four prominent Russian Mennonites toured the United States. One of them, Bernhard Warkentin, Jr., the son of a Berdiansk miller and grain shipper who was originally from the Molochna colony, decided to stay; he would later make a substantial impact on wheat production, milling, and marketing in the United States. Early in 1872, the Molochna Mennonites presented a petition to the British and American consuls in Odessa asking if they could obtain free land and "entire exemptions" from military service. They also sought advice on sending an advance

274. Smith, *Coming of the Russian Mennonites*, pp. 44–47.

"scouting" delegation.[275] The American consul relayed these requests to the legation in St. Petersburg.

Schuyler, then in charge of the mission in Curtin's absence, immediately responded, stating that military service was not compulsory, that the Homestead Act and railroad grants made plenty of land available, that Congress might provide additional settlement aid, and that a delegation was indeed advisable "to see what could be done, and to select a site for the colony." He stressed to consul Smith that in communicating with the petitioners, he should not alarm local Russian authorities.[276] The British-Canadian response was similar, setting up a competition between the two countries. William Hesperer, a Canadian immigration agent, actually visited the Mennonite colonies in south Russia in the fall of 1872 in an effort to spur emigration to his country.[277]

Schuyler also obtained an interview with Westmann, who consulted with Gorchakov but remained uncertain whether there would be any modification of policy in response to the Mennonite predicament. The liberal Russian press was at first opposed to any special status for the Mennonites: "By admitting the right of the colonists to exemption from military service, it so much the more admits the right to the same exemption of the Russian nobility, mercantile class, etc."[278] But within a month, after additional pressure from the British ambassador, the Russian government had agreed both to letting the Mennonites leave freely and to granting special privilege. Schuyler understood that the Commission on the Law of Compulsory Military Service "resolved to make an exception in favor of the Mennonites and others whose consciences forbid them to bear arms. They will not be exempted from military service entirely, as that is considered unjust to the rest of the population, but will be exempted from *carrying arms*, and will be assigned other duties." Schuyler added, "I do not know how far these statements are true, nor whether an exemption of this kind will be satisfactory to the Men-

275. Timothy Smith to Curtin, 7/19 March 1872, DPR, Russia, vol. 4434 (misc. received), RG 84, NA.

276. Schuyler to Smith, 29 March 1872 (c), DPR, Russia, vol. 4534 (notes sent), RG 84, NA.

277. Smith, *Coming of the Russian Mennonites*, pp. 49–50. A valuable survey of initial efforts to attract these settlers is "The Mennonites," Omaha *Daily Herald*, 15 January 1876. "Russian Emigration," Boston *Globe*, 13 May 1872, is a surprisingly accurate description of the Mennonite situation, probably "planted" by the Santa Fe railroad.

278. Schuyler to Fish, 6 April 1872, and enclosed translation of an article from *Russkii Mir* of 24 March/5 April 1872, DUSM, Russia, vol. 24 (roll 24, M 35), RG 59, NA.

nonites."[279] It is not clear if American and British interest in the Mennonite cause helped soften Russian policy, but, in any event, the change was not widely publicized.[280]

After these initial contacts and following Schuyler's recommendation, the Mennonite communities selected twelve of their most respected elders to go to North America to scout for land and discuss terms during the summer and fall of 1873. Unwittingly, the Russian government furthered the cause of resettlement that same year by deporting Cornelius Jansen of Berdiansk, a strong supporter of emigration who still held Prussian citizenship. He first settled in Ontario but moved in early 1874 to Nebraska, from where he devoted much effort to encouraging other Mennonites to join them.[281]

The Mennonite investigating delegation, traveling in three separate parties, was interested in guarantees of religious freedom and exemption from military service, good quality land in large blocs available free or at a low price, the right to live in closed communities with their own separate schools, and advances to cover transportation expenses. All of these were quickly granted by the Canadian government, but efforts to secure the same privileges in the United States ran into bureaucratic and political obstacles. One group, accompanied by railroad agent Michael Hiller, even managed to secure an interview with President Grant at his summer home in August 1873 and presented to him a petition seeking exemption from military service for fifty years, control over their own schools, and immunity from service on juries.[282] Although they understood from American brethren that military exemptions could be purchased for $300, according to Civil War practice, they feared that such payments would be difficult, considering the costs of their resettlement.

In forwarding the petition to Secretary of State Fish, the president noted, "Of course, no privileges can be accorded to foreign born citizens not accorded to all other citizens. But it may be proper to state to these people that it is entirely improbable that they will ever be called upon to perform invol-

279. Schuyler to Fish, 4 May 1872, ibid.

280. In fact, alternative service, quite progressive for the times, was eventually approved in 1874. It allowed the Mennonites to work under their own supervision in the state forests, and none ever served unwillingly in the military forces of the empire.

281. Gustav E. Reimer and G. R. Gaeddert, *Exiled by the Czar: Cornelius Jansen and the Great Mennonite Migration, 1874* (Newton, Kans.: Mennonite Publication Office, 1956), pp. 72–77.

282. Jay Cooke (Philadelphia) to U. S. Grant, letter of introduction, 31 July 1873; petition, 8 August 1873 (original), vol. 96, Fish Papers, LC. A version of the petition, published by Smith, *Coming of the Russian Mennonites*, pp. 72–73, is misleading as it is poorly translated from a German diary of one of the delegates, Paul Tschetter.

untary military service."[283] Fish demurred, noting that only Congress could
approve such an exemption and that it would be dangerously misleading to
forecast an absence of war. He also observed that matters relating to schools
and courts were under state jurisdiction.[284] When Hiller inquired about the
petition, Fish replied in the same vein.[285]

Another major problem was finding large tracts of good land available
cheap and near railroads. This automatically reduced most opportunities to
the government grants of land to railroads. However, in order to preempt
speculation, Congress had authorized that only the alternate sections of
land (640 acres per section) be awarded to the railroads for extending tracks
and depots across the Great Plains. The result on the map was a checkerboard pattern about thirty miles wide with the nonrailroad sections open
for homesteading (160-acre limit for each family) through land offices. Yet
the incoming Mennonites wanted guarantees of complete access to these
other sections so that they could form contiguous colonies.

The matter was subsequently pressed in Congress by American Mennonites
and powerful railroad interests. Prodded by Lancaster Mennonites, Senator Simon Cameron of Pennsylvania, a former minister to Russia, sponsored a bill to
grant the Mennonite wishes. Other support came from Indiana and Illinois
and from some of the new Plains states. A long debate ensued in April 1874
over what had become a heated sociopolitical issue. Many congressmen
thought that promoting the settlement of large groups who would resist assimilation and so avoid the "melting pot" was contrary to the spirit of America.
Anxious to move on to other business, the Senate finally voted to close debate
without acting on the bill.[286] Thus the Russian Mennonites were faced with the
prospect of escaping Russification only to succumb to Americanization.

Still, most of the Mennonite scouts recommended settlement in the
United States. A warmer climate, access to water, and less remote lands close

283. Grant to Fish, 9 August 1873 (c), Hamilton Fish file, MinnHS, original at Columbia University.
284. Fish to Grant, 13 August 1873, ibid.
285. Fish to Hiller, 5 September 1873, ibid. Apparently, on the same date Fish wrote
directly or through Hiller to the Mennonite delegation. It is unlikely, in the light of
other documents, that he penned, "It is true, however, that for the next fifty years we
will not be entangled in another war in which military service will be necessary," as
cited by Smith, *Coming of the Russian Mennonites*, p. 74, from Tschetter's papers.
286. Smith, *Coming of the Russian Mennonites*, pp. 83–90. The Philadelphia *Inquirer*
(1 May 1874), in covering the debate, criticized the opposition: "If we can estimate the
Russian Mennonites by the German Mennonites in Pennsylvania, we should say that
the doors ought to be thrown wide open for the reception of such a population."

to railroads were particular advantages. But also crucial was the influence of the prosperous American Mennonite communities, which organized in Summerfield, Illinois, a Board of Guardians to assist and support migration. No less consequential was the salesmanship of the land agents of the Santa Fe (C. B. Schmidt), Kansas Pacific (Adam Rodenheimer), Burlington (A. E. Touzalin), and Northern Pacific (Hiller), which all competed for the new settlers.[287] In fact, about 450 Mennonites from south Russia did not wait for the return of the delegates and set off for new homes in 1873, founding small settlements in Minnesota, the Dakotas, and Kansas.[288]

The real wave came in 1874, spearheaded by the Krimmer (Crimean) Mennonites[289] and the Molochna village of Alexanderwohl,[290] which had prior connections with both Jansen and Warkentin. By this time the Russian government had awakened to the fact that a major exodus of first-class farmers was about to get under way, and in the spring of 1874 General Eduard Totleben, a German-speaking Crimean War hero, hurried to the Molochna district. He went directly to Alexanderwohl to attempt to convince that group to stay, but he met only complaints about delays in obtain-

---

287. The most successful of these was Schmidt, who managed to woo most of the initial migration to Santa Fe lands in Kansas and subsequently visited the colonies several times. Hiller, however, contended that the scouting delegation hired him to make travel arrangements in Europe. American authorities, meanwhile, became concerned that these efforts were arousing the hostility of the Russian government. Hiller assured Jewell, "It is not my desire to induce these people to leave their country nor do I wish to induce anybody else to do so, this part of the business has been done by the Russian Government by depriving the Mennonites of their privileges, which were granted to them forever, and leaving it to their option, either to submit to the new rules or to emigrate." Hiller (Berlin) to Jewell, 23 May 1874, DPR, Russia, vol. 4435 (misc. received), RG 84, NA.

288. Smith, *Coming of the Russian Mennonites*, pp. 92–93; Offenberg to Westmann, 2/14 May 1874, f. 133, op. 470, d. 144 (1874), AVPR. Offenberg stressed, citing a private letter from Odessa, that 10,000 were expected to leave for America in 1874. Many Mennonites seriously considered Canada because there they would be under a steady monarchical hand rather than in the unpredictable chaos of democracy that they thought prevailed in the United States.

289. On this group, see David V. Wiebe, *They Seek a Country: A Survey of Mennonite Migrations with Special Reference to Kansas and Gnadenau* (Hillsboro, Kans.: Mennonite Brethren Publishing House, 1959). Much of their heritage is preserved in Hillsboro at the Adobe House Museum, a restored "Ukrainian" farmstead.

290. This village was founded in 1820 by later immigrants from the Danzig area. On their trek to Molochna they happened to meet Alexander I on his way to Taganrog; he gave them his best wishes, hence the name. The history of these and other Mennonites who settled in Kansas is preserved by the Mennonite Heritage Center in Goessel and the Kaufman Museum at Bethel College, North Newton.

ing their passports.[291] Not long after that nearly the whole Alexanderwohl community, about 220 families, with some others joining them from neighboring villages, left for America, traveling by three chartered trains to Hamburg and then on two immigrant ships to New York. Other, smaller groups left from Molochna, the Crimea, and Volynia about the same time.

The main Alexanderwohl party leisurely journeyed westward with stopovers in Elkhart, Indiana, and Summerfield, Illinois. Chaperoned by agents of the Santa Fe Railroad, they were housed temporarily in Topeka, Kansas, in the company's bridge shops, while they chose land to purchase—some sixty sections at three dollars an acre of the best agricultural area in the state, stretching across three counties north of Wichita. Then, they and their newly purchased livestock and equipment were transported free to that tract, where they stayed the first winter in large "immigrant houses" erected by the Santa Fe.[292]

The purchase of the alternate railroad sections of the giant checkerboard, however, meant that the Mennonites were much more spread out and had larger farms than in Ukraine, resulting at first in unusual L-shaped villages, most of which survived only a few years. They eventually homesteaded or bought out most of the farmers in the intervening sections. In the middle of all these, within bell sound of the hamlets, the large Alexanderwohl church was built, containing the records of baptisms, marriages, and deaths in the community since its departure from Friesland in the sixteenth century.

Another of the Alexanderwohl contingents went first to Lincoln, Nebraska, through the influence of Jansen, but they also scouted for land in Kansas. A joint meeting was finally held with agents of the Burlington (Nebraska) and the Santa Fe (Kansas). The Mennonites found fault with the proposed Nebraska site because a sandy area separated them from the main line of the railroad. The agent promised to construct a sturdy plank road. After further objections, such as relative scarcity of water, the Burlington offered them 100,000 acres absolutely free of charge, as well as free freight, seed, and supplies.[293] But the Mennonites de-

291. The American minister, however, was led to believe by sources in St. Petersburg that the mission was a success and that most of the Mennonites would stay in Russia; Jewell to Fish, 20 May 1874, DUSM, Russia, vol. 26 (roll 26, M 35), RG 59, NA.

292. For more details, see Saul, "The Migration of the Russian-Germans to Kansas," *Kansas Historical Quarterly* 40, 1 (Spring 1974): 38–62. The Mennonites attracted considerable newspaper attention, for as one reported on the Alexanderwohl land purchase, "this is largest land sale [150,000 acres] ever made in the West to one people." New York *Times*, 24 September 1874.

293. Smith, *Coming of the Russian Mennonites*, pp. 118–19; Reimer and Gaeddert, *Exiled by the Czar*, pp. 119–20.

cided to purchase land in Kansas, although the Santa Fe agent was quite prepared to match the Burlington offer gratis. The railroads viewed the Mennonites as good future customers and magnets for other settlers because of their reputation for setting down roots, being peaceful, and having good agricultural sense. These would not be the typical itinerant homesteaders. The railroad companies were also especially desperate for business after the 1873 depression and the 1874 Great Plains drought.

Some Russian Mennonites did settle in Nebraska and other states, but the largest number during the first immigrant years chose Kansas.[294] Everywhere they were welcomed as a stable influence during economically precarious times on the American frontier. They were followed in even larger numbers, beginning in 1875, by German Lutherans and Catholics from the Volga region. The Volga Germans in general endured more difficulties than the Mennonites, because they were poorer to begin with and came later, after much of the choicest land was taken. But they too stayed to farm vast areas of the Great Plains and to take jobs in developing "frontier" towns such as Topeka, Lincoln, and Greeley. The Black Sea Germans followed, spreading out especially through the Dakotas.

Confusion as to the real identity of these immigrants from Russia existed from the beginning and persisted for generations. The Mennonites were already divided ethnically—Dutch, Swiss, and German—and by religious differences; the Volga Germans, who had uniquely preserved eighteenth-century local German dialects and customs in their separate and remote parish villages, experienced some friction when they settled in closer proximity in the United States. All the groups from Russia were looked upon as very distinct from the large number of other German immigrants, because of their dialects, clothes, manners, and community consciousness. They were universally labeled "Rooshians."[295]

Many had, in fact, absorbed some Russian, Ukrainian, or Polish customs,

294. By October 1874 about 900 Mennonite families are recorded as arriving in North America, distributed as follows: 230 in Manitoba, 200 in Dakota, 15 in Minnesota, 80 in Nebraska, 315 in Kansas, and 60 in process of finding land. David Goertz, secretary of Mennonite Board of Guardians (Summerfield) to Voight, Russian chargé d'affaires, 27 October 1874, f. 170, op. 512/3, d. 125, AVPR. Goertz was responding to an inquiry by Voight and assuring him that the board was not encouraging emigration from Russia but only assisting them once they reached America. The colonies were well aware, however, that help would be available in the United States.

295. A typical example in Kansas was an initial identification of the Volga Germans as Mennonites, which was corrected as follows: "The Russians who have settled in Ellis county . . . resemble their Mennonite countrymen except in religion, they being Roman Catholics." Hays City *Sentinel*, 5 April 1876.

especially in communal pasturage, strip farming, and other aspects of community organization that resembled the Russian *mir*. These survived in varying degrees, to the astonishment and sometimes bemusement of American neighbors. Most settlers, however, adapted easily to the more progressive and independent agricultural patterns of the United States. The Alexanderwohl community, for example, was accustomed to the large stone rollers employed in the Ukraine for threshing, and upon arrival, they ordered some to be cut from a local quarry. But by the time their grain was ready to harvest the next year, they had discovered threshing machines; some of the stone rollers survive as barnyard or museum curiosities.

The impact of these Germanic settlers from Russia, reinforced by a large secondary waves of immigration in the 1890s and early twentieth century, was certainly unique and considerable but not easy to classify. From the newcomers, many Americans in the Midwest arrived at a distorted image of what was really Russian, yet the immigrants' actual imprint was no less Russian, Ukrainian, or Polish. Now overwhelmingly dependent on preexisting American economic and political structures and nudged along by the business-minded railroads and curious reporters, they assimilated fairly rapidly but seemed to retain definite "Russian" characteristics to outsiders. An early student of the Volga Germans in America began a 1909 Master's thesis on the Lutheran community in Lincoln, Nebraska, as follows:

> Standing at the corner of Tenth and O Streets . . . you may see pass by you from ten to twenty women with little black woolen shawls on their heads. Ask any citizen who they are and ninety-nine times in one hundred he will tell you they are "Russians." . . . As a matter of fact . . . his information is incorrect. . . . These people, of whom there are about 4,000 in the city . . . are Germans, not Russians; they are Teutons, not Slavs; they are Lutheran and Reformed, not Greek Catholics.[296]

What was North America's gain was Russia's loss, dramatizing the acute problem of Russia's agricultural backwardness that was never resolved but only worsened by alternating neglect and deliberate devastation in the fu-

---

296. Introduction, Hattie Plum Williams, *The Czar's Germans: With Particular Reference to the Volga Germans* (reprint; Lincoln, Nebr.: American Historical Society of Germans from Russia, 1975), p. xi. The organization that reprinted this book has promoted the cultural heritage of all Germans from Russia by publishing a journal, creating regional chapters, and hosting annual international conferences. Similarly, the Germans from Russia Heritage Society of Bismarck, North Dakota, focuses on those who came from Bessarabia and the Black Sea region.

ture. Already in 1874, some Russians perceived the danger in policies that drove the best farmers away and sharply criticized the government. The problem, one of them pointed out, was not only administrative bungling, such as sending a general to negotiate with Mennonites, but also the nationalistic, militant foreign policy that seemed to anticipate war. "Not trusting in a peaceful future, the Mennonites all the same are choosing in large numbers for emigration."[297]

Surprisingly, perhaps, the Mennonites made the quickest and most successful adjustments of the "Russian" immigrants. The Alexanderwohl and Swiss settlers became the nucleus of the General Conference Mennonites, probably the most open and progressive of all Anabaptists. They also infused American religious life with missionary and charitable pursuits, first among Indians and blacks, then later to Africa, Russia (ironically), and other parts of the world. These Mennonites were also leaders in founding colleges, with the result that many were soon moving from farming into other professions.

Above all, the Mennonites from Ukraine and Crimea are renowned for introducing Russian varieties of hard red winter and spring wheat (namely Turkey Red and Durum) that rapidly turned the United States into a great wheat-producing country—though it is largely a myth that this happened immediately in 1874 when each family planted the small bag of wheat brought over from the old country.[298] Because they were primarily grain farmers (corn being unknown to them) and, along with the Volga Germans, accustomed to dry, grassland (steppe) farming, because they retained connections with their homeland and quickly became involved in crucial milling and marketing operations, those of Russian Mennonite background were of signal importance in the swift transformation of vast areas of the American prairie to efficient and productive wheat cultivation.

Immigration was only one indication of the increasing and maturing of contacts between Russians and Americans. Reconstructing America and reforming Russia were both expanding their developed territory and imperial vision with consequent technical and military requirements. More serious travelers and business agents would seek money and laurels in serving those needs.

297. N. A. Demert, "Nashi obshchestvennyia dela," OZ 217, 12 (December 1874): 412–13.

298. Norman E. Saul, "Myth and History: Turkey Red Wheat and the 'Kansas Miracle,'" *Heritage of the Great Plains* 22, 3 (Summer 1989): 1–13.

2

War and Technology, 1870s

Most of the correspondence from Russia during the 1870s, especially after 1874, pertained not to peaceful Mennonites or to grand tours, but to war and expansion, to technology and progress. This was a period, moreover, in which conservative views within the Russian government gained steadily over the liberal positions that had dominated the reform era of the 1860s and a burgeoning Russian nationalism and Russia-centered Slavophilism or Pan-Slavism predominated. Mennonites and Volga Germans proved to be only the tip of the iceberg of non-Russian nationalities resentful of long-term discrimination, now made less tolerable by education, a sense of ethnic awareness, media exposure, and new repression.

What was especially ironic is that enough of the liberal spirit and freedoms of the 1860s remained—in the form, for example, of a relatively free press—to make people aware of and concerned about the problems. Those that most attracted the attention of American observers were the restrictions on the Jewish population, the consolidation of control over Central Asia, a new phase of the Eastern Question that erupted into the Russo-Turkish War of 1877–1878, and the growth of the revolutionary movement. Americans were especially sensitive to these issues because they corresponded to similar problems at home: the assimilation of large numbers of immigrants, western consolidation that led to a new series of bitter battles with the outnumbered Native Americans, the growth of the power of Washington through what some viewed as an imperial presidency (even using the term "czarism"), and emerging voices of protest that were spurred by local conditions, economic depression, and the import of European ideologies. The shadow of the Paris Commune of 1871 would fall over both the United States and Russia.

The Jewish Question

Since the beginning of relations between the two countries, Americans had given only casual notice to the plight of the Jewish population of the Russian Empire. Perhaps the existence of slavery in the United States restrained public or private criticism of ethnic discrimination in the empire; regardless, in the late 1860s the American press began to comment on the issue. In 1869, the New York *Times* smugly observed: "We hope the Czar will accede to the request of the Jews of Russia for an extension of their rights of worship and education. The Czar need have no fear of the Jews. In this country, for example, they have the same rights as other people, and are regarded as excellent citizens."[1]

Not long afterwards, the first on-the-spot investigation was conducted by Eugene Schuyler as consul in Reval; he blamed the geographic confinement of the Jews to the Pale (western and southwestern border provinces) on the opposition of Russian merchants and the general "fear of the evil influence of the Jews on the peasantry."[2] But he also noted that the barriers had been partly lifted. The result of this, however, was the sudden increase of Jews in the most prosperous urban centers and their spread throughout the empire, facilitated by railroad and commercial expansion.

Odessa became an especially strong magnet for the internal Jewish migration. Between 1854 and 1873 the Jewish population of the city jumped from 17,000 to over 51,000, from 19 percent to 27 percent of the total population.[3] Exaggerated economic, social, and religious fears caused anti-Jewish riots, often arising out of small incidents, and the violence was naturally reported by the American press, though its specific cause was usually left vague.[4] Initially the core opposition to the Jews was from the Greek population, which had dominated the economy of the city and now felt squeezed by the influx of Jews. This culminated in a full-scale pogrom conducted by Greeks and Russians on Jewish synagogues and businesses during Easter week of 1871. Many Jews were killed or left homeless, martial law was de-

---

1. New York *Times*, 30 July 1869.
2. Schuyler memorandum enclosed in Curtin to Fish, 6 January 1870, DUSM, Russia, vol. 22 (roll 22, M 35), RG 59, NA.
3. Patricia Herlihy, *Odessa: A History, 1794–1914* (Cambridge: Harvard University Press, 1986), p. 251.
4. See, for example, New York *Times*, 15 February 1871, for a description of early anti-Jewish riots in Odessa.

clared, and the army was brought in to restore order. In describing the event, consul Timothy Smith betrayed his own as well as Russian prejudice: "As a race [the Jews] are unproductive, averse to labor, occupying themselves from preference as go betweens, engaged in all manner of commerce."[5]

The conflict in Odessa prompted an official government investigation and inspired Schuyler to resume his own study of the problem. In September 1872 he sent a memorandum to the State Department on the situation of the Jews in Russia in which he described the legal restrictions on their movement and occupation, citing, for example, that they could not own estates. He also reported that a considerable number of exceptions had been allowed, especially in the reform period, for those of wealth or education. Schuyler listed the total Jewish population at 2,348,000, or 3.06 percent of the empire total. The great majority were still confined to the Pale, but 7,000 had moved to Siberia, which was legally closed to them, and about the same number were residing in St. Petersburg and Moscow each. Those who belonged to the first guild of merchants and paid a sizable annual assessment could essentially live in any city.[6] The motives for Schuyler's interest in the plight of Russia's Jews were mixed and in part designed for political consumption at home, to help Grant win some Jewish votes. As he explained to Fish, "I thought it might have some effect on [American Jews] if the Government gave them another proof of the interest they take in their welfare. With this idea I have prepared the paper on the legal position of the Hebrews in Russia."[7]

At that time Schuyler believed that the discrimination against the Jews was mainly economic rather than religious and based on the premise that "the Hebrew race has a natural tendency to exploit the population in the midst of which it is settled." The recent emergence of a strident Russian nationalism augured further conflict: "Now, since the spread of Slavonophile [sic] and ultra-Russian ideas, it is not unusual to find strong liberals and democrats, who are animated with the feelings of the Middle Ages toward the Hebrews, and even some of the prominent journals, such as the *Golos*,

5. Smith to Fish, 22 April 1871, DUSC, Odessa, vol. 5 (roll 3, M 459), RG 59, NA. For many years the American consulate in Odessa was monopolized by a local Greek family.

6. Enclosure in Schuyler to Fish, 29 September 1872, DUSM, Russia, vol. 24 (roll 24, M 35), RG 59, NA; published as "Memorandum on the Legal Position of Hebrews in Russia," PRFRUS, 1872, pp. 498–503.

7. Schuyler to Fish (unofficial), 29 September 1872, vol. 90, Fish Papers, LC.

are constantly attacking them."[8] He added that some liberal journals, for example *Vestnik Evropy* (Herald of Europe), still supported removing all restrictions.

Schuyler emphasized that progress was being made by the establishment of a government commission under the Ministry of Interior to investigate Jewish conditions, and he translated its first report. The commission began with the assumption that the Jews wanted only to be middlemen who "not only ruin but . . . corrupt the native population." The primary task for the government was to convert them from distillers to furniture making, from parasites to producers.[9] The commission did not cite emigration as a solution, but increasing numbers in the 1870s were taking that path. As with the Mennonites, threats to their communities, expanded possibilities of movement offered by steam transportation over land and sea, and ready identity with established populations abroad encouraged Jewish departures from Russia. Meanwhile, American diplomats, newspapers, and railroads would begin to see the potential strain this issue posed for Russian-American relations.

The Rosenstraus Case

The first instance of the American government interceding on behalf of a Jewish resident in Russia concerned the rights and privileges of Theodore Rosenstraus, an Austrian Jew who had emigrated to the United States and acquired citizenship. He later went to Russia to establish an optical service, first in Voronezh in 1863, then in Kharkov in 1865, as a merchant of the second guild. He expanded his business quietly into a general "American Store" with considerable success. Beginning in 1867, economic jealousy, provincial conservatism, and probably ethnic/religious hostility on the part of local authorities created problems for him.

8. Ibid. The literature on the Jewish problem in Russian history is vast and of generally good quality. See for example: Hans Rogger, *Jewish Policies and Right-Wing Politics in Imperial Russia* (Berkeley and Los Angeles: University of California Press, 1986); S. M. Dubnov, *The History of the Jews in Russia and Poland*, 3 vols. (Philadelphia: Jewish Publishing Society, 1916–20); Salo W. Baron, *The Russian Jew Under Tsars and Soviets*, 2d ed. (New York: Macmillan, 1964).

9. Schuyler to Fish, 15 March 1875, DUSM, Russia, vol. 28 (roll 28, M 35), RG 59, NA. An important member of the commission was an old Moscow friend of Schuyler's, Professor Grigor'ev; he also benefited from the work of Il'ia Orshanskii, a leading Russian expert on the Jews.

In August of that year, the police raided his store while he was away at the Poltava fair and confiscated eighty-one stereoscopic pictures, which were claimed to be indecent but which Rosenstraus argued "were only such as are sold in every city, and exposed to view in all shop windows where stereoscopic pictures are sold." Moreover, they had passed Customs with no objection.[10] Cassius Clay, perhaps because of his own involvement at the time in sordid affairs, did not bother to report the matter to Washington, but he did press this case of supposedly "filthy pictures" on Vladimir Westmann, who checked into it. The governor of Kharkov province duly reported that the principal of a local gymnasium had become concerned about the circulation of these pictures among his impressionable students and had complained to the police.[11] The outcome is not clear—whether Foreign Minister Gorchakov interceded as a favor to Clay or Rosenstraus bribed his way out of a jam—but the "American Store" remained in operation in Kharkov (perhaps without the "French postcards").

In fact, Rosenstraus expanded his business considerably when he became an agent for Singer Sewing Machine Company and brought over his brother-in-law, Bernhard Frankfurter, as a partner. In 1872 he tried to buy land for a repair shop but was denied permission.[12] The following year he was again in conflict with the local authorities; this time they refused to renew his license on grounds of religion, asserting that Jews did not have the right to trade in Kharkov (though he had been in business for eight years).[13] George Pomutz, acting in place of the minister, turned for recourse again to Westmann, who clearly did not want to champion a special exception for an American Jew.[14]

Marshall Jewell, coming late onto the scene in December, saw the case as a clear violation of Rosenstraus's rights as an American citizen under a pro-

10. Rosenstraus to Clay, 29 August 1867 (original), DPR, Russia, vol. 4502 (notes received), RG 84, NA; copy enclosed in Jewell to Fish, 15 December 1873, DUSM, Russia, vol. 25 (roll 25, M 35), RG 59, NA.

11. Clay to Westmann, 2/21 October 1867, and Westmann to Clay, 13/25 January 1868, copies enclosed in Jewell to Fish, 15 December 1873, DUSM, Russia, vol. 25 (roll 25, M 35), RG 59, NA.

12. Rosenstraus to Curtin, 2/20 October 1872, copy in Schuyler to Fish, 31 October 1872, DUSM, Russia, vol. 24 (roll 24, M 35), RG 59, NA.

13. Rosenstraus to Jewell, 20 September/2 October 1873, DPR, Russia, vol. 4435 (misc. received), RG 84, NA; copy in Jewell to Fish, 30 October 1873, DUSM, Russia, vol. 25 (roll 25, M 35), RG 59, NA.

14. Pomutz to Westmann, 31 October 1873 (c), DPR, Russia, vol. 4535 (notes sent), RG 84, NA; Pomutz to Fish, 30 October 1873, DUSM, Russia, vol. 25 (roll 25, M 35), RG 59, NA.

vision of the Treaty of Commerce of 1832, which stipulated that Americans have the same rights in the empire as Russian subjects. The new minister did not force the issue, leaving the government to develop an interpretation of the clause that would lead to considerable trouble in subsequent years: that American Jews had the same rights, no more, as Russian Jews, not other Russians. Rosenstraus solved his own predicament simply by joining the first guild of merchants, a generally recognized right of economically successful Russian Jews, with an additional payment of 600 rubles, which Rosenstraus probably viewed as only another form of bribery—or as simply the cost of doing business in Russia.[15]

This discriminatory settlement established a dangerous precedent, and the Jewish-American problem not only persisted but worsened. A few months after the satisfactory conclusion of this phase of the Rosenstraus affair, Jewell observed in passing that the Russian treatment of Jews was proving to be a real problem for the legation, "and everything which appears in print bearing upon the subject of the relations of the United States to the Hebrew race is read with interest and commented upon in official circles."[16] The lack of consistency in Russian national policy is worth noting: while removing in the name of equality the special privileges of colonists such as the Mennonites and Volga Germans, the government was tightening the discriminatory policies against the Jewish population.

Central Asia

One reason that Jewish affairs appeared to take a back seat for a few years after 1873 is that both Russians and Americans were absorbed in the conquest of Central Asia and in the Eastern Question, which seemed about to be solved. Eugene Schuyler, who had rapidly become the leading (and perhaps only) American expert on the Russian Jewish population, would devote most of his time in the 1870s to these other topics. In fact, American interest in them was largely shaped by Schuyler and the first American pro-

15. Jewell to Fish, 15 December 1873 and 27 January 1874, DUSM, Russia, vol. 25 (roll 25, M 35), RG 59, NA; Jewell to Westmann, 19/31 December 1873, DPR, Russia, vol. 4535 (notes sent), RG 84, NA.
16. Jewell to Fish, 13 May 1874, DUSM, Russia, vol. 26 (roll 26, M 35), RG 59, NA.

fessional correspondent to make Russia and Eastern Europe the focus of his work—Januarius MacGahan.[17]

Schuyler began his career of reporting on the Russian scene with excellent preparation. Coming from a branch of an old New York family that had settled in Ithaca, Schuyler attended Yale University and earned one of its first doctorates in 1861. He subsequently wrote articles for a number of journals, most notably for the nascent issues of the *Nation*. His interest in Russia was initially piqued, as in the case of Jeremiah Curtin, by the fleet visit during the Civil War, which occurred while Schuyler was studying law at Columbia University. He also found Central Asia intriguing; the first book he purchased was a romantic novel set there, and an early article of his dealt with the area.[18]

Schuyler also studied Russian for a brief period with the priest of the Russian Orthodox church in New York. Then, in the summer of 1867, at age twenty-seven, he received his first diplomatic assignment as consul in Moscow. Earlier that year he had translated Ivan Turgenev's *Fathers and Sons* for its first English edition, but much of this was taken from a French version. He subsequently met the famous author in Europe on his way to his post. Although his fluency in Russian was probably still poor when he arrived in Moscow, his knowledge of French and interest in literature and history, the latter sparked by George Bancroft, quickly earned him entry into the literary salons of the city, especially that of Prince Vladimir Odoevskii.[19] Through his patronage Schuyler obtained access to one of the best book and manuscript libraries in Russia and introductions to leading Russian writers.

Among those he met at these salons was Leo Tolstoy, and he not only visited him later at his Yasnaya Polyana country estate but also acquired rights to translate some of his works.[20] Schuyler is credited with helping the emerg-

17. The main sources on Schuyler and MacGahan are James Seay Brown, Jr., "Eugene Schuyler, Observer of Russia: His Years as a Diplomat in Russia, 1867–1875" (Ph.D. diss., Vanderbilt, 1971); Marion Moore Coleman, "Eugene Schuyler: Diplomat Extraordinary from the United States to Russia, 1867–1876," *Russian Review* 7, 1 (Autumn 1947): 33–48; and Dale L. Walker, *Januarius MacGahan: The Life and Campaigns of an American War Correspondent* (Athens: Ohio University Press, 1988).

18. Coleman, "Eugene Schuyler," pp. 36–37; Brown, "Eugene Schuyler," pp. 18–19; Schuyler, "The Progress of Russia in Asia," *Nation* 2 (16 April 1866): 489.

19. Brown, "Eugene Schuyler," pp. 23–32.

20. Tolstoy's "Sevastopol in 1855" was translated by Schuyler for Scribner's *Hours at Home* 8, 4–6 (February–April 1869): 328–36, 416–22, 526–31. Schuyler's writings probably benefited from the fact that his mother was a Scribner, since most of them were published by Scribner's.

ing Russian author obtain American books and other materials for his library and with introducing him to other Americans. Schuyler was also a friend of Mikhail Katkov's, noted editor and publicist, and attended his regular Sunday soirees, as well as those of Ivan Aksakov, a leading Slavophile.[21] Moscow at this time was the center of a budding Russian nationalism and Schuyler was influenced by it. The city elite was also fascinated by neomaterialism, science, and statistics, which helped foster Schuyler's geographical and botanical curiosity about Central Asia.[22] Later in St. Petersburg he regularly attended the meetings of the Russian Imperial Geographical Society.

During his Moscow assignment, Schuyler made his first extended tour into the countryside, to the Volga region and as far as Orenburg on the border of Central Asia, which he briefly described in an article published in 1869. The trip included visits to "Kirghiz" (Kazakh) villages, Schuyler's first contact with the Turkic peoples of Central Asia.[23] But the change in administrations in Washington that year brought an end to his tenure in Moscow. The support of Andrew Curtin, however, won him a new appointment as consul in Reval, from where he earned the minister's further respect in his report on the Jewish problem and was thereupon assigned to St. Petersburg to serve as secretary of legation. There he expanded his studies to include current problems of government and society, especially the intricacies of the factionalism developing over reform and nationality issues. He soon earned a reputation as one of the most knowledgeable outsiders on Russian affairs, and the many dispatches he wrote during gaps between ministers or when Curtin and Jewell were on holiday were considered authoritative.[24] In December 1872 Schuyler composed his first assessment of the Russian advance into Central Asia, reviewing its history and stressing its haphazard course.[25] This probably circulated among his contacts in Russia either before or after it was sent to his superiors. In any event, early the next year he received a formal invitation to tour Central Asia and left almost immediately.

By contrast, Ohioan Januarius MacGahan was a largely self-educated young man. Early on, he had developed an ambition to be a foreign corre-

---

21. Eugene Schuyler, *Selected Essays* (New York: Scribner's, 1901), pp. 207–8.
22. Brown, "Eugene Schuyler," pp. 51–56.
23. "On the Steppe," *Hours at Home* 9, 4 (August 1869): 319–29.
24. An article about a British group in St. Petersburg noted: "At the door we met a friend from the British embassy, who, with the exception, perhaps, of the American Chargg'e d'Affairess, Mr. Schuyler, is said to be the best informed man in the diplomatic corps of St. Petersburg." New York *Times*, 13 October 1874.
25. Schuyler to Fish, 21 December 1872, DUSM, Russia, vol. 24 (roll 24, M 35), RG 59, NA.

Andrew Curtin, minister to Russia. Harper's Weekly, *8 March
1869, courtesy of the Kansas Collection, University of Kansas
Libraries*

spondent because of his admiration for the work of William Howard Russell,
who had won fame reporting the Crimean War and the American Civil War
for the *Times* of London. By the age of twenty-five MacGahan had obtained
a job on the New York *Herald* with the help of a cousin, General Philip
Sheridan, and went to Europe with him to cover the Franco-Prussian War.
MacGahan was thus among the first on the scene to describe the beginnings
of the Paris Commune.[26] After its suppression MacGahan ventured east
through the Mediterranean and into the Black Sea, arriving at Sevastopol
in November 1871.

26. Walker, *Januarius MacGahan*, pp. 20, 36; Richard O'Connor, *The Scandalous Mr.
Bennett* (Garden City, N.Y.: Doubleday, 1962), p. 120.

During convalescence in Odessa from a fall from a horse, he met Varvara (Barbara) Elagina, whom he later married. MacGahan returned to Sevastopol to cover Sherman's Russian tour for the *Herald*, and he probably met Schuyler for the first time when the Sherman party reached Moscow. Back in Paris briefly with Elagina he met with *Herald* publisher James Gordon Bennett and received a new assignment to investigate the Russian push into Central Asia. Elagina opposed his going but traveled with him as far as Moscow, where he joined Schuyler. The two Americans were then together for the initial leg of their 1873 excursions through Central Asia. MacGahan produced a series of articles that were later collected into a book,[27] while Schuyler wrote a lengthy official report that was published in *Papers Relating to the Foreign Relations of the United States* and was later expanded into a two-volume travelogue.[28]

The United States was an unwitting catalyst for the Russian expansion into Central Asia that began in the 1860s. The interruption in the cotton supply to Europe owing to the Civil War naval blockade of Southern ports caused Russian merchants to petition the government for assistance in developing an alternative source along the rivers of Turkestan, using American cottonseed and irrigation techniques. Trade with Central Asia had been important to Russia for centuries, but now the expansion of railroads to the Volga and Russian settlement in Western Siberia increased its value and potential.[29] Russia was following a strategy of a contiguous empire, trading off, in a sense, Alaska for the Amur region and Central Asia. Certainly, the territory gained more than made up for the loss of Alaska economically.[30]

Central Asia bore some resemblance to the American West: thinly populated, mostly by nomadic peoples with indistinct borders and with a reputation for savagery but a poor match militarily against Western-style warfare.

27. *Campaigning on the Oxus, and the Fall of Khiva* (New York: Harper and Bros., 1874).

28. Enclosure, Jewell to Fish, 10 March 1874, DUSM, Russia, vol. 25 (roll 25, M 35), RG 59, NA; *Turkistan: Notes of a Journey in Russian Turkistan, Khokan, Bukhara, and Kuldja*, 2 vols. (New York: Scribner, Armstrong, 1877); enclosure, Jewell to Fish, 10 March 1874, PRFRUS 1874, pp. 816–31.

29. For a survey of Russian expansion in Central Asia, see Helene Carrere d'Encausse, "Systematic Conquest, 1865 to 1884," in *Central Asia: A Century of Russian Rule*, ed. Edward Allworth (New York and London: Columbia University Press, 1967), pp. 131–50; for an outline of the history and culture of Central Asia, see Geoffrey Wheeler's introduction to the abridged reprint of Schuyler's *Turkistan* (New York: Frederick Praeger, 1966), pp. xi–xxxvi.

30. It is questionable whether Russia could have sold Alaska so easily without a simultaneous expansion in another direction.

Although Schuyler would compare Tashkent to Denver, a major difference was the survival in Central Asia of permanent, indigenous commercial and cultural centers in the three khanates of Kokand, Bokhara, and Khiva, ruled by absolutist dynasties. The area was thus divided into the mainly nomadic people, largely Kirghiz or Kazakh, people on the arid high steppe and the long-settled—and watered—urban civilization ito the south, Turkestan proper. The thought of "manifest destiny" was surely in many Russian and American minds during the conquest of Central Asia, since converting these "backward" people to Western "civilization" was viewed as a Russian mission. The continued existence of slavery (mainly military captives or hostages) in the khanates was much condemned in Russian and American publications and provided one additional justification for their destruction. At least some Russians saw themselves as taking up the "white man's burden."

But other factors played a role: the end in 1859 of the long Caucasian struggle against Russia led by Shamil that had tied up Russian military forces, especially cavalry; the greatly exaggerated fear that Britain would preempt the region; and independent actions by nationalistic generals in search of glory and territory. The United States was, of course, too preoccupied in the 1860s with internal problems to pay much attention to Central Asia. In the early 1870s there were the protracted negotiations with Britain over the *Alabama* claims, culminating in the Treaty of Washington, and other absorbing concerns—such as the 1873 *Virginius* affair, when Spain captured an American merchant ship running guns to Cuban rebels and authorities in Santiago brutally executed some members of the crew.[31] These were the events that consumed the country's international attention while Russian troops were galloping into Central Asia.

A crucial Russian campaign against the Turkish-speaking, Muslim khanates of the region was launched in 1864 and ended with the seizure of the important commercial center of Tashkent in June 1865 by a force under the command of General Mikhail Cherniaev. This set off a debate in St. Petersburg, for the Russian foreign office was pursuing a cautious, noninterventionist peace policy at the time. Gorchakov was thus the chief spokesmen for a moderate, restrained policy toward Central Asia and for restoring independence to Tashkent, which would nevertheless become more and more reliant on Russia. Conservative interests supported Cherniaev's desire to annex the area. As the Russian bureaucracy moved slowly to find a

31. For an outline of the *Virginius* affair and the resulting crisis in Spanish-American relations, see Allan Nevins, *Hamilton Fish: The Inner History of the Grant Administration*, 2 vols. (New York: Dodd, Mead, 1936), 2:667–94.

compromise solution, Russian control of the region was being consolidated by the army on the spot and by invading merchants.[32] As Gorchakov foresaw, the Russian expansion annoyed Britain, and another spate of alarmist Russophobic articles and books quickly surfaced in English.[33]

By 1868, as Schuyler observed, Orenburg had become a cotton-trading hub. The cotton came by camel caravan, mainly from the Khivan area, was hauled by wagon from Orenburg to Samara, then barged up the Volga to Nizhni-Novgorod, where it was sold and loaded on trains for Moscow and other cotton-milling centers. The Russian occupation of Bukhara and Samarkand meant that the cotton grown there was now free of any customs duties. And railroads were soon being planned to Samara and to Orenburg and on into Central Asia, encouraging further development.[34] Although Schuyler recognized this as a threat to American commercial interests, little concern was yet expressed in the American press. A New York *Times* editorial of 1869 illustrated a typical American perspective that sympathized with the Russian course of expansion:

> The trade of Central Asia, then, is the rather large plum which Russia is after, and there seems no reason why she should not get it. Wiser than England in India, she seeks not to possess but to use these great inlying territories, to make them tributary to her by force of mutual interest, and, while amply protecting herself and her own interests, by arms if need be, to enforce no rule or policy save that of freedom of commerce—for herself.[35]

Britain held a decidedly different view, especially after a new wave of Russian military campaigning began early in 1873 under the aegis of the gover-

32. The story is best told by David MacKenzie, *The Lion of Tashkent: The Career of General M. G. Cherniaev* (Athens: University of Georgia Press, 1974).

33. The more the British warned about Russian penetration of Central Asia and the threat to Afghanistan and India, the faster Russia moved to forestall the possibility of a British presence. The result was the Eastern Question in reverse; in Central Asia weak, divided states were brought into an overexpanded Russian Empire while an enfeebled Ottoman Empire was breaking up into small, dependent states. Instead of a multitude of players, there was really only one power in Central Asia. Ironically, just when Russia was trying to re-form into a more homogeneous and "Russified" state (all under one law), it annexed more people of different cultural, ethnic, and religious backgrounds.

34. Schuyler to Seward, 27 June 1868, DUSC, Moscow, vol. 1 (roll 1, M 456), RG 59, NA. He enclosed samples of Central Asian cotton, which are still preserved in the diplomatic files of the National Archives.

35. New York *Times*, 27 January 1869.

nor general of Russian Turkestan, General Konstantin Kaufman.[36] This phase started when twenty-one Russian soldiers and merchants were captured and sold into slavery by forces of the still-independent Khivan khanate. In response, Kaufman launched a punitive expedition against Khiva, as two American observers arrived in the region. MacGahan, viewing his role as a war correspondent, attempted to join Kaufman's army, while Schuyler, seeking to cover as many of the sights and scenes of Central Asia as possible from a Tashkent base, continued to the east to Kuldja in Chinese Turkestan (temporarily under Russian occupation). As Americans, both were given friendly receptions and access to places and people that would have been closed to most other foreigners.

Like an early Lawrence of Arabia, MacGahan successfully crossed a large desert by camel to reach Khiva and Kaufman's army, winning renown for his efforts. His article-letters, published after his departure from the area, captured the exotic flavor of the region and the excitement of conquest. In the book that followed he included a number of sketches based on the art of Vasily Vereshchagin, which stressed the oriental character of Central Asia. Although definitely pro-Russian in his description of the campaign, MacGahan was not without sympathy for the native cultures being subdued.

Schuyler also was partial to the Russian cause, but he was very critical of Kaufman's light-handed administration of the territory, such as his tolerance of free-wheeling actions by subordinates against the natives. Yet he had only praise for Kaufman's chief military rival, Cherniaev. In this bias against the "German," he was probably influenced by the Russian nationalism that had surrounded him in Moscow.[37] Schuyler's impressions circulated in St. Petersburg in both oral and written form and were generally commended and welcomed for their frankness. Few individuals in the United States at that time would privately find fault with or deny the following:

36. The American press dismissed these British fears as greatly exaggerated: "All talk of a Russian invasion of India is moonshine." "England and Russia," *New York Times*, 28 January 1873. (German Baltic names pose special problems as they become Russianized; other variants for the general are Fon-Kaufman, von Kauffmann, and Kaufmann.)

37. Brown, "Eugene Schuyler," pp. 168–81. Brown concludes, "A re-examination of the facts shows that Schuyler's evaluation of Cherniaev was naive, and his attack on Kaufmann, whatever his very real faults, was curiously bitter" (p. 203). See also the articles by David MacKenzie, "Kaufman of Turkestan: An Assessment of His Administration, 1867–1881," *Slavic Review* 26, 2 (June 1967): 265–85; and "Schuyler: Honorable but Misled," *Slavic Review* 27, 1 (March 1968): 119–30.

In spite of the bad administration, the people are on the whole well contented with the Russian rule, finding it so much better than anything which has gone before, and their discontent is chiefly against individuals—officials and others, who harass and injure them, but it is evident that a continued series of such occurrences cannot but awaken general distrust towards the administration. . . .

On the whole, the Russian influence is beneficial in Central Asia, not only to the inhabitants, but to the world, and it certainly is greatly for our interest that a counterpoise should exist there against the extension of English dominion in Asia. Having once taken possession of the Country, it will be almost impossible for the Russians, with any fairness to the natives, to withdraw from it.[38]

Though labeled confidential, Schuyler's report was published in the State Department's annual collection of diplomatic papers, much to the astonishment of Schuyler and the Russians.[39] It was an embarrassment to have criticism of a leading Russian official in print, and Kaufman complained personally to Gorchakov. To Schuyler's surprise, Gorchakov made it clear that Schuyler was no longer welcome in Russia as an official American representative. Debated openly in the Russian press, the report created a public sensation and led to the suspension of a major paper, *Russkii Mir* (Russian world), for applauding it.[40] Meanwhile, Schuyler remained comfortably at his post in St. Petersburg through May 1876, until he was reassigned to Constantinople as consul general. Gorchakov obviously did not want to press the issue and replay the Katakazi affair in reverse.

A number of Russian officials, moreover, such as Minister of Interior Petr Valuev and the head of the Asiatic Department, Dmitri Osten-Saken, continued to support and encourage Schuyler. They hoped to get a "Central Asian Committee" appointed to investigate his charges.[41] Schuyler must not have been too concerned about the Russian reactions; even before sending his official report, he had been planning a detailed and illustrated publica-

38. Quoted from Schuyler's official report that was enclosed in Jewell to Fish, 10 March 1874, DUSM, Russia, vol. 25 (roll 25, M 35), RG 59, NA.

39. PRFRUS 1874, pp. 816–31.

40. Schuyler was under the impression that Gorchakov initially had defended his right to publish the report; Schuyler to Jewell, 11 and 27 March 1875 (c), Schuyler Letterbook, LC. In the first of these private letters to Jewell, he admitted "how much the Govt. dislikes to have people who know Russian who can understand what is going on."

41. Schuyler to Jewell, 13/25 January 1875, Schuyler Letterbook, LC; Brown, "Eugene Schuyler," pp. 181–85.

tion and had foreseen the propriety of resigning his Russian post before its issue.[42] Even the tsar became personally concerned about the publicity and asked his American military agent, Gorlov, to provide a detailed review of both McGahan's and Schuyler's writings.[43]

The news of Gorchakov's displeasure eventually reached the American press, which sharply objected to the Russian government's evident intolerance of criticism.

> The fact is, the Russians believe, or affect to believe, that if a man receives the slightest civilities at their hands, he is bound for that reason to speak well of everything in Russia. . . . Mr. Schuyler is doubtless looked upon at this moment as a monster of ingratitude, because, after being permitted, as a particular favor, to visit the Russian possessions in Central Asia, he has presumed to find fault, here and there, with what he saw. . . . But the Russians are barbarous in this sense, that they are strangers to that political civilization which allows and even implies freedom of criticism for foreign as well as for home institutions.[44]

In any event, American observations had no visible effect on Russian policy. Consolidation of the territory continued in rather erratic and brutal fashion, and Kaufman remained in charge of it until his death in 1882, when he was finally replaced by Cherniaev. Away from Russia, Schuyler was free to refocus the criticism in his book on the general waste of the whole enterprise, agreeing with Sherman's judgment that the conquest and attendant administration were not worth the money and effort but once begun could not be stopped until the entire area was under Russian control.[45]

Although more intent on covering the military action, MacGahan did reflect briefly on the broader scope of what he had seen:

42. Schuyler to John Murray (London publisher), 25 February 1874 (c), and to Hamilton Fish, 8 July 1874 (private) (c), Schuyler Letterbook, LC; Schuyler to Fish, 22 June 1874, DUSM, Russia, vol. 26 (roll 26, M 35), RG 59, NA. Assuming his post as minister while Schuyler was still in Central Asia, Jewell was at first dismayed, judging that Schuyler "*can* be of great service to a Minister but it is necessary to be *here* to be of service." Jewell to Fish, 10 October 1873, vol. 97, Fish Papers, LC. But he later defended the time his secretary spent on the book: "Here he can have access to authorities on that country better than elsewhere. . . . I see no objection to his writing it while connected with the Diplomatic Corps unless he criticises the Government in regard to which I have no knowledge." Jewell to Fish, 18 November 1873, vol. 98, ibid.
43. Gorlov to Alexander II, n.d., f. 677, op. 1, d. 491, TsGAOR.
44. New York *Times*, 25 March 1875.
45. *Turkistan* (Praeger ed.), pp. 283–84.

I am not of those who believe in a traditional policy of aggression on the part of the Russians in Central Asia. The Russian advances have been made rather through the ambition of military chiefs, who were only too glad to take advantage of the blunders and perversity of Central Asian despots to distinguish themselves, or win a decoration. Nor do I believe that the Russians have any immediate designs on India. But they see that there is a certain amount of territory lying between the English and Russian possessions which must sooner or later fall into the hands of either power. I think they are disposed to seize as much of this territory as they conveniently can; and this comprises their whole policy at present.[46]

After returning to the United States, he told Russian minister Offenberg that Russian military institutions were the best in Europe, lectured positively on Russian Central Asia to the Geographical Society of New York, and received the imperial decoration of St. Stanislas.[47] Both Schuyler and MacGahan would soon be even more pro-Russian in covering another battle scene in the Balkans.

In general, Americans saw the Russian expansion in Central Asia as paralleling their own manifest destiny, as part of the natural advance of Western Civilization, and as of no danger to other powers. They were not surprised by alarmist British hysteria about a threat to their interests but generally concurred with the New York *Times* comment that "no one who has visited Central Asia could long retain any faith in . . . the possible advance of Russia upon India."[48]

Military Exchanges

At a more professional level, the United States and Russia cooperated more than ever in military assistance programs. American army and navy missions were enthusiastically welcomed in Russia, while Russian officers had carte blanche in the United States.

American Military Missions to Russia, 1867–1880

| David Farragut | naval squadron | August 1867 |
| William B. Franklin | army | December 1869 |

46. MacGahan, *Campaigning on the Oxus*, p. 425.
47. Offenberg to Westmann, 31 January/12 February 1874, f. 133, op. 470, d. 144, AVPR; Philadelphia *Inquirer*, 7 September 1874.
48. New York *Times*, 13 August 1877.

John G. Barnard	army engineers	September 1870
Edward Simpson, Joseph Marvin	naval ordnance	April–May 1871
Jonathon Guest	naval squadron	July 1871
William Sherman, Joseph Audenreid, Frederick Grant	army tour	April–May 1872
Thomas Mallery	army	October 1872
L. L. Laidley	army ordnance	Summer 1874
George Crawford, Marcus Reno, Walter Schuyler	army	July 1875
John Worden	naval squadron	July 1875
Emory Upton, George Forsyth, William Sanger	army	April, July–August 1876
Francis V. Greene	observer, attaché	1877–1878
Thomas O. Selfridge, Jr.	naval squadron	July 1879

American visits ranged from lavish courtesy calls to fairly specific inspections of particular facilities. Most missions, however, were not dispatched just to Russia but included other European (and occasionally Asian) countries and ports.[49] The naval visits were especially harmonious, since the American fleet was viewed as one of most technically advanced and as a potential check to British dominance at sea, and a tradition of purchasing warships in the United States extended back to 1830. Whenever Grand Duke Constantine was in St. Petersburg, he could be counted on to host an opulent reception; and admirals Lesovskii and Pos'et, veterans of long stays in the United States, would demonstrate the particularly warm hospitality of the Russian navy for their American visitors. Such was the case for the call of Admiral David Farragut in August 1867. One contemporary American source described the final parade of this great Civil War hero: "The crowned heads and titled nobility of Europe seemed to vie with their humblest subjects in doing honor to this noble specimen of the American naval officer."[50]

49. Upton entered Russia first through Persia, crossed the Caucasus to Constantinople, and after touring Europe came to St. Petersburg. Peter S. Michie, *The Life and Letters of Emory Upton* (New York: D. Appleton, 1885), pp. 375, 379–84.
50. Lewis R. Hamersly, *The Records of Living Officers of the U.S. Navy and Marine Corps*, rev. ed. (Philadelphia: J. B. Lippincott, 1870), p. 9.

But Alexander II, resting on the Black Sea, entertained the tourist ship *Quaker City* instead.

Usually, however, as upon the visit of the *Franklin* and *Alaska* in 1875, Alexander II would inspect the squadron and then host a luncheon or dinner at his summer palace, Tsarskoe Selo. This particular port call was especially cordial, since it corresponded with an army mission and a Swedish royal tour, and the ranking officers were accompanied by their wives.[51] Joseph Loubat, who had been to Russia with Gustavus Fox in 1866, also came with his impressive yacht to participate in the sea festivities and to escort the imperial family from squadron to squadron.[52]

The army tours were usually of a technical nature involving inspections of fortifications and ordnance. The purpose of General John Barnard's mission of 1870 was to examine the use of iron armor plating for coastal defenses.[53] Three of the American officers—Edward Simpson, Emory Upton, and Francis Greene—published detailed accounts of their visits, but little, if anything, of Russian origin can be said to have had any great value to American military science. The army seemed to be especially interested in fortifications, while the navy had its eye on the novel, round-shaped Russian monitors—the so-called Popovkas—which were soon dismissed as a failure.[54]

The War and Navy departments were well informed about Russian developments because of the sense of trust and openness that prevailed on both sides. After his 1879 visit, Thomas Selfridge, Jr., reported, "Upon expressing my desire to inspect the torpedo defenses of the Russian Navy, except such as were considered secret, he [Admiral Kazakevich, commandant of Kronstadt] replied, 'With pleasure, we have no secrets from Americans.' "[55] In ad-

51. Schuyler to Fish, 20 July 1875, DUSM, Russia, vol. 28 (roll 28, M 35), RG 59, NA; Schuyler to Jomini, 24 June/6 July, 3/15 July, and 7/19 July 1875, DPR, Russia, vol. 4535 (notes sent), RG 84, NA.

52. Schuyler to Jomini, 24 June/6 July 1875 (c), DPR, Russia, vol. 4535 (notes sent), RG 84, NA; S. R. Franklin, *Memoirs of a Rear-Admiral* (New York and London: Harper and Bros., 1898), pp. 245–48. Captain Franklin was the escort for Princess Dagmar (Grand Duchess Maria Fedorovna), "most agreeable and cheering in every way" (p. 248).

53. Barnard to Curtin, 16 September 1879, DPR, Russia, vol. 4434 (misc. received), RG 84, NA.

54. New York *Times*, 20 October 1873, commented on the new design: "Scientific men will now have the opportunity of judging whether the Popovka is likely to be studied as a model for other vessels of the same type, or whether she is only to serve as a monument of the inventor's ingenuity."

55. To Admiral Howell, 30 July 1879, quoted in Thomas O. Selfridge, Jr., *Memoirs of Thomas O. Selfridge, Jr.* (New York and London: G. P. Putnam's, 1924), p. 233.

dition to the formal inspections, American diplomats, more often than their Russian counterparts in the United States, would visit military facilities and file reports about them. Jewell was impressed by his tour of the Kronstadt naval base in June 1874: "I was very much interested with what I saw, and was much impressed with the gigantic efforts this Government is making to become a great commercial and maritime power, and was of course pleased with the attention shown to me personally, and also with the respect paid to our flag."[56]

Military missions could entail personal connections as well. Eugene Schuyler was able to greet his brother Walter in July 1875, when he accompanied generals George Crawford and Marcus Reno on an army visit. And a special kind of alliance was formed when the daughter of Admiral Selfridge married the son of Admiral Adolf Etolin, former Finno-Russian governor of Alaska.[57]

Russian Military Missions to the United States, 1867–1880

Gorlov, Gunius, Buniakovskii	army ordnance	1867–1872
Linden	naval squadron	1870
Alexis, Pos'et	naval squadron	1871–1872
Vlas'ev	naval engineer	1872
Novosil'skii	naval engineer	1873
Zviagintsev, Mikhailov	army engineers	1875–1876
Semechkin	naval, Centennial	1876
Alexis, Butakov	naval squadron	1877
Izmailov	cavalry	July 1877
Semechkin, Grippenberg	ship construction	1878–1879

Russian military visits to the United States were longer and more intensive. Of these the most important were the extended residence from 1867 to 1872 of General Aleksandr Gorlov and his two aides, Konstantin Gunius and Vladimir Buniakovskii, who concentrated on acquiring small arms and their technology from Colt and other arms manufacturers and particularly

56. To Fish, 22 June 1874, DUSM, Russia, vol. 26 (roll 26, M 35), RG 59, NA; PRFRUS, 1874: 839. Jewell added, "The thing which struck me most forcibly was the lavish expenditure of money which this government is making for offensive as well as defensive warfare."

57. Selfridge, *Memoirs*, p. 231.

from Hiram Berdan; the naval tours associated with the two visits of Grand Duke Alexis in 1871–1872 and 1877; and the Russian warship purchases in Philadelphia in 1878. These missions generated other contacts of a private business nature.

The Berdanka

The Colt factory in Hartford, which remained a center for small-arms production in the United States after Samuel Colt's death in 1858, attracted the most Russian interest because of its earlier, especially Crimean War, connections with Russia. Gorlov was attached to this factory for about five years beginning in 1867, and in fact a substantial Russian rifle order placed in 1868 helped the Colt enterprise to recover from a disastrous fire. With subsequent modifications and improvements, this rifle, labeled the "Berdanka," was officially adopted by the Russian army after trials before the tsar in the summer of 1869; it became the principal Russian infantry weapon for many years and was still in use through World War I and the Russian civil war.[58]

Hiram Berdan was an American Civil War officer and gun mechanic who had achieved some fame for organizing "Sharps' Shooters" and for the conversion of Springfield muzzle loaders to breechloading with a locking mechanism. A new weapon, manufactured by the Colt works in Hartford, incorporated Berdan's improvements into a simplified 42-caliber rifle, modified by Gorlov to Russian specifications. Berdan and the Russian specialists also invented a reliable center-fire metallic cartridge, which was initially produced at the Union Metallic Cartridge Company in Bridgeport. With Berdan's subsequent addition of sliding bolt action, the Berdan System 2 (or Berdanka) became one of the most accurate and durable infantry weapons of its day, though the United States Army never adopted it and usually referred to it as "the Russian rifle." Both Berdan and Gorlov thought its American

58. Correspondence from St. Petersburg of 3 August, New York *Times*, 22 August 1869. See also Joseph Bradley's pioneering study, *Guns for the Tsar: American Technology and the Small Arms Industry in Nineteenth-Century Russia* (DeKalb: Northern Illinois University Press, 1990), pp. 104–11; and Alexander Tarsaidze, " 'Berdanka,' " *Russian Review* 9, 1 (January 1950): 30–36. Schuyler reported that delivery of the rifles produced by Colt had begun by March 1869; to Seward, 10 March 1869, DUSC, Moscow, vol. 1 (roll 1, M 456), RG 59, NA.

trials against the Springfield, Sharps, and Remington rifles were unfairly conducted.[59]

The Berdanka was soon entirely Russian-made, because the Russian small arms commission was unhappy with what they considered the poor quality of American steel barrels. Equipped with American machinery and partly financed by the Nobel brothers, the Izhevsk Small Arms Factory in the Urals was producing over 60,000 Berdankas a year by 1875, and during the Russo-Turkish War the combined production of the three major armaments plants—Izhevsk, Tula, and Sestroretsk—reached 1,000 Berdankas a day. By 1879 the Russian army was almost fully equipped with that rifle, with over 1 million in service.[60]

Anticipating more imperial favors, Berdan had left for Russia in 1869 and spent most of the next three years with his family in St. Petersburg working on modifications and improvements. Unfortunately, he benefited little from his inventions, as top European arms manufacturers were soon producing clones of the Berdanka. Although rewarded to some extent by Russia, he encountered obstacles, as the family governess witnessed:

> An inventor, pushing his invention with governments, has a hard time. All he gains from one contract is spent in pushing another invention. The Russian commissioners regularly refuse every improvement the general offers them, and as regularly, after waiting some months, take it. The general spent three months before he could obtain permission to make his No. 5 gun *at his own expense*. . . . Now the Russians have adopted it. It takes just so long for every opening wedge to begin its way. Not to mention that patent laws everywhere seem to be constructed so as to give an inventor as much trouble and expense as possible, and as little benefit.[61]

Another beneficiary of Russian orders was the Gatling Gun Company. Twenty of these early machine guns were sold in 1868, and after formal

59. Bradley, *Guns for the Tsar*, p. 112; for a good contemporary description of the Berdanka with detailed sketches, see Francis V. Greene, *Report on the Russian Army and Its Campaigns in Turkey in 1877–1878*, 2 vols. (New York: D. Appleton, 1879), 1:53–56.

60. Bradley, *Guns for the Tsar*, pp. 161–62; Tarsaidze, " 'Berdanka,' " 35; Greene, *Report*, 1:56–57; Liubomir Grigor'evich Beskrovnyi, *Russkaia armiia i flot v XIX veke: Voenno-ekonomicheskii potentsial Rossii* (Moscow: Nauka, 1973), pp. 305–10; Petr A. Zaionchkovskii, "Perevsoruzhenie russkoi armii v 60-70-kh godakh XIX v.," *Istoricheskie Zapiski* 36 (1951): 97–100; Robert W. Tolf, *The Russian Rockefellers: The Saga of the Nobel Family and the Russian Oil Industry* (Stanford, Calif.: Hoover Institution Press, 1976), pp. 28–29.

61. Sarah Hagar (St. Petersburg) to Kate (sister), 16 May 1871, Hagar Papers, University of Vermont Library.

adoption, Gorlov ordered several hundred more to be made by the Colt factory at $1,500 each, again altered to 42-caliber and to other exacting Russian requirements. Lewis Broadwell, who had spent several years at Kronstadt modifying naval guns for breechloading, returned to Russia in 1871 representing Gatling, but an agreement that allowed the Russians to produce their own versions ended further sales.[62] The guns were almost immediately put to use in the Khivan campaign in Central Asia, where they were transported by camels.[63] More Gatling guns were made in Russia by American workmen with imported Gatling machinery. Since no revolvers were mass-produced in Russia before the 1890s, these weapons were purchased almost wholly in the United States during this period. Although seemingly committed to Colt, Gorlov recommended Smith and Wesson, and over 130,000 were acquired during the 1870s.[64] Russian officers in the Russo-Turkish War thus carried American arms on the battlefields.

Because of the secrecy and rumor-mongering that pervaded munition sales and production, many details of the arrangements remain sketchy or unverified. Schuyler, with all of his high-placed connections, knew little about Berdan's relations with the Russian government, even though the Curtin and Berdan families were socially intimate. The secretary, however, despised Berdan's pompous parading around St. Petersburg in a general's uniform, his falsifying or exaggerating his Civil War record, and his insistence on being "presented" at court, which opened all doors to Russian high society.[65]

Another American effort to sell arms to Russia involved a member of the Augustine Heard family, which had been doing business with Russia in the Far East for many years. Albert Heard made three trips to Russia (in 1877,

62. Philadelphia *Inquirer*, 29 August and 8 December 1870; Broadwell (St. Petersburg) to Curtin, 14/26 May 1871, DPR, Russia, vol. 4434 (misc. received), RG 84, NA; Paul Wahl and Donald R. Toppel, *The Gatling Gun* (London: Herbert Jenkins, 1966), pp. 39–41.

63. Bradley, *Guns for the Tsar*, p. 116; Wahl and Toppel, *Gatling Gun*, pp. 65–66; Philadephia *Inquirer*, 29 August and 8 December 1870. The Gatlings produced in Russia were often referred to as "Gorlovs." Russia's was the second army, after that of the United States, to adopt machine guns, and the first in Europe to deploy them—as artillery—on the battlefield.

64. Beskrovnyi, *Russkaia armia*, pp. 309, 319; Bradley, *Guns for the Tsar*, pp. 115–16.

65. Schuyler to Fish (confidential), 18 November 1874 (c), Schuyler Letterbook, LC. Nor did Berdan win friends among Americans during a later residence in Berlin, incurring in particular the enmity of Nicholas Fish, the son of the secretary of state; Bancroft Davis to Fish, 12 October and 3 November 1874, vol. 104, Fish Papers, LC. Berdan did have the advantages of a well-connected wife (sister of Levi Morton, a very prominent New York banker), and a beautiful daughter.

1878, and 1879) on behalf of the Lowell Manufacturing Company and in search of buyers for a "battery" machine gun designed by De Witt Farrington. Although he met with a good reception from Grand Duke Constantine, admirals Lesovskii and Pos'et, and other ranking officials, he encountered frustrating delays getting samples through Customs and then problems in their performance during winter demonstrations. Another difficulty was that his guns could not use the Russian greased bullets. Apparently about twenty Farringtons were purchased by Russia, but the enterprise soon folded.[66] A common Russian practice was to accept display samples and design proposals and keep them for study without remuneration or acknowledgement of their source—just as Western inventors and manufacturers habitually stole each others' patents.

Ironically, and perhaps prompted by the escalation in military technology, Alexander II led an effort to moderate and regulate the conduct of war in 1874. A conference of the key military powers of Europe met in Brussels to consider a "Project of an International Declaration Concerning the Laws and Customs of War," which resembled the Geneva Convention of many years later.[67] But conflict and friction prevented the required unanimity, with Britain's refusal to participate being the main obstacle to agreement. The humanitarian motives that had inspired the attempt soon receded to the background.

Balkan Problems

The spread of new weapons of mass destruction—breechloading rifles, machine guns, and bursting (shrapnel) artillery shells—was certainly a contributing factor to the especially violent wars of the 1870s. The rise of national consciousness seemed to trigger an aggressive response in people in all levels of society. By attempting to rally Slavs beyond Russian borders under the wing of an aggressive Pan-Slavism, Russia naturally strained relations with the Ottoman Empire. Yet its conquest of Central Asia and its restored naval strength on the Black Sea—a diplomatic by-product of the Franco-Prussian War (1870–1871)—gave Russia confidence in its renewed status as a great power in the area. Gorchakov's receptivity to Bismarck's offer of a Prussian alliance, along with a less cordial one with Austria-Hungary, seemed to pave

66. Letterbook, Heard Company Papers, HL-52, and Heard diary, HP-3, Baker Library, Harvard University; Tarsaidze, " 'Berdanka,' " 34; F. W. A. Hobart, *History of the Machine Gun* (New York: Drake, 1972), pp. 23–24.
67. Schuyler's reports in PRFRUS 1875, 2:1017–23.

the way for Balkan action. Great Britain was the only worry; France was still crippled, physically and morally, by military defeat and the Paris uprising, and the United States remained friendly toward Russia and not very fond of Turks.[68]

In fact, as far as the Eastern Question was concerned, the United States was often perceived as floating in the wake of Russia. The two relatively minor American interests in the area—missionary and naval—were not in conflict with Russian interests but ran into opposition from France in the first case and from Britain in the second. Shrewd manipulators such as ambassador Nikolai Ignat'ev were able to take advantage of weak American appointees in the Ottoman capital. Though George Boker was apparently a fair match for the Russian, he observed that in his predecessor's time, "the American Legation was little more than a bobtail to the Russian kite."[69] But Boker also felt that Russia still was successfully using its friendship with the United States to bolster its side of the Eastern Question: "The suspicion of our being the secret ally of Russia is something that is forever coming to the surface in the diplomacy of this place, and Ignatieff always encourages the idea by innuendos, and by the affectation of affection for me that is at times overpowering. At all this you will smile, and well you may; but of such stuff is the forever-active diplomacy of Constantinople."[70] The Russian ploy was to lead Ottoman authorities to believe that in any conflict situation Russia held an American card—a threat of naval war against Britain, which would keep that pro-Turkish power neutral. What remained was for Balkan Slavs—and two Americans covering the scene—to produce the timing and the setting for a real war.

In the spring of 1876, Serbs, Montenegrins, and Bulgarians, the latter still firmly under Turkish administration, fomented with the aid of Russian Pan-Slavists a series of revolts in the Rumelian and Bosnian provinces of the Turkish Empire. Although the Serbs—with Russian assistance—were able to hold out in the war that erupted, the Bulgarians were no match for the

---

68. For a thorough, detailed study, see B. H. Sumner, *Russia and the Balkans, 1870–1880* (Oxford: Clarendon Press, 1937).

69. To Fish, 15 January 1875, vol. 105, Fish Papers, LC.

70. To Fish, 1 March 1875, vol. 106, Fish Papers, LC. Boker's private, as opposed to his official, correspondence provides interesting reading, as might be expected from a genuine poet. For example, "It is said the Russian protection extends over ten thousand families in Constantinople, not one member of which ever smelt Russian air. This abuse the Russian ambassador wishes neither to have disturbed nor inquired into. To Fish, 15 December 1873, vol. 99, Fish Papers, LC.

Turkish forces, newly equipped with American Peabody rifles. The bloody reprisals that followed in June became known as the "Bulgarian horrors."

One of the first reporters on the scene was Januarius MacGahan, who had been adventuring in Spain and the Arctic since his 1873 tour of Central Asia. Before leaving for Bulgaria, however, he met in London with publisher James Gordon Bennett of the New York *Herald* to clear the Balkan assignment. A big blow-up occurred over Bennett's objections to MacGahan's overt Russophilism and his failing to mention Bennett or the *Herald* in his book on Central Asia. The result was that MacGahan, determined to go to the Balkans immediately, quit the *Herald* and joined the staff of the London *Daily News*, which was already in the bad graces of the British government for criticism of its Turkish policy.[71]

MacGahan rushed off to Constantinople, arriving in July 1876 to find his old friend Schuyler just established in the post of American consul general. With the backing of minister Boker, they quickly received travel permits for the Balkan provinces. Schuyler knew enough Bulgarian to allow direct interviews with the people, and the gory details were soon flowing to the *Daily News* and to other papers.[72] MacGahan's reports of Turkish atrocities against *Christian* Slavs were thus first published for a British audience and were clearly a factor in swaying public opinion there against the Ottoman Empire. More important, they convinced a leading politician, William Gladstone, of the futility of British support for such an ally; his powerfully written book gave momentum to an anti-Turkish trend in Britain. MacGahan's accounts complemented Schuyler's adamantly hostile official reports, which were leaked to the press for publication and left few Americans willing to oppose an "exercise" of Russian justice in the Balkans.[73] An Ottoman demand for Schuyler's recall only solidified American opinion. Thus by the end of 1876, a combination of circumstances, fanned by MacGahan and Schuyler, opened the door for Russian liberation of the Balkans from Turkish rule.

Alexis Sails Again

The second trip of the Grand Duke Alexis to the United States came with less warning and with a specific military goal—to get a squadron of the Rus-

71. O'Connor, *Scandalous Bennett*, pp. 124–25; Walker, *Januarius MacGahan*, p. 167.

72. Petar Sopov, "Eugene Schuyler—Distinguished Politician, Statesman, Diplomat and Scientist," *Bulgarian Historical Review* 11, 2 (1983): 68–69.

73. Schuyler's observations, following on the heels of MacGahan's, delivered an effective one-two punch and, according to the American minister in London, were crucial to Gladstone's opposition to Turkey. Gladstone's book was entitled *Bulgarian Horrors and the Questions of the East* (London: Murray, 1876). See also Edwards Pierrepont (London) to Fish, 6 November 1876, vol. 118, Fish Papers, LC.

sian navy out of European waters and into the security of American harbors while war was brewing in Europe. Even with Britain partially neutralized by the Turkish "horrors," Russia had good historical reasons not to trust perceptions of British docility toward any Russian military ventures, especially with Prime Minister Benjamin Disraeli sounding a Russophobic trumpet.

The situation was reminiscent of previous crises in Europe: during the Crimean War when the Russian fleet was confined to its bases, and during the Polish revolt of 1863 when part of the Baltic fleet sailed to New York. This time, however, the Baltic fleet was kept at home while a squadron on a winter cruise in the Mediterranean was ordered to safer American waters. Nor was there any mystery about the purpose, which was to allow the navy more freedom of movement in case of war—or, in other words, to be in position to raid British commerce more effectively.[74] George Boker, now transferred to St. Petersburg, reported his conversation with Alexander II: "He said that in case of war between Russia and England, it would be better to have his fleet free to act upon the Atlantic, with friendly ports behind it, than to have it bottled up in the Mediterranean, and unable to act at all." The American minister was surprised at the emperor's vehemence against Britain "and in a style that a democratic orator of the old school might have envied when he was brimful of fourth of July and of whisky." He quoted him as saying in reference to Disraeli, "But what can you expect of a government conducted by a Jew, save that it will be Jewish?" Although Boker tried to appease Alexander's fear of a general war, the emperor was convinced that such a conflict would produce severe internal hardships and inflict real damage on the cause of reform in Russia, "laying all the blame at the door of England."[75]

Perhaps because of its point of origin, the Mediterranean squadron of four ships—*Bogatyr, Nazimov, Askold,* and the venerable flagship *Svetlana*—headed for Charleston rather than New York. After a brief inspection, it sought more commodious surroundings in Hampton Roads, thus making Norfolk its winter headquarters for its mid-January to mid-May 1877 so-

74. Boker to Fish, 18 November 1876, telegram and letter, DUSM, Russia, vol. 30 (roll 30, M 35), RG 59, NA.

75. To Fish, 21 November 1876, vol. 117, Fish Papers, LC. The envoy also reported that being summoned by the emperor elicited much comment in court circles. Boker concluded this private letter by pointing out to the secretary of state: "You know that the Grand Duke Alexis will accompany the fleet to America, in his character as an officer of the Navy; I hope that something may be done in official circles to let the Emperor know that this time his son is most heartily welcome. I deem it to be of real importance that this matter should not be overlooked."

*George Boker, minister to Russia. Harper's Weekly, 16
December 1871, courtesy of the Kansas Collection, University of Kansas Libraries*

journ in the United States. And, as in 1863, San Francisco received a simultaneous visit from the Russian Pacific squadron.

The Atlantic squadron was under the command of Admiral Aleksandr Butakov but among its officers were Grand Duke Alexis, who had risen to the rank of captain of the flagship *Svetlana*, and his cousin, the young Grand Duke Constantine. Americans were naturally excited about the return of "their" duke and prepared to welcome him accordingly, but because the purpose of this visit was mainly business, his movements were cloaked in greater privacy. The squadron was dutifully met by Russian minister Nikolai Shishkin, who established a headquarters for the grand dukes at the Atlantic Hotel in Norfolk.[76]

76. "The Russian Fleet," Norfolk *Virginian*, 13 January 1877.

At first Alexis was none too happy about returning to the United States, having learned upon arrival the depressing news that his good friend George Armstrong Custer had been "killed and scalped by Indians."[77] To his mother he worried over Constantine's health and the reports of approaching war, and he complained about the slowness of the mails and the fuss the local women made over his "noble" officers. He wrote facetiously, "Here is a real republican country where they so value titles."[78] But Alexis was still able to rise to the occasion.

For the people of that Virginia port the grand ducal presence created great excitement through rounds of dinners, balls, excursions, and salutes. The *Svetlana*'s band was kept busy entertaining daily tours of the ship, which had been refitted since its last visit with imposing nine-inch Krupp breech-loaded guns.[79] Alexis was often seen walking his white bulldog, brought from Malta, on the streets of Norfolk, thus inspiring a local craze for bulldogs.[80] He also enjoyed tidewater duck hunting and is credited with bringing down four with one shot.[81]

The climax of the "Russian season" in Norfolk was a grand ball on 8 February, which the local paper reserved three columns to describe:

It was not only the most fashionable gathering that Norfolk has for a long time boasted of, but it was most admirably and systematically conducted, and the pleasant, courteous and social intermingling of friends and newly-made acquaintances, of distinguished officers of the American and Russian nations, of Northern and Southern ladies, of the gallant men who "wore the blue and the grey" in past bitter struggles upon bloody fields of battle, brought vividly to one's mind the great blessing of friendship and union.

Three bands played, the Horticultural Department in Washington furnished flowers, locomotive headlights from the Atlantic railroad lit the

77. Alexis to his mother, 3 January 1877, f. 641, op. 1, d. 34, TsGAOR.
78. To his mother, 30 January 1877, ibid.
79. "Grand Duke Alexis," Norfolk *Virginian*, 16 January 1877.
80. "The latest novelty of pets in the dog line is 'the white bull-pup.' The fashion was introduced in this country by the Grand Duke Alexis, whose ugly little brute our people became familiar with during the visit of the Russian fleet to Norfolk." Norfolk *Virginian*, 11 May 1877. Alexis sent his mother a picture of himself and "his wonderful dog," taken in New York, but it was not kept with the letter; to his mother, 19 February 1877, f. 641, op. 1, d. 34, TsGAOR.
81. "Royal Hunting Party," Norfolk *Virginian*, 3 February 1877.

scene, and "each corner of the room was occupied by a beautiful Gatling gun, mounted."[82] A few days later the grand dukes returned the favor with a gala all-day reception on the *Svetlana*.[83] Not all was peace and tranquility, however. Seamen from the Russian ships were the focus of incidents on shore; in one case a policeman attempting to quell an unruly group was set upon and badly beaten.[84]

Another problem was the status of relations with the outgoing Grant administration. Old wounds had still not healed, and though Hamilton Fish tendered a formal invitation to Grand Duke Alexis to visit the White House, it was refused on the excuse that the grand duke was bound by his duty as a naval officer to stay with his ship.[85] The real reason was lack of assurance that the president would make a return visit. According to Alexis, Shishkin reported that Fish said Grant would not reciprocate because when his son was in St. Petersburg Alexander II did not call on him. "After this, Shishkin got up and left—*adorable*," the grand duke noted.[86] When Alexis accepted private invitations to revisit New York, he therefore bypassed Washington, going by coastal steamer to Baltimore to meet a special train, arranged again by Frank Thompson.[87]

Gorchakov hoped to use the naval visit to mend diplomatic fences and asked through Boker in St. Petersburg for some pledge of normal reciprocal treatment in Washington. Fish's curt undiplomatic answer was, "Certainly not." So Alexander II telegraphed strict instructions to Alexis to avoid Washington.[88] The feud ended, however, as soon as Grant and Fish left office in March and the new administration promptly made amends. Shishkin invited Alexis to join him at the inauguration, but he declined. This would have been a bit too much of an affront to Grant. Cousin "Kostia" went instead—without fanfare.[89] At the end of that month the Russian squadron

82. "The Naval Ball," Norfolk *Virginian*, 9 February 1877.

83. "Alexis, the Grand Duke as Host," Norfolk *Virginian*, 14 February 1877. Alexis complained about having to collect a lot of oysters and barrels of whiskey for the occasion; to his mother, 30 January 1877, f. 641, op. 1, d. 34, TsGAOR.

84. "Disorderly Russian Sailors," Norfolk *Virginian*, 6 March 1877.

85. Shishkin to Fish, 1 February 1877, NRL, vol. 8 (roll 6, M 39), RG 59, NA.

86. Alexis to his mother, 30 January 1877, f. 641, op. 1, d. 34, TsGAOR. The last word was in Latin script.

87. New York *Times*, 17 February 1877.

88. Boker to Evarts, 19 and 26 March 1877, DUSM, Russia, vol. 31 (roll 31, M 35), RG 59, NA.

89. Alexis to his mother, 19 February/3 March 1877, f. 641, op. 1, d. 34, TsGAOR. Alexis added that his cousin "was very happy to be playing first fiddle."

sailed into New York harbor for a more ostentatious port call, the highlight of which was a public Russian Easter feast aboard the *Svetlana*.[90]

On the morning of 18 April Grand Dukes Alexis and Constantine, along with minister Shishkin and Admiral Butakov, were cordially received at the White House by President Rutherford Hayes and his cabinet. That afternoon the president and Secretary of State William Evarts returned the call at the Russian legation.[91] The next night a ceremony "of unusual magnificence" was held at the White House with General Sherman and Admiral Porter at the table and the Marine band playing in the vestibule. A delicate situation arose at this first Hayes state dinner, however, "Mrs. Hayes being conscientiously opposed to having spirits on her table, but she yielded upon this occasion to the arguments of Secretary Evarts, who was of the opinion that foreigners were accustomed to dine with wine, and would not enjoy the dinner without it."[92] As a compromise, no glasses were placed at her place or the president's, which must have made toasting awkward.

The less-heralded Russian squadron that put into San Francisco around mid-January 1877 consisted of seven warships assembled under Admiral Konstantin Pauzino. Although led by the impressive steam corvette *Baian*, most of the ships were small and old and badly in need of repairs after crossing the Pacific. Nevertheless, they caused quite an alarm to the British, who realized the vulnerability of the practically undefended Canadian Pacific coast.[93] Anchored at the Mare Island repair yards, they were barely operational until May, by which time the immediate war scare had passed.

The Russo-Turkish War

Following the Slav revolts in the Balkans and their bloody suppression by the Turks, Pan-Slavist agitation mounted in Russia. It took time, however, to get the army assembled and on the border. Diplomatic pressure forced Rus-

90. "Kissing the Grand Duke," Norfolk *Virginian*, 11 April 1877; "The Russian Fleet's Easter," New York *Herald*, 9 April 1877.

91. "The Russian Princes," New York *Times*, 19 April 1877.

92. "State Dinner at the White House," New York *Times*, 20 April 1877. Newspapers predictably had fun with this: "We would like to see the Grand Duke induced to sign the temperance pledge, but we doubt the propriety of inveigling him to the dinner table as a guest, and then forcing him to drink his royal father's health in a glass of cold water." "The Dinner to the Grand Duke," Norfolk *Virginian*, 22 April 1877.

93. Glynn Barratt, *Russian Shadows on the British Northwest Coast of North America, 1810–1890: A Study of Rejection of Defence Responsibilities* (Vancouver: University of British Columbia Press, 1983), pp. 77–80. The twenty-year-old *Baian* had been built by an American shipyard.

sia to work with the other Great Powers toward a peaceful resolution, but when their proposals were rejected by the Ottoman government in December 1876, the way was essentially clear. Even so, Russia wisely waited until spring to begin the offensive. New Anglo-Russian stipulations, known as the London Protocol, were also turned down in early April; and the tsar's declaration of war against the Ottoman Empire was duly released on 24 April. The main Russian armies moved cumbersomely across the border, through Rumania, and then over the Danube into Bulgaria, where initial Turkish resistance in July was quickly overcome.

Russian opinion at the beginning was enthusiastic in support of the war but more so in the Slavophile center of Moscow than in cosmopolitan St. Petersburg. Nearly everyone expected that the Russian army would have an easy march through Bulgaria to Constantinople and that the war would soon be over, on the pattern of the Franco-Prussian War a few years earlier. Having little empathy with the Turks, Americans anticipated and hoped that they would be taught a lesson as all Christians were freed from their control. Alexander II was popularly depicted in the guise of a brave crusader.[94] But the prognosis of a short, easy victory over a weak foe would soon change as the tenacious Turkish army dug in for long, hard, bloody battles at Plevna and Shipka Pass.

The United States authorized a blow-by-blow account. On 20 June Sherman, as army chief of staff, designated Lieutenant Francis Greene as an official observer on the Russian side. The secretary of state then gave Greene diplomatic status as an attaché who would report to him as well as to the War Department. "As such you will seek for military and scientific facts that may be useful or valuable to the government of the United States."[95] By the end of the month Greene was already on his way across the Atlantic. He reached St. Petersburg on 20 July and received immediate permission to join the advancing, "victorious" Russian army in the field.[96]

Reaching the Russian encampments in Rumania, Greene's first impression was one of chaos and illness; nearly the whole Russian staff was sick.

> I can not but think that it is due, more than to anything else, to the defective—or rather the total lack of—sanitary precautions about the camp. . . . There *are no sinks or latrines whatever* for the officers or men;

94. For example, Thomas Nast's cartoon, *Harper's Weekly*, 26 May 1877, pp. 408–9.
95. Evarts to Greene, 23 June 1877, DI, Russia, vol. 16 (roll 138, M 77), RG 59, NA.
96. Greene to Evarts, 8/20 July 1877, DUSM, Russia, vol. 31 (roll 31, M 35), RG 59, NA.

Alexander II as a Crusader, Thomas Nast cartoon.
Harper's Weekly, 26 May 1877, *courtesy of the Kansas*
Collection, University of Kansas Libraries

and independent of the odor of the stables which are in and among the
houses and tents, the streets and lanes of the village are filled with human excrement, which is never covered and which gives forth at night
a stench of the most unhealthy nature.[97]

In his first battle reports the attaché was shocked at the carnage dealt by the
Turkish Peabody breechloading rifles, made in Providence, Rhode Island,
and at least as good as the Berdanka. What made the death toll worse was
the "admiration of the Russians for the bayonet and their indifference to the

97. Greene (Bucharest) to Evarts, 2/14 August 1877, DUSM, Russia, vol. 32 (roll 32,
M 35), RG 59, NA. Greene's letters are much more detailed, spontaneous, and critical
than his subsequently published *Report.*

spade."[98] Greene wondered why the Russians had learned no lessons from the American Civil War—"of our use of earthworks they know nothing."[99] And he deplored the lack of coordination or strategic planning on the part of the Russian command.[100]

Meanwhile, Boker recorded the changing sentiment in the capital, as costly assaults failed to dislodge the Turks from the mountain passes.

> It was thought, even by not over-sanguine men, that a campaign against Turkey, meant nothing more than a promenade of the Russian army to Constantinople; that Turkey must fall at the mere unsheathing of the sword; or if she resisted, that she must be crushed at the first serious motion of Russia's vast military power. . . . Fight your enemy where you find him, seems to be the maxim of both parties; while the simplest rules of strategy are completely disregarded.[101]

Enthusiasm for the war, he noted, was flagging sharply in St. Petersburg, where there was some appreciation of its financial repercussions.

The war, once set in motion, continued through one bloody frontal assault after another, until the Turkish army was worn down and defeated. The Russians pursued the remnant enemy but halted on the approaches to Constantinople in February 1878 to discuss peace terms. The Ottoman Empire agreed by the Treaty of San Stefano to grant full independence to Serbia, Rumania, and Montenegro, territorial concessions in the Caucasus, a large indemnity, and autonomy for a redrawn Bulgaria that would include Macedonia and a coastline on the Aegean. It would be occupied for two years by the Russian army—in other words, be a Russian protectorate.

The other powers, especially Austria and Britain, were concerned about the extent of these changes and secured the intervention of Prince Otto von Bismarck as "the honest broker." A congress of the Great Powers (omitting, of course, the United States) met in Berlin in June to redraw the Balkan map, mainly to divide Bulgaria into three parts: a northern area that would

98. Greene to Evarts, 15/27 August 1877, ibid.

99. Greene to Evarts, 9 October 1877, ibid. Green later sent eighteen copies of his published final report for distribution to the top Russian generals, Greene to Hoffman, 1 October 1879, DPR, Russia, vol. 4437 (misc. received), RG 84, NA.

100. Greene included more technical details in his letters to Sherman while writing more candidly about conditions to his parents. Greene-Sherman letters, box 2, and to parents, box 3, Greene Papers, NYPL.

101. Boker to Evarts, 28 September 1877, DUSM, Russia, vol. 32 (roll 32, M 35), RG 59, NA.

have autonomous status under Russian protection, and two other sections, eastern Rumelia and Macedonia, under a reorganized Turkish administration.[102] Austria was appeased with a military protectorate over Bosnia and Hercegovina, and Britain obtained a similar status over Cyprus. The result was a considerable diplomatic setback for Russia, but as Greene pointed out, its army had lost the strong position it held at the beginning of the armistice, while the Turkish defenses around Constantinople had been strengthened.[103] There was no other course than to accept terms that were despised by most Russians, liberals and conservatives alike.

Behind the scenes, and apparently on his own initiative, Boker's replacement, Edwin Stoughton, lobbied for the Russian-Christian cause, obtaining interviews in London with Gladstone and John Bright. He reported to Gorchakov: "If they [the Christians] are not protected from further outrages by the Turks, it will be due to the efforts of England to preserve a power in Europe which is doomed soon utterly to disappear."[104] American sympathy remained very much with Russia.

The war was well covered in the American press, thanks to MacGahan, Schuyler, Greene, David Ker, Edward Maxwell Grant (an American writing for the London *Times*), Archibald Forbes, Donald Mackenzie Wallace, and artist-reporters Francis Millet (New York *Herald*) and R. C. Woodville (*Harper's Weekly*).[105] As never before, people far from the scene could imagine the battles as they unfolded—the piles of dead and wounded soldiers, the dirt and disarray, and the generals with all their decorations. Although not uncritical of the conduct of the war, the reporters generally supported the Russian, "Christian" side. Shishkin, the Russian minister, was pleased to inform St. Petersburg of the favorable press reaction to the terms of San Stefano.[106] And General Sherman summed up American opinion in a letter to Greene:

102. For a good, brief synopsis, see A. J. P. Taylor, *The Struggle for Mastery in Europe, 1848–1918* (Oxford: Clarendon Press, 1954), pp. 228–54. Even more concise is Mrs. Ulysses Grant's recollection; when she asked Bismarck at a dinner during the congress what it was all about, he answered, "Well, to tell the truth, Russia has eaten too much Turkey, and we are helping her to digest it." *The Personal Memoirs of Julia Dent Grant*, ed. John Y. Simon (New York: G. P. Putnam's Sons, 1975), p. 246.

103. Greene (San Stefano) to Evarts, 16 May 1878, DUSM, Russia, vol. 33 (roll 33, M 35), RG 59, NA.

104. Stoughton (London) to Gorchakov (Berlin), 29 June 1878, f. 133, op. 470, d. 54 (États-Unis 1878), AVPR.

105. According to Walker, *Januarius MacGahan*, p. 195, the Englishman Forbes, MacGahan, and the Russian general Mikhail Skobelev formed a close-knit triumvirate.

106. Shishkin to Gorchakov, 23 February/7 March 1878, f. 133, op. 470, d. 120 (1878), AVPR.

The "Jaws of Death" of the Russo-Turkish War, Thomas Nast cartoon. Harper's Weekly, *2 February 1878, courtesy of the Kansas Collection, University of Kansas Libraries*

"I always felt that a Russian victory was in the interests of Civilization."[107] Yet the horrors of war seemed to overshadow allegiances, and a fitting epitaph for the whole affair was a featured Nast cartoon that portrayed a forlorn pyramid of skulls on a desolate battlefield.[108]

The war was also visually brought home to the Russian capital in the summer of 1878 through an exhibition of paintings by a young Russian artist, Vasily Vereshchagin, who had been on the battlefields. An American observer thought his work influenced a popular feeling for peace, "portray-

107. Sherman to Greene, 13 January 1878, Letters from Sherman, Greene Papers, NYPL.
108. *Harper's Weekly,* 2 February 1878.

ing with a most terrible realism the reverse side of the 'glorious war' just lived through by the nation. Everybody rushed to the exhibition; groups of depressed people remained for long hours together standing motionless, bewildered, before Verestchagin's pictures; some women in mourning had to be carried away in a deep faint."[109] The exhibition went on to Paris, Berlin, London, and eventually New York, while the artist continually added more gory battle scenes.[110]

The lives of the American observers were subject to the fallout of war. Having emerged from the conflict as the hero-founder of an independent Bulgaria and intending to cover the Congress of Berlin, MacGahan succumbed to typhus in Constantinople in May 1878 at age thirty-three.[111] Perhaps the best tribute to him—besides a statue in Sophia—was offered by his friend and companion, Francis Greene: "No man of his age has in recent years done more to bring honor on the name of America, throughout the length and breadth of Europe, and far into Asia."[112] Schuyler, after recovering from a serious bout with typhoid fever and despite his unique experience and ability, was shunted off to the American consulate in Birmingham. The press observed: "Mr. Schuyler has, I suppose, an unrivalled knowledge of Russian and Turkish politics. He is a Russian scholar, speaks three or four European languages, knows Asia, has written the best book on that central part of it just now in dispute, and has withal a European reputation as a diplomatist. Hence we send him to a midland manufacturing town in England to certify invoices."[113] At first contemplating a biography of MacGahan,[114] Schuyler made use of idle time and enhanced his reputation as a Russian scholar by writing one of Peter the Great.

Greene recuperated from an incapacitating leg ailment in St. Petersburg

109. "War Is a Thing Desired," St. Petersburg letter dated 3 January 1878, New York *Times*, 31 January 1878, p. 7.

110. For a description of these works and their reception, see Vahan D. Barooshian, *V. V. Vereshchagin: Artist at War* (Gainesville: University of Florida Press, 1993), pp. 56–93.

111. Walker, *Januarius MacGahan*, p. 297. Schuyler and Greene were also seriously ill at the same time—but recovered.

112. Greene, *Sketches of Army Life in Russia* (New York: Charles Scribner's Sons, 1880), p. 162.

113. *Harper's Weekly*, 18 January 1879, p. 43, quoting the New York *Tribune*. Schuyler's diplomatic career continued with an appointment as minister to Greece and a brief stint as assistant secretary of state. He spent much of his time writing, lecturing, and traveling, until he too died tragically in Cairo of malaria in 1890. Schuyler, *Selected Essays*, pp. 152, 170.

114. Schuyler to Greene, 30 September 1879 and 13 July 1880, box 1, Greene Papers, NYPL.

during the summer of 1878, then he returned to the United States to reflect on his experience, publish two books on the Russian army, and pursue a distinguished professional career. His book on the Russo-Turkish War is a meticulously detailed account, that draws interesting conclusions on the course of modern warfare. In Greene's view this war was of a new type, in which defense definitely triumphed over the offense, presaging World War I. The change was produced by the breechloading rifle, in this case, the American-inspired Berdanka and the Peabody. "The combination of trench and breech-loader attained such a perfection that the whole campaign may be said to have consisted—tactically—of the attack and defense of more or less hastily fortified positions."[115]

Greene calculated that with the new breechloading rifles, 400 men in twelve minutes could deliver 24,000 shots, twelve times more than in 1863 at Gettysburg. Furthermore, considering the greatly increased range and accuracy over muzzleloaded weapons, the ratio of casualties created by the same number of men would be 1,200 to 90.[116] This volume of firepower made the cavalry practically useless, and the increase in effective range pushed the field artillery off the battlefield. "But all other weapons are dwarfed before the breech-loading musket, firing easily 5 to 6 shots a minute and carrying to a range of a mile and a quarter. Therefore the infantry is now *more than ever* the arm of the service upon which all the hard fighting devolves, which inflicts and receives the greatest damage, and to which all other parts of an army are merely subsidiary."[117] Interestingly, there was no mention of any special role for the machine gun, which was usually deployed with the artillery to create a confusing deluge of "soft" bullets. Greene credited the young general Mikhail Skobelev, a hero of the capture of both Khiva and Plevna, for devising the best offensive tactic to meet the infantry's defensive strength—skirmishing on the ground from close-dug trenches. Ironically, the war also revealed that heavy armor, mines, and torpedoes were making naval warfare more distant. Seldom would sailors again fight eye to eye.

American Ships for the Russian Navy

Before the war commenced, Russia had already been considering how to take advantage of American friendship in the approaching "Eastern crisis."

115. Greene, *Report* 1:422.
116. Ibid.
117. Ibid., 455.

Captain Leonid Semechkin, aide-de-camp to Grand Duke Constantine, was assigned to the Centennial Exposition in Philadelphia at the time of Alexis's second visit, and on behalf of Gorchakov, he investigated the possibility of acquiring commerce-raiding cruisers in the United States. The Russian minister relayed the information from Semechkin that as many as twelve could be purchased or built within six months and even suggested that crews could be sent over disguised as Mennonite immigrants.[118] Employing American-manned privateers by issuing letters of marque was also seriously considered by the tsar himself.[119]

As in the time of the Crimean War certain Americans were quick to jump on the Russian bandwagon. Shishkin forwarded to St. Petersburg a petition of Irish nationalists, headed by J. B. Conover and Martin Foran, appealing for Russian assistance for their cause and expressing the view "that the Irish people at home and abroad would be pleased to see both Turkey and India pass into the possession of Russia, believing that the changes would be for the best interests of those countries, of humanity, and of Ireland."[120] Prominent diplomat John Kasson, the American minister to Austria-Hungary, actively supported the idea of allowing Russia to issue letters of marque—in order to weaken the British merchant marine and revive the American.[121]

Shishkin also advised his government that the United States would be less cautious than during the Crimean War, when southern sympathy for Britain had created some reserve. He thought that ten to twelve corsairs could be contracted for $500 each through the support of manufacturing interests in Boston and Providence. And the Fennian movement in Canada could also be used effectively against Britain.[122] After Russia and Britain cooperated in diplomatic moves (the London Protocol) in early 1877, however, the sense of a British threat diminished; then the focus of international attention shifted to the military campaign in Bulgaria.

As the Russian armies approached the straits in early 1878 and the possibility loomed that the Ottoman Empire would follow Poland into geopoliti-

118. Shishkin to Gorchakov, 12 November 1876, f. 133, op. 470, d. 131 (1876), AVPR.
119. Boker to Fish, 21 November 1876, vol. 117, Fish Papers, LC, reporting his conversation with Alexander II.
120. Shishkin to Gorchakov, 25 October/6 November 1876, f. 133, op. 470, d. 131, AVPR.
121. Edward Younger, *John A. Kasson: Politics and Diplomacy from Lincoln to McKinley* (Iowa City: Iowa State Historical Society, 1955), pp. 284–85.
122. Shishkin to Gorchakov, 18/30 November 1876, f. 133, op. 470, d. 131, AVPR.

cal oblivion, British anti-Russian hysteria peaked again. A direct military confrontation threatened when a British naval squadron entered those waters on the pretext of defending British citizens.[123] Admiral Stepan Lesovskii, a veteran of the 1863 naval visit to the United States, immediately sent Semechkin back to the United States with a party of engineers in April on a secret mission to purchase ships for commerce raiding. To emphasize its importance Alexander II instructed Semechkin personally, and the American legation was informed of its purpose as well as the fact that in case of war the emperor would not be bound by the Treaty of Paris (1856) but would issue letters of marque to privateers.[124]

Without waiting for American concurrence, 66 officers and over 600 sailors were quickly assembled and dispatched from Port Baltic (near Reval) on board the *Cimbria*, an immigrant steamer chartered from the Hamburg-America line. They actually reached their destination—the remote fishing village of South West Harbor in Maine—on 28 April, creating confusion and alarm until Semechkin arrived by way of New York. The latter made immediate arrangements through Wharton Barker, a young Philadelphia Quaker banker and investor, who had handled Russia's Centennial exhibit finances, for the purchase of the *State of California* (1,922 tons) for $400,000 from William Cramp and Sons Ship and Engine Building Company.[125] The company was to outfit the passenger steamer as a "cruiser" at an additional cost of nearly $100,000. Within ten days two more ships, the *Columbus* (1,401 tons) and the *Saratoga* (1,745 tons), were acquired through Barker and Charles H. Cramp, and subsequently an order was placed for construction of a fourth, the *Zabiaka* (668 tons) at the Cramp shipyards. Altogether, counting various supplies and armaments, the Russian government spent

123. In retrospect, and especially considering the ample publicity about the human costs of the land campaign, it seems highly unlikely that Britain was prepared to stage any sort of invasion of the Balkans to confront directly a Russian army. The British press, moreover, emphasized the losses sustained by the attacker—as did the British attaché to the emperor in the Balkans. See Frederick A. Wellesley, *With the Russians in Peace and War: Recollections of a Military Attaché* (London: Eveleigh Nash, 1905).

124. Wickham Hoffman to Evarts, telegrams of 20 April and 24 April 1878 (confidential), DUSM, Russia, vol. 33 (roll 33, M 35), RG 59, NA; G. P. Kuropiatnik, *Rossiia i SShA: Ekono-micheskie, kul'turnye i diplomaticheskie sviazi, 1867–1881* (Moscow: Nauka, 1981), pp. 311–13; Leonid I. Strakhovsky, "Russia's Privateering Projects of 1878," *Journal of Modern History* 7, 1 (March 1935): 25–27.

125. Semechkin to Barker, 15 May 1878, Correspondence, box 1, Barker Papers, LC. Under the direction of Charles H. Cramp, this Philadelphia shipyard had emerged from the Civil War as the leading builder of war vessels for the American navy. Augustus C. Buell, *The Memoirs of Charles H. Cramp* (Philadelphia and London: J. B. Lippincott, 1906), pp. 55–63.

over $1 million in the United States for the navy in 1878, not counting the handsome fees paid to Barker for his services.[126] The total, including army purchases, probably exceeded $2 million, more than the value of the regular, reported trade between the two countries.

Once converted, these vessels were intended for duty as commerce destroyers, the real goal being to deter the British from taking action in support of the Turks that would provoke a general war. Naturally alarmed by this surprise development, the British kept a close watch on the proceedings and alerted Canadian defenses.[127] The British naval attaché reportedly visited the shipyards disguised as a workman but was caught and ushered out. The Washington *Capital* commented caustically: "He will hold his job. He deserves to. He has done what no American has ever been able to do since the collapse of the Rebellion. He has discovered a navy—an actual, real, live navy—in the United States. The fact that it is a Russian navy and not an American one, humiliating as it may be to us, is a huge feather in the cap to him."[128]

The purchase of these American ships was also related to a larger scheme of augmenting the regular navy with government-subsidized merchant ships. The "Russian Society for the Formation of a Volunteer Fleet" promoted the idea that the additional ships would be deployed commercially in foreign waters but would be capable of immediate conversion to armed cruisers in time of war. Several ships were acquired from the Hamburg-America line for this purpose, and the "Russian Volunteer Fleet" served as auxiliary to the Russian navy through the civil war that followed the revolution of 1917.[129]

But the buying trip to the United States was poorly planned, a veritable comedy of errors. Although the apparent purpose of landing at a remote location in New England was to maintain secrecy and avoid detection, the appearance of a large ocean steamer in a fishing village attracted more notice than it probably would have in New York, blending in among a number of immigrant vessels. The papers were soon filled with sensational headlines. Secretary of State Evarts, having been forewarned by a cable from his lega-

126. Estimate based on the orders and memoranda in the Barker Papers, box 1, LC.
127. Barratt, *Russian Shadows*, pp. 100–106.
128. As quoted in Buell, *Memoirs of Charles H. Cramp*, p. 219.
129. Hoffman to Evarts, 9 July 1878, DUSM, Russia, vol. 33 (roll 33, M 35), RG 59, NA. In a way the volunteer fleet filled a vacuum left by the demise of the Russian America Company, as initially its main business was hauling tea from China. Konstantin Skal'kovskii, *Russkaia torgovlia v Tikhom Okeane* (St. Petersburg: Suvorin, 1883), p. 479.

tion in St. Petersburg,[130] immediately summoned the Russian minister, who knew nothing about what was going on because Semechkin had not yet arrived with his instructions. Shishkin told Evarts frankly that he could only guess that it involved the purchase of ships and wished that his government had kept him informed so that he could have cleared it in advance. "He could see no way by which war could be avoided. England had been, and still was, making such great preparations that she would probably be unwilling to forego an encounter."[131] When the question of American neutrality was raised, Shishkin assured Evarts, wrongly, that no privateering from American ports would be considered by Russia.

A few days later, after Semechkin briefed him on Russian strategy, Shishkin told Evarts that large steamships were indeed to be bought and outfitted as cruisers. "If arming them here were not permitted, they might be armed at sea, or at (say) Santo Domingo."[132] Evarts concluded that he could not prevent sales to Russia when war had not been declared.[133] An important issue in United States neutrality was raised by the precipitous Russian action. In the meantime, Cramp and Sons in Philadelphia became a beehive of activity, as Russian naval construction officers supervised the remodeling of the ships (essentially gutting and refurbishing the interiors) and a swarm of newspaper reporters and British spies scrambled for information. Since secrecy was obviously pointless, Semechkin and K. K. Grippenberg, the leading Russian ship architect, started giving regular press interviews on the progress.[134]

Under pressure from the British ambassador and after studying more closely the 1818 act of Congress that attempted to define neutrality, Evarts again summoned Shishkin to the State Department in early June. He wanted a formal statement from Russia about its intention of arming these ships. "The secretary did not consider it suitable to the sovereignty of a country to allow the creation of a public warship within its own dominions, thus to become extra-territorialized and part of the dominion and authority

130. Evarts to Hoffman, 28 April 1877, DI, Russia, vol. 16 (roll 138, M 77), RG 59, NA, acknowledging receipt of information on the *Cimbria*.
131. Evarts memorandum of conversation with Shishkin, 6 May 1878, NRL, vol. 8 (roll 6, M 39), RG 59, NA; Shishkin to Gorchakov, 27 April/9 May 1878 (very confidential), f. 133, op. 470, d. 120, AVPR.
132. Memorandum of conversation, 11 May 1878, NRL, vol. 8 (roll 6, M 39), RG 59, NA.
133. Shishkin to Gorchakov, 11/23 May 1878, f. 133, op. 470, d. 120, AVPR.
134. See "The Vessels for Russia," Philadelphia *Inquirer*, 14 and 28 May 1878.

of a foreign nation." The ships must be understood to be commercial. "At no time before leaving our ports should the public quality as a ship of war be assumed or pretended."[135] The problem was that the real Russian intentions were common knowledge.

Section three of the 1818 act forbade any military support to be furnished to a foreign country that was specifically intended to be used against another country then at peace with the United States. Literally applied, whether or not the ships purchased by the Russians were armed, they were being knowingly sold and altered for military use against a clearly designated foe. Barker and Cramp especially were in violation of the law. Or were they? It was unclear if this section held in peacetime, that is, when all affected parties were not formally engaged in hostilities. Evarts would not make a ruling until a state of war existed,[136] and the threat faded with the convening of the congress in Berlin in June. The three purchased vessels, now neutrally named the *Evropa, Aziia,* and *Afrika,* departed in late 1878, unarmed but still to be armed; in diplomatic terms, it could be contended that no particular immediate enemy then existed for Russia, and that the ships were simply acquired through normal peacetime contracts.[137] The announced excuse for not arming them before departure was that adequate heavy cannon had to be purchased from Krupp in Germany, but this may have only been a cover to safeguard American neutral sensitivities.[138]

The United States economy obviously gained from the Russo-Turkish War in the sale of ships and other weapons. The cutting off of Russian exports from the Black Sea ports raised the price of grain and the proportion of European imports from the United States, while the war increased the demands for American copper (in the form of brass for cartridges), petroleum, and tools.[139] And there was some carryover from the war; Cramp continued to court Russian business with modest success, primed especially by a meet-

135. Memorandum of conversation, 10 June 1878, NRL, vol. 8 (roll 6, M 39), RG 59, NA. Shishkin confirmed this understanding; to Gorchakov, 31 May/12 June 1878, f. 133, op. 470, d. 120, AVPR.

136. Shishkin to Giers, 31 May/12 June 1878, f. 133, op. 470, d. 120 (1878), AVPR.

137. Small steamers took some lighter arms to load on the ships outside of territorial waters, but the big guns were installed by Krupp in Germany. The *Zabiaka,* built entirely by Cramp, left quietly as a fully furnished warship early in 1879.

138. Buell, *Memoirs of Charles H. Cramp,* p. 220.

139. Boker to Evarts, 3 May 1878, DUSM, Russia, vol. 33 (roll 33, M 35), RG 59, NA. Cartridges and revolvers had been purchased in the United States for the Russian army for delivery in 1877 by a mission headed by Captain Kushekevich; Gorchakov to Shishkin, 15 November 1876 (c), f. 133, op. 470, d. 131, AVPR.

ing with Naval Minister Grand Duke Constantine when both were in Paris in 1880.[140]

The war revived to some extent the traditional American Anglophobia that had abated since the settlement of the *Alabama* affair in 1872; at least most Americans were certainly aware of British anti-Russian fears. Francis Greene summarized the American perspective: "The greatest of these [British] imaginary dangers is the idea that Russia covets the possession of India for herself. . . . There is every reason to believe that Russia has no such ambitions. . . . It was this anxiety about India that made England see a hidden purpose in every step that Russia took in regard to Turkey."[141] The war also awakened and encouraged the rise of antigovernment sentiments throughout the world because of the carnage delivered on poorly defended soldiers and helpless civilian populations by brutal war machines. In the United States it is credited with reviving interest in the American Red Cross Society and other international relief efforts.[142] Not surprisingly, as in the case of the Crimean War, Americans offered to serve as doctors for the Russian army, but this time they were not needed as much because of the number of Russian surgeons available. In fact, to qualify for regular service and pay, foreigners had to be graduates of a Russian medical school and able to speak and write Russian. Serving in a volunteer capacity in the Russian Red Cross was still possible, but there is no evidence that any American did so.[143] A small group of Americans, led by Jack Ketch of Galveston, Texas, did fight as sharpshooters with the Russian army in Bulgaria and were decorated and praised for their heroism.[144]

A Canadian Plan

One curious side effect of American "involvement" was a scheme hatched by Wharton Barker to secure the annexation of Canada with Russian assistance. The idea was inspired by the threat of a British attack on Russia and the purchase of the cruisers in May 1878 and was abetted by the Russian na-

140. Buell, *Memoirs of Charles H. Cramp*, pp. 222–25.
141. Greene, *Sketches of Army Life*, pp. 308–9.
142. Elizabeth Brown Pryor, *Clara Barton: Professional Angel* (Philadelphia: University of Pennsylvania Press, 1987), pp. 187–88.
143. Boker to Evarts, 21 November 1877, DUSM, Russia, vol. 32 (roll 32, M 35), RG 59, NA.
144. "American Sharpshooters in Russia," St. Louis *Missouri Republican*, 1 February 1879, citing the New York *World*.

val agent Semechkin. Even after the Congress of Berlin, Barker continued to pursue this objective. Thinking probably that the Russian government would be especially grateful for his recent assistance in purchasing the ships, Barker spent the summer of 1879 in St. Petersburg exploring the prospects of Russian support for the plan in conversations with Semechkin and the assistant (and acting) foreign minister, Nikolai Giers. He envisioned a situation whereby Canada would be forced into a commercial dependency on the United States that would turn into a political union. In a detailed proposal to Gorchakov, he asked for £20,000 to subsidize an annexationist movement in Canada and for the authorization to build more cruisers for Russia to bolster its capabilities in case war broke out.[145]

The following year, Barker sounded out and received encouragement from Secretary of State Evarts and potential presidential candidate James Garfield for his annexationist schemes.[146] He then pressed them again on Giers:

America can never forget her treatment at the hands of England during the dark days of the Rebellion and only waits a proper time for action, and that time will be when Russian cruisers are destroying English commerce by sinking ships and causing rise of rates of insurance on British shipping. . . . The feeling of good will now so strong between Russia and the United States would be lasting.[147]

He also promised American support for Russian seizure of "Turkey and Asia Minor." Barker asked again for financial assistance, upping the amount by £10,000 for use in influencing the next presidential election, and he repeated his request to Grand Duke Constantine.[148]

For over two years, Barker persisted with his ambitious plan in correspondence and wherever he met Russians. Giers finally refused to respond and instructed the Russian minister in Washington to not receive Barker "and

145. Barker to Gorchakov, 30 December 1879 (c), box 1, Barker Papers, LC. Semechkin returned to the United States in early 1879 on an unknown mission; Shishkin to Evarts, 25 January 1879, NRL, vol. 9 (roll 7, M 39), RG 59, NA. In a brief reminiscence of his visit to Russia, Barker is silent on this scheme. "The Secret of Russia's Friendship," *Independent* 56, 2886 (24 March 1904): 645–49.
146. Evarts to Barker, 1 March 1880, and Garfield to Barker, 9 May 1880, box 1, Barker Papers, LC.
147. To Giers, 6 July 1880 (c), box 1, Barker Papers, LC.
148. To Constantine, 7/19 July 1880 (c), ibid.

put an end to these compromising conversations."[149] Although obviously nothing came of it, influential Russians and Americans took the idea seriously and encouraged it. Barker's strange connections with Russia were not finished, however, and would continue beyond the 1917 revolution.

Grant Visits Russia

The close military relationship between the United States and Russia as the Russo-Turkish War came to an end may have contributed to the former president's decision to make a surprise visit to Russia. Ulysses Grant and his wife were indeed on a world tour and may simply have wished to leave no major country untouched. Certainly the new minister to Russia, Edwin W. Stoughton, a wealthy New Yorker and Hayes campaign backer, could be counted on for appropriate hospitality. But the tsar's bad feelings toward Grant for snubbing his son Alexis the previous year could not have been forgotten. Boker, the outgoing minister, had personally tried to convince Grant not to go, explaining to him that Gorchakov had advised against it "in a manner that was almost menacing."[150] Grant persisted.

The visit is memorable since it was the first by a former president (though President Polk's widow was there in 1874) and the last until Richard Nixon's over a hundred years later. The party, which included an official recorder, John Russell Young, was met by Stoughton and Greene on 30 July 1878 and spent the next two weeks seeing the sights of St. Petersburg and Moscow. The former president really seemed to enjoy himself in Russia. Greene, who accompanied him most of the time, reported that "the general seems very fond of going off incog. with me and wandering about the streets looking at the people or stopping at a garden to get a glass of beer."[151]

On 2 August Grant was "presented" at Tsarskoe Selo. Alexander II, apparently willing to forget and forgive, greeted him politely: "Since the foundation of your Government, relations between Russia and America have been of the friendliest character, and as long as I live nothing shall be spared to continue this friendship." Grant replied with an obvious truth, "That although the two Governments were very opposite in their character, the

149. Giers (Livadia) to Bartolomai, 10/22 November 1880 (secret and in code), f. 133, op. 470, d. 183, AVPR.
150. Boker to Adam Badeau, 4 May 1887, Autograph File, Houghton Library, Harvard University.
151. Greene to mother, 4 August 1878, box 3, Greene Papers, NYPL.

great majority of the American people were in sympathy with Russia, which good feeling he hoped would long continue."[152] Grant would retain fond memories of his imperial reception in retirement.[153]

Boker, who was not present, claimed that the Grants were treated with civility but of "the damndest commonest kind" with no balls or dinners given in their honor, but this is partly contradicted by Greene.[154] Although it is true that Alexander II hosted only a formal reception, cordiality prevailed, and elsewhere the Grants had the best of Russian hospitality: the imperial yacht for a visit to a "Popovka" monitor, *Peter the Great*, which gave Grant a fifteen-gun salute; the imperial railway car for the trip to Moscow, where they dined with the governor; a lavish reception arranged by Admiral Lesovskii; and a dinner at the legation attended by several ministerial dignitaries—Giers (foreign), Alexander Jomini (foreign), Lesovskii (navy), Samuel Greig (finance), and Dmitri Nabokov (justice).[155] Otherwise the Grants seemed to enjoy themselves in typical American style by sightseeing, shopping, and socializing;[156] to one observer they appeared rather "spooney," with Julia Grant always chattering away, oblivious to whether anyone could understand her.[157]

Information Exchange

Although military technology, anchored by the American Civil War and the Russo-Turkish War, was foremost in the exchanges of information be-

152. John Russell Young, *Around the World with General Grant: A Narrative of the Visit of General U. S. Grant, ex-President of the United States, to Various Countries in Europe, Asia, and Africa, in 1877, 1878, 1879* (New York: Subscription Book Department, 1880), p. 468.

153. "Gen. Grant's Recollections," New York *Times*, 14 March 1881. The former president was interviewed by a reporter about the assassination of Alexander II.

154. Boker to Badeau, 4 May 1887, Autograph File, Houghton Library. Greene thought Grant was pleased by his reception, "for so many people had advised him not to come here on account of reminiscences of misunderstandings about Alexis and Catacazy—and he hesitated a long while about it himself." Greene to parents, 8 August 1878, box 3, Greene Papers, NYPL.

155. Details of the Grants' visit are well covered by Young and in two diaries: Mary Stoughton (wife of minister), NYPL; and Louise Stoughton (niece of minister), A-67, Women's Archive, Radcliffe College, Harvard University.

156. Young, *Around the World*, pp. 470–93; *Personal Memoirs of Julia Dent Grant*, pp. 251–54.

157. Louise Stoughton diary, 29 July/10 August 1878, Radcliffe College. The Grant family would have another Russian connection when a granddaughter married into a prominent Russian noble family.

tween the United States and the Russian Empire, it was far from holding a monopoly. The number of other visits and contacts having the pursuit of specific knowledge in mind was especially impressive in the period from 1867 to 1881. Russians were spurred not only by the spirit of modernization accompanying the reform era but also by a reawakened individual curiosity. This was indeed the beginning of a new age in science, as manifested by the invention of the breechloading rifle, Thomas Edison's quest for Russian platinum for light bulb experiments,[158] and the close, mutual involvement of the two countries in the development of modern petroleum industries.

A major initiative for seeking information and developing exchanges with Russia was taken by the American government's Smithsonian Institution and its able "founding" secretaries, Joseph Henry and Spencer Baird. The Smithsonian's involvement beginning in 1865 with the Western Union Telegraph Expedition to Alaska and Siberia established a solid base. By 1867 a wealth of data and mineral and plant specimens were flowing into Washington from the scientists attached to the mission. Seeking further contacts, in April 1867 Henry wrote through the American legation to Admiral Friedrich (Fedor) Lutke, noted explorer and president of the Academy of Sciences, that the Smithsonian wanted to acquire the complete published works of the academy.[159] At the same time he requested any available information, published or archival, on Alaska, which had just been purchased. Cassius Clay, who was especially interested in mechanical advances, assured Henry of his cooperation "in the development and expansion of all sciences." The materials were to be sent through a professional intermediary, Dr. Felix Flugel of Leipzig. Within nine months, Henry wrote to say that he was very much indebted for the large quantity of nearly complete Russian serials, "which form one of the most prominent features in the Library of the Smithsonian Institution,"[160] the basis of America's first public Russian collection.

Henry forwarded another special "want list" of Russian publications on Alaska to a St. Petersburg bookhandler, Watkins and Company, for search and purchase.[161] Their success and Flugel's persistent complaints about diffi-

---

158. Edison (Menlo Park) to Stoughton, 19 July 1879, DPR, Russia, vol. 4437 (misc. received); Hoffman to Giers, 23 July/4 August 1879 (c), DPR, Russia, vol. 4535 (notes sent), RG 84, NA.

159. Henry to Lutke, 12 April 1867 (c), vol. 6, p. 421, RG 33 (outgoing correspondence), SA; Henry to Clay, 3 April 1867, DPR, Russia, vol. 4502 (notes received), RG 84, NA.

160. Henry to Lutke, 20 January 1868 (c), vol. 9, pp. 145–46, RG 33, SA.

161. Clay to Henry, 28 January 1868, vol. 69, p. 272, RG 26 (incoming correspondence), SA.

culties in getting materials through Customs convinced the Smithsonian to seek a more reliable and regular channel.[162] The number of requests for American publications, especially from Russian institutions, grew along with the trend for agencies in all modern countries to gather information and publish it in a coherent, systematic fashion. The bureaucratic paper industry thrived, since every group wanted a complete series of publications of comparable agencies in other countries for *their* library.

On behalf of the Smithsonian, Baird explored with Andrew Curtin the possibility of centralizing the dissemination of materials in St. Petersburg and asked if a Russian government agency or Watkins and Company could do it. He noted that he had five cases ready to send to various Russian destinations and wanted to ease the problem of distributing them within Russia.[163] Although Watkins was consequently designated as the regular intermediary, this did not end the problems. Watkins observed, for example, that it was best to let materials pile up during the summer for distribution in the winter when receipts could be more easily obtained.[164] Bills of lading still had to go through the legation, "as by this means *alone* do the boxes escape being sent to the Censor's office where *every parcel* would be opened and examined."[165]

Once a regular shipping routine had been worked out, the exchanges proceeded apace and with increasing volume and variety. Besides serials, pamphlets, and books, they included mineral samples, natural history specimens, and plants and seeds. Especially active on the Russian side were noted scientists Karl Maksimovich, director of the Imperial Botanical Gardens who especially coveted dried plant specimens from the Rocky Mountains region, and zoologist Johann (Fedor) Brandt who was interested in comparing European and North American bison.[166] Most materials, in consignments of four to six cases, were carried at cost or free of charge on ships belonging to Ropes and Company to and from Kronstadt; Watkins and Company handled distribution within St. Petersburg. Some items that were more impor-

162. Henry to Watkins and Company, 8 July 1868 (c), vol. 11, p. 103, and to Lutke, 10 November 1868 (c), vol. 12, p. 105, RG 33, SA.

163. Baird to Curtin, 9 July 1870, DPR, Russia, vol. 4434 (misc. received), RG 84, NA; Henry to Watkins, 5 June 1871 (c), vol. 24, p. 232, RG 33, SA.

164. Watkins to Smithsonian, 2/14 October 1871, vol. 121, p. 9, RG 26, SA.

165. Watkins to Smithsonian, 12 November 1871, vol. 121, p. 10, RG 26, SA.

166. Maksimovich to Henry, 21 September/3 October 1867, vol. 78, pp. 16–17; Brandt to Henry, 5/17 May 1867, vol. 93, p. 496; and Maksimovich to Henry, 15/27 October 1872, vol. 127, p. 197, RG 26, SA.

tant or more urgent went by diplomatic pouch direct to the legation and then were hand-delivered to the Russian destination.[167]

Finally, in 1876, a new law by Congress created a system of automatic ordering of government publications that was "intended to secure for the National Library everything relating to the legislation, jurisprudence, finance, political economy, geology, natural history, statistics, etc. of foreign nations, as far as published officially."[168] Each side would pay the shipping costs of what they sent to the post of the consul general, in Russia's case to New York. To simplify Russian acceptance, Henry stated, "It is of course not necessary that the question of equivalence of value be settled, all we ask is the receipt of everything published from time to time whether it be much or little."[169] Giers, in responding favorably to the proposal, noted that the volume of requests was expanding so fast that a special commission was being appointed to handle them.[170] The Russian minister pledged his cooperation. "I would be glad to see such exchanges take place, knowing how anxious my Government is of providing itself with all public documents relating to the administration and legislation of foreign countries."[171] In 1879 Spencer Baird, succeeding Henry as Smithsonian secretary, wrote to the American minister in St. Petersburg that he was quite satisfied with how the exchange was working.[172]

Besides official government documents, the Smithsonian also acted on behalf of American individuals and organizations such as universities, academies, and libraries. Their requests were usually very specific and are not easy to trace. Additionally, not all materials were handled by the Smithsonian. Government agencies engaged in direct exchanges, as, for example, that between the Russian Ministry of State Domains and the Department of Agriculture, and agencies on both sides initiated special searches for particular items. Individuals were often instrumental in establishing exchanges. For instance, Dr. Evgenyi Pelikan visited the United States on a medical mission in 1869. The long-time U.S. surgeon general

167. At times, this service went only as far as Hamburg, especially for botanical specimens; Fish to Henry, 23 December 1872, vol. 128, p. 92, RG 26, SA. The legation directly handled the exchanges of the growing number of diplomatic publications for the State Department. See Schuyler to Fish, 2 November 1874, DUSM, Russia, vol. 27 (roll 27, M 35), RG 59, NA.

168. Henry to Hoffman Atkinson, 9 September 1876, DPR, Russia, vol. 4436 (misc. received), RG 84, NA.

169. To Boker, 21 July 1876, DPR, Russia, vol. 4436 (misc. received), RG 84, NA.

170. To Boker, 11/23 December 1876, DPR, Russia, vol. 4505 (notes received), RG 84, NA; copy enclosed in Boker to Fish, 26 December 1876, DUSM, Russia, vol. 30 (roll 30, M 35), RG 59, NA.

171. Shishkin to Henry, 31 December 1877, vol. 171, p. 217, RG 26, SA.

172. To John Foster, 8 June 1879, DPR, Russia, vol. 4437 (misc. received), RG 84, NA.

(1863–1882), Dr. Joseph Barnes, was especially interested in forming international connections in pursuit of library and resource development, and Russia was naturally high on his list. With the sponsorship of Pelikan and Barnes, samples of medical instruments were soon passing back and forth between the two countries.[173] Consul general Bodisko in New York also collected information for Russian agencies. Under his prompting the Ministry of Ways and Communications sent an engineer in 1875 to study the canal system in the United States.[174] In fact, wherever Russians and Americans met, papers and items of various kinds were usually exchanged or requested and sent later.

The director of the Imperial Public Library (later Saltykov-Shchedrin), Ivan Delianov, energetically pursued direct library exchanges. In 1874 he notified the legation that he was sending thirteen boxes of books to the Boston Public Library.[175] Although some were printed in Russian, many were published in other, more universal languages—French, German, or English. Nonetheless, they were probably of limited circulation or use on the American end. The potential benefit was mainly on the Russian side, but daunting bureaucratic, and perhaps security hurdles often had to be surmounted to gain access to the incoming American materials.

Personal Contacts

The most successful and lasting contacts occurred when individual experts traveled to the other country on specific missions. The military expeditions and the visit of Dr. Pelikan noted previously are typical examples. Another instance was the 1872 inspection of American prisons and study of penal reform legislation by Vladimir Soldatenkov, a prominent and wealthy Moscow merchant.[176] That same year a delegation of eight Americans, three of them government-sponsored, attended the first International Statistical

173. Westmann to Schuyler, 6/18 July 1870, DPR, Russia, vol. 4503 (notes received), RG 84, NA.

174. "Russia Studying America," New York *Herald,* 1 September 1875.

175. To Jewell, 1 May 1874, DPR, Russia, vol. 4504 (notes received), RG 84, NA.

176. Philadelphia *Inquirer,* 31 January 1872; scrapbook clippings, Madison *Wisconsin,* 16 January 1872, box 23a, Jeremiah Curtin Papers, MCHC. Curtin served as guide for Soldatenkov's Wisconsin tour, met his future wife during it, and saw the Russian scholar frequently while in St. Petersburg; box 19, Curtin Papers, MCHC; Curtin, *Memoirs,* pp. 207–9, 218, 223, where the name is given as "Solijenkoff." For this Old Believer family's prominence, see Thomas C. Owen, *Capitalism and Politics in Russia: A Social History of the Moscow Merchants, 1855–1905* (Cambridge: Cambridge University Press, 1981), pp. 48, 51, 81, 90–91, 208.

Congress in St. Petersburg, where their Russian hosts provided their housing and local transportation.[177] The elder Grand Duke Constantine delivered a closing address to the 300 assembled Russian and foreign delegates; the Americans reported excellent progress in improving communication and coordination and a definite interest in future meetings.[178]

One of the best-known Russian scientific visits to the United States was that of Aleksandr Voeikov, who would become a world-famous meteorologist. Early in his career, in late 1872, he journeyed to America and spent several months at the Smithsonian Institution and traveling around the United States as far west as Denver and Pike's Peak. A close association developed between the thirty-year-old Russian and the seventy-five-year-old Joseph Henry. Through Henry's sponsorship, Voeikov wrote an article on Russian meteorology that was published in *Smithsonian Reports* for 1873. He also studied with James Coffin, a noted specialist on winds, at Lafayette College. While on an extended tour of South America, he received news of Coffin's death and returned in 1875 to complete some of Coffin's unfinished works with Henry's support and encouragement.[179] He later published a number of valuable scientific studies of his own.

Voeikov also sought out Cleveland Abbe, who had studied a few years before at the Pulkovo Observatory near St. Petersburg and whose innovations in the telegraphic transmission of weather reports were of special interest to Russia. In part because of Abbe's sojourn at Pulkovo in the 1860s, close relations were maintained between Russian and American scientists in the field of astronomy. Under the direction of Otto Struve, the staff of Pulkova had achieved a high reputation, and American astronomers sought to draw from their expertise and win international recognition for themselves. Abbe naturally kept up a correspondence with his Russian associates; this expanded to other American scholars and to regular, direct exchanges of scientific papers. Abbe's American mentor, Asaph Hall, led a delegation to Pulkovo in

177. Philadelphia *Inquirer*, 5 September 1872. Representing the United States officially were Edward Young, William Barnes, and E. M. Snow. Others attending were Julius Clarke and E. H. and N. L. Derby, all of Boston; Alexander Delmar of Washington, D.C.; and Charles Gorham, American minister to The Hague. Schuyler to Fish, 24 August 1872, DUSM, Russia, vol. 24 (roll 24, M 35), RG 59, NA.

178. Schuyler to Fish, 31 August 1872, DUSM, Russia, vol. 24 (roll 24, M 35), RG 59, NA.

179. Grant Konstantinovich Tsverava, "Iz istorii russko-amerikanskykh nauchnykh sviazei v XIX v.: Dzhozef Genri i Aleksandr Ivanovich Voeikov," *Priroda* 7 (July 1979): 79–85; Vadim Pokhishevskii, *Povest' o znamenitom russkom geografe Aleksandre Ivanoviche Voeikove* (Moscow: Gosizdatslit, 1955), pp. 58–65.

1870, carried on a regular correspondence with Struve, and was a member of a team that visited Vladivostok in 1874 to observe a close approach of the planet Venus.[180] Russian counterparts, such as Sergei Glazenap, were attracted to the work of Simon Newcomb, the best-known American astronomer, who visited Pulkovo in 1871 and was duly honored with election as a corresponding member of the Russian Academy of Sciences in 1875. Two other American astronomers, Hall and Benjamin Gould, soon joined him in that elite circle.

The high point of Russian-American astronomic cooperation came with Otto Struve's four-month tour of the United States in 1879. He stayed with prominent American astronomers along his route from the Washington Naval Observatory through Chicago to San Francisco.[181] Struve, with Newcomb's help, ordered a new, thirty-inch lens for a Pulkovo telescope from renowned opticians, Alvan Clark and Sons, of Cambridgeport, Massachusetts. Costing $32,000, the lens was the largest in the world at the time and would take over three years to produce.[182] One of the sons, Alvan G. Clark, accompanied Struve back to Europe to arrange for special mountings, bringing considerable attention and fame to the Cambridge firm.[183]

The Centennial Exhibition

Other important points of contact between Russians and Americans were the international expositions that were held regularly in the last half of the nineteenth century. Russian participation outside their own borders, however, was usually quite modest, as was American, and few foreigners attended those held in Russia. When the official invitation to participate in the grand celebration of one hundred years of American independence was first tendered to Russia, it was politely declined on the grounds that it came

180. Kuropiatnik, *Rossiia i SShA*, pp. 164–67.
181. Ibid., p. 169.
182. "A Great Project: The Russians Still Ahead in Astronomical Science," St. Louis *Missouri Republican*, 16 June 1879; "The Pulkovo Telescope," New York *Times*, 5 September 1879; Simon Newcomb, *The Reminiscences of an Astronomer* (Boston: Houghton Mifflin, 1903), pp. 143–45.
183. Alvan Clark and Sons (Cambridgeport) to Villamov (chargé, Washington, D.C.), f. 170, op. 512/3, d. 142 (1880), AVPR. "[This] is not only a high tribute to their skill and accuracy in such delicate work, but a matter of congratulation to Americans in general and the people of this neighborhood in particular"; as "The King of Glasses: The Thirty-Inch Objective Ordered by the Czar," St. Louis *Missouri Republican*, 27 September 1879. Struve returned in 1883 to test the finished glass at the Clark facility.

too soon after an exposition in Vienna.[184] Minister Jewell explained to the president of the Centennial Commission, "The Russians consider America much farther off than Americans do Russia. They are neither a traveling or commission people, nor are they a manufacturing one to any considerable extent."[185]

After additional American pressures and Russian second thoughts, an official commission was formed within the Ministry of Finance to plan a large-scale Russian exhibit. Alexander Jomini and Fedor Osten-Saken, officials of the foreign ministry, also placed participation high on the agenda in October 1875, and dispatches were soon flying back and forth with information.[186] The restoration of harmony following the Katakazi debacle happened to coincide with a rising interest in mechanical and folk arts, both of which were to be prominently featured in Philadelphia.[187] The Russian government couched their delayed acceptance in honorific terms—that their exhibition was simply to recognize an important American celebration. Only in December, after the arrival of a special investigator, V. A. Benitskii, did the Russians realize that it was too late to erect their own building. A scramble for available space then ensued.[188]

Golos, a voice of liberalism in Russia, used this opportunity to produce a series of articles extolling Russian-American friendship and American society and its progress.

A refusal to take part in the international exhibition might have the character of a demonstration against the national festivities of the Americans, and might be considered by them as, to say the least, an unfriendly act. . . . If we have in view the sincere friendship and mutual good relations which have constantly existed between Russia and the

184. Jewell to Gorchakov, 2 December 1873, DPR, Russia, vol. 4535 (notes sent), RG 84, NA. This miffed the American press; the New York *Times*, 1 September 1875, contrasted Russia with spunky Bermuda, which was making a great effort to participate.

185. To J. R. Hawley, 17/29 January 1874, DPR, Russia, vol. 4484 (misc. sent), RG 84, NA.

186. Shishkin to Osten-Sacken, 2/14 October 1875, f. 170, op. 512/3, d. 124, AVPR.

187. Alexander Jomini, embarrassed that he had to ask the American minister for a new invitation, was instrumental in reversing the Russian decision. Boker to Fish, 14 October (t) and 21 October 1875, enclosing Jomini to Boker, 2/15 October 1875 (t), DUSM, Russia, vol. 29 (roll 29, M 35), RG 59, NA.

188. Shishkin to A. V. Jackson, 2/14 December 1875 (c), f. 170, op. 512/3, d. 124, AVPR, asking for plans of the grounds, "with the scheme allotted to *all* countries that participate in the Exhibition marked on it."

United States, it is impossible to believe that our country will be absent from the Philadelphia Exhibition; but, on the contrary, that it will be among the most honored and dearest guests of the American people.[189]

Taking the United States as a progressive political model for Russia, *Golos* reflected the relative optimism of the mid-1870s.

Nowhere has the principle of self government had such triumph as in the United States, and in no other country has the government been so closely and inseparably bound up with the community. . . . We were drawn together by the common character and contemporaneity of the internal struggle, the great social and political revolution, in the name of the high idea of the abolition of slavery and serf labour.[190]

Starting so late, however, and contending with the usual bureaucracy and great distances, Russia could not put together an exhibit in Philadelphia by the time the Centennial kicked off with a brilliant display on 10 May. Nonetheless, the Russian diplomatic corps (Shishkin, Bodisko, Nikolai Voigt, Georgi Bakhmetev, and their families) turned out for the grand opening that featured President Grant's address—which Shishkin observed was widely criticized for borrowing words and diction from Abraham Lincoln.[191] Alexander II formally extended his warmest congratulations on the anniversary occasion, to which Grant responded appropriately.[192]

By the next big celebration day, the Fourth of July, the Russian exhibits were in place, scattered in sections through the main halls and including a large variety of articles. The "Russian Bazaar" emphasized costumes, art and design, and other objects that illustrated native traditions. The malachite section, featuring a fireplace mantel valued at $6,500, was especially popular. Other exhibits were devoted to artillery and naval guns, practical mechanics, porcelain, embroidery, silver, gold, rare minerals, leather crafts, etc. The machine hall had such Russian items as a ship's compass, lanterns, stoves, a

189. Translation of article, probably by Schuyler, from *Golos*, 8/20 October 1875, in Boker to Fish, 21 October 1875, DUSM, Russia, vol. 29 (roll 29, M 35), RG 59, NA.

190. Translation from *Golos*, 12/24 October 1875, in Boker to Fish, 25 October 1875, DUSM, Russia, vol. 29 (roll 29, M 35), RG 59, NA. For a detailed Russian account of preparations for the exhibition: "Vsemirnaia vystavka v Amerike," OZ 225, 3 (March 1876): 169–98.

191. Shishkin to Gorchakov, 7/19 May 1876, f. 133, op. 470, d. 131 (1876), AVPR.

192. Grant to Alexander II, 28 July 1876, f. 133, op. 470, d. 50 (1876), AVPR. It was signed, "Your Good Friend."

pontoon bridge, model docks, and printing machines.[193] Clearly, the Russian commission had endeavored to present the progressive best of the country. *Harper's Weekly* summarized the universal praise of the Russian displays by the press: "The representation of Russia at the Centennial Exhibition rivals in completeness and magnificence that of any other country."[194]

At least twelve Russian experts came with the exhibit to help set it up, to scout the other displays, and to explore what America had to offer in their respective fields. Technological skills predominated. The most important of these official Russian representatives were Modest Kittary, a professor of mechanics at the Imperial Polytechnic Institute in Moscow; Nikolai Petrov, a machine engineer who taught at the army's Nikolaevskii Academy; and Leonid Semechkin, who helped supervise the mechanics section.[195] Others such as Pavel Kushelov and Konstantin Skal'kovskii (trade and commerce) were just starting their careers, while Dmitri Mendeleev had already won fame for chemistry textbooks. A number of other Russians, perhaps as many as one hundred, traveled to Philadelphia for the centennial observances; at least six worked on the construction of the exhibition buildings.[196]

Mechanical Training

In one area—a demonstration of the workshop method of formal technical training—the Russian exhibit had a direct impact on American pedagogy. The president of the Massachusetts Institute of Technology, John Runkle, was extremely impressed, as he wrote to a friend:

> Russia has taught us a grand lesson. You know that the workshop problem, as part of the course for mechanical engineers, has been a difficult one,—so difficult that we have compromised on a mechanical laboratory. The Worcester Institute, Cornell University and the Illinois University have built up shops, but always from the manufacturing side and idea, and not from the teaching side. They have not analyzed ma-

193. Shishkin to Giers, 2/14 July 1876, f. 133, op. 470, d. 131 (1876), AVPR; E. M. Dvoichenko-Markova, "Uchenye Rossii na mezhdunarodnoi vystavke v Filadelfii v 1876 g.," *Novaia i Noveishaia Istoriia* 4 (July 1975): 151–53; M. M. Vladimirov, *Russkii sredi Amerikanstsev: Moi lichnyia vpechatleniia kak tokari, chernorabochago, plotnika i puteshestvennika, 1872–1876* (St. Petersburg: Obshchestvennaia pol'za, 1877), pp. 322–31.
194. 21 October 1876, p. 855.
195. Dvoichenko-Markova, "Uchenye Rossii," p. 151.
196. Vladimirov, *Russkii sredi Amerikanstsev*, pp. 269–74.

chines, and found . . . forms which the student should be taught to work out in a systematic way. . . . This the Russians have done in a complete and inexpensive way, in shops, each adapted for some particular kind of work. Beginners have not been put into expensive shops, fitted with large machines, tools and power before they are at all qualified to enter such work. . . . Presidents White, of Cornell, and Gregory, of the Illinois University, visited the Russian exhibit with me. . . . If we are wise we shall at once reap the experience.[197]

Runkle published an article the next year on "The Russian System of Mechanical Art Education." In 1878 another American science educator, C. M. Woodward, commented simply: "To Russia belongs the honor of having solved the problem of tool instruction. Others had admitted that practice in using tools and testing materials should go hand in hand with theory; but Russia first conceived and tested the idea of analyzing tool practice into its elements and teaching the elements abstractly to a class. In their hands, manual tool instruction has become a science."[198]

On Runkle's initiative, the MIT Corporation adopted the Russian method in August 1876, moving rapidly perhaps because the Russian supervisors in Philadelphia had offered to help them set up the shops.[199] Runkle also wrote to Victor Della Vos, director of the school in Moscow, and to the American vice-consul there, asking for instructional models, which in due course were forwarded through the American legation.[200] Worcester Polytechnic, the University of Pennsylvania, and the St. Louis Manual Training School (Washington University) eagerly followed the MIT-Russian pattern. Charles Thompson, who visited the Moscow school in 1882, announced the adoption of its

197. J. D. Runkle to Mrs. William Barton Rogers, 5 July 1876, in *Life and Letters of William Barton Rogers*, edited by his wife, vol. 2 (Boston: Houghton Mifflin, 1896), pp. 335–36. Rogers founded the Massachusetts Institute of Technology in the mid-1860s; Runkle held the first chair of mathematics, succeeding Rogers upon his illness in 1870. Rogers resumed the presidency in 1878.

198. As quoted in Charles Alpheus Bennett, *History of Manual and Industrial Education 1870 to 1917* (Peoria, Ill.: By author, 1937), p. 322. Bennett appropriately devoted his first chapter to Russia.

199. Runkle's letter in *Life of Rogers* 2:336. Semechkin and N. E. Serebrikov, both engineers, were visiting Boston in October and November of that year; *Frank Leslie's Illustrated Newspaper*, 11 November 1876, p. 159.

200. Runkle to Boker, 16 October 1876; Henry C. Young (vice-consul, Moscow) to Atkinson (secretary, St. Petersburg), 13 November 1876; and Della Vos (Moscow) to Boker, 10 October 1877, DPR, Russia, vol. 4436 (misc. received), RG 84, NA; and Boker to Oldenburg, 8/20 November 1876 (c), DPR, Russia, vol. 4535 (notes sent), RG 84, NA.

training system when he became president of Rose Polytechnic Institute the next year.[201] Few similar instances can be found where Americans so expeditiously and completely embraced a Russian practice.[202]

Petroleum Engineering

An example of vital technology flowing in the opposite direction involves another symbol of the new age of science, the oil industry. A resinous substance, often referred to as "naptha," had oozed from the ground along the western coast of the Caspian Sea for as long as anyone could remember, and by 1829 eighty-two so-called pits were in operation. However, the traditional date for the birth of the Russian oil industry is 1859, when the first refinery, distilling a clear kerosene from the black crude, began operation. Coincidentally, that is also the year the oil boom in the United States commenced from the successful drilling of an oil-producing well in northwestern Pennsylvania. What was most remarkable in America was the rapid development of associated technology: storage, refining, transportation, and marketing. Eventually, two of the greatest capitalist empires—Rockefeller and Nobel—would dominate the oil resources of the United States and Russia, respectively.

For a number of years the advantage would be definitely on the American side because of inventive workmen, capital deployment, and a ready market. Although at least four Americans were heavily involved in the early stages of the Russian oil business in the 1860s, they had limited success. Green Clay, the nephew of the minister, and John Gowen, who had cleared the harbor of Sevastopol of sunken ships after the Crimean War, had introduced some of the early American oil-drilling practices, though these did not work very well in the different geologic conditions of the Caucasus region. St. John Constant built and managed refineries on the estates of Arkadi Novosiltsev near Taman, in the Kuban region, beginning in 1866.

201. Bennett, *History*, pp. 42–50; New York *Herald*, 13 September 1877.
202. Marshall Jewell, the American minister, achieved nearly the same result by stealing the "secret" of the unique, yellowish, high-quality Russian leather. Jewell, a Connecticut manufacturer, simply visited Russian tanneries, inquired about the process, and then shipped back to the United States several barrels of the special birch-bark tar that gave Russian leather its much-sought-after hue and perfumed character. "In every American tannery [Jewell] is now regarded as the ablest diplomat and noblest patriot our country has ever produced." "Jewell's Quest," New York *Times*, 11 February 1877.

This was brought to a temporary halt by Novosiltsev's death in 1873 and the insolvency of his estate.[203] By this time Laslo Chandor, who had pioneered the use of coal oil for street lighting in Russia, was drilling for oil in Samara province.[204]

In the meantime, American production was forging ahead recklessly through boom-and-bust cycles and charting new directions in international markets. The big problems on the Russian side were fragmentation of production into small units, inadequate oil field technology, and the limited means of transportation. The cost of carrying oil from Baku to St. Petersburg, for example, was greater than carrying it from Pennsylvania. Russian production, therefore, stagnated at around 54 million pounds annually, while by 1873 Russian imports from the United States had risen to twice that amount.[205] All of this was soon to change. Getting the abundant oil out of the ground was not the issue; new drilling technology produced gushers in the 1870s that amazed the world, though much of the petroleum was wasted by seepage into the soil or spills into the Caspian Sea. The major obstacle was transportation—from well to refinery and refinery to market.

The main reason for Dmitri Mendeleev's assignment to the Russian Centennial exhibit was to investigate the American oil industry. After brief stops in New York and Washington, he arrived in Philadelphia at the end of June, but he found little on display at the exposition that related to oil. Believing that transportation was the key to Russian advances, he visited the Empire Transportation Company in Philadelphia, which brought oil from the Pennsylvania fields for export. He also made an intensive tour of the "Atlantic" refinery near the city, one of the largest producers of kerosene.[206] Intrigued by the exhibit on the use of oil in lamps, Mendeleev decided to visit its sponsor, the Aladdin factory of Karn City.

To do this and at the same time escape the Fourth of July crowds in Philadelphia, he and his assistant and interpreter, Valeri Gemilian, journeyed west to Pittsburgh and then north into the oil country. They toured Karn

203. Constant (Taman) to Jewell, 27 April 1873, DPR, Russia, vol. 4435 (misc. received); Jewell to Constant, 31 October 1873 (c), DPR, Russia, vol. 4484 (misc. sent), RG 84, NA.

204. G. M. Hutton (acting consul) to State Department, 8 November 1880, DUSC, St. Petersburg, vol. 15 (roll 10, M 81), RG 59, NA.

205. William H. Edwards to William Hunter, 18 November 1878, DUSC, St. Petersburg, vol. 14 (roll 9, M 81), RG 59, NA.

206. Mendeleev, "Neftanaia promyshlennost' v Severo-amerikanskom shtate Pensil'vanii i na Kavkaze," originally published in 1877, reprinted in *Sochineniia*, vol. 10 (Leningrad-Moscow: Nauka, 1949), pp. 91–110.

City, Parker, Oil City, Millerstown, and Petrolia, the heart of the American petroleum industry. Mendeleev was surprised at how little most of the American entrepreneurs seemed to know about the chemistry and geology of oil but how much they had accomplished on the practical side—storage, transportation, advertising, and marketing. Herbert W. C. Twiddle was an exception. Manager and director of the Aladdin plant, he was also "a scholar and a chemist." The two seemed to strike up a friendship, as Twiddle went out of his way to accommodate the Russians and to explain the inter-linking of pumping, pipelines, storage, and refineries.[207] By the time Mende-leev went on to Lake Erie and Niagara Falls to complete his American visit, an important oil connection between Russia and the United States had been forged. Twiddle and a crew of Pennsylvania oilers were soon in Russia trying to put the Caucasus oil fields on the right track.

Meanwhile, in 1873, Robert Nobel, a son of a Swedish entrepreneur who had pioneered in Russian manufacturing with very limited success, arrived on the Caucasus scene.[208] Impressed by what he saw around Baku, he bought one small refinery. This impulsive act attracted the attention of his more business-minded brother Ludwig, who in 1876 began the investments that would revolutionize the industry. Borrowing from American practices with the help of Alex Bary, an engineer from Philadelphia, he imported the first pipe from Scotland in 1877. Bary was soon producing it in a Moscow factory. Linking field to refinery and refinery to port, the pipelines resulted in a phenomenal reduction in transportation costs over the traditional bar-rel and cart, though the local opposition of the latter interests had to be fought off by hired Cossacks.

The next step, for which Ludwig Nobel himself can claim the major ini-tiative, was developing tanker ships to carry the refined product from Baku across the Caspian and through the river and canal waterways to St. Peters-burg. In 1878 he financed another Russian inspection team, headed by Bary, to tour American oil refineries on the East Coast and acquire the most mod-ern machinery for drilling and pumping wells. Bary hired George Adams of

207. Ibid. 10:115–24; Henry M. Leicester, "Mendeleev's Visit to America," *Journal of Chemical Education* 34, 7 (July 1957): 331–33. The only known publication by Twiddle (also spelled Tweddle) was the purely technical "Petrzcene and Its Products," *Journal of the Franklin Institute* 102, 3 (September 1876): 204–8.

208. Tolf, *Russian Rockefellers*, pp. 44–45. The best-known Nobel brother, Alfred, had already put the family name into the industrial hall of fame by the successful and effi-cient mass production of dynamite in Sweden. This gave the "Russian" Nobels psycho-logical incentive and practical financing.

Oil City for $5,000 a year to supervise this equipment and other American technicians in the Nobel oil fields.[209]

After the State Department requested more information about these new developments, Leander Dyer, the consul in Odessa, made a trip through the region during the summer of 1880. Although he saw much with his own eyes, he acknowledged that key observations came from Adams, who by this time had spent a year at Baku and another in the Kuban region, from Twiddle, and from D. R. Peacock, vice-consul at Poti. What he reported was an industry in rapid transition and expansion, wells as shallow as 6 feet competing with new ones of up to 560 feet in depth, with production expected to reach 2 million barrels that year.[210] New refineries sprang up, as Russia rapidly entered the kerosene age and created a new market of its own by converting steamships and locomotives to the use of petroleum fuel.[211]

A genuine oil rush occurred during the late 1870s with Germans, Swedes, and English joining Americans and many new Russian and Cossack settlers. Over $15 million was invested in refineries, mainly by the Nobel brothers, and barge transportation over the Caspian and up the Volga expanded.[212] In the Baku region the Nobels improved and consolidated much of the refining and marketing, but the field production remained largely in the hands of numerous small Russian companies.[213] The American expertise was concentrated in the Kuban, where over 1.5 million acres, mostly Cossack lands but also including the Novosiltsev estates, were leased for twelve years to "Twiddle and Company." By 1880 Twiddle had six American drills and crews working, employed as many Russians who were transforming the

209. "Russian Oil Territory," Philadelphia *Inquirer*, 24 April 1878. Little information is available on Bary's successful industrial pursuits in Russia, which continued until his death in 1913. An interview by DeWitt Clinton Poole in 1952 with Bary's son provides only a sketch. Notes, 3 March 1952, f. 10, box 7, Poole Papers, SHSW.

210. Dyer to Hunter, 17 August 1880, DUSC, Odessa, vol. 6 (roll 3, M 459), RG 59, NA; a summary was published as "The Petroleum Wells of Russia," in CR (1880):137–40. Another source, giving the production figures in the Russian pood (36 pounds) measurement, shows the dramatic increase in Russian oil production during the 1870s (in rounded figures): 1871—1.5 million; 1873—4 million; 1876—12 million; 1878—20 million; 1881—41 million. A. Beeby Thompson, *The Oil Fields of Russia and the Russian Petroleum Industry* (New York: D. Van Nostrand, 1904), pp. 5–6.

211. According to Lewis Emery, a Pennsylvania oilman who inspected the Russian fields in 1879, 75 percent of the Russian petroleum was used as fuel oil; "Oil in the Old World," New York *Times*, 20 February 1880.

212. Tolf, *Russian Rockefellers*, pp. 44–55, 79–80.

213. V. A. Samedov, *Neft' i ekonomika Rossii (80-90-e gody XIX veka)* (Baku: Elm, 1988), pp. 12–19.

ethnic diversity of the region, and placed a large refinery in operation in Taman. As Dyer observed,

> It is proper to say . . . that the American foremen, who have been there from Pennsylvania, have taught those people very much in regard to the business, a fact that is freely acknowledged by operation managers and all concerned. . . .
> [Twiddle's] new enterprise was organized last year on a system that has had no precedent in this country and work will not perhaps proceed without interruption and with economy and energy that will deserve success.[214]

Dyer also pointed out a number of remaining problems. Many of the American and British experts did not stay long because of disgust with the workmen under them. "The price is so low, the system of work so bad, the operators so careless and inexperienced that a very large quantity goes to waste and the wells are not worked to their capacity."[215] G. M. Hutton, acting consul general in St. Petersburg, was even less sanguine in his long, 225-page report. Twiddle, with the support of Konstantin Bodisko, who was now working in the Ministry of Finance, proposed building a pipeline from Baku through the Kuban to Poti on the Black Sea in return for a forty-year monopoly guarantee on the transport of oil through it. Many others in the industry feared a dependency on Twiddle, and the plan was rejected in favor of a government contract for a new railroad between Tiflis and Baku.[216] By the next year, however, a trans-Caucasus pipeline was under construction on the American design with the backing of Ludwig Nobel.[217]

Hutton noted the difficulties encountered with the lower quality Russian crude and the oversupply and cutthroat competition that discouraged other investors. "Thus those engaged in the naptha industries in the Russian territories are continually complaining that their business relations have arrived at a state almost bordering upon disaster."[218] The new consul in St. Peters-

214. Dyer to Hunter, 17 August 1880, DUSC, Odessa, vol. 6 (roll 3, M 459), RG 59, NA.

215. Ibid.

216. To Hunter, 8 November 1880, DUSC, St. Petersburg, vol. 15 (roll 10, M 81), RG 59, NA; V. A. Nardova, *Nachalo monopolizatsii neftianoi promyshlennosti Rossii: 1880-1890-e gody* (Leningrad: Nauka, 1974), pp. 62–65.

217. Stanton to Hunter, 2 December 1881, DUSC, St. Petersburg, vol. 16 (roll 11, M 81), RG 59, NA; Tolf, *Russian Rockefellers*, pp. 51–56.

218. Hutton to Hunter, 8 November 1880, DUSC, St. Petersburg, vol. 15 (roll 10, M 81), RG 59, NA.

burg, Edgar Stanton, was one of the first to perceive the irony of this American involvement in Russia.

> The extension of the Russian [oil industry] means war on the American petroleum trade, and although the crude Russian does not yield so great a percentage of illuminating fluid as the American article, its excessive abundance and cheapness justifies the belief that such a war must terminate disastrously for the American article as far as a European trade is concerned.
>
> It is therefore to my mind, questionable patriotism, when Americans embark their talents and capital in foreign enterprises, whose successful issue must involve a partial, if not the total, destruction of a great American export trade.[219]

Hence, one of the early warnings that a technology transfer might not be in the American national interest involved Russia and came at a time when Russia was increasingly wary of foreign dependency.

Agriculture

As in the petroleum industry, a number of Americans were involved in ventures to modernize Russian grain transport and storage, which could have made it more competitive in the European market. Despite these efforts, Russian grain handling remained backward, wasteful, and inefficient. To many American visitors this was an obvious business opportunity. Already in the 1860s Cassius Clay and Nathan Appleton had developed plans for grain elevators. Even Jeremiah Curtin in 1873 tried unsuccessfully to per-

219. To Hunter, 2 December 1881, DUSC, St. Petersburg, vol. 16 (roll 11, M 81), RG 59, NA. He applied the same analysis to those wanting to sell grain elevators: "In both cases, success can be obtained only at the expense of the American trade, and such undertakings tend only to develop the resources of America's greatest rival in the grain and petroleum trades."

For an emphasis on international competition over oil but without any mention of American assistance for Russian development, see Alexander A. Fursenko, *The Battle for Oil: The Economics and Politics of International Corporate Conflict over Petroleum, 1860–1930*, trans. and ed. Gregory Freeze (Greenwich, Conn., and London: Jai Press, 1990).

suade a wealthy Moscow merchant to finance this type of enterprise in Russia.[220]

One of the most interesting schemes involved American consul general George Pomutz, New York businessman S. W. Torrey, and George Kennan. Torrey visited Russia in the spring of 1874 and returned again in early 1876, after he had secured capital from other American businessmen, led by Jesse Hoyt. The plan was to form a joint-venture stock company in Russia with exclusive rights to elevator construction in all seaports and grain-producing areas. After much time and effort by Torrey, Pomutz, and their Russian partners to acquire government privilege by means of an initial bribe of 110,000 rubles, Torrey said he had to check with Hoyt before signing—and after delays and confusion, Hoyt backed out of the arrangement. Pomutz then turned to Kennan and some upstate New York associates of his.[221]

The consul general, anxious about the effect of the failed negotiation on his own reputation, declared that everything was ready to sign in Russia. But Kennan's main contact, Edwin Evans of Buffalo, was cautious and saw little to be gained in any capital investment in Russian elevators: "At no *sea* port in Russia can an elevator be safely built, so that a vessel can lay alongside of & be loaded from it. This would make elevators of no use excepting at such points where grain is transferred from boats to cars or from cars to boats. The question is are there in Russia points of this kind where sufficient grain passes through to make elevators profitable? I am afraid there are not."[222] Evans believed that grain elevators could only be built in Russia in conjunction with improved rail transport. Another plan by John Gowen to construct an elevator in the Odessa port in 1878 also came to nothing.[223]

Finally, the Russian government sent one of its foremost agricultural economists, Robert Orbinskii, a professor at an Odessa university, on an inspection tour of the United States. Landing in New York in July 1879, he visited Chicago, Milwaukee, Minneapolis-St. Paul, and St. Louis, where he was interviewed by a local newspaper. "He stated his object principally was to obtain information respecting the grain trade and the workings of our elevators and other matters pertaining to the tariff and rates of

---

220. Jeremiah Curtin, *Memoirs of Jeremiah Curtin*, ed. Joseph Schafer, Wisconsin Biography Series no. 2 (Madison: State Historical Society of Wisconsin, 1940), p. 207; Alma Curtin to her mother, 21 April 1874, Curtin Papers, MCHC.

221. Pomutz to Kennan, 4 June 1876, box 1, Kennan Papers, LC. This long letter contains a fascinating description of doing business in Russia.

222. Evans to Kennan, 2 July 1876, ibid.

223. "A Distinguished Russian Visitor," St. Louis *Missouri Republican*, 22 August 1879.

transportation. . . . He is astonished at the low rates that grain is conveyed to the seaboard."[224] The only grain elevator in Russia, the professor reported, was a model one at Kronstadt. Orbinskii was also amazed and perplexed by the commodity exchange he visited in St. Louis. Russians never seemed able to fathom Western middlemen operations.

In a letter to the same paper, the Russian observed that he had warned his government of the American challenge to Russian grain exports, and he sized up the current and future situation:

> We are competitors then, America and Russia, but I never met a competitor so gentlemanlike and so noble as your country. Every information I wanted was given to me with a courtesy I could never hope to find. There was nothing of the vile jealousy between rivalizing trade people, which we are accustomed to read in every history of commerce. And indeed America has nothing to fear from her generous and frank proceedings. We have endless to learn from her; we will make, I hope, some progress in her way; but I think not that we will become her equal. All the advantages that nature and will of man can give, are on your side, and all I wish is that my country could follow your example for the benefit of mankind, asking for cheap bread.[225]

On his return to Russia, Orbinskii pushed for American-style agricultural modernization, especially for the chief grain-exporting city, Odessa, and stirred up a rousing debate over the comparison of the United States with Russia in this sphere.[226] But apathy prevailed, and an elevator was not built in Odessa until the 1890s. The Russian grain market had no Nobel.

Russia also evinced an interest in the American cotton industry, again concentrating on transportation and handling. Konstantin Pos'et gathered information on this topic while chaperoning Grand Duke Alexis through Memphis and New Orleans in 1872. Not long after that, Vasilii Samdevskii, a special agent of the Ministry of State Domains, toured the southern states during the summer of 1875. His visit was apparently comprehensive, and he

224. Ibid.

225. "A Russian View," Orbinskii letter to editor, St. Louis *Missouri Republican*, 23 August 1879.

226. Orbinskii, *Ot Khlebnoi torgovlie Soedinennykh Shtatov Severnoi Ameriki* (St. Petersburg: Trenke i Fusno, 1880), and *Iz otcheta R. V. Orbinskogo o nastoiashchem polozhenii khlebnogo vyvoza iz Odessy* (Odessa: N.p., 1881), pp. 13–15; Robert V. Allen, *Russia Looks at America: The View to 1917* (Washington, D.C.: Library of Congress, 1988), pp. 124–35; Herlihy, *Odessa*, pp. 208–9, 223–24.

even arranged to import samples of blue corn grown by the Pueblo Indians in New Mexico.[227]

Almost all Russian visitors commented on transportation systems and their relationship to economic progress. Some, such as Orbinskii and Eduard Tsimmerman, gave transportation professional attention, and a few Russians were specifically sent to America to study it. For example, in 1875 Pos'et, then Minister of Ways and Communications, dispatched two "engineers" to investigate canals, rivers, dams and locks, and river and canal boats in the United States. One of them, Zviaginstev, was interviewed by the New York *Herald* as he passed through the city on his way to Petersburg (Virginia), Louisville, and New Orleans. He also intended to tour the Erie Canal.[228]

Machines and Tools

Many American-manufactured items were coming into Russia in the 1870s, but none had established monopolies. The January 1871 issues of *Moskovskiia Vedomosti*, a leading newspaper, carried advertisements for Johnston reapers (from Brockport, New York), Howe sewing machines, Lamb stocking knitters, American washing machines and oil lamps, and Wheeler and Wilson sewing machines. Buckeye and Dyke tractors were powering steam-threshing machines in Estonia by 1870.[229] Obviously, Singer and McCormick did not yet dominate in their fields. Although some of these items were sold by American concerns, such as those of Samuel Young and John Lehrs in Moscow, G. M. Hutton in St. Petersburg, and Theodore Rosenstraus in Kharkov, most were distributed by Russian and other foreign houses. They preferred to order in small lots from Western European distributors. As the American consul general noted, "Natural causes seem to exercise an important influence in cementing these customs and consequently in checking any movement looking to the development of direct trade with the merchants of the United States. . . . This unwise and uncalled for exportation and demand for quick sales exercises a damaging influence on our export trade."[230] He also pointed out the growing awkwardness of St.

227. Thomas Janes (Atlanta) to Shishkin, 30 May 1876, f. 170, op. 512/3, d. 125 (1876), AVPR.

228. New York *Herald*, 13 September 1875, p. 10.

229. Juhan Kahk, "The Spread of Agricultural Machines in Estonia from 1860 to 1880," *Agricultural History* 62, 3 (Summer 1988): 37–38.

230. Edwards to Hunter, 27 September 1879, DUSC, St. Petersburg, vol. 14 (roll 9, M 81), RG 59, NA.

Petersburg-Kronstadt as a point of entry; because of ice part of the year and the need to transship from Kronstadt, it compared favorably with the more regular year-round rail connections from Western Europe.[231] The increasing use of European transport also made it impossible to gauge with any degree of accuracy the indirect importation of American goods into Russia.

American machinery was apparently popular in Russia, since one of the major obstacles to its expanded sales was large-scale counterfeiting, that is, the use of American brand names on cheaper Western European products. This practice continued despite a declaration protecting trademarks signed between the two countries in 1874.[232] Unfortunately, at about the same time Russia imposed a differential tariff assessing sugar, wine, and "tools" at a higher rate in they entered by sea than if imported overland. Vociferous complaints by American ministers about the discriminatory nature of this tariff and claims that it violated the terms of the 1832 commercial treaty were to no avail. The foreign affairs officers, perhaps not wishing to tangle with the Finance Ministry, responded unhelpfully that American tools could avoid the higher tariff simply by coming in overland.[233]

Another, probably lesser problem was that certain American design characteristics met resistance because of local superstition or clash with tradition. Regarding sewing machines, an American consul found that "the growing popularity of the German machine is said to be due to the widespread belief that it is injurious to the health to work the American foot machine."[234] But he also accused American businesses of a lack of zeal in pushing sales in Russia; this was especially true in the case of the Singer Company, which was hard-pressed in the 1870s to meet demand at home and took a cautious approach to foreign sales.[235] After Scottish and Austrian factories were established, George Neidlinger of Hamburg made significant sales in Russia on behalf of Singer. An American consul thought that if American exporters would exhibit and demonstrate their machinery in Rus-

231. Edwards to Hunter, 7 February 1879, DUSC, St. Petersburg, ibid.

232. New York *Times*, 29 March 1874.

233. Boker to Evarts, 12 October 1877, and to Giers, 19 November 1877; Stoughton to Giers, 16/28 March 1878, PRFRUS 1878; pp. 747, 752, 756. Stoughton pointed out the obvious—that it would be more costly to transport American products overland than to bring them directly to a port.

234. Edwards to Hunter, 7 February 1879, DUSC, St. Petersburg, vol. 14 (roll 9, M 81), RG 59, NA.

235. Fred V. Carstensen, *American Enterprise in Foreign Markets: Studies of Singer and International Harvester in Russia* (Chapel Hill and London: University of North Carolina Press, 1984), pp. 28–31.

sia, "the country would be as well stocked with improved tools of husbandry and other American machinery as it is with American arms."[236] Although he seems to have missed the point that the Russian government placed a high priority on weapons, a salesman in the field identified another obstacle—the Russian peasant's natural distrust of machinery.[237]

The most ambitious American project for the development of Russia during this period failed to bear fruit. Wharton Barker, hoping to reap profits from Russian appreciation of his service during the Russo-Turkish War, interested a consortium of American businessmen in the building of a large metallurgical industry in the south of Russia. A number of field agents, headed by Henry Vezin, investigated the region during the summer of 1880 and brought back ore samples to be tested at the University of Pennsylvania. The scheme, initially backed by government officials such as Grand Duke Constantine, involved establishing coal mines on the Dolgorukii estates, extracting iron ore from the Perekop Peninsula, constructing new rail lines, improving the Azov port of Berdiansk, and building a large steel complex in the Donets Basin to produce for export and on government contract.[238] Probably the sheer scale of the enterprise, the demand for a guaranteed government contract, and the loss of position of its Russian backers in 1881 doomed the project.

The North Pacific

While Russian attention was turned toward Central Asia and the Balkans, one area that had been a focal point of Russian-American relations for many years was left very much to its own devices. In the 1860s Russia had shifted its development interest southward away from Alaska and northeast Siberia to Vladivostok and the waters around Korea and Japan, and to Blagoveshchensk along the upper Amur and on the Manchurian border. Nikolaevsk, near the mouth of the Amur, declined rapidly after the administra-

236. Edwards to Hunter, 7 February 1879, DUSC, St. Petersburg, vol. 14 (roll 9, M 81), RG 59, NA.
237. George Hume, *Thirty-Five Years in Russia* (London: Simpkin, Marshall, Hamilton, Kent, 1914), p. 60. He concentrated instead on sales in the Mennonite colonies in Ukraine.
238. [Barker, comp.], *Reports and Correspondence Relating to Projected Coal and Iron Industries in Southern Russia* (Philadelphia: By author, c. 1880), pp. 1–116.

tive offices for the region were moved to these new cities.[239] With the withdrawal of the Russian America Company, the northern outposts of Petropavlovsk and Aian were even more depressed and isolated. In addition, the Russian government promoted the business activities of Russians over foreigners in the Far East, though Americans such as Enoch Emery and James Crowley, who were already established along the Amur River, were allowed to continue operations.[240]

The shift of emphasis in the Russian Far East was at least partly the result of technology: the reliance on coal-burning steamers for the navy and for coastal and river commercial vessels made voyages into the Bering Sea not fuel efficient by comparison. A primary reason that Russia secured Sakhalin Island by treaty with Japan in 1875 was to gain sole rights to the coal deposits there. An American company based in Shanghai was operating the island's mines and selling to a variety of Far Eastern customers. After 1875, they became exclusively Russian. But another reason for taking Sakhalin was to locate a more isolated penal colony on the island. Foreigners were strictly excluded, and the mines were run largely with prison labor.[241]

In other ways the North Pacific was affected by technological change. After the sale of Alaska and with it the ships of the Russian America Company, Russia rarely had commercial sailing ships on the Pacific, except for those transporting prisoners. And despite efforts to establish a regular steamship line from San Francisco to Siberian waters, commerce and especially fishing and seal hunting in the North Pacific remained dependent on aging sailing barks.[242] At the same time, the former big business of the area, whaling, went into a sharp decline because of the replacement of whale oil by cheap kerosene and gas in lighting.

Far to the south in the Amur valley, Russian companies still relied on

239. By 1880 the population of Nikolaevsk had fallen below 3,000, while that of both Vladivostok and Blagoveshchensk were nearly 9,000. Aleksandr Kirillov, *Geografichesko-statisticheskii slovar' Amurskoi i primorksoi oblastei* (Blagoveshchensk: D. O. Moken, 1984), pp. 62, 73, 103.

240. Schuyler to Fish, 16 December 1874, DUSM, Russia, vol. 27 (roll 27, M 35), RG 59, NA.

241. New York *Herald*, 27 July and 22 September 1875. The "treaty," which also recognized Japanese jurisdiction over the southern Kuriles, took Europe by surprise, since Sakhalin had generally been thought to belong to Japan—and a substantial native Japanese population remained there.

242. There is little information on the impact of the shipping revolution in the Pacific. It would appear from scattered records that the American vessels that continued to bring supplies to Petropavlovsk and plied the Siberian coast in the 1870s were becoming decrepit and more vulnerable to storms, running aground, etc.

Americans for imports and technical assistance. In 1875 a former Mississippi riverboat captain and steamship innovator, Simon Few, agreed to provide two new steamers for the Amur. His experience illustrates the enduring and novel problems in the area. An old San Francisco vessel carrying the disassembled boats ran aground at the mouth of the Amur on its way to the Nikolaevsk port, and many pieces were jettisoned in trying to free the ship.[243] Out of what remained, Few and his American foremen were able to put together one boat and the next year to build another from local materials. Among the difficulties he encountered in the process were the nonchalance of the Russian contractors, the desertion of Nikolaevsk, and lackadaisical Russian attitudes toward work.[244] After over a year of frustrations, Few was happy to retire to his farm in Leavenworth County, Kansas.

When the Amur commercial agency at Nikolaevsk, founded by Perry Collins in 1856, was closed in 1874, its last superintendent recommended that a regular consular office be opened at the new port of Vladivostok.[245] But Russia did not welcome foreign consuls at what was still essentially a military outpost, even though the naval operations there generated quite a bit of commercial business, mostly American. The United States did not press the issue but instead established an unrecognized consulate at Petropavlovsk on the Kamchatka Peninsula with a long-time resident American merchant, H. G. O. Chase, as consul.[246] After this post was abandoned in 1878, there was no official American representative in the Russian Far East for twenty years, when a Vladivostok consulate was finally opened.

In a long report of 1875, Chase drew a depressing picture of Russian neglect and American exploitation of the Far East. That summer a Russian naval steamer cruised the northeast coast in an attempt to curtail illicit American trade in the area. Off the Chukchi coast it encountered an old American brig, which, despite the captain's denial, was trading liquor for walrus teeth. The latter were seized and returned to shore. On further inves-

---

243. Few (Nikolaevsk) to his sons (George and Abner), 29 June 1875, folder 2, Simon Few Papers, Jackson County Historical Society.

244. Few to sons, 2/13 November and 4 December 1875, ibid. In the latter Few commented in phonetic English, "They go about there work rite rong end first we think. They think American ways of work is all rong."

245. Schuyler to Fish, 30 June 1874, DUSM, Russia, vol. 26 (roll 26, M 35), RG 59, NA.

246. Chase had been in Petropavlovsk first in the 1850s, but when the Amur region opened up he transferred to Nikolaevsk and served as acting commercial agent for nine years; Chase (Vladivostok) to Fish, 18/30 August 1876, DUSC, Petropavlovsk, vol. 1 (roll 1, T 104), RG 59, NA.

tigation the Russian authorities uncovered evidence of an extensive network of smuggling as Americans traded with the native Chukchi, offering commodities such as sugar, spirits, and tobacco for furs, bone, and teeth. The Chukchi in turn exchanged some of these goods for furs in Alaska and the Kurile Islands. Chase concluded, "Complaints are too numerous to be agreeable, of lawless acts within the Russian territories of this quarter, of Adventurers, always described by the Russians as Americans—and there is but too much reason to fear that these charges are not without foundation in truth, though perhaps often exaggerated."[247]

The Russian authorities and others concerned about Russian national interests awoke gradually to what had occurred and instigated additional inspections of the territory in the late 1870s. What they discovered was indeed shocking. The external trade of the Kamchatka-Chukchi area was basically under American control. The only flags seen at Petropavlovsk—and displayed quite prominently—were American. In the whole region not a single Russian flag was to be found. Observers reported that "the Russian national consciousness in the people is much weakened." And the native attitude was: "If government has forgotten us, better to be given to the Americans."[248] The 421 people counted in Petropavlovsk and its chief merchant, Alexander Phillipeus, survived mainly because of American commerce. Although the rich salmon and cod fishing grounds in nearby coastal waters were monopolized by American vessels working with Japanese crews, at least this enterprise helped sustain the local economy.[249] For all intents and purposes northeast Siberia, Kamchatka, and outlying islands had become as much American as Alaska, given that Alaska was itself neglected and Sitka, like Petropavlovsk, had become only a "faded shadow" of its former self.[250] The Russian reaction to this American ascendancy on their territory was predictably a series of edicts that attempted to curtail foreign (that is, Ameri-

247. Chase to Fish, 18/30 September 1875, DUSC, Petropavlovsk, vol. 1 (roll 1, T 104), RG 59, NA. To dramatically illustrate one of the problems, this dispatch was received by the State Department on 17 June 1876—nine months in transit.

248. *Sbornik glavneishikh offitsial'nykh dokumentov po upravleniiu Vostochnoiu Siber'iu,* vol. 3, no. 1 (Irkutsk: I. P. Sinitsyn, 1882), pp. 38–42.

249. Ibid., p. 56. Phillipeus (or Fillippeus) was a Russian citizen of Finnish background, but the president of the Petropavlovsk town council was an American merchant named Sandolin. When news of the fishing situation reached St. Petersburg, the secretary of legation thought that a treaty regulating it might desirable; Hoffman to Evarts, 10 June 1878, DUSM, Russia, vol. 33 (roll 33, M 35), RG 59, NA.

250. "The Alaska Troubles," Boston *Herald,* 20 March 1879, described a very grim, depressing picture of Sitka and the native inhabitants of the coastal region.

can) commerce in the established ports where they exercised control, thus promising further damage to the economic life of the region.[251]

One bright spot, ironically, was the continued, even expanded presence of the Russian Orthodox church in the settlements of the former Russian America Company, thanks to a substantial subsidy from the Russian government. A visitor to Unalaska in the Aleutians in 1879 found the church flourishing under the direction of a native priest and a school continuing to teach the Aleuts in the Russian language. The community was largely self-sufficient except for fuel, the local wood supply having been depleted, and depended on coal brought by the Alaska Commercial Company from Nanaimo (Vancouver Island).[252]

After the withdrawal of all American military forces from Alaska, residents appealed to Britain for protection. There were suggestions that the United States give Alaska back to Russia, though the latter was unlikely to accept the burden. The editor of the St. Louis *Missouri Republican* eloquently summed up the situation:

> The government should do one of two things with Alaska: Treat it as other national territory is treated, or abandon it altogether. If we cannot afford to keep a military force there sufficient to maintain good order, and if the same cause prevents the employment of a naval vessel for the same purpose, let us make Russia a present of the whole establishment, fold up our little flag and silently steal away. Thus far we have only succeeded in showing our incapacity or unwillingness to take the commonest care of a possession which cost us a large sum of money when we could least spare it, and our indifference toward those citizens who were tempted to live there by our promises. There is not a mud bank or coral reef in mid-ocean which, if England owns it, has not had more and better attention than the United States has bestowed upon Alaska. . . . Shall we take care of Alaska, or give it up?[253]

Dmitri Zavalishin, the old Decembrist who had been exiled for many years in Siberia and who had publicly and vehemently opposed the sale of Alaska, helped awaken the Russian imperial consciousness to the situation in northeast Siberia. Writing in a leading newspaper, he predicted that the

251. Chase to Evarts, 1/13 December 1878, DUSC, Petropavlovsk, vol. 1 (roll 1, T 104), RG 59, NA.

252. "Among the Aleutians," St. Louis *Missouri Republican*, 16 August 1879, citing the Pittsburgh *Dispatch*.

253. Editorial, "Alaska," St. Louis *Missouri Republican*, 21 February 1879.

United States would annex Canada and would combine with Japan to drive Russia completely out of the area. He quoted an American visitor (possibly Wharton Barker) as saying, "Canada will soon willingly or unwillingly unite with us and then we will reign over the northern part of the Great Ocean; it must be exclusively our sea." Zavalishin ominously traced the steady growth of American influence since Perry Collins's Amur projects of twenty-five years earlier.[254]

Politically, however, Russia feared more the opposition of Britain and considered the United States a useful ally. Gorchakov, in his draft instructions to Shishkin, stressed: "This country has, therefore, a great value for us on the grounds of general policy, where we must desire to have it more for us than against us, and even more so, when we are forced to have contact with it in the Far East."[255] His diplomatic representatives in Washington duly kept one eye on the Pacific, reporting in detail about American plans for a base at Pearl Bay on Oahu, the increasing American presence in China, and various projects for a Central American canal.[256] Russia in general supported these developments and bowed to American pressure regarding the rights of its vessels along the Siberian shores.[257]

The Jeannette *Disaster*

The distant waters of Alaska and northeast Siberia held one special attraction for Americans—the quest to reach the North Pole. In fact, by the 1870s an international race was on to reach the pole. Most explorers adhered to the view of a German geographer, August Petermann, that the polar cap was

254. Dmitri Zavalishin, "Po povodu usileniia nashei eskadry na velikom okeane," *Moskovskiia Vedomosti*, 19 May 1882. Born in 1804, Zavalishin maintained extraordinary consistency in his expansionist ideas—beginning with a plan for a Caribbean outpost to strengthen the Russian navy in 1824—until his death in 1892. He and his much-younger second wife lived in Moscow after 1863; a daughter, born in 1876, lived until 1956. S. V. Mironenko, comp., *Dekabristy: Biograficheskii spravochnik* (Moscow: Nauka, 1988), p. 69. For Perry Collins in the Amur region, see Norman E. Saul, *Distant Friends: The United States and Russia, 1763–1867* (Lawrence: University Press of Kansas, 1991), pp. 361–64.

255. 5 August 1875, f. 133, op. 470, d. 108 (1875), AVPR.

256. Voigt to Gorchakov, 14/26 March 1875, and to Jomini, 18/30 June 1875, f. 133, op. 470, d. 108 (1875); and Shishkin to Gorchakov, 19 June/1 July 1879, f. 133, op. 470, d. 150 (1879), AVPR.

257. Evarts to Shishkin, 9 May 1877, and F. W. Seward to Shishkin, 17 August 1877, f. 170, op. 512/3, d. 141 (1880), AVPR.

open water warmed by currents and that the main problem was finding a channel through the ring of ice around it. The *Polaris* expedition, launched in 1870 under the command of Charles Hall, had attempted to locate it by sailing along the west coast of Greenland and Baffin Island but became marooned in the ice. Hall died mysteriously, and part of the crew was rescued before the Navy Department sent two ships in 1873 to find the remainder of the party. One of these carried a steam launch, the *Little Juniata*, that, commanded by the young lieutenant George Washington De Long, managed to penetrate even farther to the north and return, to great public fanfare.[258]

While obtaining valuable experience, De Long caught the "polar disease." He had also become a national hero, courtesy of the New York *Herald* reporter who had been on board. De Long was soon in contact with the publisher, James Gordon Bennett, who knew that exploring stories sold newspapers. But it was several years before another American expedition was organized. Meanwhile, in 1876, a British party pushed north of De Long's line before being forced to turn back. Bennett by now was determined that the United States should win the race and, after conferring with De Long and Petermann, purchased the schooner *Pandora* in Scotland. Bennett then used his considerable Washington influence to gain Navy Department assistance, putting the ship, rechristened the *Jeannette*, officially under the American flag. In an odd arrangement, the navy assigned personnel, headed by De Long, and the crew and ship were formally under navy rules and regulations, but the entire expense, including extensive alteration and strengthening of the *Jeannette*, was borne by Bennett to guarantee exclusive coverage by the *Herald*.

After partial refitting was completed under De Long's supervision in Britain, the *Jeannette* set sail for San Francisco in the summer of 1878. But as De Long rounded Cape Horn on his way to search for a Pacific-Arctic passage, the route preferred by Petermann, Swedish explorer Nils Nordenskjold was making his way east from the top of Scandinavia. Bennett now had visions of a sensational "Stanley-Livingstone" encounter at the North Pole. A number of other costly alterations to the *Jeannette* were made in San Francisco, delaying departure to 8 July 1879.[259] Besides De Long, the complement of thirty-three men included executive officer Charles Chipp, who had been

---

258. Leonard F. Guttridge, *Icebound: The Jeannette Expedition's Quest for the North Pole* (New York: Paragon House, 1988), pp. 16–20.

259. The Bennett-Navy Department arrangement caused additional bureaucratic problems; Guttridge, *Icebound*, pp. 42–55.

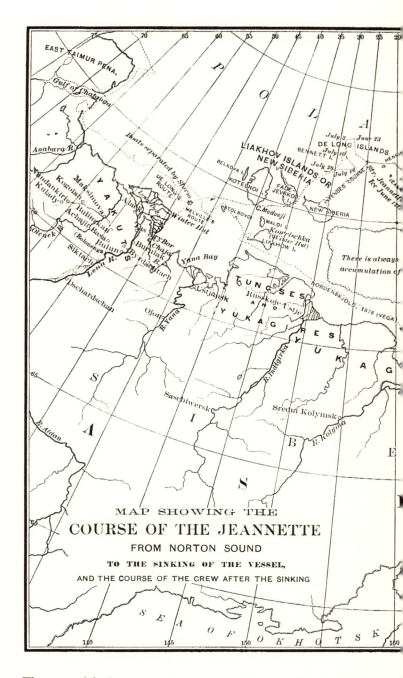

The route of the Jeannette. *From George Melville,* In the Lena Delta *(18*

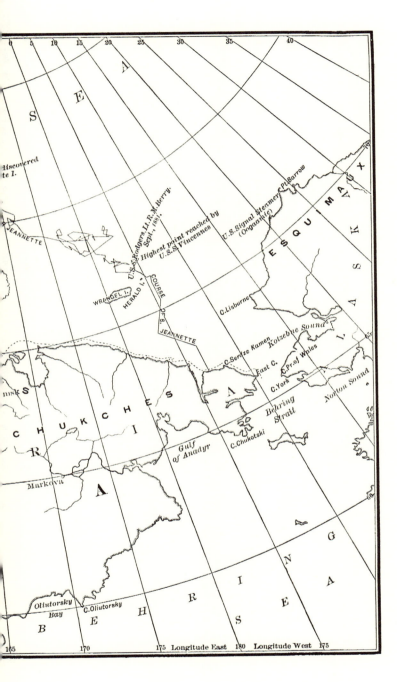

S   E   A

0   5   10   15   20   25   30   35   40

liscovered
te I.

JEANNETTE

WRANGEL I.   HERALD I.   COURSE OF S.

U.S.S. Rodgers, Lt. R. M. Berry.
Sept., 1881.

Highest point reached by
U.S.S. Vincennes

JEANNETTE

U.S. Signal Steamer Pt.Barrow
(Oogaamie)

E S Q U I M A U X

A   L   A   S   K   A

C.Lisburne

Kotzebue Sound

C.Serdze Kamen

East C.   C.Pr.of Wales

C.York

Norton Sound

msk   S

Behring
Strait

C   H   U   K   C   H   E   S

I

A

R

Gulf
of Anadyr

C.Chukotski

Markova

A

G

N

Oliutorsky
Bay   C.Oliutorsky

B   E   H   R   I   N   E   S   A

165   170   175   Longitude East   180   Longitude West   175

on the *Little Juniata*; Master John Danenhower as navigation officer; and George Melville as chief engineer.[260]

The heavily laden *Jeannette* steamed slowly through the Bering Strait in August and turned northwestward into the Arctic Ocean, but it was soon surrounded by ice and frozen fast. For almost two years the expedition was adrift above Siberia, out of sight of land, surviving on the well-planned provisioning, the naval discipline of De Long, and the ingenuity of Melville. But with supplies running short, relief unlikely, and, most of all, the pressure of the ice threatening to break up the ship, De Long decided in the late summer of 1881 to chart a hazardous trek toward the mouth of the Lena River, traversing the ice and open water alternately by sledges and boats.[261]

The last stage, maneuvering over icy and stormy seas in three boats, proved to be the most painful and risky part of the venture. Forced apart by the weather, two of the parties reached the uncharted barren islands of the vast Lena delta; the third, commanded by Lieutenant Chipp, totally disappeared. The one headed by Melville and Danenhower was fortunate to land near the east side of the delta in mid-September not far from a Tungus village, where the men found shelter. De Long's group, however, came ashore many miles to the northwest at the northern tip of the delta, from where they tried to make their way southward over a treacherous maze of land, water, and ice as winter set in and food ran out. Except for two crewmen sent ahead in search of relief, the intense suffering through cold and hunger for the others lasted only until the end of October.[262]

Melville, not wanting to put his exhausted men at further risk and discouraged by the natives from traveling at that time of year (before all waterways were solidly frozen), put off a search for the other parties. For this delay he was later criticized.[263] The two scouts from the De Long contingent finally reached a Tungus settlement but had difficulty communicating. When Melville learned of their presence, he quickly set out to meet them and

260. Danenhower was soon incapacitated by a serious eye ailment. At least this was De Long's ruling, a matter of later dispute, complicated by Danenhower's history of mental illness.

261. The details of the expedition were preserved by De Long's sense of history and habit of keeping and preserving journals. George Washington De Long, *The Voyage of the Jeannette: The Ship and Ice Journals*, ed. Emma De Long (Boston: Houghton Mifflin, 1883).

262. Guttridge, *Icebound*, pp. 215–39.

263. Guttridge in ibid. (pp. 225–39) refers to Melville's caution as "a fatal delay." For Melville's side, see George W. Melville, *In the Lena Delta: A Narrative of the Search for Lieut.-Commander De Long and His Companions* (Boston: Houghton Mifflin, 1885), pp. 116–76.

The Jeannette *leaving San Francisco for the North Pole, 1879. From George Melville,* In the Lena Delta *(1885)*

A Jeannette search party, 1882. From William Gilder, Ice Pack and Tundra *(1883)*

then, on 5 November, led a native search party northward that managed to find the records De Long had so carefully preserved but not the men themselves. As sketchy information filtered down the river, Russian authorities mistakenly telegraphed the news from Irkutsk of De Long's survival. Melville set off through Verkhoyansk to the administrative center of Yakutsk, where the thirteen survivors of the *Jeannette* reassembled at the end of 1881. But there Melville received an order from the secretary of the navy to resume the search for the twenty still missing.

In the meantime, other relief efforts had been organized. After a prolonged debate in early 1881, Congress authorized the purchase of a steam whaler, the *Rodgers*, to search for the *Jeannette*. Because the commander was instructed to exercise caution, the ship turned back as soon as it encountered extensive ice fields.[264] The Russian government pledged full cooperation for this expedition, offering supplies and safe harbors, as well as for Melville's last search in February 1882.[265] Taking two other survivors, two Russian interpreters, a Swede from Nordenskjold's party, and natives to drive the dogs and reindeer, Melville covered the ground more thoroughly and in due course found the frozen, snow-covered bodies of De Long and his companions. They were properly entombed on a prominent hill marked by a large cross. After a fruitless search for the Chipp party, Melville began his long journey home.

Troubles were far from over for the survivors, though the expenses of their sojourn in Russia were graciously provided by the Russian government, and they were welcomed as heroes on arrival in the United States. From Irkutsk John Danenhower had vented sharp criticism of De Long and Melville, while at home Siberian veteran George Kennan sniped away, especially about Melville's failure to launch a prompt search. The squabbling of the wives of De Long and Melville added another sordid dimension and ended only when Melville's spouse was incarcerated in an insane asylum.[266] Newspaper muckraking and sensation seeking—even going so far as a journalist-led and Bennett-sponsored Siberian safari that broke into De Long's tomb for some macabre sketches of the corpses and a search for papers—continued through an acrimonious naval court of inquiry in 1883.

More appropriately, the Navy Department dispatched two able officers,

264. Guttridge, *Icebound*, pp. 166–70.
265. Giers to Hoffman, 20 April/2 May 1881, DPR, Russia, vol. 4506 (notes received), RG 84, NA.
266. Emma De Long devoted the rest of her life (to 1940) to the memory of her husband and the *Jeannette*. See her *Explorer's Wife* (New York: Dodd, Mead, 1938).

Giles Harber and William Henry Schuetze, to conduct a thorough search of the Lena delta during the summer and winter of 1882–1883 for the lost party and to bring home the bodies of De Long and his men for a proper burial. Russian cooperation again left nothing to be desired—except efficiency.[267] After accomplishing this mission, the United States sent Schuetze back to Siberia in the winter of 1885–1886 to distribute gifts, including a jewel-encrusted sword from Tiffany's for the governor of Eastern Siberia. These trips helped keep the *Jeannette* affair and Siberia newsworthy for several years.

No one directly connected with the *Jeannette* came out looking very good, except the natives and Russians who rendered assistance. Those suffering the most in reputation, however, were Danenhower, the publisher and staff of the New York *Herald*, and the Navy Department. The De Long tomb, minus its bodies, still survives on what natives refer to as "American Mountain" in the Lena delta. Although Melville managed to resurrect out of the debacle a distinguished naval career—mostly behind a desk in Washington as chief of the Bureau of Steam Engineering—the unstable Danenhower committed suicide in 1887, after running the famous old training ship *Constellation* aground in Hampton Roads.[268] The *Jeannette* expedition was not without its scientific value, having proved once and for all the impossibility of sailing on open water to the North Pole.

267. "The Russians are the slowest people imaginable, of the if-I-don't-come-to-day-I-will-to-morrow kind." Schuetze (Irkutsk) to his mother, 5 April 1882, in *William Henry Schuetze* (Chicago: Lakeside Press, n.d.), p. 91.
268. Guttridge, *Icebound*, pp. 327–33.

3

Close Encounters, 1867–1880

The period from the end of the American Civil War to 1881 witnessed not only territorial change and expansion and technological advances in the two countries but also an explosion of knowledge. This was in part due to a broadening literacy combined with improvements in transmission of information, mainly by telegraph, abundant supplies of cheap paper, and inexpensive and rapid printing. In the United States every small town had a press and usually more than one. Where the railroad went, the telegraph and printing press followed, both in the United States and in Russia. Of particular significance, the countries were no longer so remote from each other. The Atlantic cable provided almost instantaneous communication between Washington, D.C., and St. Petersburg, as the quick ratification of the Alaska purchase agreement demonstrated.

Travel also became easier. Regularly scheduled and relatively comfortable, safe, and cheap transportation by ship and train made extended journeys within the means and consideration of more than the especially adventurous and wealthy. There was still plenty of opportunity for the latter, however, on the exotic frontiers of Central Asia and Siberia or in the American West and Alaska. Along with a substantial increase in the volume of travel came better facilities such as full-service hotels, decent restaurants, and convenient, inexpensive local transportation—and an appreciation of tourism. These facilities were now available in the larger "westernized" cities of Russia as well as the small towns of the American West.

A sense of kinship also helps explain why so many Americans traveled to Russia, and vice versa, during this period. A tradition of friendship and absence of serious conflict, similarities in growth and development, corresponding periods of reform and progress, and a shared hostility toward the "older" European powers helped produce a strong mutual attraction. Publicity about the Russian fleet visits of 1863–1864, the 1866 Fox mission, the sale of Alaska, and the tour of Grand Duke Alexis in the United States, accounts of Russian expansion in Central Asia and of the American conquest of the West via transcontinental railroads, the drama of the Russo-Turkish War and its war correspondents, and the purchase of warships all heightened interest and invited curiosity.

The increased numbers and circulation of newspapers and periodicals in both countries opened many more avenues for describing experiences and created a new journalistic industry. "Special correspondents" were soon reporting from the other country. What is particularly fascinating about the writing of this period (the 1870s) is that the authors were on the whole very forthcoming and blunt about expressing their views. Although some definitely had biases, were writing for profit, or had a particular audience in mind, they tended to be frank without fear of retribution or lawsuit. Such satirical and critical blasts would naturally offend feelings, whether of officials of the respective governments, or of fellow citizens. An early example is this American depiction of the 1866 mission to Russia: "Fox is not only a vulgar brute himself, but he has a bushy tail of attendants, not one of whom ever utters a word without making Europe grin from ear to ear. There is, particularly, a Captain Murray, who expiates on the days of his childhood, when his 'young America heart' throbbed with the high hope of one day witnessing an alliance between Russia and America."[1]

Getting Acquainted with Russia

Whether businessmen, reporters, diplomats, or ordinary tourists, Americans could easily prepare themselves for a visit to Russia. Plenty of information was readily available from articles and reviews in the major newspapers and on the pages of the new pictorial weeklies, but they were naturally spotty in coverage and, though often entertaining, slanted in viewpoint. Prospective travelers could also consult a good guidebook, such as the one assembled by W. Pembroke Fetridge for *Harper's*. In sixty columns this early Baedeker provided basic geographical and historical information on Russia and especially about the main tourist attractions, including a room-by-room plan of the Hermitage galleries in St. Petersburg. Besides the usual palaces in

1. Moncure Conway, "London Letter," Boston *Commonwealth*, 13 October 1866.

and outside the city, Fetridge recommended the foundling hospital, the public library, the carriage museum, and the view from the top of St. Isaac's Cathedral. Beyond the capital, Moscow received primary attention, but also covered were medieval Novgorod, the Nizhni-Novgorod fair, and a route through Tula, Kharkov, and Poltava to Odessa, and thence to the Crimea.[2]

Those who desired a familiarity with Russian words and phrases could refer to Agapius Honcharenko's *Russian and English Phrase Book,* which was advertised for "traders, travellers and teachers" and was inspired by the promise of increased contacts on the Asiatic coast of Russia after the purchase of Alaska.[3] Visitors to Russia could also consult a number of new accounts by people who had lived or traveled there. These varied widely in accuracy and readability. One of the best, *Sketches of Russian Life,* though probably not commonly available in the United States, was written by an anonymous English businessman and was unusually optimistic about the prospects for Russian progress.[4] Another, more biased British account that received wider distribution was William Hepworth Dixon's *Free Russia.*[5] Its emphasis was on the diversity of religions and customs, the unique "communism" of the Russian village, and "dissenting politics," by which was meant the Old Believers (church schismatics). One reviewer, probably Eugene Schuyler, was extremely critical: "This new 'sensational' book of Mr. Dixon's is almost too absurd for sober criticism, and were it by an obscure author we should pass it without notice. . . . I cannot undertake to correct the errors of the book, for it is one vast error." He claimed that it was full of "wild and wrong-headed theories" and indicated surprise that the author had not learned anything from his traveling companion, Andrew Mitchel, secretary of the British embassy and a friend of Schuyler's.[6]

Two other books of British origin received better notices from the same reviewer. The first by "H. C. Romanoff," the English wife of a Russian living in the Urals region, consisted primarily of translations of historical articles from the Russian press. Herbert Barry, director of the Shipilov Iron Works near Vladimir, wrote his book mainly because he was anxious to correct Dixon's errors. Barry presented a good, straightforward description of con-

---

2. W. Pembroke Fetridge, *Harper's Hand-Book for Travellers in Europe and the East . . . in Three Volumes,* 17th ed., vol. 3 (New York: Harper and Bros., 1878), pp. 1198–1255.

3. (San Francisco, Calif.: A. Roman, 1868), reviewed in *Nation* 7, 159 (16 July 1868): 326–27.

4. Henry Morley, ed., *Sketches of Russian Life Before and During the Emancipation of the Serfs* (London: Chapman and Hall, 1866).

5. (New York: Harper and Bros., 1870).

6. "Hepworth Dixon on Russia," *Nation* 10, 259 (16 June 1870): 387–88.

temporary Russian life, with sympathy and optimism regarding the conditions of the peasants.[7]

Translations of books by European authors also served American needs around 1870: *Modern Russia* by Julius Eckhardt and *Voyage in Russia* by Theophile Gautier led the way but were inferior to old standbys from the previous generation. A sophisticated review, probably again by Schuyler, of Eckhardt's work emphasized the importance of knowing the author's frame of reference, that he was an exiled Baltic German who had a very negative view of Russian reforms. Responding to his criticism of the peasant commune, the reviewer noted: "May not an entire absence of property be better than great wealth in the hands of a few?"[8] Gautier was a prolific and popular French romanticist whose works virtually monopolized second-level French reading lessons in Britain and the United States. So his *Russia* probably gained a wide readership within a select group.

Americans were more likely to pick up rather superficial accounts by their own well-heeled world travelers, who at least wrote for an American audience: for example, J. Ross Browne, Samuel Prime, Edna Proctor, and Alice Gray. Although Browne posed as a colorful "knapsack" tourist, under contract to *Harper's Weekly*, he brought a long experience of writing and travel to bear on Russia. Many of his scenes of Russian life, such as the rigors of railway travel and poverty in the countryside, were far from inviting, but Browne reassured the reader of the naturalness of Russians:

> It appeared to me that in this respect at least they are more like Americans than any people I had seen in Europe; they do pretty much as they please; follow such trades and occupations as they like best; become noisy and uproarious when it suits them; get drunk occasionally; fight now and then; lie about on the grass and under the trees when they feel tired; enjoy themselves to their heart's content at all the public places; and care nothing about the police as long as the police let them alone. I rather fancied there must be a natural democratic streak

7. "Two Books on Russia," *Nation* 13, 318 (3 August 1871): 75; the titles were *Historical Narratives from the Russian* (London: Rivingtons, 1871) and *Russia in 1870* (London: Publishing Company, 1871), respectively. Of the latter, the review stated: "We cordially recommend it as the best book on that country that has been published within the last ten years, and hope that it will find many readers." A follow up book by Barry, *Ivan at Home, or Pictures from Russian Life* (London: Publishing Company, 1872), was not as successful; *Nation* 14, 365 (27 June 1872): 427.

8. *Nation* 10, 245 (10 March 1870): 161.

in these people, for they are certainly more free and easy in their manners, rougher in their dress, more independent in their general air, and a good deal dirtier than most of the people I had met with in the course of my travels.[9]

The book also contained forty-two of Browne's own well-drawn illustrations of Russian life.

Samuel Prime, a noted Presbyterian minister, offered basic information for the average person.[10] He made interesting comparisons of Russia with Spain, emphasizing the gap between rich and poor in both. During his ten-day visit to St. Petersburg and Moscow with his son in June 1867, Prime disapprovingly observed drunkenness, street beggars, and the bad water in St. Petersburg, but he praised the bread as very good and nutritious. In a diary he kept at the time, he also described peculiarities that many later visitors would also encounter.

> On entering any home, dwelling, restaurant, shop, office or place of business, even a steamboat or railroad office on a pier or elsewhere, they remove the hat from the head instantly, and strangers are expected to do the same. . . . On entering a dwelling or any office where you are about to transact business, as at the bankers, if you have an overcoat on, you are expected to take it off in the anteroom, and leave it in the company of the servants.[11]

Edna Proctor's "journey" was one of her series of travel books that may have prompted more women to travel. She tended to wax poetic; as one review observed, she always found the last country visited the most delightful.[12] Alice Gray's brief account of her 1871 excursion to St. Petersburg and Moscow was also encouraging to the cautious traveler. She thought St. Petersburg was especially easy to manage, "for this city can be done in true American style, and by an American better than by another, for to him there are no puzzling contrasts, no need of change in the channels of thought. No previous knowledge is necessary; there are no antiquities, no

9. J. Ross Browne, *The Land of Thor* (New York: Harper and Bros., 1870), p. 30.

10. Samuel Irenaeus Prime, *The Alhambra and the Kremlin: The South and the North of Europe* (New York: Anson D. F. Randolph, 1873).

11. "Etiquette of the Bears," added notation, Prime Diary, Speer Library, Princeton Theological Seminary.

12. Edna Dean Proctor, *A Russian Journey* (Boston: James R. Osgood, 1872); *Nation* 14, 343 (25 January 1872): 62.

historical associations, no romance; all is glaring—new as Broadway."[13] Others might oppose this view, but it is an interesting analogy and fits with a recurring perception that both countries were young nations in comparison with Western Europe.

Contrasting the two main cities, St. Petersburg and Moscow, was a common theme in the popular literature on Russia with Proctor especially evocative in declaring Moscow the real Russia: "Moscow, set in her high, rolling plains, is the true metropolis of Russia. St. Petersburg may keep the court, but Moscow will still be the seat of power behind the throne; the heart-home of the Slavonnic [sic] people to whom the sea is alien, and who are content with steppe and stream. . . . After cold, misty Petersburg, the air seems warm and the sky clear."[14] But she also asserted that St. Petersburg was best seen in winter: "Colossal Works on every side, power, splendor, novelty; yet the misty skies, the low sun, which gives always the semblance of waning day, the dull tints of sea and shore, the melancholy wind blowing through the broad, level, monotonous streets, make it a sombre city during the milder half of the year." Yet when the Neva is frozen and the theaters are open, "then St. Petersburg is brilliant, imposing, unrivaled, the Miracle of the North."[15]

Another, anonymous writer-traveler was more sophisticated and politically oriented in depicting the Russian "tale of two cities":

Those two antagonistic political influences or parties which struggle for ascendancy the world over may also be found in Russia, though Russia is not a constitutionally governed state. One of them has its seat at St. Petersburg, the other at Moscow. . . . The one, fully aware that progress cannot be improvised, seeks to overcome obstacles gradually: the other expects at once to realize Utopia. . . . In a word, at St. Petersburg men reason, at Moscow they dream: in the former intelligence and moderation dominate, in the latter, visionary dreams and precipitation. . . . Moscow is ready to sacrifice everything, even Russia, for its visions of the great Slavic Empire of the future.[16]

13. Alice Gray, "My Russian Friends," *Galaxy* 13, 2 (February 1872): 230.
14. Edna Dean Proctor, "Moscow and Southern Russia," *Scribner's Monthly* 5, 6 (April 1873): 669.
15. "Northern Russia and St. Petersburg," *Scribner's Monthly* 5, 1 (November 1872): 21.
16. W. P. M., "St. Petersburg and Moscow," in "Our Monthly Gossip," *Lippincott's Magazine* 8 (September 1871): 313–14.

The same writer critically examined the Russification policies of the Young Russia party, centered in Moscow, and asserted that they hurt Russia both internally and abroad. "It is this party, so intensely patriotic, which has labored more effectively in the Prussian interest than Prussia itself."[17]

Norton Dodge, who had first visited Russia during the Crimean War and returned in 1871, saw in St. Petersburg "everything constructed for effect," constantly falling down and being rebuilt. The variety of people on the streets "make St. Petersburg seem more like a rendezvous for the hostages of an enemy than quarters for soldiers of a single country."[18] Obviously, Peter the Great's imperial capital struck people differently. A correspondent for the Boston *Herald* was emphatic that everyone must see it before they die, that nothing rivals a June night in St. Petersburg.[19] And the New York *Times* chipped in with its fluffy comment: "The city, with its bustle and noise, much resembles New York; but the stores and private residences are not so elegant as those which are to be met with in that great metropolis."[20] As a result of these contrasting descriptions, Americans would tend to believe that one could not really experience Russia without visiting both cities.

The Correspondents

The period after the American Civil War was probably the first great age of newspapers, when mass circulation dailies had tremendous power and influence, not only in their own cities but often throughout the country. Before copyright laws and syndications exercised restrictions, many of the small-town newspapers copied the larger ones, and even the major papers cited one another freely.

17. W. P. M., "Young Russia," *Lippincott's Magazine* 7 (January 1871): 105. (One suspects Eugene Schuyler as the author since he displayed similar insights—but would he have written for Scribner's rival?) "Young Russia" adherents wanted to protect Russia and Slavic culture from liberal Westernization, especially the French and British varieties—hence their pro-Prussian views in foreign policy.

18. N. S. D., "Last Winter at St. Petersburg," New York *Times*, 26 November 1871. For details Dodge was not a reliable guide; in another article he confused the summer palace at Tsarskoe Selo with the Winter Palace. "The Palace and Tombs of the Czars," *Overland Monthly* 8, 2 (February 1872): 125.

19. E. C. B., Letters from St. Petersburg, dated 20 and 28 June and 2 July, in Boston *Herald*, 7, 21, and 28 August 1869. These letters, copied by other newspapers, provide one of the best, detailed guides to the two Russian cities and may have been as useful to tourists as any of the publications available.

20. New York *Times*, 16 August 1868.

The foreign "correspondents" themselves were most often simply that—people who wrote letters from abroad describing their travels and reacting to events, not regular staff members of the newspaper. Many of them remain anonymous behind a byline such as "St. Petersburg Correspondence." For this they received very modest honoraria, usually arranged in advance by an understanding with a publisher, as for Twain's 1867 visit; but sometimes they wrote gratis, as a public service or in hopes that a newspaper or journal article would lead to a more lucrative (or at least less anonymous) book or serial publication. Some of these amateur journalists were engaged in business or on official duty, which might promote the desire to remain unidentified.

Writing was also a way of supporting residence abroad and travels to exotic places. Being nonprofessional, the correspondents were free to grind axes and spin yarns, exaggerate, reveal prejudices, and be reckless with sources. Such was the case with Mark Twain, who naturally included his Russian adventures in his San Francisco columns. Another tendency of these self-styled reporters was to comment on all and sundry regardless of their particular expertise. Moncure Conway, a Unitarian minister from Washington, spent much time abroad giving lectures and writing articles. In 1866, the Fox mission prompted him to lash out from his London base at the apparent Russian craze in the United States. Under the heading "Russia and America," Conway described Russia as "the most gigantic despotism of the old world." Noting the speculation about a Russian-American alliance, he recalled how American support for Hungarian revolutionaries was suppressed by Russian forces in 1849. "American liberals have no right to forget that in the great system of oppression of nationalities in Europe—which is, after all, the European slavery—Russia is still the greatest of sinners. . . . I fear that the nearer we get to Russia the less reason shall we find to go into raptures over her standard of internal or international righteousness."[21]

In an expanded version for the British *Fortnightly Review,* Conway traced American friendship toward Russia to the Crimean War and the mutual hostility toward England and pointed out the irony that the strongest support for Russia came from the slave states. During the Civil War, the situation was reversed, and the North welcomed any overtures of European amity. "Yet it is impossible in the nature of things that any regular alliance can be formed between Russia and America. . . . It was not a new Russia that

21. "Mr. Conway's Letters," 5 September 1866, Boston *Commonwealth,* 29 September 1866.

the *Mayflower* fought its way across the ocean to establish, but a new England."[22] This famous quote would be repeated for decades.

Surprisingly, after a sightseeing excursion in 1869 to St. Petersburg and Moscow (where Schuyler served as his guide), Conway changed his tune about Russia. As he recounted: "I made sufficient acquaintance with Russia and its people to feel ashamed for the English that prejudice should blind them so generally to this great country whose character and social conditions are of phenomenal interest. . . . Instead of finding an oppressed people, I found a people enjoying a personal liberty unknown either in England or America."[23] He even went so far as to write: "The Russian peasantry impressed me as the happiest I had seen in any country" and "the Russians [are] the most slandered people on the face of the earth."[24] Schuyler's introductions to English-speaking Russian families and special tours through peasant villages may have been responsible for this turnaround, but it was apparently not divulged in print to contemporaries. Conway was not the only American to write knowingly about Russia before actually visiting it. Among others, Eugene Lawrence, a literary critic and popular historian, included Russia in his widely distributed columns.

Echoing the general spirit of friendship, Sarah Jane Clarke Lippincott, pen name Grace Greenwood, wrote for the New York *Times* in 1868: "The bond which unites Russia and America is gradually growing stronger and stronger, and the day is not far distant when they may be looked upon as brothers. Everywhere Americans are treated with civility and respect. . . . We are glad to be among the Russians, and shake them by the hand."[25] Probably the same correspondent—simply known as "G"— filed a series of reports from the Russian capital early the next year that indicated a long-time familiarity with the scene. In February, he or she noted: "The present season here is more than usually brilliant and interesting. In social circles there is

22. Moncure D. Conway, "Russia and America," *Fortnightly Review* 6 (15 August–1 December 1866): 663–65.

23. Conway, *Autobiography: Memories and Experiences*, vol. 2 (Boston: Houghton Mifflin, 1904), p. 180. Conway was able to travel so extensively abroad because of income from accumulated investments at home. Mary Elizabeth Burtis, *Moncure Conway, 1832–1907* (New Brunswick, N.J.: Rutgers University Press, 1952), p. 197.

24. Conway, *Autobiography* 2:183.

25. "St. Petersburg letter, from our own correspondent, Greenwood," 26 July 1868, New York *Times*, 16 August 1868. The identification of the writer as American seems to rule out Frederick Greenwood, editor of the *Pall Mall Gazette*; John Hohenberg, *Foreign Correspondence: The Great Reporters and Their Times* (New York and London: Columbia University Press, 1964), p. 103.

more animation than has been seen for a number of years, while the questions of home and foreign politics are so numerous and of such importance as to occupy not only the more serious minds, but almost all classes of people in this Northern Palmyra, as St. Petersburg has not unaptly been called."[26] According to this source, the building and ownership of railroads was the foremost political and economic issue. "G" was also impressed with the expansion of coal mines for fueling the new locomotives and industry. "Russian iron is as famous as Russian leather; both are well known in America—the one for its fine and durable polish, in the form of sheet iron and stove pipes, the second in bookbinding."[27]

Praising Russian expansion in Central Asia, "G" thought that British fears of a threat to India were ridiculous, but that the Russians were much more at home in Central Asia than the British were in India.[28] This view became a fairly common one in the United States. Charles Morris, beginning a long career as a one-man "Book of Knowledge" and popular historian, wrote in 1870:

> The Russian is in great measure an Asiatic, and is far better adapted to deal with his fellow-Orientals than is any full-blooded European. He meets the sons of the Orient with their own smiling suavity and endless prudence, glides through the net of diplomacity [sic] without displaying an angle in his body, enters into their modes of thought, conforms to their customs, and allows them to delay and prevaricate to their hearts content. But when once a point is gained he is utterly unyielding. . . . [He] thoroughly understands Asia and how to deal with her.[29]

This, many Americans felt, helped explain the unreasonable British hostility toward Russia.

The Boston *Globe*'s "own correspondent," identified only as "C," entered Russia through Odessa early in 1872 and provided a colorful account from that vantage point.

> Russia to an American must be an interesting country. There is no classic ground here, but on the other hand it has some advantages over the

26. Letter of 20 February, New York *Times*, 3 April 1869.
27. Ibid.
28. Letter of 3 March, New York *Times*, 11 April 1869.
29. Charles Morris, "Russia in Central Asia," *Lippincott's Magazine* 6 (July 1870): 111.

faded and worn out kingdoms of the old world. Like our own, Russia is a new country, and resembles very much our own. If there is an advantage, Russia possesses it, because she has worked her way to civilization and magnificence from a state of absolute barbarism, while we sprang into being with the advantage of all the lights of the old world. There are still many subjects of comparisons and emulations between us; but nowhere in all Russia is there a more proper subject to begin with than Odessa. . . . We are both young, and both marching with gigantic strides to greatness, but we move by different roads.[30]

"C" enjoyed Odessa society and took in a production of "The Barber of Seville" in which "the company were in full undress." After visiting a experimental farm with a friend, he or she attended a party and met "Madam M," who was described as a popular writer. "At dinner she talked with much interest of the United States, and called us a model nation; she expressed the hope, though not much expectation, of one day visiting it." In the library "C" noticed books by James Fenimore Cooper, Washington Irving, George Bancroft, and W. H. Prescott.[31]

Probably the same correspondent, but now identified as "Alex," was soon writing from St. Petersburg regarding the controversy between Britain and the United States over the *Alabama* affair: "Russia is too well pleased to see England brought to task; and in case of an open rupture between the two nations America would find she had a warm and powerful friend in the empire of Russia. . . . There is no disguising the fact that Russia dislikes England as cordially as she likes America."[32] Similar refrains are found in other columns of "our own correspondents."

The best American reporters of the Russian scene in this period confined themselves mainly to the more exotic regions—Siberia, Central Asia, the Caucasus, to which few other Americans would venture. They include Thomas Knox, George Kennan, Januarius MacGahan, and Eugene Schuyler. Assigned by the New York *Herald* to cover the Western Union telegraph

30. "Russia," from Odessa, dated 8 February 1872, Boston *Globe*, 16 March 1872. "C" has not been identified; both Curtins are accounted for—Jeremiah was helping entertain the grand duke at home and Andrew was in Nice. One possibility is Januarius MacGahan, who was in Odessa about that time.

31. Ibid.

32. "Russia," from St. Petersburg, dated 20 February/3 March 1872, Boston *Globe*, 28 March 1872. "Alex" might be Alexander Delmar, who attended the International Statistical Congress in St. Petersburg that year, though the meeting did not begin until August.

expedition, Knox related his adventures crossing Siberia in the winter of 1866–1867 for the newspaper, in articles, and in a book, *Overland Through Asia.* He described the sights and peoples he encountered in generally glowing terms.[33] Knox was one of the first to analyze the Siberian exile system, stressing, however, that the hardships of banishment were compensated by the rareness of the death penalty and the positive accomplishments of many of the exiles in Siberia. Political prisoners, he declared, were proportionally few and seldom faced hard labor in the mines.[34]

Knox's book and Kennan's more colorful and intimate account of his experiences in Eastern Siberia were published the same year and received high praise.[35] Based on earlier articles in *Putnam's* magazine and especially popular among a broad cross-section of the American people, Kennan's *Tent Life* was reprinted several times, reaching its fourteenth edition by 1893. Besides his stirring adventures with the telegraph expedition, Kennan described the history, geography, and ethnic culture of Siberia. The prison system was treated benevolently, in contrast to his later views. The book also had a fairly wide readership in Russia in the original English edition and in Russian translation. Consul general George Pomutz gave Kennan what must have been welcome news about his book:

> I sincerely congratulate you upon its success at home, and must compliment you, as all our friends here unanimously do, upon the marvellous power of description, the clear and vivid style of expression, and the happiest humorous vein you had at your command. You make the reader at once your friend, and the lively interest he is brought to feel in the subject of your narrative will not permit him to lay the book aside—before he arrives to the last word of the last page.

33. For example, "To and Upon the Amoor River," *Harper's New Monthly Magazine* 37, 219 (August 1868): 289–306; "Traveling in Siberia," idem, 37, 220 (September 1868): 449–66; "A Sleigh-Ride Through Eastern Russia," idem, 38, 225 (February 1869): 289–305; and "The Conquest of the Amoor," *Frank Leslie's Illustrated Newspaper*, 13 November 1869, one of a series for that publication. A typical comment from the latter is: "American emigration moves Westward; that of Russia is toward the East, and greets the rising as ours the setting sun."

34. Thomas W. Knox, "Siberian Exiles," *Atlantic Monthly* 22, 131 (September 1868): 273–85.

35. Knox, *Overland Through Asia: Pictures of Siberian, Chinese, and Tartar Life* (Chicago: F. S. Gilman, 1870); and Kennan, *Tent Life in Siberia and Adventures Among the Koraks and Other Tribes in Kamchatka and Eastern Siberia* (New York: G. P. Putnam's, 1870); for a review of the latter, see "Kamchatka," *Nation* 13, 322 (31 August 1871): 145–46.

George Kennan in Siberia. From George Kennan,
Tent-Life in Siberia *(1889)*

The little book, like its restless author, is wandering from hand to
hand, from family to family;—in fact, after I got through reading it, it
never came back and keeps on wandering. All like it and its author's
name is growing popular.[36]

Kennan returned to Russia in 1870 to tour the Caucasus as a roaming vagabond,[37] but he did not fulfill his intention of writing another book, settling

36. Kennan, *Stepnaia zhizn v Sibiri: Stranstviia mezhdu koriakami i drugami plemenami
Kamchatki i Severnoi Azii* (St. Petersburg: M. Khana, 1871). Pomutz to Kennan, 20 February 1872, box 1, Kennan Papers, LC.
37. Frederick F. Travis, *George Kennan and the American-Russian Relationship,
1865–1924* (Athens: Ohio University Press, 1990), pp. 43–47.

instead for a couple of articles.[38] While retaining his interest in Russia, Kennan began instead to strive—in vain as it turned out—for successful careers in banking and insurance.

One cannot mention George Kennan's activities during this period without noting the role of lecturing to inform the American public. This media dimension was completely lacking on the Russian side of the equation. Following in the footsteps of Bayard Taylor, Kennan crisscrossed the country after his inaugural talk in January 1869.[39] Although it is true that other writers—certainly Taylor, Browne, Knox, and Proctor—lectured on Russia, Kennan was the most indefatigable in pursuit of an audience, covered more of small-town America, and made his Russian experiences his only topic.[40] His failing, however, was his tendency to exaggerate and sensationalize in both writing and speaking.

The stature of Januarius Aloysius MacGahan, the farm boy from Ohio, looms larger than life because of his knack for being in the right place at the right time, his impressive appearance (tall with a full black beard), his dramatic style of writing, his sense of adventure, and his tragic end. He thus deserves a place as one of the real pioneers among professional foreign correspondents, the American version of William Howard Russell. From his camel ride across the deserts of Central Asia to his tour of devastated Bulgarian villages, he earned a wide and influential reputation among the general public and with military men and politicians.[41]

Eugene Schuyler

Still, in terms of informing the American public on the variety of Russian life, the 1870s belongs to Eugene Schuyler. With considerable personal sacrifice, he devoted much of his energy to an understanding of Russia. Although at times hurried and careless in his writing, there is no question

38. "The Mountains and Mountaineers of the Eastern Caucasus," *Journal of the American Geographical Society of New York* 5 (1874): 169–93; and "Unwritten Literature of the Caucasian Mountaineers," *Lippincott's Magazine* 22 (October 1878): 437–46, and 22 (November 1878): 571–81.

39. Travis, *George Kennan*, pp. 38–39. Bayard Taylor had around seventy speaking engagements booked for the winter of 1869–1870, but it is not clear how many dealt with Russia; *Frank Leslie's Illustrated Newspaper*, 6 November 1869.

40. For a brief account of a 1874 lecture tour, see Kennan to Fanny Clark, 22 December 1874, Kennan Papers, Rush-Rhees Library, University of Rochester.

41. He is featured in Hohenberg, *Foreign Correspondence*, pp. 114–20.

Eugene Schuyler. From Eugene Schuyler: Selected
Essays *(1901)*

about his dedication to the cause. He had the advantages of an Ivy League
education, social position, and publisher connections, and he used them to
the utmost, while also serving his country almost continuously as a "professional" diplomat. Because of his occupation, however, he often wrote under
a pseudonym or left his works unsigned, so his contributions cannot all be
easily identified.

As already mentioned, Schuyler first learned Russian during the 1863–
1864 fleet visit to New York and launched his career in Russian studies with
a translation of Ivan Turgenev's *Fathers and Sons* in 1867. In accomplishing
this feat, he benefited from his mother's relationship to the Scribner publishing family. Schuyler also took a shortcut by translating at least part of
the work from the French edition, which he thought was excusable since it
was the author's own French version.[42] But he took a beating from the critics
in any event. While at his consular post in Moscow, he translated, fresh
from the Russian and in less haste, portions of Leo Tolstoy's fictionalized
reminiscences of the siege of Sevastopol during the Crimean War for issues

42. *Nation* 5, 129 (19 December 1867): 496.

of a Scribner's periodical.[43] He also sent "letters" to newspapers in hopes of picking up some extra money. After one such dispatch, he asked a friend to check to see if it was published. "If it is will you be kind enough to put on that bland and persuasive manner, which you know so well how to assume, and see if they will pay me anything for it."[44]

Schuyler soon ventured more seriously into print with his own colorful vignettes of life in Moscow and in the region of Orenburg on his first trip to Central Asia.[45] He also wrote anonymously a series of articles and many book reviews for the *Nation*.[46] The most interesting in retrospect was on "Russian Universities."[47] In plain language he described not only the establishment of nine universities and their strengths (Kazan, oriental languages; St. Petersburg, mathematics; Kiev and Kharkov, medicine; Moscow, history; and so on) but also his own personal experiences at the University of Moscow. For example, he heard legal historian Boris Chicherin lecture on Rousseau's social contract just before he was forced to resign for his liberal views. He found students attentive to lectures but also discovered names of French ballerinas whittled into the desks.

Schuyler was quite critical of the few opportunities for writing or speaking in the university. "Few people are more disposed to talk than the Russians, and few are more wordy, but . . . every educated man [needs] to express his opinions on a variety of subjects in a clear and concise way, both orally and in writings." He lamented the absence of student unions, debating societies, and an internal university life, and he deplored the repressive atmosphere that prevailed. The students wore hair long ("like in our Western colleges") and were generally dirty and careless in dress. They were adopting Slavophile ideas, donning peasant clothes and living in communal "digs," where disorder, dust, scattered books, and cheap tobacco smoke reigned. "It is the poor students who give the tone, because they are in the majority: they are very democratic, regard all as their equals, despise gloves, neckties, and other belongings of aristocracy, and look with contempt on

43. *Hours at Home* 8, 4–6 (February–April 1869): 328–36, 316–22, and 526–31.

44. Schuyler (Moscow) to Burton Harrison, 25 December 1867/6 January 1868, box 8, Burton Harrison Papers, LC.

45. "The Russian Peasant," *Hours at Home* 9, 1 (May 1869): 313–20; and "On the Steppe," ibid. 9, 4 (August 1869): 319–29.

46. Schuyler reviewed almost every book written on Russia between 1867 and 1880. His articles in the *Nation* included ones on Russian railroads (7, 144 [2 April 1868]: 271), cooperative societies (7, 182 [8 October 1868]: 287–88), and Turgenev (9, 222 [8 September 1869]: 271–73).

47. *Nation* 9, 227 (4 November 1869): 384–86.

the 'aristocrats' unless they will share in some way their mode of life."[48] The emancipation of women was a favorite topic, and several professors had even announced special courses for women along with opportunities to take examinations.

Schuyler also wrote articles, letters, and notes, describing Russian scenes and events and several reviews for *Athenaeum: Journal of Literature, Science, the Fine Arts, Music, and the Drama*.[49] Fortunate to be in Russia during a time of reform and openness, Schuyler met many people on his travels and in the course of diplomatic business. His duties and his concentration on producing *Turkestan*, a biography of Peter the Great, and a translation of Tolstoy's *The Cossacks* occupied most of his time in the mid-1870s. After covering the Russo-Turkish War as an official agent, Schuyler wrote another series of article-reminiscences for *Lippincott's Magazine* in 1878. In one on the "Russian Press," he observed, "Like many other native institutions, Russian journalism is merely a fine fragment. Russia has a multitude of ships but no navy; a number of ministers but no government; a host of journals but no press." He characterized the official newspapers as "National Music."[50]

Schuyler's biography of Peter the Great, written in the heroic, narrative style of Thomas Macauley and serialized in the *Century*, was probably the first widely recognized American contribution to Russian history. Based on primary materials, including a number of rare documents that Schuyler had collected in Moscow and St. Petersburg, and finished during the leisure of a consular posting in Birmingham, it withstood the scrutiny of time until the works of Russian and German historians became available in translation and new emphases on economic and social factors provided corrective interpretations. Its publication demonstrates that there was a definite market in the United States for Russian history, a market that was also served by a new edition of John Lothrop Mottley's earlier but much weaker biographical study of the great tsar-reformer. Nothing they or any other American produced, however, could compete for broad interpretive scope and intimate detail with Alfred Rambaud's *History of Russia* or British journalist Donald

---

48. Ibid., 385. One begins to wonder if Schuyler was reporting on the sixties of another century.

49. "My Russian Letter" recounted a meeting of the Imperial Russian Geographical Society, discussed William Ralston's *Songs of the Russian People*, and noted the celebration of the 200th anniversary of the birth of Peter the Great; *Athenaeum* 2331 (29 June 1872): 815.

50. D. K., "The Russian Press," *Lippincott's Magazine* 22 (September 1878): 382–83. Internal evidence in one of the articles suggests that D. K. was Schuyler.

Mackenzie Wallace's *Russia*, both of which had sizable audiences in the United States and were stocked in public libraries across the country.[51]

Although Schuyler never managed to collect his own reports and views of Russia in a comprehensive volume, he rose to his highest stature as a journalist in a series of articles for the New York *Times* in 1880, called "Pictures of Russian Life." While revisiting his old stomping grounds in St. Petersburg that year, he described the capital with a number of editorial flourishes. The city, he wrote, was not Russia: "It is simply the vices of Western Europe neatly bound in Russian leather." And though he had just completed a biographical work, he complained "that the history of Russia is still to be written. What we now possess is a history not of Russia but of a few distinguished Russians."[52] From Moscow, Schuyler passed on a stirring account of the Battle of Borodino from an old general who had participated in it, reminisced about the Volga area, and helped Turgenev unveil a famous statue of Alexander Pushkin.[53]

His frankest comments Schuyler reserved until after his departure. He foresaw a severe upheaval ahead for Russia. "Circumstances are forcing on Russia a transformation for which she is utterly unprepared. Hitherto all her troubles have arisen from the fact of her being an Empire of the nineteenth century under a Government of the fifteenth." The real threat, he believed, was the absence of a strong middle class, which dominated the governing bodies of other countries and had "everything to lose and nothing to gain by revolution." Peasant emancipation and new modes of transportation he

51. After the original French edition was published in 1876, a number of English editions appeared, the standard one being the translation by Leonna Lang: Alfred Nicholas Rambaud, *History of Russia from the Earliest Times*, 3 vols. (Boston: Estes and Lauriat, 1879–1882). The first volume was considered by one reviewer (possibly Schuyler) to be surprisingly sympathetic and objective; *Nation* 28, 722 (1 May 1879): 306.

A review of Wallace's *Russia*, 2 vols. (New York: Holt, 1877), perhaps by George Kennan, noted: "The great merit of the book is its thorough analysis of the phenomena with which it deals. . . . In reading it we are conscious only of a feeling of absorbing interest, but the impression which it leaves is that of a fullness of knowledge and clearness of comprehension such as few persons could pretend to possess in regard to the countries with which they are best acquainted whether through the description of others or their own observations." *Lippincott's Magazine* 18 (May 1877): 643–44. The book went through five American editions the first year, solid evidence of its popularity.

52. Dateline, from St. Petersburg, dated 17 May 1880, New York *Times*, 14 June 1880. Although foregoing a byline, Schuyler betrayed himself by stating that his hotel near St. Isaacs was the place where he had dined with MacGahan before leaving for Khiva in 1873.

53. "Moscow and Its Suburbs," "Moscow's Sparrow Hills," and "A Popular Russian Poet," New York *Times*, 21, 27, and 28 June 1880.

saw as challenging traditional social structures. "The danger now threatening Russia is of a different kind—that of a collapse of the Present before the Future is ready to replace it. . . . Her traditional system of surveillance and espionage has manifestly run its course, and is now wholly insufficient to deal with the new circumstances which confront it."[54] Schuyler doubted, however, that representative government would ever work in Russia, and in fact, he saw no clear way out of the dilemma.

For a comprehensive history of Russia, Americans would have to depend on foreign works, especially French and German, translated into English. It was not that there was no interest but rather that the task was too formidable. Besides Schuyler, John Bacon, a former secretary of legation in St. Petersburg (1858–1859) from South Carolina, considered tackling the project of recounting Russia's history—"I mean its real history"—and sought help from the Russian minister. "The histories of Russia in this country are for the most part English compilations and of a very partial and partisan view."[55] Finally, Mary Robinson responded in 1882 with a superficial distillation of Russian history that at least showed a demand existed.[56]

Russian Literature

Until 1867 Americans were largely ignorant of Russian literature. In contrast, educated Russians during the first half of the nineteenth century were quite familiar with American writers—Irving, Cooper, Harriet Beecher Stowe, Nathaniel Hawthorne, Herman Melville, Edgar Allan Poe. It was no accident that Eugene Schuyler, who had perhaps the best insights and knowledge of Russia of any American of that time, helped to prompt interest in Russian literature and to usher in the "age of Turgenev" with his translation of *Fathers and Sons* in the summer of 1867. It received only a modest public reception at first, mainly as a "Muscovite" curiosity.[57]

The favorable critical response to this novel, however, and even more to *On the Eve*, sparked a general interest in Russian literature. Thomas Sargent Perry and A. C. Dillman led the way with their reviews in 1871, pre-

54. "A Great Empire's Burden," from Liverpool, dated 9 August 1880, *New York Times*, 22 August 1880.

55. Bacon to Offenberg, 17 May 1873, f. 170, op. 512/3, d. 110 (1872), AVPR.

56. "History of Russia," *Chautauquan* 3, 1 (October 1882): 10–14, and seven successive issues, totaling only about thirty pages.

57. Royal Gettman, *Turgenev in England and America*, Illinois Studies in Language and Literature vol. 27, no. 2 (Urbana: University of Illinois Press, 1941), pp. 39–40.

ceding the much-ballyhooed visit of Grand Duke Alexis.[58] A veritable Turgenev craze ensued among New England literati, as they absorbed each fresh translation—*Smoke*, *A Sportsman's Sketches* (which was viewed as the Russian equivalent of *Uncle Tom's Cabin*), and *A House of Gentlefolk*. The fact that Turgenev was much more popular in the United States than in Britain can be indirectly ascribed to the friendlier relations between the two countries and the wide publicity given to the grand duke's visit. More important, American audiences responded easily to Turgenev's idealism and character depiction, and influential New England writers such as William Dean Howells. Henry James, and Cornell professor Hjalmar Boyesen all strongly praised and recommended Turgenev's works.[59] Their promotion no doubt inspired better and more frequent translations.

Turgenev did his part by evincing an interest in American literature and republican ideals. As one analyst noted, "There seemed to be an occult connection between the Russian novelist and the young post-war Americans, both men and women."[60] The writer, in fact, was often referred to in Russian circles as "the American," and he seemed proud of it. For literature, Turgenev liked Hawthorne's work best of all, but he also admired Henry Wadsworth Longfellow, Walt Whitman, Bret Harte, James Russell Lowell, Howells, and Harriet Beecher Stowe. Although he never realized his ambition to visit the United states, unlike most other Russian writers he was readily accessible in Paris, where he was sought out by Stowe, Lowell, William Bailey Aldrich, and Boyesen, and from where he corresponded with Howells and Henry and William James. Finally, in 1879, he met Mark Twain. To Boyesen, Turgenev remarked: "There is a man who at last conforms to my notion of what an American ought to be. Your other friends here—and yourself, too, for that matter—are typeless cosmopolitans; you might be almost anything. But this man has physiognomy; he has the flavor of the soil.[61]

58. Reviews by Perry, *Atlantic Monthly* 27 (February 1871): 265; and Dillman, "Ivan Tourgenef, the Novelist," *Lippincott's Magazine* 7 (May 1871): 494–502. This corresponded with the appearance of *On the Eve* and was followed by a new edition of Schuyler's *Fathers and Sons* translation in 1872.

59. Gettman, *Turgenev*, pp. 44–49; Alexsandr Nikoliukin, *Vzaimosviazi literatur Rossii i SShA: Turgenev, Tolstoi, Dostoevskii i Amerika* (Moscow: Nauka, 1987), pp. 87–97; and Per E. Seyersted, "Turgenev's Interest in America, As Seen in His Contacts with H. H. Boyesen, W. D. Howells and Other American Authors," *Scando-Slavica* (Copenhagen) 11 (1965): 25–39.

60. Van Wyck Brooks, *New England: Indian Summer, 1865–1915* (New York: E. P. Dutton, 1940), p. 233.

61. As quoted in Seyersted, "Turgenev's Interest in America," 39.

Ivan Turgenev, 1868. From Letopis' zhizni i tvorchestva I. S.
Turgeneva *(1934)*

Turgenev and contemporary American writers idealized women and,
along with especially Henry Adams, depicted the men of their society as failures. As Van Wyck Brooks has observed, "the young American men were
the victims of conditions that resembled in part the conditions of Turgenev's
Russia."[62] This common theme inspired much of the mutual admiration.
That is not to say Turgenev was not criticized, since Perry and others found
a number of flaws in the novels—for example, contrived tragedies. But it is
also clear that Perry and Howells viewed Turgenev's works as an important
step forward in improving the quality of the American public's tastes, as
books and characters with messages, not the light summer reading so often
preferred by Americans.[63]

Although the focus on Turgenev inspired some interest in neglected Russian writers of the past—Pushkin, Nikolai Gogol, Mikhail Lermontov—

62. Brooks, *New England*, p. 234.
63. Gettman, *Turgenev*, pp. 58–59.

Americans leaned toward the present. For that reason the "historical" books of Leo Tolstoy—*Sevastopol Tales*, *The Cossacks*, and *War and Peace*—received little public attention. These works also had their supporters, however. George Kennan, in reviewing Schuyler's rendering of *The Cossacks*, recommended it while delivering a classic coup de grâce to the translator: "That the book should produce such an impression in a translation so uncouth and blundering as Mr. Schuyler has given is a strong testimony to its merit. It is usually thought that a translator ought to be tolerably familiar with two languages, but readers of *The Cossacks* will be forced to doubt if Mr. Schuyler is acquainted with one."[64] Poor translation was still one obvious obstacle to an American appreciation of the finest Russian literature of the time. Kennan himself was convinced of this but was largely unsuccessful in trying his own hand at Tolstoy.[65] He nonetheless lamented the American focus on Turgenev to the neglect of equally good writers such as Ivan Goncharov, Fedor Dostoevsky, and Tolstoy, although he did share with the public his own fascination with Caucasian folk literature.[66] The key problem was that with the glaring exception of Kennan and Schuyler, very few Americans understood the historical and social settings of these contemporary Russian works.[67]

Turgenev had a considerable influence on American literature and literary criticism of the 1870s and 1880s, especially on James, Whitman, Perry, Howells, Longfellow, and Adams,[68] but his broader impact on the American view of Russia at this time is not easy to measure. Fiction certainly provided one more dimension of a perspective on Russian life. Perhaps the literature of

64. *Lippincott's Magazine* 22 (November 1878): 646. Although unsigned, the review certainly reflects the expertise and the tone of Kennan, who had his own article in that issue. Kennan was even more strident in his criticism in "Russian into English," New York *Tribune*, 27 July 1878. Lamentably, America's two leading Russian experts in this period—Schuyler and Kennan—despised each other and never met or cooperated in any way, although Jeremiah Curtin corresponded with both.

65. Travis, *George Kennan*, pp. 79–80.

66. See his "Unwritten Literature of the Caucasian Mountaineers." *Lippincott's Magazine* also provided a similar sampling of Ukrainian lore; Sarah B. Wister, "Ballads and Bards of the Ukraine," 16 (December 1875): 724–29.

67. This is a point that Dorothy Brewster stresses in analyzing the fascination of Howells and James with Turgenev; *East-West Passage: A Study in Literary Relationships* (London: George Allen and Unwin, 1954), pp. 94–96.

68. For an excellent appraisal, see Nikoliukin, *Vzaimosviazi*, pp. 98–103. A number of other Russian scholars—A. A. Elistratova, T. L. Morosova, G. A. Gvozdeva, L. N. Funso, and G. Grubman—have dwelt on the interconnection of Henry James and Ivan Turgenev.

Russia allowed more character identification in the United States than in other countries, but affinity did not go so far as to inspire the formation of Russian studies at universities. That would await the next generation.

Editorial Opinion

Russia was a frequent subject of unsigned columns on the editorial pages of American newspapers in the 1870s. Their appearance typically corresponded with particular events such as the tour of Grand Duke Alexis and the Russo-Turkish War. To analyze all of them, even just those of the leading newspapers and journals, would require a book in itself. Suffice it to say that Russia received much more press attention during this period than ever before, in part at least because editors were much better informed by their correspondents and probably made direct use of their material from time to time.[69] There may also have been the belief, especially during and after the visit of Alexis, that Russia sold newspapers.

A considerable maturation can be detected over the course of the 1870s, which started with rather optimistic and naive perceptions of Russian developments. Influenced by Russian reform and evident advances, editors saw harmony in government and society leading to progress and power. "For the Empire of the Czar is not merely a dynasty—it is a civilization; not merely a great Power, but the embodiment of a great principle and the promise of a social revolution." The isolated, Asian character of Russia was an obstacle that could be overcome by salutary expansion, such as the taking of Constantinople: "Russia would enter the fraternity of European powers, as she can never thoroughly do while her head is hidden among the clouds and snow of the far north. Turkey is an Asiatic barbarism that apes western civilization. It is past being patched."[70]

Russia often still emerged as different, mysterious, imponderable. "Russia

69. Editorials often coincided with and elaborated on correspondence columns.

70. New York *Times*, 1 October 1870. Another interesting suggestion on how to make Russia more Western was offered by an American engineer who had toured Russia: connect the Caspian Sea to the Black Sea by canal. The Caspian would over time be raised and enlarged, creating a "new Mediterranean" in Central Asia that would change the climate and become the geographic and economic equivalent of the Great Lakes. "Such a great triumph of a nation over Nature would be far the greatest conquest in the annals of human material progress." Henry C. Spalding, "The Black Sea and the Caspian," *Van Nostrand's Eclectic Engineering Magazine* 15, 92 (August 1876): 122–27.

is the historical enigma of modern times, the Sphinx who will solve her own riddle, but who will, nevertheless, see others destroyed in the vain attempt to solve it for themselves."[71] The same editor, however, saw hope in the relatively relaxed censorship of the period:

> The press in Russia enjoys already a tolerable amount of freedom, and is manifesting also the power of that public opinion whose growth almost keeps pace with an increasing strength of the Executive. These powers are, under the present relations of political parties in Russia, of a kind to balance each other, not to tend toward active conflict. . . . It is precisely this alliance between the throne and all the social and political aspirations of the thinking class of the Russian people that properly constitutes the greatness of its coming influence and the magnitude of its ultimate destiny.[72]

Russian efforts to improve education received special praise in Philadelphia.

> Russia has for some time past been the scene of a great contest, though a peaceful one. In the march of progress upon which the nation has entered, the first step was the enfranchisement of the serfs. Naturally the next was the education of the masses. . . . All were agreed as to the necessity of education, but as to the system that should be adopted the greatest diversity of opinion prevailed. In time, however, all minor differences came to be merged into two divisions, one party contending for the classical and the other for the technical system. But the fiercer the battle waged the less chance there seemed to be of any satisfactory result. Seeing this, the Czar, assuming his right as the Father of his People, stepped in and settled the matter in favor of the classicists. . . . While to more advanced nations the advantages of the technical system preponderate, yet to the Russians in their semi-barbarism the scale

71. New York *Times*, 26 December 1871.

72. Ibid. The *Nation*, perhaps adopting Schuyler's words, presented another view of the Russian press: "The character of the daily press of St. Petersburg and Moscow is in perfect keeping with the peculiarity of the Russian public; it is extremely fickle, flighty, and inconsistent; it treats the most insignificant matters with the same zeal and emphasis as the most important subjects." "Russian Newspapers and Magazines," *Nation* 7, 158 (9 July 1868): 28.

turns in favor of the intellect [, the] developing, refining influence of the classical. One thing is quite certain, it will bring Russia into sympathy with European civilization, which is undoubtedly founded on a classical basis.[73]

The paper repeated its optimism over a year later.

Despite the rigidly despotic character of her government, Russia is moving steadily forward on the broad and shining path of popular education. The authorities are encouraging free libraries in the large cities; schools are being established throughout the length and breadth of the Muscovite domain, and the system of education will be made a compulsory one we may well rest assured. . . . Where Alexander II's praiseworthy and exceptionable system will lead time alone can tell, but that it will tend to elevate and improve the masses of the too-long benighted Russians is certain.[74]

American editors also admired Russian progress in affirmative action, in opening up opportunities for women in education and employment, noting that women served as physicians, surgeons, chemists, and telegraph operators. A female accountant even worked in the tsar's own chancellory. "What will our young medical students, who hissed lady scholars at colleges in this city [Philadelphia] two years ago, say to this? Tyrannical Russia is certainly more tolerant and progressive than themselves; and those older members of the profession, who cannot consult with physicians that recognize female practitioners, will they be content to lag behind Russia in the march of progress?"[75]

During the tour of Grand Duke Alexis, geniality mostly prevailed in the American press, but interspersed were a few complaints about all of the toadying to royalty and comments on the obvious irony of a democracy fawning over a symbol of autocracy.

If Russians prefer an absolute monarchy—and very certainly this form of government has made Russia powerful, rich and prosperous, and popular intelligence rapidly progressive—we have no right to

73. Philadelphia *Inquirer*, 5 August 1871.
74. Ibid., 18 November 1872.
75. Ibid., 13 October 1871.

object. . . . We do not revere a crown in attesting our respect for him who wears well and worthily a crown. But we do have a high respect for kings and presidents who fill their high offices wisely, justly and as statesmen should.[76]

The popularity of Alexander II in the United States was obviously shaped in some quarters by editorial scorn for the Grant administration.

In these press samplings can be found glimmers of fresh insight on Russia, but some writers recognized and bemoaned their superficial knowledge.

Now that travel, politics and M. Tourgenieff's novels are constantly bringing Russia before us are we not all struck by our ignorance of that country? Some few of us may have been to St. Petersburg and brought away curious fairings from Nijni Novgorod: some few may know the short history of the czars back to Peter the Great, who by an effect of chronological perspective looks about as distant as Charlemagne.[77]

This state of affairs could explain the harmony in the relations between the two countries.

It has often been said that Americans and Russians are natural friends. We seem such because we are so ignorant of one another. We have almost nothing in common; and having nothing in common, we have no conflicting interests; . . . Russia has a totally different language, a different religion, different traditions, different government, different destiny. . . . We can be counted on . . . to sympathize with Russia in any of her wars, at least until we get better acquainted.[78]

On the other hand, editors were sometimes carried away by Russian achievements that seemed to foster American interests. This was especially the case with the defeat of the Turks.

Russia is indeed now the great power of the East. Her future growth will, in all probability, be in Asia. When at length she wins Constantinople, as she is sure to do, she will be the intermediate power between Asia and Europe. She will connect as Byzantium did, the great chan-

76. Memphis *Daily Appeal*, 5 February 1872.
77. S. B. W., "Royal Manners of Old Russia," *Lippincott's Magazine* 14 (September 1874): 381.
78. "Our Feeling Toward England," New York *Times*, 12 May 1878.

nels of trade between Central Asia and Asia Minor and Southern and
Eastern Europe. Wherever she extends her territory, she will substitute
military order and law for barbarism and disorder.[79]

But 1878 also signaled a switch in opinion toward Russia.

Somewhat excessively absorbed in the course and outcome of the Russo-
Turkish War, American editors, especially those of the New York *Times*,
turned to a more critical appraisal of Russian social and political conditions.
The new development that was watched with interest and sometimes sympathy was generally referred to by the Turgenevian label, "nihilism." After
virtually ignoring the populist movement in Russia that culminated in the
1874 exodus of radical-liberal students "to the people," or more exactly to
the Russian peasant villages, Americans seemed to become obsessed with
the violent strain of nihilism that arose in the wake of the Russo-Turkish
War under the quasi-organized direction of the "People's Will," a terrorist,
conspiratorial wing of the broad, radical Russian populist movement. The
episode that galvanized American attention was the arrest of Vera Zasulich,
of a prominent noble family, for the shooting of the St. Petersburg chief of
police, Fedor Trepov, early in 1878. Those Americans who had read
Turgenev or who questioned law and authority could relate to her deed, to
the dramatic account of her trial, acquittal, and refuge in Western Europe.[80]

The New York *Times* revealed a new level of sophistication in its treatment of nihilism in Russia. In an editorial in early 1879, entitled "Two
Plagues in Russia," the paper blamed poor sanitary conditions and poverty
for the rapid spread of an epidemic along the Volga.

> The other plague, for which the Government is still more directly re-
> sponsible, is of a political and social order. The time has come when the
> Imperial Government, with its merciless bureaucratic machinery of re-
> pression, cannot hold in complete subjection a people who will persist
> in learning something of the principles and the advantages of freedom,
> and thereby make themselves discontented. So hopeless does the con-

79. "The New Power in the East," ibid., 18 March 1878.
80. The Russian revolutionary movement has been well covered. For this period, see
especially Franco Venturi, *Roots of Revolution: A History of the Populist and Socialist Move-
ments in Nineteenth Century Russia* (New York: Grosset and Dunlap, 1966); Adam B.
Ulam, *In the Name of the People: Prophets and Conspirators in Prerevolutionary Russia* (New
York: Viking Press, 1977); and the chapter, "The Bomb: Russian Violence," in James H.
Billington, *Fire in the Minds of Men: Origins of the Revolutionary Faith* (New York: Basic
Books, 1980).

dition of things appear that Socialism itself can scarcely find anything to work upon. . . . Destruction is the only thing that to them seems practicable, and their thoughts do not reach to the more difficult tasks of construction. They would tear down and destroy, clear the ground for a new start, and think of rebuilding only when existing institutions have been overturned in ruins. Hence, Nihilism is the form that desperate agitation takes in Russia.[81]

The writer correctly saw that the educational institutions were the core of the movement. If the university students "chafe against restraints or presume to make a protest, no matter on what ground, they are liable to be treated as dangerous conspirators against authority, and summarily graduated to the high degrees of Northern Siberia."[82]

A number of other editorial columns the same line in covering the punishment of religious dissenters, the Rostov revolt of April, Siberia as a prison, and "Russia's reign of terror against Nihilists." One writer pessimistically predicted upheaval and revolution.

Every new announcement of the fierce unrest in Russia and the frantic effort of the Government to smother it into stillness by a fresh exercise of despotic power, makes it more and more evident that the great Empire of the Czars is destined to undergo a revolution in the character and methods of its administration. . . . A violent and wide-spread political conflagration involving the destruction of the autocratic dynasty of the Romanoffs, may yet be avoided by timely concessions to the more reasonable demands of the moderate and sober among the opponents of its course, demands which they dare not formulate at present. . . . But no symptom of a disposition to concede anything whatever has yet appeared. On the contrary, the policy of repression is made more and more severe with every demonstration of discontent, and with the new restrictions upon personal freedom, the increased vigilance of exasperating espionage, the extension of arbitrary power in the hands of subordinates of the Czar, the spirit of revolt must spread in area and become more intense and desperate.[83]

81. New York *Times*, 8 February 1879.
82. Ibid.
83. "The Russian Revolution," New York *Times*, 3 May 1879. George Kennan may have been the author, since he was in New York and had recently contributed to the paper.

Another sharp analysis followed in the next issue: "Were any six ordinary men called upon to define Nihilism, five of the six would probably describe it as an association of Russian Republicans for the purpose of superseding absolutism by popular government. But this definition would be wholly wide of the truth. . . . Nihilism is the present of Socialism, without the future."[84]

A midwestern editorial encapsulated the current situation:

It is no longer Nihilism, Panslavism, nor any other "ism" or party that menaces the imperial authority, but the whole enlightened portion of the nation. It is well understood that the chief among the incentives to the Turkish war was the hope of turning into another channel the dangerous forces which imperilled the Romanoff dynasty, and thus creating a diversion at home. But the hope proved delusive. The lame and impotent conclusion of a war which cost the country so much blood and treasure has greatly increased the discontent and thrown the whole people into a state of sullen fermentation.[85]

Even the old adage about the United States and Russia being the young, progressive nations of the world was falling into disrepute.

There is one popular fallacy in regard to Russia which ought to be abandoned. We mean the theory that Russian growth and development are the natural results of the awakening energy of a youthful nation; a nation rude and uncultured, indeed, but full of that vitality and ambition which age chills and checks. The truth is that the most serious disadvantage under which Russia labors is age. In everything which constitutes political health and strength, she is not nearly so young as Germany, France, Italy or England. She is far behind her European neighbors, not because she is too young, but because she is too old. The varnish of modern civilization and the reviving influences of modern thought do not extend beyond the circle of court and aristocracy. . . . Scratch the rural Russian and you find a Tartar—not very greatly improved by Christianity. The manners, customs, ideas, social institutions and traditions are of the most primitive sort; and any

84. "Russia's Nemesis," New York *Times*, 4 May 1879.
85. "Restless Russians," citing correspondence of the Chicago *Times*, St. Louis *Missouri Republican*, 1 January 1879.

change, however beneficial, is looked upon with distrust and treated with contempt.[86]

At least some of the American press rose to the occasion to describe Russia's seething internal affairs after the Russo-Turkish War. The editorials were surprisingly insightful and prescient, obviously taking advantage of close reading and perhaps direct advice from individuals such as Schuyler and Kennan. Clearly frustrated by the Russian resort to repression, they aptly marked 1879 as a major turning point in Russian history and presaged the rejection of the dominant traditional views of Russian-American relations—well before the assassination of Alexander II or George Kennan's exposé of conditions in Siberian prisons.

Undiplomatic Views

Apart from Schuyler and to a lesser extent Wickham Hoffman, the American diplomatic and consular agents in Russia in the 1870s published little on their experiences. Even their official correspondence, whether concise or meandering, was largely centered on business. Two likely reasons were that they did not trust State Department officials and channels of communication and that their tenures were generally too short to form impressions or have many substantive Russian experiences. Some, of course, were sensitive to their positions and careful to be "diplomatic." Still, more filtered back to family, associates, and friends at home than is usually recognized. As prominent politicians or businessmen, the ministers were also asked to give talks after their return in which their views of Russia were revealed.

Occasionally, a private conversation or communication would become public, as in the case of a letter that William Jewell wrote to a friend in Rochester. Boasting that he had twenty-four servants who spoke a variety of languages, Jewell decried the ostentation and disrepute of society in the capital. " 'Russia has its own code of morals, I suppose,' continued the Governor, 'which the people live up to. From our point of view there are no morals.' He says he likes being in St. Petersburg 'some' but wouldn't like to spend his life there. 'In all the elements of strength and greatness America is so far ahead of Europe that the contrast is painful.' "[87] Jewell's successor, George Boker, a well-known poet and writer, demonstrated his potential for blunt commen-

86. "Russian Affairs," editorial, St. Louis *Missouri Republican*, 9 March 1879.
87. *Harper's Weekly*, 25 April 1874, p. 355.

tary in letters to Hamilton Fish. Perhaps sad at missing the Centennial in his hometown, Boker wrote in the summer of 1876: "I wish you had sent me to a place where the women are less ugly. My God! To look at them only gives one an organic dejection. . . . I think of importing a woman from France just to look at. The D. S. [Department of State] should furnish her out of the contingency fund."[88] Boker became quite depressed over his failure to secure another diplomatic assignment and basically retired from both politics and literary pursuits after his return to the United States.[89]

His successor, Edwin Stoughton, was virtually his opposite, being an active businessman, wealthy, and politically conscious. Stoughton brought an extended staff and set up his own diplomatic court on a sophisticated standard not displayed by an American since Henry Middleton's tenure in the 1820s. Many American friends and associates—including the Grants—sought out the Stoughton hospitality in St. Petersburg and reported on the luxurious lifestyle. One noted, "The troika owned by the Stoughtons was the best-looking one in St. Petersburg, drawn by three beautiful horses abrest [sic] and having grooms with plumes in their hats."[90] It excited notice everywhere and seemed to symbolize that the United States had come a long way since the legendary penury of John Quincy Adams. The diaries of Stoughton's wife and niece attest to the active social life that swirled about them and the number of Americans who came to partake of it.

But they also recorded signs of transition and change. On the terroristic activity of the nihilists, Louise Stoughton wrote, "It is a danger which seems spreading in every country. . . . I would rather be almost anyone I know than the Emperor of Russia."[91] The minister, perhaps predictably, defended the established order in Russia and, in an interview with a reporter during a

88. To Fish, 24 July 1876, vol. 108, Fish Papers, LC. Boker also advised the secretary of state on how to pronounce the name of a new Russian minister: "Try to say *Christ's Church* while you are coughing and sneezing together with influenza, and you have it."

89. "Having sacrificed his art at the call of the country, he felt doubly cheated, now that his public career was arrested. He felt that the years had left him void." Edward Sculley Bradley, *George Henry Boker, Poet and Patriot* (Philadelphia: University of Pennsylvania Press, 1927), p. 314. For the revival of interest in Boker's verse plays in the 1980s, see Oliver H. Evans, *George Henry Boker* (Boston: Twayne, 1984). Boker was hampered in both St. Petersburg and Washington, D.C., by the fact that his wife was a Virginian and a Democrat and made sure everyone knew it; Hoffman to Fish, 4 January 1878, vol. 120, Fish Papers, LC.

90. Mary Ames Cushman, *She Wrote It All Down* (New York: Charles Scribner's Sons, 1936), p. 66.

91. Louise Stoughton Diary, 1 September 1878, A-67, Women's Archive, Radcliffe College, Harvard University.

visit home, criticized the sympathetic attention that the American press was giving to the revolutionaries. He later published an article of his own on the subject,[92] which caused some strong press reaction:

> Minister Stoughton's opportunities for obtaining accurate information concerning the revolutionary party in Russia have been exceedingly limited. He has hardly been outside of St. Petersburg, and there his associations have been mainly with the diplomatic corps and the court circle. He has breathed only an aristocratic and imperial atmosphere. The popular air has never touched him, and could not one in his position. . . . Had he been at Versailles in 1788 he probably would have thought, from all he could see and hear, that the BOURBON dynasty was destined to last forever.[93]

This illustrates the cloud obscuring the American grasp of Russia. Many Americans who had the opportunity to reside in the country had their perceptions distorted by their political or business positions. Others, like John Foster, who replaced Stoughton as minister in the early stages of a distinguished public career, were obstinately "diplomatic." Foster recalled that "notwithstanding the climate, we found our residence in St. Petersburg very enjoyable, and we left it with the most pleasant memories of our intercourse with its people."[94] Yet he was there during the upheaval of 1881! The understated minister also expressed regret at having to cancel a planned cruise down the Volga that year because of the Garfield assassination.

Occasionally a glimmer of brilliance would surface amid the tedium of official dispatches. G. M. Hutton, sitting in as consul in early 1881, just before the assassination of the tsar, introduced a long, detailed description of the Russian economy with a very modern observation: "Russia advances on the road to progress not in the sure and steadfast way which is to be noticed in the developments of other nations, but rather by a series of spasmodic efforts and gigantic struggles succeeded in every instance by relapse and exhaustion. The present moment partakes of the nature of such a crisis."[95]

92. Edwin W. Stoughton, "Popular Fallacies About Russia," *North American Review* 283 (June 1880): 523–46.

93. "Stoughton on Nihilism," editorial, St. Louis *Missouri Republican,* 13 June 1879.

94. John Watson Foster, *Diplomatic Memoirs,* 2 vols. (Boston: Houghton Mifflin, 1909), 1:215.

95. Hutton to Hunter, 24 February 1881, DUSC, St. Petersburg, vol. 15 (roll 10, M 81), RG 59, NA.

Although obviously not a diplomat, Clara Kellogg, who spent the winter of 1880–1881 as a lead singer for the St. Petersburg opera, remembered the social tension at the end of the reign of Alexander II. In particular, she found the vigilance and coldness in the theater appalling: "Everything in Russia is numbered. There are no individuals there—only units. I used to feel as if I must have a number myself; as if I, too, must soon be absorbed into that grim Monster system, and my feeling of helplessness and oppression steadily increased."[96]

Private persons traveling or residing in Russia wrote letters home that at least in some cases had wide hand-to-hand circulation, such as those of the Berdans' governess. Unfortunately, much of this material is lost or not yet publicly available. A random piece might surface in the public arena—for example, the detailed letter of James Vincent Swann, dated 1 January 1870 from Moscow, read at that year's annual meeting of the Missouri Historical Society.[97] Occasionally, a revealing view of Russia would survive thanks to the fame of the author. For a proposed Russian translation of *Leaves of Grass*, Walt Whitman wrote:

You Russians and we Americans;—our countries so distant, so unlike at first glance—such a difference in social and political conditions, and our respective methods of moral and practical development the last hundred years;—and yet in certain features, and vastest ones, so resembling each other. . . . The idea, perennial through the ages that they both have their historic and divine missions—the fervent element of manly friendship throughout the whole people, surpassed by no other races—the grand expanse of territorial limits and boundaries—the unformed and nebulous state of many things, not yet permanently settled, but agreed on all hands to be the preparations of an infinitely greater future—the fact that both peoples have their independent and leading positions to hold, keep, and if necessary fight for, against the rest of the world—the deathless aspirations at the inmost centre of each great community, so vehement, so mysterious, so abysmic—are certainly features you Russians and we Americans possess in common.[98]

96. Clara Louise Kellogg, *Memoirs of an American Prima Donna* (New York and London: G. P. Putnam's Sons, 1913), p. 339. It is, of course, possible that her memories were shaped by subsequent events.

97. "Missouri Historical Society," St. Louis *Missouri Republican*, 4 February 1870.

98. To John Fitzgerald Lee, 20 December 1881, in Edwin Haviland Miller, ed., *Walt Whitman: The Correspondence*, vol. 3, *1876–1885* (New York: New York University Press, 1964), p. 259.

Pictorial Presentation

The American journalistic views of Russia in the 1870s differed in one significant respect from earlier times and from Russian views of America: Many were illustrated. It is safe to say that every American who could see, whether literate or not, whether living in the city or on a farm, or in a remote mining camp, knew what Grand Duke Alexis looked like and was exposed to stirring images of the Russian army on the attack in Bulgaria. Such was the wide distribution of the new illustrated weeklies, *Harper's* and *Frank Leslie's*, but pictures also appeared in many of the books, pamphlets, newspapers, and in shops for sale. Depictions of Russian royalty, statesmen, and generals revealed that they looked very much like white Americans, whereas ordinary Russians, unless they had the unusual opportunity of seeing for themselves, persisted in thinking of Americans as either red or black.

The sources of the printed sketches are not always clear and obviously owed much to the imagination of the artist. Many, however, were derived from photographs or people on the spot or were freely copied from European publications. Ordinary travelers also tried their hand at pen or pencil sketches to decorate their letters and diaries with Russian exotica. Almost every issue of *Harper's Weekly* had some sort of picture relating to Russia with an accompanying descriptive text: scenes of holidays, celebrations, military maneuvers, weddings, peasant life, buildings, Nevskii Prospect, the Kremlin, royal family and leading officials of government, etc. Ultimately, the subject matter extended to the revolutionary movement, showing arrests, executions, and prisoners in transit to Siberia. Some scenes, such as that after a nihilist bomb attack on the Winter Palace, are unique and still of value to Russian studies today.[99]

The Russian Image of America

Although media reports reached almost everybody in the United States, the Russians who were informed about Americans were a much more select and exclusive group. The people who were able to travel to the United States were the most knowledgeable, but this was a rather small number. Turgenev personified a larger group; traveling extensively or living for periods in Western Europe, they came into contact with Americans directly or indirectly through literature and art and publications that were more commonly avail-

99. *Harper's Weekly*, 3 April 1880, p. 209.

Jeremiah and Alma Curtin. From Memoirs of Jeremiah Curtin *(1940)*

able there. Americans in Russia may have had a greater impact than their tiny numbers would suggest because of their tendency to be more open to contacts with people; yet American weakness in foreign languages frequently restricted social intercourse. Exceptions, such as Eugene Schuyler, Jeremiah Curtin, and George Kennan, could make a substantial impression, not only because of their language ability but also because of the length or frequency of their stays and the extent of territory they covered. For example, Curtin and his wife spent most of four years (1872–1876) living and traveling in Russia.[100]

As noted, pictorial representations were generally absent in Russian pub-

100. A Russian told Alma Curtin "that there never was a person who was not a regular Russian who spoke as my husband did." To her mother, 27 November(?) 1872, box 19, Jeremiah Curtin Papers, MCHC.

lications,[101] but some Russians may have had access to Western materials and even to some of the original works or copies of George Catlin and August Bierstadt. Minister Jewell was authorized to dispose of Catlin portfolios left behind by Andrew Curtin,[102] and the Academy of Fine Arts conferred an honorary diploma on Bierstadt in 1870.[103]

The primary source of information about the United States remained, as in earlier periods, literature. The old standbys, James Fenimore Cooper and Washington Irving, continued to enjoy success in Russia in the 1870s. Numerous editions of "complete" (usually the most popular) works were issued, especially by publisher M. O. Wolf, who owned one of the best bookstores in St. Petersburg.[104] Hawthorne and Stowe were also in demand, judging by the number of their works that appeared in Russian. After "The Song of Hiawatha" was partially translated in 1866 and more completely in 1868, Longfellow attracted much attention in the literary journals, promoted especially by Dmitri Mikhalovskii. Edgar Allan Poe, though known and discussed by Russian literary critics before 1867, first won popularity in this period, especially with the publication of a Russian version of *Annabelle Lee* in 1878, and is considered to have had a formative influence upon Dostoevsky.[105]

The most important "new" American writer of this period for Russians was Bret Harte. A short story appeared in 1872, followed by "The Outcasts of Poker Flat" in 1873.[106] Harte immediately received favorable critical note, and his stories were published regularly in the leading literary journals. His narrative style suited the Russian preference for serialization in journals and for colorful descriptions of people and places of foreign lands; the first vol-

101. An exception was *Niva*, which began publication in 1870 but contained very little on America, mostly concentrating on Russian historical and allegorical themes.

102. Louise Catlin Kiney to Jewell, 17 March 1874, DPR, Russia, vol. 4435 (misc. received), RG 84, NA.

103. Tserev to Curtin, 15 February 1871, DPR, Russia, vol. 4503 (notes received), RG 84, NA.

104. Jeffrey Brooks, *When Russia Learned to Read: Literacy and Popular Literature, 1861–1917* (Princeton, N.J.: Princeton University Press, 1985), p. 112.

105. Details are from the valuable collection of American literature in Russian compiled by Valentina Abramovna Libman, *Amerikanskaia literatura v Russkikh perevodakh i kritike bibliografiia 1776–1975* (Moscow: Nauka, 1977). Dostoevsky wrote the preface to the first translation (by Mikhalovskii) of Poe short stories published in 1864; Aleksandr Nikoliukin, ed., *A Russian Discovery of America* (Moscow: Progress Publishers, 1986), pp. 250–52; see also Joan Delanay Grossman, *Edgar Allan Poe in Russia: A Study in Legend and Literary Influence* (Würzburg: Jal-verlag, 1973), p. 52.

106. Libman, *Amerikanskaia literatura*, pp. 77–83; Nikoliukin, *Vzaimosviazi*, pp. 289–91. For the emphasis of one important journal on Americana, see V. E. Bograd, *Zhurnal "Otechestvennye zapiski," 1868–1884: Ukazatel' soderzhaniia* (Moscow: Kniga, 1971).

ume of his stories in Russian was published in 1874.[107] Several prominent Russian writers—Nikolai Shelgunov, Grigori Danilevskii, and Nicholas Chernyshevsky, still active in exile—extolled Harte to the Russian audience. He was also well-served by translators such as Anna Engelhardt and A. N. Pleshcheev.[108]

Other American authors, for reasons that may or may not be evident, were slower to appear in Russian: Melville, Henry David Thoreau, Ralph Waldo Emerson, Whitman, and Twain. The latter's first translation (1874) into Russian was *The Gilded Age*, written with Charles Warner, and by 1877 Twain achieved star billing in a leading Russian literary journal.[109] His better-known novels, *The Prince and the Pauper* and *The Adventures of Tom Sawyer*, did not appear in Russian until 1883. Although Whitman and Emerson were known and translated in small excerpts, Russian editions of their major works were not produced until the end of the century.[110] In contrast to the 1870s, however, the rate of Russian publication of American literature in the early 1880s was significantly lower because of the change in political climate. Even so, the Russian exposure to American literature was probably greater than to British and second only to French, thanks especially to the Russian preference for Cooper over Walter Scott, for Longfellow over William Wordsworth or Robert Browning.

The America Craze in Russia

Russians, however, were not as dependent on fiction to form their perceptions of America in the 1870s. The relatively liberal censorship of the reform era had made current, descriptive material on American life available in the Russian language, primarily in journals and books and to a lesser extent in newspapers. There is also no question that within Russian liberal, radical, and even some conservative circles, the United States held a special allure in

107. Bret Harte, *Razskazy, ocherki i legendy*, ed. by A. N. Pleshcheev (St. Petersburg: A. Nakhimov, 1874).

108. Nikoliukin, *Vzaimosviazi*, pp. 290–97.

109. M. Tven, "Iumorist-amerikanets ob Amerike," trans. P. I. Veinberg, OZ 232, 6 232 (June 1877): 411–38; *Mishurnyi vek: Roman Mark Tveina i Charl'za Uarnera*, trans. M. K. Tsebrikova (St. Petersburg: A. A. Kraevskii, 1874).

110. Libman, *Amerikanskaia literatura*, pp. 244, 252. It should be noted that Russians were not as dependent on translation as Americans, since they could read American literature in the original English—or in French and German versions. Such was the case with Tolstoy's early interest in Emerson; Nikoliukin, *Vzaimosviazi*, pp. 139–40.

this period. Simply put, almost anything about America sold well in Russia. In fact, it is not unlikely that some of the best and most revealing accounts of American life in the 1870s are found in these Russian writings, little of which has been translated.[111] One ironic and important contrast is apparent: American descriptions of Russia were mainly of high society, key cities, and exotic terrain but reached a wide cross-section of the population; Russian accounts of the United States covered a wide range of American society, city and country, north and south, but were intended for a much more limited, elite audience. In other words, the common people of the United States were exposed to images of an aristocratic society and idealistic revolutionaries, while the Russian nobility read about the slums of Chicago and practical factory work.

As they appraised the United States during this period, Russians could draw on a historical tendency to look to the West. Indeed, the preceding generation of Russian "intelligentsia"—Vissarion Belinsky, Alexander Herzen, Nicholas Chernyshevsky—had already focused discussion and debate upon the United States, its checkered past and promising future. And over them still loomed Alexis de Tocqueville, whose analysis remained compelling for forty years after its publication. Another French traveler, Louis Laurent Simonin, provided a more contemporary and down-to-earth description, especially of progress in the West, that was influential in drawing Russians into the American hinterland.[112] William Hepworth Dixon, who would write about Russia for a British audience, earlier surveyed the United States; his *New America* of 1867 was translated into two Russian editions and critically evaluated in leading journals.[113]

Continuing in the tradition of Belinsky and Chernyshevsky were translator-critics Dmitri Mikhalovskii and Ernst Vatson and the populist Peter Lavrov. As in the case of their predecessors, they were not able to visit the United States themselves but demonstrated nevertheless a keen interest in that country. Mikhalovskii pioneered and promoted the works of a number

111. For a few excerpts, see Nikoliukin, *A Russian Discovery*, pp. 285–387.

112. *Le grand-ouest des États-Unis* (Paris: Hachette, 1867); this was expanded into *Le monde américain: Souvenirs de mes voyages* (Paris: Hachette, 1876) and other editions. An English translation of the former is *The Rocky Mountain West in 1867*, trans. and annotated by Wilson O. Clough (Lincoln: University of Nebraska Press, 1966). Excerpts were published in Russian—for example, "Kolonizatsiia v Amerike," *Nedelia* 38 (1875): 1235–42.

113. For Dixon's influence, see Robert V. Allen, *Russia Looks at America: The View to 1917* (Washington, D.C.: Library of Congress, 1988), pp. 37–40.

of American authors, but in the 1860s and 1870s he focused on translations of Longfellow and Harte. Most of these were initially published in *Otechestvennyia Zapiski* (Fatherland notes), beginning with "The Song of Hiawatha" in 1848.[114] He turned to the poems of Harte in 1853 and his first translation of a short story by that writer appeared in 1874.[115] In his commentaries Mikhalovskii used a general knowledge of the United States to draw the reader in.

Vatson, the thoroughly Russianized son of a Scottish physician who practiced in Russia, graduated from the University of Moscow and began his career as an understudy and assistant to Chernyshevsky on *Sovremennik* (Contemporary). He quickly became a leading political correspondent for the journal in the 1860s, during its last years. One of his best-known contributions was a historical essay on Abraham Lincoln, written on the occasion of his assassination in 1865.[116] He continued to reflect on international affairs for a number of journals and newspapers through the 1880s, providing much commentary on the United States.

While rivaling Chernyshevsky and Herzen as a populist thinker, Peter Lavrov demonstrated a particular fascination for the United States in articles he wrote from provincial exile and from Western Europe for *Otechestvennyia Zapiski*. Writing on a popular subject also allowed him to secure funds to escape abroad, where he founded *Vpered* (Forward), the foremost radical journal of the period, in Zurich, later moving it to London. In many ways he was the successor to Herzen for the emigré community and as a vocal dissenter. His *Historical Letters*, published in 1870, competes with Herzen's *My Past and Thoughts* in its influence on Russian progressive thought.[117]

Lavrov's most important works on the United States are "North American Sectarianism" and "Civilization and Wild Tribes," which featured historical description (from the Puritans to the Mormons, and from initial settlement to frontier warfare) and critical commentary on these particular

114. "Pesnia o Gaiavate," OZ 177, 5 (May 1868): 1–16; 177, 6 (June 1868): 263–72. Mikhalovskii's version was assessed and critiqued by the next Russian translator, Ivan Bunin; Nikoliukin, *A Russian Discovery*, pp. 427–29.

115. OZ 213, 3 (March 1873): 79–82; 217, 12 (December 1874): 385–408.

116. Ernst K. Vatson, *Etiudy i ocherki po obshchestvennym voprosam (s portretom i biografiei avtora)* (St. Petersburg: Skorokhodov, 1892), pp. v, 224–44.

117. For an excellent analysis of Lavrov's place in Russian history and philosophy, see James Scanlan's introduction, "Peter Lavrov: An Intellectual Biography," in Peter Lavrov, *Historical Letters* (Berkeley and Los Angeles: University of California Press, 1967), pp. 1–65. See also Philip Pomper, *Peter Lavrov and the Russian Revolutionary Movement* (Chicago and London: University of Chicago Press, 1972).

traits of the New World.[118] His perspective on the United States is illustrated by an often-quoted passage from *Vpered* of 1876, about the flight of people "to America, which has swallowed up without trace so much fresh force, so many noble intents in the creation of that republic of humbug, that kingdom of the dollar, which we see there today."[119] Because of his reputation as a leading political thinker, Lavrov's comments on life in the United States must have had wide circulation and a large impact.

Although perhaps less influential than Lavrov, a number of other well-known Russian radicals of this period demonstrated an interest in the United States. They include Peter Tkachev, who concentrated his effort on American prisons; Nikolai Shelgunov, who wrote more impressionistically on American history; and Mariia Tsebrikova, who furnished a women's viewpoint in her portraits of early American leaders.[120] Perhaps most important of all was Lev Mechnikov, given his colorful career as a volunteer with Garibaldi, his friendship with both Herzen and Bakunin, and his long editorial and journalistic pursuits at home and abroad. His writings on the United States focused on its agriculture and economy.[121]

Journals such as *Otechestvennyia Zapiski*, *Delo* (Affair), *Slovo* (Word), and the popular and the progressive *Nedelia* (Week) maintained a regular and thorough coverage of American political, economic, and social affairs until 1881. Their subjects included Johnson's impeachment, protectionism, the Ku Klux Klan, Mormons, railroad monopolies, the passage of the Fifteenth Amendment, the Pomeroy scandal in Kansas, agricultural issues, colonization and settlement, Indian affairs, growth of cities, Reconstruction, schools

118. "Severo-Amerikanskoe sektatorstvo," OZ 177, 4 (April 1868): 403–70; and "Tsivilizatsiia i dikie plemena," OZ 188, 5 (May 1869): 107–69.

119. Nikoliukin, *A Russian Discovery*, p. 338. On the recent civil conflict in the United States, Lavrov blamed the Southern minority for desregarding the "best" constitution, but argued that the North's military suppression could only be justified if it improved the lot of the black majority. For a detailed analysis, see David Hecht, *Russian Radicals Look to America, 1825–1894* (Cambridge: Harvard University Press, 1947), pp. 142–95.

120. Tkachev, "Amerikanskie tiur'my," *Delo* 3, 2 (1867): 137–50; Shelgunov, "Ocherki iz istorii severoamerikanskogo soiuza," *Delo* 11, 1 (1867): 95–137; 12, 1 (1867): 60–99; Tsebrikova, *Amerikanka XVIII veka* (St. Petersburg: Sushchinskii, 1871) and *Istoricheskie razskazy* (St. Petersburg: Vospitanie i obuchenie, 1881).

121. "Emigratsiia v Ameriku," *Delo* 10, 2 (1876): 88–101; "Khlebnyi vopros v Amerike i Evrope," *Delo* 5, 1 (1880): 49–87; 6, 1 (1880): 133–75; "Protektsionizm v Amerike," *Delo* 7, 1 (1880): 299–335; 8, 1 (1880): 86–117. His brother was the noted bacteriologist Il'ia Mechnikov. For an examination of Lev Mechnikov's revolutionary life, see Martin A. Miller, *The Russian Revolutionary Emigrés, 1825–1870* (Baltimore and London: Johns Hopkins University Press, 1986), pp. 153–55, 193–95.

and education, the grand duke's visit, the "women's question," the Centennial, and the temperance movement. Most are written anonymously, though the overall quality and contemporary feel of the material seems to suggest Vatson or Lavrov, one or more of the Russian visitors to the United States, or Western press translations. The volume and persistence of attention to the United States certainly indicates readership demand.[122]

Russians See America

The dominant and most interesting of the Russian publications about the United States were written by people with firsthand experience, though it must be emphasized that these Russian visitors were from the rather small and elite educated portion of the society. Many were also dissidents, unhappy with the course of reforms in Russia but free to leave and (usually) to return. Some were disillusioned by European civilization in general and hoped to find a better one in the New World.

One of the first to publish his impressions was Ivan Ivaniukov, who graphically described his visit to Cambridge, Massachusetts, in 1867. He was surprised by the scramble for seats on the train and struck by the contrast of the openness and quiet of the countryside with the noise and bustle of New York City. Ivaniukov noted that in the university town, as in New York, apple pie was the national dish, but other menu items were different—beans and cod predominating. He was impressed by neat gardens, good streets, and Harvard, where students paid $100 tuition and professors received $2,000 a year. Of the 500 students, Ivaniukov informed the Russian readers, two were Negroes; he also reported the political divisions among the professors, namely twenty-two Republicans and twenty Democrats.[123] His broader survey also offered a sound explanation of the roles of county, city, state, and federal governments.

Pavel Ogorodnikov was a young army officer who got into trouble for reading populist literature in 1862, escaped to Western Europe, and then

122. The University of Illinois at Champagne-Urbana has one of the best collections of serials for this period, mostly in microform. Besides *Nedelia*, *Delo*, and *Otechestvennyia Zapiski*, *Moskovskiia Vedomosti*, *Russkoe Bogatstvo*, *Morskoi Sbornik*, *Golos*, *Istoricheskii Vestnik*, and *Vestnik Evropy* were surveyed for this period. For a thorough examination of *Delo* and *Slovo*, see Irina Mal'kova, "Istoriia i politika SShA na stranitsakh russkikh demokraticheskikh zhurnalov *Delo* i *Slovo*," in *Amerikanskii Ezhegodnik 1971* (Moscow: Nauka, 1971), pp. 273–94.

123. "Iz Ameriki, pis'mo pervoe," OZ 179, 8 (August 1868): 180–86.

made his way to America in 1869. He saw and reported the contemporary scene comprehensively but with a critical eye, capturing the flavor of the underside of American cities—New York, Chicago, and San Francisco—where he lived in small Russian communities. His pictures of the beer hall, bordello, and soda shop do not gloss over the corrupt doctors taking kickbacks from pharmacies, the sordid prostitution, immigrant poverty, tenements, and slums.[124] Crossing the country by train, apparently the first Russian to traverse the continent, Ogorodnikov related in detail what he saw from the windows and at stopovers, digressing into accounts of railroad development and Indian history. He was impressed with the hotels, farms, and the cheerfulness and kindness of the people he met.[125]

Yet Ogorodnikov's emphasis was on the harshness of immigrant life. In Chicago he met a starving student of the University of St. Petersburg who was too proud to beg or accept a handout from his landlord. He had worked on a farm in New York and at a sawmill in Michigan but found the labor too demanding. The writer quoted the student's reaction to American society: "In Russia a middle-grade schoolboy has more learning than is possessed here by some rich man who may become a mayor, a judge or even the president. He knows how to read and write, but that is all, and he is vulgar and without any idea of respect for others or of what constitutes reasonable freedom!"[126] Now the young man was destitute, extremely unhappy, and without the means to return to Russia. Ogorodnikov offered to carry an appeal for him to the consul general in New York. One important repercussion of this episode in Ogorodnikov's description of his travels is that Fedor Dostoevsky relied heavily on it for a dark portrait of America through the eyes of the character Shatov in *The Possessed*.[127]

Ogorodnikov actually saw the brighter side of the equation: fraud and corruption balanced by self-government; freedom of speech only partly diverted into religious frenzies; excessive wealth promoting economic progress;

124. *V Strane svobody*, 2 vols., 2d ed. (St. Petersburg: Rossiiskoi bib., 1882), 1:64–109. Ogorodnikov's travel account was first serialized in the journal *Zaria* in 1870 and then published in book form as *Ot N'iu Iorka do San' Frantsisko i obratno v Rossiiu* (St. Petersburg: Kolesov and Mikhin, 1872).

125. *V Strane svobody* 1:114–80.

126. Nikoliukin, *A Russian Discovery*, p. 295. Ogorodnikov's Chicago stay is available in this translation (pp. 288–99). Unfortunately, Nikoliukin's valuable contribution is limited by his choice of mostly negative selections; Ivaniukov, Linden, and Tsimmerman, for example, are omitted.

127. Hans Rogger, "America in the Russian Mind—or Russian Discoveries of America," *Pacific Historical Review* 47, 1 (February 1978): 38–40.

a sense of self-esteem preserved through hardship and servile labor; discrimination amid rising opportunities for immigrants, women, and blacks. His may have been a perplexing tapestry for Russians to unravel, but it no doubt held their interest.

In historical perspective, perhaps the most compelling part of Ogorodnikov's detailed narrative is his description of the new Russian immigrants in San Francisco and their problems. Especially good are his character sketches of Nikolai Goncharenko (Honcharenko), the radical, Pan-Slavist Ukrainian Cossack who published a small newspaper; Botelman, who had successfully moved his cigarette factory from Sitka to San Francisco; and other former imperial subjects displaced by the sale of Alaska. According to the writer, they spent most of their time reminiscing about the good old days in Alaska, complaining about the injustices of the sale (such as a woman who got rich selling the company's vodka), disparaging the United States and especially the corruption in San Francisco, and squabbling among themselves. Also criticized were the practices of the Russian America Company and Hutchinson, Kohl, and Company, which they believed made $3 million in the first two to three years through unscrupulous operations, and the alleged financial scams of the last Russian governor, Maksutov.[128]

Another account of San Francisco at this time (1870) is by a naval officer who was familiar with the region from earlier ship calls. He recited the history of Nikolai Rezanov's early visit, the establishment of Fort Ross, and the area's rapid development after 1849. The bustling city is pictured in all its diversity—many nationalities, workers and miners, hoodlums and loafers. A Russian, "Count N.," goes to a hotel just to ride the elevator; popular minstrel shows are described with enthusiasm.[129] His is a less one-sided and more attractive depiction of a changing California than Ogorodnikov's.

In 1869–1870, Eduard Tsimmerman (Zimmerman) retraced a journey he had made twelve years earlier to underscore the rapidity of change and progress in the United States. In his flattering survey, he focused on agricultural development on the Great Plains, and he reviewed in detail the Homestead Act and its effects. Returning to Omaha, Columbus, and Grand Island, Nebraska, he convincingly portrayed the growth of frontier towns, local government, agriculture, and an excellent transportation system. In Columbus he found that a man whom he had known as a menial laborer in 1857 had

---

128. *V Strane svobody* 1:251–308, 2:3–22.

129. Lt. Linden, "Zametki o Kalifornii i Sandvichevykh ostrovakh," *Morskoi Sbornik* 118, 1 (January 1872): 75–95.

become a wealthy farmer with a two-story house.[130] As a missionary of liberalism, Tsimmerman stressed the importance of personal freedom and initiative for "the extraordinary significance of the American, free system of settlement."[131] He highlighted the role of government in fostering agricultural expansion by railroad land grants and the Homestead Act.

Tsimmerman returned to this theme a few years later in a strongly worded plea for Russia to follow the American example, arguing (apparently against the dominant view) that much of its agrarian program could apply to Russia. He even insisted that Russia had advantages over America— better soil and proximity to Western European markets. Citing and comparing the Mennonite experience in south Russia with the settlement of the Great Plains, Tsimmerman showed how these same Mennonites and others had transformed "Bleeding Kansas" into a flourishing region. A prosperous agriculture could be achieved in Russia by using the existing communal base and encouraging settlement in new territories in the Amur region and south Russia, by building an integrated transportation system, and by promoting the development of regional market towns. Russia, he concluded, must move along the American path of agricultural progress.[132]

As part of his self-appointed pedagogic mission, Tsimmerman undertook one of the first objective efforts at outlining the history of the United States as an adjunct to publicity about the Centennial Exposition in Philadelphia.[133] Thus his writings were noteworthy attempts at public education, for which comparable equivalents are rare among American musings about Russia, and they received wide circulation during the height of interest in Americana.

130. Eduard R. Tsimmerman, "Votchinnyi zakon v Amerike i nashi stepi," *OZ* 234, 9 (September 1877): 148–49; see also his *Puteshestvie po Amerike v 1869–1870 g.* (Moscow: Grachev, 1871). Several sources, including Dmitri Mendeleev, attested to Tsimmerman's impact on the Russian reading public; Nikoliukin, *A Russian Discovery*, p. 344.

131. "Osnovye novykh shtatov v Amerike," *OZ* 199, 12 (December 1871): 374. This refrain is repeated by others at this time, for example, Mikhail Butin, *Pis'ma iz Ameriki* (St. Petersburg: Demakov, 1872).

132. "Votchinnyi zakon v Amerike i nashi stepi," 109–66. Tsimmerman reportedly earned 30,000 rubles from his writings on America; New York *Sun* interview with Father Bjerring, as quoted in "Russians in the United States," St. Louis *Missouri Republican,* 9 October 1879.

133. Tsimmerman, "Stoletnaia godovshchina v S. Amerike: Ocherki iz istorii Soedinennykh shtatov," *OZ* 225, 4 (May 1876): 667–89; 226, 6 (June 1876): 421–52; 228, 9, (September 1876): 91–120; 228, 10, (October 1876): 549–66; 229, 12, (December 1876): 349–84.

The New York Russian Circle

Paralleling Ogorodnikov's emphasis on urban life but concentrating on New York and the Russian exile community are the fascinating "letters" of Nikolai Slavinskii, serialized in *Otechestvennyia Zapiski* in 1872 and published as a separate book the next year.[134] A nobleman from south Russia, Slavinskii had come to America in 1869 to visit his sister, Mary Frey, who had accompanied her husband in a quest for free communal experimentation.[135] Colorful and detailed, his writings cover virtually all aspects of New York City life from the Bowery to Williamsburg to Thompson Square, where Russians congregated, and is one of the most intimate portrayals extant of the emerging metropolis. He digressed at length on a number of subjects: the American press, with particular focus on the *National Police Gazette* and *Harper's Weekly*; markets and food distribution, including a vivid description of Fulton Market; the new Chinatown; the medical profession and especially the role of women in it; police and crime; arson and the fire departments; cheap and efficient transportation systems; political rallies and parades (such as St. Patrick's Day); and minstrel halls, theaters, and concerts. He deplored the general ignorance about Russia that he encountered but was surprised by a reasonably accurate portrayal of Peter the Great in a new play, *The Tsarina*, performed at a theater in Brooklyn.[136]

Slavinskii seemed to be particularly interested in popular culture, visiting the San Francisco minstrel and other music halls, the Cooper Union lectures, the Beethoven Jubilee at the American Institute Coliseum with 3,000 singers and an audience of 13,000, and the skating rinks and beer gardens. He noted that California wines were just entering the market, though whisky, ale, and beer were still dominant; described ice cream sodas (like ones in Odessa but better); and recorded that "Shoo-Fly, Don't Bother Me" was the most popular song of 1870. He was amazed by the number of female employees, the monopoly of domestic housework by African-Americans and Irish immigrants, the bustle and intensity of all work, insurance policies being sold on trains, the rapid ups and downs of personal fortunes, and the high level of crime and violence.

Like most Russians, Slavinskii was intrigued by American Indians and devoted two "letters" to the subject. He considered that their individual treat-

134. *Pis'ma ob Amerike i Russkikh pereselentsakh* (St. Petersburg: P. P. Merkulev, 1873).
135. Slavinskii was apparently assisted by his brother-in-law, William Frey, who later claimed authorship of some of the letters; *Progressive Communist* 1, 4 (April 1875).
136. OZ 199, 1 (January 1872): 117–18.

ment was better than he had expected to find but bemoaned their collective, violent exploitation. Of special interest is his narrative of the visit that an Indian delegation led by Chief Red Cloud made to New York. He attended a theater presentation for the party and thought that the emphasis on military power in the performance was purposely to overawe the Indians. But at Red Cloud's Cooper Union appearance, Slavinskii was impressed with the chief's cool dignity and his quiet but dramatic retelling of the Fetterman massacre of 1866.[137]

Slavinskii's main contributions, especially for his Russian audience, were his stories of the Russian community in New York, which numbered thirty or more. Centered around "Dr. M." from south Russia (perhaps a Dr. Moritz mentioned by Ogorodnikov) who had served with Garibaldi, the "circle" was attempting to fill a void by serving as an immigrant aid society for the increasing number of visiting Russians. Dues were collected from those who could pay to help Russians upon arrival or in dire need. Although encouraged by the support of consul general Osten-Saken and by the building of a new Russian Orthodox church under Father Bjerring in 1870, the members still quarreled among themselves, primarily because they represented a varied and contentious lot of unhappy political misfits, as Slavinskii illustrated. The portraits reveal an interesting spectrum of both Russian and American life. While noting that most of the Russians in New York used pseudonyms, he generally referred to them by initial.

For example, "Z." went into business as an agent of a St. Petersburg firm, selling caviar, malachite, and papirosi (Russian cigarettes) but was disappointed that the malachite did not sell. He then went west to enter the grocery business in Omaha but was called home by the death of his father.[138] Another, Lev Bel'skii, had been a postmaster at Kronstadt, and opened a "private letter office" in New York that specialized in "erotic" mail—actually a lonely hearts club, with a newsletter distribution of 10,000 copies—but he got into trouble for opening mail and taking out money. After being attacked and wounded by one of his customers, he recuperated in Bellevue, married a wealthy woman, took her money, and returned to Russia, where he posed as an American and lectured on the country.[139]

Others found odd jobs: seasonal work in Pennsylvania forests, cleaning streets, giving French and Russian lessons, selling fireworks on the Fourth of

137. OZ 205, 5 (May 1872): 250–58.
138. *Pis'ma ob Amerike*, pp. 198–99, 223.
139. Ibid., pp. 226–28. Slavinskii cites the *National Police Gazette* as a source of information.

July, miscellaneous printing that led in one case to arrest for counterfeiting. Many became dejected and disappointed about life in the United States and returned home. Slavinskii considered that the time spent in America had not been wasted but had been a "practical school." Not only could the community provide only limited help, but little sympathy could be expected from Americans who considered poverty a sign of laziness. The generally higher-class Russian immigrants were frustrated by an inability to make use of their "intellectual talents" in the United States.[140]

Slavinskii reached the level of comic opera in describing the arrival on the New York scene in late 1869 of the Russian choral group led by Dmitri Agrenev-Slavianskii and the havoc it produced in the Russian community.[141] The defection of the two leading female singers, who eloped with local residents, caused sharp divisions within the New York enclave, threats and costly lawsuits, and decisions to return home.[142] Slavinskii must have been relieved to leave New York in the spring to visit the Missouri communal society where his sister and brother-in-law had temporarily settled.

A Russian American Commune

Many of the Russians[143] who came to the United States after the American Civil War were followers of some aspect of the broad Russian dissent movement known as *narodnichestvo*, or populism. Influenced by Western social thinkers, especially Charles Fourier, and Russians such as Herzen and

140. *Pis'ma ob Amerike*, p. 225.

141. See chap. 1. A brief excerpt from Slavinskii's description of the Agrenev troupe performances has been translated in Nikoliukin, *A Russian Discovery*, pp. 301–4. Agrenev-Slavianskii seemed very surprised by the business-mindedness of the United States: "The whole life of America is money. . . . Workers and professors laboring over new discoveries think not so much about their use, about what they will do for mankind, but about what can be gained from them." As quoted from letter of 22 February 1870 in *Golos*, in A. Khitrovo, *Dmitrii Aleksandrovich Slavianskii i ego deiatel'nost'* (Tver: F. S. Murav'ev, 1887), p. 30.

142. Slavinskii, *Pis'ma ob Amerike*, pp. 218–25. The Russian legation in Washington, D.C., tried to keep track of these Russian communities in America—for its own particular reasons—but usually found they were divided within and without and relatively harmless. For example, Offenberg to Westermann, 31 December 1873/12 January 1874, f. 133, op. 470, d. 144, AVPR.

143. Although they generally referred to themselves as "Russians," a large number were from south Russia and were probably Ukrainian or of German, Jewish, or mixed backgrounds. In New York, they concentrated around Thompson Square, which is still a predominantly Slavic neighborhood in the East Village.

Chernyshevsky, they idealized the communal features of the Russian peasant village, the *mir*. Given the restrictions on freedom of action and publication in Russia, many left Russia for European exile, and some naturally looked to the United States as a land of opportunity for social experimentation.

The best example is Vladimir Geins (Heinz) of a Russian-German noble family with a tradition of military service. Following the family pattern, he attended a cavalry officer's school but then became a teacher of higher mathematics and a coastal surveyor in the army. Exposed to the ideas of both Russian and Western reformers, by 1862 he was a budding nihilist. He became discouraged, however, by its turn toward violence and, after reading excerpts of Dixon's *New America*, decided in 1868 to seek a new environment across the Atlantic.[144] Believing firmly in careful preparation, the thirty-year-old Geins married the teenage Mariia Slavinskaia shortly before departing. He also changed his name to conform to his new quest for freedom—Wilhelm Frei, which would soon be Americanized. William and Mary Frey entered the country in April 1868 at Jersey City, where they eked out an existence for a few months, then joined another Russian exile family (pseudonym Brooks) in an attempt to find better work in St. Louis. By the summer of 1869 the Freys, now with a baby daughter, were back east in a Russian furniture cooperative and boarding house in the Williamsburg section of Brooklyn.[145] Meanwhile, William contributed to Russia's understanding of the United States with a long, sophisticated analysis of the election of 1868.[146]

Frey was also making a systematic study of utopian societies in the country that naturally led him to the Oneida community, though he was discouraged from joining by a Russian resident there, Ivan Debogorii-Mokrievich. He came in contact with a small journal, *Communist*, published by Alexander Longley in Missouri, and after an extended correspondence, the Freys set off to join Longley's new settlement, the Reunion community,

144. Avrahm Yarmolinsky, *A Russian's American Dream: A Memoir on William Frey* (Lawrence: University Press of Kansas, 1965), pp. 1–8. This valuable source is based on the extensive diaries and letters of the Freys in the NYPL.

145. Yarmolinsky, *A Russian's American Dream*, pp. 11–13. Slavinskii most likely visited the Freys before they left New York and perhaps picked up information from them for his own description of America; OZ 299, 1 (January 1872): 104–5.

146. V. K. Geins, "Prezidentskaia kampaniia v Amerike," OZ 184, 2 (February 1869): 415–53. He was probably also the "W. F.," author of an article on the "woman question," "Zhenskii vopros v Amerike," OZ 302, 4 (April 1872): 503–38, which contained a particular reference to Kansas, where he was living at the time.

*William and Mary Frey, ca. 1880. From Avrahm
Yarmolinsky,* A Russian's American Dream
(1965)

in southwest Missouri in early 1870.[147] In January 1871, a dispute among its
twenty-five members prompted the Freys and Stephen Briggs and his wife to
split off. They founded their own utopian society by homesteading recently
confiscated Osage Indian lands near Cedar Vale in southern Kansas.[148]

With heroic effort and despite unusual practices for that period, such as
vegetarianism and hydropathy, the Freys persisted for eight difficult years.
In its early stage Frey's "Progressive community" was joined by the Brookses

147. Longley gave directions and asked Frey to bring money; Longley to Frey, 2 and
25 December 1869, box 1, files 1 and 3, Frey Papers, NYPL. The Missouri commune is
described by Slavinskii, *Pis'ma ob Amerike*, pp. 265–69.
148. Briggs and Frey each staked homesteads, a total of 320 acres, on rough land
near the Oklahoma (Indian Territory) border and erected a "walnut shanty." Frey to
Longley, 19 April 1871, box 1, file 3, Frey Papers, NYPL.

and eccentric J. G. Truman, who described himself as "a crank, a spiritualist and a nudist." Together they survived on rather crude attempts at farming, by working for neighbors, and on irregular remittances from Frey's family in Russia. William corresponded extensively with members of other communistic groups in the United States, such as Oneida, Icaria, the Amanas, Shakers, and others. In a typical early response, T. G. Garner of Saranas, Michigan, sought more information on railheads and markets, "for communists have to deal largely in fruits and vegetables so that they can get the greatest amount from the smallest land."[149] Frey also wrote about his personal philosophy in Lavrov's *Vpered* in 1874.

Frey's commune reached its zenith in 1875, after William had acquired newsprint and was editing a monthly newsletter called the *Progressive Communist*.[150] In the first issue, he cited John Stuart Mill and Pierre-Joseph Proudhon in describing his objective: "Our ideal is a net of communities, scattered throughout the world. They may unite among themselves for the sake of convenience in work; retaining always the supremacy in the arrangement of their internal life, without interference from outsiders. In short, communism must not be stationery [sic], but progressive and subject to the same innumerable differentiations as everything else."[151] Frey also acknowledged the influence of Lavrov and *Vpered* and explained his reason for coming to the United States:

> The laws of this country protect the freedom of speech and the freedom of action more than anywhere else. The Atlantic keeps it safe from those regularly organized banditti, which are commonly called European governments; and this government, having no pretext to keep a large army, is comparatively weak and cannot display much despotism against us. Besides, the disposition of the masses here is quite different from that in Europe.[152]

149. To Frey, 27 January 1872, box 1, file 2, ibid.

150. The journal had a very small circulation; copies are preserved in the Frey Papers, NYPL, and on microfilm at the Kansas Historical Research Center in Topeka. Frey learned typesetting and printed the journal himself on the presses of the newspaper in the nearby town of Elk Falls, which gave him some free publicity: "There seems to be a settlement of Communists a few miles east of Cedarvale in this county, and the *Progressive Communist* is published monthly at 50 cents per year and is devoted to the interests of the Commune." "The Progressive Communist," Elk Falls *Howard County Ledger,* 14 January 1875.

151. "What 'Progressive' Means," *Progressive Communist* 1, 1 (1 January 1875).

152. Frey, "A Letter About Communism," ibid. 1, 3 (March 1875).

By this time the small, poor Kansas commune was well-known in both the United States and Russia and attracted a number of visitors and temporary members.[153] Among the Russians were Vladimir Dobroliubov, brother of the famous critic associated with Chernyshevsky; the flamboyant Vladimir Muromtsev; the sculptor Fedor Kamenskii; the later well-known socialist revolutionary Nikolai Chaikovskii; Aleksandr Malikov, a Christian pacifist; Grigori Machtet, a literary-minded Ukrainian; and others who hid their identities under such aliases as "Right" and "Small." Although a similar variety of Americans drifted in and out, the total number of residents probably never exceeded fifteen at one time, including children.

The community favored shared duties, including the upbringing of children, vegetarianism, women's and children's equality, monogamy with easy divorce, environmental preservation, and organized self-criticism; members were nonetheless assigned, or took, definite jurisdictional responsibilities (Frey was in charge of cooking, Briggs fruit and vegetable raising). One practical problem the erstwhile farmers had was digging a well that was not tainted by oil.[154] From the beginning tensions erupted because of the varied personalities and philosophical viewpoints; some of the Americans, for example, were adherents of spiritualism. Mary Frey, to the consternation of her husband, had affairs with Machtet and Muromstev (with whom she had another child) and left the commune for a while. She returned to accompany her husband to London but eventually settled in New York.

In 1875, William Frey reorganized the Russian members into the "Investigating community" which used the same common facilities but slept in a separate building.[155] At that time Frey had real rivals in Chaikovskii and Malikov, and they argued intensely over Frey's domination of the community, vegetarianism, and religion. Malikov, who subsequently became a disciple of

153. It was described by New York publisher Charles Nordhoff in *The Communistic Societies of the United States* (New York: Harper and Bros., 1875) and by Grigori Machtet, "Russkaia sem'ia v Kanzase," *Nedelia* 31 (1875). An excellent translation of the latter is in Olga Peters Hasty and Susanne Fusso, eds. and trans., *America Through Russian Eyes, 1874–1926* (New Haven, Conn., and London: Yale University Press, 1988), pp. 60–76.

154. "The 'Progressive Communists' has 'swarmed,' and a new society is called the 'Investigating Community.'" Elk Falls *Howard County Ledger*, 5 August 1875. See also *Progressive Communist* 1, 7 (July 1875), which includes a separate page, "The Social Investigator," and Hecht, pp. 206–10.

155. A. Faresov, "Odin iz 'Semidesiatnikov': Ocherk," *Vestnik Evropy* 39, 9 (September 1904): 225–60. This article is a tribute to Malikov, based mostly on the author's interview with Malikov about his Kansas experiences shortly before the latter's death in 1904.

Leo Tolstoy's, was especially critical in later life of his uncomfortable (physical and mental) Kansas experience.[156]

Frey continued to write about the United States for the Russian audience—and to make money to support his impoverished community.[157] He and Briggs somehow remained steadfast partners until the farm and its livestock and equipment were sold in the fall of 1879;[158] their collection of books had already been given to the Cedar Vale Public Library.[159] Briggs settled in Florida, while Frey moved on for a few years to another, much larger "Russian-Jewish" experimental farm, the New Odessa community in Oregon.[160] Then, turning from practicing communism to philosophical positivism, Frey moved to London, from where he carried on an extensive correspondence with Tolstoy and even visited the writer at Yasnaya Polyana in 1886 on his one return trip to Russia. Frey died in London in 1889 and would have been disappointed to know that his beloved daughter, Bella, rebelled against social utopianism and became an ardent Roman Catholic.[161]

Russians and the American West

For the majority of Russians attracted to the Frey settlement, the American frontier was simply a place to test utopian socialist ideas. For one of the temporary members of Frey's commune, however, the American prairie became more than

156. The property was later the site of one of the richest oil wells in the region. "Hit Oil in Kansas," Topeka *State Journal*, 17 May 1919, based on an interview with Nikolai Chaikovskii in London, in Immigration Clippings, vol. 1, KSHS.

157. For examples, V. K. Geins, "Prezidentskaia kampaniia v Amerike: Poiavlenie tret'ei partii," OZ 230, 2 (February 1877): 415–53; "Rastrata obshchestvennykh zemel' amerikanskim kongressom," OZ 233, 5 (May 1877): 81–97.

158. "Progressive Community is about dissolved. They have sold out, and are in a squabble among themselves, and there is no telling how it will end." Chautauqua *Journal*, 18 September 1879.

159. Chautauqua County *Times*, 10 and 31 January 1879. The books included those of Hume, Macauley, Gibbons, Rollins, Josephus, Abbott, Mill, and Spencer. Assessing the contribution as worth thirty dollars, the paper commented (31 January): "Would that some of our citizens had the public spirit and benevolence of the Russian Community. There is no way of promoting the morality and intelligence of a community equal to the circulation of good, healthy reading matter among its members."

160. Briggs (Jacksonville) to Frey, 11 February 1881, box 2, file 1, Frey Papers, NYPL. The letter was mainly about taxes still owed in Kansas. For more on the Oregon Russian commune, see Helen Blumenthal, "Odessa Colony," Master's thesis, Portland State University, 1967.

161. Faresov, "Odin iz 'Semidesiatnikov,'" 253–54; V. Frei, *Pis'ma V. Freia k L. N. Tolstolu* (Geneva: M. Elpidine, 1887).

Grigori Machtet. From Machtet, Sobranie Sochineniia
(1902)

a backdrop for social experimentation. Grigori Machtet came from western Ukraine to drink from the fountain of liberal-radical ideas in the late 1860s as part of a Kievan radical circle. He and several other "Kievans" came under the influence of Vladimir Debogorii-Mokrievich and his brother and cousin. Like Frey and others, they viewed America as the land of freedom to practice their socialist ideals. They even called themselves "Amerikantsy," the Americans, and began to save money to go there.[162] In the meantime and despite his radical record, Machtet managed to obtain a teaching position near his home.

According to Debogorii-Mokrievich, the particular catalyst for the departure of three of the group—Machtet, Ivan Rechitskii, and Aleksandr Roman'ko-Romanovskii—for the United States was the celebrated Nechaev affair of the winter of 1869–1870. Sergei Nechaev was a young Russian radical who believed that the way to forge a bond among revolutionaries was to carry out the collective murder of a member of his own terrorist group. Publicity about this event naturally created considerable notoriety and controversy

162. Vladimir Debogorii-Mokrievich, *Vospominaniia* (Paris: J. Allemane, 1894), pp. 10–11.

within and outside the radical circles, especially since it was soon immortalized by Dostoevsky in *The Possessed*, serialized in *Russkaia Vedomosti* in 1871. The reaction of the Kievan "Americans" was that the corrupted atmosphere in Russia had caused this demoralization, and they had to escape from it.[163]

The twenty-year-old Machtet, who anglicized his name to George Mansted, arrived with his friends in New York in the summer of 1872, and after a few grim weeks within the Russian circle there, they headed westward, like the Freys, to the Kansas prairie. Although obviously aware of the commune there, the Mansted party, joined by Ivan Linev, struck out on their own, at first earning their way by working at a tree nursery near Troy in the northeastern corner of the state. When the planting of prickly Osage orange hedgerows ceased for the winter, the four Russians were lent a wagon and team of horses and given the task of clearing some land belonging to a Russian-born nurseryman about a hundred miles west, near Marysville.[164] Their eventual goal was to found their own communal farm, but on the journey a fateful accident occurred.

About halfway the travelers stopped for dinner by a stream near Seneca. While resting, Rechitskii pulled out an old pistol that he had recently acquired and attempted to shoot a bird. In the process of investigating why it failed to fire, it went off and mortally wounded Alexander Room (Roman'ko-Romanovskii). The cries of consternation attracted the attention of some nearby woodcutters, whereupon, in quick succession, Rechitskii was arrested by the local sheriff, a coroner's jury was summoned in Seneca, and Rechitskii was exonerated (mainly on Machtet's testimony). The funeral and burial of Room was attended by most of the townspeople.[165] The remaining Russians now separated: Rechitskii to return home with the effects of the deceased; Linev to go his own way, ultimately into Siberian exile; and Machtet to stay on in Marysville, where he settled in town and went to evening classes in English. The next spring he journeyed southward to join the Frey

163. Ibid., p. 9. For background on Nechaev, see Venturi, *Roots of Revolution*, pp. 354–88; Billington, *Fire in the Minds of Men*, pp. 397–400; and Ulam, *In the Name of the People*, pp. 143–55, 187–211.

164. "Preriia i Pionery," *Nedelia* 8, 47 (1875): 1710–16. For a translation of some of his pictures of Kansas, see Hasty and Fusso, eds., *America Through Russian Eyes*, pp. 16–82; and for more details, see Norman E. Saul, "Through Curious and Foreign Eyes: Grigori Machtet Chronicles the Kansas Frontier, 1872–1873," *Kansas History* 17, 2 (Summer 1994): 76–90. For a complete compilation, see G. A. Machtet, *Polnoe sobranie sochinenii: Pervoe posmertnoe izd.*, 12 vols. in 6 (Kiev: V. K. Fuks, 1902), vol. 2, and *Polnoe sobranie sochinenii*, 12 vols. (St. Petersburg: Prosveshchenie, 1911–1913).

165. "Sad Accident," Seneca *Courier*, 15 November 1872, which noted that "Room" "received the decent attention due from a civilized community."

community, but after about eight months of communal life (including a love affair with Mary Frey), he set off for home. His later participation in the "to the people" movement in 1874 earned him years of prison and exile.[166]

The most important aspect of Machtet's wanderings over the Kansas prairie is that he logged much of it for publication in a popular Russian liberal weekly, *Nedelia*. Although revealing the youth and immaturity of the writer, these American stories foreshadowed the popular poet and writer that he would become. He was interested, more than any other Russian writer, in the nuances and features of the American heartland and in sympathetically sketching its inhabitants. Russian readers could thus gain a unique insight into provincial American life and its concerns in the 1870s.

Machtet provides yet-another description of the New York Russian community and a critical view of urban America,[167] but he waxes most eloquent in describing what he heard and saw around Troy, Seneca, Marysville, and Independence, Kansas, and at the Progressive communist community near Cedar Vale. His humane portrayal of the Kansas countryside served as a counterweight to the more negative assessments of the United States from the pens of other Russian visitors. His vignettes included town meetings, the mass murder of a farm family, a night séance at a farmer's house, the sophistication of frontier town life, classroom experiences and conversations with the teacher on education, the court proceedings connected with the accidental shooting, political scandals in Kansas, the debate over herd law versus fence law, train travel through the West, and, of course, a critical appraisal of the Frey commune.

Unlike most Russian travel writers, Machtet described his American environment in colorful detail and imagery rather than obsessively recording what was happening to him. As a result his "snapshots" should be of interest to all students of 1870s America. For example, in relating local lore, he would retain particular idioms and figures of speech in original, phonetically spelled English in the Russian text, thereby allowing direct insight into everyday speech patterns of the 1870s on the Great Plains.

Another Russian subject of already recognized artistic talent arrived in Kansas about the same time as Machtet. Fedor Kamenskii had, in fact, re-

---

166. V. A. Gol'tsev, "G. A. Machtet," in *Polnoe Sobranie* (Kiev), 12:v–xii; T. G. Machtet-Iurkevich [his daughter], introduction in Machtet, *Izbrannoe* (Moscow: Gosizkhudlit, 1958), pp. 4–6. "To the People" was the 1874 climactic movement of this generation of Russian revolutionaries. Its goal—to motivate peasants to revolt—failed, and most participants were arrested.
167. Translation in Nikoliukin, *A Russian Discovery*, pp. 321–36.

ceived the patronage of Alexander II for his works of sculpture and looked forward to a promising future in the medium, but in 1871, he threw it all away and emigrated to the United States. He settled for several years as a farmer in Kansas and was briefly with the Frey commune. Although he apparently wrote nothing about his life, he was interviewed by a Chicago newspaper while visiting the World's Fair in 1893. Kamenskii revealed that he had first moved from Kansas to Florida, where he worked in orange groves and resumed his sculpturing in a house he built overlooking a bay; the last four years he had been living in New York City under the name of Mao Dak.[168]

Kurbskii and Vladimirov

About the same time that Machtet was immersed in the Kansas prairie, two other Russians were seeing another America from the ground level. A. S. Kurbskii, a former landowner, arrived in 1871 specifically to study and write about American life and work. Following in the footsteps of Ogorodnikov, Kurbskii absorbed the immigrant experience, first in the New York community and then in Chicago, where he lived among Germans and worked in a sawmill on Clark Street and then at a brickyard north of the river. Discouraged by the hard labor but impressed by the equality of workers and bosses, Kurbskii learned of an opportunity for employment during the summer on a broomcorn plantation in Arkansas.[169] There he worked side-by-side with blacks and described their optimism and prevailing spirit of freedom amid poverty and oppression. Kurbskii saw the United States as the archetypical land of opportunity, citing as proof his own rise from menial laborer to a foreman on the plantation and bragging that in one season he saved $700.[170] The plantation owner then made him the chaperone for his son, who was traveling with his brother by train into Indian Territory (Oklahoma). During the trip Kurbskii noted the changes in dress and speech of the passengers as they progressed westward.

Kurbskii's writings, first published in *Vestnik Evropy* in 1873 and 1874 and

168. "His a Strange Life," Chicago *Inter Ocean*, 14 May 1893, p. 1. According to the *Granat Encyclopedia*, Kamenskii died in 1913.

169. A. S. Kurbskii, "Russkii rabochii u Amerikanskago planatatora: Razskazy i vospominaniia," *Vestnik Evropy* 7, 7 (July 1873): 46–53.

170. Ibid. 8, 9 (September 1873): 160–63.

then in book form,[171] emphasized the variety, opportunity, and openness of American life, presenting a much more flattering picture than that of Ogorodnikov. He also perceived a Russian affinity with Americans:

> In the character of the Russian there are certain features which resemble the character of Americans and are but rarely met with in other Europeans, this being, as I believe, the root of that sympathy which Americans evoke in Russians who come into contact with them. The same ability to accustom oneself quickly to any new circumstance and adapt to it, the same rapid and precise understanding of large and complex undertakings, the desire to do everything on a grand scale, and a dislike of pettiness and penny-pinching.[172]

After his adventures in Arkansas and Oklahoma, Kurbskii returned to Chicago in the fall of 1871 to a more comfortable existence as a partner in a hardware store. He was actually on a short trip south of the city to buy stoves when the great fire started on 8 October. The Russian then related, graphically and emotionally, his return to the burning city and his harrowing passage through it, just barely crossing through the tunnel under the Chicago River to the north side. His is perhaps one of the best eyewitness accounts of the great conflagration, as well as of old Chicago in general.[173]

Mikhail Vladimirov was another idealistic young Russian who ventured to the United States. Growing up in Saratov on the Volga, he became interested in America from reading about it in novels and journal descriptions. Somewhat sobered by maturing experiences in the Caucasus and in St. Petersburg, he made the voyage across the Atlantic, arriving at Hoboken in August 1872. Working his way around the country, Vladimirov would probably see more of the United States than any other Russian visitor of this period.[174]

After the mandatory few weeks with the Russian community in New York, Vladimirov journeyed south through Savannah to Jacksonville, Florida, where he began his toils in a flour mill, then at a sawmill. He moved on

171. Kurbskii, *Russkii rabochii u Amerikanskago planatatora* (St. Petersburg: A. Khomikovskii, 1875).

172. From Nikoliukin, *A Russian Discovery*, pp. 305–6.

173. Translation in ibid., pp. 309–17.

174. M. M. Vladimirov, *Russkii sredi Amerikanstsev: Moi lichnyia vpechatleniia kak tokari, chernorabochago, plotnike i puteshestvennika: 1872–1876* (St. Petersburg: Obshchestvennaia pol'za, 1877), pp. 2–11; Nikoliukin, *A Russian Discovery*, pp. 368–82; for reviews, see *Nedelia* 10, 22 (May 1877): 751–53; and OZ 233, 8 (August 1877): 272–76.

to Tallahassee early in 1873 to work at a convent and on a farm. He then jumped from job to job, with the longest stint as a stevedore in Appalachicola and Pensacola, before finally making his way to New Orleans in the summer of 1873. Affected by the depression that year, he went north to St. Louis, shoveled dirt for a tunnel project, and took odd jobs as a carpenter and bricklayer.[175]

Taking to the road again, the itinerant Russian tried his luck in Chicago. There he was befriended by a long-time Russian settler and northern general in the Civil War, Ivan Turchin (Turchaninov), who was then in the real estate business and establishing a Polish immigrant colony at Radom in southern Illinois. Vladimirov was hired to repair streets there during the winter of 1873–1874. By April he was once more on the move—to San Francisco, through Kansas City and Omaha. Crossing Nebraska, he visited a Mennonite family near Hastings who had recently arrived from the Ukraine. He hopped freight trains through Wyoming, ran completely out of money, and was forced to join a railroad work crew in Utah in order to eat. By June he had reached California, where he found pleasanter and more lucrative employment as a tutor for children of a Russian-Alaskan family. Now able to sightsee at leisure, Vladimirov toured the state during the eighteen months he spent there, visiting the Bay Area, Yosemite, the redwood forests, and Fort Ross.[176]

Vladimirov saved enough money for a train ticket all the way to Boston, via Detroit and Niagara Falls, and for an extended tour of the East Coast— New Haven, New York, Washington, Baltimore, and Philadelphia—from September through December 1875. In the capital he witnessed the funeral of Vice-president Henry Wilson, visited the White House and met President Grant, attended sessions of Congress, and toured Mount Vernon. Again out of money, in Philadelphia he found work as a carpenter on Centennial buildings and stayed on to examine the exposition before departing for home.[177]

Vladimirov's book about his far-flung adventures did not glorify America since his focus was on the underside, the impoverished and depression-afflicted part of society. Yet he balanced the desperation of unemployment with the variety of jobs available, poor pay with the cheapness of housing, exploitation with the generally good relations between bosses and workers. Everywhere he found educational opportunities and personal successes as

175. Vladimirov, *Russkii sredi Amerikanstsev,* pp. 17–62.
176. Ibid., pp. 77–95, 97–129, 139–86.
177. Ibid., pp. 188–254, 269–337.

well as dejection and failure. In conclusion, he did not regret the experience but would not recommend it to others; there was no place like home. Vladimirov and Kurbskii both illustrate the difficulties that educated Russians from the nobility had in enduring ordinary, solitary life and work at the lower rungs, but also the diversity and variety of Americans and American life during the 1870s.

A Woman's View

While Vladimirov was helping to erect the Centennial buildings, a young woman from St. Petersburg was enjoying an edifying but still stressful life in Philadelphia. Adelaida Lukanina (also known as Paevskaia) had first sought an opportunity for medical training in 1872 in the relatively progressive atmosphere of the University of Zurich, where a number of other Russians—as well as several Americans—were studying. When the Russian government recalled the students in 1873, fearing their radical corruption, she stayed behind to finish her education. Completing the course but concerned about retribution at home, Lukanina came to Philadelphia in early 1875 with Swiss friends and armed with letters of introduction from her Zurich professors, including the American Susan Dimmock. She lodged at first with a companion's brother in an immigrant section of Germantown, while she sought a position as an intern in a hospital. Since that was not possible for a woman, she was befriended by Rachel Bodley, dean of the Women's Medical College of Pennsylvania, and placed in the clinic there.

The detailed account of her experiences, published a few years later, provides interesting insights into this foundational period for women studying medicine in the United States.[178] Lukanina worked a few months at the women's college in Philadelphia, then through Fanny Brandeis and Maria Zakrzewska, a noted medical pioneer from Prussian Poland, she was invited to be an intern at the New England Hospital for Women and Children in Boston. During August and September 1875, she worked in the hospital dispensary and at a clinic in the center of the city that served the Irish slums

178. Adelaida N. Lukanina, "God v Amerike: Iz vospominanii zhenshchiny-medika," *Vestnik Evropy* 16, 8 (August 1881): 621–66; 16, 9 (September 1881): 31–78; 17, 4 (April 1882): 495–538. See also Jeannette Tuve, *The First Russian Women Physicians* (Newtonville, Mass.: Oriental Research Partners, 1984), pp. 34–43. Lukanina's seminal study has been ignored by most Russian and American scholars, though it was apparently reprinted in 1892: A. N. Paevskaia, *God v Amerike: Iz vospominanii zhenshchiny-vracha* (St. Petersburg, 1892); a copy cannot be found in the United States.

and the black poor. In her memoirs she paints a harrowing picture of the most destitute people of Boston, observing that the Irish immigrants, while generally gay and God-fearing, were dirty and filthy, living in worse conditions and with less self-respect than the blacks.[179]

Returning to the hospital in the fall, Lukanina met another Russian student, a young, aristocratic woman who had studied at the University of Michigan but who was soon dismissed for being too inexperienced.[180] She was struck by the fact that medical education in the United States was more experimental than in Europe, yet American women doctors were more conservative and religious than their European counterparts. Lukanina praised the selfless dedication and sacrifice of her American supervisors, but she finally left the hospital because of what she considered too much time devoted to routine tasks and too little for study.[181] Back in Philadelphia, she formally enrolled at the Women's College of Medicine, which she found more open and tolerant than the hospital in Boston. The college had a varied faculty and student body that included several nationalities, a few blacks such as Rebecca Cole, and those of different beliefs, including Quakers, Mormons, and nonbelievers. She especially admired Dean Bodley and Bodley's successor, Clara Marshall; Frances Emily White, who taught anatomy; and Emmeline Cleveland, an earnest practitioner and ground-breaking ovarian surgeon as well as teacher of obstetrics. Her friends included fellow students Alice Bennett and Alice Bigelow, who would both rise to prominence in hospital administration. Lukanina's sketches of these and other American women doctors are vivid and forthright, essential reading for anyone studying the early history of professional American women.[182]

Lukanina passed her examinations in March 1876, took part in the graduation ceremony—in the new Agricultural Hall on the Centennial grounds—and was invited to become a resident physician at a local hospital. But, leaving before the grand opening of the Centennial, she revisited Boston and departed for Europe, where she apparently practiced medicine for a number of years and then returned to Russia shortly before her death in 1905.[183] Her critical commentary on American women and medicine singled

179. Lukanina, "God v Amerike," 63–72.
180. Ibid., 74–75. Lukanina described the other Russian student as only eighteen, "very pretty but awkward."
181. Ibid., 78.
182. The best study is Regina Markell Morantz, *Sympathy and Science: Women Physicians in American Medicine* (New York and Oxford: Oxford University Press, 1985).
183. Tuve, *Russian Women Physicians*, p. 43.

out the nonrecognition of midwifery, but she also focused her sharp eyes on the woman's domestic role, giving minute descriptions of American family life and especially the typical middle-class Philadelphia home—hot and cold running water, central steam heat from a basement furnace, and excessive static in the rugs.[184]

Although Lukanina evidently enjoyed her American experience (about fifteen months) and presented a fairly attractive image of life there for women, very few emancipated Russian women would follow in her footsteps. Yet two who did settle in the United States in the 1870s managed to put their imprints on the age. Elena Petrovna Blavatskaia, better known as Madame Blavatsky, created a considerable stir in the growing spiritualist movement in New York. Interaction with American leaders such as Henry Olcott would lead to the foundation of the Theosophical Society, which became a worldwide movement in the 1880s.[185] Famous for her unique lifestyle, flamboyant dress, and pet monkeys, Zenaida Ragozin wrote oriental histories for Putnam's *Our Nation* series and tutored select New York pupils in languages and music. Her favorite student and godchild, Elizabeth Reynolds, would become Columbia University's first teacher of Russian and a leading American authority on Russian drama.[186]

Critical Eyes

Other Russians published less complimentary observations about the United States. Konstantin Skal'kovskii, trained as a mining engineer and already an experienced traveler, came as an official representative to the Centennial and took advantage of the opportunity to tour the country: Washington, New York, Niagara Falls, Chicago, San Francisco, St. Louis. Although he claimed to be a scholar, his views, first appearing in the conservative *Novoe Vremia* (New times) and then in book form, were too esoteric and disdainful to merit the distinction.[187] He emphasized such Americana as

184. Lukanina, "God v Amerike," 512–15. In Philadelphia, Lukanina stayed with an old friend, identified only as "Vera Iakovlevna B."

185. See Marion Meade, *Madame Blavatsky: The Woman Behind the Myth* (New York: G. P. Putnam's Sons, 1980), pp. 101–92.

186. An extensive correspondence between Ragozin and members of the Reynolds family is in Norman Hapgood-Reynolds Family Papers, LC.

187. K. Skal'kovskii, *V strane iga i svoboda: Putevyia vpechatleniia* (St. Petersburg: Obshchestvennaia pol'za, 1878). He also wrote a more technical book about American mining laws.

hot corn bread, ice tea, fans for the stifling heat in summer, clubs as drinking societies, Decoration Day, black minstrels, and the infatuation with freemasonry. The most negative features were a dull social life, the filthy streets of New York, Indian suppression (with some attention to the Battle of Little Big Horn), racial discrimination, and political parties and favoritism; on the Russian side, but he was critical of how unrepresentative the Russian centennial exhibit was (too much malachite) and how the former Alaskans in San Francisco had succumbed to drunkenness and prostitution.[188]

On the other hand, Skal'kovskii was impressed by the varied scenery, the quick rebuilding of Chicago, huge public projects, and the partiality for labor-saving machines. On balance, he concluded that American society with all of its faults was still better than that of Europe. While complaining of American ignorance of Russia—one school atlas placed Tiflis (the capital of Russian Georgia) in Persia—he committed some careless errors himself, describing, for example, Columbus as the capital of Indiana.[189]

Nikolai Tsaknii, another runaway radical populist, could find little to praise in the America he saw, though his exposure was apparently brief. Tsaknii's United States was a land of the most extreme capitalist exploitation: large factories with poor workers and huge farms employing "coolie" labor. Women and children had to work to feed the family. He was impressed, however, with the availability of information in the public media about these conditions and the freedom of workers to organize and strike about grievances.[190] His aim was clearly to dispel any Russian myths about an idyllic America.

The writing of Aleksandr Lopukhin took a different approach, making pathetic observations in episodic fashion. One of his articles examined the Chinese settlement in New York with clarity and understanding; unlike most other immigrants, "they are peaceful people who do not spend their money in beer halls."[191] Like the bulk of Russian visitors, he was especially interested in the Russian community in New York. While noting the difficult adjustments of many, Lopukhin described a simple sailor who had risen to be a "two-story American gentleman" and who spoke both cultivated En-

188. Ibid., pp. 283, 388, and passim.

189. Ibid., p. 400.

190. Nikolai Tsaknii, "Kartiny polozheniia truda v Soedinennykh Shtatakh," *Slovo* 3, 2–3 (February–March 1880): 23–38; "Pis'ma ob Amerike," *Slovo* 3, 10 (October 1880): 37–49; *Slovo* 4, 1 (January 1881): 116–30. Portions are translated in Nikoliukin, *A Russian Discovery*, pp. 383–87.

191. Aleksandr Lopukhin, "Travlia nebesnikov," *Nedelia* 20 (1880): 641. The book was entitled *Zhizn' za okeanom* (St. Petersburg: Dobrodeev, 1881).

glish and his original "gutter" Russian.[192] Lopukhin stressed to his Russian audience the friendship of Americans to Russians and their interest in Russia. He attended a musical comedy in New York set during the Russo-Turkish War, which depicted Russian officers as romantic heroes conducting a mission of civilizing the Turks. He contended that it was the most popular stage production in New York and that the repeated use of some Russian words, such as *gospodin* (mister), *chort vosmi* (devil take it), and *shchi* (cabbage soup), led to their inclusion in ordinary street conversation.[193]

These three observers all went on to distinguished careers in Russia: Skal'kovskii as an essayist, critic, and historian; Tsaknii as a liberal newspaper editor in Odessa; Lopukhin as a theologian.[194]

Other Writings on America

Many more articles and editorial comments appeared in the Russian press about the United States, usually by unidentified authors who had not seen the country and were writing on the basis of reading and opinion. They generally reflect the range of views offered by the travel literature but are sometimes more extreme either in support of or in opposition to American politics and society. An example is an editorial in the conservative and nationalistic *Russkoe Bogatstvo* (Russian wealth) in 1879.[195] Its main point was that out of friendship Russia had done much for the United States, such as giving up Alaska, but had received very little in return. The United States supplied arms to Russia during the Russo-Turkish War but also to the other side to its great benefit: "Such is friendship, friendship for trade—trade!"[196] The article highlighted the vigilante justice, the lack of respect for marriage, the absurdity of the temperance and free love movements, the unholy power of religion, blacks being turned away from major hotels, and the sudden rise of flamboyant capitalists such as John Jacob Astor and Cornelius Vanderbilt. Although not expressing a particularly fresh outlook on the United States, this editorial was a harbinger of much more to come.

To measure the impact in Russia of these fairly extensive commentaries on

192. Lopukhin, "Za okeanom (pis'mo iz N'iu-Iorka)," *Nedelia* 2 (1880): 67.
193. "Russofil'stvo amerikantsev," *Nedelia* 4 (1880): 125–29.
194. Allen, *Russia Looks at America*, pp. 184–85, 201; Nikoliukin, *A Russian Discovery*, pp. 383, 496.
195. E. Gizhitskii, "Soedinennye Shtaty v nastoiashchee vremia," *Russkoe Bogatstvo* 1 (January 1879): 84–98.
196. Ibid., p. 84.

American life is not easy. During the reform era of Alexander II, publications were relatively uncensored, and liberal and constitutional societies, especially that of the friendly United States, could be discussed openly. Articles appeared in leading journals and then were usually compiled in book form, providing a second and more durable exposure, but their readership would naturally be limited to the small percentage of the population that was literate and receptive. The portrayals were varied and complex, perhaps confusing to the Russian reader. This may account for the fact that they failed to promote a noticeable increase in Russian emigration or travel to the United States; and they were probably not a significant factor for Jewish, Polish, and German emigration.

Americans were generally unaware of their close surveillance by Russians for the obvious reason that so few read Russian. The publications of Tsimmerman, Slavinskii, and Ogorodnikov were given token notice. A correspondent to the New York *Times*, probably Eugene Schuyler, described in more detail the observations of Kurbskii: "The writer was much struck by the good impression produced in America by Russia's former criminals while the representatives of the highest classes of Russian society, large numbers of whom live in New York and San Francisco, are a laughing stock to their neighbors, on account of their quarrels among themselves and their general inability to get on."[197]

The Russians who stayed in the United States were an odd assortment and, for the most part, had unsatisfactory experiences. In 1879 a reporter of the New York *Sun* visited the Russian Orthodox church in the city and was surprised to find the service conducted in English. The reason, he was told by one of the congregation, was "because he [Father Bjerring] does not understand Russian. He is no more a Russian than an American." This person gave the visitor a rundown on the number of Russians in the United States during the 1870s: New York thirty, Kansas thirty, Florida twenty, Virginia five, and California over thirty. But, he added, "the Kansas Communists, or nearly all of them, have returned to Europe to look after their revolutionary propaganda, and so have the Virginia and Florida settlers."[198] The *Sun's* source claimed that the New York community did not have common interests to hold them together.

197. "Russian Notes," correspondence from St. Petersburg, 10 December 1874, New York *Times*, 5 January 1875.
198. As quoted in "Russian in the United States," St. Louis *Missouri Republican*, 9 October 1879.

To the Russians of New York can be applied the old saying that whenever three Russians meet there are four different opinions. Some Russians after returning to Russia have made money by publishing books about their travels in this country; for example, Zimmerman made over 30,000 rubles; Slavinsky, Vladimiroff and some others made a few thousands apiece. You see the Russians take a great interest in the Americans, whom they speak of as "our trans-Atlantic friends."

Next came an interview with a Russian druggist.

"This is not the country for Russians to make money in," he said; "they are different from the Yankees—too unpractical. . . . Seven years ago I came here with my hands and head as my sole capital, and now I may be worth ten thousand. There are a few other Russians who make a living. The great majority of Russians who come here bring money, spend it and return disappointed. The trouble with my countrymen here is that they don't get rid of their Russian notions and ways, and so they fail. . . . The Russians, with their aristocratic socialistic ideas, are not fitted to succeed in this country, where a knack for money-making commands the highest respect."

The reporter then asked if any Russian peasants had settled here: "'That's funny. A moojik in New York! Why, a Russian peasant in full dress would be arrested as soon as he showed himself on the streets collecting a crowd. Perhaps Barnum might bail him out, and make a few thousand dollars by putting him on exhibition. Luckily the Russian government sees to it that the peasants don't leave the country. What an idea. A moojik in New York!' "[199] Yet Mennonites and Volga Germans had arrived in large numbers looking very much like Russian peasants, and there would soon be many more of the poor, downtrodden non-Russian peoples of the Russian Empire coming to the United States. And their presence would eventually affect the course of Russian-American relations.

199. Ibid.

4

Crime and Punishment, 1880s

As Russian-American relations entered the 1880s, the portents appeared excellent for an even closer understanding between the two nations. The striking differences in their political and social characters seemed to be diminishing as Russian reforms and a definite if slow-paced Westernization occurred. The United States on the other hand was becoming more "imperial," more mindful of national interests in the global arena, and consequently more appreciative of the quasi-alliance with Russia. Business and technical exchanges were also advancing and fostering the image of stable and continuing harmony. Russian interest in the United States had never been higher, as demonstrated by the quantity of publication and contacts, while the United States could now boast of genuine Russian experts, not only Eugene Schuyler, Jeremiah Curtin, and George Kennan, but new faces, such as Nathan Haskell Dole, David Ker, and Isabel Hapgood.

In 1880 the Russian Empire seemed to be headed for another round of reforms, to include a Western-style but limited constitution and a national representative "advisory" body, under the guidance of Minister of Interior Mikhail Loris-Melikov. The time was propitious after military victory in the Russo-Turkish War and an at least temporary resolution of the Eastern Question at the Congress of Berlin. Alexander II could now move his attention back to the domestic scene with the knowledge that foreign affairs were secure under the management of his respected and pacific, though aging, chancellor and foreign minister, Alexander Gorchakov. Speaking fluent English with no accent, Gorchakov impressed all of his many American visitors, not least among them being former president Ulysses S. Grant.[1]

Prodding these leaders were the proponents of the earlier reforms, Minister of War Dmitri Miliutin and Americanophile Minister of Navy Grand Duke Constantine, the latter increasingly reliant on his chief assistant, the even more Americanized Admiral Stepan Lesovskii. In addition, two other key ministers promoted modernization and were admirers of the United States: Admiral Konstantin Pos'et, the minister of transportation (ways and communications) who had accompanied Grand Duke Alexis, and the progressive minister of finance, Aleksandr Abaza, whose father had been one of the primary Russian advocates of and investors in the venture to connect America and Russia by telegraph in the 1860s.[2]

Also of significance, American diplomatic relations were now in more professional hands. Gone were the uproarious times of Cassius Clay and Konstantin Katakazi. Nikolai Shishkin had steered quietly through the morass of Washington politics since his arrival in 1875 and then switched places with the minister to Greece, Mikhail Bartolomai, in 1880. The caliber of American representatives in St. Petersburg was also improving. Edwin Stoughton, who had defended the Russian regime's handling of nihilist opponents in the New York press, was replaced in 1879 by John W. Foster of Indiana, one of the most esteemed American diplomats of the late nineteenth century. He was followed by William Hunt of New Orleans, Alphonso Taft of Cincinnati, George Lothrop of Detroit, Lambert Tree of Chicago, and Charles Emory Smith of Philadelphia. In the frequent and extended gaps between their tenures, the secretaries of legation, Wickham Hoffman and George Wurts, matched and at times exceeded the standard of professional competence and knowledge of Russia set by Eugene Schuyler in the previous decade. Hoffman pointed out a disadvantage placed on American diplomacy in Russia: "It is a pity our Government changes its ministers here so often. This is a personal Government and personal influence has every weight."[3] All, however, were respected and conscientious servants.

Despite the generally positive outlook for Russian-American relations in

1. "Gen. Grant's Recollections," New York *Times,* 14 March 1881, p. 1.

2. Rumors circulated early in 1881 of a closer financial connection between Russia and the United States through a new economic program supported by a large loan. *Frank Leslie's Illustrated Newspaper,* 19 February 1881, pp. 407, 411.

3. To J. C. Bancroft Davis, 31 May 1882, as quoted in George Sherman Queen, "The United States and the Material Advance in Russia, 1881–1906" (Ph.D. diss. University of Illinois, 1941), p. 61.

the 1880s, signs of change had appeared on the horizon, causing a number of politically conscious members of the Russian nobility, such as former Minister of Interior Petr Valuev, to become quietly pessimistic.[4] Chief among these omens was the rise of Russian nationalism and conservative Pan-Slavism, especially manifest during the Russo-Turkish War and then intensified by the results of the Congress of Berlin. Among the leaders were General Mikhail Cherniaev, a hero of the conquest of Central Asia and the suppression of Balkan revolts in the 1870s, influential Moscow publisher and editor Mikhail Katkov, and the new procurator of the Holy Synod and director of religious affairs, Konstantin Pobedonostsev. As an intellectual conservative and tutor to the future Alexander III, the procurator held an especially influential position at court. By the end of 1880 these individuals represented a formidable internal opposition to liberal reforms and to flexible international policies.[5] Russian government and official society had become sharply divided into ideological camps.

Two widely publicized developments of the late 1870s opened the door for Russian conservatives and captured the attention of Americans: the Russian radical socialist movement, especially its terrorist practices, and the Jewish Question. Stimulated by such celebrated cases as the attempted murder of the St. Petersburg chief of police and the subsequent trial, acquittal, and escape of Vera Zasulich in early 1878, Americans grew increasingly sympathetic to the cause of Russian political, social, and religious justice. The various organized acts of violence by members of the "People's Will," beginning in 1879, might be condemned by the American press, but they struck a romantic and responsive chord in Americans, particularly as the daring exploits continued against great odds.[6]

Some Americans were disturbed at possible complicity in Russian terrorist acts. W. W. Hanes of Cincinnati thought his improved grenades and bombs had fallen into the hands of "nihilists, socialists and communists" and wanted to go to St. Petersburg to warn authorities.[7] Such dramatic inci-

4. For revealing discussions of this important period, see W. Bruce Lincoln, *The Great Reforms: Autocracy, Bureaucracy and the Politics of Change in Imperial Russia* (DeKalb: Northern Illinois University Press, 1990), pp. 173–83; and G. M. Hamburg, *Politics of the Russian Nobility, 1881–1905* (New Brunswick, N.J.: Rutgers University Press, 1984), pp. 71–84.

5. See the chapter "1881" in Robert F. Byrnes, *Pobedonostsev: His Life and Thought* (Bloomington and London: Indiana University Press, 1986), pp. 139–64.

6. For background on the Peoples' Will, see Deborah Hardy, *Land and Freedom: The Origins of Russian Terrorism, 1876–1879* (Westport, Conn.: Greenwood Press, 1987).

7. To Russian legation, 5 May 1879, f. 133, op. 470, d. 183, AVPR.

dents as the March 1880 bombing of the Winter Palace, graphically depicted in the American illustrated weeklies, naturally created an outcry for a tougher stance among American supporters of traditional authority in Russia.[8] The romance of Russian causes would be dampened when Americans began to feel the "nihilist" heat themselves.

The Opening of the Jewish Question

The Jewish Question was more complex. The reform era of the 1860s and 1870s had left intact most of the legal restrictions on the Jewish population that dated to the partitioning of Poland in the eighteenth century, but their enforcement had been considerably relaxed. Many Jews took advantage of an opportunity to move out of their overcrowded original ghettos into other towns and villages, especially throughout the southern provinces of the empire. The new influx naturally disturbed the traditional economic, social, and religious life of these predominantly Slavic (but non-Russian) communities. Moreover, Jews often engaged in high-profile occupations such as tavernkeepers, vodka dealers, and moneylenders to the lower classes of town and country. Resentment festered. Already in 1871, a serious pogrom had shaken Odessa, the third largest city and key grain port of the empire, but on the whole law and order prevailed through the decade.

Russian-American relations were affected in two ways by the Russian Jewish problem. Many Jews who had resettled in cities such as Odessa, Minsk, and Kiev decided to emigrate, with the United States becoming the new promised land. In the United States, the past grievances and and with punishments of increasing severity for those caught the obvious state of poverty of their Russian cousins roused the resident Jewish population to call attention to the restrictions that were still applied in Russia, thus awakening the sensitivities of Americans generally to issues of inequality in religious and economic activities in Russia.[9]

In addition, a number of Russian and non-Russian Jews who had become naturalized American citizens were drawn to Russia by business opportunities. But they soon discovered that the discriminatory Russian laws against Jews applied to them regardless of their American citizenship, as illustrated

8. The Russian legation received a warning from an American who overheard two Russians speaking German talking about planting nitroglycerine in the plumbing of the Winter Palace; William Seafort (Detroit) to Shishkin, 22 May 1879, ibid.

9. For background, see Hans Rogger, *Jewish Policies and Right-Wing Politics in Imperial Russia* (Berkeley and Los Angeles: University of California Press, 1986).

previously by the recurring difficulties of Theodore and Herman Rosenstraus, shopkeepers of Kharkov. Naturalized Jewish-American men of Russian (usually Polish) birth who returned, often simply to visit relatives and attend to family affairs, found themselves vulnerable to prosecution for leaving Russia without permission in order to evade military service, especially if they had left as children after 1874. The number of cases that involved the limited protective capability of American diplomats and consuls in Russia naturally rose as visits increased, especially when the Russian government stiffened its enforcement during and after the Russo-Turkish War.

The fact that the Russian government tended to be lenient and make exceptions for "American" Jews added to the confusion. A case in point is that of Henry Pinkos, who came to St. Petersburg on business at the beginning of 1880. In May he ran afoul of an order restricting the residence of newly arrived foreign Jews to brief periods, but he was able to obtain a liberal extension to arrange business affairs and transportation. When his departure from Kronstadt was finally scheduled, he and his family were refused exit permission because their documents were not in order. Then they were threatened with arrest for having overstayed the legal limit.[10]

That same year an agent of an American textile firm, Marx Wilczynski, was deported from St. Petersburg so quickly that he could not even communicate with the legation. Protesting the Russian action through diplomatic channels from Berlin, he was granted permission to reenter Russia for a six-month visit.[11] Consistency was blatantly missing from Russia's policy toward foreign Jews. These cases finally produced a pointed rejoinder from Secretary of State William Evarts:

> If the meaning of this [policy] is that a citizen of the United States has been broken up in his business at St. Petersburg simply for the reason that he is a Jew rather than a believer in any other creed, then it is certainly time for this Government to express itself. . . . It should be made clear to the Government of Russia, that in the view of this Government the religion professed by one of its citizens has no relation whatever to that citizen's right to the protection of the United States; and that in the eye of this Government an injury officially dealt to Mr. Pinkos in St. Petersburg on the sole ground that he is a Jew, presents

10. Hoffman to Evarts, 7 May and 21 July 1880, DUSM, Russia, vol. 34 (roll 34, M 35), RG 59, NA.
11. Hoffman to Evarts, 21 October 1880, ibid.; and Foster to Evarts, 30 December 1880, DUSM, Russia, vol. 35 (roll 35, M 35), RG 59, NA.

the same aspect that an injury officially done to a citizen of Russia in New York for the reason that he attends any particular church there, would to the view of His Majesty's Government.[12]

Proceeding on these instructions, Foster had a revealing conversation with the acting foreign minister, Nikolai Giers, who admitted "that the Russian government had found the Jewish question a very vexatious and disagreeable one, both as to the internal relations and the treatment of foreign Jews." He asserted, however, that Jews were "a bad class of society, largely engaged in smuggling and illegal commercial transactions. Of late years they had been active participants in revolutionary conspiracies and plots against the life of the Emperor, and had shown a restless and disloyal inclination."[13] Regardless, the foreign minister noted that a commission had been appointed to recommend changes in the Russian laws regarding Jews.

The American minister agreed that the situation was complex, especially when information was so difficult to obtain. He guessed that there were at least 30,000 Jews then living in St. Petersburg instead of the official figure of 2,000. Foster also underscored to Giers the broader aspects of the question.

> I stated that while the object . . . was to obtain proper recognition of the rights of American Jews, my Government took a deep interest in the amelioration of the condition of the Jewish race in other nations. . . .
>
> Mr. de Giers said he sympathized fully in theory with the view taken by my Government, as most in consonance with the spirit of the age. But in Russia the subject could not be treated as an abstract question. A long series of legislative acts and regulations, the strong prejudices of the Russian people, the bad character of great numbers of the Jewish race, and various other political and social circumstances had to be taken into consideration.[14]

In response, Evarts recognized the intricacies of Russia's Jewish problem and wanted to limit American involvement as much as possible.

> Russia's treatment of her own Jews, or of other foreign Jews resorting thither, may, in determinate cases, attract the sympathy of the Ameri-

12. To Foster, 4 September 1880, DI, Russia, vol. 16 (roll 138, M 77), RG 59, NA.
13. Foster to Evarts, 30 December 1880, DUSM, Russia, vol. 35 (roll 35, M 35), RG 59, NA.
14. Ibid.

James G. Blaine. From Theron Crawford, James G. Blaine
(1893)

can people, but the aim of the government of the United States is the specific one of protecting its own citizens. If the hardships to which Russian and foreign Jews are subjected involves our citizens, we think we have just ground for remonstrance and expectancy of better treatment.

Acknowledging Russia's efforts to settle those cases, the secretary of state instructed Foster further: "It is not the desire of this Government to embarrass that of Russia by insistence upon these points with any degree of harshness, when the disposition reported in your despatches is so conciliatory."[15]
The crux of the issue was the Russian interpretation of the commercial treaty of 1832, which stated that Americans were to have equal rights with citizens of Russia. Unfortunately, not all of the tsar's subjects had the same

15. To Foster, 3 March 1881, DI, Russia, vol. 16 (roll 136, M 77), RG 59, NA.

rights, and it thus seemed unfair and illegal for Americans of such a distinctive group as Jews to have more privileges than their Russian counterparts. Russian officials contended, therefore, that to determine the legal status of foreign visitors or residents, their religious faith had to be ascertained and a discriminatory judgment made that ran counter to the basic American principles. This debate would plague Russian-American relations until religious distinctions were removed in the revolution of 1917—and even beyond.

Another development contributed to the Jewish Question. The Russian reforms had encouraged mobility and increased educational as well as economic opportunities for the large Jewish population of the empire, drawing a number of young Jews to universities in Odessa, Kiev, and Warsaw and even to the better-known ones in St. Petersburg and Moscow. Some of these students, mindful of their own oppressed background, converted to the cause of social and political revolution, both to the urban-centered terrorism and to the more moderate course of working among the people on a long-term basis. This factor, exaggerated by the conservative press, heightened the public perception of a growing Jewish "threat" to traditional Russian institutions and values, especially since it was coupled with increasing unrest among other repressed minorities such as Poles and Ukrainians. As this multifaceted situation was evolving, a cataclysmic event shook the country. Ethnic and revolutionary tensions escalated hand in hand into the 1880s.

The Assassination of Alexander II

Since soon after the "People's Will" was formed in 1879, it had pronounced as its main goal the assassination of Alexander II, the chief symbol of the repressive state that it was determined to overthrow. Its spiritual leader was Vera Figner, who was from a Russian-German noble family (though many enemies may have wished her to be Jewish). Membership included a variety of people but mostly former university students from the provinces, a surprising number of whom were women.[16] The organization's activities were naturally centered in and around St. Petersburg, where the emperor and his family lived during most of the year. Several dramatic attempts were made

16. For biographies of leading women, see Margaret Maxwell, *Narodniki Women: Russian Women Who Sacrificed Themselves for the Dream of Freedom* (New York: Pergamon, 1990).

on the life of the tsar. Finally, a group led by Sof'ia Perovskaia and Andrei Zheliabov prepared multiple methods of attack early in 1881, including planting mines in a tunnel under a street over which the tsar often passed. The police, however, had almost caught up with the plotters and in fact arrested Zheliabov in February.[17]

On 13 March 1881 the tsar made the usual routine visits around the capital, riding in his special bomb-proof carriage and accompanied by mounted guards. On his way back to the Winter Palace, the entourage carefully avoided the mined street because of rumors of danger there. But on the most obvious alternate route along the Catherine Canal, members of the conspiracy were stationed with grenades. One was thrown under the imperial carriage as it passed, wounding a couple of the guards but leaving Alexander II unharmed. The tsar then made a fatal mistake in getting out to inspect the damage. Another assassin, Ignat Hrynievicki (Grinevitskii in Russian), approached and dropped an explosive at the tsar's feet, blowing off both his legs.[18] Alexander II lived only long enough to reach his bed in the palace, and the assassin was also killed by the blast. Six of the ringleaders were soon under arrest, including Gesia Gelfman (Jessie Helfman), from whose apartment the operation was staged.

The public outrage that followed assumed a nationalistic tone, since a Pole had perpetrated the assassination and a Jewish woman, Gelfman, had helped organize it. Most historians agree that the event was a decisive turning point in Russian history because of the ensuing reaction, which became embedded in Russian political life for many years. Reports that Alexander II was about to sign a constitutional arrangement for a parliamentary assembly made the timing of the deed seem even more tragic. Thrust so suddenly into the limelight, the new tsar was ill-prepared and probably personally unsuited to the leadership tasks ahead. He was easily influenced by the rising conservative clique, led by his former tutor, Pobedonostsev, and a recently appointed and powerful "minister of court" and chief of security, Illarion Vorontsov-Dashkov. The latter quickly helped organize an ultrana-

---

17. For basic background and details, see Adam B. Ulam, *In the Name of the People: Prophets and Conspirators in Prerevolutionary Russia* (New York: Viking Press, 1977); James H. Billington, *Fire in the Minds of Men: Origins of the Revolutionary Faith* (New York: Basic Books, 1980), pp. 386–418; and W. Bruce Lincoln, *In War's Dark Shadow: The Russians Before the Great War* (New York: Dial Press, 1983), pp. 135–90.

18. American officials were first informed by cable with the details following; Foster to Blaine, 13 March and 14 March 1881, DUSM, Russia, vol. 35 (roll 35, M 35), RG 59, NA.

tionalist, quasi-secret "Sacred Band," whose missions were to protect the new tsar and his family, root out terrorists, and promote Russian patriotism.[19]

The American response to the assassination was what might be expected from a still-friendly power and one that had suffered a similar shock sixteen years before. The Senate immediately dispatched a resolution of sympathy to the Russian legation, which returned its appreciation.[20] General Grant, apparently having buried his ill feelings about the past, related in an interview his fond memories of his 1878 conversation with Alexander II.[21] The New York *Times* led an attack on the Russian revolutionaries: "Now, if never before, Nihilism unmasks and stands revealed as the chief foe of the liberty of the Russian people. . . . It is Nihilism which has retarded the growth of Russian liberty in its very infancy, and which has now perhaps dealt it a blow from which it will not recover in a generation."[22]

When Russian exiles and sympathetic socialists met in New York on the evening of 15 March for a celebration of the revolutionary success in Russia, they were sharply chastised by the press as a bunch of "adventurers and lunatics" who were more interested in drinking beer than in serious discussion.[23] A solemn requiem was held a week later at the small Russian chapel on Second Avenue, attended by patriotic Russians, curious onlookers, foreign consuls, and local dignitaries, including former minister Edwin Stoughton. The tall and impressive Father Nicholas Bjerring was reportedly very uncomfortable with conducting the service before such an unfamiliar, impolite, and jostling crowd, about a third of whom had to remain outside in the street.[24]

In Washington, a service was held at noon on 15 March in an improvised chapel in the Russian legation with the diplomatic corps and secretaries of state and war in attendance. The Russian minister, however, was upset that a grand ball at General Edward Beale's house was held as scheduled that eve-

---

19. For more analysis of the beginnings of the reign of Alexander III, see Heide W. Whelan, *Alexander III and the State Council: Bureaucracy and Counter-Reform in Late Imperial Russia* (New Brunswick, N.J.: Rutgers University Press, 1982).

20. Bartolomai to Blaine, 17 March 1881, NRL, vol. 9 (roll 7, M 39), RG 59, NA.

21. "Gen. Grant's Recollections," New York *Times*, 14 March 1881, p. 1.

22. "What the Nihilists Have Done," New York *Times*, 14 March 1881, p. 4. A cartoon depicting the grave of Alexander II was captioned "The Remedy Is Worse than the Evil." *Harper's Weekly*, 2 April 1881, p. 221.

23. New York *Times*, 16 March 1881, p. 4.

24. "In Memory of the Czar," ibid., 21 March 1881, p. 5.

ning, especially since the host was the father-in-law of a Russian diplomat.[25] Elsewhere, Andrew Dickson White, as minister to Germany, participated in a similar ceremony in Berlin and recalled that the last time he held a candle was at the funeral of Nicholas I in the Peter and Paul Church in St. Petersburg. To his current colleague there he reflected,

> I have always cherished a kind of tenderness for him [Alexander II] and feel now that a man who has emancipated forty millions of serfs deserved a better fate. It is a curious thing in history that such men as Louis XVI, Abraham Lincoln, and Alexander II who really emancipated millions of their people have died violent deaths, virtually in consequence of such emancipations.[26]

The official note of sympathy from Secretary of State James G. Blaine was in a similar vein, recalling Alexander II's assistance to the Union during the Civil War, "even at the risk of plunging his own empire into war."[27]

Whether the trend toward national conservatism would have continued under Alexander II or a new spirit of constitutionalism ushered in by Loris-Melikov would have prevailed, the reaction following the assassination settled the issue. The speedy execution of five of the convicted plotters (excepting the pregnant Gesia Gelfman) presaged the new era. Among the approximately 100,000 spectators was secretary of legation Hoffman, who described the universal indignation at the "stupidity and brutality of the chief executioners" as the rope broke twice in trying to hang one of them. "I am confident that they came away so disgusted with the barbarity of the spectacle, that hereafter they will be indifferent to, if they do not connive at, its overthrow." Hoffman added a philosophical assessment of the general situation:

> It appears to me that the condition of this country is going from bad to worse. The late Emperor, when he gave the serfs their liberty, should

25. Bartolomai to Giers, 5/17 March and 23 March/4 April 1881, f. 133, op. 470, d. 154 (1881), AVPR. On the marriage of Mamie Beale and Georgi Bakhmetev in Vienna, see New York *Herald*, 26 March 1877.

26. To John W. Foster, 15 March 1881, Foster Papers, LC.

27. To Foster, 13 April 1881, DI, Russia, vol. 16 (roll 138, M 77), RG 59, NA. Russians would soon have an opportunity to repay respects when President James A. Garfield died of complications from an assassin's attack in September. Admiral Avraam Aslambegov, who was commanding the Russian Pacific squadron on call in San Francisco, appeared before the commander of the Presidio in his full dress uniform and ordered his ships cloaked in black; Hoffman to Giers, 10/22 October 1881 (c), DPR, Russia, vol. 4536 (notes sent), RG 84, NA.

Alexander III upon his ascendancy to the throne. Harper's Weekly, *2 April 1881, courtesy of the Kansas Collection, University of Kansas Libraries*

have followed it with a constitutional government. When one man is absolute master of the liberty of all his subjects, and can imprison them indefinitely, or send them into exile, without process of law, freedom of the serf is illogical. Slavery is the necessary concomitant of arbitrary government, as freedom is of a constitutional government.

In the meantime, the Emperor shuts himself up in his palace, or rather fortress, of Gatchina. . . . and notwithstanding all these precautions, anonymous letters are found from time to time in the palace, warning the emperor that unless he complies with the demands of the conspirators, his son will be kidnapped, and he and the Empress will share the fate of his father.[28]

28. To Blaine (confidential), 19 April 1882, DUSM, Russia, vol. 35 (roll 35, M 35), RG 59, NA. An artist's contemporary rendition of the execution scene is in *Harper's Weekly*, 28 May 1881, p. 216.

Such was to be the tenor of the new reign. With the rise in influence of Pobedonostsev and successive interior ministers, Nikolai Ignat'ev and Dmitri Tolstoi, the remaining "liberals" resigned their positions: Melikov and Abaza in April, Miliutin in May, and Grand Duke Constantine as president of the State Council in July. Foster, having shortened his vacation in Italy, wrote, "These events are interpreted as a plain indication of the Emperor's resolution to allow no diminution of his autocratic power, to encourage the conservative element and to seek to restore confidence and order by rigorous and repressive measures. The effect has been very marked and generally unfavorable."[29] But he still believed that there might be reforms.

Adding to the despair and melancholy surrounding the loss of the liberator tsar was economic depression, driven especially by a widespread drought the previous year.[30] Foster noted that "the past winter has been a season of great suffering in large sections of the country, owing to the failure of crops, and just now many industries and manufactories are suspended or employ only a limited number of hands, and idle and hungry people add to the complication, of which it is feared the nihilists will be too ready to profit."[31] And certainly that fear amplified the government's security precautions. It even prompted concern about "revolutionists" who had escaped for the freedom of America, especially Leo Hartman (Lev Gartman), implicated in an assassination attempt in 1880. Blaine reported unofficially, "The Russian Minister has expressed to me the belief that the Nihilist Conspirators have an efficient bunch of cooperationists in New York—the objective point being the murder of Alexander III."[32]

29. Foster to Blaine, 23 May 1881, DUSM, Russia, vol. 35 (roll 35, M 35), RG 59, NA. One of the best "eyewitness" accounts of the period is Evgenii M. Feoktistov, *Vospominaniia E. M. Feoktistova: Za kulisami politiki i literatury, 1848–1896*, ed. Iu. G. Oksman (Leningrad: Priboi, 1929; reprint, Newtonville, Mass.: Oriental Research Partners, 1975), pp. 196–238.

30. Foster warned that "whole provinces, embracing millions of people, are threatened with famine during the present winter." To Evarts, 19 November 1880, DUSM, Russia, vol. 34 (roll 34, M 35), RG 59, NA. The famine was concentrated along the Volga in Samara and Saratov provinces and along the Black Sea. Calling this a year of "manifold misfortunes," Dyer in Odessa reported that because of the sharp drop in grain exports, American grain supplied the Russian Mediterranean market, and only 5 percent of Britain's imports came from Russia. To Hunter, 25 March 1881, DUSC, Odessa, vol. 6 (roll 3, M 459), RG 59, NA.

31. Foster to Blaine, 23 May 1881, DUSM, Russia, vol. 35 (roll 35, M 35), RG 59, NA.

32. To Foster (private and confidential), 29 June 1881 (c), Foster Papers, LC.

The Impact on the Jewish Population

The 1880s was bound to be a difficult period for the Jews of Russia, regardless of revolutionary attempts against the government. The growth of conservative nationalism, which was often hostile to Jews and other non-Russians, the harsh economic times, and the upward and outward mobility of the Jews encouraged resentment. But no one anticipated the degree of violence that would be directed against this segment of the population in the wake of the assassination.

A wave of pogroms occurred in 1881, mainly in April and May but continuing through August; there were irregular outbreaks for many years. The predominant historical explanation was for many years that the Russian government, including a number of vocal anti-Semites in leading positions, deliberately instigated and directed the horrible violence against the Jews. Recent scholarship has convincingly shown, however, that authorities, both at the central and local levels, were not directly responsible for the pogroms, though they were usually slow and half-hearted in responding.[33] The "riots" were instead the product of rumors, long-standing grievances, ignorance and superstition, religious emotion, and pent-up anger erupting locally. A particular trigger was the circulation of a rumor that Alexander III, upset about Jewish revolutionary involvement in the death of his father, had signed an *ukaz* calling for vengeance against the Jews. As popularly understood, this allowed complete freedom to pillage Jewish property for a period of three days, the normal length of a pogrom. All told, the extent of the destruction and loss of life was obviously enormous, yet an exact assessment is impossible given the tendency of both the authorities and the Jewish communities to hide the evidence.

The assassination was considered by many people as a blow against Slavic national tradition and culture, despite the irony that Alexander II was mostly of German blood and Western in orientation. Consequently, the attacks generally followed Christian religious holidays, especially Easter.[34] The perpetrators were mainly Ukrainian and Polish because of their predomi-

---

33. See especially I. Michael Aronson, *Troubled Waters: The Origins of the 1881 Anti-Jewish Pogroms in Russia* (Pittsburgh, Pa.: University of Pittsburgh Press, 1990); Rogger, *Jewish Policies and Right-Wing Politics*, pp. 25–31; and John Klier, "The Russian Press and the Anti-Jewish Pogroms of 1881," *Canadian-American Slavic Studies* 17, 2 (Summer 1983): 199–221.

34. For the calendar of pogroms and specific examples of their course, see Aronson, *Troubled Waters*, pp. 43–61.

nance in the districts inhabited by Jews. Since the earliest and most brutal of the pogroms occurred in cities and towns, such as Elizavetgrad, Kiev, and Warsaw, business competitors of recently established Jews may have played a leadership role. The economic depression also meant that the number of people owing money to Jewish lenders had risen, and many were unable to pay their debts.

Local authorities were on the whole incapable or unwilling to deal with the ferocity and mob nature of the violence, though both clergy and officials can be credited with efforts to stem the tide; some of the rioters were even arrested and punished.[35] More often, the authorities viewed the events from the perspective that "they had it coming to them" and enforced the restrictive laws more severely. This compounded the hardships for the Jews, who were then forced to abandon their homes and property and return to their place of origin or to a few larger cities, such as Odessa, Warsaw, and Minsk. Large-scale emigration from these cities was thus a direct result of the attacks and Russian policy.

Unfortunately, American representatives were not in a good position to observe the situation. The consulship in Odessa, a key point in the region, was in a state of transition, Leander Dyer having left for an extended leave in February.[36] In St. Petersburg, Foster was frequently absent and hamstrung by contradictory information, but he did report that every Jewish dwelling in Kiev had been damaged during the rampage there: "Indiscriminate pillage became so much feared that Christians chalked their houses with crosses or exhibited holy images with lighted lamps before them to save themselves from the fury of the rabble. The acts that have been committed are more worthy of the Dark Ages than of the present century."[37] But it was nine months before Hoffman reported the extent of the riots in Warsaw, based on a consular report of 1 February 1882. Over a thousand Jewish shops had been ransacked in clearly ethnic targeting. Hoffman, however, epitomized the American willingness to accept Russian official explanations, for he thought that the damage had been exaggerated by the Jewish community and that the hatred was justified because Jews (virtually repeating the words

35. Fortunately for Russia, 1881 turned out to be the best crop year since 1874; Godfried Hoglund (Taganrog) to Foster, 7 July 1881, DPR, Russia, vol. 4438 (misc. received), RG 84, NA.
36. Dyer to Foster, 2 February 1881, ibid.
37. To Blaine, 24 May 1881, DUSM, Russia, vol. 35 (roll 35, M 35), RG 59, NA. The early pogroms were directed more toward destruction of property than the Jews themselves.

of Giers) "demoralize and oppress the lower classes by usury and fleecing them in all possible manners, instead of setting to work in an honest way."[38]

Apparently Americans on the scene did not know exactly what to believe or do and were influenced by their own prejudices. Hoffman was only trying to excuse inaction. In any event, a stronger stance was difficult, if not dangerous diplomatically; the British ambassador, for example, had received a negative official and public reaction to his moderate diplomatic protest against the attacks.[39] The Russian government made it clear that its internal affairs were not to be a subject of international discussion, so, to Giers's relief, Foster remained silent.[40] Another consideration was the friendly cooperation, especially from Ignat'ev, on the *Jeannette* rescue missions and the genuine expressions of regret when an assassin mortally wounded President Garfield. In fact, the lingering death of the president kept Blaine on hold as secretary of state. This no doubt contributed to American foreign policy paralysis. In August, Hoffman, acting on instruction, appeared at the Foreign Ministry to read Blaine's dispatch concerning the treatment of American Jews; Giers would not listen to it, but he did take a copy.[41]

In a circular of 13 September 1881, the Russian government banned public discussion of the Jewish problem and authorized even sterner legal enforcement of the restrictions. The directive blamed the Jews for their own difficulties, focusing especially on their expanded economic role outside the original Pale. Although there was some effort to stop the violence, the clearly anti-Semitic posture of the government did little to douse the pogroms, which continued, though with less intensity, well into 1882.

The American public was also slow to react. One traveler compassionately mentioned the Jewish plight in describing his visit to Warsaw,[42] the American news media provided short accounts,[43] and pictures of the Kiev pogrom, probably from British sources, were published in July.[44] It was not long, however, before more details became available through Jewish chan-

---

38. To Frelinghuysen, 14 February 1882, DUSM, Russia, vol. 36 (roll 36, M 35), RG 59, NA.

39. Foster to Blaine, 24 May 1881, DUSM, Russia, vol. 35 (roll 35, M 35), RG 59, NA.

40. Giers to Bartolomai, 8 July 1881, f. 170, op. 512/1, d. 6, AVPR.

41. Hoffman to Blaine, 29 August 1881, DUSM, Russia, vol. 35 (roll 35, M 35), RG 59, NA.

42. James W. Buel, *Russian Nihilism and Exile Life in Siberia* (St. Louis, Mo.: Historical Publishing Company, 1883), pp. 492–93.

43. See, for example, New York *Times*, 14 May 1881.

44. *Leslie's Illustrated*, 9 July 1881, p. 312, and 16 July 1881, p. 328.

nels and from new immigrants. The belated American response was shaped by the obvious downtrodden appearance of Jews fleeing Russia and by the increasingly conservative direction of Russian policy. Sympathy for persecuted Jews and revolutionary nihilists could thus be combined, as in the case of Hartman, whom Russia wanted returned to face charges. *Harper's Weekly* rose to his defense:

> There is no question as to the existence of a most cruel, arbitrary, and oppressive despotism in Russia. Whatever may have been the motives which inspired the late Emperor in his experiments of reform, the experiments themselves have almost wholly failed. The emancipation of the serfs from the control of their masters is an accomplished fact; but they have passed to another servitude, which is all the more galling because they are no longer protected from it by the interposition of their lords.[45]

Finally, in April 1882, Blaine's replacement, Frederick Frelinghuysen, summarized what he believed to be the position of the United States:

> The prejudice of race and creed having in our day given way to the claims of our common humanity, the people of the United States have heard, with great regret, the stories of the sufferings of the Jews in Russia. . . . You will, if a favorable opportunity offers, state with all proper deference that the feeling of friendship which the United States entertain for Russia prompts this Government to express the hope that the Imperial Government will find means to cause the persecution of these unfortunate fellow beings to cease.

But he added a definite note of caution; "However much this Republic may disapprove of affairs in other nationalities, it does not conceive that it is its right or province officiously and offensively to intermeddle."[46]

Perrin and Rosenstraus

Diplomatically, attention was centered on the repercussions of the pogroms and Russian restrictions on the status of two naturalized American Jews

45. *Harper's weekly*, 13 August 1881, p. 558.
46. To Hoffman, 15 April 1882, DI, Russia, vol. 16 (roll 138, M 77), RG 59, NA. It may be relevant to note that the new secretary of state served simultaneously as president of the American Bible Society during 1884–1885.

who were businessmen in Kharkov. Alexis Victor Perrin, an ambitious twenty-eight-year-old traveling salesman, had arrived in Moscow early in 1879 with the object of establishing an independent dealership in American agricultural implements and other manufactured goods under the name of "Associated Industries of the United States in Russia."[47] His first but unsuccessful effort was to sell locomotive headlights to the Tambov-Saratov railroad. The next year Perrin settled in Kharkov as agent of the McCormick Harvesting Machine Company under the nominal direction of its chief representative in Russia, George Freudenreich, who was headquartered in Odessa. With little encouragement from Freudenreich or McCormick,[48] he planned to rapidly expand his agency, marry a local woman, and settle down with what promised to be a profitable enterprise in the heart of Russia's breadbasket.

In early July 1881, while exhibiting reapers in a field near Kharkov, local authorities questioned Perrin's right to conduct business in the area and accused him of being a Russian-born Jew who had fled Russia to escape military service. Perrin, whose original name was apparently Pravin, was sufficiently frightened to leave immediately for Odessa. He hurriedly escaped the country through Rumania, after sending strong protests to the legation in St. Petersburg. In turn, Freudenreich claimed considerable losses for his company in Russia and accused business competitors in Kharkov of forcing Perrin out. The incident, in fact, discouraged McCormick from seeking more Russian business at this time.[49]

The charges were probably correct according to Russian law, since Perrin had left Russia when he was seventeen without permission. However, he claimed that he was no longer Jewish, having converted to Orthodoxy in 1871, and that he had verbal permission from the minister of interior (Loris-Melikov) to reside in Kharkov. Perrin also contended that he did not know of his Jewish origins and that the charges were instigated by a rival suitor to his bride-to-be. But the scrutiny of Jewish residents in 1881 and Perrin's own

47. Perrin (Moscow) to Hoffman, 22 March 1879, DPR, Russia, vol. 4437 (misc. received), RG 84, NA. In this letter Perrin describes a two-month tour through the central and southern provinces of Russia and takes issue with Hoffman's article about Russian business prospects in the *American Exporter*.

48. Fred V. Carstensen, *American Enterprise in Foreign Markets: Studies of Singer and International Harvester in Russia* (Chapel Hill and London: University of North Carolina Press, 1984), pp. 121–22.

49. Ibid.; Freudenreich (Odessa) to Hoffman, 3 August 1881, DPR, Russia, vol. 4438 (misc. received), RG 84, NA. Freudenreich emphasized that this was an especially sensitive time when the agent was to collect payments from the previous year's business.

loud behavior had no doubt aggravated the situation.[50] Hoffman took up the case immediately with government officials but found little sympathy for it.[51] After interviews with Giers and Ignat'ev, Hoffman advised Perrin that the latter was "not disposed to relax one iota of the severity of the laws in relation to foreigners in Russia and above all in relations to former Russian subjects, returning here, with, as it may be supposed, different notions of government from those they had when they went away."[52]

Perrin still hoped to be able to settle his business and romantic affairs in Kharkov. From London he wrote Hoffman: "My business in Russia is of such important a nature that I cannot resist the idea of being deprived of visiting that country, even if worse comes to worse and I am condemned to colonization to Siberia."[53] He even pressed the minister of interior directly to give him special permission to return, much to the annoyance of Hoffman.[54] And on a brief visit to the United States, Perrin managed to ingratiate himself with the New York press.[55] He was finally told that he was clearly in violation of Russian law regarding evasion of military service and the American government could do nothing more.[56]

The Rosenstraus affair had a happier outcome but, developing at about the same time as Perrin's, gave the impression of an incipient Russian onslaught against resident American Jews. Theodore Rosenstraus, originally from Württemburg, had emigrated to the United States and was naturalized in New York before entering retail trade in Kharkov in the 1860s. The business flourished, especially because of demand for Singer sewing machines

50. To Hoffman, 2 December (New York) and 22 December 1881 (London), DPR, Russia, vol. 4438 (misc. received), RG 84, NA.

51. Hoffman to Blaine, 10 August 1881, DUSM, Russia, vol. 35 (roll 35, M 35), RG 59, NA; Hoffman to Giers, 20 July/1 August and 29 July/10 August 1881, DPR, Russia, vol. 4536 (notes sent), RG 84, NA.

52. Hoffman to Perrin, 25 August 1881, DPR, Russia, vol. 4484 (misc. sent), RG 84, NA. To Freudenreich Hoffman wrote, "The russian gov't. is exceedingly unwilling that its former subjects, who have become familiar with a different and more liberal form of gov't. should return to spread their new ideas in this country." 9 August 1881, ibid.

53. Perrin to Hoffman, 6 January 1882, DUSM, Russia, vol. 36 (roll 36, M 35), RG 59, NA.

54. Hoffman to Frelinghuysen, 31 January 1882, ibid.

55. "Subject or Citizen: Naturalized in America and Arrested in Russia," New York *Herald*, 5 December 1881, p. 10. He was quoted as saying, "It seems strange that Russia should be the only place where an American is not a free man, but if he is not to be protected there it will be a good thing to find out."

56. Perrin (Paris) to Hunt, 9 October 1882, DPR, Russia, vol. 4438 (misc. received); Hunt to Perrin, 20 October and 13 November 1882, DPR, Russia, vol. 4484 (misc. sent), RG 84, NA.

and despite periodic badgering by local officials. By 1880 he had brought his brother Herman to Russia, opened more branches, and employed a number of relatives as clerks. He was now ready to retire (though only in his fifties) to Germany and leave the successful business in the hands of Herman. His attempt to transfer his first-merchant guild status to his brother at the end of 1881 alerted authorities and perhaps competitors as well. The Rosenstrauses were informed that as American Jews they had no right to live in Kharkov and were ordered to leave.[57] The American legation was again summoned into action.

In St. Petersburg Hoffman immediately appealed to Ignat'ev and won a temporary extension. He argued that Americans were being clearly discriminated against, as Russian and other foreign Jews were still allowed to conduct business in Kharkov.[58] But the matter devolved on a recent law that foreign Jews in Russia could not hire clerks even though they were Jewish relatives. To Hoffman and new minister William Hunt, this violated the stipulation in the 1832 treaty that Americans be accorded the same treatment as Russians, but they wavered in pressing this point with Russian ministers in 1882 for fear of causing an even sterner backlash and in hopes that disregard might lead to nonenforcement. Hoffman advised this latter course in a telegram and follow-up letter to Rosenstraus.[59]

Not satisfied with this, Herman Rosenstraus went to St. Petersburg to make a personal appeal and wrote directly to President Chester A. Arthur in April, thus prodding the Department of State and its representatives in Russia to further exertions.[60] Approaching the minister of interior, the reactionary Dmitri Tolstoi, Hoffman obtained an extension until 15 October but no final resolution. He then learned that, as in earlier difficulties, Herman Rosenstraus had "arranged things" with the authorities in Kharkov.[61]

---

57. H. Rosenstraus to legation, 30 December 1881 (old style), and T. Rosenstraus to legation, 3/15 January 1882, DPR, Russia, vol. 4438 (misc. received), RG 84, NA. Herman noted: "While writing this it almost breaks my heart at the idea, that a free American citizen who means to be upright and honest, should be dealt with in such a way and only for the mere reason because it pleased the Lord to have him born a Jew."
58. To Ignat'ev, 5/17 January 1882, DPR, Russia, vol. 4536 (notes sent), RG 84, NA.
59. Telegram to Rosenstraus, 13 April 1882 (c), and letter, 8 May 1882, DPR, Russia, vol. 4484 (misc. sent), RG 84, NA.
60. Frelinghuysen to Hunt, 26 June 1882 (c), DI, Russia, vol. 16 (roll 138, M 77), RG 59, NA.
61. Hoffman to Frelinghuysen, 15 and 19 July 1882, and Hunt to Frelinghuysen, 15 September and 1 November 1882, DUSM, Russia, vol. 36 (roll 36, M 35), RG 59, NA; Tolstoi to Hunt, 5/17 July 1882, DPR, Russia, vol. 4507 (notes received), RG 84, NA.

Rosenstraus remained in a tenuous situation with only temporary extensions, which made business planning awkward if not impossible. He became increasingly embittered by the whole affair: "I think it a great wrong that I, as an American citizen should be haunted [sic] like a criminal while my fellow American citizens who are protected by the same flag are left in peace and this is done because the God you and I and we all offer our prayers to had me born a Jew."[62] Nevertheless, probably through the age-old custom of bribery, the Rosenstrauses operated in Kharkov for several more years, although Herman left in 1888.[63] As he explained to the New York *Times:* "I left Russia . . . for I didn't feel satisfied to stay in a country where I was only tolerated. I landed in this free country in June, 1888, and believe me I feel at home again." Theodore, however, was still doing business in 1890.[64]

The Rosenstraus and Perrin cases, though occurring in the same place at about the same time and involving Jewish businessmen of naturalized American citizenship, differed in two important respects. Perrin was born in Russia, the Rosenstrauses in Germany. The latter conducted a long-established business and were accustomed to dealing with local authorities; Perrin was a newcomer easily scared away. The results were typical of several cases that came before the American diplomatic service in Russia.[65]

Jewish Emigration

The 1881 pogroms and stricter enforcement of legal restrictions by the Russian government promoted a significant wave of emigration to the United States. Jews in south Russia must have known about the successful flight of Mennonites, Volga Germans, and some Jews and Poles in the 1870s. Many forced to flee from their pogrom-battered districts went to Odessa, where

62. Rosenstraus (Kharkov) to Hunt, 6 October 1883, DPR, Russia, vol. 4439 (misc. received), RG 84, NA.

63. H. Rosenstraus (Kharkov) to Lothrop, 29 April 1888, DPR, Russia, vol. 4443 (misc. received), RG 84, NA. Hounded again by the authorities, he now only requested permission to take out household effects without paying any duties; Wurts to Blaine, 2 March 1890, DUSM, Russia, vol. 41 (roll 41, M 35), RG 59, NA.

64. H. Rosenstraus (New York) to editor, 14 November 1890, "One of the Persecuted Jews," New York *Times,* 16 November 1890, p. 11; T. Rosenstraus to Wurts, 16/28 February 1890, DPR, Russia, vol. 4444 (misc. received), RG 84, NA.

65. Among other cases involving Americans, Joseph Moses, the stable director for a circus, was also threatened but managed to come to an understanding with the police. Like Rosenstraus, he was born in Germany and naturalized in the United States. Hoffman to Blaine, 9 January 1882, DUSM, Russia, vol. 36 (roll 36, M 35), RG 59, NA.

Russian-Jewish immigrants arriving in New York City in 1882. Harper's Weekly,
*18 February 1882, courtesy of the Kansas Collection, University of Kansas
Libraries*

transport could be more readily arranged. Publicity given to their plight had
also awakened philanthropic instincts among prosperous Jews abroad, who
provided financial support for emigration and settlement. Adolph Sanger
founded an organization for that purpose in New York in September 1881,
and the first Russian pogrom refugees arrived later that month.[66]

To use an apt cliché, the trickle soon became a flood. A temporary American agent in Taganrog was startled to find in April 1882 that suddenly all
Jews in his area wanted to emigrate to the United States to purchase land
and become farmers.[67] By June, 1,500 of the 6,000 resident Jews of Moscow
were reported to have left the country, and the total boarding ships in
Odessa that month was placed between 20,000 and 25,000. This naturally
caused strains and hardships. Whereas the earlier emigration of Mennonites
and Volga Germans had been well-planned and by routed train to German
port cities, the Jewish emigration was hastily arranged, larger in scale, and
initially mostly through Odessa. A consequence was that many were
stranded for intervals in refugee camps or shelters in France and elsewhere.[68]
The American consul general noted that Russian public opinion supported

66. New York *Times*, 15 September 1881, p. 2, and 28 September 1881, p. 1.
67. Hoyland to Hoffman, 3/15 April 1882, DPR, Russia, vol. 4438 (misc. received),
RG 84, NA.
68. A Russian source in Paris emphasized the hardships for large families; *Voskhod*
(Ascent) 1, 2 (8 January 1882).

emigration, as did wealthy Russian Jews who wanted to get rid of their poorer brethren.[69]

By the beginning of 1882, steady streams of immigrants were arriving at New York, Philadelphia, and Baltimore, calling more and more attention to their sufferings in Russia. Over 2,500 had arrived in New York by March, and Philadelphia greeted one of the largest single contingents—325 debarking from the *Illinois*—on 23 February.[70] At Chickering Hall in New York on 1 February, a mass meeting was held to protest the Russian abuse and the continuing though sporadic pogroms in Russia, and another was organized a month later at the Academy of Music in Philadelphia.[71] Sympathizers specifically called for United States government intervention. By April a resolution had reached the floor of the House of Representatives asking the president to appeal to the tsar in regarding the treatment of the Jews, but it was referred to the Committee on Foreign Relations.[72] One of the leaders of the protest, Myer Isaacs, circulated a pamphlet on the "Persecution of Jews in Russia" that complained of the lack of diplomatic pressure. It even found its way to Russia and no doubt helped to inspire Frelinghuysen's instruction cited previously.[73]

By July 1882 the flow of Jewish refugees from Russia was severely taxing the abilities of the Jewish aid societies. The New York organization had found employment for 6,470, but 2,200 remained destitute on Ward's Island.

69. Stanton to Hunter, 19 June 1882, DUSC, St. Petersburg, vol. 16 (roll 11, M 81), RG 59, NA. He also reported that non-Russian residents were becoming alarmed by the Jewish exodus. "The opinion of the *foreign* element is decidedly with the oppressed party the more so as the whole movement is considered the precursor of future movements against all foreigners especially the Germans."

70. New York *Times*, 16 February 1882, p. 3, and 23 February 1882, p. 5. The Russian chargé in Washington, Villamov, may have misled his government at this time by reporting that Jewish immigration was of no importance and that the protest meetings were politically inspired, much to-do about nothing; Villamov to Giers, 21 January/2 February and 11/23 March 1882, f. 133, op. 470, d. 105 (1882), AVPR. However, Karl Struve, who arrived on the scene in April, took the matter more seriously; Struve to Giers, 7/19 May 1882, ibid.

71. New York *Times*, 2 February 1882, p. 4, and 5 March 1882, p. 2; "The Jewish Persecution in Russia," *Harper's Weekly*, 11 February 1882, p. 83. Admitting that the United States was not free from incidents against Jews, the latter article concluded: "But honorable and humane men here and everywhere join in the indignation which the present spectacle arouses, and wonder whether the Russian Government means to show itself savage or civilized."

72. "The Condition of Russian Jews," New York *Times*, 9 April 1882, p. 1.

73. A copy is in DPR, Russia, vol. 4438 (misc. received), RG 84, NA. Though undated, it is filed between letters of 20 May and 8 June 1882, which may indicate the time it was received in St. Petersburg.

Over $140,000 had been collected for organizing resettlement at the rate of a thousand each month.[74] By this time the total number of refugees had reportedly reached 15,000, still a small portion (6 percent) of the total Jewish population of the United States at that time.[75]

Insufficient charity was not the only problem. In contrast to many other immigrants, this group was less inclined toward agricultural settlement, more communally oriented, aroused resentment from other immigrants, and could not even speak proper German, let alone any English. Most were also very orthodox in religious practices, unlike their American benefactors. Some fears were voiced in New York that the influx might draw public attention to and hurt the successfully established Jewish communities. How widespread this feeling was is not clear, but efforts were definitely directed to moving these people out of the cities, mainly to the West and into farming.[76] Just as some German-American activists had shunned the Volga German immigrants, many American Jews at first preferred to have nothing to do with their impoverished and different kindred from Russia—or at least wanted to hurry them out of sight.

Dissatisfaction was the natural result. Agricultural land was not wisely chosen, usually remote and left over from previous ventures, and the process of settlement was slow and costly. In general the new immigrants from Odessa were accustomed to urban life, not to farming. They also lacked resources for tools, construction, and seeds, mainly because there were no local sponsors such as railroads. Although there were some lasting successes, such as the New Odessa colony in Oregon, most of the settlements soon failed, and their members found other work or returned home, some within a few months of their arrival.[77] For example, on 7 August 1882, a disgruntled group of 300 demonstrated in front of the Hebrew Aid Society in New York, demanding to be sent home.[78] An initially promising colony in Middlesex County, Virginia, founded by the Baltimore aid society, was abandoned after a year. As an editorial conjectured, "It may be that the spirit of our institutions is unfavorable to the maintenance of separate colonies on American soil."[79] Unfortunately, these migratory Jews would face even worse situations in Russia—and perhaps flee again as refugees.

74. "Work of the Hebrew Aid Society," New York *Times*, 18 July 1882, p. 8.
75. Ibid., 16 July 1882, p. 8.
76. "The Hebrews from Russia," ibid.
77. Fifty-one families returned to Russia in July 1882; ibid., 15 July 1882, p. 3.
78. "Discontented Russian Jews," ibid., 8 August 1882, p. 8.
79. "American Colonial Failures," ibid., 8 December 1883, p. 4.

For a time the exodus from Russia subsided. As a new consul, Fulton Paul, reported from Odessa:

Emigration to the United States from South Russia has received a check, in consequence of news received from some of those who departed hence a few months since as to the condition of affairs there, an impression having prevailed here that the United States government would furnish each capital or land that could be converted into ready money to each male immigrant, and as but few of them are agriculturists or accustomed to hard labor their disappointment can be realized, and many have expressed a desire to return here.

For example, a Jewish grain dealer who had lived in the United States had returned and was now discouraging others from leaving by arguing that more money was to be made in Russia.[80]

The Coronation

The Jewish immigrant presence in the United States helped substantiate the negative public opinion of Russia in the United States on the eve of what was expected to be a grandiose spectacle of crowning the new tsar. But more newsprint was devoted to the hardships endured by the large number of real and suspected revolutionaries who were being incarcerated in Siberia in the postassassination wave of repression. Observing three Russian warships packed with convicts pass through the Suez Canal on their way to Sakhalin, David Ker proclaimed this practice the "application of fifteenth century principles to nineteenth century facts. Any system, even if tolerable enough in itself, may become a monstrous absurdity through mere lapse of time."[81]

The cloak of secrecy that descended on the court and the government following the assassination affected the coronation and prompted speculation about its probable date, if it would be private, or if there would even be one. A year into his reign, Alexander III was still isolated in his country palace. An American newspaper reported: "The czar is represented to lead a pitiable life in the prison-palace of Gatchina. He is said to be stupefied by captivity. He is afraid to accompany the czarina for outdoor exercise, and

80. To Hunter, 3 July 1882, DUSC, Odessa, vol. 6 (roll 3, M 459), RG 59, NA.
81. "Peasants and Nihilists" from Suez Canal, dated 20 May, New York *Times*, 2 July 1882, p. 4.

spends his daily [sic] with the children in the gymnasium, climbing rope ladders and turning somersaults."[82] Uncertainty about the crowning of the tsar persisted through most of 1882.[83] Finally, the date was set for May 1883 for the traditional ceremonies in Moscow, and grand preparations were soon under way.

Security measures tightened along with an increase in revolutionary threats. Both factors reduced the number of foreign observers—at least in comparison with the last coronation in 1856. The United States would again, however, be well represented. Heading the official party was the minister, William L. Hunt, his wife, daughter, and son. As special ambassador from Washington came Rear Admiral Charles Baldwin, commander of the Atlantic squadron. On board the *Lancaster* was a large naval staff, including William L. Chandler, the son of the secretary of navy, as Baldwin's personal secretary, and an impressive retinue of officers, led by distinguished and worldly Captains Bancroft Gherhardi and Alphonse Baptiste.[84]

Playing the Samuel Colt role of 1856 in representing the American public in the official party was John Mackay, the California forty-niner and "silver king," accompanied by his wife. He furnished the special car that carried the American group to Moscow and seemed to be the only one who really enjoyed the occasion.[85] Baldwin was miffed at being left off the formal invitation list to the coronation ceremony; Giers personally and hurriedly corrected this, and the admiral reluctantly attended. Although the snafu became the subject of an official protest, Baldwin was appeased by a chatty conversation with the new tsar at the diplomatic reception that followed—as well as by personal gifts of a handsome snuff box and a gold medal.[86]

Also on hand were reporters from the New York *Herald* and New York *Times*, who described the Moscow extravaganza in excruciating detail. The *Herald* reporter was even one of five newsmen to gain admittance to the climactic ceremony, "to the just disappointment of many other worthy col-

82. *Leslie's Illustrated*, 1 April 1882, p. 91.

83. "The Czar's Coronation," New York *Times*, 22 September 1882, p. 4.

84. Hunt to Giers, 23 April/7 May 1883, DPR, Russia, vol. 4536 (notes sent), RG 84, NA.

85. Mary King Waddington, *Letters of a Diplomat's Wife, 1883-1900* (London: Smith, Elder, 1905), p. 37. For background on Mackay, see John Russell Young, *Men and Memories: Personal Reminiscences* (New York and London: F. Tennyson Neely, 1901), 2:440–53.

86. Giers (in his own hand) to Hunt, 16/28 May 1883, DPR, Russia, vol. 4507 (notes received), RG 84, NA; Hunt to Frelinghuysen, 18 June 1883, DUSM, Russia, vol. 37 (roll 37, M 35), RG 59, NA; "Americans at Moscow," New York *Herald*, 3 June 1883, p. 15.

leagues."[87] Although the triumphal entry of the tsar into the city was eclipsed in New York papers by the grand celebration for the opening of the Brooklyn Bridge, readers were primed for coronation gush: "No such magnificent spectacle has been witnessed anywhere in Europe in modern times as the glorious and impressive service of to-day. The most gorgeous that I have ever seen sinks into insignificance compared with that which has just been brought to an end."[88] The *Herald*'s man on the scene, however, could not resist the temptation to recall a well-known Hans Christian Andersen story: "The Russian application of the fable is obvious. Heralds, chamberlains, courtiers, are busily dressing the Czar in the attributes of immortality, and though much of the week has passed in safety there is still a constant foreboding of the hour when his subjects shall learn that he has nothing on."[89]

The Americans in Moscow were in the Russian eye. Mackay's wealth was the subject of some speculation in the Moscow press as he was expected to spend 3 million rubles during his visit.[90] Admiral Baldwin was the only foreign naval representative and made sure that all St. Petersburg knew it by ordering the *Lancaster* to answer the postcoronation salute in Moscow "gun for gun."[91] As on similar occasions, American women produced the most singular impression for their country. Of eleven ladies attending the diplomatic reception, eight were American: Hunt's wife and daughter, Mrs. Baldwin, Mrs. Mackay, Mary King Waddington (wife of the special French envoy), and the wives of the Belgian, German, and Dutch ministers.[92] Although Mrs. Hunt suffered "diplomatic fatigue," her pretty daughter was

87. "Crowned," dated 27 May, New York *Herald*, 28 May 1883, p. 3 (whole page). The other reporters at the ceremony were from the London *Times*, Paris *Le Figaro*, Prague *Politik*, and Berlin *Vorsiche Zeitung*.

88. Ibid. Not long afterwards two of the American witnesses, Admiral Baldwin and Mrs. Waddington, debated whether the United States could produce such a display, with the admiral insisting on the affirmative but Waddington denying it: "I stuck to my guns, and said that certainly not all the intelligence, energy, education and money of America could produce such a pageant. What was so wonderful was the contrast. All the modern life and luxury grafted upon the old half-Eastern, half-barbarian world." Waddington, *Letters*, p. 137.

89. "Proclaiming the Coronation," New York *Herald*, 25 May 1883, p. 6. *Harper's Weekly*, 9 June 1883, p. 354, put it in plain English: "The tragedy of the Czar's position is that he stands really alone."

90. "Alexander III," New York *Herald*, 27 May 1883, p. 11 (whole page).

91. "Americans at Moscow," New York *Herald*, 3 June 1883, p. 15.

92. Mary King Waddington was the granddaughter of Rufus King and the sister-in-law of Eugene Schuyler. The German ambassador was married to Anna Jay, a descendant of another noted American family. Waddington, *Letters*, pp. v, 37–39.

the belle of the coronation. As the *Herald* noted, "The presence of so many and so charming American ladies in the diplomatic corps with the special embassies now in Moscow was the source of considerable comment."[93] They attracted the special attention of the empress, the emperor, and, of course, all the grand dukes, led by the experienced Alexis. Democratic America again came close to stealing the imperial show.

In general, the *Herald* scooped the *Times* with its liberal use of long cablegrams, but the latter's correspondent was far more knowledgeable and observant. Although these "letters" were without attribution, they were probably written by David Ker, who knew Russian and was an experienced traveler in the country.[94] Especially interesting were his comments on the dejection and pessimism in 1883 Russia in contrast to the hopes and optimism perceived during a visit three years earlier. Conservatism and Slavophilism were definitely in ascendance.[95]

> On my return to Russia this time I was struck by the change which had taken place in the disposition of society. Russians are very sociable by nature, and like to talk over men and things in their family circles, when many friends and acquaintances gather around the tea-table, drinking innumerable glasses of tea, smoking Turkish cigarettes, and discussing all subjects of interest in the presence of the ladies, who are just as well informed on all questions of social and political importance as are their husbands and brothers. Now, however, there is scarcely any animated conversations carried on in private houses, while public speeches are almost entirely prohibited, unless they be purely official ones.[96]

Foreign Affairs

Although the reign of Alexander III (1881–1894) is noted for political repression at home, it implemented significant bold shifts in foreign policy. Already in June 1881, Nikolai Giers laid the cornerstone of his tenure as foreign minister with a secret alliance with Germany and Austria—the Dreikaiserbund or Three Emperors' League—for a three-year term. Short,

93. New York *Herald*, 3 June 1883, p. 15.
94. The author mentions being in Central Asia in 1873.
95. "Men of Power in Russia" (letter of 7 May 1883), New York *Times*, 25 May 1883, p. 5.
96. "Russian State Affairs" (letter of 18 May 1883), New York *Times*, 4 June 1883, p. 2.

thin, and unimpressive, with hair and beard streaked with grey, Giers was from a German family that had moved to Russia in the eighteenth century to perform government service. Married to Gorchakov's niece, he was groomed as his assistant and successor; then, during the chancellor's prolonged illness after 1878, he was acting foreign minister, to which post he finally succeeded in 1882.[97]

In contrast to his predecessor, however, Giers was definitely in the shadow of the German chancellor, Otto von Bismarck, now styled a "prince" and generally acknowledged to be the mastermind of rapidly rising German power and authority in Europe. Bismarck's primary goals were to keep France on the defensive, dominate Austria, buy off Britain with trade, and cajole Russia into pacificity. By the German connection Russia hoped to gain solidarity and stability in the quest for security, peace, and conservatism and indeed received some of each, enough to agree to a three-year renewal of the arrangement in 1884.

The 1880s was a volatile time in international politics. The situation in the Balkans remained unsettled from the wreckage of the 1870s and the Congress of Berlin. Russia's recognized protectorate over the fledgling, "autonomous" Bulgaria was upset by a combination of Bulgarian nationalism and the ambitions of Alexander of Battenberg, who had been designated its guiding prince with Russian and German blessing. With Britain taking a more militant stance against Russian expansion, a crisis erupted in 1885 when Alexander of Battenberg moved to unite the provinces and to create a larger, more independent Bulgaria. This threat of war, intensified by political machinations, popular opinion, and jingoist presses, was a setback for the Russian Pan-Slavist cause.

A minor incident occurred in an American port during the tension that served to lighten parlor conversation. A small Russian sloop of war, *Strelok*, sought refuge at Norfolk in May 1885, but it was pursued and then held under observation by a much larger British ship, the *Garnet*. Moored near each other for several weeks, the officers of both ships were feted on shore by local citizenry and the United States Navy and apparently on outwardly friendly terms. The Russian commander, however, prepared surreptitiously to leave. When a number of fruit boats were observed going back and forth, the queried Russians answered that since there was so little fruit at home, they were

---

97. "M. de Giers Hard Road," New York *Times*, 7 July 1882, p. 2. For background on Giers's life, see Barbara Jelavich and Charles Jelavich, *The Education of a Russian Statesman: The Memoirs of Nicholas Karlovich Giers* (Berkeley and Los Angeles: University of California Press, 1962).

eating all they could. The boats were really carrying coal. Then one night lights were placed on sticks in the water as a decoy for the ship while the officers attended an opera on shore, but as soon as they returned the darkened ship silently weighed anchor. At dawn the *Garnet* sat alone in the harbor.[98]

Another potential tinderbox was in Central Asia, where Russian consolidation and expansion was matched by British advances into Afghanistan. The perception of British hostility to Russia in the international arena, despite flourishing trade relations, also extended to the Far East, as Russia increased its military and naval strength in the Vladivostok region and along the Amur River boundary, as well as its diplomatic position in China and Japan.

These conflicts encouraged anti-German sentiments among Russian observers within and without court circles, who became increasingly critical of Giers and his apparent subservience to German interests. They were led by the ever-influential publicist Mikhail Katkov, former patriot schemer Ilia Tsion (Elie Cyon), who had taken up residence in Paris,[99] and the Russian thorn in the side of America, Konstantin Katakazi. The latter renewed his connections with Katkov and sought in vain another diplomatic appointment in conversations with Giers and Pobedonostsev in St. Petersburg during the winter of 1883–1884.[100] Back in France, Katakazi continued to pursue an official connection, criticized the new Russian ambassador to France, predicted Germanization of the Balkans, and published Pan-Slavic letters in the French press under the name of Constantine Gavrilov.[101]

Aided and abetted by a similar cast of French writers and political activists, these partisans campaigned against the German alliance and in favor of one with France. Strange and egotistical personalities, they often clashed with one another. According to Tsion, Katakazi, disappointed in the rejection of his overtures but still a police agent, switched sides in 1886 and accepted payment from Bismarck to circulate compromising documents but

98. "Under the Garnet's Nose," New York *Times*, 21 August 1892, p. 17.
99. Tsion's role is emphasized and detailed by George F. Kennan and by the contemporary account of Feoktistov in *Vospominaniia*, pp. 268–91. For his own version of events, see Elie de Cyon, *Histoire de l'entente Franco-Russe, 1886–1894: Documents et souvenirs* (Paris: A. Charles, 1895).
100. Katakazi (St. Petersburg) to Giers (personal), 16 January 1884, referring to conversation the previous day, f. 133, op. 470, d. 22 (correspondance de Catacazy 1884), AVPR. Not surprisingly, the foreign ministry kept a separate file on Katakazi.
101. Katakazi to Giers, 25 August/6 September, 17/29 October, 20 November/2 December, and 18/30 December 1884, ibid.

was soon ignominiously exposed.[102] Nevertheless, a decisive swing toward this unlikely marriage of convenience between Russia and France occurred between 1886 and 1888, manifested by the weaker "Reinsurance Treaty" with Germany of 1887, by the failure of that arrangement to be renewed in 1890, and by French willingness to finance Russian industrialization.

The continuance of friendly relations with the United States served Russia in three main ways during this period: an assurance of an ability to broaden its international position in the wider world; an example of harmony with a government of quite different foundations, useful vis-à-vis the French Republic; and as a continued check on British aggression, especially in the Far East where American interests were rising. The able caretaker of the Russian mission in Washington, D.C., during most of the 1880s was Karl Struve, the son of the prominent Russian astronomer who had visited the United States a few years before. Significantly, Struve came in 1882 from Japan, where he had been minister for ten years; he would remain officially at his new post for another decade.[103] The large Struve family, in contrast to a number of their predecessors, fit in well and were highly regarded in society. Unfortunately, his popular Russian wife became ill and went home with her five children for treatment in 1885; Struve was thus often absent from his post.[104] Already that year he had requested a transfer to Europe.[105]

American Missions

The Americans and their families assigned diplomatic and consular duties in Russia underwent generally unhappy experiences in the 1880s. After John Foster of Indiana retired from the legation in 1882, William Hunt and

102. Cyon, *Histoire*, pp. 322–23. He describes Katakazi as having "a remarkable spirit of intrigue" and as "greedy as a merchant in the Constantinople bazaar." The source might be suspect, except that it was published in France soon after the events.

103. Struve's predecessor, Mikhail Bartolomai, was being removed quietly after a short tenure, and with the mutual agreement of both countries, for some apparent indiscretions of his wife, who was of British origin. Details are not clear. Wickham Hoffman assured Blaine that the new minister's wife was "a Russian lady agreeable and highly connected" and that no one in the government knew the reason for the change except Jomini, Giers, and Alexander III. Hoffman to Blaine, 8 October 1881, DUSM, Russia, vol. 36 (roll 36, M 35), RG 59, NA.

104. Lavish praise was bestowed on her at her death in 1889; "Death of Mrs. de Struve," New York *Times*, 14 August 1889, p. 1.

105. To Giers (private), 23 April/5 May 1885, f. 133, op. 470, d. 105, AVPR.

his wife and daughter from New Orleans took up residence in St. Petersburg. Although they all spoke French, adjusted well to the Russian social
scene, and were acclaimed at the coronation, the family suffered from the
climate and the repressive political atmosphere. They were also inconven-
ienced by poor housing, a common problem of American diplomats on a
stringent budget. As Wurts wrote Hunt while he was recuperating at Karls-
bad after the coronation: "This Maison Petit is little better than an assigna-
tion house. It has long been inhabited by French actresses and other persons whose reputations have left much to be desired."[106] Sadly, Hunt's tenure
was cut short by his death in February 1884.[107]

With rare good sense the vacancy was filled by transferring Alphonso Taft
of Cincinnati from Vienna, but after less than a year, he became very ill of
typhoid fever, and this talented diplomat and administrator was forced to
leave the scene.[108] His appointment was apparently congenial to the entourage that included his second wife and daughter; as a visitor noted, "The
Tafts enjoy St. Petersburg very much and have surrounded themselves with
a charming circle there. Fanny has a little dancing party every Monday evening under pretext of 'practicing the Mazourka.' "[109]

The new Cleveland administration appointee was also from the Midwest:
George V. N. Lothrop of Detroit, certainly a novice in diplomacy and something of a surprise selection.[110] After a grand Michigan send-off, the
Lothrops and their two attractive daughters headed to Russia with few
expectations—"I suppose we shall hardly know any Russians, as I have
heard they do not care for foreigners, least of all for Americans."[111] The family survived three Russian winters, cushioned by living in style and hosting
receptions and dinners. Giers and future foreign minister Alexander Iz-

106. Wurts (St. Petersburg) to Hunt, 14 July 1883, reel 2, Hunt Papers, LC.
107. Russia was earning a reputation as a "killer" post. An obituary for Edwin
Stoughton indicated that he had been in "enfeebled health" since he returned from
Russia; Harper's Weekly, 21 January 1882, p. 43.
108. Bayard to Taft, 13 May 1885, DI, Russia, vol. 16 (roll 138, M 77), RG 59, NA;
Lewis Alexander Leonard, Life of Alphonso Taft (New York: Hawke Publishing Company, 1920), pp. 183–88; Isabel Ross, An American Family: The Tafts—1678 to 1964 (Westport, Conn.: Greenwood Press, 1964), p. 95.
109. Moncure Conway to John Kasson, 5 February 1885 (c), Conway Correspondence, Columbia University Library; original in Dickinson College library.
110. New York Times, 9 May 1885, p. 4.
111. Almira Lothrop letter of 3 October 1885, in The Court of Alexander III: Letters
of Mrs. Lothrop, ed. William Prall [son-in-law] (Philadelphia: John C. Winston, 1910),
p. 30.

volsky even attended the Thanksgiving celebration in 1887.[112] According to one source, Lothrop spent $15,000 above his salary ($17,000).[113] Finally, ill and tired of his duties, Lothrop resigned in July 1888. He had nonetheless become an enthusiast of Russia: "Russia is a country so enormous and so remote that we are likely to have many erroneous notions about her. But let us not forget in America that she has always been our friend, and that in some great national exigencies this friendship has been of great value."[114]

Lambert Tree of Chicago was the next minister but served only a month at the Russian capital before a new administration was installed in Washington. Secretary George Wurts, facing another tedious arrangement of housing and staff, had advised Tree to await the results of the election before coming, as his late appointment and expected short tenure was much criticized in the Foreign Ministry. Wurts noted that if Cleveland failed to win reelection, Tree would not be able to make a friend in the place.[115] Even so, the secretary kept up an active correspondence with Tree after his departure.

A number of people solicited the Russian post from President Benjamin Harrison, including an old Civil War comrade-in-arms and veteran of the Russian scene, the eighty-year-old Cassius Clay.[116] The choice was again a surprise: Allen Thorndyke Rice, the wealthy publisher of the *North American Review*. A fellow editor commented:

Mr. Thorndyke Rice will probably not have a good time at St. Petersburg, where the climate has been extremely hard on nearly every American minister for several years. The work, however, is light, the honor is considerable, and arrangements as to leave of absence are always liberal. If the duties of the mission were likely to be serious we hardly think Mr. Rice's appointment would be approved, because it is extremely difficult to take him seriously under any circumstances.[117]

A storm was threatening in the Senate over his confirmation when Rice

112. Ibid., p. 139.
113. William P. Harrison diary, "Tour of the Globe," 18 July 1887, printed copy, Carter Harrison Papers, Newberry Library.
114. Detroit letter, quoted in "Social Conditions in Russia," New York *Times*, 11 November 1888, p. 3.
115. Wurts to Tree, 22 September 1888, Tree Papers, Newberry Library.
116. Rosen to Giers, 22 March/3 April 1889, f. 133, op. 470, d. 96 (1889), AVPR.
117. "Diplomatic Appointments," New York *Times*, 28 March 1889, p. 4. Wurts was elated: "Rice is very clever, a thorough man of the world, but with literary tastes, has a good fortune and doubtless speaks French and German as well as his own language." To Tree, 5 April 1889, Tree Papers, Newberry Library.

died unexpectedly. The post was then vacant over a year before Charles Emory Smith of Philadelphia reached St. Petersburg. During this and other lapses between appointments, the United States was fortunate again to have a dedicated and experienced secretary of legation—George Wurts, who had replaced Wickham Hoffman in 1882—to perform the routine diplomatic chores. Because of an increasing workload, in 1890 Wurts secured the budding European historian, Archibald Cary Coolidge, as an assistant.

Consular Squabbles

One of the major tasks confronting the legation had little to do with Russia but rather was overseeing and refereeing a parade of itinerant consuls and vice-consuls. In St. Petersburg the general consular office suffered from instability. Since the benign administration of George Pomutz (who died in 1882), a number of consuls and acting consuls assumed responsibility for the duties. Edgar Stanton was his official replacement but was absent much of the time. The most diligent of the caretakers was George Hutton, son of a long-time resident merchant. During those years, 1882–1885, some useful commercial reports were forwarded to Washington from an office in the Hutton business, but Hutton was not averse to using the legation for purposes such as importing duty-free bottles of perfume for a lady friend.[118]

The subsequent brief tenures included another local businessman, George Henry Prince (of Ropes and Company), Pierce M. B. Young of South Carolina, James Swann and William Henry Dunster (also business residents), and Charlton Way from Savannah. Their collective service did little more than cause recriminations among them about office accounts, the extra expenses of moving to other locations, and acquiring new sets of furniture.[119] No one seemed to really want the job, as Almira Lothrop commented regarding Young's departure after nine months: "He has never liked his office here, and besides says he has never felt well; thinks this is a dreadful climate."[120] Finally, John M. Crawford brought the situation under control in the summer of 1889.

Most of the blame for the state of negligence and transience in consular affairs in St. Petersburg falls on Washington. The situation was somewhat

118. Hutton to Hunt, 29 May and 2 June 1883, reel 2, Hunt Papers, LC.
119. For an example of such charges, see Swann to State Department, 18 August 1886, DUSC, St. Petersburg, vol. 18 (roll 13, M 81), RG 59, NA.
120. Lothrop, *Letters*, p. 126.

different in Moscow, where the American reputation was reduced to shambles by unscrupulous conduct at the scene, following a pattern set by John Hatterscheidt in the 1860s. At least part of the problem was the reliance by the St. Petersburg legation, itself in disarray, on American resident merchants in Moscow who in the 1880s included August Weber, John Lehrs, Eccles Gillespie Van Riper, Samuel Smith, William Hauflein, and August Hoffman.

In 1884 Van Riper, a seller of pumping machinery and a buyer of platinum, wrested the consulship from Weber and proceeded to consort with August Hoffman, who was designated vice-consul. Together they arranged exhibits in 1884 for a number of Moscow merchants and artisans at an exposition in Hoffman's native New Orleans. For a fee of 200 rubles, Van Riper and Hoffman would guarantee handsome medals and a prize from an American exhibit was considered quite a plum by Muscovites. The venture was successfully promoted by Van Riper's wife, who spoke Russian and was an effective saleswoman for the medals.[121]

All might have gone well except for the delays in receiving the medals, which angered the Moscow merchants, and a falling-out between Hoffman and Van Riper over shares of the spoils, which, according to one source, had reached 40,000 rubles ($20,000).[122] The whole operation became public in September 1885, when Hoffman filed a suit in a Moscow court against Van Riper and released correspondence about the scam.[123] Van Riper issued a countersuit, and soon most of Moscow was choosing up sides, though embarrassed by the whole affair.[124] After some delay, Van Riper and Hoffman were dismissed from their shared consulship, and August Weber was summoned back to the position.[125]

Van Riper, however, prevailed in court and resumed his Moscow business, much to the dismay of the medal-less Muscovites. Then in May 1887, he was arrested at his dacha, hauled off to jail, and summarily escorted by the police to the frontier, leaving his family stranded in Moscow.[126] Incensed at his treatment, especially since he was on the verge of bidding on a contract

121. "Consul Van Riper's Ways," New York *Times*, 27 November 1887, p. 12.

122. Ibid.

123. Lothrop to Bayard, 5 October 1885, DUSM, Russia, roll 38 (roll 38, M 35), RG 59, NA.

124. Lothrop to Bayard, 5 and 27 November 1885, ibid.

125. Wurts to Vlangaly, 7/19 April 1886, DPR, Russia, vol. 4536 (notes sent), RG 84, NA.

126. Van Riper (Moscow) to Lothrop, 8/26 May 1887, and Van Riper (Carlsbad) to Lothrop, 28 May 1887, DPR, Russia, vol. 4442 (misc. received), RG 84, NA.

for pumps for the Moscow water system, Van Riper demanded action from the minister in St. Petersburg.[127] Lothrop was obviously reluctant to get involved and departed for the summer, leaving Van Riper out in the well-deserved cold. Despite frantic appeals by his wife, Van Riper's Moscow operation came to an ignominious conclusion.[128]

The Moscow informant for the New York *Times* attributed the outcome to the likelihood that the authorities felt "in duty bound to protect the sheep in its care from further shearing by unscrupulous exponents of new methods in trade and industry."[129] The situation was so bad that consul general Charlton Way could not recommend any local American to replace Van Riper.[130] And when a British acting consul was forced to resign, he suggested that a German, Nicholas Wertheim, take his place. "Of the very few American citizens residing in Moscow, there is not one who is eligible for the post of a Consular officer."[131]

Van Riper was not the only American businessman to be expelled from Russia in 1887. On the surface, the other important American consulate in Russia, at Odessa, was in relatively good shape under the professional direction of Fulton Paul and then, after 1884, Thomas Heenan. Far removed from St. Petersburg and Moscow and unaffected by the problems there, the Odessa consulate went about its own business, tranquil and serene—except for the stir created by an unusually venturesome and aggressive Mennonite.

The Strange Case of Abraham Thiessen

Although few Americans would long remember the trouble caused by Abraham Thiessen, he was a veritable loose cannon on the Ukrainian steppe. Born in the Ukrainian/New Russia colony of Molochna in 1839, Thiessen became by 1869 a leading spokesmen for the poor, landless Mennonites, a Mennonite *narodnik* (populist). In response to this pressure the Mennonite

127. Van Riper (Carlsbad) to Lothrop, 2, 5, 6, and 16 June 1887, ibid. In the letter of 5 June, Van Riper thought Lothrop was being too diplomatic: "I know the Russian character perfectly, it is always 'tomorrow' with them, and 'tomorrow' means next week or month, if you do not pursue them with vigor." He also claimed, "I committed no fraud, and wronged no one, in my connection with N. O. Exposition."

128. Lothrop to Weber (Moscow), 28 November/10 December 1887, DPR, Russia, vol. 4571 (letters sent), RG 84, NA.

129. New York *Times*, 27 November 1887, p. 12.

130. Way to Porter, 13 October 1887, DUSC, St. Petersburg, vol. 18 (roll 13, M 81), RG 59, NA.

131. N. W. Hornstedt to Avery Adee, 25 January 1889, DUSC, Moscow, vol. 3 (roll 2, M 456), RG 59, NA.

elders agreed to set aside a special tract of land to be divided among the landless, but about 300 families, including Thiessen's, were left out. After vain efforts to bring Russian authority to bear on the case in audiences with the minister of state domains in St. Petersburg, first with Aleksandr Zelenoi in 1870 and then with Petr Valuev in 1873, Thiessen led a local demonstration and physical occupation of land in 1874. This resulted in his arrest and incarceration in prison at Kaluga "for raising agricultural questions and exciting the Mennonites to emigration."[132]

In 1876 he escaped from prison and made his way first to Switzerland, where he published an account of Mennonite-Russian injustices, and then to the United States to an immigrant colony founded that year by Cornelius Jansen near Fairbury, Nebraska.[133] There he duly became a naturalized citizen and pressed without success for a state subsidy for a nascent silk industry pioneered by Jansen.[134] Permanent settlement on the American plains was not to his taste, however, and remembering his unfinished business in Russia, he appeared in St. Petersburg in 1886 to appeal again to officials, lay out his case to Lothrop, and write letters of protest to the *Petersburger Herold*. He had also purchased agricultural equipment from David Bradley and Company of Chicago and intended to accept delivery in Odessa and set up business in Halbstadt, the chief Molochna administrative center and market town.[135] His real purpose was to resume the fight against what a number of

132. Governor of Odessa to Heenan, 14/26 January 1888, DUSC, Odessa, vol. 8 (roll 4, M 459), RG 59, NA. Supportive material in Thiessen memorial, Peabody, Kansas, enclosed with Vlangaly to Wurts, 17/29 December 1888, DPR, Russia, vol. 4509 (notes received), RG 84, NA; Cornelius Krahn, "Abraham Thiessen: A Mennonite Revolutionary?" *Mennonite Life* (April 1969): 73–75. The "memorial," written in good English and in the third person, is undated, but Thiessen was in Peabody only from October 1887 to June 1888. Bound in a volume of the Diplomatic Post Records for Russia, the pages are out of order. Other materials relating to the case are also in disarray.

133. Jansen, like most of the Mennonites in Russia, orginally came from the Danzig area. He served as Prussian consul in the Azov port of Berdiansk and was expelled from Russia in 1873 for advocating emigration. Gustav E. Reimer and G. R. Gaeddert, *Exiled by the Czar: Cornelius Jansen and the Great Mennonite Migration, 1874* (Newton, Kans.: Mennonite Publication Office, 1956), pp. 123–32.

134. Reimer and Gaeddert, *Exiled by the Czar*, p. 128; Peabody *Gazette*, 20 October 1887. Thiessen apparently came with or joined relatives, for the original settlers of the town of Jansen, founded in 1886, included John P. Thiessen, who operated a hardware store; Reimer and Gaeddert, *Exiled by the Czar*, pp. 138, 205.

135. Thiessen claimed that "it was his intention to introduce improved methods of agriculture represented by these implements, among his Mennonite friends, not alone for the purpose of benefiting them, but also for the purpose of opening an additional foreign market for this class of American manufactures." Thiessen memorial, DPR, Russia, vol. 4509 (notes received), RG 84, NA.

poor Mennonites believed were frauds in land grants.[136] Lothrop advised against this course: "I warned him that he would be likely to stir up enemies and if he went into South Russia they might give him trouble."[137]

Apparently under the impression that he was covered by a general amnesty decreed by Alexander III in 1881, Thiessen proceeded to the Molochna colony, where he was at once arrested on 9 November.[138] Although courting trouble by his arrogant attitude, he suffered severe and untoward punishment. Taken to Berdiansk, he was allegedly kept in an unheated cell for a month, clothed in only an undershirt; he nearly died of exposure. He was then loaded on an open wagon and carried in the direction of Siberia for three days in temperatures of thirty below zero, after which he was brought back to Berdiansk.[139] Thiessen managed, through friends, to contact Heenan and Lothrop, who immediately protested to Giers.[140]

Under orders to turn him over to the American consul in Odessa, the provincial police guided him along a thirty-five-day roundabout journey through Melitopol and Kharkov seemingly in hopes he would die. But the durable Thiessen survived and on 25 February finally reached Odessa, where he was released to Heenan's custody. To the consul's dismay, Thiessen insisted on returning directly to Berdiansk, Halbstadt, and St. Petersburg to recover his equipment and protest his treatment. Heenan revealed his disgust to Lothrop: "[You] must be weary of the everlasting Thiessen case."[141] But he was also sensitive about performing his duties. "I was utterly opposed to Thiessen and his object in coming to Russia, and had but little sympathy with his efforts to shield himself in his attack on Russian officials, behind his American citizenship; nevertheless, I do not believe that I displayed a lack of energy in my efforts in his behalf."[142] He managed to get Thiessen safely escorted across the border by the end of March.

Returning to the American prairie, this ambitious Mennonite secured a post as superintendent of the state-subsidized Kansas Silk Station in Pea-

136. Lothrop to Bayard, 23 February 1887, DUSM, Russia, vol. 39 (roll 39, M 35), RG 59, NA.

137. To Heenan, 28 November/10 December 1886, DUSC, Odessa, vol. 8 (roll 4, M 459), RG 59, NA.

138. Thiessen memorial, DPR, Russia, vol. 4509 (notes received); Heenan to Lothrop, 25 January 1887, DPR, Russia, vol. 4442, (misc. received), RG 84, NA.

139. Thiessen memorial, DPR, Russia, vol. 4509 (notes received), RG 84, NA.

140. Lothrop to Giers, 28 November/10 December 1886 (c), DPR, Russia, vol. 4537 (notes sent), RG 84, NA.

141. Heenan to Lothrop, 7 March 1887, DPR, Russia, vol. 4442 (misc. received), RG 84, NA.

142. Heenan to Lothrop, 8 March 1887, ibid.

body.[143] Thiessen quickly became an active promoter of this experimental industry that relied on Ukrainian Mennonite expertise and published a number of letters and pamphlets during his brief tenure.[144] While in Peabody, he also drafted a long, wordy "memorial" about his recent adventure, claiming $8,000 in damages from the Russian government. The Russian authorities were naturally deaf to this appeal, which finally ceased when Thiessen himself was laid to rest on the family's Nebraska farm in May 1889.[145]

Commercial Relations

Given the state of the American consular corps in Russia, it was fortuitous that direct shipping trade had declined to a new low. In the 1870s the number of American vessels entering St. Petersburg averaged about ten, the most being fourteen in 1879. But the average for the 1880s was only two or three; in 1882 only one American ship entered St. Petersburg, compared to 663 British steamers.[146] Lothrop noted that in 1885 not a single American commercial ship entered Russian waters: "Were it not for the Legation and Consulate . . . and the occasional visit of a vessel of the American Navy, the American flag would never be seen here."[147] Although the American merchant marine had declined, the continental European railroad net had expanded, providing alternative access to Russia. The main port of St. Petersburg was now awkwardly placed for reaching the Russian market, even though a new channel was dredged to make the city proper more accessible to oceangoing vessels. Most of the incoming cargoes, moreover, were raw materials for industry or luxury goods for well-to-do residents.

The overall exchange is even more misleading than for previous periods.

143. Peabody *Gazette*, 20 October 1887; "Kansas Silk Industry," Topeka *Mail*, 28 October 1887. The station was established in April 1887, and already by July Thiessen was making inquiries about it. Marion County (Kansas) *Anzeiger*, 22 July 1887, cited in Krahn, "Abraham Thiessen," 77.

144. Peabody *Gazette*, 20 October and 17 November 1887, and 21 January, 7 and 14 April, and 21 June 1888.

145. Vlangaly to Wurts, 17/29 December 1888, DPR, Russia, vol. 4509 (notes received), RG 84, NA; Krahn, "Abraham Thiessen," 77. The memorial probably passed through the State Department on its way to Russia; Bayard to Wurts, 30 October 1888 (c), DI, Russia, vol. 16 (roll 138, M 77), RG 59, NA.

146. Stanton to Hunter, 26 December 1882, DUSC, St. Petersburg, vol. 16 (roll 11, M 81); and 9 October 1884, DUSC, St. Petersburg, vol. 17 (roll 12, M 81), RG 59, NA.

147. To Bayard, 16 September 1885, DUSM, Russia, vol. 38 (roll 38, M 35), RG 59, NA.

Less raw cotton was being imported, since Russia now relied on its own Central Asian production and on finished goods from Britain. Yet many other American products were crossing the Russian border as reexports, primarily through Germany, though these were often counted as "German" goods. Russian statistics nevertheless recorded a substantial gain for direct American imports, rising from seventh place in 1881 to a distant third in 1884—Germany 113 million rubles, Britain 79 million, United States 24 million.[148] This ranking would hold for the next two years. Most of the imports consisted of assorted manufactured goods such as sewing machines and agricultural equipment.

Improvements in transportation and expansion of industry, along with the continued backwardness of agriculture, inspired at least some Americans to see golden opportunities. One casual business traveler, after emphasizing the difficulties encountered in an archaic bureaucracy, added, "I believe there is an opportunity to make money in Russia by intelligent foreigners, owing to the absence of a middle-class."[149] Consul General Way was more specific.

> There are vast probabilities of the extension and development of American trade with Russia. There is no other country so sure of yielding a rich harvest to the American Exporter. . . . But it is useless to flood Russia with circulars and catalogues; they go into the waste-basket as fast as they are received. The goods must be presented by samples and they must be pushed with American vigor and energy.[150]

The problem was that American foreign traders would rather use trustworthy European middlemen, and businesses such as Ropes and Company, already established in Russia, were content with their small-scale operations. Conservative Russia was less inclined to seek American business and more likely in the 1880s to redress British dominance with German trade. Instead, Russia and the United States were now perceived more and more as rivals, especially in the marketing of one old and one new product—grain and oil. Yet both offered opportunities for American ventures.

148. Stanton to Hunter, 9 April 1883, DUSC, St. Petersburg, vol. 16 (roll 11, M 81), RG 59, NA; and Way to Rives, 31 March 1888, DUSC, St. Petersburg, vol. 18 (roll 13, M 81), RG 59, NA.
149. Charles F. Cutting, *Glimpses of Scandinavia and Russia* (Boston: Thomas Groom, 1887), p. 92.
150. To Rives, 31 March 1888, DUSC, St. Petersburg, vol. 18 (roll 13, M 81), RG 59, NA.

Kerosene and Bread

The substantial American involvement in the initial development of the Russian oil industry in the Caucasus ended with the consolidation of operations under the Nobel enterprises. More and deeper wells, expanded refining capacity, and cheaper transportation drove American oil out of the St. Petersburg market by 1881. Three years later, fifty-eight of the most productive wells in Baku and vicinity were owned by the Nobel firm.[151] Its hold on refining and transportation was even more complete. Dubbed the "Rothschilds of Baku," the Nobels were soon competing on the international market with the chief American oil interests headed by John D. Rockefeller.[152] This development naturally awakened considerable American notice.

A difference of opinion existed, however, regarding Russian oil potential. Although some observers continued to predict that it would soon take over the German and Mediterranean markets,[153] others were less sanguine. A few American oil products (such as sewing machine oil) were still imported because of their superior quality.[154] The heavy Caucasian crude combined with the dearth of skilled workers in the region also resulted in much waste. The American consul in Odessa commented after a tour of Baku in 1883 that most American specialists had left "as they find it difficult to work satisfactorily with the class of men furnished to them as helpers."[155]

But the primary obstacle was still transportation. Despite the completion of a rail line from Baku to Tiflis, which connected with Batum on the Black Sea, handling the liquid products remained tedious and expensive. Discussions about a proposed direct pipeline from Baku to the Black Sea led to nothing

151. David Ker, "Baku and Its Petroleum," New York *Times*, 15 November 1884, p. 3. This reporter spent a month investigating the region and recording the horrible waste and pollution that accompanied the exploitation of natural resources.

152. A British source noted that of 100 million hectoliters of kerosene produced in 1887, 64 million were American, 25 million were Russian. "Russian Petroleum," New York *Times*, 29 October 1888, p. 4. On the Nobel rise, see Robert W. Tolf, *The Russian Rockefellers: The Saga of the Nobel Family and the Russian Oil Industry* (Stanford, Calif.: Hoover Institution Press, 1976).

153. For example, Wurts to Frelinghuysen, 12 May 1884, DUSM, Russia, vol. 37 (roll 37, M 35), RG 59, NA. In 1887, Lothrop reported, "It will be seen that the entire expulsion of American petroleum from the European markets is confidently looked for," that abundance and cheapness of Russian oil would overcome its poor quality; Lothrop to Bayard, 6 October 1887, PRFRUS 1888, p. 1397.

154. Bornholdt commercial report from Riga, 1 October 1883, DUSC, St. Petersburg, vol. 17 (roll 12, M 81), RG 59, NA.

155. Fulton Paul to State Department, 12 July 1883, DUSC, Odessa, vol. 7 (roll 4, M 459), RG 59, NA.

for the time being, in part because the government insisted that pipe and machinery be manufactured in Russia.[156] The few American traveling businessmen who were drawn to the scene were impressed by the expansion and progress and chilled by the miserable conditions of work they witnessed.[157] With the simultaneous emergence of Nobel and Rockefeller as dominant figures in world oil by 1886, the battle was joined for global competition. Early that year a petroleum expert, James B. Chambers of New York, was appointed special agent at Batum to keep an eye on Russian expansion in this industry for both the American government and Standard Oil.[158]

What intrigued Chambers and American visitors the most was the Russian use of petroleum fuel to power Volga River steamers and railroad locomotives. Americans were soon making similar experiments while acknowledging the Russian precedents.[159] Regardless, the one great consumer item that connected Russian village to American farm was kerosene for lighting and heating.

As in the case of oil products, the United States and Russia ruled the export grain market, and in about the same proportions. There were other similarities. Just as much of the heavier Russian crude was burned at home in steamers and locomotives, so most of the grain was rye, barley, and millet grown for domestic consumption. Although Russia produced more total grains, the United States on average raised twice as much wheat, the variety most in demand for export. And because of superior soil, farming skills, machinery, and transportation, the proportion of American wheat in the export market grew steadily. The American consul in Odessa reported that while British grain imports from Russia had dropped from 18 percent of the total in 1878 to 5 percent in 1880, those from the United States rose from 56 percent to 67 percent.[160]

The Russian government was keenly aware of the situation but did little

156. Heenan to State Department, 15 February 1888, and Chambers report, 1 March 1887, DUSC, Odessa, vol. 8 (roll 4, M 459), RG 59, NA.

157. Samuel Sullivan Cox, *Diversions of a Diplomat in Turkey* (New York: Charles L. Webster, 1893), pp. 155–70; William P. Harrison diary, "Tour of the Globe," p. 87, Carter Harrison Papers, Newberry Library.

158. Heenan to Porter, 28 January 1886, DUSC, Odessa, vol. 7 (roll 4, M 459), RG 59, NA; "Reaching Out to Europe," New York *Times*, 5 April 1886, p. 2.

159. New York *Times*, 8 December 1882, p. 4.

160. Paul to Frelinghuysen, 25 March 1881, DUSC, Odessa, vol. 6 (roll 3, M 459), RG 59, NA. America's export success became a matter of concern to the Russian foreign office as well; Giers to Rosen (in code), 20 February 1889, f. 133, op. 470, d. 96 (1889), AVPR. In 1887 American wheat production was about double the Russian, and together they accounted for 70 percent of the world's wheat trade. "The World's Wheat Harvest," *Nation* 47, 1216 (18 October 1888): 306.

to remedy it. One problem was the frequency of bad crop years in the 1880s: 1880, 1882, 1884, 1885, 1889 were all poor. Even in good years, such as 1888, storage and transportation difficulties limited exports.[161] Again, the climate was a factor: the damp, cold autumn dogged the harvesting of grain, which had to be planted in the spring because of the severe winters. The need for American-style elevators at railheads and in the ports was widely recognized, both by American observers and Russian officials, but no action was taken. Yet at the highest level industrialization was given priority.

In the related area of agricultural mechanization, more progress was discernible thanks to enterprising salesmen and initially low duties on imports, and Americans were among the chief beneficiaries. Germany, however, held a virtual monopoly on the primary agricultural implement, the plow, while British threshing machines and steam engines, because they were more durable, kept most American models out of the competition.[162] The few that were sold in Russia were purchased mostly by the nobility and especially in the Baltic provinces. A small number of American harvesters were brought back to Ukraine from the United States by returning Mennonites.[163] One source claimed that a new duty on iron was driving Russian implement makers out of business, thus boosting demand for imports in the early 1880s.[164]

In mowers, reapers, binders, and hayrakers, however, American machinery clearly dominated the market, and one estimate of 1882 listed annual sales of 800 to 1,000. These were unevenly distributed, with most reaching the Baltic states and Ukraine. As consul Stanton observed, "It is seldom that a German colonist at Molotschansk, with 100 acres of arable land, does not possess a mowing machine, and he finds that it pays even though the machine works but 5 or 6 days during the year."[165] Because of the special

161. Secretary of legation Wurts summed them up: "The grain of this year is represented to be of fine quality, but it is well known that, owing to carelessness in its storage, immense quantities often heaped 'mountains high' at railway stations awaiting transportation, . . . without any protection from the weather, much of the grain of Russia reaches destination in a damaged condition or is lost altogether." To Bayard, 7 September 1888, DUSM, Russia, vol. 40 (roll 40, M 35), RG 59, NA.

162. George Scott to Hunter, 28 May 1885, DUSC, Odessa, vol. 7 (roll 4, M 459); and Heenan to Wharton, 25 July 1889, DUSC, Odessa, vol. 9 (roll 5, M 459), RG 59, NA. For the experiences of a British thresher salesman, see George Hume, *Thirty-Five Years in Russia* (London: Simpkin, Marshall, Hamilton, Kent, 1914).

163. Paul to Hunter, 28 May 1885, DUSC, Odessa, vol. 7 (roll 4, M 459), RG 59, NA. He noted that the durability of machines "is essential to the Russian farmer because he takes little care of them."

164. Stanton to Hunter, 22 March 1882, quoting a letter from the owner of an iron foundry in south Russia, DUSC, St. Petersburg, vol. 16 (roll 11, M 81), RG 59, NA.

165. Ibid.

sales efforts of the McCormick company and its Russian headquarters in Odessa, this market control held for many years. Already by 1884 the company was doing more business in Russia than in any other foreign country, except New Zealand.[166] The biggest sellers were the simplest machines, and the more sophisticated self-binders had limited appeal. According to an Odessa consul, "The lack of money among the people and the cheap state of the labor market are among the principal causes why self-binders are not more in demand."[167]

With the death of Cyrus McCormick and the succession of his son in 1884, more emphasis was placed on expanded production for foreign sales. By 1888 McCormick had a number of dealers concentrated in the south of Russia selling his products as well as those of others. Average annual sales of 250 mowers and 250 reapers were threatened, however, by higher duties and competition from new Russian factories. George Freudenreich foresaw a mixed picture.

> While we are without doubt apparently entering upon an era of better times here in Russia, still we cannot hope to increase our special trade very much, on account of the prosperity of the South Russian factories, of which there are quite a number now whose trade is increasing with every year to our detriment of course, as they are able to sell much cheaper than we are on account of the high duties we have to pay.[168]

Other problems, such as a failure to adapt binders to be pulled by oxen in Crimea, lost customers.[169] Freudenreich thought that in any event economic and social backwardness limited agricultural mechanization in Russia, but he admitted that his cautious extension of credit, usually only granted until the next harvest, also reduced potential sales.

166. George S. Queen, "The McCormick Harvesting Machine Company in Russia," *Russian Review* 23, 2 (April 1964): 164; Heenan to Rives, 25 July 1889, DUSC, Odessa, vol. 9 (roll 5, M 459), RG 59, NA. Heenan noted that 1888 was the best year so far for imports of American agricultural implements; to Rives, 26 March 1890, DUSC, Odessa, vol. 9 (roll 5, M 459), RG 59, NA. In the 1880s, besides McCormick, American brand names included Johnston, Wood, Advance, Deere, and Champion; Scott to Hunter, 28 May 1885, DUSC, Odessa, vol. 7 (roll 4, M 459), RG 59, NA.

167. Scott to Hunter, 28 May 1885, DUSC, Odessa, vol. 7 (roll 4, M 459), RG 59, NA.

168. George Freudenreich (Odessa) to Cyrus McCormick, Jr., 21 September 1888, box 112, 2C, McCormick Company Papers, SHSW.

169. Freudenreich (Budapest) to McCormick, 20 October 1888, ibid.

The company's new European manager knew that McCormick, who was visiting Europe in the summer of 1888, was particularly interested in expansion in Russia. Calling Freudenreich too inconsistent and conservative, he advised the agent's removal.

All that Freudenreich says about the difficulties of the Binder business such as the apathy of Agents, the want of intelligence on the part of farmers and labourers, and the disinclination of the landed proprietors to use Binders, fearing to disturb their relations with the villagers, is identical with what we have been hearing in this Country [Britain], and in France and Italy for years, and it is, in fact, the history of the Binder trade, so far as I know anything about it. But for all that, Binders are making their way every year in increasing number, and I expect things [in Russia] will follow much the same course.[170]

McCormick reorganized the Russian agency six years later.[171]

Some other American machines, such as cornshellers, entered the Russian market, but opportunities were often missed because of shipping delays and lack of information about demand.[172] The consul in St. Petersburg repeated the standard saw: "The vast body of the population is too ignorant and too poor to appreciate and purchase our manufactures, and the proximity of England and Germany give those countries such advantages in this market as to render successful competition on our part almost impossible."[173] Yet the McCormick experience seemed to offer a different lesson on the American commercial capability in Russia.

One visitor to Ukraine commented on where the adoption of American modern equipment might lead: "What if American energy and its agricultural machines should take hold of these vast grain-fields? . . . What hindrance is there to Russia rivaling America in its grain product? Is it not Russian dreariness in transportation and our labor-saving machines? May not these impediments be obviated in time, and then where is our vaunted supremacy!" But he concluded patriotically that "the co-operation, skill, con-

170. Percy Lankeston (London) to McCormick, 1 September 1888, ibid.
171. European matters were complicated in 1888–1889 by the bankruptcy of a dealer in Budapest that involved Freudenreich. McCormick had planned to visit Russia but returned home because of illness. McCormick to Freudenreich, 19 September 1888, ibid.
172. Paul to Blaine, 20 March 1881, DUSC, Odessa, vol. 6 (roll 3, M 459), RG 59, NA.
173. Stanton to Hunter, 12 December 1883, DUSC, St. Petersburg, vol. 17 (roll 12, M 81), RG 59, NA.

centration and economy of the American cannot have a rival."[174] A similar observation might have been made about the Russian purchase of cotton seed through Francis Vogel of San Antonio in 1886. Despite American seed, typical Bokhara cotton was inferior in quality, usually requiring a mixture of American or East Indian for shirting.[175]

But the United States borrowed seed from Russia's cupboard that would prosper on the American central plains. "Turkey Red" wheat probably first arrived in the United States in the baggage of Mennonite immigrants from the Crimea in 1874, but it did not become generally known in American agriculture until the late 1880s. After plot testing in Missouri and Kansas, its adaptive potential was fully realized: this hard-grained wheat could be planted in the fall to take best advantage of the snow melt and spring rains on the prairie. Steel rollers for milling were imported from Canada, and the switch to a "middling," sifting process made large-scale production of hard-wheat flour feasible. This, coupled with a high-demand market from newly arriving immigrants and export possibilities, prompted a series of Russian field surveys, especially pioneered by Bernhard Warkentin, a miller of Mennonite background from Newton, Kansas. There was also a large import of seed wheat.[176] Turkey Red and its several mutant strains thus became the dominant wheat for the Great Plains through the 1940s, until hybridization produced shorter stem varieties better adapted for combining.

The Mennonite immigration also inspired a silk experimental station in Kansas, influenced by the modest success of ones in the Ukrainian Molochna colony and subsidized by the state. Neither the American nor Russian efforts were long lasting or of national economic significance. However, another product of the Russian steppe—wool—remained a key import from Russia, mainly for the manufacture of rugs. The trade was predominantly handled by foreign brokers and was considered somewhat irregular by both Russian authorities and the local American consuls.[177]

174. Samuel Sullivan Cox, *Arctic Sunbeams, or From Broadway to the Bosphorus by Way of the North Cape* (New York: Putnam's, 1882), p. 326.

175. "The Czar's Lastest Scheme," New York *Times*, 27 April 1886, p. 1; Weber to Lothrop, 5 October 1887, DPR, Russia, vol. 4442 (misc. received), RG 84, NA.

176. Norman E. Saul, "Myth and History: Turkey Red Wheat and the 'Kansas Miracle,'" *Heritage of the Great Plains* 22, 3 (Summer 1989): 1–13. *Krasnaia turetskaia,* as it was called in Russia, had a restricted range of planting in Russia because of its vulnerability to winter kill. It was probably of Albanian or Bulgarian origin and introduced into Russia by Crimean Tatars, hence its name.

177. Heenan to James Porter, 10 July 1886, DUSC, Odessa, vol. 7 (roll 4, M 459), RG 59, NA.

Russians continued to be enamored of and concerned about American agricultural progress and made special efforts to keep informed. A detailed study published in 1883 attributed American success to virgin soil, cheap land, wide use of machinery, the farmers' highly developed technical skills, constant expansion of the area cultivated, and increasing population.[178] By 1887, Russia had attached a permanent "technical agent," Aleksandr Rutkovskii, to its diplomatic mission in Washington.[179] The huge American machinery section at the Paris Exposition of 1889, which made quite an impression on a Russian inspector, reinforced perceptions of American supremacy.[180]

Economic Expansion

Americans were quick to realize several other opportunities in Russia. Some were familiar lines of business, such as the trading houses established by Enoch Emery along the Amur River in Siberia and the efforts to build ships for the Russian navy by William Webb and Charles Cramp.[181] New ventures were sometimes abortive, as in the case of the attempt by George Eagle of Chicago to sell a telephone franchise to Russia in 1881.[182] This was a clear indication, however, of the rapid spread of new technology advanced by American business initiatives abroad—led by McCormick, Singer, Bell, Edison, and Westinghouse—and more slowly realized in Russia.[183]

More auspicious beginnings came in life insurance, a new enterprise dominated by two American companies. Sidney Schmey broke the ground for Equitable early in 1887, and Paul Moeller followed in 1890 for New York Life.[184] They soon had a network of agents and rapidly rising volume of poli-

178. "K voprosy o khlebnoi konkurentsii Rossii s Ameriki," OZ 269, 8 (August 1883): 171.

179. Struve to Giers, 13/25 January 1887, f. 133, op. 470, d. 106 (1888), AVPR.

180. S. M. Bogdanov, *Zemledelie na Parizhskoi vsemirnoi vystavke 1889 goda* (St. Petersburg: Demakov, 1889), pp. 30–34.

181. Hunt to Admiral Shestakov, 25 October/5 November 1882 and 25 June 1883 (c), DPR, Russia, vol. 4536 (notes sent), RG 84, NA; Augustus C. Buell, *The Memoirs of Charles H. Cramp* (Philadelphia and London: J. B. Lippincott, 1906), 222–26.

182. Foster to Eagle, 3 June 1881, DPR, Russia, vol. 4484 (misc. sent), RG 84, NA.

183. William H. Becker, "American Manufacturers and Foreign Markets, 1870–1900: Business Historians and the 'New Economic Determinists,'" *Business History Review* 47, 4 (Winter 1973): 466–81; Queen, "The United States and the Material Advance in Russia, 1881–1906."

184. Lothrop to Ivan Vyshnegradskii (minister of finance), 26 January/7 February 1887 (c), DPR, Russia, vol. 4537 (Russia notes); Calvin Wells (Pittsburgh) to Smith, 5 May 1890, DPR, Russia, vol. 4444 (misc. received), RG 84, NA.

cies, despite the suspicions of government officials and many of the conservative public that insurance was fraudulent financial scheming.

As another example of a profitable Russian connection, in 1883 Charles L. Tiffany of New York initiated, through H. A. Spaulding, a private showing of glass and jewelry to the imperial family.[185] Henry Hiller was then appointed the company's regular Russian agent in 1884. Married to a Russian and with many years of experience in the Siberian trade, Hiller made annual trips to Russia to buy gems, porcelain, malachite, and other luxury items, usually arranging for the stones to be cut and set in Moscow.[186] His wife, who specialized in linen and lace, often joined him, and the trips then included extended visits with her relatives.

In the summer of 1891 Tiffany sent a trained geologist-gemologist, George F. Kunz, to the fair at Nizhni-Novgorod to acquire a variety of Russian objects, including a number of copper-alloy icons and crosses. That holiday season Tiffany's mounted an exhibition of these items and attracted considerable attention at the Union Square store in New York. The Smithsonian Institution purchased some of the icons and crosses the following year; a century later, the museum finally gave them special recognition.[187]

The most successful and enduring of all enterprises were sales of American-made sewing machines, which at first included a number of brands: Singer, Wheeler and Wilson, Howe, and Davis. Singer soon dominated the market thanks to the development of a network of sales agents and repair and supply shops, the granting of convenient payment terms, careful supervision from the independent Hamburg enterprise of George Neidlinger, and less competition that allowed higher prices.[188] Agents, mostly Germans trained by Neidlinger, could count on ample supplies because of a new Singer factory at Floridsdorf, near Vienna. The biggest prob-

185. C. L. Tiffany (New York) to Hunt, 7 February 1883, and H. A. Spaulding (Paris) to Hunt, 20 June 1883, reel 2, Hunt Papers, LC.

186. For an example of buying instructions, see C. L. Tiffany to Hiller, 4 September 1886, box 1, folder 3, Hiller Papers, Mystic Seaport Library. In 1887, Tiffany's son Bernard went along; Tiffany to Hiller, 19 March 1887, ibid.

187. Richard Eighme Ahlborn and Vera Beaver-Bricken Espinola, eds., *Russian Copper Icons and Crosses from the Kunz Collection: Castings of Faith*, Smithsonian Studies in History and Technology no. 51 (Washington, D.C.: Smithsonian Institution Press, 1991). A clipping on the 1891 exhibition is found in box 1, Kunz Papers, LC.

188. Carstensen, *American Enterprise*, pp. 28–33; Neidlinger (Moscow) to George McKenzie, 15 April 1882, box 84, Singer Sewing Machine Company Papers, SHSW. Neidlinger was not simply a Singer agent but a prominent Hamburg businessman and investor who had a monopoly contract for distribution of Singer machines on the European continent; he also handled Remington typewriters.

lems were cultural suspicions of machinery, acute economic fluctuations in the 1880s, and the counterfeiting of American models by German companies, to which Singer was especially vulnerable since most of the American imports came through Germany.[189]

The Siberian Exile System

Russia's governance by autocrats rather than by elected representatives had always tempered American affinity with Russians. Vague reports of the harsh treatment of Russian political dissidents had occasionally surfaced, but the differences between the two countries were largely obscured by the absence of conflict and the presence of common interests—until the 1880s. Now the real debate over Russian repressive policies and American opposition to them began, and it would continue for more than a century. The chief instigation was the Russian reaction following the assassination of Alexander II that increased the use of internal exile as a form of punishment.

This and publicity about the *Jeannette* tragedy raised awareness of Siberia. George Kennan, who disapproved of the handling of that affair, proposed in 1881 to several New York newspapers a thorough investigation of Siberian exiles, but without success.[190] He was not the first to catalog the evils associated with this "system," only the best-known and most eloquent. Henry Lansdell, an English clergyman who toured Siberia in 1881, exposed this Russian style of criminal justice—with assistance from a review in the *Nation*: "Whatever the cause may be, there is no doubt that the phrase 'transportation to Siberia' is generally associated with the idea of exceptionally inhuman, though not very clearly defined, punishment, administered by irresponsible and brutal officials."[191] The American reviewer considered

189. Because of this great German connection, Singer was often considered a German company in Russia. Mindful of growing Russian nationalism, Neidlinger advised his German agents in Russia to become Russian subjects. Neidlinger (Hamburg) to Singer Company, 7 February 1888, box 84, Singer Sewing Machine Company Papers, SHSW.

190. For example, Kennan to C. A. Dana (New York *Sun*), 22 July 1881, box 3, Kennan Papers, NYPL. See also the excellent study by Frederick Travis, *George Kennan and the American-Russian Relationship, 1865–1924* (Athens: Ohio University Press, 1990), pp. 88–90, 106, n. 68.

191. "New Light on Siberia," *Nation* 34, 872 (16 March 1882): 230, review of Henry Lansdell, *Through Siberia*, 3d ed. (Boston: Houghton Mifflin, 1882).

Lansdell's account "frank and unprejudiced." Although critical of their treatment, Lansdell naively tried to dispel rumors about their numbers, claiming that only 72 out of 20,000 were there for political reasons.

In connection with his critique of the loss of the *Jeannette*, and perhaps influenced by a reading of Lansdell, Kennan gave a lecture in February 1882 to the American Geographical Society on conditions in Siberia, describing the treatment of prisoners in lively detail—a technique he had mastered during numerous speaking tours. Kennan carefully examined the Russian system but concluded that its hardships had been greatly exaggerated. If he were faced with a choice, he would rather be in Siberia than Sing Sing.[192]

The debate over the oppressiveness of the Russian government started in earnest in 1884, when William Jackson Armstrong delivered a series of lectures in Washington, D.C., strongly condemning Russia. Kennan was present at the first one but maintained his silence. After Kennan himself continued to proclaim a milder stance in a speech of January 1885, Armstrong attacked him in print. Kennan dismissed his opponent as incompetent to speak on the subject, but he faced a stronger challenge from James Buel, who had traveled through Siberia and published a critical commentary, also based on firsthand observation.[193]

Kennan, however, had already made plans for his own, more sweeping investigation. Having established a connection with *Century* magazine by his article on the Caucasus, he convinced its editor to sponsor his journeys to Russia. The first, in the summer of 1884, to European Russia was a preliminary scouting of the feasibility for achieving access to people and places. Encouraged by this and provoked by his encounter with Armstrong, Kennan returned in the summer of 1885 to embark on his study.[194] This would take him over a year, ten months of which was in Siberia. The result was a series of articles for *Century*, beginning in November 1887, that would color the American perception of Russia for over a hundred years.

192. An expanded published version is "Siberia—The Exiles' Abode," *Journal of the American Geographical Society of New York* 14 (1882): 13–68. For contemporary views of the lecture, see New York *Herald*, 25 February 1882, and "The Exiles of Siberia," *Harper's Weekly*, 11 March 1882, p. 147. See also Travis, *George Kennan*, pp. 73–84.

193. Travis, *George Kennan*, pp. 87–89; Buel, *Russian Nihilism*; W. J. Armstrong, *Siberia and the Nihilists: Why Kennan Went to Siberia* (Oakland, Calif.: Pacific Press, 1890). Armstrong's volume includes his two principal letters that were printed in Washington newspapers early in 1885.

194. The journalist had no difficulty securing American blessing and Russian permission for his travel; Bayard to Taft, 27 April 1885, DI, Russia, vol. 16 (roll 138, M 77), RG 59, NA; Vlangaly to Taft, 4/16 June 1885, DPR, Russia, vol. 4508 (misc. received), RG 84, NA.

None of this would probably have happened without the foundation of an intense American curiosity about Russia and other exotic lands. For example, Albert Bickmore, a noted naturalist, offered a series of lectures for schoolteachers in January 1887 at the American Museum of Natural History in New York. For his talk on a trip across Siberia the auditorium was filled so well in advance that the sponsors took advantage of the occasion to circulate a petition to build a larger hall. Bickmore, in contrast to Kennan and Armstrong, was optimistic about the future and thought new developments in Russia "promise to make the Russian Empire the source of supplies for modern Europe and the most formidable power on the eastern continent."[195] Such publicity could certainly awaken publishers and editors to money-making opportunities.

The American appetite for adventure stories of Siberia had already been whetted by Lansdell and Buel and the De Long expedition, and in the 1880s, another man with personal knowledge was stirring up imaginations. Sergei Kravchinskii had gained infamy by assassinating the head of the Third (political police). After escaping to the West, he wrote several books under the pseudonym of Stepniak. He soon discovered that the sympathy of British audiences for Russia's political misfits easily extended to America. Although reckless with historical facts and inflammatory in the use of English vocabulary, Stepniak definitely warmed up readers for Kennan. One review of *The Russian Storm-Cloud* found him "prone to color and exaggerate with the recklessness of a fanatical patriot and combatant, but not to invent and deceive."[196]

The soil was ready for Kennan's sowing. The impact of his series of articles was indeed greater than the renowned work of the Marquis de Custine of fifty years earlier, partly because it came from the pen of one who had been considered a friend to Russia. In addition, Kennan's audience was larger, because the series was carried in a popular monthly journal (with circulation of about 200,000) in every issue over a two-year period (November

195. "Professor Bickmore on 'Russia,'" New York *Tribune*, 30 January 1887, p. 2.
196. *Nation* 43, 1097 (8 July 1886): 41. Kennan, however, thought that Stepniak had toned down his exaggerations in this book; as he wrote to reformer William Dudley Foulke, "The public won't give as much credit to the assertion of a man who is evidently carried away by strong feeling as they will to those of a man who clearly has himself in hand and doesn't appear to be straining his case to the utmost in order to produce an effect." To Foulke, 4 February 1888, box 3, Foulke Papers, LC. For an excellent appraisal of Stepniak's impact, see Jane E. Good, "America and the Russian Revolutionary Movement, 1888-1905," *Russian Review* 41, 3 (July 1982): 175-79.

Russian Populist revolutionaries: Nikolai Chaikovskii and
Sergei Kravchinskii (Stepniak) seated in front left to right.
From William English Walling, Russia's Message *(1910)*

1887 to November 1889) and was reinforced by extensive lecture tours by
the author himself.

The charges that Kennan's harsh views of Russia were molded by a lucrative contract with a magazine that wanted to sell copies or simply by his belated recognition of his own error can be easily refuted. This is not to say
that Kennan was the model of objectivity in his depiction of Siberian prison
conditions. He was clearly affected by his intensive personal experiences of
Siberian life and travel, and his fluency in Russian enabled him to speak
freely with prisoners, hard-labor miners, guards, officials, and a number of
people sympathetic to the liberal cause in Russia. In short, Kennan underwent a major conversion to a virulent opposition to established authority in
Russia and, like many later defectors from communism, became doubly devoted to his new cause. The result was a certain selectivity and exaggeration

that, while making his "sermons" more colorful and sensational, provoked some reverse reaction. Kennan himself now became a subject of debate.

George Kennan's journals and private correspondence clearly reveal the scope of his change of heart and the conditions under which he labored in Russia. In a New Year's Eve letter to Theodore Dwight from Irkutsk, he summed up succinctly his Siberian experience: "It was I think without exception the hardest journey of my life."[197] The visit to the Nerchinsk silver mines was apparently the nadir as far as observation of cruelty was concerned, but Kennan noted privately that none of the exiles there were "politicals." "The tools and machinery are of the rudest and most primitive description. . . . Their condition is everywhere *bad—very bad—*but I have not time or space in a letter to go into the extensive question of their treatment." But the trip had its lighter moments. In Chita, at a tea, "after drinking about a gallon of everything *except tea,* you ought to have seen me dance Siberian quadrilles! . . . I was so dizzy that I couldn't have told you whether I was the band, or the cold lunch, or merely a copper cent twirled for drinks!"[198]

In another letter Kennan remarked on the difficulties of carrying excess baggage in the person of George Frost, who went along to sketch pictures for the articles but who suffered a mental derangement that worsened to severe paranoia in Siberia. This certainly did not make Kennan's task any easier, yet he wrote Dwight that he had enough notes for two books. "If it can't be worked up so as to produce a very deep impression then I am no judge of material. I shall be disappointed if my book is not translated into every language in Europe."[199] And eventually it would be.

Century, from the very inception of the illustrated series, was committed but defensive about publishing the articles: "These criticisms proceed from a country whose relations with Russia are particularly cordial. They are printed in a periodical where 'The Life of Peter the Great' did much to increase the amicable interest of Americans in the affairs of Russia, and they are from a hand that has shown conspicuously its friendliness toward the Russian Government."[200] The editorial concluded that Russian liberals "desire freedom of speech, freedom of the press, security for personal rights, and

197. Kennan to Dwight, 31 December 1885/1 January 1886, Dwight Autograph Collection, 1880–1886, MassHS.
198. Ibid.
199. Kennan (St. Petersburg) to Dwight, 20 March 1886, ibid.
200. "America Is Not Russia," *Century* 35, 3 (January 1888): 484. "The Life of Peter the Great" was Eugene Schuyler's article, but it was published in *Scribner's Monthly,* the predecessor to *Century.*

a constitutional form of government. America, above all nations of the world, means these very things."[201] In this and in Kennan's writings one observes strident moralizing; the "liberty bell" was ringing loud and clear.

Kennan's personal mission was evident in a letter he wrote to Indianan William Dudley Foulke, a prison reform advocate, as the series began: "I have written under strong self-control and have tried not to let my emotion run away with my judgement or lead me into exaggeration. I believe everything that I have thus far written to be strictly and absolutely true and not overstated, . . . because these sufferings are to me vividly real." One declared goal was the defeat of a proposed extradition treaty with Russia: "And yet we Americans to whom the fighters for freedom in Russia have every right to look for encouragement and sympathy are so indifferent that we allow the most important phases of this conflict to pass without a word or comment and even discuss the advisability of surrendering to the despotic Government of that country the few strugglers for liberty who happen to reach our shores."[202]

Kennan was aware of the one-sided view that he nonetheless presented. To the Hoosier reformer he declared that he intended to include the government's case against the terrorists, "but the *Century* people wanted to get to the *pictures*," so he postponed indefinitely an examination of the other side of the question.[203] The "pictures" that accompanied Kennan's text were sketches made from photographs taken by Kennan and others, anonymous and attributed sketches picked up during his tour, and those of Frost. They no doubt did help to promote the series—and sales of *Century*.

The editors stipulated that Kennan delay his planned lecture tours until the series had run its course, except for a few select audiences. Mark Twain attended one of these exclusive appearances in March 1888 before the Washington Literary Society, and he is reported to have been moved to rise and exclaim, "If dynamite is the only remedy for such conditions, then thank God for dynamite!"[204] This was a taste of things to come. In February 1889 Kennan began his verbal campaign to expose Russian conditions to audiences in New England and the Midwest and generally attracted large

201. Ibid.

202. Kennan (Washington) to Foulke, 4 February 1888, box 3 (1888 folder), Foulke Papers, LC.

203. Kennan to Foulke, 15 February 1888, ibid.

204. As quoted in Travis, *George Kennan*, p. 178. Another source puts the location at the Lowell Institute; Louis J. Budd, "Twain, Howells, and the Boston Nihilists," *New England Quarterly* 32, 3 (September 1959): 351.

crowds. For change of pace, he also included on the playbill his earlier talks on "tent life" and the Caucasus. As powerful as his articles had been, Kennan's personal appearances were even more effective and dramatic. Especially gripping were his character sketches of people such as Ekaterina Breshko-Breshkovskaia whom he met in "the system."[205]

The next season Kennan had 200 engagements traveling as far west as Denver, something of an endurance test. Already on 9 January he wrote a friend from Monroe, Michigan, that he was exhausted from "getting up at unearthly hours in the morning, waiting half a day at a time for trains at dreary railway junctions and talking myself blind every night."[206] A man with a mission, Kennan added new material whenever he could; for example, he used news of a reported massacre of prisoners in Yakutsk to gain nationwide publicity while lecturing in Chicago.[207]

Everywhere his fame preceded him, and his lectures were well covered by the local press. The Kansas City *Star* reported on 24 March: "The most prominent man in town today is George Kennan, the great Siberian explorer and lecturer, who has probably seen more persecution, seen more hardship, and found more danger than any other living American in times of peace." The series of four lectures, sponsored by the Women's Christian Temperance Union (WCTU), began with his talk on the Caucasus before a responsive audience.

When the announcement was made that George Kennan would lecture in Kansas City no little interest was created and the public in general looked forward to evenings spent with the famous Russian traveler with much pleasure. Delightful as were the promises of a rare treat to be afforded, it was plain that the many in attendance last night at the Warder Grand Opera house were given a greater pleasure than they had expected.

The name of George Kennan has attracted attention throughout the civilized world as the first to give to other nations the story of Russian atrocities as obtained from personal observation, yet the impressions left upon his hearers was that not half had been told of the man who

205. See Jane E. Good and David R. Jones, *Babushka: The Life of the Russian Revolutionary Ekaterina K. Breshko-Breshkovskaia (1844–1934)* (Newtonville, Mass.: Oriental Research Partners, 1991), pp. 67–70.
206. To W. Hallitt Phillips, 9 January 1890, Phillips-Meyers Papers, UNC.
207. "Men Shot Down Like Dogs," New York *Times*, 8 February 1890, p. 5.

stood before them reciting in a clear resonant voice, talks of life in the mountains of the Caucasus.[208]

No wonder the house was filled the next evening for "Russian Political Exiles." After shifting into low gear the following afternoon with "Vagabond Tales," the *pièce de résistance* came that night when Kennan appeared in ragged garb, fettered with chains, on a dimly lit stage—as he explained, convict miners were never allowed to see daylight.[209]

By the time he reached Denver, with 142 appearances behind him, Kennan swore he would never do it again.[210] But having cleared approximately $20,000, enough to buy a new summer home on the Cape Breton, Nova Scotia, shore, he was back on the road the next year. A sampling from the brief journal that Kennan kept reveals practical proselytizing: Lynn, Massachusetts—camp life, "unresponsive"; Haverhill—convict mine, "sympathetic audience"; Bridgeport, "rain and wind, hard to speak, paid $250" (apparently the maximum); Boston, "larger audience and lecture well received, gave Kropotkin's escape first time with blackboard diagram"; Paterson, New Jersey—convict mine, "large audience but hall in bad and malodorous condition from German ball the previous night." In the Midwest the emphasis was more on university and college towns—Madison, Wisconsin; Minneapolis; Grinnell, Iowa; Iowa City; Terre Haute; Delaware, Ohio—but he was ill by the time he reached Toledo at the end of February and canceled the rest of the tour.[211]

The two-volume compilation of the articles, *Siberia and the Exile System*, that appeared in late 1891 was a disappointment in sales, probably because the local market was now saturated with the gory details of Siberian exile from Kennan, Buel, Stepniak, and others. Much of the compilation had already appeared in three Russian editions, published by emigré presses, and in German and French, but his earlier *Tent Life* was revived in reprintings. Kennan's position as an expert on Russia was now well established. To his wife he later reflected, probably with the license of hindsight: "If you had opposed my going to Siberia in 1885, I never would have gone and life would have taken a different course. I might have been prosperous, but I should perhaps have had little reputation in the world at large, because it

208. "Tales of the Caucasus," Kansas City *Star*, 25 March 1890, p. 4.
209. Kansas City *Star*, 27 March 1890, p. 1.
210. To Phillips, 2 April 1890, Phillips-Meyers Papers, UNC.
211. Diary, 1889–1890, box 20, Kennan Papers, LC.

was that trip that gave me my start in literature and in the lecture field. . . . I shall be remembered—in Russia at least—long after I am dead."[212]

Kennan's devotion and dedication cannot be questioned. His writing, public speaking, and personal correspondence with a wide range of Russian, American, and British sympathizers had a substantial, if not easily measured, influence on public and private opinion. American perceptions of Russia were already changing, but Kennan gave the shift a decided push and a degree of permanence. For many in the English-speaking world, Russia became the model of despotism. Hoosier author Lew Wallace summed up the new mood in 1888: "So few people understand what the Russian power represents. A vague idea of gratitude prevails in our country—gratitude to the Czar, and for what? For nothing disinterested. And then—my God, the horrible brutality of the imperial administration! Russian ideas of government once dominate, and progress ends. In that day, Heaven help the world!"[213]

But Kennan's effect was even broader. It helped inspire Theodore Roosevelt's civil service changes, gave impetus to prison reform throughout the world including Russia, highlighted international opposition to despotism, and propelled American moral consciousness and missionary impulse. From that time almost everyone traveling in or writing about Russia had to measure their perceptions against Kennan's. One of the first was Englishman Lionel Gowing, who followed Kennan through Siberia in 1886 and concluded that he was close to the truth.[214] Kennan's work was a lasting standard for future reference, so to missionary Arthur Judson Brown, writing in 1917, "George Kennan exposed the real Russia."[215]

There were, of course, those who took issue with Kennan's portrayal of Russia. By concentrating on articles and giving lectures, Kennan escaped a reviewer's formal critique for some time, but at least one American, the minister in St. Petersburg, issued a rebuttal. In a letter released in Detroit, George Lothrop considered

Mr. Kennan's statements to be in the main correct, but . . . the impression conveyed by them is calculated to give a mistaken idea of the social conditions of Russia. That idea is that the people of Russia live in a wretched condition of fear, cowering and cringing under a cold and

212. To E. W. K., 11 February 1912, box 15, Kennan Papers, LC.
213. Wallace (Crawfordsville) to Foulke, 5 January 1888, box 3, Foulke Papers, LC.
214. Gowing, *Five Thousand Miles in a Sledge* (New York: D. Appleton, 1890), p. ix.
215. Brown, *Russia in Transformation* (New York: Fleming H. Revell, 1917), p. 48.

cruel despotism with fear lest they may at any time be seized and condemned to the horrors of Siberian exile. . . . Russian civil society is no more oppressed with fears of Siberian exile than is society in New-York with fears of Sing Sing.[216]

Only after the combined impact of articles and lectures had fully registered and the book had finally appeared did Kennan face expert evaluation. The most important was from Isabel Hapgood, who had also traveled widely in Russia (though not in Siberia). In the *Nation* she accused Kennan of having preconceived views and of being as thoroughly hoodwinked by Russian exiles as earlier writers had been by government officials. She attacked his bias with a clever compliment: "It is the commonest of practices to state only one side of a question, but the knack of doing so in a manner which shall leave the reader utterly unconscious that another side exists, is a rare gift."[217] Kennan denied that he saw everything in the bleakest light and cited a number of positive aspects, but this only earned a further editorial rebuke: "It is an undeniable fact that not one in a thousand of Mr. Kennan's readers even notices his mention of those extenuating circumstances to which he now aids us in calling attention, owing to the unrelieved blackness of the descriptions to which we objected."[218]

Aftershocks of the Kennan exposé went in various directions. Ironically, Englishmen led the counterattack. Harry De Windt, after a tour of Siberian prisons made specifically to check Kennan's details, reported from what he saw that major reforms must have been made in a very short time, but his analysis suffered from obvious partisanship and Russian patronage.[219] The few private advocates of the Russian government abroad, such as Olga Novikova, were again labeled as spies for defending their country and for supporting the efforts of De Windt and others.[220]

Also joining the fray were a number of rebellious Irishmen. While not de-

216. Lothrop, "Social Condition of Russia," New York *Times*, 11 November 1888, p. 3. Nevertheless, Lothrop had agreed to serve as a conduit for exile communications with Kennan; Anastasi Petrunkevich (Tver) to Lothrop, 31 December 1886/12 January 1887, DPR, Russia, vol. 4442 (misc. received), RG 84, NA.

217. Hapgood, "Kennan's Siberia—I," *Nation* 54, 1385 (14 January 1892): 37–38.

218. Hapgood, "Mr. Kennan and Siberia," *Nation* 54, 1389 (11 February 1892): 109.

219. Harry De Windt, *Siberia As It Is* (London: Chapman and Hall, 1892), pp. 469–73; Travis, *George Kennan*, pp. 175–76. The *Nation* (48, 1239 [28 March 1889], p. 273) dismissed William T. Stead's *Truth About Russia* (London: Cassell, 1888) as "amusing and naive."

220. For earlier charges, see "The Russian Spy System," New York *Times*, 23 October 1887, p. 17.

nying the accuracy of Kennan's descriptions, they countered that British prisons were far worse.[221] An Irish-American, writing privately to the Russian minister in Washington, explained that Americans were guilty only of being duped by Britain in order "to escape notice of her diabolical record in connection with Ireland" and suggested that Russia mount a campaign of exposing British abuses in Ireland. He enclosed an article from the Detroit *Tribune*, inspired by a Kennan lecture, to serve his purpose of obtaining a Russian consular position in that city and money to bribe the local press.[222]

Russian officials were naturally unhappy about the stir created by Kennan, but their response only made the situation worse. Kennan's articles were cut out of copies of *Century*, and the censorship received wide publicity, though Hapgood asserted that plenty of intact copies were circulating in St. Petersburg.[223] Although some Russian officials looked on the United States with renewed suspicion, radicals both at home and abroad discovered an unexpected defender. Kennan himself reported that prisoners in St. Petersburg celebrated the Fourth of July by burning candles and hanging red, white, and blue rags out of their cell windows.[224] The timing of the radical turn to the United States was particularly auspicious, since France, the customary "safe house," was closing its doors as it courted an alliance with the tsar.

Many years later a Russian-American exile, reflecting on the prerevolutionary atmosphere, would lament:

> What knowledge Americans might have had of Russia was at this time overshadowed by the impression made by a series of articles running in one of the magazines. They were written by Mr. George Kennan, whose vivid and accurate pictures of the miseries existing in the overcrowded and unsanitary prisons, the long agonizing journeys of the Siberian exiles after leaving the railroad and before reaching their destination, the brutal treatment they there received, focussed attention on one partic-

221. "British vs. Russian Imprisonment," *Nation* 54, 1389 (11 February 1892): 109.

222. Thomas J. McCormick (Detroit) to Struve, 27 April 1890, f. 170, op. 512/1, d. 43 (1890), AVPR.

223. "My Experiences with the Russian Censor," *Nation* 51, 1321 (23 October 1890): 318–21. This had already become a general practice, with even *Harper's Monthly* coming under the knife in Odessa; Heenan to Rives, 9 July 1888, DUSC, Odessa, vol. 8 (roll 4, M 459), RG 59, NA.

224. Interview, Kansas City *Star*, 27 March 1890, p. 4.

ular feature of Russian life and government, while the better aspects were disregarded. Everything in Russia was held in horror.[225]

At least this was the impression in Russia outside of Siberia. What Kennan reported—and large numbers of Americans grasped—may have been true but was not the whole truth.

The Jewish Refugee Problem

Although Russia's treatment of the Jewish population would have continued to concern many Americans in the face of mounting official anti-Semitic policies, the Kennan exposé reinvigorated the issue. The public perceptions of the conditions of Jews and of Siberian exiles (a few were both) tended to go hand in hand, each bolstering the other. A case in point is that of the anarchist and would-be assassin Leo Hartman, who became an American citizen in 1886 and served as agitator for both causes.[226] The number of Russian Jews who became active in American radical and socialist movements helped cement the identification of Jews with political exiles.

The Russian policy of restricting the emigration of exiles but encouraging Jews to leave the country complicated the diplomatic situation. So did the adamant refusal to acknowledge the rights of American Jews, especially those of Russian origin such as Israel Muller and William Jamaiker, who went back to Russia to invest in business only to be driven out. The government politely resisted American pleas based on the 1832 treaty by claiming it was only treating all Jews equally.[227] But the recharged anti-Semitism of Russian officials as well as of the general public made exceptions for Americans more problematic. As minister Lothrop noted on the case of Muller, "I may mention that the difficulty is much aggravated by the intense anti-Jewish feeling that seems to exist throughout Russia."[228] Another dispatch, however, was less sympathetic. He considered Muller one of those Jews who "go to the United States to obtain naturalization and protection, and return intending to permanently remain here, claiming to be treated as American

225. Emma Cochrane Panafidine, *Russia—My Home: An Intimate Record of Personal Experiences Before, During and After the Bolshevist Revolution* (Indianapolis: Bobbs-Merrill, 1931), p. 25.

226. "An Anarchist Citizen," New York *Times*, 25 October 1886, p. 4.

227. Giers to Taft, 29 December 1884/10 January 1885, DPR, Russia, vol. 4508 (notes received), RG 84, NA.

228. To Bayard, 13 August 1885, PRFRUS 1885, p. 671.

citizens and as such to have rights, which, if admitted would give them great advantages over their brethren of the same faith."[229] Jamaiker resolved the problem by formally converting to the Lutheran faith.[230]

The reverse of the few Americans wanting to stay in Russia was the mass exodus that was stimulated by government policy, popular anti-Semitism, bad economic conditions, sectarian division, and increased pressure for military recruitment from the 1880s war scares. These factors coalesced in the sensitive border province of Bessarabia, with the result that over 40,000 Jews poured out of there through Odessa in 1888, almost all headed to the United States.[231] This was the beginning of a flood that reinforced Kennan's depiction of persecution and nearly overwhelmed immigration authorities and relief societies in the United States. A perception took hold that immigration patterns had dramatically altered: "Their [German] place was filled by Italians and Russians, who still dominate in the army of newly arriving citizens. The term Russian in this regard is somewhat of a misnomer, it being true politically and not ethnologically. Nearly all the subjects of the Czar who enter our gates are Hebrews, who are flying from the bigotry and oppression which mark orthodox Muscovy."[232] The Hebrew Sheltering House on Madison Avenue in New York did its best to cope with the tide.[233]

Confusion reigned in settlement ghettos, among politicians in Washington and St. Petersburg, and in Western Jewish circles. As the American government tightened admission, Jewish leaders—with the help of Baron Maurice de Hirsch, a prominent and wealthy British Jew, and his Jewish Colonization Association—sought other solutions, channeling the Russian refugees to Brazil, Mexico, Canada, and, finally, Palestine, campaigning for relief for the population in Russia in hopes of slowing the migration, and re-

229. To Bayard, 14 June 1885, DUSM, Russia, vol. 38 (roll 38, M 35), RG 59, NA.

230. Heenan to Lothrop, 20 May/1 June 1888, DPR, Russia, vol. 4443 (misc. received), RG 84, NA.

231. Heenan to Rives, 17 September 1888, DUSC, Odessa, vol. 8 (roll 4, M 459), RG 59, NA. A religious awakening, stirred by Rabbi Joseph Rabinowitz but with Christian aspects, had intensified and complicated unrest in the area of Bessarabia annexed by Russia in 1878. For contemporary publicity, see John F. Hurst, "The Christian Revolt of the Jews in Southern Russia," *Chautauquan* 5, 4 (January 1885): 218–20.

232. "A Scene in Castle Garden," *Harper's Weekly*, 2 February 1889, p. 86.

233. "The Jews in Russia," New York *Times*, 14 December 1890, p. 9. Compared with total immigration for the 1880s, the number of Russian Jews entering the country is not that impressive. Of a total of 5,246,613, only 193,021 were Jewish, 135,003 from Russia. The proportion of Russian Jews would rise in the next decade with smaller total immigration: 279,811 out of 3,687,564. The count is subject to underreporting, because some Russian Jews went to other countries before migrating to the United States.

doubling efforts to assist people in transit and upon arrival.[234] The United States was still the destination of choice, often promoted by those with vested business interests in immigrant traffic. For example, an attractive booklet on Jewish life in America published in Russian, stressing availability of assistance, was subsidized by advertisements of the North German Lloyd and Hamburg-America steamship lines.[235]

Alarmed by the charges issuing from the Western press—and perhaps mindful of the need to appease French-Jewish bankers—Russian officials took the initiative in trying to break the diplomatic impasse that had resulted from Russia's own policies. After discussing the matter with Alexander III on 9 February 1891, Giers summoned the American minister, Charles Emory Smith, to clarify the Russian position. He was emphatic that no new measures had been enacted, that only old laws had been stiffened, and that the issue was not religious but social and economic. The problem, Giers said, was that Jews monopolize saloons and mills and rent land to Christians. According to Smith, the foreign minister was too candid in explaining why Jews were restricted: "The Hebrews were an intellectual race— more alert mentally than the ingenuous people by whom they were surrounded—and if they had free and unlimited access to the highest opportunities of education they would absorb the professions within themselves."[236]

At the same time, the American government was carefully choosing its words in response to the situation. In a long dispatch, Acting Secretary of State William Wharton explained to Smith:

> The hospitality of a nation should not be turned into a burden. And, however much we may sympathize with wanderers forced by untoward circumstances to quit their homes, and however ready the disposition to relieve the deplorable condition into which they may be cast by the application of the laws of their native country, the Government and people of the United States cannot avoid a feeling of concern at the enforcement of measures which threaten to frustrate their efforts to minister to the wants and improve the condition of those who are driven to seek a livelihood within their borders. . . .

234. "The Hebrew Exodus from Russia," *Harper's Weekly*, 5 September 1891, p. 671.
235. G. M. Praisa [George Moses], *Russkie Evrei v Amerike: Ocherki iz istorii, zhizni i byta russko-evreiskikh emigrantov v Soedinennykh Shtatakh Sev. Ameriki s 1881 g. po 1891 g.* (St. Petersburg: Landau, 1893).
236. To Wharton, 10 February 1891, DUSM, Russia, vol. 42 (roll 42, M 35), RG 59, NA.

The Government of the United States does not assume to dictate the internal policy of other nations, or to make suggestions as to what their municipal laws should be or as to the manner in which they should be administered. Nevertheless, the mutual duties of nations require that each should use its power with a due regard for the results which its exercise produces on the rest of the world. It is in this aspect that the conditions of the Jews in Russia is now brought to the attention of the United States, upon whose shores are cast daily evidences of the suffering and destitution wrought by the enforcement of edicts against this unhappy people.[237]

The sheer weight of numbers had overwhelmed the vestiges of official sympathy.

Smith's conversation with Giers about this dispatch was important enough to attract the notice of the latter's assistant, Vladimir Lamzdorf, who observed that the foreign minister had difficulty understanding it because of his weak knowledge of English.[238] The effort in any case was of no avail. Smith believed that Russia actually tightened restrictions, thus causing an even larger emigration in the spring of 1891: "Since then it has gone on in a strong and steady current, and it becomes a question of special importance to us whether this movement and the causes which lie behind it can be influenced and modified."[239] After another interview with Giers, Smith requested from Washington specific information on the number of Russian Jewish immigrants to the United States and was quickly informed that during a six-month period of 1891 (May to November), 49,616 had entered.[240] A consul in Moscow later recalled that the midnight train from Moscow to Brest was used "to carry them away by the hundreds" in the spring of 1891, "when every means was devised to get rid of as many of the Jews as possible."[241]

237. 18 February 1891 (c), DI, Russia, vol. 16 (roll 138, M 77), RG 59, NA.

238. Entry of 7 March 1891, Vladimir Lamzdorf, *Dnevnik, 1891–1892*, ed. by F. A. Rotshtein (Moscow-Leningrad: Academia, 1934), p. 70.

239. Smith to Blaine, 20 October 1891, DUSM, Russia, vol. 42 (roll 42, M 35), RG 59, NA.

240. Smith to Blaine, 24 December 1891 (letter and telegram), ibid., and Blaine to Smith, 5 January 1892, DI, Russia, vol. 17 (roll 139, M 77), RG 59, NA. Indirect migration makes such exact figures suspect. For example, a group of Russian Jews spent the summer of 1892 encamped at Lyons in France before they were allowed to go to Boston; "Russian Jews in Camp," Cleveland *Plain Dealer*, 25 August 1892, p. 6.

241. Hornstedt to White, 28 January 1893, DPR, Russia, vol. 4447 (misc. received), RG 84, NA.

American Jewish leaders such as Jacob Schiff and Oscar Straus were pursuing a quiet lobbying effort in Washington but becoming increasingly distressed by what they perceived as governmental indifference.[242] Finally, in the summer of 1891 an official commission of inquiry into emigration from Russia was sent from the United States, which included among its members Walter Kempster and John Weber. Its findings during a tour through the Pale certainly did not help Russia's case. Acknowledging that "the Jew may breathe in more than one place if he reaches a certain educational standing," Weber found nothing but injustice and contradiction in Russia's treatment of the Jews. The effect, he thought, was to destroy business enterprise and stifle intelligence. "I hold that Russia is not civilized nor Christianized," he angrily concluded.[243] But another investigator, Joseph Pennell, asserted that conditions for Jews were no worse in Russia than in Austria. He accused the sensationalist press of building up hysteria, though he conceded that the Russian hatred of Jews was indeed intense. He saw swarms of Jews crowding into cities looking for hand-outs—and the West unquestioningly taking up their cause.[244] The American contradiction in the Jewish refugee problem was that there were determined attacks on the Russian claim that the issue was only social and economic and not religious, yet there was just as determined opposition to any large-scale migration.[245]

The Extradition Treaty

Russian officials often declared that one justification of the ill-usage of Jews was that many of them were nihilists, a charge taken up by the defenders of both in the United States. In fact, the number of radical revolutionaries among the Jewish immigrants was a proverbial drop in the bucket. The belief, real or contrived, tended to bond the two causes together, especially in the face of the threat of extradition posed by the negotiation of a treaty be-

242. See Gary Dean Best, *To Free a People: American Jewish Leaders and the Jewish Problem in Eastern Europe, 1890–1914* (Westport, Conn.: Greenwood Press, 1982), pp. 6–54.

243. John B. Weber, *Autobiography of John B. Weber* (New York: J. W. Clement, 1924), pp. 112, 124, quoting from a speech, "Russia in 1891."

244. Joseph Pennell, *The Jew at Home: Impressions of a Summer and Autumn Spent with Him* (New York: D. Appleton, 1892), pp. 11, 73, 103.

245. Herman Adler, "Russian Barbarities and Their Apologist," *North American Review* 153, 420 (November 1891): 518–22. Adler rejected the Russian assertion that the issue was not religious, answering a defense of that position in the same journal by Goldwin Smith.

tween the two countries to claim fugitives from justice. Opposition to such an agreement became a theme of Kennan's lectures, a campaign of periodicals promoting the exile cause, such as *Free Russia* and *Darkest Russia*, and the *raison d'être* of antitsarist organizations.

Meetings in April 1887 of the Russian American National League, composed mostly of Jews, with Leo Hartman as featured speaker, won the support of the Knights of Labor against the treaty then under consideration by the Senate Committee on Foreign Relations.[246] The fear was that Russia would use the agreement to reclaim for punishment a wide variety of so-called political criminals, such as the huge number of Jewish immigrants who were considered to have evaded Russian military service. Kennan refused to join the league, though he spoke at a meeting and led, with Foulke, a private campaign aimed at individual senators.

Although political criminals were supposedly exempted from extradition, article three of the draft treaty specified those involved in "the willful or negligent killing of the sovereign or chief magistrate of the State or of any member of his family, as well as an attempt to commit or participate in the said crimes." The latter phrase could unlock the door to a Russian demand for the return of any political refugee. Another objection was the absence of open, public, and fair trials in Russia for those accused of crimes, making it impossible to determine the justice of a government case criminal or political. Kennan especially argued for rejection on this point. To Foulke he wrote, "I am opposed to *any* treaty of that kind even although it contains the most explicit stipulation that *all* political offenders shall be excepted from its provisions."[247] Kennan explained why he did not do more at this time to fight the treaty:

I have not taken any active part in opposition to the proposed treaty—that is publicly—and have not written to the newspapers about it simply because I desire to preserve an attitude of fairness and impartiality in my magazine articles and to make it impossible for the defenders of the Russian Government to point to any action of mine and say "Mr

246. "Not Liking the Treaty," New York *Times*, 3 April 1887, p. 7; and "Russian Americans in Politics," New York *Times*, 14 April 1887, p. 8.

247. Kennan to Foulke, 20 December 1887, box 3, Foulke Papers, LC; Travis, *George Kennan*, pp. 208–9. Foulke recalled, somewhat inaccurately: "Russia wanted the United States Government to declare that the revolution movement in Russia had no political meaning, and that any attempt which should endanger the Czar's life, even for the purpose of obtaining constitutional government, should be regarded as simply a plot to commit murder." Foulke, *A Hoosier Autobiography* (New York: Oxford, 1922), p. 95.

Kennan's articles are prejudiced and not to be depended upon—you see he is siding with regicides nihilists and bomb-throwers, and does not want even murderers to be punished."[248]

After more than a year of intensive propaganda, the treaty was apparently permanently stalled in committee. The movement it generated was now ready to refocus on something else. Another Kennan lecture, in November 1889 in Philadelphia, inspired the Siberian Exile Petition Movement, a broad-based effort to raise the visibility of the plight of Russian political prisoners and to use American public opinion to improve conditions and perhaps achieve release or extradition.[249] Like a pyramid scheme, this spawned other short-lived organizations—such as the Russian Exile Relief Committee and the United States Siberian Exile Humane Society.[250]

Activism peaked with the publication of an American edition of the London-based and Stepniak-inspired *Free Russia* in August 1890 (with Kennan as editor) and the formation of the American Society of Friends of Russian Freedom, generally known as the Free Russia movement. Even the blasé Russian minister felt he should be alarmed about such developments, but he reasoned that Americans organize clubs, circles, and societies to seek philanthropy for all kinds of things.[251] He would soon have a more serious concern, when Kravchinskii/Stepniak arrived on American soil in December 1890 and drew large audiences during his two-month lecture tour. Following in the steps of Kennan, he was there ostensibly to raise money for the revolutionary cause by portraying Russian radicals as American liberals—and was becoming quite wealthy in the process.[252]

Other Missions

Jews were not the only religious minority in Russia that was considered a menace to Russian society. The members of the Congregational Anglo-American church in St. Petersburg had for many years promoted the circulation of bibles and other religious tracts with support from the American

248. To Foulke, 4 February 1888, box 3, Foulke Papers, LC.
249. Alfred J. P. McClure, "The Siberian Exile Petition Movement of Philadelphia," *Century* 40, 4 (August 1890): 636–37.
250. Travis, *George Kennan*, pp. 197–98.
251. Struve to Giers, 13/25 February 1890, f. 133, op. 470, d. 104 (1890), AVPR.
252. Ulam, *In the Name of the People*, pp. 294–95; Good, "America and the Russian Revolutionary Movement," pp. 177–79.

Bible Society. Direct efforts of agents of this society, even though concentrated on non-Russian areas of the empire such as Estonia and the Caucasus, ran into difficulty and became the subject of diplomatic protests.[253]

American and especially British activities resulted in the foundation in 1876 of the Russian Tract Society, which soon achieved wide notoriety because of the fanaticism of its Russian leaders, Vasily Pashkov and Modest Korf. The two men were accused of ties to nihilism and came under increasing scrutiny from authorities. Some members of the Congregational Anglo-American church were involved in the society's activities, and by 1884 one of the oldest American residents of the city, George H. Prince, had assumed its presidency. But in that year it was suppressed by the government. In attributing this to the influence of Pobedonostsev and Dmitri Tolstoi, secretary of legation Wurts observed: "It is said that not only are the teachings of the Pashkoffsky at variance with those of the established church, and therefore should not be tolerated, but also that owing to its workings having been taken advantage of by the nihilists for the distribution of their own publications, its suppression is but a prudent measure of the police for the preservation of order."[254] Needless to say, Pashkov and Korf joined the list of convicted exiles.

Prince and the Congregational Anglo-American church, however, remained unmolested. In fact, in December 1890, when it celebrated its fiftieth anniversary, a number of Russian dignitaries, including Foreign Minister Giers, were in attendance, probably because the American minister presided and homage was paid to James Buchanan's role in the church's founding.[255] Even the emperor made special note of the event at the New Year's Day diplomatic reception, and according to Smith, the rarity of this type of public occasion provoked much comment in St. Petersburg society.[256]

The Seventh Day Adventist movement also faced difficulties in Russia at this time. The foreign missions of this American-based church were begun by a converted Polish Catholic priest in Switzerland in 1866. From a base in Basel, Amer-

253. Isaac Bliss (St. Petersburg) to Hunt, 1 December 1882, DPR, Russia, vol. 4438 (misc. received), RG 84, NA; Frelinghuysen to Hoffman, 27 May 1882 (c), DI, Russia, vol. 16 (roll 138, M 77), RG 59, NA.
254. Wurts to Frelinghuysen, 25 June 1884, DUSM, Russia, vol. 37 (roll 37, M 35), RG 59, NA.
255. Alex Francis (minister of the church) to Smith, 23 November 1890, DPR, Russia, vol. 4444 (misc. received), RG 84, NA; Smith to Blaine, 23 December 1890, DUSM, Russia, vol. 42 (roll 42, M 35), RG 59, NA.
256. Smith to Blaine, 14 January 1891, DUSM, Russia, vol. 42 (roll 42, M 35), RG 59, NA.

ican missionaries spread out into Central and Eastern Europe.[257] In Russia they were careful to confine their work to the non-Orthodox population, mainly the Lutheran and Mennonite German communities. Elder Charles Richard Louis Conradi won converts and established a church at Berdebulat in Crimea during the summer of 1886, but he was soon arrested and confined at Perekop. Minister Lothrop, in successfully interceding on his behalf, was careful to explain that Conradi was not Jewish.[258] The same year another American Adventist, C. Laubhan, organized a church in the Volga German Lutheran town of Shcherbakovka (Tscherbakowka). His success in evading suppression encouraged Jacob Klein, from Kansas, to work in a neighboring village, Krestovyi Buderak, and in his hometown of Frank in the fall of 1889. In 1890, Klein was arrested on his way to Samara, apparently on the complaint of a Lutheran pastor. Both he and Laubhan were forced to leave the region, despite diplomatic intercession.[259] Conradi maintained, however, that the churches were flourishing with over 400 members, and the Adventist leader was back touring the Mennonite areas in 1894.[260]

As dramatized by the Jews, Mennonites, and Volga Germans, resettlement was the choice of many who confronted Russian social, religious, or ethnic discrimination. The rise of the conservative Orthodoxy of Pobedonostsev in the 1880s exerted new pressure on the even larger Roman Catholic population of the empire in Poland, Lithuania, and western Ukraine. The result would be a large-scale emigration that changed permanently the ethnic composition of a number of large American cities. Russification policies in the Lutheran Baltic provinces of Latvia, Estonia, and Finland had a similar but less dramatic effect.

Orthodoxy in America

The Russian Orthodox church in the United States was having its own problems. After a promising beginning under Father Nicholas Bjerring

257. John Norton Loughborough, *The Great Second Advent Movement: Its Rise and Progress* (Washington, D.C.: Review and Herald Publishing Company, 1909; reprint, New York: Arno Press, 1972), pp. 403–6.

258. Ibid., p. 409; Lothrop to Vlangaly, 6/18 August 1886, DPR, Russia, vol. 4537 (Russia notes), RG 84, NA.

259. Conradi (Hamburg) to Rice, 12 June 1890, DPR, Russia, vol. 4444 (misc. received), RG 84, NA; Smith to Klein, 20 October 1890, and to Conradi, 5 March and 9 December 1891 (c), DPR, Russia, vol. 4572 (letters sent), and Conradi to Smith, 23 February 1891, DPR, Russia, vol. 4445 (misc. received), RG 84, NA.

260. Conradi (Kharkov) to White, 7 October 1894, DPR, Russia, vol. 229 (misc. received), RG 84, NA.

(since 1870) and a flurry of attention given it at the time of the assassination of Alexander II, the little New York church closed early in 1883. A local journal commented: "The Rev. Mr. Bjerring, formerly priest of the Greek chapel in New York, which the Russian government decided to discontinue, has applied for membership in the presbytery of this city, and it is expected that his application will be favorably entertained."[261] Probably the conservative and Russian nationalist Pobedonostsev, who was directly in charge of religious affairs, could not be very pleased with a cleric who was a former Catholic priest of Danish origin and could speak little Russian. Bjerring's role in founding a local benevolent society that assisted all Russians, regardless of politics or beliefs, was also viewed as intolerable. A new, official parish—St. Nicholas on Second Avenue—was finally consecrated in 1892.[262]

With the purchase of Alaska, the United States gained several thousand Russian Orthodox adherents. To serve them the Holy Synod created in 1870 an autonomous diocese under Bishop Ivan (Stefan Mitropolskii) at Sitka. But several of these Russian-Alaskans left to join a Russian community in San Francisco. Following the advice of a famous Alaskan missionary, Ivan Veniaminov, now Bishop Innocent of Moscow, the see was moved to that city in 1872, where the Alexander Nevsky Cathedral was erected on Pierce Street.[263] Although financed by the Russian Holy Synod, the new diocese remained in precarious condition—as did Alaska, where a few dedicated priests were left to hold their remote parishes together, dependent on the Alaska Commercial Company for communications.

Bishop Ivan was recalled in 1876, but his replacement, Nestor (Nikolai Zakkis), did not arrive until 1880. At least he had some experience in the United States—as chaplain on one of the Russian ships that visited New York in 1863—and made serious attempts to visit his far-flung flock. Unfortunately, he drowned in the Bering Sea in 1882 during a tour of his active churches. After another awkward gap, Vasily Sokolovskii was named Bishop Vladimir in 1888. He reorganized the bishopric, built a new, larger cathedral on Powell Street, instituted services in English (since the church was also

261. *Harper's Weekly*, 24 February 1883, p. 115. The official history of the church in America, though quite kind to Bjerring, says simply that the closure was "for unknown reasons." Constance J. Tarasar, ed., *Orthodox America, 1794–1976: Development of the Orthodox Church in America* (Syosset, N.Y.: Orthodox Church in America, 1975), p. 39.

262. Olarovskii to Struve, 2/14 June 1892, f. 133, op. 512/1, d. 56 (1892), AVPR.

263. Tarasar, ed., *Orthodox America*, p. 29. The text of Veniaminov's letter of 1868 to Pobedonostsev is in *Alaskan Missionary Spirituality*, ed. Michael Oleksa (Mahwah, N.J.: Paulist Press, 1987), p. 251. See also the biographical sketch of Veniaminov by Andrew Kashevarov in ibid., pp. 341–62.

serving Greeks and other Slavs), and translated the liturgy into Aleut and Eskimo for the northern parishes.[264] This outgoing and enlightened leadership was continued by his successor, Nicholas (Mikhail Ziorov), in the 1890s.

By 1892, parishes had been founded in Portland, Seattle, Chicago, Minneapolis, and several sites in Pennsylvania. Some of these resulted from the crossover of Uniate congregations, whose members recognized the papacy but conducted services in a Slavic language and were mostly western Ukrainian or Galician and Slovak. They were apparently unhappy about their neglect by the Roman Catholic church in the United States, which was dominated by German, Irish, and Italian immigrants and did not accept vernacular liturgy performed by married priests. An example is the case of Father John Toth in Minneapolis who had a falling-out with the St. Paul Catholic archbishop in 1889 and approached Bishop Vladimir in San Francisco. After a protracted tug-of-war, Toth's congregation was formally welcomed into the Russian Orthodox fold in 1892.[265] Toth convinced kindred settlements in Pennsylvania to follow suit. Immigration and isolation seemed to reinforce bonds of Slavic brotherhood, and the Orthodox church heeded the missionary potential in the United States.

In the meantime, the sizable Russian-creole community that survived in Alaska resorted to appeals for help through the Russian minister in Washington, D.C., as if they were living in a foreign country, and in exasperation to Canadian authorities in Vancouver.[266] The absence of government, the blurred Russian-American boundaries in the North Pacific, and the autonomous nature of the region is best illustrated by two rather different men who made a definite mark on this period of Alaskan history: Henry W. Elliott and Sheldon Jackson.

Elliott was a naturalist and, like Kennan, a veteran of the Western Union telegraph expedition to the area. He argued that Alaska needed some benign government support, but overall it had nothing to offer white men, and its natives should therefore be left alone as much as possible. Jackson, on the other hand, was an ambitious and successful Presbyterian missionary who saw in Alaska new ground and people to conquer and set off in 1877 to establish the first Protestant mission at Wrangell to serve miners. This expanded under Hall Young and John Brady to Sitka, where an industrial school was formed for the local population, native and creole. With the ar-

264. Tarasar, ed., *Orthodox America*, pp. 30–35.
265. Ibid., pp. 45–53.
266. Shishkin to Gorchakov, 16/28 February 1879, f. 133, op. 470, d. 150, AVPR.

St. Michael's Church in Sitka in the 1930s.
From Iubileinyi Sbornik *(1944)*

rival of an indefatigable teacher, Fannie Kellogg, and her marriage to Brady, mission work in Alaska achieved a degree of permanence by 1880, despite much local opposition.[267] Jackson, meanwhile, campaigned vigorously for more government funds and oversight, presenting more than 900 lectures over a six-year period (1878–1884) in which he urged the Americanization of Alaska through education and development.[268] For years, however, a money-conscious Congress adopted an extreme hands-off version of Elliott's position. As one historian observes, finally, in 1884, "after *seventeen* years of ne-

267. Sheldon Jackson, *Alaska and Missions on the North Pacific Coast* (New York: Dodd, Mead, 1880), pp. 187–205. A visitor in 1888 noted that, despite a flourishing school, the missionaries had been unsuccessful in instilling a sense of modesty and morality among the Indians; Abby Johnson Woodman, *Picturesque Alaska* (Boston: Houghton Mifflin, 1889), pp. 149–61.

268. Ted C. Hinkley, *The Americanization of Alaska, 1867–1897* (Palo Alto, Calif.: Pacific Books, 1967), pp. 111–18.

glect and delay, a limited form of territorial government was provided for Alaska."[269]

The Sealing Controversy

The primary business operation in the North Pacific, killing and skinning seals, ignored most of the mainland territory. Fur hunting had brought the Russians to America in the first place, but now the prey was seals rather than sea otter. In 1868 the San Francisco-based Hutchinson, Kohl, and Company had negotiated with the Russian authorities a twenty-year lease for exclusive rights to hunt seals on the Kommandorskii (or Copper) Islands, near the Kamchatkan coast. Another California company, the Alaska Commercial Company, had already obtained similar rights for the Pribylov Islands in the Bering Sea, which had been acquired along with Alaska. When the two companies merged in late 1868, the new enterprise obtained a monopoly over seal hunting on land.[270] By 1880 the company, led by William Hutchinson, had reorganized and expanded its operations by employing native (Chukchi and Aleut) hunters who lived on the Kommandorskii Islands during the summer.[271] It had also established bases for coal, water, and other supplies on the Siberian mainland and at Unalaska. Although the company cleared an average of $400,000 a year from the Kommandorskii Islands alone, by contract Russia received only 10 percent, or 80,000 rubles (about $40,000).

The company obtained even greater income from the Pribylovs. There the annual "catch" was limited to 100,000, for which the United States Treasury received $55,000 in annual "rent" and a $2.62 "tax" for each skin.[272] A

269. Robert Laird Stewart, *Sheldon Jackson* (New York: Fleming H. Revell, 1908), p. 342.

270. Alaska Commercial Company minutes, 21 October and 30 December 1868, reel 2, CHS.

271. By this time the major investors were Louis Gerstle (president), Louis Sloss (vice-president), William Kohl, Tuburico Parrott, the Jonathan Parrott estate, Jonathan Miller, the H. M. Hutchinson estate, and Charles A. Williams; box 1, William Windom Papers, MinnHS.

272. An act of Congress of 1870, amended in 1873, placed responsibility for the proper utilization of this resource in the secretary of the Treasury. By some (American) accounts, the selective culling of 100,000, mostly males, would not deplete the herd, and the United States government netted around a quarter of a million dollars each year, far more than the administrative outlays for Alaska. H. H. McIntyre (Pribylovs) to Alaska Commercial Company, 16 July 1889 (c), ibid. For more background, see William R. Hurt, *Arctic Passage: The Turbulent History of the Land and People of the Bering Sea, 1697-1975* (New York: Charles Scribner's Sons, 1975), pp. 224-45.

serious international problem developed, however, as sealskins became more fashionable in the 1880s, because demand triggered the growth of pelagic (deep sea) hunting mainly by Canadian interlopers, who tracked the long winter migration of the seals and slaughtered them in open waters.[273] An outcry was raised by the company, which considered such activity illegal poaching, but also by others who predicted the rapid extermination of these animals by such indiscriminate hunting.

The interception of seals by natives along the Aleutians and the British Columbian and Alaskan coasts had been going on for ages. More active, commercial "poaching" probably began when some seals were netted along with cod by fishermen plying the same route. In fact, there had been accounts of hundreds of thousands of seals descending on a cod bank at one time. International issues arose over where and how the pelagic hunting was done. The legal area was off Vancouver Island within the three-mile coastal waters of British Columbia, yet increasingly sealing schooners not only breached the three-mile limit in the North Pacific but also entered the Bering Sea in the summer and corralled seals not far from the Pribylovs.[274]

Russia was also quick to raise an alarm by sending a special investigator from its islands to San Francisco and Alaska in 1885 to discuss the swift decline of the seal population.[275] Continued poaching then led to a series of American seizures of offending foreign vessels by Treasury revenue cutters, especially in 1887, and culminated in the much-publicized taking of the Canadian schooner *Black Diamond*.[276] Because this policy was inconsistent, the

---

273. Raw sealskins from these waters were sold at biannual auctions in London; after dressing and finishing, about three-quarters were delivered to American furriers, thus adding another complex international dimension to the business. In 1870, when the leasing began, the London price was $5.25 for a skin, but in 1888, the last year of a full quota from the Pribylovs, the company realized $1,867,095.46, or $18.67 apiece, from the auction. Wm. MacNaughton's Sons (New York) to T. B. Bradford, 9 February 1889 (c), and C. A. Williams to Windom, 20 January 1890, ibid. William Windom, as secretary of the Treasury, was collecting information regarding a new lease.

274. The actual sales from poaching, easily traced through the same London market, seldom exceeded 25,000 skins a year, but whether firearms or spears were used, pelagic hunting could not distinquish male from female, or old from young, which resulted in many wasted kills. Intercepting pregnant females off the islands caused multiple deaths as pups in the rookeries would starve.

275. *Leslie's Illustrated*, 4 April 1885.

276. "The Behring Sea Dispute," *Harper's Weekly*, 17 August 1889, p. 642. Further annoyances were the reported use by foreign poachers of isolated Alaskan ports for salting, packing, and transshipping the skins and evidence that at least some of the vessels were financed from London; McIntyre to Alaskan Commercial Company, 16 July 1889, box 1, Windom Papers, MinnHS.

Department of State ordered them released when a formal diplomatic protest was made. Finally, in 1889 these apparently fruitless seizures ended, their only benefit being the public attention they called to the region, more than anytime since 1867.

Investigations, conducted by Henry Elliott on behalf of the Smithsonian in 1890 and 1891, determined that the seal herds had been reduced to little over a million (from about 5 million in 1874) and that as many as 60,000 may have been "intercepted" during migration in May and June of 1891. The fur seals were divided into two main "herds"—the superior grey-black seals who used the Pribylov Islands for birthing and raising their young and those of the Kommandorskii Islands. Furs of the latter were worth about half as much as those of the former and therefore were less sought by the poachers.[277] This is why the sealing controversy centered on Alaska and the United States rather than on Russia, though Russia was an interested observer. Britain backed the Canadians for obvious political reasons but also to defend the principle of free and unlimited access to international waters. But just as the white man's decimation of the great buffalo herds had devastated the Plains Indians, so the liquidation of vast numbers of seals entailed similar disaster for Native American and Siberian peoples.

As bilateral negotiations opened in 1890, the United States and Britain took diametrically opposed positions. The former claimed that the seals belonging to the Pribylovs were the property of the United States wherever they chose to go. As a company agent put it, "When the seals on which the British are now poaching are found in the Pacific, they are simply astray but are, nevertheless, either our property or that of Russia, and should be respected and protected as such."[278] Britain advocated that all land killing be stopped and that the breeding grounds come under international protection but that hunting at sea be open and unrestricted to everyone.[279] Other proposed solutions were even more unrealistic: declaring at least the Bering Sea an American lake that had been purchased from Russia along with Alaska; or ending the poaching and the problem by a deliberate extermination of all seals.

To complicate matters, the administration in Washington was certainly

277. "The Alaska Fur Seal," Cleveland *Plain Dealer,* 7 February 1892, p. 4. Elliott was originally from Cleveland, and the leading newspaper there paid close attention to his activities.

278. McIntyre to Alaska Commercial Company, 16 July 1889, box 1, Windom Papers, MinnHS.

279. Foster to Wurts, 12 August 1892, and to White, 1 November 1892, DI, Russia, vol. 17 (roll 139, M 77), RG 59, NA.

not a disinterested party, and the foremost concern was for loss of revenue as the seals declined and the lease became less attractive. Moreover, both President Harrison and Secretary of State Blaine were closely connected to the owners of the American sealing company. With no agreement in sight, Blaine finally relented in March 1891 to a British-backed moratorium on all hunting, while secretly allowing the company to continue its operations. Elliott was so disgusted with the outcome that he went public with what was happening and quit his Smithsonian position.[280] In the meantime, resolution of the dispute awaited the ruling of a court of arbitration in Paris.

In making its case the United States hoped to win active Russian support. As Blaine cabled Smith in May 1890, "It is of the utmost importance that we cordially cooperate with Russia in the policy touching our joint interest in the Behring Sea. Omit no proper opportunity to impress this view upon the Russian Government. Any difference between the two Powers will inure to the advantage of Great Britain."[281] In fact, this goal may have cooled official American pressure on behalf of the Jewish population in 1890–1892. Russia responded in kind with its own efforts to police the region. The captain of a British Columbia ship seized by the Russians in the summer of 1892 claimed he overheard crewmen saying that they were only doing this to help the United States in its case against Great Britain.[282]

This temporary common cause helped the Americans maintain a monopoly over Russian as well as American seals on the Kommandorskii Islands when the lease came up for renewal in 1890. Since Russia preferred to award the contract to a Russian enterprise, the Americans formed a pseudo-Russian concern, the North American Commercial Company, through a St. Petersburg agent and secured twenty-year renewal of the agreement.[283]

By this time, other resources of the waters of Alaska were being harvested by both Americans and Canadians, especially in the netting of cod, herring,

---

280. James T. Gay, "Harrison, Blaine, and Cronyism," *Alaska Journal* 3, 1 (Winter 1973): 13–17. Indeed, the controversy sparked one of America's first endangered species crusades, with author Lew Wallace spearheading it; "The Seal Should Be Saved," letter to editor, New York *Tribune*, 26 March 1892, p. 4. Apart from the seals, public exposure also raised questions about the right of the federal government to foster and protect a private monopoly, then allow it to use only foreign markets. Solutions ranged from complete government withdrawal and free unregulated sealing to an entirely government-run operation.
281. 10 May 1890(1), DI, Russia, vol. 16 (roll 138, M 77), RG 59, NA.
282. "Russia in Bering Sea," Cleveland *Plain Dealer*, 28 September 1892, p. 7.
283. Smith to Blaine, 6 December 1890, DUSM, Russia, vol. 42 (roll 42, M 35), RG 59, NA.

and salmon. The codfishermen usually took their catch and ran it home for drying and processing into oil, but the salmon fishing produced a local canning industry that grew rapidly in the 1880s. By 1889 over 3 million salmon were being canned annually at the Karluk River area of Kodiak alone. This business was managed primarily by outsiders employing Chinese laborers, and so, like the sealers, it deprived natives of their usual catches.[284]

Alaska Rediscovered

In the late 1880s, Alaska once more became a general target of venturesome travelers and reporters. Kate Field, a favorite of American literati, recorded the desolate scene in Sitka for *Harper's Weekly* in 1888. Only about 200 creoles were left there, who were "apt to possess the vices of both races, . . . prone to sell bad spirits and beer to the natives." She observed that none spoke English and that the local priest still administered the oath of allegiance to the tsar while the American administration looked the other way.[285] Her guide, George Kostromitinov, a nephew of a long-time Russian consul in San Francisco, deserves credit for reawakening the American public to Alaska. He also served as consultant and interpreter for a New York *Times* reporter in 1889, who noted that few Americans knew what Alaska was or how much it had been neglected and suggested that a congressional committee go there to see for itself.[286]

The American rediscovery of Alaska was promoted by other newcomers on the scene, chiefly miners, missionaries, and explorers. The former, coming in large numbers already in the 1870s, were at first mostly Canadians interested in easy access through Juneau to the gold-bearing streams in the mountains of the Cassior region. Canadians wandered back and forth across the border in search of gold and furs, at times encountering hostile natives who naturally resented these exploitive foreign intrusions. At least one account of the disappearance of a mining party took the side of the Indians and blamed a tactless administration.[287] And gold found along the bound-

284. Hinckley, *Americanization of Alaska*, pp. 123–28.
285. "A Trip to Southeastern Alaska," *Harper's Weekly*, 8 September 1888, p. 681.
286. "The Alaska Seal Islands," New York *Times*, 5 March 1889. A Senate committee actually did visit the territory that year; "Mission Work in Alaska," New York *Times*, 19 January 1890, p. 6.
287. "Hostile Alaska Indians," New York *Times*, 26 February 1892. With such conflicts in mind, a House committee had suggested in 1890 that the capital be shifted from Sitka to Juneau; ibid., 8 May 1890, p. 4.

ary between Canada and Alaska instigated lengthy discussions of the border's exact placement, which involved tedious and largely fruitless searches of Russian archives.

More missionaries also descended on the territory, annoying the Indians, the established Russian Orthodox churches, and especially the smugglers of liquor whom they were determined to curb. A Moravian venture to the western coast in 1884 found that the Eskimos "had been utterly neglected by the government and the Christian churches of the United States."[288] The Presbyterian mission at Sitka had difficult beginnings despite Jackson's efforts, while Quakers from Iowa and Kansas were initially successful on Douglas Island, and the Jesuits made inroads along the Yukon from Canada.

By 1890, however, Bishop Vladimir was cooperating with the Presbyterians in the conduct of a training school and orphanage for natives in Sitka. But rampant thievery and prostitution, encouraged by native indifference and the lack of law enforcement, were formidable obstacles. "There is no legislative body of any kind in the territory, no Indian agencies and no local municipal government or authority," complained one observer.[289] In a celebrated 1892 case involving smugglers, a noted Quaker missionary, Charles H. Edwards, was killed and another was tarred and feathered. A report about this incident stated that there were fewer than a dozen people in Alaska with authority to make arrests—and none were made.[290]

After assuming his post in San Francisco, Bishop Nicholas painted a grim picture of disease and death among the natives, but he now saw the solution in a greater American presence, asking for warships, medical relief, assistance in recovering church property, and subsidies for schools.[291] Both missionary and a few government-sponsored schools aimed mostly at the native population began to appear but had limited success and were resented by the creole Russian Orthodox schools. The confused situation and the need for more information to persuade the government to intervene finally inspired the first serious effort at census taking of the territory in 1890.[292]

Other noteworthy projects in the region included Sheldon Jackson's plan, with Washington's blessing, to transfer a sizable herd of Siberian rein-

288. *Harper's Weekly*, 3 May 1884, p. 283.

289. "Mission Work in Alaska," New York *Times*, 19 January 1890.

290. "Lawlessness in Alaska," New York *Times*, 7 June 1892.

291. Nicholas (San Francisco) to Shilling (secretary of legation, Washington), 28 October/7 November 1892, f. 370, op. 512/1, d. 55, AVPR.

292. A census of Sitka was taken by the army in 1870; see appendix 2, in R. N. DeArmond, ed., *Lady Franklin Visits Sitka, Alaska 1870* (Anchorage: Alaska Historical Society, 1981), pp. 93–125.

deer to Alaska. The first large contingent of 177 reached Port Clarence on the western coast on the revenue cutter *Bear* in September 1892.[293] The idea was to turn the Eskimos into Lapplike reindeer herders. A more important Russian development that helped stir American interest in the North Pacific at this time was the publicity about the beginning of construction on the Trans-Siberian Railroad, which inspired wild ideas of an intercontinental rail link over or under the Bering Sea. By this time, Alaska could at last be considered part of the United States because of the establishment of regular twice-monthly mail service between Seattle and Sitka—with extended delivery to four other designated offices "by whoever chances that way."[294] But this was still truly America's last frontier.

The 1880s was indeed a decade of new and complex developments in the Russian-American relationship. In some ways it resembled the beginning of a "cold war" over Russian treatment of certain classes of its citizens, especially since the shift from reform toward caution and reaction in one country was matched by the rise of moralistic fervor, nationalistic pride, and aggressive philanthropy in the other. Although a few people saw the hypocrisy in American outrage about repression in Russia, many other Americans sought rational business objectives and, if convenient, selfless humanitarian goals from a base of increasing international economic and political strength.

293. Wharton to Smith, 17 March 1892, DI, Russia, vol. 17 (roll 139, M 77), RG 59, NA; "Reindeer in Alaska," New York *Times*, 19 October 1892. A few were apparently brought ashore in the summer of 1891; Hinkley, *Americanization of Alaska*, p. 199.

294. "Some Far-Away Post Offices," New York *Times*, 15 July 1892. Jackson claimed credit for the first irregular mail delivery in 1883, simply taking mail along on his annual tour of missions; Stewart, *Sheldon Jackson*, p. 338.

5

Bread and Sympathy, 1890–1898

The negative view of Russia inspired by Kennan's writing and lecturing and by the Jewish persecution and emigration did little to slow the traffic of Americans into Russia. In fact, the extensive publicity may have encouraged more people to want to see for themselves and, after Kennan's success, prompted editors and publishers to seek and produce more books and articles about Russia. But other factors were important. The American outlook was becoming more international, signified by such events as the inauguration and immediate success of the *National Geographic Magazine*, which kindled quests for the new and exotic, at home and abroad.[1] Merchant capital and industrialization produced comparative affluence and more leisure time. On the receiving end of telegraphic dispatches from distant quarters of the globe, daily newspapers brought the world into upper- and middle-class parlors.

Travel itself had become easier and safer than ever before with the advent of luxury liners, Pullman sleeping cars, commodious stations, and posh hotels. And to link everything together were better guidebooks, tour agents, and interpreters. Everywhere Baedeker went, Americans would follow.[2] Besides much-publicized geographical monuments and such marvels of the new age as the Eiffel Tower and the Brooklyn Bridge, famous people beckoned. Leo Tolstoy was one of the sights to see for enterprising American

1. Gardiner G. Hubbard, "Russia in Europe," *National Geographic Magazine* 7, 1 (January 1896): 3–26. The presidential address of 1895 featured Russia.
2. The first Baedeker guide to part of Russia was published in 1883, but the edition that would become standard—Karl Baedeker, *Russland: Handbuch für Reisende* (Leipzig: Baedeker, 1888)—came out five years later. Although a French version was available by 1897, an English translation did not appear until 1912.

tourists to Russia, and at least thirty managed to meet and converse with him, a few extensively and more than once.

Americans, awash with national pride and newfound imperialism, were now more prone to compare Russia unfavorably with the United States or Western Europe and to sympathize with the downtrodden, whether Jews, Poles, nihilists, or Russian peasants. This high moralistic tone came from clergymen and missionaries, idealistic social reformers, and wealthy philanthropists. For example, Methodist minister James Monroe Buckley stressed in 1886, ante Kennan, the low morality of Russians, deplorable living conditions, excessive press censorship, and the dismal fate of "unhappy Poland."[3]

Representing an increasing number of women tourists and their point of view was Lilian Leland:

> Russia is dirty, her people are likewise, Moscow is especially so. But it is a holy land and a pious people. There are plenty of rich churches and poor people. Religion, poverty, ignorance and dirt, go hand in hand— might be called concomitants of each other. . . . America is the most radical and the most civilized country in the world. Russia, Ireland and Italy are but little in advance of heathendom.[4]

But she also reported that Russia was as safe for a woman to visit as any other country.

Other travelers of these years betrayed Kennan's influence either in preconceptions or in what they looked for in Russia. For veteran globe-trotter Lee Meriwether, "Russia is like a vast prison. . . . Walls—that is, offices— meet you at every turn."[5] Francis Sessions observed that he and his wife "did not feel very comfortable in a strange country, . . . to have so many of the police and detectives about us."[6] Another midwestern visitor probably expressed a common feeling: "An American will never forget the strange sensation which possesses him as he crosses the frontier and enters Russia."[7]

3. Buckley, *The Midnight Sun, the Tsar and the Nihilist: Adventures and Observations in Norway, Sweden and Russia* (Boston: Lothrop, 1886), pp. 280, 297, 327, 372–76.

4. Leland, *Traveling Alone: A Woman's Journey Around the World* (New York: American News, 1890), p. 275.

5. Meriwether, *A Tramp Trip: How to See Europe on Fifty Cents a Day* (New York: Harper and Bros., 1887), p. 207.

6. Sessions, *From the Land of the Midnight Sun to the Volga* (New York: Welch, Fracker, 1890), p. 122.

7. Perry S. Heath, *A Hoosier in Russia: The Only White Tsar—His Imperialism, Country and People* (New York: Lorborn Publishing, 1888), p. 7.

And Presbyterian minister William Wilberforce Newton reported that one of his traveling companions on his European tour always spoke in a whisper while in Russia.[8]

Still, Russia had its defenders, or at least visitors who leaned over backwards to give it the benefit of the doubt. Newspaperman and future ambassador Curtis Guild presented a balanced, colorful view of the country,[9] while Charles Cutting attacked the critics of Russia directly: "Indeed, our whole Russian experience has been most enjoyable in every way. The stories one hears of the surveillance and difficulties of travelling in the Empire are almost as absurd as some of the ideas stay-at-home English have of America."[10] Similarly, John Bouton blamed British prejudices for influencing Americans. "Englishmen can not be trusted to treat Russia fairly. John Bull hates Ivanovitch."[11] A more widely read observer, Charles Augustus Stoddard, looked to the future: "Slowly but surely this great Russian nation is awakening from its sleep. It is a giant ignorant of its enormous strength, like a blind Samson, or an elephant led by a man with a javelin. But when once it begins to learn and to know its power, its progress must be amazing. . . . Give the Russians time, education, and a full sense of their power, and they will overcome everything."[12] Russia, it seems, was in the eye of the beholder.

Those attracted to Russia for exotic experiences formed a parade to Central Asia. They included the wealthy plumbing supplier of Chicago, Charles R. Crane (1891), Archibald Cary Coolidge (1891), Odessa consul Thomas Heenan (1892), Theodore Child (1892), veteran traveler Frank Vincent (1893), Benjamin Thurston (1894), Michael Shoemaker (1894), Harold Jefferson Coolidge (brother of Archibald, 1894), St. Louis businessmen Gus and Frank Brecht (1895), and Thomas Stevens (1896). Most adventurous of all were Thomas G. Allen and William Sachtleben, recent graduates of Washington University of St. Louis, who arrived in late 1891 on the Persian-Russian border with bicycles to cross the Eurasian continent. Shocked at

8. Newton, *A Run Through Russia: The Story of a Visit to Count Tolstoi* (Hartford, Conn.: Student Publishing Company, 1894), p. 66. The person was identified only as "Lord Byron," another clergyman.

9. Guild, *Britons and Muscovites, or Traits of Two Empires* (Boston: Lee and Shepard, 1888).

10. Cutting, *Glimpses of Scandinavia and Russia* (Boston: Thomas Groom, 1887), p. 90.

11. Bouton, *Roundabout to Moscow: An Epicurean Journey* (New York: D. Appleton, 1887), p. 11.

12. Stoddard, *Across Russia: From the Baltic to the Danube* (New York: Charles Scribner's Sons, 1892), p. 86.

Russian police; sketch by Frederic Remington, 1892.
From Poultney Bigelow, Borderlands *(1895)*

the drunkenness, gambling, social laxity, and bad roads, they abandoned their original plan of traversing Siberia and went directly from Central Asia into China.[13] Although the experiences of these hardy travelers made little lasting impression on either country, the same could not be said for two notable troublemakers.

A dilettante sportsman, yachtsman, and world traveler, Poultney Bigelow had made a hiking and boating tour of the Ukraine and Poland in 1890, and decided in late 1891 to put Kennan's Russia fully to the test. Armed with a commission from the United States government to inspect coastal erosion

13. Allen and Sachtleben, *Across Asia on a Bicycle: The Journey of Two American Students from Constantinople to Peking* (New York: Century, 1897); Allen to Wurts, 7 June and 5 July 1892, DPR, Russia, vol. 4447 (misc. received), RG 84, NA. For a résumé of the trip, see Mary Ellen Benson, "Riding the 'Devil's Cart' Across Asia," *Washington University Magazine* 61, 2 (Summer 1991): 28–33.

Poultney Bigelow. From Bigelow, Seventy Summers *(1925)*

and a contract from *Harper's Monthly,* he set off for Russia in the spring of
1892, bringing along a former Yale classmate, Frederic Remington, to provide on-the-spot illustrations.[14] They sent ahead two sailboats modified for
paddling and manipulating currents, with the intention of surveying by water the entire Baltic coast from St. Petersburg south to the German border
and then inland on the border streams. Despite the novelty of the plan and

14. Bigelow to American legation, St. Petersburg, 20 May 1892, DPR, Russia, vol.
4447 (misc. received), RG 84, NA; copy enclosed in Wurts to Foster, 27 August 1892,
DUSM, Russia, vol. 43 (roll 43, M 35), RG 59, NA. Bigelow, son of diplomat John Bigelow, had plenty of time to reminisce over his exploits, since he lived to the age of
ninety-nine, to 1955. See his *Seventy Summers,* 2 vols. (New York: Longmans, Green,
1925), in which (1:307) he describes himself as a chaperone for Remington. The contract with *Harper's* provided $750 per article and $250 for each illustration. Peggy Samuels and Harold Samuels, *Frederic Remington: A Biography* (Garden City, N.Y.: Doubleday, 1982), p. 170.

the fact that the route would take them through several naval bases and within yards of strategic fortresses, Bigelow and Remington expected immediate approval by the Russian government and to accomplish their goal within a few weeks. What actually happened caused headaches for Russian and American officials and a sensation at home because of the fame of this unusual pair.

That the proposed tour bore striking resemblance in miniature to the Kennan-Frost exposé mission of five years earlier could escape no one and was later confirmed by the dedication of the eventual book to Kennan.[15] Clearly, Bigelow and Remington did their best to call attention to themselves. After making a scene in crossing the frontier, they dallied in Warsaw with known Polish revolutionaries and taunted the police on their tail. They finally arrived in St. Petersburg on 6 June and secured secretary of legation Wurts's reluctant assistance in applying for the official passes, which they expected to receive the next day. They encountered trouble getting the boats through Customs and then became irritated at the delays, blaming Wurts as well as the Russian authorities.[16]

With the help of a secretary of the Russian legation in Washington who was on leave, the boats were safely transported to Kovno on the Russian-German border. So, after only a few days in Russia proper, the American duo departed for Kovno to await authorization for their trip. Remington, meanwhile, made himself unwelcome by sketching soldiers and other local characters and retreated into brandy and depression. Bigelow summed up their mood: "There is nothing much sadder than Russia, and Remington's reference to it once as 'the sad gray land' seemed more and more apt the more I saw of this mournful empire."[17] Although Bigelow slipped off to visit a friend in Novgorod, they actually saw little of Russia before impatiently crossing to the German side, where Bigelow claimed, wrongly, that they had

15. Poultney Bigelow, *The Borderland of Czar and Kaiser: Notes from Both Sides of the Russian Frontier* (New York: Harper and Bros., 1895), frontispiece.

16. Bigelow, *Borderland*, p. 71; Wurts to Shishkin, 25 May/6 June 1892, DPR, Russia, vol. 4538 (notes sent), RG 84, NA; Wurts to Foster, 27 August 1892, DUSM, Russia, vol. 43 (roll 43, M 35), RG 59, NA; Samuels and Samuels, pp. 173–74. *Remington, The United States was again between ministers at the time. Bigelow later wrote Andrew Dickson White: "The behavior of Mr. Wurts towards Remington and myself was what we might have expected had we been two disorderly sailors brought up before a consular court. He seemed to regard the credentials of our Secretary of State as of a value equal to but not greater than the seal of a college debating society." Roll 59, White Papers, Cornell University.

17. Bigelow, *Borderland*, p. 27.

been expelled.[18] Actually, permission to explore the Russian frontier was duly granted and reached Bigelow in Berlin two weeks later.[19]

For Remington the few days spent in Russia were obviously an ordeal. To Julian Ralph he wrote:

> Bigelow and I have been chased all over Russia and finally fired bodily out of the country—we left St. Petersburg and instead of crossing at the R. R. point we stopped at Kovno and took a steamer down the Neiman and then a Jew with a funny cart. These Russians are a frightful lot of barbarians and their police espionage is something you cannot imagine. We dodged the police telegrams and got off with our notes and sketches—the canoes are in Russia and God knows whether we will ever get them. . . .
>
> I have been as lonesome as a toad in a well—can't talk the d—— language and its a grand error if one supposes that Russians can talk English. One can't even read the letters of the signs—sort of Greek Russian characters.
>
> Some people think they know about vermin—lice and fleas but they don't—no one but Russians understand.[20]

Nevertheless, Remington left a legacy of his visit in some fine sketches of Russian soldiers and peasants.[21]

Popular Culture

American purveyors of the "lower arts" also targeted Russia. Perhaps the first was Theodore Leut, a naturalized American who made a modest living in Russia exhibiting freaks, especially bearded ladies, and had become the proprietor of the

18. Wurts to Foster, 27 August 1892, DUSM, Russia, vol. 43 (roll 43, M 35), RG 59, NA; Bigelow, *Seventy Summers* 1:323; Ben Merchant Vorpahl, *Frederic Remington and the West: With the Eye of the Mind* (Austin and London: University of Texas Press, 1972), pp. 129–33.

19. A more docile Bigelow acknowledged he had not been expelled and thanked Wurts for his service, but "Remington has run home in disgust and bankruptsy and cholera stare me in the face." To Wurts, 18 August 1892, DPR, Russia, vol. 4447 (misc. received), RG 84, NA.

20. 11 June 1892 (photostat copy), personal misc. file, Remington Papers, NYPL.

21. "Frederick [sic] Remington's Exhibition of Painting," *Harper's Weekly*, 7 January 1893, p. 7. Over one hundred pictures of German and Russian scenes were displayed at the American Art Association galleries during the 1892–1893 winter. One expert considered "Blue-China Cossack" the best of the lot; Vorpahl, *Remington and the West*, p. 135.

Russian soldier; sketch by Frederic Remington, 1892. From Poultney Bigelow, Borderlands *(1895)*

Passage Museum in St. Petersburg before his death in an insane asylum in 1885.[22] Equestrian artists Davis Richards and Richard Conrad performed in the Russian circus in the 1870s.[23] Minstrels Hannah Edwards and Julia Thompson from Philadelphia toured the country in 1882 with Harry Clifton's "American Original Colored Jubilee Singers."[24] And Joseph Johnson, under the more exotic name of Charles Leroux, made news when his hot air balloon took a sudden dive into the sea off the Baltic coast and he drowned.[25]

American horses, horse trainers, and drivers were particularly in demand

22. Swann to Hunter, 1 August 1885, DUSC, St. Petersburg, vol. 17 (roll 12, M 81), RG 59, NA. Leut was married successively to bearded sisters, Louise and Maria Pastriani.

23. Pomutz to Edwards, 9 March 1879, DUSC, St. Petersburg, vol. 16 (roll 11, M 81), RG 59, NA.

24. Clifton (Rostov) to Foster, 28 August 1882, DPR, Russia, vol. 4438 (misc. received), RG 84, NA.

25. Crawford to Wharton, 10 October 1889, DUSC, St. Petersburg, vol. 19 (roll 14, M 81), RG 59, NA.

in Russia. For many years Joseph Moses, using the less Jewish name of James Moscow, managed the stable of the Moscow circus and imported American trick horses and acts. An American tourist encountered two sets of brothers by the names of Caton and Raymer driving sulkies at the race track.[26] Finally, Fred Whitney's "Wild America" show appeared on the Russian-Polish frontier in 1890, creating some new problems for the legation. After the Russians initially refused admission, Wurts successfully pleaded its educational value.[27] Then, to simplify customs inspection, Native Americans and animals were listed on one bulk-inventory passport. The show, featuring diving horses along with the usual cowboy and Indian acts, played to enthusiastic crowds in Warsaw and St. Petersburg.[28]

The Whitney precedent eased the way for a similar customs clearance for Buffalo Bill's star-filled troupe during a Black Sea cruise in 1892. It apparently only performed in Batum and Sevastopol, where Colonel Cody picked up a new act: a group of Cossacks led by a descendant of Mazeppa, a famous Ukrainian rebel during the reign of Peter the Great. They would be a highlight of his Chicago world's fair show.[29] Buffalo Bill also left behind a memento of the visit in the form of an American Sioux Indian named Humper Nespar, or Wadded Moccasin.

Allegedly discharged at Sevastopol for drunkenness, Humper Nespar, or Hampa as he was known in Odessa, remained in Russia for several years performing, or on exhibit, in circuses in the south of Russia. As this employment was unsteady and Hampa had succumbed to alcoholism, he soon came to the attention of the American consul in Odessa, who befriended him but then pleaded for reimbursement of his expenses. "The fellow is, I fear, a confirmed drunkard, else he might do very well in the show busi-

26. John A. Logan, Jr., *In Joyful Russia* (New York: D. Appleton and Co., 1897), p. 230.

27. The company was at first mistaken for Buffalo Bill's better-known one; Whitney (Warsaw) to Wurts, 14/26 April 1890, DPR, Russia, vol. 4444 (misc. received), and Wurts to Vyshnegradskii, 16/28 April, 19 April/1 May, and 3/15 July 1890, DPR, Russia, vol. 4537 (notes sent), RG 84, NA. There had been another "wild" American intrusion on that frontier the year before, when P. T. Barnum transported eight elephants from India overland through Russia; Newton, *A Run Through Russia*, p. 12.

28. For a description of the Whitney show, see Don Russell, *The Wild West, or A History of the Wild West Shows* (Austin, Tex.: Steck-Warlick, 1970), pp. 37–38.

29. Ibid., p. 40; Wurts to Shishkin, 18/30 April 1892, DPR, Russia, vol. 4538 (notes sent), and Shishkin to Wurts, 5/17 May 1892, DPR, Russia, vol. 4510, (notes received), RG 84, NA. At the 1893 Chicago exposition, ten cossacks from Ozuget performed under the direction of Prince Ivan Macheradze, identified as one of Mazeppa's clan; "Cossacks and Uhlans," Chicago *Record*, 14 April 1893, p. 5.

ness."[30] Hampa did not have an American passport, and Indians from reservations were not considered citizens—nor could they be naturalized except by act of Congress or by leaving a reservation and adopting "the habits of civilized life." Consequently, Hampa's precise status mystified American officials in Russia until a clarification was finally received from Washington: "Even if he has not acquired citizenship, he is a ward of the Government and entitled to the consideration and assistance of our diplomatic and consular officers."[31] He was then provided with a certificate in Russian:

> To Whom it May Concern: The bearer of this document is a North American Indian whose name is Hampa. This Indian is a ward of the United States and is entitled to the protection of its consular and other officials. He is not, however, entitled to a passport as he is not a citizen of the United States. This consulate has the honor to request the Russian authorities to grant Hampa all necessary protection during his stay in Russia and grant him permission to depart when he requires it.[32]

A Russian official might well have seen the irony in this document, coming from a country that took such an interest in some of Russia's mistreated subjects. No other information could be found on America's "wandering ward" in Russia.

Literature and the Arts

During the last fifteen years of the nineteenth century, the impact of Russian culture on the United States increased dramatically, perhaps reaching its all-time apex. This mitigated to some extent the critical assessments of Kennan and many travel writers, who in fact usually made exceptions to their unfavorable comments in respect to Russian literature, art, music, and science. The American age of Turgenev that was particularly pronounced in the 1870s overlapped with that of Tolstoy, and Eugene Schuyler paved the

30. Heenan (Odessa) to Breckinridge, 15 March 1896, DPR, Russia, vol. 4452 (misc. received), RG 84, NA. In bringing Breckinridge's successor up-to-date and repeating claims for reimbursement, Heenan emphasized that the affair was more complicated because other Americans "were civilized beings." To Rockhill, 7 May 1896, DPR, Russia, vol. 4450 (misc. received), RG 84, NA.
31. John Sherman to Breckinridge, 5 April 1897, DI, Russia, vol. 17 (roll 139, M 77), RG 59, NA.
32. Copy in Heenan to Rockhill, 7 May 1896, DPR, Russia, vol. 4450 (misc. received), RG 84, NA.

way for both. His new third edition and improved translation of Tolstoy's *Cossacks* appeared in 1887 and received good reviews.[33] He also had the distinction of being the first (and possibly only) American to visit both Turgenev and Tolstoy.

Eighteen eighty-six constituted the real breakthrough for Russian literature available in English translation. The list that year included a number of Nikolai Gogol's short stories as well as *Dead Souls* and *Taras Bulba*, Dostoevsky's *Crime and Punishment*, Krylov's *Fables*, and two of Tolstoy's major works, *Anna Karenina* and *War and Peace*. Even Nicholas Chernyshevsky's *What Is To Be Done* rated two new American editions. The leading translators of these classics, Isabel Hapgood (Gogol and Tolstoy), Nathan Haskell Dole (Tolstoy and Chernyshevsky), and Jeremiah Curtin—promoted them along with their own books on Russian cultural accomplishments. Hapgood's *Epic Songs of Russia* especially met with critical acclaim.[34]

The new interest which has begun to manifest itself in Russian things could have no more significant illustration than that supplied by Miss Hapgood's felicitous experiment in the translation of the epic Russian song. Ten years ago it would have been impossible to issue a volume like this, such was the wide-spread incredulity, even among educated readers, concerning native Russian literature, . . . a new and original intellect, saturated with the learning of the West, yet full of the freshness of the Eastern life.[35]

The reviewer ascribed the "new interest" to intensive political discussion.

Dole, on the other hand, was initially less well-received because he translated mainly from French editions; even his general book on Russian literature was mostly a translation of Ernst Dupuy's.[36] Hapgood herself criticized

---

33. Count Leo Tolstoy, *The Cossacks: A Tale of the Caucasus in 1852* (New York: Gottsberger, 1887); Aleksandr Nikoliukin, *Vzaimosviazi literatur Rossii i SShA: Turgenev, Tolstoi, Dostoevskii i Amerike* (Moscow: Nauka, 1987), pp. 166–68. Schuyler continued to review books about Russia and translations of literature in the 1880s, but he was mainly occupied with diplomatic affairs until his death in Venice in July 1890. His friends at *Nation* bitterly castigated the government in Washington, D.C., for "rejecting his nomination as Assistant Secretary to Mr. Blaine, . . . and its grudging him the appointment to Cairo in which, we think we may say, he sacrificed his health and his life." *Nation* 51, 1308 (24 July 1890): 73.

34. Hapgood, *The Epic Songs of Russia* (New York: Scribner's, 1886).

35. "Epic Russia," *Atlantic Monthly* 58, 349 (November 1886): 704.

36. "The Great Russian Masters," *Nation* 43, 1113 (28 October 1886): 354.

his rendering of *Anna Karenina*.[37] Nevertheless, as literary agent for publisher Thomas Crowell, Dole did his share of promoting Russian literature to the popular audience with commentaries and homey translations that expurgated any racy, immoral, or overly philosophical material. Turning to more serious literary criticism, he presented a series of lectures in April 1888 at the Berkeley Lyceum in New York that treated of Gogol, Turgenev, and Tolstoy.[38] His 1889 *War and Peace* was more successful, but to Curtin he showed a becoming modesty: "*Voina i Mir* will be published this week. It makes four large volumes—of about four hundred pages each. Do you know, Mr. Curtin, after I have been guilty of publishing a translation, I feel like hiding my head, like an ostrich, as if I had committed some crime! I feel so ignorant; I am certain that I have *perverted* my author. Oh! I am very humble as a translator."[39]

Curtin's accomplishment, *Myths and Folk-Tales of the Russians, Western Slavs and Magyars*, first published in 1890, would be the standard work on the subject for many years.[40] Although he translated Gogol's *Taras Bulba* in 1888,[41] it was not until 1896 that he tackled what became the most popular literary work in America written by a Slav, *Quo Vadis* by Henryk Sienkiewicz, who was not a Russian but a Polish resident of Russia.[42] Repeated editions and a lucrative contract for his other works firmly established Curtin's linguistic reputation and provided funds for his real love—cultural anthropology.[43]

37. Letter to the editor, *Nation* 42, 1082 (25 March 1886): 259–60. And William Schuyler (possibly another name used by Eugene) pointed out that a whole chapter, the ethical key to the book, had been omitted from *Anna Karenina*; "Tolstoi and His Translations," *Nation* 48, 1249 (6 June 1889): 468.

38. *Harper's Weekly*, 7 April 1888, p. 243. Dole was an avid promoter of a wide range of "exotic" literature and introduced Americans to Omar Khayyam.

39. 23 September 1889, box 8, Curtin Papers, MCHC. Dole also revealed the publisher's concern about printing these Russian epics: "Mr. Crowell is groaning in spirit at the expense of bringing out this big work. The very name 'Russian novel' is like a red rag to a bull. He puts down his horns and shakes his head and his eyes take on a gory expression. 'Anna Karenina' is the only one of the many that he has published from the Russian that has proved a good investment."

40. For a laudatory "first" review, *Nation* 52, 1337 (15 January 1891): 52.

41. John Alden to Curtin, 28 August 1888, box 7, Curtin Papers, MCHC.

42. Jeremiah Curtin, *Memoirs of Jeremiah Curtin*, ed., Joseph Schafer, Wisconsin Biography Series no. 2 (Madison: State Historical Society of Wisconsin, 1940), pp. 530–31. Curtin's own boast—"No man not of our people is as dear to our people as Sienkiewicz"—was perhaps excessive; to Dr. Berni, n.d. (c), box 7, Curtin Papers, MCHC.

43. Sienkiewicz, of course, benefited, as did Polish national pride in the United States; Sienkiewicz (Warsaw) to Curtin, 27 December 1898, box 7, ibid.

After 1886 and through the 1890s a cascade of reprints, new editions, and fresh translations flowed from American presses. Besides Hapgood, Dole, and Curtin, almost anyone with a working knowledge of Russian or fluency in French could try their hand—Aline Delano, Mary Cruger, Benjamin Tucker, Clara Bell, Laura Kendall, and by 1894 the most prolific of all translators from Russian, the Englishwoman Constance Garnett. Tolstoy was easily the favorite Russian author, but others, new and old, received due attention: Alexander Pushkin, especially *The Captain's Daughter*; Gogol, *The Inspector General* (1892); Vladimir Korolenko's short stories; Dostoevsky, *The Idiot* (1887) and *Poor Folk* (1894); Aleksei Tolstoy, *Prince Serebrianyi* (1892); and Russia's first prominent woman writer, Sofia Kovalevskaia, *Reflections of Childhood*.[44] Harriet Preston observed in 1887 that Americans seemed to be consumed with two passions—German opera and Russian romance. She credited the works of Gogol as path breaking and stated that Turgenev, like Stowe, had on his side "the immense power of exact opportunity."[45]

The Tolstoy Craze

What can account for the sudden and sustained popularity of Russian literature in the United States? One reason has already been covered: the simultaneous political discussion about Russia, generated especially by Kennan.[46] Another is that the leading Russian author, Tolstoy, was involved in that debate; witness his much-publicized reception of George Kennan in 1885, his subsequent interest in Kennan's writings about Siberia, and his effort to obtain uncensored copies of the *Century*.[47] Yet Tolstoy envisioned another di-

44. The list is derived from Nikoliukin, *Vzaimosviazi*, pp. 330–35, and Valentina Abramovna Libman, *Amerikanskaia literatura v Russkikh perevodakh i kritike bibliografiia 1776–1975* (Moscow: Mauka, 1977).

45. Preston, "The Spell of Russian Writers," *Atlantic Monthly* 60, 358 (August 1887): 199, 208.

46. Curtis Guild observed in 1888 that "Russian novelists just now . . . are the fashion in American literary circles, and information about this great nation and its people will on that account be more sought for and more generally disseminated than ever before." *Britons and Muscovites*, p. 138.

47. Kennan, "A Visit to Count Tolstoy," *Century* 34 (June 1887): 252–65. The interview received wide publicity in the United States and even in Russia: "Amerikanets v gostiakh u L. N. Tolstogo," *Nedelia* 28 (12 July 1887): 889–91. Kennan attempted to get Tolstoy's support for his campaign on behalf of the exiles, but Tolstoy abstained from any action that might provoke conflict.

rection for Russia's future, and messianic crusade meshed with the pious spirit of WCTU America.

The Tolstoys basked in this foreign adoration. His wife, Sofia, wrote in her diary in June 1887: "Today we had a number of letters from America, along with Kennan's article in *The Century* about his visit to Yasnaya Polyana and his conversation with Lev Nikolaevich, and also a review of L. N.'s translated works. All very flattering and favorable. How extraordinary and marvellous to find that people in these faraway places have such a genuine understanding and sympathy for his work."[48] Tolstoy's writings struck a chord with Americans also because the author himself had been influenced by American literary giants such as Nathaniel Hawthorne, Ralph Waldo Emerson, and especially Henry Thoreau.[49] American readers were thus, to some extent, rediscovering their own older romantic themes—civil disobedience, nonviolence, and back-to-nature—through a Russian prism. A leading modern authority, Aleksandr Nikoliukin, places particular emphasis on this connection to explain the American susceptibility to Tolstoy.[50]

William Dean Howells led the scramble of American literati onto the Tolstoy bandwagon, beginning in 1886.[51] The following year a friend wrote about Howells, "You know how deep he is in Tolstoi. Tolstoi has really troubled him, because he does not know but he ought to be ploughing and reaping."[52] By that time Tolstoy clubs were springing up at Harvard and around the country, further evidence of the mystifying nature of the author's challenge. Tolstoy reciprocated by reading Howells, as well as Walt Whitman, though he had little use

48. *The Diaries of Sofia Tolstaya*, trans. Cathy Porter (London: Jonathan Cape, 1985), p. 82.

49. After a 1900 visit to the sage of Yasnaya Polyana, Curtin wrote, "Tolstoi takes a profound interest in America; he says that he owes more to the thought of great American writers: Channing, Theodore Parker, Emerson, Garrison, Lowell, Thoreau, and others than to any other source." *Memoirs*, pp. 784–85. Curtin dictated his memoirs late in life to his wife, Alma, who referred for details to her notes, letters, diaries, and own published writings. Although Curtin spoke privately in Russian with Tolstoy for some time, he discussed the content of the conversation with his wife. See Alma Curtin diary, 15 June 1900, box 22b, and her "Visit with Count Tolstoy," Bristol, Vermont, newspaper clipping, n.d., box 8, Curtin Papers, MCHC.

50. Nikoliukin, *Vzaimosviazi*, pp. 134–50.

51. Louis J. Budd, "Twain, Howells, and the Boston Nihilists," *New England Quarterly* 32, 3 (September 1959): 352–53. Budd contends that Howells, unlike Twain, paid no attention to Russia before 1885.

52. Edward E. Hale, Jr., to his wife, 28 May 1887, *Life and Letters of Edward Everett Hale*, 2 vols. (Boston: Little, Brown, 1917), 2:328.

*Leo Tolstoy; photograph by Burton Holmes, 1903. From
Holmes,* Travelogues *(1908)*

for most contemporary American writers.[53] He was much more interested in recent social and economic ideas expressed by such people as Henry George and
Alice Bunker Stockham.[54] A number of prominent "ordinary" Americans
were apparently fascinated by Tolstoy as well. Dakota rancher and future president Theodore Roosevelt read *Anna Karenina* while chasing cattle rustlers
down a river in 1886. He wrote to his sister: "I took 'Anna Karenine [sic]' along
on the thief catching trip and read it through with much more interest than I
have any other novel for I do not know how long. Tolstoi is a great writer. . . .
Anna had a character so contradictory, unbalanced, melancholy and fiercely

53. In particular, he remarked on *The Rise of Silas Lapham* and *The Undisovered
Country*; R. F. Christian, ed., *Tolstoy's Letters* (New York: Charles Scribner's Sons, 1978),
p. 464.
54. Robert V. Allen, *Russia Looks at America: The View to 1917* (Washington, D.C.:
Library of Congress, 1988), pp. 60–64; Curtin, *Memoirs*, p. 785.

passionate that she can hardly be perceived as being other than partially insane." He went on to read *War and Peace* during the spring roundup.[55]

Similarly, John Fiske, a well-known Harvard philosopher-historian, read *War and Peace* on an 1887 cross-country train ride. "It is one of the most powerful stories I ever read, and on about as gigantic a scale as 'Les Miserables.' Somehow the story fitted the landscape, and both worked upon me at once."[56] In 1888, the Russian agent for Cyrus McCormick, Jr., recommended Kennan's articles to his boss: "It will give you an insight into the dark history of Russia, which will serve as a great contrast to Tolstoi's novels which you have been reading."[57] Nor did one need to read the novels to be influenced by Tolstoy. When asked which of them had impressed him the most, William Jennings Bryan replied, "Oh, I have not read Tolstoy's works; but I have read a great many articles in the magazines and the Sunday newspapers about him."[58] Biographers agree that Tolstoy had a considerable impact on Bryan's developing pacifism, especially after his extended visit to Yasnaya Polyana in December 1903.

The real herald of Tolstoyism in the United States, however, was Isabel Hapgood, the author's guardian angel, promoter, and translator of many of his writings. She tried to interest publishers in *War and Peace* and *Anna Karenina* as early as 1881 but, according to her, was told, "No one in Russia knows how to write except Turgenev, and he is far above the heads of Bostonians."[59] After the breakthrough in 1886, Hapgood soon had her bags packed for Russia. She reached St. Petersburg in the fall of 1887 but apparently did not visit Tolstoy until the following year. She then spent most of two years in Russia writing articles, translating, and occasionally corresponding with, visiting, and advising the Tolstoy family.

55. 12 April 1886, *Letters from Theodore Roosevelt to Anna Roosevelt Cowles, 1870–1918* (New York and London: Charles Scribner's Sons, 1924), pp. 72, 83–84.

56. Fiske (Portland, Oregon) to his wife, 3 June 1887, in John Spencer Clark, ed., *The Life and Letters of John Fiske*, 2 vols. (Boston: Houghton Mifflin, 1917), 2:359. Fiske was somewhat preconditioned to the Russian outlook: he was the stepson of Edwin Stoughton and had received a number of letters from his mother while she was in Russia. He was also a friend and classmate of Jeremiah Curtin's and had begun to learn Russian in 1878. "As soon as I get to reading it easily I think I can work up a good book of Folk-Lore out of a big mine of russian stuff out in the Harvard Library." Fiske to his mother, 15 November 1878, in Ethel F. Fisk, comp., *The Letters of John Fiske* (New York: Macmillan, 1940), p. 375. See also Curtin, *Memoirs*, pp. 52–53, 60–61, 242–44.

57. Freudenreich to McCormick, 2 November 1888, box 112, 2C, McCormick Company Papers, SHSW.

58. As quoted in Paolo E. Coletta, *William Jennings Bryan: Political Evangelist, 1860–1908* (Lincoln: University of Nebraska Press, 1964), p. 318.

59. Hapgood, "Tolstoi's 'Kreutzer Sonata,' " *Nation* 50, 1294 (17 April 1890): 313.

Described by one Russian as a very large woman with a loud, masculine voice who insisted on speaking bad Russian even when the listener was fluent in English,[60] Hapgood had other interests than Tolstoy to pursue. She had already earned plaudits for her translation of Victor Hugo's *Les Miserables*, but now made Russia in general her *cause célebrè*. In attempting to mitigate the damage caused by Kennan, she commented regularly for American journals on Russian cultural, political, and social affairs.[61] Hapgood's relations with Tolstoy cooled, however, over her refusal to translate *The Kreutzer Sonata* in 1890 because "the whole book is a violent and roughly worded attack upon the evils of animal passion."[62] Hapgood manifested a possible limit to the American infatuation with Tolstoy, in that many Americans might not fancy, at least publicly, the sexual emphasis in his writings.

The Tolstoy craze thus abated somewhat in the early 1890s, partly because of the scandal over this one novella and partly because he wrote little else during the period. Viciously exposing his own marriage in the book, Tolstoy preached sexual abstinence in wedlock, a message undermined by his wife's pregnancy. *The Kreutzer Sonata* was, despite local banning and Hapgood's opposition, published in four separate English editions in 1890, no doubt facilitated by Tolstoy's renunciation of his rights, which left the work in the public domain.[63]

The Tolstoy enigma still cast a giant shadow across the United States. Mark Twain probably expressed a common American view at the time when he remarked to an acquaintance who had visited Tolstoy in 1891: "Lucky Dog, you have broken bread with the man who commands, and almost monopolizes, the thought of the world."[64] The Tolstoy family's efforts in famine

60. Ivan Ianzhul, *Vospominaniia I. I. Ianzhula o perezhitom i vidennom v 1864–1909 gg.*, 2 vols. (St. Petersburg: Stoikovyi, 1910–1911), 2:15. Secretary of Legation Wurts also found Miss Hapgood rather tiring and referred to her as "our spinster compatriot." To Lambert Tree, 18 February 1889, Tree Papers, Newberry Library.

61. Hapgood, "My Experience with the Russian Censor," *Nation* 51, 1321 (23 October 1890): 318–21; see also her "Passports, Police, and Post Office in Russia," *Atlantic Monthly* 72, 420 (July 1893): 42–49. Many of these essays were collected in *Russian Rambles* (Boston: Houghton Mifflin, 1895), which was dedicated "to Russia and my Russian friends."

62. Hapgood, "Tolstoi's 'Kreutzer Sonata,'" 313–15. In notes on the presentation of a Tolstoy letter to the New York Public Library, dated July 1911, Hapgood reflected that "a black cat ran between us." Hapgood Papers, box 4, NYPL.

63. This could not have endeared him to fellow writers. For the atmosphere around the Tolstoy family's most troubled times, see Louise Smoluchowski, *Lev and Sonya: The Story of the Tolstoy Marriage* (New York: Paragon, 1987).

64. Henry W. Fischer, *Abroad with Mark Twain and Eugene Field: Tales They Told to a Fellow Correspondent* (New York: Nicholas Brown, 1922), p. xix.

relief in 1891–1893 again boosted his reputation among Americans, and American humanitarian aid in turn warmed the feelings of Tolstoy toward the United States.

Despite his moody depressions, Tolstoy seemed to be always available to visiting Americans, interrupting a visit to an estate of a friend north of Moscow in 1889 to entertain a group of American clergymen.[65] He even sought out Americans, much to the surprise of educator-diplomat Andrew White. They spent most of two days together in Moscow, after which White concluded to a friend, "Tolstoi is certainly one of the most amazingly original men I have ever met. He suggests new lines of thought; but that he is a safe guide is by no means so certain."[66] The fascination with Tolstoy also worked the other way, helping visiting Russians break the ice in America. Ivan Ianzhul, a friend of Tolstoy's who visited the United States, reported that a letter of introduction from him opened all doors in 1893 and that he was the main topic of conversation with the Americans he met.[67]

The sage of Yasnaya Polyana put on such a show for Jane Addams in 1896 that "a horde of perplexing questions, concerning those problems of existence of which in happier moments we catch but fleeting glimpses and at which we even then stand aghast, pursued us relentlessly on the long journey through the great wheat plains of South Russia." Addams was so impressed by Tolstoy's lunch of only black bread, kasha, and kvas and by his comment that there was enough material in the sleeve of her dress to clothe a small girl that she read everything of his available in English, French, or German translation. Although she vowed "upon return to Hull-House . . . to spend two hours every morning in the little bakery," this schedule lasted only a short time.[68]

65. Newton, *A Run Through Russia*, pp. 154–65. A partial list, since known visitors were often accompanied by others, is as follows: 1868—Schuyler; 1885—Kennan; 1888—Hapgood; 1889—Hapgood, William Wilberforce Newton, Alice Bunker Stockham; 1891—Hapgood, James Creelman; 1892—Charles Emory Smith, Rudolf Blankenburg, Henry Fischer, Charles Reeve, Julian Hubbell; 1893—John Bellows; 1894—Andrew Dickson White, Rabbi Joseph Krauskopf; 1895—Hapgood; 1896 Jane Addams; 1898—Rosalie Norton; 1900—Alma and Jeremiah Curtin, William Rainey Harper, Charles Crane; 1901—Albert Beveridge, Burton Holmes; 1902—Edward Steiner; 1903—William Jennings Bryan, Creelman; 1906—Kellogg Durland; 1907—Samuel June Barrows.

66. To Holls, 30 March 1894, White letters, Holls Papers, Columbia University. Another American simply considered Tolstoy "a great national treasure." James Creelman, "A Visit to Tolstoi," *Harper's Weekly*, 16 April 1892, p. 380.

67. Ianzhul, *Vospominaniia* 2:16.

68. Jane Addams, *Twenty Years at Hull House with Autobiographical Notes* (New York: Macmillan, 1914), pp. 274, 275–76. Addams's visit with Tolstoy naturally received wide notice at home—for example, *Frank Leslie's Illustrated Newspaper*, 22 October 1896, p. 263.

For mental, family, and other reasons, Tolstoy never accepted any of the many invitations to visit the United States. To William Wilberforce Newton he said that he was afraid that his hosts "might overpower him with kindness."[69] Americans were still able to track him down after the turn of the century, even though in old age he became increasingly reclusive. To Senator Albert Beveridge's 1901 inquiry, Tolstoy responded, "I am not at home to all the world; above all I am not at home for interviews; but an American can always find me."[70] Although Tolstoy lived to become a legend in his own time, the person who replaced Hapgood in carrying the American torch at the beginning of a new century—thus assuring the sage of continuing American visibility—was Edward Steiner. This disciple not only made three separate trips to see Tolstoy but also sought additional insights from Tolstoy's friends; Steiner wrote one of the best contemporary analyses of the man and his works.[71]

Tolstoy was also instrumental in gaining permission and sponsoring the emigration in 1898–1899 of a persecuted Old Believer sect, the Dukhobors—though their search for cheap and more isolated living space took most of them to western Canada rather than the United States. Tolstoy was assisted by Pobedonostsev, whom he detested, and on the American end by Peter Demens (Tverskoi), who tried to entice the Dukhobors to move to California after they encountered hardships in Canada.[72] The same situation would befall the migrating Molokans sect of south Russia in 1903, though more of them did find homes in California or Hawaii through Demens.[73]

In contrast to Russian literature on the American scene and to earlier periods in Russia, relatively little contemporary American writing surfaced in Russian translation. Leading the list were Howells, Bret Harte, Edward Bellamy (especially *Looking Backward*), Mark Twain, and George Washington Cable.[74] But none of these authors approached the stature of Tolstoy in the United States.

---

69. As quoted in Newton, *A Run Through Russia*, p. 170.

70. Burton Holmes, *Travelogues*, vol. 8 (New York: McClure, 1910), p. 184. Holmes accompanied Beveridge and brought a large, sixty-millimeter movie camera to take some footage of Tolstoy (now apparently lost); see Irving Wallace's introduction to *The Man Who Photographed the World: Burton Holmes Travelogues, 1886–1913*, ed. Genoa Caldwell (New York: Harry N. Abrams, 1977), p. 18.

71. See Edward A. Steiner, *Tolstoy the Man* (New York: Outlook, 1904).

72. Demens to Ernest Crosley, 10 February 1900, box 3, Demens Papers, LC. The papers include several letters to Tolstoy on the Dukhobors.

73. Demens to J. B. Custler, 16 April 1906, box 2, ibid.

74. For Russian literary criticism for this period, see Valentina Abramovna Libman, comp., *Russian Studies of American Literature: A Bibliography*, trans. Robert V. Allen (Chapel Hill: University of North Carolina Press, 1969).

When asked if he had a message for the American people in 1900, Tolstoy emphasized his appreciation for William Lloyd Garrison, Theodore Parker, Ralph Waldo Emerson, Henry David Thoreau, William Ellery Channing, John Greenleaf Whittier, and Walt Whitman.[75] Current American literature simply did not offer much to Russians, and all Western literature was officially discouraged to some extent because it was considered a threat to Russia's autocratic and theocratic institutions and Pan-Slavic mission. The architect of that policy, Pobedonostsev, was himself an avid reader of American "classics" and frequently quoted Emerson to impress visitors and in his correspondence.[76]

Russia in American Literature

One of the remarkable trends, perhaps inspired by the close attention given to Russia in the United States, was the appearance of Russian settings and characters in popular American fiction. Two experienced reporters of the Russian scene, Thomas Knox and David Ker, were among the first to produce colorful and descriptive books aimed at young people.[77] Another writer, Mary Van Rensselaer Cruger of New York aristocracy, using the nom de plume of Julienne Gordon, imagined an elderly diplomat's romantic winter escapades in St. Petersburg and drew from a personal visit to enliven the story with details. A Russian character provides an opportunity for an unflattering portrait of Americans in general: "I am told these Americans are very respectable, correct, and well-bred people. I take little interest, however, in the nation they represent; their traditions are *nil*, and their institutions

75. Tolstoy to Edward Garnett, 21 June 1900, in Aleksandr Nikoliukin, ed., *A Russian Discovery of America* (Moscow: Progress Publishers, 1986), p. 431.

76. Robert F. Byrnes, *Pobedonostsev: His Life and Thought* (Bloomington and London: Indiana University Press, 1986), p. 346. Andrew White cultivated Pobedonostsev and reported that he especially liked American literature and that Emerson had more influence on him than any other writer. To Holls, 9 January 1893, Holls Papers, Columbia University. See also Andrew Dickson White, "A Statesman of Russia: Constantine Pobedonostzeff," *Century* 56 (1898), pp. 114–16.

77. Ker, *From the Hudson to the Neva* (Boston: D. Lothrop, 1883), and *Cossack and Czar* (New York: Tait, 1893), a fictionalized account of the struggle between Peter the Great and Mazeppa; Knox, *The Boy Travellers in the Russian Empire* (New York: Harper and Bros., 1886), and *The Siberian Exiles* (New York: R. Bonner's Sons, 1893). Ker was British, but after a contract dispute with the London *Daily Telegraph* over the publication of his reports from Central Asia in 1874, he moved to the United States; Ker, *On the Road to Khiva* (London: Henry S. King, 1874), p. viii.

intensely antipathetic to me. . . . However, I will go to their legation for fifteen minutes tomorrow. Civility costs little."[78] In their even more direct effort to explain Russia to Americans in fictional guise, Barbara MacGahan and Lydia Pimenov Noble had the advantage of being Russians writing in English.[79]

More prolific and influential in serving the American market with adventure stories set in Russia was the popular writer Richard Henry Savage. His plots included intriguing settings, mystery, travel, and romantic Russian-American liaisons.[80] Savage's works circulated widely and at least did offer readers fairly accurate lessons in geography, culture, and society. Some reviewers, however, were disdainful of such authors who wrote knowingly about Russia but had never been there: "The popularity of everything Russian has called into existence a mass of worthless books which profess to enlighten and amuse the public."[81]

Art

The visual arts paralleled literature, but on a much smaller scale. Again, the flow was mainly from Russia to the United States and was dominated by one person, Vasily Vereshchagin. Truly the Tolstoy of Russian painting, his works ranged from pastoral to grandiose, from battlefield to church, from exotic to spiritual. His realistic depictions of the Russo-Turkish War broke on Russia and Europe like a storm and spread in various copies and sketch versions across the pages of American journals and books. The first major exhi-

78. Cruger, *Diplomat's Diary* (Philadelphia: Lippincott's, 1890), p. 38. Cruger, also a translator of Russian literature, visited Russia during the winter of 1887–1888 and was received by the imperial family; Lothrop to Giers, 7/19 January 1888, DPR, Russia, vol. 4537 (notes sent), RG 84, NA.

79. MacGahan, *Xenia Repnina: A Story of Russia To-day* (New York and London: George Routledge and Sons, 1890), and Noble, *Before the Dawn: A Story of Russian Life* (Boston: Houghton Mifflin, 1901).

80. Savage, *My Official Wife: A Novel* (New York: Home Publishing, 1891); *The Masked Venus: A Story of Many Lands* (New York: American News, 1893); *Lost Countess Falka: A Story of the Orient* (Chicago: Rand, McNally, 1896). According to a biographer, Remington read *My Official Wife* in preparation for his ill-fated Russia tour; Samuels and Samuels, *Remington*, p. 173.

81. *Nation* 54, 1433 (15 December 1892): 461. Savage may have visited Russia, for a "Mr. Savage" is mentioned by ambassador Hitchcock as a bothersome American tourist; to brother Henry, 9 July 1898, box 22, Hitchcock Papers, RG 316, NA.

bition of his work in the United States was held in November 1888.[82] Sponsored by the American Art Association in New York, it caused a public furor. Not only was the response similar to the reception of Tolstoy's writing, it was interwoven with it. "There is this peculiarity about Verestchagin's work, that it continually proposes a problem to the spectator, and a problem which sternly demands an answer and brooks no evasion, no graceful shirking, no temporizing, no trifling with world-questions."[83]

In March 1891 Vereshchagin came to the United States and settled in a studio in Washington for a few weeks, but he was apparently out of his element. Although befriended by Jeremiah Curtin, he was ill, temperamental, and unhappy, and he soon departed.[84] Curtin continued to pursue American sales of his paintings, and the artist even returned in 1901 to attend a special exhibition at the Chicago Art Institute that featured his recent work in the Philippines. Regardless, Vereshchagin failed to achieve lasting popularity in the United States, probably because of the overwhelming ascendancy of the French impressionists.[85] The same is true of other prominent Russian artists, such as Konstantin Makovskii, who visited the United States in 1893 (and managed to sell one portrait for $3,000), and Ivan Aizovskii.[86] The dedicated promoters of these artists, and of the up-and-coming "quiet and gentle genius," Ilia Repin,[87] were Curtin, Hapgood, Halsey Ives of Washington University, and Theodore Child. The latter visited

82. "The Verestchagin Exhibition," *Nation* 47, 1221 (22 November 1888): 423. Familiarity with the artist was facilitated by Hapgood's translation of a book by his brother that included family history; Alexander Verestchagin, *At Home and in War, 1853–1881* (New York: Thomas Y. Crowell, 1888).

83. "The Verestchagin Exhibition at the American Art Galleries," *Critic* 10 (17 November 1888): 246. The review stressed the Russianness of the works displayed: "The word *narodnost* (nationality) seems written in letters of gold upon these mysterious, baffling canvases, each of which form one stone in the kaleidoscopic mosaic of the exhibition." On the same occasion, Valerian Griboedov, a Russian resident in the United States, noted, "Like Russia's foremost novelist, Verestchagin has set our people thinking." "A Russian Apostle of Art," *Cosmopolitan* 6, 4 (February 1889): 311–26.

84. Curtin, *Memoirs*, pp. 445–46; Vereshchagin (Washington) to Curtin, March 1891, box 7, Curtin Papers, MCHC.

85. Curtin, *Memoirs*, pp. 857–59, citing especially Vereshchagin's personality disorders. The artist earned some final respect from Americans when in 1904 he went down with a battleship at Port Arthur, while trying to depict the horrors of another war.

86. A. S. Suvorin, *Dnevnik A. S. Suvorina*, ed. Mikhail Krichevskii (Moscow-Petrograd: L. D. Frankel', 1923), p. 49.

87. A number of excellent sketches by Repin, including one of Tolstoy, were featured in two of Hapgood's articles: "A Russian National Artist," *Century* 45, 1 (November 1892): 3–12; and "The Nevsky Prospekt," *Scribner's Magazine* 12, 2 (August 1892): 301–22.

Vasily Vereshchagin, a Russian artist. Harper's Weekly, *17 November 1888, courtesy of the Kansas Collection, University of Kansas Libraries*

Russia especially to study early and modern Russian art and to write about it with some expertise. Among other things, he acquainted the American reader with the riches of the Tretiakov Gallery in Moscow.[88]

Scattered information is available that Russian art may have been better known in the United States than is generally recognized. For example, Henry Sheldon, one of the founders of the Newberry Library in Chicago, revealed that all the pictures in his dining room were Russian, most of which he had picked up during an 1876 tour of the country.[89] Nearly every traveler collected folk art. Hapgood struggled through the difficulties of importing a

88. "The Kremlin and Russian Art" and "Modern Russian Art," in Theodore Child, *The Tsar and His People, or Social Life in Russia* (New York: Harper and Bros., 1891), pp. 289–390.
89. To Lambert Tree, 17 October 1888, Tree Papers, Newberry Library.

number of native peasant costumes in 1893.[90] Icons, of course, were featured in the growing number of Orthodox churches in America.

Music

In another area of cultural exchange the Russian impact on the United States in the 1880s was considerable, and, even more than in other spheres, the field was defined by one man—Peter Tchaikovsky. After Anton Rubenstein's tour of 1872 had primed American audiences for Russian compositions, Tchaikovsky rapidly earned popularity on the concert stage. A prominent New York conductor, Leopold Damrosch, was an early advocate of his music, promoting it through the 1880s and corresponding directly with the composer.[91] Thus, ironically, by 1890 Tchaikovsky was probably more popular in the United States than in Russia. As in the case of Tolstoy in literature, the variety and magnitude of his work—symphonies, opera, ballet, concertos, sonatas, and choral music—and the emphasis on Russian national and religious themes suited the American taste for the exotic, mystical, and romantic. Some major works, such as the Piano Concerto no. 1 and Violin Concerto, were in fact first performed in the United States. It was therefore quite natural that Walter Damrosch, who had succeeded his father as director of the New York Symphony, should suggest that the Russian composer be invited to highlight the opening in 1891 of a grand new music hall that had been financed largely by Andrew Carnegie.

Sailing from Havre, Tchaikovsky arrived in New York on 26 April 1891. Although already homesick and disliking his fourteen-story hotel, he enjoyed all the fuss made over him, the flattery of Damrosch, the quality of the orchestra at rehearsals, and the lavish hospitality of the elite cultural patrons of the city— Carnegie (who reminded Tchaikovsky of the Russian playwright Alexander Ostrovsky), Morris Reno, and Francis Hyde. At the opening concert on 5 May he conducted his Marche Solonnelle after the first intermission to a receptive audience and good reviews.[92] The third concert featured his Suite no. 3, and the fourth, two choral pieces. Despite some grumbling about the unfamiliarity of these works, reviewers warmed to the occasion: "His two a capella choruses, heard for the first time in America, are wonderfully fine compositions, full of deep religious feeling, at times assuming the gorgeous pomp of the Greek ritual,

90. Ianzhul, *Vospominaniia* 2:15.
91. Elkhonon Yoffe, *Tchaikovsky in America: The Composer's Visit in 1891* (New York and Oxford: Oxford University Press, 1986), pp. vii-13.
92. Ibid., pp. 57–86. "Noble music" was the comment of one knowledgeable person: 5 May 1891 entry, *The Diaries of Andrew Dickson White*, ed. Robert Morris Ogden (Ithaca, N.Y.: Cornell University Library, 1959), p. 308.

again the mysticism which shrouds the Eastern church and anon the simplicity of the Russian peasant's childlike faith."[93] The final, matinee performance of the Piano Concerto no. 1, featuring the brilliant young Adele Aus der Ohe, satisfied everyone. One commentator provided a fitting encomium: "Let us salute Peter Ilyich Tchaikovsky. He does not compose like Bach, Beethoven, nor yet Wagner, but he has given us new thoughts, a broader vision, a new gleam of beauty from that wonderful ocean called music."[94]

Tchaikovsky now had time for a quick trip to Niagara Falls, weekends at "dachas" along the Hudson, and a visit to Washington. There he was comfortably hosted by the Russian legation and minister Struve and pleasantly surprised to discover that the secretary was an accomplished pianist.[95] He concluded his tour by conducting the piano concerto in Baltimore and Philadelphia and was serenaded by cavalcades of music at the Composer's Club and in the Metropolitan Opera House in New York. Tchaikovsky embarked for Europe on 20 May with much fanfare and was plied with invitations to return. Although at the time another tour seemed likely, his dislike of travel and public appearances and then his premature death in 1893 prevented it.[96]

Russian music drew more and more attention in the United States and was included on many concert programs. Part of this was because of the American taste for the new and different combined with simple curiosity. For example, prominent Republican banker Frederick Holls obtained sheet music of Russian masses and choral work, especially that of Dmitri Bortnianskii, which he and his wife played on their organ and piano. "It is exactly the music which I wanted and the existence of which I was not absolutely certain."[97]

Famine Relief

Eighteen ninety-one was a bad year for Russians, especially for the great majority who lived in the villages. Problems with the food supply in Russia had been worsening in the last two decades of the nineteenth century; from 1879

93. From *Morning Journal*, 9 May 1891, in Yoffe, *Tchaikovsky*, p. 101.
94. *Musical Courier*, 20 May 1891, in ibid., p. 149.
95. Ibid., pp. 131–52.
96. The composer was also disappointed that his American trip had netted him only 1,000 rubles; ibid., p. 163. Upon Tchaikovsky's death, Carnegie had a commemorative statue placed in the music hall in New York and offered a duplicate to the Moscow Conservatory of Music; Breckinridge to Shishkin, 2 May 1895, DPR, Russia, vol. 4538 (notes sent), RG 84, NA.
97. To White, 17 April 1893, roll 60, White Papers, Cornell University.

to 1889, six years saw poor harvests.[98] The primary cause was drought, but this was apparently exacerbated by colder and shorter summers, insect infestations, soil exhaustion, and population growth. Moreover, the development of railroads, improved tax collection, and the export emphasis of large estates moved grain out of the countryside with greater efficiency, leaving less behind in reserve. Thanks to the introduction of some modern machinery and government pressure, more marginal land had been converted to cash crops and additional areas of the eastern steppe had been brought under cultivation, so that exports had tripled since the 1860s to serve the markets of urbanizing Western Europe. Between the 1870s and the 1890s, the basic food crops of rye (black bread) and buckwheat (kasha) declined, while the primary export grains—wheat, barley, and oats—increased.[99]

One of the worst crop failures occurred in 1891 in provinces fanning from Odessa on the Black Sea northeast through the Volga region. The magnitude of the disaster was slow to be realized both inside and outside Russia because of the reluctance of local officials to report it and of the central government to acknowledge it for market and budgetary reasons. Grains, especially wheat, continued to be shipped out of the country as usual.[100]

Anyone who had been reading American dispatches from Russia should have been prepared for impending catastrophe. Although the consular service was often in disarray, its best and most thorough reports concerned agriculture, for the obvious reason that the United States was especially interested in its chief rival in a key export market. Already in 1883 Consul General Stanton had advised that "Russia had not been able to hold its own against American competition," pointing out the weakness in transportation, poor quality of product, and insufficient care in handling.[101] Some actions were taken to improve the situation, but mainly on the larger estates, not on the village lands. Heenan reported from Odessa in 1890:

The majority of the peasantry farm in a primitive and slovenly manner, the result is that the large proprietors who farm in the modern im-

98. This information is collected from American consular reports.

99. John Crawford, "Russia," 7 January 1894, CR 44, 162 (1894), p. 557. For a detailed study by region, see Aleksandr S. Nifontov, *Zernovoe proizvodstvo Rossii vo vtoroi Polovine XIX veka: Po materialam ezhegodnoi statistiki urozhaev Evropeiskoi Rossii* (Moscow: Nauka, 1974).

100. The figures for 1891 and 1892 for Russian wheat exports were 176,097,000 (above average) and 81,446,000 poods, respectively; CR 44, 162 (1894): 560.

101. To Hunter, 12 December 1883, DUSC, St. Petersburg, vol. 17 (roll 12, M 81), RG 59, NA.

proved manner realize in many instances twice the yield from their lands, than does the neighboring peasant. The large proprietors take better care of their grain and keep their land cleaner than does the peasant. They are also able to make a better bargain for their grain than does their less intelligent neighbor.[102]

He added ominously that there had been a considerable reserve of grain in the country but that it was now exhausted. This situation had evolved as a consequence of the long-drawn-out serf-peasant emancipation, which had legally separated the peasant population from the noble landlord class. No longer were the provincial nobility very concerned about the livelihood of "their" peasants, who had now become the wards of the government.

Although indications of a significant crop failure were obvious in the summer, details were not publicly disclosed until October.[103] More information circulated in Europe through private channels, especially from British-born St. Petersburg grain dealer John C. Blessig who had connections in Saratov, but the extent and degree of the disaster were still not apparent. Tragically, rumors that grain exports would be halted caused a massive scramble in ports such as Odessa to ship as much as possible.[104] The order belatedly came at the end of November.[105] One reason for the slow reaction was that Alexander III and his ailing chancellor, Giers, were preoccupied with foreign affairs—a momentous shift to a French alliance—and were away from the court and ministerial communications much of the summer and fall. By December the Odessa consul reported that the government was making large purchases of grain for the army because of heightened tension with Germany and Austria-Hungary,[106] which certainly did not help matters.

The first graphic details of suffering, particularly on the Volga and in Tambov province, reached the West through the missionary activities of the Congregational Anglo-American church in St. Petersburg and the closely linked English Society of Friends, which sounded the alarm across the Atlantic.

102. Heenan (Odessa) to Wharton, 26 March 1890, DUSC, Odessa, vol. 10 (roll 5, M 459), RG 59, NA.
103. Smith to Blaine, 22 October 1891, DUSM, Russia, vol. 42 (roll 42, M 35), RG 59, NA.
104. Heenan (Odessa) to Wharton, 21 November 1891, DUSC, Odessa, vol. 10 (roll 5, M 459), RG 59, NA.
105. Smith to Wharton, 28 November 1891, DUSM, Russia, vol. 42 (roll 42, M 35), RG 59, NA.
106. Heenan to Blaine, 24 December 1891, DUSC, Odessa, vol. 10 (roll 5, M 459), RG 59, NA.

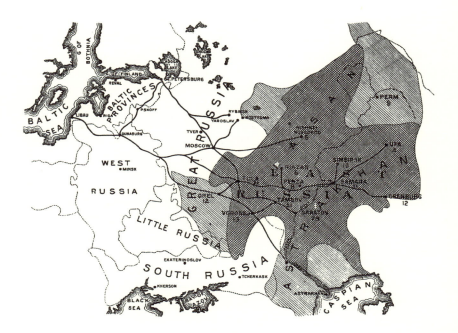

*The Russian famine area, with severity of famine indicated by intensity of shading.
From William Edgar,* The Russian Famine *(1892)*

Those who should receive credit for initiating relief programs include Alexander Francis of the St. Petersburg church, who by December had visited the Volga Tambov regions twice; James Bezant, a British resident of Samara; William Barnes Stevens of the Society of Friends; John Blessig; and Leo Tolstoy. The latter was naturally interested in the peasants for humanitarian reasons and could rally support from both inside and outside of the country.[107]

The magnanimous American offering of large quantities of food and money came as something of a surprise and still lacks full explanation, especially considering the highly negative views of Russia that had been, and still were, circulating in the country. That in itself suggests one answer: many Americans were condi-

107. Hapgood later claimed that she had given Tolstoy the idea of leading a relief organization and had helped him set it up. Yet she had traveled extensively in the Volga region during the summer of 1891 and had reported no problems. Notes of July 1911, box 4, Hapgood Papers, NYPL; "A Journey on the Volga," *Atlantic* 69, 412 (February 1892): 231–40; and "Harvest-Tide on the Volga," *Atlantic* 69, 413 (March 1892): 314–27.

tioned to think of helpless, downtrodden Russians, whether in Siberian mines, as Jewish refugees, or in general. Others were alienated by all the recent anti-Russian publicity and eager to hark back to days of friendship and harmony. While American missionary spirit and church leadership were influential, also important was the growth of humanitarian organizations such as the Red Cross and the surfeit of philanthropic new wealth. Another motivating factor was certainly business expedience, since there was a huge grain surplus that year. And politics had a role, as famine relief coincided with renewed Anglophobia, mainly over the sealing dispute.

American and Russian officials were obviously crucial actors in the unfolding crisis. Charles Emory Smith, the minister in St. Petersburg, was at first reluctant to respond to the situation because of the resistance of the Russian government to outside aid, suspicion that the conditions in distant provinces might be exaggerated, and that large stocks of grain still in Russian ports could be sent back to the countryside.[108] By early December, however, after conversations with Alexander Francis, Smith began a campaign to solicit American contributions.[109] As the publisher/editor of a Philadelphia newspaper, Smith was in an excellent position to alert the public. To his friend and editor of the New York *Times* he emphasized the "extreme gravity of the situation."[110] And he added a personal note to a long report on the famine, advising that it be released to the Associated Press.[111] He then postponed a planned leave of absence and, along with his experienced secretary, George Wurts, an able Consul General, John Crawford, and a willing vice-consul in Riga, Niels Bornholdt, devoted much time and energy to the reception and distribution of donated American food and money. This was not easily done, as Smith noted privately to a friend, "without wounding the sensibilities of the Government and with its approval and cooperation."[112]

On the Washington end, Blaine and his State Department staff assisted the aid effort. In late December, he informed Smith, "It gives me pleasure to

108. Smith to Wharton, 22 October and 28 November 1891, DUSM, Russia, vol. 42 (roll 42, M 35), RG 59, NA. For this section, the author is indebted to the work of Carlyse Marshall, "Famine in Russia and American Charity, 1891–1893," Master's thesis, University of Kansas, 1994.

109. Smith, "The Famine in Russia," New York *Tribune*, 24 December 1891, p. 2.

110. To Charles S. Smith, 29 December 1891, DPR, Russia, vol. 4572 (letters sent), RG 84, NA.

111. To Blaine, 11 January 1892, DUSM, Russia, vol. 42 (roll 42, M 35), RG 59, NA. This request seems to have been readily granted, since newspapers began citing Smith's famine reports—for example, "About the Russian Famine," New York *Tribune*, 2 February 1892, p. 3.

112. To Elijah Halford, 26 March 1892, misc. letters, box 1, Halford Papers, LC.

state that generous efforts have been initiated in the grain producing centres of the West aided by the Red Cross Association of the United States, for co-operation in this humane work."[113] And later, in a more formal statement meant for public consumption, Blaine observed,

> The American people, always quick to answer such an appeal, do so on this occasion . . . with an appreciative sense of the opportunity afforded them not only to share their plenty with their less fortunate fellow-men in Russia, but at the same time to evince once more their good-will toward the people of a nation whose relations with the United States have been marked for so many years with so many mutual proofs of friendly regard.[114]

The press covered the famine with as much detail as they could muster and using pictures with long descriptive captions.[115]

At first the Russian government was unwilling to acknowledge the scope of the problem and to accept aid from outside, especially when the initial offers came from British agencies. A cruel caricature of the tsar denying the existence of the famine whetted this sensitivity.[116] But secondary complications also hindered early relief efforts; fifty barges loaded with grain were stranded because of the extraordinary low water levels of the Volga, and severe bottlenecks occurred in rail shipments. In any event, the first formal offer of substantial American assistance, received by the Russian legation in Washington by mid-November, was forwarded promptly to St. Petersburg, and a cabled acceptance returned on 4 December—a fast turnaround for bureaucratic Russian officialdom.[117]

In the interval, a Special Committee for famine relief, headed by heir to

113. Blaine to Smith, 23 December 1891, DI, Russia, vol. 17 (roll 139, M 77), RG 59, NA.

114. To Smith, 30 January 1892, ibid.

115. See especially *Leslie's Illustrated* for the first half of 1892.

116. An official in the Foreign Ministry could not understand why a copy was sent so that it would necessarily be preserved in its archive. Vladimir Lamzdorf, *Dnevnik, 1891–1892*, ed. F. A. Rotshtein (Moscow-Leningrad: Academia, 1934), 9 January 1892, p. 229.

117. Greger to Shishkin, 13/25 November 1891, and Shishkin to Struve, 22 November/4 December 1891, f. 133, op. 470, d. 100, AVPR; Harold F. Smith, "Bread for the Russians: William C. Edgar and the Relief Campaign of 1892," *Minnesota History* 42, 2 (Summer 1970): 54–55. Several of the communications pertaining to famine relief have been published in " 'Eto vopros ne politiki, eto vopros gumannosti': Dokumenty o pomoshchi amerikanskogo naroda vo vremia goloda v Rossii 1891–1892 gg.," ed. V. I. Zhuralev, *Istoricheskii Arkhiv: Nauchno-Publikatorskii Zhurnal* 1 (1993), pp. 194–209.

the throne Grand Duke Nicholas, met for the first time at the end of November. Influential in getting the Russian government on the relief track were one of its members, Minister of Court Illarion Vorontsov-Dashkov, who happened to own an estate in hard-hit Tambov province, and a prominent Americanophile, Andrei A. Bobrinskoi.[118] They took charge of coordinating American relief on the Russian end. A large amount of money, though certainly far from enough, was made available through the Ministry of Interior as loans to hard-pressed local governments to buy grain and for the development of public works projects in the most affected provinces.[119]

The first organized American response came not from the commercially prominent East Coast cities but from far-off Minnesota, where William C. Edgar, the editor of the *Northwestern Miller*, accepted the challenge. Apparently aroused to action by reports from European agents, Edgar mobilized the local milling industry, the largest and most prosperous in the United States. After receiving the go-ahead on 4 December in a telegram from Aleksandr Greger, secretary of the Russian legation, Edgar forged a crucial alliance with Governor William R. Merriam, a popular and powerful Republican politician, and launched a drive that cited Russian assistance to the United States during the Civil War and called on the traditional Christmas spirit. Edgar sent 5,000 circulars to wheat flour millers throughout the country, and Merriam issued a proclamation, "An Appeal to the People of Minnesota!"[120]

118. Bobrinskoi (modern variant, Bobrinskii) was a great-grandson of Catherine the Great. He is usually referred to as A. A. Bobrinskoi in contemporary sources, creating confusion in identification, since his brother Aleksei, head of the Imperial Archaeological Commission, was more famous. Their father, Aleksandr A. Bobrinskoi, had been a strong proponent of railroad construction and progress in the reign of Nicholas I, and the family had large estates in famine areas. Although the whole Bobrinskoi family was involved in relief efforts, Andrei was a member of the special Russian commission, and his knowledge of English made him a valuable liaison with the American relief groups. William C. Edgar, *The Russian Famine of 1891 and 1892* (Minneapolis: Millers and Manufacturers Insurance, 1893), p. 24 and pictures; Andrei Bobrinskoi to Edgar, 3/15 January 1893, box 7, Edgar Papers, MinnHS. Bobrinskoi accurately summarized American relief for the Russian public: "Amerikanskaia pomoshch' v 1892 i 1893 godakh," *Russkii Vestnik* 39, 2 (February 1894): 252–64.

119. For more details on the Russian government efforts, see Richard G. Robbins, Jr., *Famine in Russia, 1891–1892: The Imperial Government Responds to a Crisis* (New York and London: Columbia University Press, 1975).

120. Edgar, *Russian Famine*, p. 6; Merriam (St. Paul) to Horace Boies (Des Moines), 26 December 1891, vol. 1, correspondence of Iowa State Famine Relief Committee, ISHS. Edgar was personally well-known to many leading millers because of his editorial position and because he had served as secretary and organizer of an industry-sponsored tour of the British Isles the previous summer. For more on the American relief campaign, see Marshall, "Famine in Russia and American Charity."

By 25 December they had secured pledges for one million pounds of flour, mainly from large millers such as Pillsbury and from Charles Reeve of the Holly Flour Mill in St. Paul. Merriam's pressure on the railroads assured free transportation to an eastern port.[121] This was still far from the target of six million pounds needed to fill a ship. With a preliminary deadline of 20 January for the dispatch of trains to New York, Edgar reached out to other states, especially Iowa.[122] That state, however, was organizing its own relief effort focused on corn, while Edgar insisted on sending wheat flour: "What the United States should send to Russia is neither money or corn. It is flour and flour only. A good wholesome low grade flour is exactly suited to the Russian peasant's needs, and this is what should be sent him."[123]

Nebraska proved to be more cooperative and willing to join the Minnesota effort but, like Iowa, had a greater surplus of corn to offer. Edgar finally accepted several carloads and had it ground into meal in Akron, Ohio, on the way to the port. Gathering grain and flour from greater distances and managing small shipments on a large number of railroads naturally took time, and only in early March did the cars clear the terminals for the East. Arranging for a ship was also not easy. At first it was hoped that Congress or the Russian legation would provide this transportation, and the latter did make a commitment of last resort.[124] Fortunately, a large American shipping company, the Atlantic Transport line, donated the use of the *Missouri*.

It now turned out that the midwestern flour and corn meal ready for loading in New York in March still did not fill the ship. Money collected in New York City and a fee for carrying a consignment of cattle to Britain were then used to buy more flour locally. The total cargo for Russia thus reached 5,250,000 pounds of flour and 250,000 of corn meal, valued by Edgar at $125,000.[125] Edgar, Reeve, and prominent Minneapolis merchant Edmund Phelps boarded a passenger ship to be on hand when the *Missouri* docked on

121. Edgar, *Russian Famine*, p. 6; Smith, "Bread for the Russians," 54–57. The railroads would recoup their losses by transporting people to the Republican convention in Minneapolis that summer.

122. Edgar to Boies, 24 December 1891, and to Benjamin Tillinghast, 2 January 1892, vol. 1, Iowa State Famine Relief Committee, ISHS.

123. *Northwestern Miller* 33, 9 (26 February 1892).

124. Greger to Blaine, 11 December 1892 (c), vol. 1, Iowa State Famine Relief Committee, ISHS.

125. Edgar, *Russian Famine*, pp. 12–16. Edgar argued, however, that this was based on the millers' cost and that transportation, wholesale and retail markups, and famine inflation brought the value of this one shipment up to $600,000 at delivery in the Russian provinces. The Russian consul in New York priced the cargo more precisely at $138,541; Olarovskii to Struve, 3/15 March 1892, f. 133, op. 512/1, d. 56, AVPR.

The Missouri *at Libau. From William Edgar,* The Russian Famine *(1892)*

8 April at the Russian Baltic port of Libau, the only one open that early in the season.[126]

In the meantime, following an example set in London, a "Russian Famine Relief Committee of the United States" was organized in Washington, D.C., under the chairmanship of John W. Hoyt, former governor of Wyoming Territory and leader since the 1870s of the national university movement.[127] En-

126. Bornholdt, a Danish merchant serving as American consul in Riga, offered to unload the ship at his own expense; Smith to Blaine, DUSM, Russia, vol. 42 (roll 42, M 35), RG 59, NA.

127. Hoyt to Shilling, 18 December 1892, f. 133, op. 512/1, d. 56, AVPR. In recapping to the Russian diplomat his involvement in the relief effort, Hoyt wrote: "My interest in Russia was greatly deepened by my journeys in the Empire a quarter of a century ago and has strengthened with the years. Glad indeed that we have been able to do something for the relief of those of your people who suffered. I only regret that we could not have done more."

The Missouri *leaving New York harbor loaded with Minnesota flour. From William Edgar,* The Russian Famine *(1892)*

listed as honorary members were former president Rutherford Hayes,[128] Vice-president Levi Morton, Chief Justice Frederick Fuller, Cardinal Gibbons of Baltimore, Senator John Sherman, and an assortment of governors and civic and church leaders. In cooperation with Clara Barton and the American Red Cross, it produced circulars, advertised in major newspapers, and promoted the formation of state and city relief committees.

One of the first tasks was to lobby for government funding for transportation of the food relief. Although backed by President Harrison and approved by a solid majority in the Senate, the bill to appropriate $100,000 was defeated in early January by the House. The members cited an absence of precedent and an interpretation of lack of authority. Some saw this opposition as "an open bid for the Jewish vote next year."[129]

In spite of this setback and even before the *Missouri* sailed, Philadelphia rose to the occasion behind the noted reformer and future mayor Rudolph

128. For his part, the former president wrote to a friend on 19 December 1891, "My wish is to do what is sensible and best." Charles Richard Williams, ed., *Diary and Letters of Rutherford Birchard Hayes*, 5 vols. (Columbus: Ohio State Archeological and Historical Society, 1926; reprint, New York: Kraus, 1971), 5:39.

129. "Relief for Russia," Cleveland *Plain Dealer*, 7 January 1892, p. 3, a special report from Washington, D.C. For details of the debate, see Merle Curti, *American Philanthropy Abroad: A History* (New Brunswick, N.J.: Rutgers University Press, 1963), pp. 103–8.

Blankenburg, a Quaker businessman who had contacts with the English Society of Friends. His prominent and wealthy friends included John Wanamaker, Robert Ogden, Francis Reeves, William Grundy, Anthony Drexel, and Edward Biddle. Learning of the Minnesota and Iowa campaigns, they rapidly collected a large sum of money with the obvious goal of beating the *Missouri* to Russia. Recent experience with relief for Johnstown flood victims, as well as the historic Quaker impulse and the fact that Charles Emory Smith hailed from Philadelphia, also contributed to the special role of this city. To further the cause, Blankenburg published a persuasive and shaming pamphlet, "Shall Russian Peasants Die of Starvation?: A Question for Prosperous America."[130]

With cash donations used to purchase flour, the transport *Indiana* was quickly loaded and earned the distinction of being the first relief ship to arrive at a Russian port, on 16 March.[131] It was met with great fanfare at Libau by its own welcoming committee—Blankenburg, Drexel, Biddle, and Grundy, who had gone ahead by a more comfortable ship—American consuls, and an assortment of Russian dignitaries led by Andrei Bobrinskoi. Finally, after time-consuming (and somewhat embarrassing) ceremonies and parties, trains set off for the famine areas bedecked with Russian and American flags and carrying 4,186,830 pounds of foodstuffs. As Smith noted, "There is no doubt that the manner, spirit and substance of the American donations have made a marked impression in Russia."[132] After additional funds were collected, the Philadelphia committee dispatched a second vessel, which reached Riga on 13 May.

A number of American cities without the means or organization to sponsor their own shiploads of food were soon responding to the call for assistance with monetary contributions. In New York Charles S. Smith, chairman of the Chamber of Commerce, organized a relief committee whose treasurer was none other than financier J. Pierpont Morgan.[133] But, according to Isabel Hapgood, the New York drive had no momentum until she formed her own relief group on Tolstoy's behalf and then joined forces with

130. Blankenburg autograph collection, case 19, box 14, Society Misc.—Blankenburg Papers, HSP.

131. Lucretia Blankenburg, *The Blankenburgs of Philadelphia, by One of Them* (Philadelphia: John C. Winston, 1929), pp. 35–36; Smith to Blaine, 23 March 1892, DUSM, Russia, vol. 42 (roll 42, M 35), RG 59, NA; "Russians Express Gratitude," New York *Tribune*, 21 March 1892, p. 1. Blankenburg, a German-born merchant-reformer, was later referred to as "Old Dutch Cleanser."

132. To Blaine, 23 March 1892, DUSM, Russia, vol. 42 (roll 42, M 35), RG 59, NA.

133. "To Aid Starving Russia," New York *Tribune*, 6 February 1892, p. 4.

the Chamber of Commerce.[134] The highlight of the campaign was a benefit concert staged by Julia Butterfield at Carnegie Hall on 12 March that featured a "Who's Who" of American opera singers and the New York Symphony orchestra performing the works of Tchaikovsky and Rubenstein. It added $7,000 to the $40,000 already raised from the city.[135]

Kidder, Peabody served as the collection agency in Boston. Although the Boston relief commission included some illustrious names—Joseph Quincy, William Lloyd Garrison, Oliver Peabody, and Edward Everett Hale—it ran into more opposition than in most other cities.[136] Mistrust of the Russian government and questions about the reliability of information regarding famine conditions were the main obstacles.

Meanwhile, individuals in smaller towns or on farms responded directly to the national committee, the Russian legation, the American legation in St. Petersburg, the consulate in Moscow, the State Department, the Congregational Anglo-American church, or Leo Tolstoy, whose private relief effort was gaining wide recognition. From Charleston, South Carolina, for example, the *News and Courier* forwarded through the State Department over $3,000 in four separate checks, while the Mennonite Relief Fund of Elkhart, Indiana, used a New York agent.[137] By mid-April the American legation in St. Petersburg had received $77,000 from such sources.[138]

In Cleveland, James R. Garfield, a son of the former president, formed a relief committee in February and managed the solicitations; publicity in the

134. Hapgood to Tillinghast, 5 February 1892, vol. 2, correspondence of Iowa State Famine Relief Committee, ISHS.

135. Daniel Butterfield to Smith, 26 February 1892, DPR, Russia, vol. 4446 (misc. received), RG 84, NA; "Singing for Starving Russians," New York *Tribune*, 13 March 1892, p. 6; "For the Russian Sufferers," New York *Times*, 14 March 1892, p. 5. The Butterfields had visited St. Petersburg during the summer of 1890; Smith to Vyshnegradskii, 21 May/2 June 1890 (c), DPR, Russia, vol. 4537 (notes sent), RG 84, NA.

136. Kidder, Peabody to Smith, and Hale to Smith, 29 January 1892, DPR, Russia, vol. 4446 (misc. received), RG 84, NA. Hale noted, "To you personally, I ought to say that the reason why this contribution is so small is that there is a general distrust here of the officials of the Russian government."

137. Wharton to Smith, 17 March, 2 April, and 17 May 1892, DI, Russia, vol. 17 (roll 139, M 77), RG 59, NA; Smith to John Funk, 7 April 1892 (c), DPR, Russia, vol. 4572 (letters sent), RG 84, NA; Funk to Mabel Boardman, 6 April 1903, box 59, American Red Cross Papers, RG 200, NA. The public schools of Florence, South Carolina, sent a check for $11.51; Blaine to Wurts, 31 May 1892, DI, Russia, vol. 17 (roll 139, M 77), RG 59, NA. Hoyt acknowledged twenty-one such contributions on a single day in March; John Hoyt letterbook, box 59, American Red Cross Papers, RG 200, NA.

138. Smith to Blaine, 16 April 1892, DUSM, Russia, vol. 43 (roll 43, M 35), RG 59, NA.

local paper was once more an effective prod to charity.[139] Printed "subscription papers" were sent to businesses, factories, schools, churches, and fire and police stations, and the First National Bank and *Plain Dealer* served as collection points. Patrolmen went house to house on their beats, and in most cases the individuals signed donation forms, preserving a fairly complete list of contributors. For example, the Second Police Post collected $83.05 from around 250 individuals, an average of thirty-three cents apiece.[140] By 15 April, when subscriptions were closed, Cleveland relief totaled $4,962.02, including $300 raised from passing the hat in the state legislature in Columbus.[141]

The only recorded resistance came from the Jewish community. A rabbi wrote a terse note to Garfield that his congregation already had fifty families of the tsar's subjects to care for, but the local agent of Northwestern Mutual Life was more explicit:

> I am not charitable enough to assist, when I think of the great number of my co-religionists who by persecution have been driven away from the home of their birth and the number of poor starving wretches that are in our own midst not through any fault of their own, but because of their religious faith. These people have been quite a tax upon the Jewish community, and I feel that it is a great[er] charity to help here at home than to send this money to a country where there is so much danger that the thieving officers of the Russian Government will prevent these funds . . . of aiding the sufferers.[142]

Another problem facing Garfield and the Cleveland relief committee was where to send the money. Tolstoy was the initial choice, but Hoyt and Greger recommended the Russian Red Cross while Crawford from St. Petersburg advocated the Great Benevolent Society of Russia, of which he was a

139. On 24 January 1892, the Cleveland *Plain Dealer* carried a four-column article on the famine, entitled "Millions Starving," and suggested that donations be sent to Leo Tolstoy at an address in Moscow.

140. A file of returned subscription papers is in box 105, Harry A. Garfield Papers, LC. Harry was the brother and law partner of James R. Garfield. Of a total of 280 subscription forms sent out, 105 were returned with names and money, and 22 came back blank. A number of other donations were received without the forms, for a total of 225 collective donors. "Report of the Russian Relief Committee of Cleveland, Ohio," ibid.

141. Garfield to William T. Clark (Columbus), 29 March 1892, ibid., "The Russian Fund," Cleveland *Plain Dealer*, 15 April 1892, p. 4.

142. Kaufman to Garfield, 3 March 1892, box 104, Garfield Papers, LC.

member.[143] Crawford also asserted, in strictest confidence, that the Russian Red Cross could not be trusted and advised against Tolstoy, because "his ideas on social and domestic life are either unsound, or are a long way in advance of the age." He did concede that "in some respects his ideas of coming to the practical relief of the sufferers are good, and his 'soup kitchens' are meeting with general approval with other relief organizations."[144]

Garfield finally committed to Tolstoy, and the first check for $1,500 was dispatched to the St. Petersburg legation on 24 March, just a month after the Cleveland campaign began.[145] On the signed receipt, dated "Moscow, 2/14 April," Tolstoy added in English, "with heartfelt thanks to the generous contributors."[146] In sending the third and last installment, Garfield wanted Tolstoy to know that $627.07 of the $5,000 "came from the children of the public schools of this city."[147] Surprisingly, the chief midwestern city, Chicago, contributed very little; the explanation given by the Illinois governor was "that the immense work and outlay of *time* and *money* involved in the preparation for the great Columbian Exposition so absorbs the energies of the City."[148]

Money donations, such as Cleveland's, had definite advantages. They could be channeled more quickly and selectively to charities and to afflicted regions and so could provide greater flexibility in dealing with the situation. The Tolstoy fund and Blessig's Russian Famine Relief Fund, for example, furnished medical supplies, other kinds of sustenance, clothing, portable bakeries, transportation, relief workers, seed potatoes, boards for coffins, and, what became crucial in the summer of 1892, the replacement of horses that had perished or been sold. Crawford also recommended money contributions, since they could be more easily sent to the hard-hit Volga Germans and could be used for desperately needed horses, cattle, and seed.[149] In fact,

143. "Aid for Starving Russia," Cleveland *Plain Dealer*, 26 February 1892, p. 4; Hoyt to Garfield, 5 March 1892, and Crawford to Garfield, 26 March 1892 (confidential), box 105, Garfield Papers, LC.

144. Crawford to Garfield, 26 March 1892, box 105, Garfield Papers, LC.

145. Garfield to Smith, 24 March 1892, ibid.

146. Enclosure, Smith to Garfield, 19 April 1892, ibid. Smith observed that Tolstoy thought the printed form was "too cold," so he had delivered the Cleveland check personally.

147. Garfield to Wurts, 14 May 1892 (c), ibid. A delay occurred in the transmittal of this contribution, because Garfield forgot to sign the check! Wurts to Garfield, 28 May 1892, ibid.

148. William Stackpole to Tillinghast, 6 February 1892, vol. 2, Iowa State Famine Relief Committee, ISHS.

149. Crawford to Garfield, 26 March 1892, box 105, Garfield Papers, LC.

Leo Tolstoy, 1892; photographed by Francis Reeve in Moscow. From Reeve, Russia Then and Now *(1917)*

by the time the first relief ship had arrived, the American legation and consulates had distributed $65,000.[150]

Why all aid was not delivered in the form of money was because of fear that food stocks were too low in Russia and would be further depleted by purchases; concern that the availability of such funds would only encourage speculation and cause prices to rise in Europe;[151] a belief that distribution could be better controlled through managed delivery; a desire to obtain maximum publicity while unloading a surplus and stabilizing domestic

150. Smith to Elijah Halford, 26 March 1892, misc. letters, box 1, Halford Papers, LC. On occasion cash contributions were earmarked, as in the case of an American Red Cross transfer of funds specifically to supply nurses to famine areas. Hubbell (Washington, D.C.) to Wurts, 23 August 1892, DPR, Russia, vol. 4447 (misc. received), RG 84, NA.

151. Prices for winter wheat and rye did almost double in 1892; Peter Gatrell, *The Tsarist Economy, 1850–1917* (New York: St. Martin's Press, 1986), pp. 132–33.

prices; and easier collection in grain-producing areas of contributions in kind.

Iowa Corn

Grassroots support was especially pronounced in Iowa, where a campaign was mounted that surpassed Minnesota's. Benjamin Franklin Tillinghast, a Davenport newspaperman and state Red Cross promoter, led the drive to collect corn from farmers. He was apparently inspired by another Davenport resident, authoress Alice French, who learned about the famine from a local Unitarian pastor.[152] The governor cooperated in forming a famine relief commission and in backing this truly "populist" effort. The state was divided into thirteen regions, corresponding to congressional districts, with collection agents designated for each county. Another distinguishing characteristic of the Iowa campaign was the leading role taken by women, especially French, who headed an auxiliary Women's Relief Committee; Dr. Mary Weeks Burnett of Chicago; Isabel Hapgood; and Clara Barton and the American Red Cross, whose field agent, Julian Hubbell, was a prime mover.[153] The involvement of these people and agencies and the problems of canvassing the countryside during a wet and muddy winter caused coordination problems and slowed the Iowa collections.[154] The suitability of corn also raised questions, especially since it was publicly opposed by the Russian consul in New York and the Philadelphia and Minnesota relief groups.[155]

Encouraged by the presence in Russia of noted corn promoter Charles Murphy, by support from a new Russian consul in Chicago, and by authori-

152. "Miss French used to say . . . 'I started Mr. Tillinghast, and he started everybody in Iowa!' " Evelyn Schuyler Schaeffer, "A Ship-Load of Iowa Corn," *New Peterson Magazine* 1, 5 (May 1893): 472. Schaeffer was Eugene Schuyler's sister; she lived in Iowa and participated in the campaign.

153. Ibid., p. 474; Elizabeth Brown Pryor, *Clara Barton: Professional Angel* (Philadelphia: University of Pennsylvania Press, 1987), pp. 267–69; "The Women's Gift to Russia," *Harper's Weekly*, 23 April 1892, p. 402.

154. Ogden (Philadelphia) to Smith, 12 February 1892, DPR, Russia, vol. 4446 (misc. received), RG 84, NA.

155. Ogden to Hoyt, 15 February 1892, box 112 (roll 83), Barton Papers, LC. Besides its unfamiliarity to Russian peasants, arguments against corn included the possibility of meal spoiling in shipment, the absence of grinding facilities in Russia, and the appearance that the United States was using the famine for commercial advertising. Tillinghast, however, thought that opposition was plotted by Edgar and Reeve and that their actions were "selfish and commercial, under the cloak of charity." Tillinghast to Barton, 6 March 1892, ibid.

Clara Barton. Harper's Weekly, *1 February 1896, courtesy of the Kansas Collection, University of Kansas Libraries*

tative assurance that there were small mills able to handle corn near every village, Tillinghast became more confident that hungry Russians would learn to eat it and overcame Clara Barton's misgivings.[156] After an agonizing debate, the Iowans decided against trading corn for flour, because they owed it to the farmers to prove their case. They also elected to send shelled corn instead of meal since it would ship better and to grind it into meal would cause delays.[157] The Iowans consoled themselves that the corn, if rejected as human food, could be fed to animals or perhaps planted as seeds.

As in the Minnesota relief effort, Tillinghast convinced the railroads to ship the corn free to an eastern port, and by the second week of February carloads were leaving the state bearing colorful Red Cross placards.[158] De-

156. Tillinghast to Barton, 28 February 1892; Thal to Tillinghast, 9 March 1892 (c), ibid.
157. French to Barton, 30 December 1891, ibid.
158. Tillinghast to Barton, 14 February 1892, ibid.

layed en route, they began arriving in New York in early March, where Hubbell superintended storage at elevators in Brooklyn. Tillinghast, who wrote as many as a hundred letters a day, had taken up the cause with a vengeance, spurring his county agents and peppering his newspaper friends (especially those in Chicago) with assorted columns, letters, and appeals, thus stirring up donations from Illinois and other midwestern states.

That the collection of corn was ultimately successful and that so many individual Iowa farmers contributed can be attributed to their having been on the receiving end of relief a few years before, to bumper crops in 1891, and to the recent birth and political successes of midwestern populism. As Hubbell and newspaperman Frank Carpenter of the Washington *Evening Star* sailed ahead to Russia, the *Tynehead*, chartered by the Red Cross with $12,000 donated from the Washington area, weighed anchor somewhat embarrassingly under a British flag. Accompanied by the smaller *Borodino*, the ships finally delivered 117,000 bushels of Iowa corn, 731 sacks of flour, 400 sacks of cornmeal, and small amounts of canned goods, bacon, and medical supplies to Riga on 20 June.[159] According to a draft of Hubbell's final report, the Russian carloads of corn were distributed as follows: Samara 103, Saratov 49, Perm 22, Kazan 21, Tambov 19, Riazan 15, Orenburg 9, and Simbirsk 6—that is, most of it to the Volga region. He also claimed from personal observation in the field that the corn was indeed consumed as food by the peasants and that they liked it and wanted more.[160]

The Iowa relief thus created a sideshow to the Russian famine—the distribution of unfamiliar corn instead of wheat flour. By coincidence, Secretary of Agriculture Jeremiah Rusk, a Wisconsin corn farmer, had just launched a campaign to sell corn to Europe and had commissioned Charles Murphy for that purpose. While in Berlin trying to sell cornmeal to the German army, Murphy heard of the Russian famine and sent off samples of white and yellow cornbread to St. Petersburg.[161] He was soon lobbying publicly for the in-

159. Wurts to Wharton, 21 June 1892, DUSM, vol. 43 (roll 43, M 35), RG 59, NA; Schaeffer, "Ship-Load of Iowa Corn," p. 476.

160. Undated draft, box 112 (roll 83), Barton Papers, LC. Slightly different figures are in the published version, also undated, in Clara Barton, *The Red Cross: A History of This Remarkable International Movement in the Interest of Humanity* (Washington, D.C.: American National Red Cross, 1898), pp. 180–94. Hubbell went on to represent the United States at an international conference of the Red Cross in Rome.

161. Murphy (Berlin) to Smith, 21 November 1891, DPR, Russia, vol. 4445 (misc. received); Smith to Murphy (Berlin), 4 December 1891, DPR, Russia, vol. 4572 (letters sent); Murphy (Berlin) to Smith, 29 January 1892, vol. 4446 (misc. received), RG 84, NA.

clusion of corn in famine relief; on the Washington end, Rusk eagerly supported the Iowa corn drive.[162]

With the blessing of the Department of Agriculture, Murphy was soon on his way to St. Petersburg, where he met with Minister of Interior Ivan Durnovo and other Russian officials. He contended that he encountered opposition from the American United Millers Association but was encouraged by the interest of the Russian government.[163] Murphy was soon back in Berlin arranging for the distribution of corn recipes and "corn kitchens" in Russia. Through contacts with Blessig, he took a personal humanitarian interest in obtaining relief for the Volga Germans but also saw an opportunity in the Iowa shipment to advance his own mission: "The Indian corn propaganda will be always coupled with this Russian famine business, which will do more than anything I know of to rivet the attention of the people of Europe to this corn question."[164] In the public debate that ensued over corn versus flour, a Des Moines source claimed that corn could keep a Russian peasant alive for six months for half the cost of flour.[165]

Besides the Iowa corn, the *Leo* docked at St. Petersburg on 14 July with 3 million pounds of flour. The sponsor was Brooklyn evangelist T. De Witt Talmage, whose rapidly growing tabernacle adherents and widely circulated newspaper, the *Christian Herald,* had designated Russia a special mission in 1892.[166] His efforts were chastised by other relief groups as belated and self-promoting.[167] More helpful and duly noted by the Russian press were the donations from Americans resident in Russia.[168]

162. Rusk (Washington) to Tillinghast, 29 December 1891, vol. 1, Iowa State Famine Relief Committee, ISHS.

163. Murphy (Berlin) to Smith, 3 and 14 February 1892, DPR, Russia, vol. 4446 (misc. received); and Durnovo to Smith, 11/23 March 1892, DPR, Russia, vol. 4510 (notes received), RG 84, NA.

164. Murphy to Smith, 4 April 1892, DPR, Russia, vol. 4446 (misc. received), RG 84, NA. Isabel Hapgood was another proponent of sending cheaper corn and provided her own recipes in Russian to be included in each sack. "The Suffering in Russia," *Nation* 54, 1392 (27 February 1892): 168; "Missouri to Sail on Tuesday," New York *Tribune,* 13 March 1892, p. 1.

165. "Aid for Starving Russia," *Nation* 54, 1390 (18 February 1892): 129; Schaeffer, "Ship-Load of Iowa Corn," p. 477.

166. *T. De Witt Talmage: His Life and Work,* ed. Louis A. Banks (London: O. W. Binkerd, 1902), pp. 199–200.

167. Crawford (St. Petersburg) to Edgar, 25 August 1892, box 7, Edgar Papers, MinnHS. "You sized that pile up just right, for we were mortified to death by the unreasonable demands of the Christian Herald people." Talmage wanted his shipment to take priority over others.

168. *Russkie Vedomosti,* 8 May 1892.

*Consul Niels Bornholdt, Captain James Spencer, Consul-General
John Crawford, and Francis Reeve after the arrival of the* Cone-
maugh *at Riga. From Francis Reeve,* Russia Then and Now *(1917)*

Overall, American relief was divided into a number of separate, uncoordinated campaigns that generated some rivalry and friction but still managed to achieve their goals. Clara Barton was upset that all foodstuffs did
not go under the Red Cross flag and especially annoyed with the Philadelphia group that stole her thunder.[169] Edgar and Tillinghast, however,
patched up their wheat-corn rivalry for the good of the cause.[170]

169. Barton to Tillinghast, 8 February 1892, vol. 2, Iowa State Famine Relief Committee, ISHS. This eight-page letter is very revealing of the trials and tribulations of a
Red Cross administration that adhered to the principle of accepting only goods and service but no money.
170. Edgar to Tillinghast, 4 February 1892, vol. 1, Iowa State Famine Relief Committee, ISHS; Tillinghast to Barton, 11 June 1892, box 112 (roll 83), Barton Papers, LC.
Alice French later invited Edgar to come down to Davenport "to talk over the 'Russian
campaign' " with her and Tillinghast; French to Edgar, 12 May 1893, box 1, Edgar Papers, MinnHS.

Impact of Russian Famine on Russian-American Relations

The Russian famine of 1891–1893 was undoubtedly one of the greatest human disasters to afflict European civilization in the nineteenth century. The closest comparisons in Russian history are the Napoleonic invasion of 1812 and the cholera epidemic of 1830–1831. During the latter about 250,000 perished over the whole empire.[171] Deaths from the famine are not easy to calculate because it was accompanied by another cholera outbreak, though this epidemic was concentrated south of the main famine areas in Central Asia and the Caucasus. Statistics from the rural provinces are also difficult to track. Contemporary estimates were about 750,000 direct deaths, but more recent analysis places the famine toll at around 400,000 with an additional 300,000 succumbing to disease and the elements.[172] The famine left many more weakened and vulnerable to later illness and was devastating ecologically, since few domesticated animals, game, fish, or even trees survived in the famine areas.

For the United States, the relief campaign was easily the greatest humanitarian effort to date and set a standard for the future. Because of the diversity of cash and kind contributions, number of avenues used, and people involved, the total American aid cannot be accurately measured. The first shipload of flour was valued at $79,000 and the second at $138,000 by the legation.[173] Using that as a rough basis and including transportation and service costs (but not the time of the sponsors), the American contributions probably surpassed $1 million, with some cash donations continuing into 1893.[174] Although much of the food arrived after the famine had peaked, it was crucial in putting communities back together again. As in the case of lend-lease during World War II, an important aspect was psychological, bolstering the Russian will to survive. This relief program for a country with a

171. Roderick E. McGrew, *Russia and the Cholera, 1823–1832* (Madison: University of Wisconsin Press, 1965), pp. 98–99. Cholera generated more sensation and greater fear because it hit the major cities, Moscow and St. Petersburg, especially hard, whereas famine was mainly confined to the countryside.

172. Robbins, *Famine in Russia*, pp. 170–71. Many also suffered from cold and exposure while traveling to seek food or because the thatched roofs of houses had been fed to animals. For a good description of the Volga area, see James W. Long, *From Privileged to Dispossessed: The Volga Germans, 1860–1917* (Lincoln: University of Nebraska Press, 1988), pp. 79–81. The great hunger in Ireland of the 1840s that extended over a longer period took about 1 million lives.

173. T. Blynor, "Food for Starving Russia," *Harper's Weekly*, 5 March 1892, p. 223.

174. A rough Russian estimate is $500,000 in foodstuffs and $100,000 in cash; Bobrinskoi, "Amerikanskaia pomoshch'," p. 263.

totally different system of government also served as a precedent for the 1921–1922 American Relief Administration assistance to Russia and for many other global humanitarian causes.

The proportionate value of the American relief is even more elusive. Much of the central government assistance through the Ministry of Interior, reportedly reaching $75 million, was in the form of loans to local governments, some of which were probably never paid back.[175] In any event, help from across the Atlantic constituted both a significant and a symbolic part of the total Russian famine relief. The private participation of American citizens probably influenced the government to allow Russians to assist independently, thus suggesting a model for private philanthropy within Russia. The campaign was also a boon for Red Cross groups in both the United States and Russia because it bolstered a new international organization and stimulated pride in volunteerism.[176]

After some initial hesitation, the Russian government readily accepted all varieties of American humanitarian aid with genuine gratitude and permitted extensive publicity.[177] Vorontsov-Dashkov expressed official opinion when he wrote Blankenburg, in English, "The friendly feelings of sympathy America shows us now, when so many of our people are in want, can never be forgotten by me or my countrymen."[178] And Grand Duke Nicholas, who chaired the Special Relief Commission, told Smith, "We are all deeply touched by the shiploads of food which are coming to us from America."[179] The government even allowed Americans to target the aid and supervise distribution. Although a number of reports about the mismanagement and corruption of government officials surfaced in the contemporary American press from British, Russian radical, and even American relief sources, recent

175. Edgar, *Russian Famine*, p. 37. Citing a Ministry of Finance report, Andrew White gave a figure of 162 million rubles ($81 million); White (St. Petersburg) to Tillinghast, 19 January 1893, vol. 2, Iowa State Famine Relief Committee, ISHS.

176. Curti, *American Philanthropy Abroad*, p. 119; Mabel T. Boardman, *Under the Red Cross Flag at Home and Abroad* (Philadelphia and London: J. B. Lippincott, 1915), pp. 217–18. A solemn march, "God Save Our Land," was inspired by the famine relief and performed at Arlington National Cemetery by John Philip Sousa on Memorial Day 1892; A. McClemment (Philadelphia) to Smith, 22 March 1892, DPR, Russia, vol. 4446 (misc. received), RG 84, NA.

177. For example, "Kak amerikantsy pomogaiut Rossii," *Severnyi Vestnik* 4 (April 1892): 94–102; 5 (May 1892): 81–91.

178. Vorontsov-Dashkov to Blankenburg, 8(/19?) March 1892, case 19, box 14, Society Misc.—Blankenburg Papers, HSP.

179. Smith to Blaine, 24 March 1892, DUSM, Russia, vol. 42 (roll 42, M 35), RG 59, NA.

scholarship demonstrates that the government at the central and local levels did a surprisingly good job of distributing relief.[180] At least few of those Americans involved complained at the time. The result was an atmosphere of friendship and harmony both in Russia and the United States that, if not a cure for "Kennanitis," placed it in temporary remission.[181]

As was apparent from the Cleveland solicitations, Jewish communities opposed relief. This was muted, however, because large numbers of Russian Jewish immigrants were receiving assistance simultaneously. There was also a mistaken early belief that the Jewish population was afflicted by the famine, and it would have been impolitic to advocate aid for one portion of the Russian population and oppose it for another.[182] A few inveterate anti-Russians did speak out: Poultney Bigelow, before his exploits with Remington in Russia, reportedly asserted in a lecture in New Haven that "not one pound of flour contributed from this country will ever reach the starving people; [there is] no such thing as an honest man in Russia."[183]

The philanthropic effort generally reflected well on the Americans involved, but there was one embarrassing public row among New York society women. Noted do-gooder Louise Thomas decided to help out on the Russian end under the cloak of the Red Cross (being an old friend of Clara Barton's). She also had a reputation for assisting Russian revolutionary exiles and in fact had initially planned to take with her Theophilia Kraemer, a Polish exile who had already become well-known for "patriotic" pro-Polish speeches. This raised the hackles of Isabel Hapgood, who alerted a Russian editor-friend and attacked Thomas behind her back.[184]

Hapgood's alarum persuaded Russian diplomats to refuse Kraemer a visa and forced Barton to any Red Cross affiliation with Thomas. The whole

180. Robbins, *Famine in Russia*, pp. 178–80; Norman Naimark, *Terrorists and Social Democrats: The Russian Revolutionary Movement Under Alexander III* (Cambridge: Harvard University Press, 1983), pp. 213–14.

181. One exception was Alexander Johnson, secretary of the Indiana Board of Charities, who wrote to Clara Barton: "Why should we spend our strength and give our money to prolong the wretched lives of these poor miserable creatures. Why not let the ravening wolves, the 'tchinovniks' of the government, devour them at once, aided by the famine. Every dollar we send to Russia means a dollar given to help support the worst possible government in the world." February 22, 1892, box 112 (roll 83), Barton Papers, LC.

182. See Allan Spetter, "The United States, the Russian Jews and the Russian Famine of 1891–1892," *American Jewish Historical Quarterly* 64, 3 (March 1975): 236–44.

183. As cited in Robert Ogden to Smith, 15 March 1892, DPR, Russia, vol. 4446 (misc. received), RG 84, NA.

184. Hapgood to Vladimir Stasov, 6 May 1892, in "Samozvanka," *Novosti i Birzhevnaia Gazeta*, 12 May 1892.

business became public fodder when Barbara MacGahan, with her Russian press connections, released Hapgood's correspondence and supported Thomas. With rumors circulating that Hapgood was a Russian spy in the pay of the government, New York newspapers had a field day interviewing MacGahan, Hapgood, Thomas, and Barton and puncturing society egos. Barton's reputation suffered as a result of this and charges of mismanagement.[185] John Hoyt summed it up: "But for the unnecessary and injudicious zeal of two lady members of the committee ambitious to render personal service in the famine districts, everything from the beginning to end would have been without friction or embarrassment."[186]

Predictably, George Kennan at first blamed the extent of famine distress on the Russian government and accused the relief campaigns of aiding despotism, thus earning the rebuke of Tillinghast during an Iowa speaking tour.[187] As a member of the board of directors of the Red Cross, Kennan was caught in a dilemma, which he resolved by curbing his attack on relief and even contributing $100 himself.[188] To an inquiry about the efforts of the American Red Cross, he responded, "As far as the work for the Russian peasants is concerned it seems to me to have been done intelligently and efficiently,"[189] and he attended the annual board meeting at which Russian relief was the main topic. Kennan's retreat and relief publicity in general contributed to the eclipse of the Free Russia movement in the United States and provided an opening for the controversial extradition treaty that was signed early in 1893.

185. Thomas to Barton, 18 and 22 April 1892; Hapgood to Barton, 19 April 1892; "Here's a Pretty Scandal," New York *Morning Advertiser*, 26 May 1892 (clipping); "Mistakes All Round," New York *Recorder*, 10 August 1892 (clipping), box 112 (roll 83), Barton Papers, LC. Tillinghast met Hapgood at the time of this conflict and remarked, "Her egotism outruns her judgement and she is utterly without business sagacity." To Barton, 24 April 1892, ibid. According to the New York accounts, two Russian editors—Stasov (*Novosti*) and Nekrasov (*Severnyi Vestnik*)—partisans of Hapgood and Thomas, respectively, were prepared to fight a duel over them. See also "Kto prav?" *Moskovskiia Vedomosti*, 15 May 1892.
186. Hoyt to White, 27 March 1893, roll 60, White Papers, Cornell University.
187. "The Famine in Russia," interview with Kennan, New York *Times*, 3 January 1892, p. 13; Tillinghast to Kennan, 11 February 1892, box 2, Kennan Papers, LC. At the other end of the spectrum, one contemporary American visitor to Russia blamed Jews for the severity of the famine because of their stranglehold over the Russian peasants, ignoring the fact that very few lived in the provinces most severely afflicted; Thomas Stevens, "Russia's Famine: The Moujiks' Evil Genius," *Leslie's Illustrated*, 21 April 1892, p. 200.
188. Tillinghast to Barton, 8 March 1892, box 112 (roll 83), Barton Papers, LC.
189. To Mrs. Parker, 8 July 1892 (c), ibid.

In Russia some opposition to receiving aid reared its head in Pan-Slavic and conservative quarters, where it was felt that the country should manage for itself. Perhaps there was nationalistic cause for concern, since arrivals of American aid, especially the flour and cornmeal, were greeted with fanfare. Following elaborate ceremonies—the one for the *Missouri* included a specially composed "Missouri March"[190]—trains flying American flags headed for designated provincial cities, where they were heralded again. When the first train pulled into Samara on the Volga, huge crowds welcomed it with cheers and singing, and a band played "Hail Columbia" and "The Star Spangled Banner" repeatedly. Then loaded carts, also carrying American flags, paraded through town, preceded by a military band.[191]

So much fuss was made over the arrivals of American aid that it engendered criticism about all the time spent celebrating while people were starving. Secretary of legation Wurts was chagrined: "It was certainly an anomaly to greet provisions sent to the starving by a flow of champagne and a series of expensive feasts in town halls."[192] And Edgar was taken aback by the attention he drew from supplicants and well-wishers in Moscow after a long interview was published in a local newspaper.[193] The last American transports, shepherded by Talmage and Louis Klopsch and assisted by Louise Thomas, came and went with less notice.

American aid was targeted to some extent. The German colonies around Saratov had been especially hard hit, yet reports circulated that they were being neglected by government relief. Community leaders there also had ways of making their wants known in the West.[194] As a result, some of the relief leaders—Blessig, Murphy, Blankenburg, Hubbell—took a special interest in their conditions, and the largest single consignment of Minnesota flour was earmarked for Saratov.[195] Diplomatic pressure was also applied with political gain at home apparently in mind: "Would not such an action [special shipment for Volga Germans] have a good effect upon our *German* fellow-

190. Printed sheet music, composed by E. Fliege, is in box 7, Edgar Papers, MinnHS.

191. James A. Bezant (Samara) to Smith, 17 March 1892, DPR, Russia, vol. 4446 (misc. received), RG 84, NA; Hubbell report in Barton, *Red Cross*, pp. 188–93; Tillinghast, "Our Gift of Corn," Davenport *Democrat*, 1 January 1893.

192. Wurts to Foster, 20 July 1892, DUSM, Russia, vol. 43 (roll 43, M 35), RG 59, NA.

193. Edgar, *Russian Famine*, p. 37.

194. Alexander Faidel (Ekaterinenstadt) to Blessig, 30 March 1892 (c), and petition to Murphy, 11 April 1892, in Murphy to Breckinridge, DPR, Russia, vol. 231 (misc. received), RG 84, NA.

195. Edgar, *Russian Famine*, p. 31.

Celebrating the arrival of the Missouri *in Libau, 1892: semi-seated on the right is William Edgar; standing far right is Andrei Bobrinskoi. From William Edgar,* The Russian Famine *(1892)*

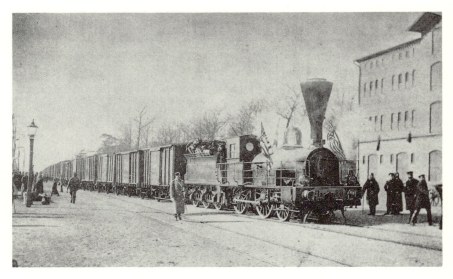

Famine relief train leaving Libau. From Edgar, The Russian Famine *(1892)*

citizens in the States?"[196] Nonetheless, both the need and response were real. Blankenburg went to see for himself and reported after a four-day tour that the "misery is indescribable."[197]

Of the Americans who reached Russia that year, Blankenburg and his friend Grundy, Julian Hubbell, Frank Carpenter, John Hoyt, and Louise Thomas inspected the Volga famine areas. They were appalled by the poverty and suffering and easily convinced that the aid effort had been worthwhile.[198] Blankenburg conferred with Tolstoy in Moscow and Hubbell tracked him down at Yasnaya Polyana, but some of those who came to superintend American relief never left St. Petersburg, partly because of fear of cholera and typhus in the countryside.[199] Edgar, who had intended to make an extensive tour, limited it to a Bobrinskoi-guided visit to Tula and Tambov provinces.[200] Consequently, the exact disposition of all the food and money is not well documented. Judging from a variety of sources and reports, Americans were generally satisfied with the reliability and sincerity of the distribution but much disturbed by evidence of the long neglect of the peasant villages.[201]

Contacts between Americans and Russian officials increased and were facilitated because of the famine. After a meeting with the future tsar, Smith reported, "During the conversation, which continued for some time, the Grand Duke referred to the visit which his uncle, the Grand Duke Alexis, made several years ago to the United States, and said that his uncle often recalled it with pleasure."[202] Even Arthur Blackstein, a young Jewish bacteriologist from Cornell, found his experimental research on cholera quite welcome in Russia.[203]

---

196. Crawford (Libau) to Smith, 11 March 1892, DPR, Russia, vol. 4446 (misc. received), RG 84, NA.

197. Blankenburg (Saratov) to Smith, 19/31 March 1892, ibid. According to his wife, "The memory left by the distress he witnessed haunted Mr. Blankenburg for months after his return home." Blankenburg, *Blankenburgs of Philadelphia*, p. 39.

198. Thomas to Wurts, 2/14 July 1892, DPR, Russia, vol. 4447 (misc. received), RG 84, NA; Hoyt to White, 27 March 1893, roll 60, White Papers, Cornell University.

199. For one such itinerary that lasted all of two weeks, see Thomas De Witt Talmage diary, 1892, box 2, Talmage Papers, LC. It included receptions given by Alexander III and the empress at Peterhof (22 July) and by Grand Duke Nicholas (17 July).

200. This was done ostensibly out of concern for the health of his wife at home; Edgar (Moscow) to his wife, 16 April 1892, box 1, Edgar Papers, MinnHS.

201. W. C. Edgar, "Russia's Conflict with Hunger," *Review of Reviews* 5, 30 (July 1892): 692–95.

202. Smith to Blaine, 24 March 1892, DUSM, Russia, vol. 42 (roll 42, M 35), RG 59, NA.

203. A. D. White to H. W. Sage, 26 December 1893, roll 59, White Papers, Cornell University.

That Russians genuinely appreciated American aid was illustrated by an unsolicited resolution that famous chemists Dmitri Mendeleev and Dmitri Konovalov sponsored:

> The United States of America in sending bread to the Russian people in time of scarcity and need gave the most affecting instance of brotherly feeling. The Russian chemists who devote themselves to the service of universal science, at their meeting of the 7/19 May, decided to ask their brethren of the Smithsonian Institution to transmit the expression of their sincere thanks to all persons or institutions who contributed to the fulfillment of this brotherly aid.[204]

Russian gratitude was also expressed formally in an elaborate, pictorial "address" prepared by the nobility of St. Petersburg at the end of 1893.[205]

A similar mood of amity existed in Washington, where the Russian legation was on the receiving end of an outpouring of American sympathy. The interest in Russia inspired by the famine obviously increased popular knowledge of the country in the United States. As French confessed to Barton, "One incidental result is a growing familiarity with the history and character of Russia . . . and I may add a growing enthusiasm and friendship for this great, misunderstood nation, as well."[206] Likewise, America was probably never so prominent in the Russian press as in 1892. Less measurable is the appreciation of the largely illiterate recipients in the countryside.[207]

Because of the weakened condition of the survivors, the shortage of seed and horses, a long and hard winter, and continued drought conditions, the famine persisted into 1893 in many areas, especially in Tula, Tambov, and Voronezh provinces and in Finland. Another American relief campaign was

204. Original in Russian and English, dated 31 May 1892 and signed by Mendeleev and Konovalov, box 58, RG 31, SA. A note indicated that copies were sent to the Associated Press, W. C. Edgar, Russian Famine Relief Committee, and the Washington *Evening Star.*

205. White to Gresham, 7 November 1893, DUSM, Russia, vol. 45 (roll 45, M 35), RG 59, NA.

206. French to Barton, 14 January 1892, box 112 (roll 83), Barton Papers, LC.

207. Perhaps the closest observer was Alexander Francis: "Daily I am in receipt of long detailed accounts showing how wide spread has been the distribution of the American flour. In all I am urgently requested to thank the good American people for the timely help and to assure them that the Russian peasants will never forget the kindness which prompted the gift: they will never cease to pray God to bless their American Friends and to grant them success in all their enterprises." Francis (St. Petersburg) to Barton, 24 August/5 September 1892, box 112 (roll 83), Barton Papers, LC.

considered but dismissed for fear of overtaxing American generosity. Bobrinskoi told Crawford that "the effect was so good, so beautiful, last spring that he would be very sorry to [see] anything less beautiful and generous this year."[208] Olga Novikova, who had become acquainted with Edgar in Moscow, wrote, "I am simply ashamed to appeal once more to public charity."[209] Still, some leftover funds were sent from American sources, especially from Philadelphia—and gratefully received.[210]

One solution to famine conditions—escape—also affected Russian-American relations. The Jewish migration continued independently, and though their main settlement areas were little affected, the deeply depressed atmosphere in the country may have contributed to a desire to leave. A renewed emigration of Volga Germans was obviously a direct result of the famine; they tended to follow the path of their predecessors into the Great Plains region. Usually too poor to buy land, they settled in cities such as Topeka and Lincoln and became workers, often in railroad shops or flour mills, or seasonal laborers in sugar beet fields in Colorado rather than independent farmers.[211] A large number of Bessarabian or Black Sea Germans, also struggling under poor yields in 1892, resettled at this time mainly in the Dakotas and Manitoba.[212] The increased exodus included many other non-Russian peoples of the empire—Finns,[213] Lithuanians, Poles, and Ukrainians.

---

208. Crawford added, "It is a fact that the Government is now well prepared to cope with the distress—very much better than last year." Crawford (St. Petersburg) to Edgar, 25 December 1892, box 1, Edgar Papers, MinnHS. And Bobrinskoi stressed the capability of local charities; Bobrinskoi (St. Petersburg) to Edgar, 3/15 January 1893, ibid. Tillinghast, for one, was ready to launch another campaign for 1893 if needed; to Andrew Dickson White, 8 December 1892, roll 59, White Papers, Cornell University.

209. To Edgar, 9 January 1893, box 1, Edgar Papers, MinnHS.

210. Vladimir Bobrinskoi (Bogorodetsk, Tula province) to Edgar, 12 March 1893, ibid.

211. For the arrival of one group, see Topeka *Mail*, 8 January 1892. See also Hattie Plum Williams, *The Czar's Germans with Particular Reference to the Volga Germans* (reprint; Lincoln, Nebr.: American Historical Society of Germans from Russia, 1975), pp. 204–10. The bags of cornmeal from Nebraska contained a notice in Russian, advising that the contents were not flour and that it came from Nebraska. One wonders if this had any connection with the movement of a large number of Lutheran Volga Germans to that state the same year.

212. Heenan to Wharton, 23 January 1893, DUSC, Odessa, vol. 10 (roll 15, M 459), RG 59, NA, reporting on a shipload leaving Odessa.

213. Finland was afflicted by both crop failures and a crisis over political autonomy during 1891–1892. See especially C. Leonard Lundin, "Finland," in *Russification in the Baltic Provinces and Finland, 1855–1914*, ed. Edward C. Thaden (Princeton, N.J.: Princeton University Press, 1981), pp. 411–18; White to Tillinghast, 28 December 1892, vol. 2, Iowa State Famine Relief Committee, ISHS.

In total, emigration from Russia to the United States doubled in 1892 to a record high of over 80,000, a peak that would not be reached again until 1900. In this decade immigrants from Russia surpassed those from Germany for the first time.[214] Many more went to Canada and South America, and some of these would later move to the United States. The key consequences of this migration were the dramatic opening of large new areas of the American plains to dryland grain and irrigated sugar beet production, greater ethnic diversity, and more abundant good and cheap labor in market towns and industrial cities.

The Extradition Treaty

Action on a draft of an extradition treaty, proposed by Russia in September 1886 and under consideration by the Senate, had been suspended after Kennan, Foulke, and others mounted an effective opposition. Although some amendments had been made to appease their fears of its use against Russian political exiles, planning and attempting assassination was still included as an extraditable crime, which was deemed unacceptable by the treaty's detractors.[215] The famine relief campaign quieted the opposition through most of 1892 as sympathy for Russia rose. Moreover, the sensational assassination attempt in July of Carnegie Steel president Henry Clay Frick by a Russian Jew, Alexander Berkman, had sparked some concern. Even so, the passage of the extradition treaty by the Senate in February 1893 came as a surprise.

Coincident to the approval and with courage bolstered by the American famine relief, a secretary of the Russian legation, Petr Botkin, took the offensive with an article, "A Voice for Russia," published in the *Century*.[216] Pointing out that prisons are not attractive anywhere, Botkin asserted that Kennan painted the Russian system in the darkest possible colors. He defended the record of his government against Kennan and stressed the substantial number of cordial inquiries that had been received by the legation about the famine. "I am convinced the disagreeable impression produced by Mr. Ken-

214. A. S. Sokolov, "Rossiiskaia trudovaia immigratsiia v Ameriku v poslednei cherverti XIX v.," *Sovetskaia Etnografiia* 2 (March–April 1986): 98–99; S. Patkanov, *Itogi statistiki immigratsii v Soedinennye Shtaty Sev. Ameriki iz Rossii za desiatiletie 1900–1909 gg.* (St. Petersburg: Nyrkin, 1911), pp. 4–7.

215. "Extradition Treaty," New York *Times*, 23 March 1892, p. 4.

216. "A Voice for Russia," *Century* 45, 4 (February 1893): 612. A draft was forwarded to St. Petersburg (f. 133, op. 512/3, d. 62 [1893], AVPR).

nan's articles . . . will altogether vanish before full knowledge of the actual facts."[217]

This Russian plea was accompanied by an editorial that underscored the significance of a Russian official speaking out in such a way.[218] A Cornell colleague of Andrew White's noted that it caused much comment in the press, "many papers, like the New York *Sun*, speaking very highly of it and taking occasion to recount the story of Russia's many tokens of friendship for America."[219] George Kennan finally responded to Botkin, point by point, basically making his case on the thinness of the evidence presented by the Russian.[220] The counterattack was part of his renewed offensive against the Russian government with the extradition treaty as the central target. His tactics included a sharply worded public letter to President Cleveland and the revitalized publication of *Free Russia*. Several Kennan and Stepniak-inspired articles against the extradition treaty appeared in the New York *Times* and charged "dirty tricks"—because the final stage was completed in strict secrecy.[221] White, while being pestered by his liberal friends, was forced to see the treaty through to its formal promulgation in early June, and the anti-extradition rhetoric was soon drowned out by economic depression and a new spirit of international accord.

The Columbian Exposition

Plans to celebrate the 400th anniversary of Columbus's "discovery" of America had progressed for several years with Chicago, a symbol of American prosperity and expansion, picked as the location. This grand, interna-

217. "A Voice for Russia," p. 613.

218. "A Word from Russia," *Century* 45, 4 (February 1893): 625.

219. U. G. Weatherby to White, 13 February 1893, roll 59, White Papers, Cornell University. White's concurrent report describing his friendly reception may have unwittingly given Botkin credence; "A Guest of the Czar," Syracuse *Standard*, 22 February 1893, clipping in ibid.

220. Kennan, "A Voice for the People of Russia: A Reply to 'A Voice for Russia,' " *Century* 46, 3 (July 1893): 461–72. Typical of Kennan, his reply was considerably longer than Botkin's original.

221. Frederick Travis, *George Kennan and the American–Russian Relationship, 1865–1924* (Athens: Ohio University Press, 1990), pp. 208–17; New York *Times*, 2 April 1893, p. 7; 11 April, p. 1; 17 May, p. 4; 26 June, p. 1. Andrew White was rather defensive about his part in it, salvaging face in making extradition of political offenders less easy; to Holls, 7 June 1893, Holls Papers, Columbia University. In fact, few cases would ever cause any public concern.

tional world's fair was to surpass those of Philadelphia in 1876 and Paris in 1889. Organizers sought out Russian participation as early as 1890, but it seemed unlikely because of strains produced by the Kennan attacks.[222] Yet St. Petersburg forwarded its formal acceptance even before Botkin made a detailed inspection of the site in June 1891.[223] In September a Russian consul, Peter Thal, was assigned to the city "greatly in view of the coming exhibition."[224] Chicago had long impressed Russians for its growth and as an agricultural center, even serving as a magnet for wandering exiles and travelers.

The development and escalation of Russian plans for the exhibition coincided with the acceptance of American famine relief in early 1892. The director of the Department of Commerce and Industry of the Ministry of Finance initially headed the exhibit arrangements commission, while the wife of minister Ivan Vyshnegradskii was in charge of a special women's committee. A preparatory delegation visited Chicago in June 1892,[225] but interest swelled after the energetic and ambitious Sergei Witte became minister of finance at the end of August. Even Pobedonostsev was intrigued by a "congress of religions" to be held in connection with the exposition.[226] By the end of the year the government had budgeted over half a million rubles (approximately $250,000) to support participation.[227] On 12 October 1892, minister Struve, along with Botkin, joined consul Thal for the festive groundbreaking ceremonies along the lake front.[228]

Witte's new director of the Department of Commerce and Industry, Vladimir Kovalevskii, added even more impetus to the Russian descent on Chicago. Among the motivations were to reciprocate famine relief, to publicize the construction of the Siberian railroad, to solidify American friendship (with the Far East particularly in mind), to demonstrate Russia's coming of

222. Smith to Blaine, 22 December 1890, DUSM, Russia, vol. 42 (roll 42, M 35), RG 59, NA.

223. Shishkin (acting foreign minister) to Struve, 14/26 June 1891 (c), and Greger to Shishkin, 27 June/9 July 1891, enclosing Botkin's report of 27 June, f. 133, op. 470, d. 100, AVPR.

224. Greger to Wharton, 13 September 1891, NRL, vol. 11 (roll 9, M 39), RG 59, NA.

225. Smith to Blaine, 9 February and 1 March 1892, DUSM, Russia, vol. 42 (roll 42, M 35), RG 59, NA; "Russia at the Fair," Chicago *Tribune*, 27 June 1892.

226. White to Foster, 5 December 1892, DUSM, Russia, vol. 44 (roll 44, M 35), RG 59, NA.

227. White to Foster, 12 January 1893, ibid.

228. Struve (Washington) to Giers (t), 13/25 October 1892, and Shilling to Giers, 16/28 October 1892, f. 133, op. 470, d. 94 (1892), AVPR.

industrial age, and, most of all, to gather technical information to advance that program. At least forty specialists were instructed to attend the exposition and report back in detail. Others came as journalists or on a private basis. And a squadron of the imperial navy, carrying yet another grand duke to America, came to participate in the Columbian naval review.

As in 1876, most of the Russian displays were not in place for the grand opening on 1 May 1893, but with a good excuse: the ships carrying them could not leave the Baltic before April because of ice, and one was lost at sea.[229] The new Russian minister, Grigori Kantakuzen, was on hand, however, along with Botkin, Thal, P. I. Glukhovskii, and his commission: Konstantin Rakussa-Sushchevskii (art section), Sergei Volkonskii (education), and Princess Liudmila Shakhovskaia, who helped open the women's building with a well-received speech in English.[230] According to Botkin, the group was mortified when President Cleveland deliberately sought out the Russian sections and found only confusion and disarray.[231]

Finally, on 17 June, Bishop Nicholas formally dedicated the sixteen Russian sections scattered throughout the exposition buildings.[232] By all accounts the Russian exhibits were very popular; taking precedence were Orlov horses, furs, and the plans and models for the Siberian railroad,[233] but other items included leather, linen, china, silver, crystal, paintings (Aizovskii, Makovskii, and Repin), folk arts, and manganese ore samples.[234]

229. Actually, few nations had completed their exhibits by the opening date.

230. Kantakuzen to Shishkin, 24 April/6 May 1893, f. 133, op. 470, d. 101 (1893), AVPR; *Niva* 24, 21 (22 May 1893): 500–502. This illustrated weekly published a number of pictures of the exposition and Chicago sights throughout the year. See especially "Kolumbiiskaia vystavka v Chikago," *Niva* 24, 31 (31 July 1893): 700, and 24, 33 (14 August 1893): 747.

231. As related to Suvorin by Botkin, *Dnevnik Suvorina*, p. 68. According to this story, Cleveland, taken aback by the number of official representatives standing in front of empty stalls, said, "I thank Russia for sending such honorable men."

232. "Blessed by Bishop," Chicago *Tribune*, 18 June 1893, p. 1. Special local guests at the reception included the Palmers, the Pullmans, and the Armours. Budding historian Mikhail Rostovtsev served as interpreter.

233. Attracting particular attention to Siberia was a model of a leper colony proposed for the Yakutsk region, designed by English reformer Kate Marsden; Chicago *Tribune*, 18 June 1893, p. 3. See her *On Sledge and Horseback to the Outcast Siberian Lepers* (London: Record Press, 1892).

234. A. S. Sokolov, "Rossiia na vsemirnoi vystavke v Chikago v 1893 g.," in *Amerikanskii Ezhegodnik 1984* (Moscow: Nauka, 1984), pp. 157–58. The art exhibit, managed by Mrs. Leonid Semechkin, was highlighted by Repin's "The Cossack's Answer," scenes of Columbus's voyages by Aizovskii, many depictions of Russian history, and portraits of Tolstoy, Rubinstein, Tchaikovsky, and Vereshchagin; "Russian Art Display," Chicago *Tribune*, 21 June 1893, p. 3.

Russian section in the Manufactures Building, Chicago World's Fair, 1893. Harper's Weekly, *28 October 1893, courtesy of the Kansas Collection, University of Kansas Libraries*

Altogether, there were 1,200 Russian exhibits; a quarter of them were agricultural, followed in emphasis by manufacturing and women's work. The crafts section was distinguished by a grotesque neo-gothic, neo-medieval facade on Columbia Avenue, the entrance flanked by two four-foot-high malachite vases and featuring a woollen shawl that contained 24.5 million stitches and weighed only eight ounces.[235] Capping the promotion of Russian wares in Chicago was the publication of *The Industries of Russia,* compiled by A. Keppen and edited by John Crawford, the American consul general in Russia.[236]

The greatest impact, however, involved what Russia took home from Chi-

235. V. V. Sviatlovskii, "Pis'ma iz Ameriki: Kolumbiiskaia vystavka v Chikago," *Russkoe Obozrenie* 23, 5 (October 1893): 895–97; "Work of Deft Russian Fingers," Chicago *Tribune,* 18 June 1893, p. 13. A double-page picture of the entrance is in *Niva* 24, 21 (22 May 1893): 488–89, and in Chicago *Tribune,* 24 July 1893, p. 8.

236. Witte to Grover Cleveland, 10/22 September 1893, NRL, vol. 11 (roll 9, M 39), RG 59, NA. In presenting a copy of the five volumes, Witte emphasized that "we owe the successful accomplishment of this work to the energetic and able assistance afforded by Mr. J. M. Crawford, . . . who kindly undertook on my invitation to conduct, revise and edit the translation of this entire series."

cago. The exposition revealed a new technological age fused with an American imperial spirit at the very time that Russia was embarking on a crash program of construction and development.[237] Or, as minister White noted at the time:

> There is evidently a feeling that the two nations are under somewhat similar economic conditions—each being vast in extent, with enormous undeveloped resources, and, that our country having taken the lead in all that pertains to material development—to say nothing of leadership in other fields—both the Exposition and the country at large are the most fitting places for the study of the leading facts. The result of this feeling is that a considerable number of Russians are making ready to visit Chicago.[238]

So many came, in fact, that one of the first Russian publications about the world's fair was a guidebook written by Nikolai Pliskii.[239] Counting delegates, caretakers and handlers, performers, reporters, naval officers, a grand ducal entourage, and tourists, probably at least 300 Russians attended the fair. Although Britain may have had a larger contingent at the exposition, Russia can claim first place in the close attention given to it.

Perhaps famine relief and international factors helped open up the Russian presses to all things American in 1893. An early visitor and publicist was Odessa engineer Nikolai Mel'nikov, who wrote about the wonders of the exhibition.[240] Having the advantage of American residence and familiarity, Barbara MacGahan, Russian-born widow of the war correspondent, contributed a number of detailed letters on the exposition for *Severnyi Vestnik* (Northern herald) in the summer and fall of 1893. She focused on professional and technical education, women's exhibits, the degree of national pride and progress on display, and how much the Russian exhibits

237. Emily S. Rosenberg, *Spreading the American Dream: American Economic and Cultural Expansion, 1890-1945* (New York: Hill and Wang, 1982), pp. 5-8; Theodore H. Von Laue, *Sergei Witte and the Industrialization of Russia* (New York: Atheneum, 1974), pp. 81-87.

238. To Gresham, 18 April 1893, DUSM, Russia, vol. 44 (roll 44, M 35), RG 59, NA.

239. *Podrobnyi putevoditel' na Vsemirnuiu kolumbovu vystavku v Chikago 1893 goda* (St. Petersburg, 1893), cited in Allen, *Russia Looks at America*, p. 192.

240. *Chudesa vystavki v Chikago* (Odessa, 1893); Sokolov, "Rossiia na vsemirnoi vystavke," p. 156.

were liked.[241] She was impressed by the confusion and vastness of the exposition and the fact that most visitors failed to follow the American caveat "not to bite off more than one can chew."[242]

Also wide-ranging in his coverage was Vladimir Sviatlovskii, a socialist exile who nonetheless wrote a series of thirty-nine reports for a leading St. Petersburg newspaper, *Novoe Vremia*, and longer articles for *Russkoe Obozrenie* (Russian review). Arriving on the Fourth of July, he thought he was in a besieged city with all the shooting and mayhem going on. He watched firemen battle roof fires throughout the night and reported that there were thirty-six casualties.[243] In contrast to MacGahan, Sviatlovskii was critical of the Russian presence—choral and orchestral performances, art selections, and exhibit—but acknowledged the popularity of everything Russian.[244] Besides the fair, he described a notorious lynching in Illinois, the harsh treatment of Native Americans, the booming petroleum industry, and labor strife at the Pullman Company.[245]

Russia's America mania of 1893 may also have inspired the writing career of one of the best-known Russian residents of the United States, Petr Dement'ev (Demens), who wrote under the name of "P. A. Tverskoi." An amazing entrepreneur and raconteur, Demens started his American adventures in 1881 in the lumber business and as a railroad promoter in Florida; there he established a port on the Gulf Coast and named it after the Russian capital. He also pioneered in citrus cultivation but by 1893 had moved on to California, where he was a prominent banker and developer. His informative and at times erudite "letters from America" first started appearing in early 1893 in the most influential Russian periodical, *Vestnik Evropy*, and continued for many years. He also wrote popular articles about his visit to

241. V. Mak-Gavan, "Pis'ma iz Ameriki, kolumbiiskaia vsemirnaia vystavka," *Severnyi Vestnik* 7, 7 (July 1893): part 2, 64–78.

242. Ibid. 7, 11 (November 1893): part 2, 62–75.

243. *Russkoe Obozrenie* 23, 4 (September 1893): 328–30. Newspapers reported many other victims of heat and traffic accidents, especially on the new cable cars, but apparently no Russians were among them.

244. Ibid. 4, 24 (October 1893): 887–909; 4, 25 (November 1893): 317–45.

245. Allen, *Russia Looks at America*, pp. 192, 308; Nikoliukin, *A Russian Discovery*, pp. 403–7, which includes a translation of the lynching story. Sviatlovskii would return to Russia to become a respected academic Marxist and professor at the University of St. Petersburg. He retained an interest in the United States and on a subsequent visit in 1908 had a narrow escape while inspecting a lava pool on Kilauea volcano on Hawaii; clipping from Chicago *Evening Post*, 6 April 1908, vol. 1, Lobdell Papers, ChicagoHS.

the Columbian Exposition for *Nedelia*.[246] Another "Russian" correspondent was Arnold Gillin, actually an American citizen who had settled in Moscow as a merchant; he was the editor of a technical journal, *Dvigatel'* (Motor), which promoted American goods.[247]

Although most of the Russian visitors to the exposition were simply lost in the crowds, one exception was Vladimir Korolenko, some of whose short stories had recently been published in the United States. He endured a fuss made over him by the American press and gathered material during his stay for some of his most popular stories, including "Death Factory," about a visit to the slaughterhouses of Chicago.[248] All this publicity for the citadel of the Midwest probably accounts for an American professor's discovery when crossing the Caspian Sea a few years later that "passengers knew nothing of New York . . . but respond to the word *Chicago!*"[249]

Praised by the media and doubtless enjoyed by fair attendees were the Russian choral group directed by Evgeniia Lineva and an orchestra led by Czech-born Voitek Glavach. For the opening of the exhibits in June, Glavach helped organize and conduct eight concerts of Russian music that included works of Tchaikovsky, Glinka, Rimsky-Korsakov, Rubenstein, Mussorgsky, and Alexander Glazunov, the latter having composed a special "Triumphal March" for the occasion.[250] Glavach and his wife Sofia stayed to direct the music for "Russia Day" on 3 August, highlighted by the surprise playing of "Marseillaise" in honor of the Franco-Russian rapprochement and Rimsky-Korsakov's new "Spanish Caprice."[251]

The specialists earned their attendance at the exposition by publishing

246. Allen, *Russia Looks at America*, pp. 152–53; Nikoliukin, *A Russian Discovery*, pp. 408–9. For his autobiography: Tverskoi, *Ocherki Severo-Amerikanskikh Soedinennykh Shtatov* (St. Petersburg: Skorokhodov, 1895).

247. Gillin (Moscow) to Breckinridge, 6/18 March 1897, DPR, Russia, vol. 4452 (misc. received), RG 84, NA. Arnold Gillin had considerable experience in popularizing American life for the Russian audience; see, for example, his *Otgoloski novago sveta: Razskazy i ocherky iz Amerikanskoi zhizni* (St. Petersburg: Slavianskoi pechetnaia, 1879).

248. Nikoliukin, *A Russian Discovery*, pp. 414–26.

249. Henry Augustus Ward diary, 26 December 1898, Diaries and Journals, 1898–1899, Ward Papers, University of Rochester.

250. "Russian Folk Songs," Chicago *Tribune*, 11 June 1893, p. 27; "Music at the Fair," Chicago *Tribune*, 20 June 1893, p. 26. Although Glavach drew some attention by playing an unusual instrument—a two-clavier harmonium—he could not really compete with Paderewski, Dvořák, and Saint-Saëns, let alone the popular side attractions of Lillian Russell and Little Egypt. Lineva, who later became a well-known authority on Slavic folk songs, left behind a memento of her appearance: *Russian Folk-Songs as Sung by the People* (Chicago: C. F. Summy, c. 1893).

251. "Russians at the Fair," Chicago *Record*, 4 August 1893, p. 3.

technical reports. Among the most notable were those of Kovalevskii (education), Stepan Gulishambarov (oil industry), Ianzhul (economics), Dmitri Konovalov (chemical industry), D. N. Golovnin (irrigation), Volkonskii (education; this was the son of the assistant minister of finance), Sergei Kareisha (railroads and elevators), Nikolai Pliskii (advertising), Charlampi Golovin (director of the St. Petersburg Technical Institute), Ottokar Aderkas (education), V. L. Kirpichev (machine building and trusts), and A. D. Gattsuk (machine tools). Representing Russia in agriculture were Ivan Rostovtsev, educator and father of the historian of ancient Rome, and Vil'iam Vil'-iams, the Russianized son of Moscow-American manufacturer Robert Williams, who served as vice-president of the agricultural section. Judging from the lavish and highly publicized reception given for the "delegates" in 1894, the Russian government considered the mission a success.[252]

Perhaps able to claim the record for the most distance traveled to reach Chicago, Nikolai Iadrintsev came from Irkutsk to represent Siberia at the exposition. Editor of a major Siberian newspaper, *Vostochnoe Obozrenie* (Eastern review) and leader of the Siberian regionalist movement, Iadrintsev was charmed by Chicago, took extensive notes, and imagined future Siberian development imitating the American. An added bonus to his trip was an opportunity to renew acquaintance with George Kennan, whom he had first met in Siberia. Unfortunately, Iadrintsev's impressions of America remain unpublished.[253]

One of the best "inside" accounts by an official representative is that of Ivan Ianzhul, who published lengthy reports stressing the connection between American education and economic development. A political economy professor from the University of Moscow and former official of the Ministry of Finance, Ianzhul was solicited by Witte in early November 1892 and received his official appointment in February 1893. He was advanced 3,200 rubles ($1,600) for his and his wife's expenses for a four-month trip and with instructions that Ianzhul thought were formidable: report on the rate and collection of all kinds of taxes and customs duties, the organization of government inspectors and who controls and supervises them, the construction and upkeep (federal, state, and city) of port facilities, the determi-

252. Allen, *Russia Looks at America*, pp. 194–215; Sokolov, "Rossiia na vsemirnoi vystavke," pp. 161–64; *Otchet general'nago kommisara russkago otdela Vsemirnoi Kolumbovoi Vystavki v Chikago Vyssochaiskago Dvora Glukhovskago* (St. Petersburg: Kirshbaum, 1895); Sviatlovskii, "Pis'ma iz Ameriki," pp. 891–95 (October 1893).
253. Information kindly provided by Helen Hundley, Wichita State University, who has worked extensively in Iadrintsev manuscripts in Irkutsk and Moscow.

nation of excise taxes, the quarantine laws, the McKinley tariff, elevators, and the cleaning, inspection, and grading of grain. All this was to be presented to the ministry in book form within a year of departure.[254]

When Ianzhul complained about the variety and extent of the demands, he was told that the ministry needed everything covered but that he could select what he wanted to report on. Sensing the importance of grain elevators but acknowledging his own ignorance, he simply hired someone else to investigate. After a quick refresher course in English, the Ianzhuls departed in early March, armed with a sheaf of introductory letters, including some from Leo Tolstoy. Delayed by side trips to Paris and Dresden and repairs to their Cunard liner, they arrived in early May at New York and obtained lodgings in the pension of a Russian emigré named Beliakov, who also operated a department store with the help of his Irish wife. He found several former students among the Jewish immigrants now working at menial labor, dined with political economist Edwin Seligman of Columbia University, and studied in the libraries. In the meantime, his wife, who was interested in education and women's issues, was guided around the city by Isabel Hapgood.[255]

Ianzhul did some research in government offices in Washington before going on to Chicago for the Russian opening in June. They stayed in the private home of a Polish Jew in the city for six weeks and visited the exposition daily, impressed by the crowds, the heat and dirt, and the squalor alongside "the beauty and richness" of the exhibition. He complained about the lack of system, categorization, and prices for items displayed, concluding that the exposition was "very good but as deformed as Chicago itself."[256] He reported that the Russian exhibits were "excellent and attract general attention," especially a Russian "office," where a sailor was installed to make tea with a samovar. Perhaps no other person examined the fair more closely.

Returning via Washington and New York, the Ianzhuls repaid Witte's confidence with a series of articles in prominent publications—*Russkie Vedomosti* and *Vestnik Evropy*—and books.[257] Ianzhul maintained his interest in the United States, publishing a few years later a psychological interpretation that stressed labor efficiency, capital investment, and speed in the transfor-

254. Ianzhul, *Vospominaniia* 2:120–28.
255. Ibid., pp. 131–35.
256. Ibid., pp. 142–45. In writing the memoirs, Ianzhul relied heavily on letters that his wife wrote to her mother, so the quotations are probably her words.
257. Ibid., pp. 146–48; Allen, *Russia Looks at America*, pp. 204–12.

mation and development of a nation—a model he concluded would have a tremendous impact on backward areas such as Asia.[258]

Sergei Volkonskii also stayed throughout most of the exposition and beyond but, in contrast to Ianzhul, spent most of his time socializing with (and studying) the North Shore elite—the Palmers, Pullmans, and McVeahys. Thanks to them, he became a popular after-dinner speaker at aristocratic gatherings.[259] The Russian presence at the fair continued through its closing at the end of October. Just how many of the 27.5 million recorded visitors examined the Russian exhibits is unknown, but one could hardly miss them. "Russia has impressed its individuality so strongly upon all the exhibits over which its colors wave in the Columbian Exposition that it would be no difficult matter to pick them out [even] if they were not especially designated as belongings of the Czar."[260] They also had a lasting influence, as most items and duplicates were sold.[261] One example is the acquisition by the Smithsonian Institution of a large piece of rock salt that was made into a natural seven-inch lens and inspired a search over several years for even larger specimens.[262] A connection may also be found between the exposition, especially in Volkonskii's social contacts, and the creation of a center of Russian studies at the University of Chicago a few years later.

Russian Naval Visit and Grand Duke Alexander

Russia also readily accepted an invitation to participate in an international naval review in conjunction with the Columbian festivities. The main problem, as mentioned, was getting the ships out of the Baltic in time for assem-

258. I. I. Ianzhul, *Iz psikhologii narodov (ekonomicheskoe znachenie 'vremeni' i prostranstva')* (Odessa: Isakovich, 1895).
259. Volkonskii, *Moi Vospominaniia* (Munich: Mednyi Vsadnik, 192?), pp. 251–61. To illustrate the American work ethic, Volkonskii related on page 257 a conversation with Pullman (spelling as in original): "Why dont you give up business, Mr. Pulman, and take up a hoby?" "But business is my hoby." Volkonskii credited his social and cultural success to Andrew White's letters of introduction; Volkonskii (San Francisco) to White, 20 December 1893, roll 61, White Papers, Cornell University.
260. "Czar Land Treasure," Chicago *Tribune*, 24 July 1893, p. 8.
261. This was one of the inducements for all exhibitors and caused problems over customs rulings that forbade early sale of duplicates. The indefinite closing date for the exposition also led to a one-day Russian strike. "Russians Are Angry," Chicago *Tribune*, 21 July 1893, p. 1; and "Russia's Storm Over," ibid., 22 July 1893, p. 4.
262. See correspondence between Herbert H. D. Pierce and J. P. Langley, box 52, RG 31, SA.

Grand Duke Alexander Mikhailovich (in white), with Russian officers and clergy, New York, 1893. Harper's Weekly, *22 July 1893, courtesy of the Kansas Collection, University of Kansas Libraries*

bly at Hampton Roads in May.[263] Of the three ships initially dispatched, the *General Admiral* and *Rynda* arrived in time to join a promenade of thirty-five ships to New York. The flagship *Dmitri Donskoi*, commanded by Vice-admiral Nikolai Kaznakov, met them off Sandy Hook, allowing full participation by the Russian officers and crews in the review by President Cleveland and the celebratory dinners and balls, including one for the sailors at Madison Square Garden.[264] Heading the Russian official party was the polished and sophisticated Grand Duke Alexander Mikhailovich, the tsar's nephew. Of the group, Kaznakov was familiar with America, having attended a maritime conference in Washington in 1889.[265]

The admiral and grand duke, accompanied by several junior officers, visited Washington, where they participated in a number of social occasions in-

263. White to Foster, 2 February 1893, DUSM, Russia, vol. 44 (roll 44, M 35), RG 59, NA.

264. Kantakuzen to Shishkin, 24 April/6 May 1893, f. 133, op. 470, d. 101 (1893), AVPR.

265. Aleksandr Mikhailovich was twenty-seven at the time, the son of the youngest brother of Alexander II. He later married a cousin, Grand Duchess Xenia, a daughter of Alexander III, thus becoming the brother-in-law of Nicholas II. They had several children from whom descend one of the two surviving lines of the Romanov dynasty.

cluding an informal breakfast with the president.[266] Accompanied by minister Kantakuzen and joined by the *Dmitri Donskoi* and *Rynda* in the Chesapeake Bay, the official party made a formal call at Philadelphia to present honors and gifts to the leaders of famine relief—Talmage, Klopsch, Blankenburg, Reeves, Biddle, Drexel, Edgar, and Hubbell. The ceremony on 15 May, the tenth anniversary of the tsar's coronation, featured words of thanks from Kantakuzen, a full salute from the *Rynda*, hymns from the Russian sailors' chorus, and fireworks and illuminations at night.[267] In June the grand ducal party made a quiet, incognito visit to the fair in Chicago.[268]

The Russian squadron, augmented by three more modern ships, used New York for its base of operations for the summer and drew much social and press attention. "Each of these vessels is a model of the most modern pattern of construction, and in their own class they present the finest examples of the ships of the third naval power in the world."[269] The grand duke, admiral, ranking officers, and Consul General Olarovskii kept ferries busy carrying them to the Butterfield, Roosevelt, Vanderbilt, and other summer homes along the Hudson, where they consumed the best that America had to offer, including fifty-year-old Kentucky bourbon.[270] The visit concluded with a week-long series of social rounds at Newport in August and a departure escort of a fleet of yachts. Perhaps summing up the atmosphere, one officer voiced a common refrain to a reporter from the New York *Times*: "You have your Wild West. We have our Wild East. You are settling up and developing the Wild West. We are doing likewise with our Wild East. Soon your Wild West and our Wild East will meet."[271]

Nor did the American dream escape Grand Duke Alexander. As he later recalled:

266. Kantakuzen to Shishkin, 1/13 May 1893, f. 133, op. 470, d. 101 (1893), AVPR.
267. Kantakuzen to Shishkin, 12/24 May and 19/31 May 1893, f. 133, op. 470, d. 101, AVPR; Kantakuzen to Blankenburg, 27 May 1893, case 19, box 14, Society misc.—Blankenburg Papers, HSP. Edgar deserved and received "first prize," an enameled tea set, especially for his book, which was widely circulated in Russia; Crawford to Edgar, 12 April 1893, and Kantakuzen to Edgar, 1 April 1893, box 7, Edgar Papers, MinnHS.
268. "As Lieut. Romanoff," Chicago *Tribune*, 20 June 1893, p. 9. Russian minister Kantakuzen also made a fact-finding tour with several Russian dignitaries in July and August that included stops in San Francisco, Minneapolis (to pay respects to Edgar and visit the Holly Flour Mill), and Chicago; Kantakuzen to Edgar, 9 July and 29 September 1893, box 7, Edgar Papers, MinnHS.
269. Griboedov, "Our Russian Visitors," *Harper's Weekly*, 22 July 1893, p. 688.
270. New York *Times*, 11, 13, 15, 16, 17 July 1893; Julia Butterfield, ed., *A Biographical Memorial of General Daniel Butterfield Including Many Addresses and Military Writings* (New York,: Grafton Press, 1904), pp. 195–96.
271. 17 July 1893, p. 1.

What was the matter with us? Why did we not follow the American way of doing things? We had no business bothering with Europe and imitating the methods befitting nations forced by their poverty to live off their wits. . . .

Here, four thousand miles away from the cockpit of European strife, stood a living example of possibilities akin to ours, if we would only put a little common sense into our policies!

Right then and there, during the remaining few minutes of my ride [up Fifth Avenue] in 1893, I commenced working out a large plan for the Americanization of Russia.[272]

In concert with a number of his countrymen, he would seek a new road to America through Asia.

The Siberian Railroad

The idea of an eastern connection with the United States was not new but was being given special emphasis in 1892 and 1893 by the Russian government's plans to build a railroad across Siberia to link European Russia with Vladivostok and other points in the Far East. Since the suspension of construction of the telegraph line from the American West Coast to Siberia—through Alaska and across the Bering Strait—the idea of a trans-Siberian communications link had been periodically revived. Contributing to this was the continued expansion and successful development of long-distance railroads, which had become the defining symbol of both agricultural settlement and industrial development. The United States was the archetype.

The Siberian railroad thus had American roots. One of the first to encourage it was Pavel Mel'nikov, who had toured the United States, brought George Washington Whistler to Russia, helped him superintend the first long-distance railroad from St. Petersburg to Moscow, and launched the Russian side of the telegraph project. After serving several years as minister of transportation in the 1860s, he published an article, "On a Siberian Railroad," in 1869.[273] Another pioneer promoter also had ample opportunity to experience the American transcontinental achievement. Admiral Konstantin Pos'et, minister of transportation from 1874 to 1888, had accompanied

272. Alexander, *Once a Grand Duke* (New York: Farrar and Rinehart, 1932), p. 123.
273. Mikhail Voronin and Margarita Voronina, *Pavel Petrovich Mel'nikov, 1804–1880* (Leningrad: Nauka, 1977), pp. 91–96.

Grand Duke Alexis on his storybook excursion across the country as far west as Cheyenne and Denver in 1872. Part of his assignment was to collect information on the connection between water and rail transportation and industrial and agricultural development. As early as 1875 he submitted the first comprehensive plan to develop Siberia by means of railroads. Pos'et's projected northern line through the Urals was stalled by proponents of a more southern route, led by Aleksandr Abaza, another railroad advocate who served as director of state economics in the Ministry of Finance.[274] Other obstacles were the obsession with accomplishing internal reforms smoothly, the interference of foreign affairs, and especially the Russo-Turkish War of 1877–1878. These all caused strains to the country's finances.

Pos'et revived his plan in 1884, but this time met strong opposition from the conservative minister of finance, Ivan Vyshnegradskii. There was some concern about the potential for disruptions to law and order, such as the view of the Ministry of Interior that facilitating the movement of people was dangerous to the state, especially in Siberia, which was prized for its remoteness. Another, more sensible argument was that the focus should be on expanding the lines in European Russia.[275] Pos'et had support from General Mikhail Annenkov, who had just supervised the successful completion of a railroad from the Caspian Sea to Samarkand and argued that one through Siberia could be built cheaper and faster than previously thought.

Although Pos'et, one of the few administrators to survive the 1881 transition, resigned his post because of an accident to the imperial train in 1888, the trans-Siberian concept was pushed by his successors, Adolf Giubbenet and Sergei Witte. The initially poor response of Russia's railroads to famine relief forced Giubbenet's departure and brought Witte, a dynamic railroad man, to the fore. He, Annenkov, and Pos'et, combined with the famine and prospects of improved finances through French-backed loans, convinced Alexander III in 1892 that the time for a Siberian railroad had finally come.

274. Steven G. Marks, *Road to Power: The Trans-Siberian Railroad and the Colonization of Asian Russia, 1850–1917* (Ithaca, N.Y.: Cornell University Press, 1991), pp. 64–67. For a less scholarly and more popular account, with pictures, see Harmon Tupper, *To the Great Ocean: Siberia and the Trans-Siberian Railway* (Boston: Little, Brown, 1965).

275. Although Russia had been building new railroads in the 1870s and 1880s, it was still behind not only the United States but also the other major European powers, in terms of total system and rate of expansion. In 1890 Russia had 30,600 kilometers of lines; the United States had 251,700, Germany 41,800, France 36,900, and Britain 32,300. Aida M. Solov'eva, *Zheleznodoroshnyi transport Rossii vo vtoroi polovine XIX v.* (Moscow: Nauka, 1975), p. 231.

Witte's shift in August from transportation to finance minister gave him added leverage.

The next question was who would build it, and the immediate and obvious answer was—Americans. After all, they helped build Russia's first major railroad and had the most transcontinental rail experience. And Russia was currently importing a substantial number of locomotives from the United States. In fact, as early as 1888 in Paris, Annenkov had mentioned this possibility to Wharton Barker, Philadelphia financier and an old friend to Russia, and rumors had circulated about it in the American press.[276] Negotiations resumed in late June 1892 between Annenkov, Frederick Holls, and Colonel T. Wilkin Cragg, a consulting engineer. Holls cabled the news to his friend Barker, who was receptive to a proposal for "an imperial concession."[277] As Holls explained in a follow-up letter, "It seems that the Czar is very anxious to have the road built at once, and he would prefer to give the concession to an *American*."[278]

Because of previous business frustrations with Russia, however, Barker wanted a firm contract guaranteed by substantial government bonds and set off for St. Petersburg to negotiate directly. "I know the Russians and business habits better than most men do and I know that exact conditions must be made and agreed to and signed under Imperial seal to make it safe to embark in business with them or under them."[279] He took on a Scottish-Russian partner, George Baird, to organize a Russian syndicate that would have a one-third share in the project, a more acceptable arrangement to the Russian government than one that was exclusively American.[280]

The crucial problem now was financing, and the promoters quickly found themselves in a Catch-22. The Russian government did not want to issue a clearly defined concession without proof of investment capability, and fi-

276. George S. Queen, "Wharton Barker and Concessions in Imperial Russia, 1878–1892," *Journal of Modern History* 17, 3 (September 1945): 205; *Leslie's Illustrated*, 24 November 1888, p. 235.

277. Holls to Barker (t), and Barker to Holls (c), 4 July 1892, box 6, Barker Papers, LC.

278. To Barker, 5 July 1892, ibid.

279. Barker to Holls, 11 July 1892, ibid.

280. Baird's Alexandrovskii steel works (the former Winans operation, which Baird had purchased from the government for iron and steel production) had been a major supplier of rails by government contract, helping Russia reduce its dependency on imports from 80 percent in the 1870s to around 20 percent in the 1880s. Solov'eva, *Zheleznodoroshnyi*, p. 135; John P. McKay, *Pioneers for Profit: Foreign Entrepreneurship and Russian Industrialization, 1885–1913* (Chicago and London: University of Chicago Press, 1970), pp. 41, 114.

nanciers did not want to commit such sums without a definite concession. As Barker wrote Baird,

> It is a hard task to get large sums of money, almost an impossible task, when the conditions of the concession are uncertain and the terms are still in doubt. . . . The Russian gentlemen in the Syndicate and in the Government also should see this and an immediate effort should be made to get an answer from the Imperial Russian Government that the concession will be granted at once when we show where the money is coming from.[281]

Back in the United States, Barker was frustrated by the reluctance of American capitalists, led by Elliot Shephard and the Vanderbilts, to make advance commitments and by indications from Baird that Russian investors were also having cold feet. "The whole enterprise is in great danger of being brought to ruin on both sides of the Atlantic because the Russians will not trust you and me as concessionaires. . . . It can be carried only as an American enterprise, whether Capital is to be found in Europe or in America."[282] One annoying difficulty was an inability to secure funds for "preliminary expenses"—the bribes, payoffs, and so forth that were the costs of doing business with Russia. As one historian has observed, "The red tape of bureaucracy and privilege in Russia had proved too thick."[283]

But other factors played a part in the failure of an American-built Siberian railroad. American investors, mindful of Jewish persecution and Siberian exiles, were wary of adverse publicity, especially when safer and more lucrative investments could be found elsewhere. Barker was not devoting full attention to the venture, since he was very much involved in Republican convention politics during the summer of 1892. Most important, Witte's new position of strength in the fall of that year, not only serving as finance minister but clearly having the tsar's absolute confidence, took the project in another direction—government financing and construction. By the end of October the American investment proposal was collapsing. Baird cabled Barker on 14 November: "Our contract with Russian syndicate cancelled."[284] A week later, Alexander III appointed a Siberian Railroad Committee, to oversee construction; it was headed by Grand Duke Nicholas.

281. Barker (London) to Baird, 6 September 1892 (c), box 6, Barker Papers, LC.
282. Barker (Philadelphia) to Baird, 4 October 1892, ibid.
283. Queen, "Wharton Barker," p. 213.
284. Baird to Barker, 14 November 1892 (t), box 6, Barker Papers, LC.

Other American overtures were firmly refused. Responding to a private inquiry from William Edgar early in 1894, Andrei Bobrinskoi wrote, "The railway is being built exclusively by the russian government on government money, with russian material, by engineers on government service, that is why I believe that it is most probable that the offer of the American railway construction will be declined."[285] Finally, in answer to a direct query, Witte flatly informed the American minister that the government would construct the railroad.[286]

Americans, nevertheless, would perceive the great Trans-Siberian Railway as a stepchild, the image of their own imperial destiny. Andrew White believed in the committee's announcement that the road would be "a work of peace and civilization in the East" and compared it directly to American manifest destiny.[287] His successor, in reporting on early progress, concluded, "That this great railway system is destined to open up a country of great richness cannot, in the light of present knowledge, be doubted."[288] The display of the plans in Chicago inspired the Transportation Museum (later the Museum of Science and Industry) to commission a much-publicized expedition across Siberia by Joseph Pangborn during the winter of 1895–1896.[289] And in the American press no railroad ever received so much free advertising, reaching a point of overkill with an extended series by Thomas Allen.[290]

The North Pacific

Publicity about Russia's rail extension eastward helped turn American eyes westward into the Pacific and to its own last frontier in Alaska.[291] There the Bering Sea controversy over sealing still simmered. The American view,

285. Bobrinskoi to Edgar, 12/24 February 1894, box 1, Edgar Papers, MinnHS (with original spelling).

286. Breckinridge to Witte, 21 November/3 December 1894 (c), DPR, Russia, vol. 4538 (notes sent); Witte to Breckinridge, 24 November/6 December 1894, DPR, Russia, vol. 4511 (notes received), RG 84, NA.

287. White to Foster, 16 February 1893, DUSM, Russia, vol. 44 (roll 44, M 35), RG 59, NA.

288. Breckinridge to Olney, 14 October 1895, DUSM, Russia, vol. 47 (roll 47, M 35), RG 59, NA.

289. Breckinridge to Shishkin, 23 November/5 December 1894, DPR, Russia, vol. 4538 (notes sent); and Pangborn (Vladivostok) to Breckinridge, 10 October 1895, DPR, Russia, vol. 4449 (misc. received), RG 84, NA.

290. Beginning naturally with "The Great Siberian Railway," the series included "The New Siberia," "A Siberian City," "Siberian Aborigines," "The Siberian Soldiery and Barracks," and "Peasant Farming in Siberia."

291. For example, Alson L. Baily to Kantakuzen, 9 March 1893, f. 133, op. 512/2, d. 62, AVPR, who boasted, "The time is coming when the two governments of Russia and America is [sic] to dominate the whole world."

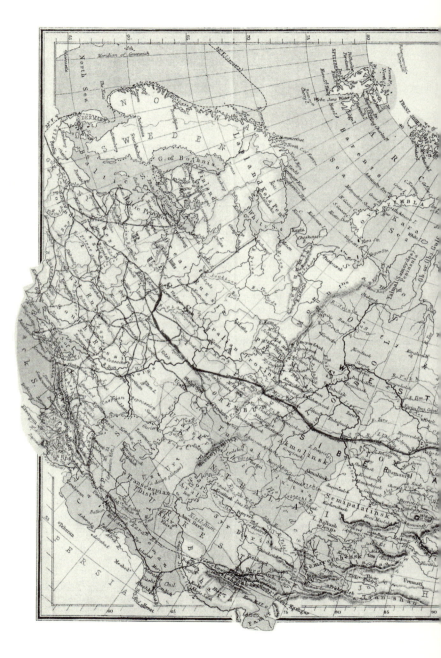

Trans-Siberian and Chinese Eastern Railroads, ca. 1900. In the author's collection

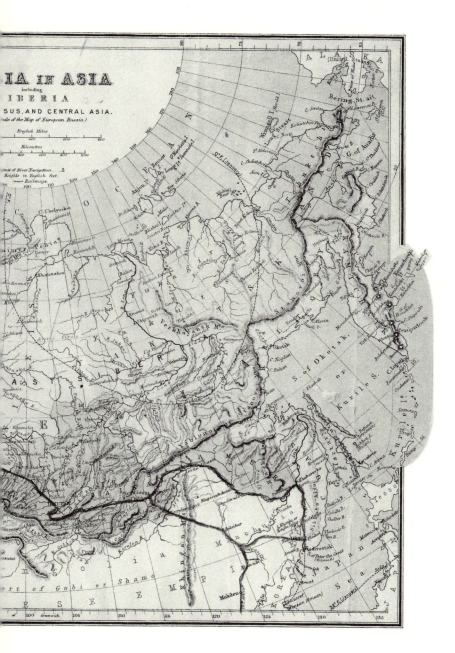

though inconsistently pursued through a rapid succession of secretaries of state from Bayard to Gresham,[292] was that the United States inherited through the purchase of Alaska and the accompanying Pribylov Islands a one-hundred-mile water right and a proprietary jurisdiction over the seals, wherever they might wander. It supported the principle of controlled hunting by the North American Commercial Company, whose profits from a new, twenty-year contract were in jeopardy. Britain and Canada stood for competitive enterprise and freedom of the seas, though they balked at a threatened extinction of the seals.[293]

Russia at first responded favorably to the American position, not only because of its own vested interest in sealing but also out of long-standing hostility to Britain. Roman Rosen, as Russian chargé d'affaires in Washington, drafted an agreement with Blaine in 1889 that would have provided for joint policing to protect the Bering Sea against interlopers, but it was opposed by legal counsel of the Ministry of Navy in St. Petersburg.[294] Thus did Russian bureaucratic procedures defeat an early effort to avoid arbitration.

In September 1892 Nikolai Grebnitskii, administrator of the Kommandorskii Islands, arrived in the United States vociferously complaining about Canadian intruders and their severe damage to the "Russian" herds, and he pressed for Russian support of the American position when he reached St. Petersburg.[295] At a time, therefore, that corresponded with famine relief shipments and the launching of the Trans-Siberian Railroad, Russia seemed prepared to cooperate with the United States in the Pacific. For example, Russia

292. Homer E. Socolofsky and Allan B. Spetter, *The Presidency of Benjamin Harrison* (Lawrence: University Press of Kansas, 1987), pp. 137–43; Matilda Gresham, *The Life of Walter Quintin Gresham, 1832–1895*, 2 vols. (Chicago: Rand, McNally, 1919), 2:717–33.

293. An investigation of the Pribylovs in 1890 by Henry Elliott found greater devastation of the herd than expected and indicated island hunting as partly responsible. Charles S. Campbell, Jr., "The Anglo-American Crisis in the Bering Sea," *Mississippi Valley Historical Review* 48, 3 (December 1961): 399–400; Herbert L. Aldrich, *Arctic Alaska and Siberia, or Eight Months with the Arctic Whalemen* (Chicago: Rand, McNally, 1889), pp. 48–51; William L. Counse, "The Bering Sea Controversy," *Harper's Weekly*, 28 February 1891, p. 164; "Seals Becoming Scarce," New York *Times*, 15 July 1892, p. 4. The new pelagic hunting also encouraged smuggling on both sides of the Bering Sea.

294. Rosen, *Forty Years of Diplomacy*, 2 vols. (New York: Alfred A. Knopf, 1922), 1:77–80.

295. Clipping from New York *Sun* of 30 September 1892 in Grebnitskii folder, f. 133, op. 512/1, d. 56, AVPR. Grebnitskii maintained that the indiscriminate killing of seals at sea not only was decimating the breeding population but was also producing crucial interruptions in the migratory patterns that in turn caused a significantly lower birth rate; White to Foster, 8 December 1892, DUSM, Russia, vol. 44 (roll 44, M 35), RG 59, NA.

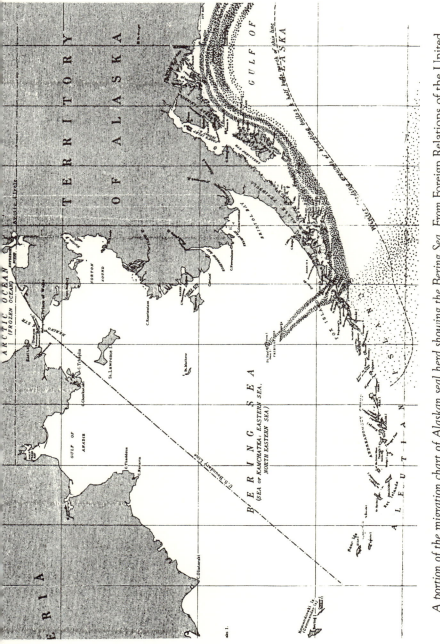

A portion of the migration chart of Alaskan seal herd showing the Bering Sea. From Foreign Relations of the United States (1893), courtesy of Government Documents Library, University of Kansas

was quick to respond positively to new American designs on the Hawaiian Islands.[296] This was in keeping with a traditionally close relationship between the two countries in Pacific naval affairs.[297]

Finally, in hopes of finding a solution to the sealing impasse and easing the mounting conflict with Britain, the United States agreed in 1892 to an arbitration conference. A commission of seven members (two from the United States, two from Britain, and one each from Italy, Sweden, and France) that notably excluded Russia met in Paris to undertake the almost impossible task of protecting at once maritime rights, business contracts, national interests, damage claims, and the seals.[298] While negotiations were under way, in early 1893 Russia proposed to Britain the establishment of a protective no-hunting zone of thirty miles around the islands as a *modus vivendi*; in return, Russia would back Britain's claims for compensation for the seized ships. The United States protested this Russian "betrayal," but Kantakuzen explained to Gresham that Russia was miffed about not being a party either to arbitration or to the development of the postulate that seals in open seas remained national property.[299] In St. Petersburg, Dmitri Kapnist of the Asiatic Department of the Foreign Ministry reassured the American minister that the agreement was only temporary, to prevent the immediate extinction of the herds.[300]

Although Britain pressed in Paris for a twenty-mile restricted hunting area around the islands, and the United States sought a one-hundred-mile limit, the arbitration settlement provided for a sixty-mile zone and the banning of hunting on the eastern side of the Bering Sea and north of 35° latitude during the summer months. It further ruled that compensation must be paid for losses entailed by the seizure of ships, the details to be worked

296. Kantakuzen to Shishkin, 16/28 February and 5/17 March 1893, f. 133, op. 470, d. 101, AVPR.

297. This cordiality included Pacific naval stations. Admiral William Emory wrote a Russian colleague in 1892 that he could count on seeing anything he wished if he visited the United States, because "we have no secrets from Russia, whom we gratefully remember, particularly our naval service." To Zinovi Rozhdestvenskii, 16 December 1892, in Rear Admiral Albert Gleaves, ed., *The Life of an American Sailor: William Helmsley Emory, from His Letters and Memoirs* (New York: George H. Doran, 1923), p. 159.

298. "Behring Sea Arbitration," New York *Tribune*, 1 March 1892, p. 1.

299. Gresham to John Foster, 14 July 1893, Foster Papers, LC; Webb to Gresham, 19 April 1894, DUSM, Russia, vol. 45 (roll 45, M 35), RG 59, NA. Another explanation for the change in Russian attitude is that Russia had similar grievances about the invasion of territorial waters by American whalers.

300. White to Foster (Paris), 17 March and 23 June 1893, DPR, Russia, vol. 4573 (letters sent), RG 84, NA.

out later between the parties concerned.[301] The American government was very unhappy with this outcome and continued its protests. Policing the agreement in such a large and foggy expanse of sea proved impossible, so the slaughter continued. By 1910 the herds were so depleted that hunting was no longer economically profitable, which saved the few remaining from extinction.

In his recollections of his diplomatic assignment in St. Petersburg, White blamed the defeat for the United States and the seals on the anti-American bias of Kapnist and of Nikolai Shishkin, a former minister to the United States who was in charge of the Foreign Ministry during Giers's illness. He also admitted the superior influence of the British ambassador, Sir Robert Morier, and the generally weak (financially and socially) position of American diplomatic service abroad, especially in Russia.[302] John Foster, who was in charge of presenting the American case in Paris, decried the crucial lack of Russian support but thought that the United States had not asserted a proprietary claim over the seals strongly enough.[303]

Alaska

Although the Alaska Territory was sadly neglected, by 1890 the American presence there was booming because of increased missionary activity, exploration, gold-seeking, and fishing. The United States government was finally allocating funds to improve the educational institutions and the economic viability of the natives of the region. Russia also stepped up its involvement. Through the influence of the powerful man behind the throne, Konstantin Pobedonostsev, by the 1890s Russia was providing direct support ($75,000 annually), appropriated by the State Council and augmented by a subsidy from the St. Petersburg Missionary Society, specifically for the Russian Orthodox church in Alaska and especially its schools and missions.[304] But Russia wanted the United States to assist financially, to restore stolen or lost

301. Foster (Paris) to White, 6 July 1893, DPR, Russia, vol. 4448 (misc. received), RG 84, NA.
302. White, *Autobiography of Andrew Dickson White*, 2 vols. (New York: N.p., 1905), 2:16–21.
303. Foster, *Diplomatic Memoirs*, 2 vols. (Boston: Houghton Mifflin, 1909), 2:46–50.
304. Metropolit Feofil, "Pravoslavie v Amerike," in *Iubileinyi sbornik v pamiat' 150–letiia russkoi pravoslavnoi tserkvi v Severnoi Amerike* (New York, 1944), pp. 123–26; Basil Bensen, *Russian Orthodox Church in Alaska, 1794-1967* (Sitka, Alaska: Russian Orthodox Church, 1967), pp. 57–59.

Nicholas, Bishop of North America, ca. 1900. From Iubileinyi Sbornik *(1934)*

church property, and to mediate differences with other missionaries, who
were descending on the area in force.

During his tenure from 1891 to 1898, Bishop Nicholas (Mikhail Ziorov)
was given wide latitude by the Holy Synod; considerably expanding the
number of priests, churches, and schools in Alaska, he also began a weekly
newspaper in both Russian and English.[305] However, Nicholas complained
that only Protestants were appointed as teachers in the new American "public" schools in Orthodox parishes. He was especially upset that the predomi-
nately Orthodox natives did not have American citizenship but endured
the same disadvantaged status as reservation Indians in the rest of the
United States. In 1898 he wrote directly to President McKinley protesting

305. Bishop Gregory (Afonsky), *A History of the Russian Orthodox Church in Alaska,
1794–1917* (Kodiak, Alaska: St. Herman's Seminary Press, 1977), pp. 83–86. Nicholas
became a prominent Russian clergyman as archbishop of Tver, bishop of Warsaw, and a
member of the State Duma after 1905.

that they were at the mercy of American commercial and religious inter-ests.[306] After receiving a communication from Pobedonostsev on these sub-jects, the American minister warned the administration in a private letter; "The Procurator General, is universally recognized, not only in Russia but throughout Europe, as a man possessing a very high degree of influence, per-haps, indeed more influence than any other person with the Emperor."[307] Although not the only factor, Russian pressure was certainly an important reason for increased American attention to the North Pacific territories.

The projects of Sheldon Jackson, veteran Presbyterian missionary and newly named federal commissioner of education for Alaska, continued apace in the 1890s. The importation of reindeer from Siberia, specifically aimed at developing the mainland Eskimo economy, began in 1892 and re-ceived additional government subsidies after 1894, not only for more rein-deer but also for stations manned by Lapps from Finland and Sweden to in-struct the Eskimo in reindeer husbandry. By 1900 an impressive 3,323 reindeer were counted in western Alaska, but the program achieved mixed results in improving Eskimo livelihood. In fact, epidemics of diseases such as measles and influenza, brought by the newcomers, reduced the population of Eskimo villages so much that they could not maintain the deer and left them vulnerable to wild dogs.[308]

Publicity about church and government activities in Alaska enticed more visitors, especially those with missionary or social welfare impulses, which in turn created even more general literature.[309] The rise of cheap and easy pho-tography boosted Alaskan visibility. Harvard historian John Fiske, for one, visited Alaska in June 1892, brought back many photographs, and gave lec-tures on its potential.[310] And Alaska, ignored at Philadelphia in 1876, was given prominence in government exhibits at the Columbian Exposition. Americans were finally beginning to recognize Alaska as an integral part of the United States.

306. Ibid., p. 85.
307. White to Gresham, 12 September 1894, enclosing a copy of Nikolai's report of 7/19 June 1894, DUSM, Russia, vol. 46 (roll 46, M 35), RG 59, NA. The bishop com-plained specifically about the anti-Orthodox bias of Sheldon Jackson.
308. Sheldon Jackson, *Tenth Annual Report on Introduction of Reindeer into Alaska . . . 1900* (Washington, D.C.: Government Printing Office, 1901), pp. 10–27; Jackson to Breckinridge, 20 August 1895, DPR, Russia, vol. 4449 (misc. received), RG 84, NA.
309. For example, Abby Johnson Woodman, *Picturesque Alaska* (Boston: Houghton Mifflin, 1889), and Eliza Scidmore, *Appleton's Guide Book to Alaska* (New York: D. Ap-pleton, 1893).
310. Clark, *Life and Letters of Fiske* 2:445; Fiske to his mother, 27 May 1892, in Fisk, *Letters of Fiske*, p. 608.

Learning Russian

The increased contacts and the heightened interest and exposure to Russian culture finally produced the first proposals for serious academic studies. Probably the Tolstoy craze supplied the most important impetus, since one of the writer's closest American acquaintances and translators broached the issue in 1892. Picking up on a suggestion in *Book News* that a chair in Slavonic studies be established, Isabel Hapgood argued that the easiest and quickest way to achieve this was to hire a professor from St. Petersburg, Moscow, or Kiev who spoke English. "There is not a single man in this country who is fitted to fill that chair even creditably. . . . Moreover, it demands a speaking and writing knowledge of Russian such as no American man possesses."[311]

Nathan Haskell Dole supported the idea of a professorship but argued in favor of an American's superior ability to teach and inspire. "Would not an American who had been educated several years in Russia be better qualified to do good work in these branches [teaching and research] than a Russian who would be disqualified from writing idiomatic English."[312] He suggested that Jeremiah Curtin would be an ideal candidate. Leo Wiener, a Russian-Jewish immigrant with a university education (Warsaw), then teaching in a Kansas City high school, joined the fray, declaring that "the Russian language is not such a bugbear as some would like to make it; it is scarcely more difficult than Greek."[313] He suggested as a candidate William Morfill of Oxford, who had recently written a Russian grammar.[314]

Hapgood retorted that Morfill's work was of poor quality and pointed out another prerequisite for Russian studies—a library. Only Harvard, Yale, and Cornell could qualify.[315] Dole, on the other hand, saw an opportunity in the innovative program being introduced at the University of Chicago and interested its new president, William Rainey Harper, in a center (with more

---

311. Hapgood, "A Russian Professorship," *Nation* 54, 1407 (16 June 1892): 447.
312. "The Russian Professorship," *Nation* 54, 1409 (30 June 1892): 484.
313. Ibid., p. 485.
314. Ibid.; William Morfill, *A Grammar of the Russian Language* (Oxford: Clarendon Press, 1889). Morfill also published many editions of popular books on Russia and Poland, as well as grammars for other Slavic languages. For a critical review, see *Nation* 49, 1271 (7 November 1889): 377.
315. "The Russian Professorship," *Nation* 55, 1411 (14 July 1892): 29. A few other universities were making a start, such as the University of Illinois.

than one professor) of Slavic studies. Harper approached John D. Rockefeller for funding, but nothing came of this for the time being.[316]

Two other circumstances governed the race for the first formal course of study in Russian. Travel and broadening expertise in their fields had inspired a number of faculty members in a variety of subjects to acquire some knowledge of the Russian language; this seemed to be particularly the case at Yale, which, at the beginning of the 1890s, probably had the best university library of Russian books and maps.[317] Another factor was the flight of faculty from Slavic Europe. A case in point was Alexander Herdler, a German from Bohemia who had attended the University of Prague and had become an instructor of modern languages at Princeton. Speaking Czech and observing the expanded interest in Slavic literature, he consulted the Russian minister in 1895 about studying Russian at the University of St. Petersburg with the goal of introducing Russian language courses in the United States.[318]

Migration from Eastern Europe was integral to the development of Slavic studies in the United States in another respect—library acquisition and management, as embodied by Alexis Babine (Aleksei Babin). Receiving a Master's degree from the Sorbonne in 1893, he served as a librarian at Cornell (1893–1896), Indiana University (1896–1898), and Stanford (1898–1901), before becoming in 1902 the founder and director of the Slavic Division of the Library of Congress. There he consolidated and made available a variety of Russian language collections and was instrumental in the purchase of new materials from abroad.[319] Acting in a mentor capacity, when he returned to Russia for the summer of 1894, Babine took Cornell student Jerome Landfield with him to study the language and people.[320]

Another method of inspiring academic interest in Russia was to host guest lecturers from Russia. One appeared in Boston in October 1893, prob-

---

316. Albert Parry, *America Learns Russian: A History of the Teaching of the Russian Language in the United States* (Syracuse, N.Y.: Syracuse University Press, 1967), pp. 46–47.

317. W. G. Sumner (New Haven) to Lothrop, 19 March 1888, DPR, Russia, vol. 4443 (misc. received), RG 84, NA. Sumner, a professor of political science, was asking for books on the Russian social and economic system, which suggests that he had learned Russian; there were already three scholars on the Yale faculty with that ability.

318. Parry, *America Learns Russian*, pp. 47–48; Herdler to Breckinridge, 21 January 1895, DPR, Russia, vol. 4449 (misc. received), RG 84, NA.

319. Vita, dated February 1924, box 1, Babine Papers, LC.

320. Landfield (Tambov) to White, 5/17 August 1894, roll 62, White Papers, Cornell University.

ably a holdover from the exposition.[321] More extensive were the lectures of Sergei Volkonskii, whose appearances at Cornell University in the fall of 1893 were arranged by White. Citing a letter from Jacob Gould Schurman, one of his successors as president of Cornell, White assured Minister of Education Ivan Delianov:

> The Prince's lectures are doing a good service, both for our own country and for Russia. It is important for us Americans to escape from provincialism and to realize that other nations are also taking their part in the work of civilization. But the lectures are perhaps of still more importance for Russia, as they give authoritative information among the chosen youth of a people of sixty-five million regarding the conditions and work of a country of which we remain in the greatest ignorance, and on which there are no lectures given at our universities.[322]

White also sent many parcels of books for the Cornell library, but he had a particular fascination with bells. He shipped a 400-pound Russian bell from Moscow to the university, and beginning in the summer of 1894, its ringing announced the library's closing time.[323]

As it happened, Harvard University was the first to inaugurate regular courses in Russian. Professor Francis Child, an expert on English and Scottish ballads, became interested in collecting Slavic folksongs and realized the need for a colleague with the appropriate language skills. Meanwhile, Dole continued to press the case, now shifting from Chicago to his alma mater: "Ought not Harvard University to have the honor of establishing the first chair of Russian language and literature on this continent?"[324] At about the same time, the university hired a new instructor of history, Archibald Cary Coolidge, who had been a secretary at the legation in Russia (1890–1891), had toured the country extensively, and had gained some knowledge of the language. In Russia he also met budding Russianist Charles R. Crane and won his moral, and perhaps financial, backing.[325] In 1894 Coolidge introduced the first regular history course that concentrated on

321. Fiske to his son James, 27 October 1893, in Fisk, *Letters of Fiske*, p. 625.

322. White to Delianov, 10/22 June 1894 (c), DPR, Russia, vol. 4538 (notes sent), RG 84, NA. Schurman described the lectures as "a great delight and profit"; to White, 6 December 1893, roll 61, White Papers, Cornell University. For the scope of Voldonskii's speeches, see his *Addresses* (Chicago: J. C. Winship, 1893).

323. White to George Burr, 14 May 1894, roll 61, White Papers, Cornell University.

324. Dole, "A Plea for the Study of Russian," *Harvard Graduate's Magazine* 3, 10 (December 1894): 184.

325. Coolidge to Crane, 8 March (Vienna) and 27 March (Cambridge) 1894, box 2, Crane Papers, BA, Columbia University.

Sergei Volkonskii. From Volkonskii, Pictures of
Russian History and Russian Literature *(1897)*

Russia.[326] The next year Wiener, who by then was teaching Germanic and Romance languages at the University of Missouri, came to Boston to study at the public library. Child and Coolidge secured his appointment to teach the first Russian language course at Harvard in 1896.[327] A contemporary source indicated that one rationale was that "our relations with Russia give promise of being somewhat closer than they have in the past," citing specifically the building of

326. Coolidge, "A Plea for the Study of the History of Northern Europe," *American Historical Review* 2, 1 (October 1896): 34–39; Robert F. Byrnes, *Awakening American Education to the World: The Role of Archibald Cary Coolidge, 1866–1928* (Notre Dame, Ind.: University of Notre Dame Press, 1982), pp. 52–53. It was fitting that Coolidge was a direct descendant of Thomas Jefferson's, since Jefferson had promoted the first official diplomatic correspondence with Russia; Harold Jefferson Coolidge and Robert Howard Lord, *Archibald Cary Coolidge: Life and Letters* (Boston: Houghton Mifflin, 1932), p. 3.

327. Parry, *America Learns Russian*, pp. 50–53; Byrnes, *Awakening American Education*, pp. 110–11; "Russian in American Universities," editorial note in *Independent* 75, 3376 (14 August 1913): 401.

*Archibald Cary Coolidge. From Harold J. Coolidge and
Robert H. Lord,* Archibald Cary Coolidge: Life and
Letters *(1932)*

the Siberian railroad.[328] With job security and institutional support, Wiener was soon in Russia acquiring books for the library.[329]

Interest, scholarship, and philanthropy worked hand in hand in advancing Russian studies in the United States. Ambassador Charlemagne Tower spent money and energy for an extensive collection of books for his hometown university in Philadelphia.[330] Within a decade a number of institutions were offering courses in Russian with qualified teachers: University of California–Berkeley, 1901 (George Rapall Noyes, a student of Wiener's, who

328. "This Busy World," *Harper's Weekly,* 18 April 1896, p. 402.
329. Wiener to Hitchcock, 20 June 1898, DPR, Russia, vol. 4455 (misc. received), RG 84, NA. Despite his conversion to Unitarianism, Wiener had difficulties getting a visa for Russia.
330. Sharlemain Tauer, *Katalog russkikh knig prinesennyi v dar universitetu v Pennsel'vanii* (St. Petersburg: N.p., 1902).

had also attended the University of St. Petersburg for two years);[331] University of Chicago, 1901 (Xenophon Kalamatiano); University of Wisconsin, 1907; University of Michigan, 1908 (Clarence Meader); and Johns Hopkins University, 1910 (Franklin Edgerton).[332] This paved the way for more Russian academic visitors, such as Prince Peter Kropotkin (Harvard, 1901) and Paul Miliukov (Chicago, 1903). Frederic Austin Ogg, who pioneered the study of Russia at Indiana University, predicted that within twenty years knowledge of Russian would be as important as French.[333] Perhaps one anonymous observer was correct, "that an essentially new art has arisen in modern times, the art of understanding peoples. . . . Emergence from this habit of treating Russia as a Scythian country rich in Slavonian marvels has naturally been slow, but the process has proved not less certain than that of growing civilization and the progressive unification of the nations."[334] It would still be a long struggle.

Kennan Reprise

George Kennan, still the leading American expert on Russia, made no direct contribution to the establishment of academic studies of that country. Moreover, two definite attitudes toward Russia had become apparent: one characterized by Kennan, and the other, a more sympathetic view arising from the interaction with famine relief, the exposition, and Russian studies. The two views naturally led to some confusion and contradiction in American perceptions and an effort to find a middle ground. As Victor Yarros wrote, "It must be constantly borne in mind that Russian life represents an anomalous compromise between civilization and barbarism, between western ideas and oriental habits of thought and feeling."[335]

Kennan, meanwhile, published little on Russia between 1893 and 1903, and nothing for the *Century* after his response to Botkin's "Voice" in 1893. He continued to make a living on the lecture circuit at home and in Britain

---

331. Alexander Kaun and Ernest J. Simmons, *Slavic Studies* (Ithaca, N.Y.: Cornell University Press, 1943), p. 229.

332. Parry, *America Learns Russian*, pp. 53–62; Uzzell, "Russian in American Universities," p. 401.

333. Ogg, "The Rise of the Russian Nation," *Chautauquan* 36, 3 (December 1902): 239.

334. "A Study of Russia," *Atlantic Monthly* 73, 436 (February 1894): 269.

335. "The Russian Periodical Press," *Chautauquan* 18, 5 (February 1894): 545.

(November–December 1893). On 24 November 1895 he wrote from Chicago to a friend that he had filled nineteen engagements in a month and had seventeen more to go.[336] Apparently, these were on the same themes as before, for he answered one inquiry that his best lectures were 1) camp life in Siberia, 2) mountains and mountaineers of the Caucasus, and 3) Siberian convict mines, in that order.[337] It is interesting that the most provocative was last.

But if Kennan himself was less active, he had powerful allies to carry on the work. James Buel issued an updated version of his attack on the Russian government, predicting that a great power struggle between the United States and Russia would culminate in the breakup of the empire.[338] One of the most influential critics was Mark Twain, whose anti-autocratic populism focused on Russia and intensified over the years. His sarcastic extremism is best illustrated by his advice "to keep the [Russian] throne vacant by dynamite until the day when candidates shall decline with thanks."[339] And from *Tom Sawyer Abroad* (1894) came the comment that Russia "ain't no more important in this world than Rhode Island is, and hasn't got half as much in it that's worth saving."[340] Even so, Twain maintained a curiosity and interest in the country.[341]

Jewish Emigration

Another concern that fed the hostile view of Russia was the fate of its Jewish population. Contrary to one interpretation, American interest was not drowned out by famine relief,[342] but it did become more diffuse and complex. Certainly many Americans were alarmed about the presence of an anarchist element among the new Russian Jewish immigrants; though the threat was greatly exaggerated, the attempted assassination of Henry Frick by a

---

336. To Phillips, 24 November 1895, Phillips-Meyers Papers, UNC.
337. Kennan to George Ramsay, 10 January 1898, Ramsay Papers, Duke University.
338. Buel, *A Nemesis of Misgovernment* (Philadelphia: Historical Publishing Company, 1900), pp. 539–43.
339. As quoted in Louis Budd, "Twain, Howells, and the Boston Nihilists," p. 355.
340. Ibid., p. 361.
341. Fischer, *Abroad with Mark Twain*, p. 143. According to one source, Twain planned to visit St. Petersburg in 1899 but became disgusted with European travel on a trip to Budapest; Herbert J. Hagerman, *Letters of a Young Diplomat* (Santa Fe, N. Mex.: Rydal Press, 1937), p. 102.
342. Spetter, "The United States, the Russian Jews and the Russian Famine," pp. 236–44.

Russian-Jewish immigrant in 1892 stood as a permanent reminder. Inhabitants of large cities, including many in established Jewish communities, continued to worry about the influx of such large numbers of Jewish immigrants, especially when the huge invasion of 1892 was followed by a troublesome economic depression. Riots, such as those that occurred in Chicago in April 1892, fueled the anxiety.[343]

Prompted by Washington and a barrage of letters from Oscar Straus,[344] Andrew White launched a thorough investigation of the Jewish Question in 1893. His detailed report was as balanced and objective as one could expect. He contended that Russia had placed no new restrictions on Jews but was enforcing previous edicts with more and more severity. Blaming this on the reactionary government and rising anti-Semitism, White found an irreconcilable difference in temperament between Russians and Jews. "The difficulty is that the life of the Israelite is marked by sobriety, self-denial, and foresight; and, whatever may be the kindly qualities ascribed to the Russian peasant—and they are many—these are rarely, if ever mentioned among them."[345] He saw "a complex of antipathies" driving Jews out of the country, particularly an intensified wave of Russification and reaction in the late 1880s and early 1890s that affected most non-Russian subjects.

Gresham's commentary on this report, however, betrayed a typical prejudice and self-righteousness on the American side:

It has been for some time evident that the measures adopted by the Imperial Government against the Jews, although professedly a domestic policy directly affecting the subjects of the Tsar, was calculated to injuriously affect the American people by abruptly forcing upon our shores a numerous class of immigrants destitute of resources and unfitted in many important respects for absorption into our body politic. And the continued enforcement of such harsh and inhuman measures, . . . necessarily driving to our shores large numbers of degraded and undesir-

343. For example, "Riotous Russian Refugees," Cleveland *Plain Dealer,* 23 April 1892, p. 8.

344. Straus had keen insight into the Jewish predicament. Admitting that occupations such as keepers of taverns and baths and moneylenders drew hostility, he believed that the Jews were forced into those positions by the authorities because they were the only people who could be trusted with the tasks. "Such is the sad lot of the Jews in Russia, that they are cursed for practices into which their persecution drove them." To White, 17 January 1893, roll 59, White Papers, Cornell University.

345. To Gresham, 6 July 1893, DUSM, Russia, vol. 45 (roll 45, M 35), RG 59, NA.

able persons who must in great measure be supported by our people, cannot be regarded as consistent with the friendship which the Russian Government has long professed for the United States.[346]

The invitation of the Statue of Liberty had apparently been lost on the secretary of state.

Despite repeated appeals, Russia would not mitigate its practices relating to its Jewish population. It did, however, initiate a new policy for American Jews, whether of Russian origin or not. Strict enforcement had already produced a number of troublesome cases and rising tensions between the two countries; the Russian government decided this could be solved by not issuing any visas to American Jews, a policy later extended to all foreign Jews. In February 1893 the Russian consul general in New York refused to grant a visa to Mrs. Minnie Lerin on the sole grounds that she was of the Jewish religion, thus opening the "passport question" that would embroil Russian-American relations for the next twenty years.[347]

When a protest was delivered to Kantakuzen in Washington, he assured the State Department that the consul was acting on instructions from St. Petersburg. William Wharton, acting secretary of state, wrote that this "presents a question as embarrassing as it is painful, when arising with a nation for whose government and people such intimate friendship has so long been manifested by the American nation." He stated that the United States cannot condone such a restriction: "The asserted right of territorial sovereignty over all sojourners in the Empire, has, to our deep regret, outweighed our friendly protests. His Majesty's Government, however, surely cannot expect the United States to acquiesce in the assumption of a religious inquisitorial function within our own borders, by a foreign agency, in a manner so repugnant to the national sense."[348] Although gallons of ink would be expended over clarifying and protesting this issue, it was probably never stated better than at the beginning.

To confuse matters, the religious restriction appeared to be in abeyance for a time. Even a prominent Philadelphia rabbi, Joseph Krauskopf, was not only admitted but allowed to tour Jewish communities in Ukraine and Poland during the summer of 1894. White had assured Witte, however, that

346. To White, 28 August 1893, DI, Russia, vol. 17 (roll 139, M 77), RG 59, NA.

347. Ann E. Healy, "Tsarist Anti-Semitism and Russian-American Relations," *Slavic Review* 42, 3 (Fall 1983): 415.

348. To White, 28 February 1893, DI, Russia, vol. 17 (roll 139, M 77), RG 59, NA.

Krauskopf was "absolutely non-fanatic."[349] As a progressive reformist, backed by influential American Jews, he discussed his plan for American financing of the resettlement of Jews elsewhere in Russia with Witte, Pobedonostsev, and Tolstoy in Moscow and expected to receive their approval.[350]

But the passport issue was revived in 1895. Fedor Osten-Saken, in a conversation with legation secretary Herbert Pierce, made it clear that any formal protest of a visa denial would meet with a firm rejection and rigid enforcement; otherwise, the policy would be applied moderately.[351] While continuing to argue that this violated the Constitution, Clifton Breckinridge, minister to Russia, feared that if pressed too hard Russia would refuse to issue visas to any Americans.[352] Aleksei Lobanov-Rostovsky, who succeeded Giers as foreign minister in 1895, stated, "The refusal of a visa is not at all an attack upon any established religion; it is the consequence of a foreign law of an administrative character, which only has its effect outside of the territory of the Union."[353] But Acting Secretary of State Alvey Adee disagreed, viewing the policy "in the light of an invidious discrimination tending to discredit and humiliate American Jews in the eyes of their fellow-citizens."[354] And so the debate went.

Russian officials tried to mollify the American opposition by allowing some discretion to consuls and pointing out that the decree of 26 March 1891, on which "the administrative practice" was based, made exceptions for prominent bankers, merchants, their staffs, and bona fide tourists.[355] Although unrelenting, Breckinridge admitted, "These conferences revealed the difficulty that even the most enlightened Russians have in realizing the nature of our institutions, and in separating a question of extraterritoriality from questions internal to themselves." But he continued to believe that "they reciprocate our desire to settle this matter in a way alike honorable and considerate to both countries." The Russians seemed mystified that a

349. Witte to White, 6/18 July 1894, DPR, Russia, vol. 4538 (notes sent), RG 84, NA.

350. White to Gresham, 9 August 1894, DUSM, Russia, vol. 46 (roll 46, M 35), RG 59, NA; White, *Autobiography* 2:34; Oscar Straus to White, 6 June 1894, and Krauskopf to White, 15/27 July (Odessa) and 15 September 1894 (Philadelphia), roll 62, White Papers, Cornell University.

351. Pierce to Uhl, 13 June 1895, PRFRUS 1895, p. 2; p. 1058.

352. To Osten-Saken, 24 June 1895, and to Olney, 24 July 1895, ibid., pp. 1062–64.

353. To Breckinridge, 26 June/8 July 1895, ibid., p. 1065.

354. To Breckinridge, 22 August 1895, ibid., p. 1067. The American side tended to ignore the fact that the restriction applied to all foreign Jews, not just American.

355. Lobanov-Rostovsky to Breckinridge, 12/24 August 1895, ibid., p. 1069.

real rival, Britain, did not object to the discriminatory policy but that a traditional friend did.[356]

It was probably frustration over this business that drove Breckinridge to exclaim at the end of a long dispatch on improving relations: "At the risk of repetition I will say that Russia is *semi*-Asiatic, the blemish of which is self adulation, and the weakness of which is to underestimate both its friends and its foes."[357] Acting Secretary of State Edwin Uhl harkened back to Wharton when he wrote that the essence of the problem was "the assumption by the agents of Russia in the United States of inquisitorial functions touching the religious faith of applicants for passports."[358]

To the charges of religious discrimination, Russian officials responded that Jews were being distinguished with special status as a national-cultural class, not as a religion. As Botkin had tried to explain in Washington,

[The Jew] is not homogeneous with us in Russia; he does not feel or desire solidarity with us. In Russia he is and remains a guest only, a guest from ancient times, and not an integral part of the community. . . . Our meek, ignorant, and easy-going peasantry fell under the control of the Jews, who, as a class, are far better educated and more thrifty, and have the aptitude for commerce and for money-getting which distinguishes their race everywhere.[359]

By extension, then, Russians would need to be protected from all Westerners—social protectionism to accompany economic protectionism. A number of American Jews, nevertheless, did visit Russia throughout these years by using false papers, by bribing notoriously corrupt officials on the Polish-German frontier, by special permission, or through Russian bureaucratic inefficiency or soft-heartedness.

The United States had its own passport problem. A number of immigrants stayed only long enough to obtain citizenship, then returned to Eu-

356. Breckinridge to Gresham, 24 July 1895, DUSM, Russia, vol. 47 (roll 47, M 35), RG 59, NA. To the acting foreign minister Breckinridge wrote as strongly as diplomatically feasible: "I trust that I have been able to make clear to Your excellency that my Government never can and never should consent to these practices. They humiliate . . . by invidious and disparaging distinctions, a class embracing many of its most honored and valuable citizens." Breckinridge to Olney, 6 December 1895, DUSM, Russia, vol. 48 (roll 48, M 35), RG 59, NA.

357. To Olney, 24 December 1895, ibid.

358. To Pierce, 23 October 1895, DI, Russia, vol. 17 (roll 139, M 77), RG 59, NA.

359. Botkin, "A Voice for Russia," enclosed in Kantakuzen to Giers, 1/13 February 1893, f. 133, op. 512/1, d. 62 (1893), AVPR.

rope under protection of an American passport. Russian officials claimed that some Russian Jews attempted to evade legal restrictions that way. The question of their passport renewal was a thorny one, since it hinged on an interpretation of motives and intent—if they planned to return to the United States or if they were pursuing and advancing an American interest abroad. The much-publicized case of David Woldenberg, who carried on a large and successful business in Russian Poland, was a test case. "It has been decided in Washington not to issue passports to persons who have remained a short time in America and secured citizenship, return to Europe and endeavor to enjoy the advantages of both countries without fulfilling their duty to either."[360] But after his appeal to the legation in person, the government relented.[361] As in the application of Russian policy, decisions often depended on the individual involved.

American Travelers

No wonder innocent Americans abroad in Russia at the end of the century were baffled and came back with contradictory impressions. Three individuals, all visiting in 1897, discovered different faces of Russia. Charles Gillis, traveling with a group of tourists, found Russia "entering upon a career which will ultimately place her among the foremost nations of the earth in civilization, as she is already in power."[362] But a member of another tour group thought the best way of dealing with Russians was to ignore them. "We saw in Moscow some of the dirtiest and most repulsive of the Russians, who, were they Tartars or otherwise, deepened our conviction that to keep such in repression required a strong government."[363] Truxton Beale, venturing into the interior on the first stage of the Siberian railroad, identified the most pronounced traits of the people as "sympathy and humanity."[364]

Evidently most Americans now visited Russia in groups, trusting safety in numbers. Also in 1897, Nicholas Senn, a professor of the Rush Medical College in Chicago, attended with three other American physicians an in-

360. White to Woldenberg, 17/29 May 1894, DPR, Russia, vol. 4573 (letters sent), RG 84, NA.
361. White to Gresham, 8 June 1894, DUSM, Russia, vol. 46 (roll 46, M 35), RG 59, NA.
362. Gillis, *A Summer Vacation in Iceland, Norway, Sweden and Russia* (New York: J. J. Little, 1898), p. 51.
363. Abbie Mason in A. V. D. Honeyman, ed., *From America to Russia in the Summer of 1897* (Plainfield, N.J.: Honeyman, 1897), p. 111.
364. Beale, "Russian Humanity," *Cosmopolitan* 24, 2 (December 1897): 111.

ternational medical congress in Moscow. The group then toured a hospital in Samara and journeyed across Siberia. Senn described a very different prison situation than Kennan had a decade earlier: "The well-behaved criminals in Siberia are soon given an opportunity to establish homes and create an independent existence, a great inducement and encouragement to better their moral condition."[365] Perhaps this included Vladimir Ilich Ulianov, better known as Lenin, who was residing fairly comfortably in Siberian exile at the time. Stephen Bonsal and Julian Ralph also went to Siberia to verify Kennan's depiction and by 1898 were waging an active revisionist campaign in the American press.[366]

Elizabeth Thomas, however, did not fare so well during her solo fact-finding mission during the winter of 1895–1896. After making numerous inquiries about prisons and their inmates, in exiting Russia she was arrested, detained, and searched, and a number of her papers were confiscated. She admitted they included letters of exiles and notes on prison conditions but continued to complain bitterly about her treatment. The American legation had little sympathy for her case, because she had clearly violated Russian law.[367]

On the other hand, Constance Cary Harrison apparently had a delightful time off the beaten path in the "exotic" Volga region: "We have just come out of a sort of dreamland of color and movement and wonderful kaleidoscopic pictures of a world utterly unlike anything in previous experience. . . . Moscow we found much more ancient and individual than Petersburg and Nizhni was a step further away from Europe. . . . It was like a succession of 'opera choruses' of the most vivid and brilliantly colored sets."[368] Another positive voice was that of Charles A. Dana, the venerable publisher of the New York *Sun*, former socialist, and inveterate traveler. Dana went from Odessa to Tiflis, then up the Volga in 1896 and extolled the people and places in a book published two years later.[369] In general, criticism and complaints were muted by naiveté, lingering famine sympathy, and the

365. Senn, *Around the World via Siberia* (Chicago: W. B. Conkey, 1902), p. 133.

366. Taylor Stults, "Imperial Russia Through American Eyes, 1894–1904: A Study in Public Opinion" (Ph.D. diss., University of Missouri, 1970), pp. 73–77.

367. Thomas (Berlin) to Breckinridge, 28 January 1896, DPR, Russia, vol. 4451 (misc. received), and Breckinridge to Thomas, 13/25 February 1896, DPR, Russia, vol. 4485 (misc. sent), RG 84, NA; Breckinridge to Olney, 4 April 1896, DUSM, Russia, vol. 48 (roll 48, M 35), RG 59, NA.

368. To Fairfax (her son) from Kiev, 4 September 1896, box 3, Burton Harrison Papers, LC. She noted that the manager of her Kiev hotel was an American Jew.

369. Dana, *Eastern Journeys: Some Notes of Travel in Russia, in the Caucasus and to Jerusalem* (New York: D. Appleton, 1898). Dana was seventy-five when he made this trip.

festive atmosphere leading up to and surrounding the coronation of Nicholas II.

The Last Russian Coronation

The death of Alexander III on 1 November 1894 brought relief and hope to those Americans who looked for reform and progress in Russia. It also raised to the throne a man who was no stranger to Americans and American affairs. In fact, Nicholas II probably was better informed about the United States than any previous Russian ruler, because of his facility in English, his practice of reading reports, his experience with famine relief and the Siberian railroad, and his conversations with uncles and cousins who had traveled there and with his worldly mother.[370] Americans in turn knew more about Nicholas as grand duke for the same reasons. His mother, the Empress Maria Fedorovna, renowned for her beauty and generally referred to abroad by her Danish name as Princess Dagmar, was the model for a popular American porcelain doll.

One of the new tsar's first acts, on the advice of Witte, was the appointment of Mikhail Khilkov as minister of transportation. Having spent several years in the United States and South America learning by practical experience about running trains and railroads, Khilkov became "the American engineer" in the government.[371] After a year and a half in office, he set off across Siberia and the Pacific, with Joseph Pangborn as guide, for a railroad inspection tour of America, the first such visit by an incumbent Russian minister.[372] As a result of these exposures to America, his home and office in

370. Lambert Tree, perhaps the first American to see Nicholas in an official capacity, was impressed with his intelligence, his eagerness to learn about America, and his fluent English; to Bayard, 4 January 1889, DUSM, Russia, vol. 40 (roll 40, M 35), RG 59, NA. But White had a different impression: "He always seemed to me a pleasant young man, but without any interest in anything whatever," adding intriguingly, "some time I will give you a curious instance of this, obtained in my own conversation with him." To Holls, 14 December 1894, Holls Papers, Columbia University.

371. V. Griboedov, "An Americanized Russian Minister," *Leslie's Illustrated*, 22 August 1895, p. 118; Nelson A. Miles, *Military Europe: A Narrative of Observations and Personal Experience* (New York: Doubleday and McClure, 1898), pp. 78–79.

372. Breckinridge to James Wilson, 14 October 1896, box 4, James Wilson Papers, LC. Breckinridge described Pangborn as a "general messenger, friend and philosopher for the Prince." As such he may have had direct influence on construction, for example, his recommendation to build a "shortcut" across Manchuria to Vladivostok; Breckinridge to Olney, 4 April 1896, DUSM, Russia, vol. 48 (roll 48, M 35), RG 59, NA.

Mikhail Khilkov, minister of transportation,
1895–1905. From Annette Meakin, A River of Iron
(1901)

St. Petersburg would always be open to visiting Americans for the ten years of his tenure.

The perception of the new tsar pursuing an American path was especially impressed upon General Nelson Miles in an interview in 1897.

> Not only was he well informed on all military matters, but he seemed to be interested chiefly in the development of his country, especially that vast wilderness of Siberia, whose condition is very much like that of our western country a few years ago. . . . I found him quite familiar with the history of the development of our western country and the advantage derived from railway communications, and that he hoped to follow our example of dividing the unoccupied land into small sections

to be given to actual settlers, and thereby producing a nation of patriotic home-builders similar to our own.[373]

Few Americans would have the opportunity of an audience with the emperor, but a number did see him at a distance.

Coronations were similar to expositions, attracting a flood of visitors for a grand festival. About as many Americans made their way to Moscow in 1896 as Russians had traveled to Chicago in 1893, but the events in Russia were more concentrated and, as a major official function, involved much diplomacy and protocol—or at least should have, if Americans had been up to it. Clifton Breckinridge was clearly out of his element in handling the situation as minister. The Cleveland administration did not help matters by designating Major General Alexander McDowell McCook, an Ohio-born Civil War hero and commandant of Fort Leavenworth, as its official representative and by sending back Creighton Webb, already infamous in St. Petersburg, to assist Breckinridge.[374] To the minister's consternation, McCook, who was already in Europe, assembled a party that would be larger and more imposing than his own: McCook's wife and daughter; his brother John with wife and daughter; Charles and Harriet Anderson; and Captain George Scriven as aide. Rear Admiral Thomas O. Selfridge, Jr., sailed from his Mediterranean station on board the USS *Minnesota* to complete the formal list.[375]

Months beforehand, Breckinridge had fretted about his diplomatic costumes and the headache of money. He justified a last-minute supplemental credit of $2,500: "I know of no means by which friendly relations are more assuredly advanced than by suitable marks of honor and respect upon occasions like this. . . . While our expenditures are as nothing compared with those of other nations with hardly greater public interests to serve, yet with discretion and economy I feel that we shall not wound the sensibilities of Russia."[376] With the help of able, Harvard-educated Herbert Pierce, Simon

373. Miles, *Serving the Republic: Memoirs of the Civil and Military Life of Nelson A. Miles* (reprint; Freeport, N.Y.: Books for Libraries Press, 1971), p. 265.

374. Olney to Breckinridge, 17 February and 22 April 1896, DI, Russia, vol. 17 (roll 139, M 77), RG 59, NA. Breckinridge acknowledged that Webb "is a hard fellow to hold down, but Gen. McCook and staff will be with me, and if necessary we will 'drum head' him and have him shot." To William Rockhill, 8 April 1896, DPR, Russia, vol. 4485 (misc. sent), RG 84, NA.

375. Breckinridge to Selfridge, 16/28 April 1896, DPR, Russia, vol. 4485 (misc. sent), RG 84, NA.

376. To Olney, 22 May 1896, DUSM, Russia, vol. 48 (roll 48, M 35), RG 59, NA.

Gordon (Baldwin agent), and Moscow consul Adolph Billhardt, Breckinridge arranged for horses and carriages and shipped them ahead to Moscow, rented suitable quarters there for the official party, and reserved special
trains to carry the Americans to Moscow.[377] The nadir was refereeing the
scramble for badge passes to key events among the fifty or so Americans
who flocked into Moscow. The minister later complained to Washington
that having seventeen Americans on the "official list" was "a most embarrassing tax already laid upon the hospitality of the Russian officials."[378]

Representing the American aristocracy were a number of women: Mary
Simmerson Logan, publisher of *Home Magazine* and widow of a prominent
Illinois senator;[379] Emily Warren Roebling, wife of the builder of the Brooklyn Bridge; Bertha Palmer, the prominent spouse of Chicago's renowned developer; Harriet Anderson, wife of an international banker; Zelia Nuttall,
an archeologist from the University of Pennsylvania; and Phoebe Apperson
Hearst, widow of a senator from California and mother of William Randolph Hearst. All were expected to—and did—spend freely; Mrs. Palmer's
one-week hotel bill in Moscow totaled $10,000.[380]

Of around ninety correspondents gathered for the show, about a dozen
were American. They included William E. Dodge Stokes, Lewis Moore
(United Press International), Henry Fischer (New York *Journal*), Aubrey
Stanhope (New York *Herald*), Maynard Butler (*Harper's Weekly*), Harriet
Hurlbert (New York *Tribune*), Helen Glenn (Cincinnati *Tribune*), Thomas
Allen (*Leslie's Illustrated*), Julian Ralph, Clarence Falk, and Richard Harding
Davis (New York *Journal* and other Hearst papers). Davis won the American
scuffle for a blue badge that admitted him and eleven other correspondents
to the actual coronation ceremony. "No one who has not been with us these
last ten days can know what we have had to do." In formal court costume,

377. Breckinridge to McCook, 7 and 17 April and 1 and 2 May 1896, box 3, Mc-
Cook Family Papers, LC; Billhardt (Moscow) to Breckinridge, 27 November 1895 and 2
May 1896, DPR, Russia, vol. 4227 (Moscow dispatches), RG 84, NA. The minister later
suffered through a messy claim for additional expenses from the landlord of the rented
apartments in Moscow; Breckinridge to Billhardt, 13 October 1896, DPR, Russia, vol.
4485 (misc. sent), RG 84, NA.
378. To Olney, 27 May 1896, DUSM, Russia, vol. 48 (roll 48, M 35), RG 59, NA.
379. For the recollections of her banker son, who accompanied her, see Logan, *In
Joyful Russia*, pp. 210–30; James Pickett Jones, *John A. Logan: Stalwart Republican from Illinois* (Tallahassee: University Presses of Florida, 1982), pp. 224–25.
380. Richard Harding Davis (Moscow) to his brother, 17 May 1896, box 3, correspondence 1893–1896, Davis Papers, University of Virginia.

he took notes on his hat. "It was the sight of the century and I was in it. . . . It was a beautiful sight, much more beautiful than I imagined possible and the empress more beautiful and more sad looking than ever before."[381]

Davis grumbled about Hearst's stinginess in paying for the cabled reports, but his efforts to get his wires sent resulted in one of the best behind-the-scenes pictures—of buttering up officials and bribing the head of the telegraph bureau.

> It is like a game of whist and poker combined, and we bluff on two flaming fours and crawl the next minute to a man that holds a measly two spot. . . . And we go dashing about all day in a bath chair with a driver in a bell hat and a blue bright gown leaving cards and writing notes and giving drinks and having secretaries to lunch and buying flowers for wives and cigar boxes for husbands and threatening the minister with Cleveland's name and flattering old McCook by listening to his stories.[382]

The sixteen-year-old Susan McCook, daughter of John, followed American precedents by becoming the sweetheart of the coronation balls. Her proud father and chaperone reported that she was constantly surrounded by officers and especially pursued by the British military attaché. "Mr. B[reckinridge] told Mrs. [Alexander] McCook that he had never seen a young lady who in beauty, manner, and dress, intelligence and character so completely realized his idea of what a young lady should be." John McCook also provided colorful descriptions of the festivities for relatives at home: the line of six elegant carriages that carried the official American party in the tsar's grand entrance parade into the city over smooth and sound-deafened, sand-covered streets; the placing of the crown on Nicholas's head to the accompaniment of the Ivan III tower bells, followed by a thousand-gun salute and the ringing of 5,000 bells throughout the city; and the fireworks at night: "I am a pretty good American but I frankly admit that we have yet to learn the first elements of illumination."[383] He was also on hand to witness the disaster on 29 May at Khodinskii field, where gifts were distributed to the common

381. To his brother, 15 May 1896, ibid.
382. To his brother, 17 May 1896, ibid.
383. John McCook to Nettie, 21 May 1896 (c), box 3, McCook Family Papers, LC.

Nicholas II's entrance into Moscow after his coronation. Harper's Weekly, *20 June 1896. Courtesy of the Kansas Collection, University of Kansas Libraries*

people with little foresight, and over 1,500 people were killed in a mob frenzy.[384]

Some Americans at the coronation ceremonies were singled out for their lack of social graces. Mrs. Breckinridge was scolded for wearing a golf cloak to receptions, the minister for being "only a schoolmaster out in Arkansas [who] did not understand Social or Court matters," and the admiral for shaking hands without taking his gloves off, while Webb managed to infuriate nearly everyone.[385] This whispered carping was omitted, however, from the many press accounts that recorded all the pomp and circumstance for an infatuated American public at home.

384. To Nettie, 30 May 1896, ibid. For other poignant eyewitness accounts, see Thomas G. Allen, "The Khodinsky Disaster," *Bachelor of Arts* 3, 4 (October 1896): 490–96, and Maynard Butler, "The Khodynsky Plain Disaster," *Harper's Weekly,* 18 July 1896, p. 706.

385. Davis noted, "The chief cause of everyone's grief is Creighton Webb who has had the insolence to come back here and work on old Breck to make him Secretary or something or other and who is on the court list ahead of the visiting commission. . . . Breck believes in him but everyone else is up hard against him and I guess it will end in a row." To his brother, 17 May 1896, box 3, Davis Papers, University of Virginia.

Back to Business

Russian-American business relations were undergoing a transition. Direct trade continued to decline in proportion to the totals of each country, both in imports and exports. Many of the traditional American imports from Russia—linen, hemp, leather, bristles, sheet iron, cordage—were now being supplied from other sources or by other products; only cotton remained significant among the featured items of Russian imports from the United States for most of the century. In 1890 it accounted for 95 percent of official American exports to Russia, most of it indirect and supplying over 60 percent of Russia's cotton needs.[386]

Manufactured goods rose in importance, chiefly from Khilkov's insistence on ordering some 500 large Baldwin locomotives for the Siberian railroad in the 1890s, 138 during the winter of 1897–1898. After a long hiatus of sales of American locomotives to Russia from 1878 to 1892, Baldwin's energetic St. Petersburg agent, Simon James Gordon, sold over 200 more for Russia's European lines between 1895 and 1898 at a price of about $4 million.[387] Gordon was also instrumental in Baldwin's establishing a locomotive factory at Sormovo near Nizhni-Novgorod, furnished with $500,000 of American machinery and managed by Walter F. Dixon of Philadelphia. The first engine constructed at this plant made its successful run in April 1888, but Baldwin sold out to a Russian company in 1900.[388]

Westinghouse also secured a large contract for equipping rolling stock with air brakes and in 1898 sent Charles R. Crane to start production in St. Petersburg with $3 million in orders from the Russian government. The plant, employing a thousand workers and managed by Crane's brother-in-law, William E. Smith, had mixed results, but New York Air Brake was suffi-

386. George S. Queen, "The United States and the Material Advance in Russia, 1881–1905" (Ph.D. diss., University of Illinois, 1941), pp. 162–68.

387. Ibid.; Gordon to Holloway, 9/21 November 1898, enclosed in Tower to Hay, 1 May 1901, DUSM, Russia, vol. 58 (roll 58, M 35), RG 59, NA.

388. "Locomotive Plant for Russia," New York *Times*, 20 April 1896, p. 12; Hitchcock to Dixon, 8 April 1898, DPR, Russia, vol. 4486 (misc. sent), RG 84, NA; Fred V. Carstensen, *American Enterprise in Foreign Markets: Studies of Singer and International Harvester in Russia* (Chapel Hill and London: University of North Carolina Press, 1984), p. 46. Gordon, however, was accused of being a wife-beater and bribe-taker in 1901 and was dismissed by Baldwin; Tower to Hay, 1 May 1901, DUSM, Russia, vol. 58 (roll 58, M 35), RG 59, NA.

ciently encouraged to follow suit with a plant near Moscow.[389] Other American manufacturers that opened offices or secured agents in Russia in the 1890s included National Cash Register, Carnegie Steel, Pratt and Whitney, and the Worthington Pumping Engine Company, the latter also represented by Smith.[390] Additionally, American companies had a small role in Russia's electrification, which proceeded slowly.[391]

A number of other American products began to make inroads in the Russian market, ranging from oatmeal to typewriters, but McCormick reapers and binders and Singer sewing machines continued to be the most significant items.[392] Sales of these were limited by famine conditions and world recession and by increased domestic and foreign competition. The most formidable obstacle on paper—laws forbidding foreign companies from operating on Russian soil without a specific bilateral treaty—was easily overcome by agents registering as guild merchants. The McCormick enterprise, concentrated in the south, was also hampered by high customs duties from the protective tariff of 1891, by dependence on local shops that represented other manufacturers, and the lack of a warehouse and spare parts inventory. George Freudenreich, who had headed the agency since 1880, blamed the backwardness and suspicion of the Russian peasant. Even so, he placed orders for 225 mowers and 250 binders for Russian delivery in 1889.[393]

Crop failures in 1891 and 1892 not only eliminated sales in large areas but also reduced demand in other parts of Russia because of the abundance of desperate, itinerant workers, many carrying scythes. In good years such as 1893 and 1894, there was increased demand for labor-saving machines from landed proprietors, since most peasants did not need to seek outside income. McCormick's chief competition was a simple reaper, called the *lobo-*

389. Hitchcock to W. R. Day, 21 May 1898, DUSM, Russia, vol. 52 (roll 52, M 35), RG 59, NA; J. M. Schoonmaker (Pittsburgh) to Hitchcock, 17 February 1898, DPR, Russia, vol. 4454 (misc. received), RG 84, NA; "Russia's Great Future," New York *Tribune*, 19 November 1899, pp. 2, 4.

390. Francis A. Pratt to White, 22 December 1893, roll 61, and Andrew Carnegie to White, 4 June 1894, roll 62, White Papers, Cornell Universtiy; W. E. Smith to Breckinridge, 12/24 March 1897, and Michael Tultchinsky (Odessa) to Breckinridge, 1 April 1897, DPR, Russia, vol. 4452 (misc. received), RG 84, NA.

391. See Jonathon Coopersmith, *The Electrification of Russia, 1880–1926* (Ithaca, N.Y., and London: Cornell University Press, 1992), pp. 42–98.

392. "Hercules Oats" tried to enter the Russian market but was thwarted when oatmeal was classified as a children's food protected by tariff; Breckinridge to Gresham, 16 July 1895, DUSM, Russia, vol. 47 (roll 47, M 35), RG 59, NA.

393. Freudenreich to McCormick, 10 August 1888, box 112, 2C, McCormick Company Papers, SHSW.

greika, developed by the Mennonites in the Ukraine. Although it required an additional worker to rake the cut grain from a platform, it was cheaper, more durable, easier to maintain, and traveled better (doubling as a wagon) than the self-raking McCormick reaper.[394]

Motivated by a reduced rate of sales growth at home, the McCormick company pushed expansion into foreign markets in the 1890s. None seemed more promising than the vast agricultural lands of Russia. George Tracy was sent to the head office in Odessa, first working under Freudenreich and learning Russian and German, then replacing him in 1895. Through his more careful selection of agents, his expansion of the sales force, and his exhibitions of implements, especially the new "Daisy" model binder, McCormick sales to Russia grew about three times in value from 1894 to 1898, to over 500,000 rubles.[395] Tracy's success was due in part to his recognition of the prospects for a new market in Siberia along the path of the new railroad; he also allied with progressive local zemstvo administrations, and opened a new central agency for north Russia in Riga. The company further benefited from a suspension of duties on imported reapers and binders obtained in 1897 by Russian agricultural interests.

Singer fortunes also rose in the 1890s, strengthened by experience in world marketing and the completion of European production facilities. Russian sales were reorganized and expanded by Hamburg-based agent George Neidlinger, who had been with the company since 1865 and had the advantages of German expertise and connections in the Russian business world.[396] The size and scope of his operations, coupled with the impression of a rapid modernization and expansion of the Russian economy, convinced the Singer Board of Directors to approve the formation of a Russian subsidiary under Neidlinger in June 1894. After three more years of preparation, "Manufakturnaia Kompaniia Zinger" was formally chartered by the tsar with central sales offices in Riga, Warsaw, St. Petersburg, and Moscow.[397] By 1899 they had a total of ninety-two retail outlets. With sales of machines in

394. For the McCormick operations in Russia, see Elizabeth Pickering, "The International Harvester Company in Russia: A Case Study of a Foreign Corporation in Russia from the 1860s to the 1930s" (Ph.D. diss., Princeton University, 1967), pp. 8–34.

395. Ibid.; Carstensen, *American Enterprise*, pp. 127–30; George S. Queen, "The McCormick Harvesting Machine Company in Russia," *Russian Review* 23, 2 (April 1964): 165–66, 177–78.

396. Robert Bruce Davies, "The International Operations of the Singer Manufacturing Company, 1854–1895" (Ph.D. diss., University of Wisconsin, 1967), pp. 97–98.

397. Neidlinger (St. Petersburg) to F. G. Bourne (Singer president), 28 June/10 July 1897, box 105, Singer Sewing Machine Company Papers, SHSW.

Russia reaching 68,188 in 1895, Neidlinger urged the company to consider establishing a factory in Russia.[398] After an extensive search, eighty-one acres were purchased in 1898 along a major rail line at Podolsk, about twenty-five miles south of Moscow, for the site of what would become a large, sophisticated, Western-owned and directed factory.[399]

American models also dominated the typewriter market, though distribution was managed by local businesses. As the Moscow consul reported, "The machine best known here is the Remington; the agency for the whole of Russia is in the hands of a firm by the name of J. Bloch, large dealers in bicycles, sewing machines, and they manage to place about 200 to 300 per annum over the whole empire."[400] The same source reported that Hammond was making inroads with fifty to sixty sold through a local stationer.

In the meantime, another large and profitable American business in Russia was under seige—life insurance. After a pioneering entry into Russia by New York Life Insurance, the Equitable Life Assurance Society of America set up an agency under Sidney Schmey in 1890.[401] Although the Russian government required a $500,000 security deposit, sales boomed, and by mid-1893 the two companies had expanded their operations in Russia to a total worth of 35 million rubles in outstanding insurance. Yet they faced increased competition from Russian companies and adverse publicity in the press and government circles for unfair practices. The main problem that the Russians had with the American companies concerned the "tontine system" of leaving dividends on policies to accumulate additional insurance; they defended their inability to understand it with charges of unethical business conduct, and a special insurance commission of the Ministry of Finance proposed a prohibition.[402]

398. Neidlinger to Bourne (Singer president), 11 July 1896 (Hamburg correspondence), box 86, ibid.
399. Neidlinger (Hamburg) to Bourne, 22 February 1898, box 87, ibid. The architect of the factory was Aleksei Miliukov, younger brother of the historian; plans, folder 7, box 155, ibid. The Podolsk site served as the main sewing machine plant in Soviet Russia under state administration; in 1995, the Singer company was considering its reacquisition.
400. Hornstedt to Munson Typewriter (Chicago), 2 November 1893 (c), DPR, Russia, vol. 4226 (Moscow dispatches), RG 84, NA.
401. R. Carlyle Buley, *The Equitable Life Assurance Society of the United States, 1859–1964*, 2 vols. (New York: D. Appleton-Century-Crofts, 1967), 1:436–38.
402. Ibid., 439–41; P. P. Moeller (St. Petersburg) to White, 5/17 May 1893, DPR, Russia, vol. 4448 (misc. received), RG 84, NA; White to Gresham, 18 June 1893, DUSM, Russia, vol. 45 (roll 45, M 35), RG 59, NA. An Equitable reply to the Russian government, defending the "tontine system," dated 21 August 1893, was sixty-six pages long; DPR, Russia, vol. 4448 (misc. received), RG 84, NA.

George W. Perkins. From Claude Bowers, Beveridge and the Progressive Era *(1932)*

The two American companies jointly brought in George Batcheller, a prominent attorney with diplomatic experience, to represent them and pressured the State Department for additional assistance.[403] Unfortunately, the protracted negotiations occurred mostly during a ministerial interlude, and secretary-chargé Webb was on poor terms with Finance Minister Witte. "He is a very cold man. Extremely difficult to approach, at war with society through its refusal to recognize his wife who was a notorious character—madly ambitious and of a nature to sweep from his path every obstacle to his success."[404] Batcheller was successful only in deferring Russian government action, but the threat remained and undermined the planned expansion of the business. Then George Perkins, working specifically as chief foreign

403. Webb to Gresham, 31 October 1893, DUSM, Russia, vol. 45 (roll 45, M 35), RG 59, NA.
404. To Gresham, 30 December 1893, DUSM, Russia, vol. 45 (roll 45, M 35), RG 59, NA.

agent of New York Life, skillfully obtained official blessings through revised policies and an additional deposit. Equitable also replaced the antagonistic Schmey as manager of its St. Petersburg office in 1894 with a Russian, Peter Popov, though the former remained the overall manager.

New York Life reorganized and consolidated operations in 1899.[405] On his visit to Russia that year, Perkins strengthened his company's position: "Imagine my actual surprise at being able to show the gentlemen in charge of the Government control of our Company that books, records and forms in use by the Insurance Department at Albany, New York, were superior to those in use here, with the result that Albany methods have been adopted . . . by the Insurance Bureau here."[406] Perkins's main objective, however, was to ward off the entry into Russia of Mutual Assurance Company, represented by Frederick Holls, and he successfully blocked the new rival with Equitable's cooperation. He also recruited a key representative of the Russia Company, the main local competition, along with fifty of his subagents. With this victory he expected gross sales to rise from 30 million rubles in 1899 to 45 million in 1900, making New York Life in Russia "a very snug little life insurance company all by itself."[407] To smooth relations with the Ministry of Finance and demonstrate confidence in Russian commercial possibilities, Perkins agreed to purchase 20 million rubles ($10 million) in railroad bonds at 4 percent.[408] Thus, by the turn of the century the American insurance business in Russia was enlarging rapidly—though one scholarly study asserts that the Equitable business there was never profitable.[409]

Obviously, the keys to American business success in Russia were, first, resident agents such as Gordon, Dixon, Neidlinger, Tracy, and Schmey, who

405. Buley, *Equitable Life Assurance* 1:439–40. Perkins became a partner of J. P. Morgan's but is best known for merging McCormick, Deering, and other agricultural implement companies into the International Harvester Company; Carstensen, *American Enterprise*, p. 164.

406. Perkins to Pierce, 21 October 1899, enclosed in Pierce to Hill, 24 October 1899, DUSM, Russia, vol. 55 (roll 55, M 35), RG 59, NA.

407. Perkins to John McCall (president of New York Life), 22 October 1899, box 4, general file, Perkins Papers, Columbia University. One Moscow agent, Gelb, easily led the company, with sales of 2 million rubles in 1899 alone.

408. Ibid.; Frank Vanderlip diary, 26 April 1901, box D-4, Vanderlip Papers, Columbia University. Perkins even considered structuring New York Life in Russia as an independent subsidiary; Perkins to Pierce, 19 November 1900 (c), box 53, Perkins Papers, Columbia University.

409. Buley, *Equitable Life Assurance* 1:441. Equitable would later regret having expanded into Russia because of long and tedious lawsuits that extended to 1943 over honoring policies that lapsed during the upheavals of revolution and civil war; ibid., 2:952.

were committed, patient, and knowledgeable about Russian practices; and second, parent managements, led by people like McCormick and Perkins, that actively pursued foreign business. Other businessmen operated independently with considerable profit as permanent Russian residents. Continuing into the third generation was William Ropes and Company, headed by John Henry Prince and Ernest E. Ropes. From the importation of American petroleum in the 1870s, the primary business had evolved into oil refining at the Petrovsky Oil Works in St. Petersburg. The company produced kerosene under the brand mark of "Caucasine," indicating the new origin of the raw product, but it continued to perform as foreign exchange and shipping agents into World War I.[410]

Similarly, Samuel and Thomas Smith maintained a wholesale supply business in Moscow that had operated successfully for thirty years and also served as occasional vice-consuls there. A business letterhead declared that Thomas was a dealer in "railway and factory plant and materials."[411] He also was a member of the local geographic society and knew prominent educators such as Mikhail Rostovtsev.[412] An even larger enterprise was that of John N. Lehrs, who inherited from his father, Henry, an import-export business in Moscow that featured cotton imports and agricultural implement sales.[413] He would remain in operation there until forced out by the upheavals following the Bolshevik seizure of power, whereupon the business moved to Riga. A similar longevity was achieved by Charles H. Smith, whose company operated in Nikolaevsk and Vladivostok for forty years, until his death in 1898. In fact, the increased business at this terminus of the Siberian rail-

410. Ernest Ropes to White, 18/30 December 1892, DPR, Russia, vol. 4447 (misc. received), RG 84, NA; Wurts to Blaine, 30 April 1892, DUSM, Russia, vol. 43 (roll 43, M 35), RG 59, NA; *Ocherki istorii Leningrada* (Moscow-Leningrad: Nauka, 1956), 3:51.

411. Thomas Smith (Moscow) to White, 17/29 December 1892, DPR, Russia, vol. 4447 (misc. received), RG 84, NA; Smith to Breckenridge, 1 July 1897, DPR, Russia, vol. 4453, RG 84, NA. In 1893 Samuel Smith was "a paralytic old man." Hornstedt (Moscow) to Webb, 2 May 1893, DPR, Russia, vol. 4448 (misc. received), RG 84, NA. Billhardt recommended Thomas Smith: "He . . . speaks Russian like a native, has a hardware store and deals in machinery intended for mechanics and somewhat in agricultural implements, making frequent trips to the interior of Russia. He knows all about Russian trade and ways, is a good talker and sharp." To Ebert (Saratov), 4 December 1894, DPR, Russia, vol. 4226 (Moscow dispatches), RG 84, NA.

412. T. Smith (Moscow) to Charles Crane, 29 November 1892, 7/19 February 1893, box 2, Crane Papers, BA, Columbia University.

413. Billhardt (Moscow) to Pierce, 25 September 1895, DPR, Russia, vol. 4449 (misc. received), and 14 January 1895, DPR, Russia, vol. 4227 (Moscow dispatches), RG 84, NA.

road led to the establishment of a consulate there at the turn of the century.[414]

Some American equipment sales to Russia occurred on the whims of consular appointees. Since they were dependent on both official and private fees for support, the consuls were often active in championed business connections. For example, Adolph Billhardt, a consul in Moscow from Upper Sandusky, Ohio, was partial to Buckeye businesses and promoted Marion steam shovels and dredges and Huber threshing machines with some success.[415] Perkins thought that having an active supporter of business, such as Herbert Pierce, in the embassy was vital. "All the splendid work you have done in Russia is only just about to bear fruit and that it would be a great loss to the commercial interests of this country to have you leave St. Petersburg in the near future."[416] The short terms of so many American diplomatic appointees certainly did not help to solidify business contacts.

Americans still tried to sell experimental new technology to Russia. One of the more interesting cooperative ventures was the use of corn stalks in the lining of armor on warships, promoted in St. Petersburg in 1898 by Henry Watts of the Marsden Company of Philadelphia, Irving Scott of the Union Iron Works of San Francisco, and H. W. Wiley of the Department of Agriculture. The fodder would not stop shells but would automatically seal up the hole to prevent leakage after being penetrated.[417] Nothing apparently came of this, probably because it would be useless against exploding shells. Another scheme connected an old family business (Ropes and Company) in Russia with new technical inventiveness. Henry Ropes Trask, who pioneered windmill irrigation in Kansas, surveyed for similar possibilities around Kazan in 1898.[418]

Americans still dominated quality dental work in late-nineteenth-century Russia, and there were American dentists in St. Petersburg, Moscow, Kiev,

414. Richard Greener (Vladivostok) to John Hay, 20 September 1898, DUSC, Vladivostok, vol. 1 (roll 1, M 486), RG 59, NA.
415. Billhardt to Marion Steam Shovel Company, 8 October 1894; to Huber, 4 December 1894; and to R. Ebert (Saratov), 15 October 1894, DPR, Russia, vol. 4226 (Moscow dispatches), RG 84, NA.
416. Perkins to Pierce, 19 November 1900, letterbook, box 53, Perkins Papers, Columbia University.
417. Holloway report, 25 July 1898, CR 58, 217 (October 1898): 216.
418. Trask (Kazan) to Hitchcock, 22 October/3 November 1898, DPR, Russia, vol. 4455 (misc. received), RG 84, NA.

Warsaw, and Baku.[419] Even so, Joseph Wassall, a Chicago dentist who was encouraged to come to St. Petersburg in 1894 by Russians at the Columbian Exposition, failed to obtain the necessary license.[420] In St. Petersburg, Henry Wollison continued the American monopoly of service to the imperial family that had belonged to Thomas Evans for a good part of the nineteenth century. Evans had operated out of Paris since 1842 and is credited with introducing gold fillings to Europe; he earned a fortune of several million dollars caring for the elite teeth of Europe.[421] Wollison apparently pioneered the use of toothpaste in Russia, but one of his American patients there complained he had "fallen into Russian ways" and was very slow in his work.[422]

Other Americans provided technical expertise on long-term contracts: Henry C. Rector was manager of the Moscow Telephone Company, a Belgian enterprise that used the Bell system; William H. Dunster was engraver for the mint of the Imperial Bank until his death in 1899; and Roy C. Fletcher superintended the American tabulating machines for the Russian census;[423] Alexander Boroday, an electrical engineer, was by origin of Kharkov nobility (Borodaevskii) but had emigrated to the United States in 1877. He worked as a draftsman in steel construction and then for six years as a Westinghouse electrical engineer before returning to Russia to work on electric railways for Alexander Bary. He ran into trouble for having left Russia illegally and had to depart in a hurry.[424]

Born in St. Petersburg in 1847, Alexander Bary arrived in Philadelphia

419. Names from various diplomatic and consular communications about passport renewals: St. Petersburg (Harvey Linn, Henry Wollison, Henry James Miller, Charles Searle); Moscow (Henry Michaels, William Regner, Will Lambie); Kiev (Herbert Clearwater); Baku (Charles Neville Wallach); Warsaw (James Levy). Wollison was granted a new passport since he paid taxes and maintained a residence in Pittsfield, Massachusetts, but Michaels was initially denied because he had reportedly come to Russia in the 1860s to evade Civil War service. Hitchcock to Sherman, 24 December 1897, DUSM, Russia, vol. 51 (roll 51, M 35), RG 59, NA; Sherman to Hitchcock, 22 December 1897 and 13 January 1898, DI, Russia, vol. 17 (roll 139, M 77), RG 59, NA.

420. Wassall to White, 2/14 March 1894, roll 61, White Papers, Cornell University.

421. Hitchcock to Sherman, 24 December 1897, DUSM, Russia, vol. 51 (roll 51, M 35), RG 59, NA. Evans died in Europe in 1897 but was buried in his home city of Philadelphia. Obituary, New York *Times*, 16 November 1897, p. 7.

422. Henry Allen diary, 8/20 December 1894, box 1, Allen Papers, LC.

423. Hornstedt (Moscow) to Webb (St. Petersburg), 2 August 1893, DPR, Russia, vol. 4226 (Moscow dispatches), RG 84, NA; W. F. Willcox to McCormick, 19 March 1904, DPR, Russia, vol. 4462 (misc. received), RG 84, NA.

424. Boroday to Breckinridge, 30 December 1895, DPR, Russia, vol. 4449 (misc. received), and Breckinridge to Boroday, 14/26 February 1896, DPR, Russia, vol. 4485 (misc. sent), RG 84, NA.

with his brother in 1870 and was employed as a construction engineer. After having earned a considerable reputation as a designer of buildings for the Philadelphia Centennial, Bary returned to Russia in 1878 and established a substantial iron foundry in Moscow. The company produced a variety of items, including pipes and pumps, for the Nobel enterprises in the Caucasus, but Bary also parlayed his skills as an architect and builder, notably for the exposition in Nizhni-Novgorod.[425]

Probably the most successful, independent American entrepreneur in Russia was Enoch Emery. Sailing from Boston to Nikolaevsk as a cabin boy around 1868, Emery gradually built a mercantile empire in Eastern Siberia with large stores in Blagoveshchensk, Khabarovsk, Nikolaevsk, and Vladivostok that prospered alongside the government development efforts in the area, doing over a million dollars of business annually.[426] By the 1890s, he had married a Russian and taken up permanent residence in Moscow, making yearly trips to inspect his eastern enterprises. One Siberian traveler reported, "Emery always favors American goods and sells immense numbers of agricultural implements and of other things in the manufacture of which America excels. This is the only great American firm in Siberia."[427] Emery himself boasted he handled almost everything from buttons to steamboats, from calico to quartz crushers, from butter to diamonds. In 1901 alone he had 600 tons of agricultural machinery on order from the United States.[428]

Emery also supplied commercial and political information to American officials and was a sharp critic of American initiatives in Russia:

> I would beg to call your attention, as a merchant who has been engaged for the past thirty years in supplying the wants of the Russian Far East, to the fact that our manufacturers are by no means alive to the

425. McCormick to Hay, 2/15 February 1905, DUSM, Russia, vol. 62 (roll 62, M 35), RG 59, NA; Logan, *In Joyful Russia*, p. 109. As in the case of Lehrs, Bary would be prominent in the Moscow business world and left an estate of $5 million to his children when he died in 1913; interview notes, W. A. Bary (son), New York, 3 March 1952, box 7, Poole Papers, SHSW.

426. Hitchcock to Sherman, 15 February 1898, DUSM, Russia, vol. 51 (roll 51, M 35), RG 59, NA.

427. Washington B. Vanderlip, *In Search of a Siberian Klondike* (New York: Century, 1903), p. 12. The American consul general noted, "Mr. Enoch Emery is an American citizen doing a very large business in Siberia chiefly in American goods and having eleven warehouses in different parts of that country east of Irkutsk." Pierce to Hay, 13 December 1898, DUSM, Russia, vol. 53 (roll 53, M 35), RG 59, NA.

428. Emery to Tower, 19 February/4 March 1901, DPR, Russia, vol. 4460 (misc. received), RG 84, NA.

Teatime in Russia, August 1896. Left to right: Henry Hiller, Charles Dana, Enoch Emery, and Dana's granddaughter. Courtesy Mystic Seaport Museum, Inc., G. W. Blunt White Library, Manuscript Collection, Henry Hiller Papers, Collection 77, box 2, vol. 5, p. 99

value of the vast market to be found there for goods of every class. Speaking from a wide experience, I can only suppose that our manufacturers are either unable, or do not care, to consider the peculiar tastes and requirements of foreign countries.[429]

But Emery's confident perspective arose from his own near-monopoly of the limited trade.

Although apparently friendly with a few other Americans in Moscow,

429. Emery (Moscow) to Hitchcock, 17/29 April 1898, DPR, Russia, vol. 4454 (misc. received), RG 84, NA.

such as Tiffany buyer Henry Hiller,[430] Emery was essentially a loner with a mean disposition and an obsession about his wealth. His wife, whom he divorced in 1895, complained of his stinginess and physical abuse. "He is a man with no moral principles at all, vain and ill-tempered, without any sense of honor and word."[431] In 1905 he became mentally unbalanced and spent the few remaining years of his life in a sanatorium near Moscow, leaving his large estate to be fought over by estranged nieces and nephews in New England.

Still, Emery set an example of business success that helped inspire a climate of high expectations for future Russian-American economic cooperation. As the American consul in Moscow advised the secretary of agriculture, "The air is at present full of all kinds of projects, building new railroads, extending others, deepening canals, and constructing new ones. Since the building of the great Siberian Railway has been commenced, a new era seems to have begun for Russia."[432] His successor, Thomas Smith, also saw many opportunities for Americans in Russia. "I wish I could say something to impress my countrymen here at home with the fact that Russia is the country of the future, and that investments are absolutely safe. There is perfect freedom there for every one if he leaves politics alone."[433] All that was needed was peace and harmony.

430. Hiller to his wife, 24 April 1897, box 2, Hiller Papers, Mystic Seaport Library, describing their nerve-shattering bicycle ride over the cobblestone streets of Moscow.
431. Eugenia Men to Breckinridge, 2 June 1895, DPR, Russia, vol. 4449 (misc. received), RG 84, NA.
432. Billhardt to J. Sterling Morton, 9 July 1895 (c), DPR, Russia, vol. 4227 (Moscow dispatches), RG 84, NA.
433. Interviewed in the New York *Tribune*, 19 November 1899, pp. 2, 4.

6

Disharmony and War, 1898–1905

The political and economic growth of the United States brought it firmly and definitely into the larger world community of the late nineteenth century, especially in economic relations. Russia, since the time of Peter the Great a major factor in the calculations of European powers, was receiving new and more guarded respect as a result of industrial progress, the building of the Siberian railroad, and the Franco-Russian alliance. The latter, though professed by Giers to indicate a policy of peace, placed the rising, expanding Germany in a pincer between the two great continental military powers of the century, thus creating a diplomatic and military tension that would finally erupt in the Great War.[1] There was, however, enough of the old Russo-German friendship—especially in the ties between the two autocrats—to permit diplomatic rumor and manipulation. Meanwhile, the United States would remain for a number of years little more than an observer of the European diplomatic scene.

More immediately, the turmoil in China, the growth of Japanese power, Russia's Siberian development program, and expanding American interest in East Asia created a fertile field for diplomatic and military maneuvering that brought Russia and the United States—and Britain—into conflict as well as cooperation. Russia was unique in being both a European and Asiatic nation, but the United States could also assert an Atlantic and Pacific heritage and destiny. Suffering distinct disadvantages in terms of distance,

---

1. Nikolai Giers was apparently sincere in his expression of peace in receiving Andrew Dickson White as minister. As White quoted him, " 'Tell your government,' he said, 'that the closer the lines are drawn which bind Russia and France, the more strongly will Russian influence be used to hold back the French from war.' " *Autobiography of Andrew Dickson White*, 2 vols. (New York: N.p., 1905), 2:32.

transportation technology, and capital, Russia would blunder into a war that would have a profound internal impact, while the United States would become truly a Pacific power through both peaceful and military means. Perhaps the contrast of the mainly military outpost of Vladivostok with the booming, cosmopolitan city of San Francisco illustrates best the respective positions of the two countries.

The change in the conduct of Russian foreign policy by the end of the century was dramatic. No longer was it steadily guided and nurtured by long-term foreign ministers who also held the dignified title of chancellor or vice-chancellor. After a lingering illness Giers died in 1895 and was succeeded by the feeble, dilettantish seventy-year-old Aleksei Lobanov-Rostovsky; after his death the following year came Mikhail Murav'ev, the minister to Denmark. Described as a "born courtier and flatterer" without ministry experience, Murav'ev nevertheless initiated a much more active policy in the Far East and toward the United States. Upon Murav'ev's sudden death in June 1900, Vladimir Lamzdorf ascended to the post.[2] A hardworking recluse who rarely left St. Petersburg, Lamzdorf was already conducting the day-to-day affairs of the ministry, since he had been groomed by Giers as his successor.

All these ministers and their assistants—the little-respected Nikolai Shishkin, the seldom available Dmitri Kapnist, the rude and pedantic Nikolai Zinov'ev, and the eccentric Fedor Osten-Saken—demonstrated meager leadership and had numerous quarrels with one another, but they were also victims of the situation in the government as a whole.[3] Although Alexander III had wielded a strong hand in foreign policy, the shy and uncertain Nicholas II was more reticent, at first leaving much of the key policymaking in the hands of two powerful inherited state servants, Sergei Witte and Konstantin Pobedonostsev. No wonder Andrew White concentrated on this pair in his memoirs. But the influence of Witte and Pobedonostsev had declined by 1900, and Witte was forced to resign his central post as minister of finance in 1903, leaving the government virtually leaderless as far as official

2. Andrew D. Kalmykow, *Memoirs of a Russian Diplomat: Outposts of the Empire, 1893–1917* (New Haven, Conn., and London: Yale University Press, 1971), p. 98; this and Iurii Solov'ev, *Dvadtsat' piat' let moei diplomaticheskoi sluzhby (1893–1918)* (Moscow-Leningrad: Gosizdat, 1928) are excellent sources for characterization of policy leadership during this period.

3. For descriptions of many of these personalities, see Dominic Lieven, *Russia's Rulers Under the Old Regime* (New Haven, Conn., and London: Yale University Press, 1989), pp. 160, 167, 198.

foreign policy was concerned and subject to a variety of counterproductive influences.

Because of similar illnesses and deaths—and an unusual number of changes effected by political elections—the Department of State in this period also lacked continuity and stability as it worked through a succession of secretaries and acting secretaries from Blaine to Hay. Although the polished and relaxed Walter Gresham and the inexperienced and cantankerous Richard Olney performed well under the circumstances, they were probably not suited for the sophisticated handling of world power diplomacy that the United States now required.[4] It was not cabinet members or political parties but the presidents themselves who now began to exercise the dominant role in foreign policy. This opened the way for cronyism or outside pressure groups, akin to the situation developing in Russia.

From Legations to Embassies

Russian ministers to the United States in the 1890s saw comparatively little of Washington, considering their short tenures, lapses between appointments, leaves at home, and summers in New England. Karl Struve finally succeeded in obtaining a transfer to the Netherlands, for the sake of his family in 1892. Grigori Kantakuzen, from a Russian-Greek family, arrived in January 1893 to handle matters through the Chicago world's fair and in 1895 was transferred to Württemburg, an indication of his diplomatic standing. His predecessor there, Ernst Kotzebue, served just over a year in Washington before being replaced in August 1897 by Artur Cassini, the Russian minister to China. His appointment resumed a tradition of connecting the American appointment to Far Eastern experience, and his stature raised the visibility of Russian-American relations.

One obvious characteristic of Russian diplomats in the United States is that most of them were of non-Russian ethnic background. Cassini, described as a "diplomat of the Gorchakov school," is reported to have spoken and written French almost exclusively, employing Russian or English only on very rare occasions.[5] Also of international background was a succession

---

4. Gerald G. Eggert, *Richard Olney: Evolution of a Statesman* (University Park and London: Pennsylvania State University Press, 1974), pp. 171–73.

5. Solov'ev, *Dvadtsat'piat'let*, p. 35.

Artur Cassini, Russian ambassador to the United States. World's Work, *April 1904, p. 4673*

of first and second secretaries—Aleksandr Greger, Roman Rosen, Petr Botkin, Aleksandr Bogdanov, Aleksandr Somov, Baron Schilling, and Grigori Vollant (de Wollant)—and consuls—Aleksandr Olarovskii, Vladimir Teplov, and Nikolai Lodyzhenskii (New York); Atsimovich (San Francisco); Tal' and Albert Schlippenbach (Chicago). They seemed to have had their full share of social problems. Greger was for a time very popular, but he and his wife scandalized Washington with their extramarital affairs;[6] Bogdanov committed suicide, and Teplov was "grossly compromised" and forced into retirement.[7] Others such as Rosen were rotated in and out of the United States with a regularity that resembled that of American diplomats in Russia. At least Rosen's varied experience came in handy in 1905 when he replaced Cassini for the Portsmouth treaty negotiations.

The diplomatic tasks became greater and more complicated because of famine relief, the extradition treaty, the sealing arbitration, the delegations to Chicago, the Jewish visa problem, increased business inquiries, and the

6. Henry Allen to White, 17 December 1893, roll 60, White Papers, Cornell University; Allen diary, 5 December 1894, box 1, Allen Papers, LC.

7. Vollant to Lamzdorf, 14/27 January and 1/14 June 1901, f. 133, op. 470, d. 106, AVPR.

need to keep an eye on Russian terrorists in the United States (usually through Pinkerton detectives). Another complication was the designation of a special agent, Aleksandr Rutkovskii, from the Ministry of Finance with responsibility for negotiating a new commercial treaty, a matter usually left to diplomats.[8] Despite handicaps, the Russian staff was diligent in reporting the complex course of American affairs through changing times and several presidencies; there was even a detailed, eyewitness account of the assassination of President McKinley in Buffalo.[9]

The American diplomats in St. Petersburg were a mixed lot in both background and temperament. Charles Emory Smith, the Philadelphia newspaperman, performed his one government appointment with skill and enthusiasm, especially considering the unusual strain of famine relief. He was followed in late 1892 by veteran diplomat and educator Andrew Dickson White, who returned to St. Petersburg after an initial stint as secretary nearly forty years earlier and exploited that experience at every turn. Already well-known for his tenure as president of Cornell University and occasional ventures into politics, his appointment and acceptance were a surprise to the American public.[10] He even survived a change in administrations in Washington and remained at his post until October 1894. Although his reports at the time were generally pro-Russian and optimistic, his later writings and memoirs were bitter and more critical.

With future publication in mind, White made the most of the opportunity for extended conversations with contrasting poles of Russian thought—Tolstoy and Pobedonostsev. White nevertheless suffered several handicaps, not least of which was an incompetent and trying secretary, Creighton Webb. He was also forced to endure as host an onslaught of prominent Americans, which in 1894 alone included Francis A. Pratt of the Pratt and Whitney Company, art historian Halsey Ives of Washington University, publisher Charles Dana, inveterate collector and author James Wilson, Slavicist Jeremiah Curtin, business-seeking Wharton Barker, eccentric Methodist minister Lawrence Alvord, Rabbi Joseph Krauskopf, Charles Crane, and Professor Herman Schoenfeld of Columbia University.[11] He was also saddled for part of his tenure with an immature older daughter and a

8. Cassini to Murav'ev, 16 February 1900, f. 133, op. 470, d. 109, pt. 1, AVPR.

9. Vollant to Obolenskii, 29 August/11 September 1901, f. 133, op. 470, d. 150, AVPR. Significantly, this was sent to the Ministry of Interior.

10. Glenn C. Altschuler, *Andrew D. White—Educator, Historian, Diplomat* (Ithaca, N.Y., and London: Cornell University Press, 1979), pp. 191–92.

11. Correspondence, rolls 61 and 62, White Papers, Cornell University.

Andrew Dickson White, minister to Russia. Harper's
Weekly, *30 July 1892, courtesy of the Kansas Collection,
University of Kansas Libraries*

new, much younger wife; a difficult and domineering woman, she presented
her sixty-two-year-old husband with another daughter during the 1893
summer retreat in Finland.[12] Frustrated by the *fait accompli* of an unpopular
extradition treaty, Russia's failure to support the United States on the sealing controversy, and the vexations of the Jewish visa problem, White sought
solace in writing a book on universal history and beginning his memoirs.

According to his army attaché, White was holding out for the rank of ambassador, which had been suggested by the United States in 1893,[13] but it

12. Henry Allen commented on the latter: "Mr. W. is for all in all one of the most
charming and excellent men I have known, and I pity him deeply for being compelled
to live with such a woman"; and on the former: "Poor Miss White seems to have the intelligence of a girl of fifteen instead of her age, 23–25 years. I really felt very sorry for
Mr. W." Diary, 20 July/1 August and 25 May/6 June 1894, box 1, Allen Papers, LC.
    13. Allen to his wife, 27 August 1893, box 5, Allen Papers, LC.

was another five years before Russia responded. The proposal, part of a general elevation of diplomatic posts, was brought to St. Petersburg by Petr Botkin, but the Russian foreign ministry was then in no position to accept, owing to the precarious shift in alliances, Giers's illness, and Shishkin's anti-American bent. At least one contemporary diarist was dismayed that Russia did not seize the opportunity to be first but trailed behind the other powers.[14]

Clifton Breckinridge finally received the ministerial plum for his support for Grover Cleveland, though his appointment to Russia occurred in spite of White's efforts to head it off.[15] His first chore in St. Petersburg was to attend the funeral of Alexander III and dutifully kiss the dead tsar's shriveled hand.[16] According to Lieutenant Henry Allen's initial impression, "the Breckinridge family arrived and presented a very sorry sight—very unlike an ambassadorial family."[17] His opinion did not change in subsequent months, especially when Breckinridge failed to introduce his staff at the annual New Year's reception and leaned on a chair while talking to the empress.[18] "They are so much out of their proper sphere and with such limited means that I really pity them."[19] Although hindered by inexperience, penury, a small staff, and his wife's difficult pregnancy and illness, Breckinridge nevertheless survived the strain of the 1896 coronation and creditably performed a variety of other diplomatic duties until the McKinley inauguration brought another change in missions.[20]

The Russian post was now becoming more desirable. Fred Grant, having attained general rank in the army, thought the return of the Republicans to the White House ensured his appointment, and General James Harrison

14. A. S. Suvorin, *Dnevnik A. S. Suvorina*, ed. Mikhail Krichevskii (Moscow-Petrograd: L. D. Frankel', 1923), 23 September 1893, p. 68.

15. White (Dresden) to Allen, 18 April 1894, box 5, Allen Papers, LC.

16. Allen, who was forced to follow suit, remarked on the belated and inadequate embalming of the body: the hands, "like his face looked like dirty marble." Diary, 2/14 November 1894, box 1, Allen Papers, LC. Mrs. Allen, observing the scene from a safe distance, remarked: "Harry and Mr. Breckinridge had the courage to go up and kiss the dead Emperor's hand but I could not do so. They say he is terribly changed and most unpleasant to look at as there is talk of his having been embalmed too late." To Bertie, 16 November 1894, box 4, ibid.

17. Diary, 15/27 October 1894, box 1, Allen Papers, LC.

18. Ibid., 1/13 January 1895.

19. Ibid., 10/22 February 1895.

20. James F. Willis, "An Arkansan in St. Petersburg: Clifton Rodes Breckinridge, Minister to Russia, 1894–1897," *Arkansas Historical Quarterly* 38, 1 (Spring 1979): 15–28. The Breckinridges won the sympathy of Nicholas and Alexandra, since they were going through the birth of their first child at the same time.

Wilson also maneuvered for it with business gains in mind.[21] Fortunately, St. Louis and Pittsburgh glass manufacturer Ethan Allen Hitchcock was appointed, although a rumor circulated that McKinley really had Hitchcock's more politically active brother Henry in mind.[22] Hitchcock was the opposite of Breckinridge—wealthy, sophisticated, dedicated, ambitious, and without congressional ties. He also had an extensive international background as a merchant in China and would have a distinguished subsequent career as secretary of the interior in the McKinley and Roosevelt administrations. He and his family settled comfortably into St. Petersburg society.[23]

Unlike many of his predecessors, Hitchcock appeared to enjoy his assignment but was typically frustrated by his small staff.

> There is no question as to American opportunity—in making the most of which however, our Legation is sadly handicapped—there being but the Minister and Secretary—whose diplomatic and social duties leave but little time for working up and pushing our Industrial interests. . . . The Embassies and Legations of most other countries are represented by a full staff—with specific duties, no small part of which is to secure, for their respective countries and countrymen, a full share of the trade and business of this country—and they are doing it, . . . while we are embarrassed for want of sufficient assistance to find out, keep track of and secure such business.[24]

Russia's surprise elevation of Cassini to the rank of ambassador in early 1898 immediately conferred the same designation on Hitchcock and the assignment of more personnel.[25]

But McKinley wanted Hitchcock in Washington, and Philadelphia financier Charlemagne Tower, who was not only well-heeled and well-traveled but even had diplomatic experience (Austria-Hungary), assumed the St. Pe-

21. Extract from Philadelphia *Ledger*, 3 April 1897, and John Foster to Wilson, 3 April 1897, box 4, Wilson Papers, LC. For more details, see Thomas McCormick, "The Wilson-McCook Scheme of 1896–1897," *Pacific Historical Review* 36, 1 (February 1967): 47–58.

22. Alexander McCook to James Wilson, 7 August 1897, box 9, Wilson Papers, LC.

23. His army attaché commented, "They are all extremely kind, I mean the natives and the American Colony is well bonded together." George L. Anderson to his mother, 18 December 1897, Anderson Papers, SHSW.

24. To John Pitcairn, 20 January 1898 (c), box 37, Hitchcock Papers, RG 316, NA.

25. Sherman to Hitchcock, 3 February 1898 (t), DI, Russia, vol. 17 (roll 139, M 77), and Hitchcock to Sherman, 4 February 1898 (t), DUSM, Russia, vol. 51 (roll 51, M 35), RG 59, NA.

Ethan Allen Hitchcock. From Herbert Hagerman, Letters of a
Young Diplomat *(1937)*

tersburg post. Tall, thin, and bald, Tower was described as "a fair, square and
just sort of man and, beneath his somewhat cold exterior, very kindly indeed."[26] His tenure from March 1899 to late 1903, when he was "promoted"
to Berlin, was the longest since that of Cassius Clay in the 1860s.

Tower's successor was Robert S. McCormick, nephew of Cyrus but a true
professional diplomat who had little to do with the family business. He
served languidly in the Russian capital into the revolution of 1905, when
George von Lengerke Meyer, a prominent Boston businessman and friend
of both William McKinley's and Theodore Roosevelt's, was transferred from

26. Herbert J. Hagerman, *Letters of a Young Diplomat* (Santa Fe, N.Mex.: Rydal Press,
1937), p. 114. His name was easy prey for quipsters; as a British newspaper reported on
a Russian holiday, "The illumination extended from the Charlemagne Tower to the
Nevsky." Maurice Boyd to Curtis Guild, 15 August 1912, DPR, Russia, vol. 4586 (misc.
received), RG 84, NA.

Charlemagne Tower, St. Petersburg, 1901. From Herbert Hagerman, Letters of a Young Diplomat *(1937)*

Rome. Despite his reputation as a sportsman and automobile fancier,[27] Meyer can claim some credit for rescuing Russia from the debacle of the Russo-Japanese War and thus indirectly from the revolution of 1905.

Besides the vagaries of the administration of Russian foreign policy, which seemed to have an almost mystical quality at the end of the nineteenth century, the American diplomats contended with an even greater assortment of tourists, businessmen, and journalists. Hitchcock complained privately to

27. Frederick T. Birchall, "Our New Ambassadors," *American Illustrated Magazine* 60, 1 (May 1905): 58–59. In the midst of war and revolution, one of Meyer's first acts in St. Petersburg was to purchase polo ponies. He wrote defensively to a friend, "I would rather you would not say anything about it, because the papers make so much talk, but I have got to have some exercise this summer and that is the only way I can get it." Meyer to Craig Wadsworth, 2/15 April 1905, box 3, Meyer Papers, MassHS.

his brother about these globe-trotters who left him little time to write; "They come in and sit and sit, and talk and talk."[28] He was particularly irate about Lilian Bell, a writer for the *Ladies Home Journal*, who forwarded her laundry addressed to him in order to avoid delays in Customs. "She is a 'smart aleck' in skirts."[29]

Secretaries—and chargés during lapses between and leaves of ministers— were especially important in maintaining continuity. Unfortunately, the competent and dedicated George Wurts was replaced in 1893 by Creighton Webb, from all accounts a complete disaster. Not only did Webb have no apparent skill in performing his duties, but he constantly gossiped about the legation staff and was outspokenly anti-Russian in conversation. He owed his appointment to the fact that his father had a distinguished Civil War diplomatic career and that his elder brother had been a Yale classmate of White's. Although notably reserved in his official reports and published memoirs, White complained privately that Webb was making a horrible mess and that, as a result, "my position here is becoming almost unbearable."[30]

One observer did not see much improvement in Webb's replacement in July 1894: Herbert H. D. Pierce "does not give the impression of being a man of keen perceptive faculties, nor is he familiar with any language except his own."[31] Luckily, Pierce survived a difficult beginning under Breckinridge, learned quickly on the job, and demonstrated his mettle by staying in St. Petersburg for over five years without a leave. In his spare time he actually learned Russian and worked on a biography of Ivan the Terrible, which was apparently never finished, though he did publish a few articles on the Russian scene.[32] Quiet and unassuming, Pierce earned the respect of both Russian and American officials, who fought against his reassignment. He was finally rewarded with a high-level appointment in the State Department in

28. 9 July 1898, box 22, Hitchcock Papers, RG 316, NA. Hitchcock averaged between four and five visits a day, made and received; Hitchcock calling book, 1899, box 62, ibid.

29. To Henry (his brother), 20 July 1898, box 22, ibid.

30. White (personal and confidential) to Allen, 16 December 1893, box 5, Allen Papers, LC. When White was in Finland for the summer, he had to give Webb precise detailed instructions on everything. Through the tension comes an unusual insight into the daily activities of the legation; rolls 60–62, White Papers, Cornell University.

31. Allen diary, 18/30 July 1894, box 1, Allen Papers, LC.

32. Jeremiah Curtin, *Memoirs of Jeremiah Curtin*, ed. Joseph Schafer, Wisconsin Biography Series no. 2 (Madison: State Historical Society of Wisconsin, 1940), p. 680.

late 1901 and became a key adviser to Theodore Roosevelt on Russian affairs and a principal in the Portsmouth peace conference.[33]

Other career diplomats—John Riddle, Spencer Eddy, Montgomery Schuyler, Basil Miles (who would become a leading American expert on Russia during the 1917 revolution and civil war), and Paxton Hibben—followed capably in the footsteps of Pierce. Because of pressure by White, Hitchcock, and others to improve the American diplomatic service, the staff was increased in 1898 to include a second secretary, Herbert Hagerman (a former student of White's); salaries and amenities were also enhanced. For the first time since Cassius Clay the American post in St. Petersburg could vie with the European powers for social ostentation; Charlemagne Tower invited 2,000 guests to a Thanksgiving Day reception at his rented palace in 1899.[34] The person who really managed affairs of this kind and held everything together through comings and goings was the long-term clerk and translator James de Freshville, a true "unsung hero" of the American Russian mission.[35]

Also enhancing the American presence in the Russian capital was the assignment of regular military attachés. For decades Russia had been a favorite destination for special American military excursions. Whether commanding a squadron of ships or as solitary agents, American officers could always count on cordial receptions in military-minded Russia. In fact, diplomats were often chagrined at the ease with which bureaucratic barriers evaporated before any American with military rank, past or present. More surprising perhaps is that the Russian uniform garnered similar respect in the United States. The hosts of these military scavengers were, of course, not slippery diplomats but honorable officers and gentlemen mindful of reciprocity.

After some unsatisfactory experiments with roving attachés in Europe in the 1880s,[36] the secretary of war designated Lieutenant Henry T. Allen the

33. Tower to Lamzdorf, 21 November/4 December 1901, DPR, Russia, vol. 123 (notes sent), RG 84, NA. Hitchcock also strongly recommended Pierce: "The Russian Court is . . . the most critical and exacting in the observance of formalities and routine procedure; an intelligent and prompt compliance with which, based upon ability and actual experience is *absolutely necessary*." To President McKinley, 28 December 1897, DUSM, Russia, vol. 51 (roll 51, M 35), RG 59, NA.

34. Hagerman, *Letters*, p. 142.

35. Freshville periodically threatened to leave for more rewarding employment; to Hitchcock, 27 April 1899, box 30, Hitchcock Papers, RG 316, NA.

36. For a critical comment on one descent on St. Petersburg, see George Wurts to Lambert Tree, 1 March 1889, Tree Papers, Newberry Library. Wurts added, "I am sure that the Administration just out of power never would have given its sanction to such an arrangement had it been made aware of its impropriety." To Tree, 16 March 1889, ibid.

American ambassador's coach, St. Petersburg, ca. 1899. From Herbert Hagerman,
Letters of a Young Diplomat *(1937)*

first regular military attaché to Russia.[37] The choice was indeed fortunate.
Having had his curiosity aroused by a tour of duty in Alaska, Allen visited
Russia privately while on leave in 1887. He subsequently served as assistant
professor of modern languages at West Point and acquired a good command
of Russian.[38] Recommended by the commandant as "one of the brightest,
most courteous, active and intelligent young officers of the army," Allen further obtained the backing of Charles Emory Smith for the appointment.[39]

For five years Allen became the rock of the American diplomatic establishment in Russia and seemed to win the respect of everyone, both socially
and professionally.[40] He probably spent more time in imperial and noble palaces and clubrooms, and certainly on hunts in the field, than any other
American.[41] After reassignment to Fort Riley in 1895, Allen escaped to an-

37. Redfield Proctor to General Drum, 28 February 1890 (c), box 5, Allen Papers,
LC.
38. Heath Twichell, Jr., *Allen: The Biography of an Army Officer, 1859–1930* (New
Brunswick, N.J.: Rutgers University Press, 1974), pp. 59–66.
39. Colonel Wilson to Smith, 12 February 1890 (c), box 5, Allen Papers, LC.
40. Twichell, *Allen,* pp. 75–77; White strongly recommended to Breckinridge that he
retain Allen because "his acquaintance with Russian society generally makes his advice
invaluable in a multitude of delicate matters besetting a new minister." 27 August 1894
(c), box 5, Allen Papers, LC. Allen's diaries and letters provide a colorful and detailed
portrait of Russian-American society in St. Petersburg during the 1890s.
41. Allen earned high marks from future president Theodore Roosevelt for his articles about hunting experiences in Russia; Roosevelt to Allen, 24 March 1894, box 27,

other attaché post at White's embassy in Berlin in 1897 and accompanied
General Nelson Miles on a Russian tour that year.[42]

Allen set an example of close relations with Russian officials that few of his
many, short-term successors could match, but Russian-American military exposure was appropriate to the times. The situation would change with the
Russo-Japanese War, when a whole platoon of "observers" swarmed into the
country. Most of the early attachés were not suited to diplomatic life or Russian society, and gaps in tenures, especially one following Allen's departure,
were taken as insults by Russia.[43] On the other side Allen was matched by the
appointment to Washington of General Dmitri Mertvago. Following him were
a number of transitory attachés, some of whom—Fersen, Butakov,
Rozhdestvenskii—later achieved prominence in the Russian navy.

Consuls, too, were improving in quality, number, and experience. John Crawford, having won the gratitude of Witte for overseeing the production of the five-
volume work on Russian industries for the Columbian Exposition, left St. Petersburg for his home in Cincinnati in 1894. "I am thoroughly tired out, due to the
constant application during all these years to the work of this office and to the continued residence in the debilitating and trying climate of this city, and speaking
personally, I am not sorry to be relieved."[44] He was replaced by Charles Jonas,
former lieutenant governor of Wisconsin, who served only eight months before arranging a trade of posts with Prague consul John Karel, also of Wisconsin. After

Allen Papers, LC. Allen had a distinguished subsequent career in the Spanish-
American War and on the western front in World War I, concluding in 1919 with his
command of American occupation forces in Europe.

42. Miles was impressed with the audience Allen arranged with Nicholas II and the
parallel the tsar drew between Siberia and the American West: "I found him quite familiar with the history of the development of our western country and the advantage
derived from railway communications, and that he hoped to follow our example by di-
viding the unoccupied land into small sections to be given to actual settlers, and
thereby producing a nation of patriotic home-builders similar to our own." Nelson A.
Miles, *Serving the Republic: Memoirs of the Civil and Military Life of Nelson A. Miles* (reprint; Freeport, N.Y.: Books for Libraries Press, 1971), p. 265.

43. His ultimate successor was described by William S. Sims, the next attaché:
"[Captain Alexander] Rodgers is a fine man, but he is almost entirely devoid of humor,
and consequently not a cheerful travelling companion." Sims to Adelaide, 15/27
March 1897, box 5, Sims Papers, LC. Sims also was clearly out of place in a diplomatic
setting but did have a sense of humor, referring privately to one of his Russian acquaintances as "Prince Wipeoffyourchinsky." Ibid., 8/20 March 1897; Elting E. Morrison, *Admiral Sims and the Modern American Navy* (New York: Russell and Russell, 1942),
pp. 49–53.

44. Crawford to Gresham, 7 April 1894, DUSC, St. Petersburg, vol. 21 (roll 16, M
81), RG 59, NA. He had, however, campaigned actively to retain his position; Crawford
to Edgar, 12 April 1893, box 7, Edgar Papers, MinnHS.

two-and-a-half years, in October 1897, William R. Holloway of Indiana succeeded Karel and lasted a full six years before earning a transfer to Halifax.[45] Ethelbert Watts then moved his wife and six children to Russia, again from Prague.

Besides the normal functions of a consulate in a world-class political and economic center, the American consuls in St. Petersburg oversaw, either in coordination or in conflict with ministers and secretaries of legation, the performance of other consuls and tried to keep track of Americans all over the vast empire. Distance and faulty and irregular communications were always problems, and there was seldom the time or inclination to make fact-finding tours. Moreover, none besides Crawford ever acquired much knowledge of Russian; most spoke French or German or depended on the language skills of a succession of part-time vice-consuls and clerks, such as local businessmen William Dunster and Paul Magnus.

The other consulates were for once on a fairly stable footing thanks to the long tenures of Niels Bornholdt (Riga) and Thomas Heenan (Odessa). Even the Moscow office, which had been plagued with problems from the beginning, kept a steady course in the 1890s under Adolph Billhardt (1894–1897) and merchants Thomas and Samuel Smith.[46] Despite his complaint that he was the tallest person in Batum and had the lowest rank, vice-consul James Chambers was really an employee of Standard Oil spying on the Russian oil industry.[47] One significant addition to the ranks was a new post at Vladivostok, opened in September 1898 by Richard Greener of Philadelphia, an intellectual and one of the first African-Americans in the foreign service. Before the Russo-Japanese War disrupted his consulate, leading to a protested dismissal, Greener learned Russian and even tried his hand at translating Pushkin.[48]

All Americans, especially those with little international experience, had

45. George Kennan described Holloway during his 1901 visit: "The Consul-general is a cordial, breezy off-hand unceremonious westerner—a gray-haired portly man about 60 years of age." To his wife, 7 July 1901, box 15, Kennan Papers, LC.

46. The Smiths had periodically served as interim consuls during the frequent lapses in appointments. In 1901 Thomas left the office in the hands of Samuel because of a conflict-of-interest rule that would not allow him to continue in business; Thomas Smith to David Hill, 17 June 1901, DUSC, Moscow, vol. 2 (roll 2, M 456), RG 59, NA.

47. Heenan (Odessa) to Hill, 22 March 1899, DUSC, Odessa, vol. 12 (roll 6, M 459), RG 59, NA. Proper Bostonian clergyman Lyman Abbott thought this was a disgrace; *Impressions of a Careless Traveller* (New York: Outlook, 1909), p. 87.

48. Greener to Frank [?], 25 December 1906, enclosing copy of "My Portrait," Greener Papers, Howard University. Understandably, Greener's appointment was controversial, but at least one visitor praised his service. "He is a loyal American, and does all in his power for his country-men who come to the city." Nicholas Senn, *Around the World via Siberia* (Chicago: W. B. Conkey, 1902), p. 171. See also Allison Blakely, "Richard Greener and the 'Talented Tenth's' Dilemma," *Journal of Negro History* 59, 4 (October 1974): 305–21.

Red Square in Moscow, 1892. From William Edgar, The Russian Famine *(1892)*

difficulty adjusting to Russia and its peculiar bureaucratic methods and social customs. Herbert Hagerman commented, "I am afraid after a residence
in this country of a year or more, I shall have to be twirled two or three
times through my orbit in order to get back into the celestial atmosphere."[49]
Unfortunately, this strange Russian environment fostered a tendency on the
part of most officials to confine their contacts to the foreign community.

Far Eastern Crisis

Tensions in East Asia[50] had been mounting for several years as a result of a
number of factors: the rise of Japan as a military-industrial power; the increased presence of Russia, especially with the growth of Vladivostok, the
development of the Amur basin, and the launching of the Trans-Siberian
Railroad; the international significance of the China trade; and the unsettled political status of much of the Oriental mainland. Influential voices
within Japan and Russia were simultaneously advocating imperialist expan-

49. To Mrs. Hope Chamberlain, 20 February 1899, Chamberlain Papers (12–A),
Duke University.
50. Although "East Asia" is the current designation in Western literature, "Far East"
is the term used by Russian sources, then and now. Here they are used interchangeably.

sion in Korea, China, and Manchuria. The chief spokesmen in Russia for an aggressive policy were Esper Ukhtomskii, editor of the powerful *St. Peterburgskiia Vedomosti* (St. Petersburg news) and the tsar's companion on his Far Eastern tour in 1891, and Petr Badmaev, a Siberian Buriat converted to Russian Orthodox nationalism. Although opposed by saner elements, especially in the Foreign Ministry, they gained the support of conservative military and business circles in the 1890s.[51]

An early skirmish occurred over a proposal, pushed by Khilkov and American expert Joseph Pangborn in the summer of 1895, for building a railroad across central Manchuria as a shortcut for the Siberian railroad. In their minds this was a rational alternative to the longer and more difficult and expensive construction along the Russian side of the Amur and Ussuri rivers.[52] With the backing of expansionists, who saw this as a stepping stone into China and Korea, they won the vital support of Witte by July. Kapnist of the Asiatic Department of the Foreign Ministry, however, argued in favor of a northern Manchurian route that would avoid the great bend of the Amur and would have fewer political repercussions. Needless to say, the central route won the favor of Nicholas II. From there, it was calculated, branch lines could reach a "warm water" port and penetrate the northern China market.

In the meantime, a contest for dominance in Korea between China and Japan reached a crisis, and Japan declared war on 1 August 1894. Within a few months, and much to the surprise of Russia and the other interested powers, Japan achieved a clear military victory, supremacy over the Yellow Sea, and occupation of the Liaotung Peninsula and Dairen, one of Manchuria's natural outlets to the sea. The Treaty of Shimonoseki on 17 April 1895 recognized Japanese control of this area. But Russia swiftly marshaled a Western, mainly French and German, opposition that forced Japan to modify the terms and withdraw from the peninsula. In return Japan received a larger indemnity, paid by China with a Franco-Russian loan and administered by a new Russo-Chinese bank that was chartered in December 1895 and held extensive powers in northern China. Russia thus emerged with a much-strengthened position in China.

---

51. For a study of Russian policy in East Asia for this period, see Andrew Malozemoff, *Russian Far Eastern Policy, 1881-1904: With Special Emphasis on the Causes of the Russo-Japanese War* (Berkeley and Los Angeles: University of California Press, 1958).

52. Pangborn was at least partly motivated by prospects of American business; *Side Lights on Management World Systems Railways*, 2d ed. (Baltimore, Md.: author, 1901), pp. 231–33.

Quick to capitalize on this diplomatic and financial victory, Witte closeted the Chinese envoy to the 1896 coronation and extracted a concession for building the railroad across Manchuria. Construction soon commenced on what was euphemistically dubbed the Chinese Eastern Railway. The dramatic pace of change in the Far East caught the United States off-guard, introducing another volatile issue besides the Jewish Question into Russian-American relations. Some Americans, such as chargé Charles Denby in Peking, saw all China threatened by the new Russian presence in Manchuria.[53] From his diplomatic vantage point, Breckinridge warned of a serious deterioration in traditional Russian friendship for the United States.[54] Assessing Russian intentions was obviously clouded by the weakness of the Russian foreign ministry in the mid-1890s.

The advent of Mikhail Murav'ev and the departure of Shishkin from the Foreign Ministry in 1897 heralded a more aggressive Russian stance in the Far East combined with an effort to appease the United States. As Breckinridge now noted, "Count Muravieff . . . impresses me as having clear and comprehensive views of the interests of his country upon this line of policy, and he seems to shape its course and invite its development with firmness, ability and tact."[55] One of his first moves as foreign minister was to shift Cassini, who had helped achieve Russian diplomatic gains as envoy to China, with the new rank of ambassador to Washington, where he would attempt to sooth concerns over Russian policy. In his instructions to Cassini, Murav'ev stressed Far Eastern developments, the need to contain Japan, and support for American control of Hawaii, for otherwise he feared this "Malta of the Pacific" would become Japanese.[56]

In the summer of 1897 Germany inaugurated another stage in great-power relations toward China. Through a series of initiatives, of which Russia was kept partially informed, Germany gained control of Kiaochow on the Yellow Sea, which revived consideration of a warm-water base for the expanding Russian navy either in Korea or China. Although a high-level con-

---

53. For an excellent study, emphasizing conflict between Russia and the United States, see Edward H. Zabriskie, *American-Russian Rivalry in the Far East: A Study in Diplomacy and Power Politics, 1895–1914* (Westport, Conn.: Greenwood Press, 1973).

54. Breckinridge (Paris) to Olney, 11 November 1896, as cited in Zabriskie, *American-Russian Rivalry*, p. 37.

55. Breckinridge to Sherman, 25 August 1897, DUSM, Russia, vol. 51 (roll 51, M 35), RG 59, NA.

56. Murav'ev to Cassini, 29 January 1898 (c), f. 133, op. 470, d. 113, AVPR. The same potential was reported six months earlier by New York *Times* reporter Bradford Colt DeWolf; St. Petersburg letter, dated 28 June, New York *Times*, 25 July 1897, p. 15.

ference called by Witte in December opposed a move at that time, Murav'ev pressed ahead anyway with the tsar's blessing, ordering a naval occupation of Port Arthur the same month. In early 1898 China signed a twenty-five-year concessionary lease for the southern part of the Liaotung Peninsula, the same territory Japan had been forced to abandon just two years before.

France could not oppose its ally, and Germany was in no position to argue against a concession from China similar to the one that it had just obtained. Britain was taken unawares but consoled by the fact that this expansion was far from the Persian Gulf and by the hope that it might keep Russia quiet in the Balkans. Mourning a sunken battleship and preparing for war against Spain, as well as the annexation of the Hawaiian Islands, the United States had little grounds for complaint about the Russian "coup." The Japanese were understandably upset and might have gone to war then except for uncertainty about the reaction of France and Germany.[57]

Moreover, for both national and personal reasons, the new ambassadors, Cassini and Hitchcock, were striving for improved Russian-American relations in 1898. Murav'ev adroitly gave Hitchcock advance warning of the "lease," explaining that it was needed as a commercial terminal for the Siberian railroad, "in place of Vladivostok where the harbor is rendered useless by physical and climatic conditions the greater part of the year."[58] Under instructions, Cassini was quick to declare for the United States against Spain. Hitchcock, in congratulating John Hay on his appointment as secretary of state, reassured him:

So far as Russia is concerned, we have nothing to fear, diplomatically or commercially, from the position she has achieved, and will maintain, in the Far East. . . .

That Russia should seek, political and diplomatic supremacy at Pekin is natural and perfectly proper, in view of her long line of territorial contiguity and in protection of the vast interests to be developed by her magnificient Siberian railway system, which is also, even now, foreshadowing enormous possibilities for our trade and commerce across the Pacific.[59]

57. Malozemoff, *Russian Far Eastern Policy*, pp. 97–109.
58. Hitchcock to Sherman, 19 March 1898 (draft, confidential, read and destroy), box 37, Hitchcock Papers, RG 316, NA. In fact, Vladivostok is kept open by icebreakers through the winter, but it is much farther north.
59. To Hay, 18 August 1898 (c), box 37, Hitchcock Papers, RG 316, NA.

At least some believed that Russian progress in East Asia was in American interest.

The Hague Peace Conference

On 24 August 1898, at the usually boring and formal weekly reception for the diplomatic representatives in St. Petersburg, Murav'ev presented each with a circular outlining "the humanitarian and magnanimous ideas of His Majesty the Emperor" for "the maintenance of general peace, and a possible reduction of the excessive armaments which weigh upon all nations."[60] The call for an international conference to discuss these matters caught everyone by surprise, especially since this occurred in late summer, normally a dormant diplomatic period. The United States was, embarrassingly, in the middle of a war but, after receiving reassurances that no discussions were intended on current situations, responded favorably to the project. The other major powers also acceded, though with some unease and few expectations.[61] Not to do so would have been a diplomatic insult.

The precise origins of the Russian proposal are not completely clear. Certainly the concepts of arms limitation and arbitration as an alternative to war were gaining currency in the 1890s, and surely Nicholas II was cognizant of them.[62] Andrew White, then ambassador to Germany and eventual head of the American delegation to the conference, thought that Pobedonostsev was behind the Russian initiative.[63] More likely, it came from the tsar himself, abetted by certain advisers: Murav'ev, who sought to reassert the dominance of the Foreign Ministry over Finance Minister Witte, and Minister of War Aleksei Kuropatkin, who was concerned about escalating arms costs.[64] Once the idea was on the table, Witte himself submitted a comprehensive plan to Murev'ev to supplant Kuropatkin's more general one.[65]

60. An English translation is in Frederick W. Holls, *The Peace Conference at The Hague* (New York: Macmillan, 1900), pp. 8–12.

61. Hitchcock to Hay, 3 September 1898, DUSM, Russia, vol. 53 (roll 53, M 35); Hay to Hitchcock, 14 September 1898, DI, Russia, vol. 18 (roll 140, M 77), RG 59, NA.

62. In 1895 Phillip Garret, representing the Peace Association, wrote to Breckinridge asking him to plead with the tsar for these causes; 25 April 1895, DPR, Russia, vol. 4449 (misc. received), RG 84, NA.

63. White, *Autobiography* 2:69

64. Andrew M. Werner, "Nicholas II," in *Biographical Dictionary of Modern Peace Leaders*, ed. Harold Josephson (Westport, Conn.: Greenwood Press, 1985), pp. 690–91.

65. "K istorii pervoi Gaagskoi konferentsii 1899 g.," *Krasnyi Arkhiv* 50–51 (1932): 64–65.

Frederick Holls, secretary to the American delegation at The Hague, hinted that the death of Bismarck in July and the Spanish-American War were the immediate incentives.[66] The world press had indeed glorified Bismarck as a peacemaker and arbiter on the eve of the Russian announcement, but whether Murav'ev, Witte, or Nicholas II had Bismarckian dreams is open to question. The Russian Foreign Ministry was also receiving long, detailed reports on the Spanish-American War direct from the United States, Spain, and elsewhere.[67] Both Cassini and his counterpart in Madrid, Dmitri Shevich, warned emphatically in June and July of an Anglo-American rapprochement, and Shevich especially underscored British attempts to mediate the conflict to its own advantage.[68] Another of the American delegates, Alfred T. Mahan, was convinced that "the immediate cause of Russia calling for the Conference was the shock of our late war, resulting in the rapprochement of the U.S. and Great Britain and our sudden appearance in Asia, as the result of a successful war."[69] Indeed, Manila had just fallen when the circular was issued. There was a sense of the international situation getting out of control and upsetting traditional alignments.

Another factor may simply have been the practical consequences of the armaments race, which Russia was finding increasingly expensive and which competed with Witte's ambitious internal development plans. Small arms were one thing—and Russia had offered 150,000 Berdanka-2 rifles for American purchase at the beginning of the war—but large, heavily armored battleships were another. The destructiveness of modern weaponry and the unknown implications of new inventions, such as exploding bombs of chemical gases and submarines, inspired appeals for limitations. But Mahan believed "that Russia has not the slightest intention either of reducing her armaments, or even discontinuing the programme for their increase."[70]

In May 1898, for example, work began on two Russian warships, destined

66. Holls, *Peace Conference*, pp. 1–7.

67. A file of reports, all on the war, from Vladimir Teplov in New York, dated between 22 May and 2 October 1898, totaled 238 pages: f. 133, op. 470, d. 113 (1898), AVPR. In addition, Major Ermolov and Captain Aleksandr Lieven were sent as special observers for the army and navy; Lamzdorf to Vollant, 1 May 1898, ibid.

68. Cassini to "my good friend," 10/22 June 1898, f. 138, op. 467, d. 170, AVPR; Shevich (Madrid) to Murav'ev, 11/23 July 1898, in "Ispano-britanskii konflikt 1898–1899 gg.," *Krasnyi Arkhiv* 60 (1933): 28–30.

69. To Samuel Ashe, 23 September 1899, in *Letters and Papers of Alfred Thayer Mahan*, ed. Robert Seager II and Doris D. Maguire, 4 vols. (Annapolis, Md.: Naval Institute Press, 1975), 2:658.

70. Ibid.

for the Pacific, at the Cramp shipyards in Hampton Roads.[71] As Hagerman reported from St. Petersburg, "They are building ships for the Russian navy as fast as they can."[72] And Heenan observed a well-armed regiment shipping out of Odessa to garrison Port Arthur and a significant expansion of the volunteer fleet for Pacific destinations.[73] Russian extension in the Far East certainly did not come cheap, especially with the construction required for a naval base at Port Arthur and for the neighboring commercial port of Dalny. As Hagerman pondered,

> I don't see how Russia could afford to go to war with anyone. It is a constant wonder to me how they can keep up their immense military establishment, keep on building railroads and canals, buying ships and rails and paying hundreds of thousands of officials. The Government is terribly hard up. . . . The natural resources are being developed, but very slowly in comparison with the huge and costly expansion that is going on.[74]

American public reactions to the Russian proposal for a general peace conference were mixed. One appreciative source noted that this "noblest exercise of imperial prerogative in all human history" came precisely at a time of renewed international rivalry in the Far East.[75] A more neutral publication was at first mystified ("What does Russia Mean?"),[76] then turned sarcastic: "The Russian Czar recently proposed an international scheme of general disarmament. Nobody seconded the motion, and he has now ordered the construction of 23 torpedo-boat destroyers of the latest type, and is ready to take the other side of the question."[77]

71. Cramp negotiated directly with Grand Duke Alexis, minister of navy, for a contract that was reported to be worth $15 million. Cramp to Breckinridge, 16 August 1897, DPR, Russia, vol. 4453 (misc. received), RG 84, NA; Hitchcock to Cramp, 2 April 1898 (c), and to Day, 12 April 1898 (c), DPR, Russia, vol. 4486 (misc. sent), RG 84, NA; "To Build Ships for Russia," New York Times, 13 May 1898, p. 5. The 12,000-ton battleship Variag and a smaller battle cruiser were launched at the end of October 1899; New York Times, 1 November 1899, p. 4.

72. Hagerman, Letters, p. 126.

73. Heenan to Hitchcock, 12 May 1898 (t), DPR, Russia, vol. 4454 (misc. received), RG 84, NA; Heenan to Hill, 16 November 1898, DUSC, Odessa, vol. 12 (roll 6, M 459), RG 59, NA.

74. Hagerman, Letters, p. 132.

75. "The Czar as World Peacemaker," Chautauquan (October 1898): 85.

76. Frank Leslie's Illustrated Newspaper, 15 September 1898, p. 202.

77. Ibid., 29 December 1898, p. 510.

Herbert Pierce, sympathetic to Russia, studied opinion in St. Petersburg and concluded that the majority of those who counted were opposed.

> To expect them now to at once respond with enthusiasm to a proposition which involves the belief that this great military establishment . . . is in fact but a drain upon the resources of the country . . . would be to require an elasticity of temperament which the national character does not possess. Nor does the humanitarian aspect especially appeal to the ordinary Russian mind. The semi-oriental influences and traditions of the people have bred in them a slight regard for the value of human life and an apathetic fatalism which does not admit of the same point of view as exists in Western peoples.[78]

Less prejudiced was his keen observation that "as this is essentially a military centre, in which the greater part of society has some individual interest in the army, any proposition looking to a reduction of the army suggests the possibility of affecting personal interests which could not be complacently regarded."[79]

Most contemporaries, in fact, did view the peace overtures with cynicism, seeing them as a crude mask for aggressive designs. The stir of patriotism and flag-waving for the relatively inexpensive American triumph over Spain also undermined the cause. But once the war ended, and a date, place, and agenda were set for the conference, American apologists became more vocal. Edward Everett Hale backed international arbitration in a much-quoted sermon at the Park Avenue Church in January 1899; Lyman Abbott praised the tsar at the Friend's Meeting House in April; and the Russian ambassador reported that President McKinley evinced a personal interest.[80] Telegrams and letters to the Russian embassy in Washington elicited appreciation from the tsar himself: "Deeply affected by the expressions which have reached him from the United States and which prove how completely the ideas of peace . . . find a warm response in this great country, His Majesty the Emperor has deigned to charge me to convey his most sincere thanks to all those who have sent his Imperial Majesty the expression of their senti-

78. To Hay, 9 November 1898, DUSM, Russia, vol. 53 (roll 53, M 35), RG 59, NA; PRFRUS 1898, p. 534. He also noted that the diplomatic community thought it "visionary and utopian, if not partaking of quixotism."

79. Ibid.

80. New York *Times*, 30 January 1899, p. 10, and 30 April, p. 5; Cassini to Murav'ev, 5 March and 2 April 1899, f. 133, op. 470, d. 110 (1899), AVPR.

ments with regard to highly humanitarian an achievement."[81] Russia had given the American peace movement a shot in the arm, and the peace conference now received its greatest popular support from the United States.

Passing over the first choice for location, Switzerland, because of the number of hostile Russian emigrés there, delegates from most of the Western countries assembled in May 1899 at The Hague. Surprisingly, the Russian delegation was undistinguished; the leaders were Georg Staal, ambassador to Britain, and the stodgy and conservative but respected authority on international law, Fedor Martens. The Americans—White, Holls, Seth Low, Stanford Newel, Mahan (navy), and Captain William Crozier (army)— concentrated on setting up an international tribunal or court of neutral judges to arbitrate claims between nations. Opposition came from the Germans, who argued that these matters should be left to traditional diplomatic procedures and that an international court would be amateurish and unpredictable. A watered-down version of the American plan was eventually approved and brought into being as a permanent court of arbitration.

The other key issue—disarmament—had few advocates, and it went down in defeat along with an old American cause—exemption of noncontraband private property from seizure at sea during wartime. Some progress was made in outlawing certain weapons, protecting civil property from pillaging, safeguarding medical services, and improving and standardizing the treatment of prisoners of war through refinements to the Geneva Convention.[82] A noble effort to limit and contain international military conflict had at least begun, and Russia could take credit for initiating it.

Open Door

Coincident with the new Russian presence in Chinese waters and in Manchuria, the United States was also becoming a true Pacific power with the annexation of the Hawaiian Islands and the acquisition of the Philippines, both of which Russia had officially supported. As the British, French, and Germans concentrated on the south and central coasts of China, the commercial sights of Russia and the United States focused on the north. There was a widespread American fear that imperialist interests, especially Rus-

81. Cassini to Hay, 5/17 April 1899, NRL, vol. 12 (roll 10, M 39), RG 59, NA.
82. For the day-to-day negotiations and agreements, see Holls, *Peace Conference*; and White, *Autobiography* 2:250–354.

Secretary of State John Hay. World's Work,
April 1904, p. 4604

sia's, would lead to exclusionary spheres of control. On 6 September 1899, a
year after Murav'ev circulated the surprise note calling for a global peace
conference, Secretary of State John Hay, in similar style, issued a call to the
diplomatic missions in Washington chiefly involved in China—Britain, Germany, and Russia—asking for recognition of an "open door" policy. While
acknowledging established regions of influence, it proposed equal rights for
all to the China market through nondifferential treatment in any harbors
and on all railroads controlled by a foreign power—free ports and free access
by land to them.

Russia was slow to respond because both Cassini and Murav'ev were absent from their posts. Although officials professed to be mystified by the language, they were actually deliberating how to maintain a special status in
"leased territories." A cautious acceptance at the end of the year ignored the
proviso that disallowed discriminatory railroad rates on goods of other

countries.[83] While Cassini warned of what he considered Hay's pro-British inclinations and saw the hand of that power behind the "open door,"[84] Murav'ev simply refused to acknowledge the validity of the term. When the United States pressed for unequivocal Russian concurrence, Cassini concluded that the United States had assumed a much more aggressive and demanding diplomatic posture after the Spanish-American War.[85] Although Russian responses had been ambiguous and dependent on the agreement by the others, Hay declared in a circular of 20 March 1900 that the concerned parties had approved the open door, which was therefore in force.

The Boxer Rebellion

The sharply increased Western and Japanese political and economic involvement in Chinese affairs was especially manifested in the building of railroads, establishment of banks, and missionary activity. The intrusion provoked a nationalistic Chinese reaction, led by a secret society known as the Boxers, whose aim was to contain and eliminate these alien influences. Beginning appropriately with attacks on trains, depots, and telegraph lines in June 1900, the rebellion spread rapidly, and as it sought to gain control over the central government, it focused its hostility on defenseless missionaries and the protected legations in Peking. Fearing commercial losses and the potential division or disintegration of China, Hay issued another circular committing military force to the defense of American interests and to the integrity of China and calling for the cooperation and participation of the other powers.

On the surface, Russia agreed with American policy, but in fact it recognized that a weak and divided China would be to its advantage, helping Russia consolidate authority in Manchuria while hurting the other powers.[86] Russian guards were withdrawn from Peking at a critical juncture, and the expansionist minister of war, Kuropatkin, argued for the immediate occupation and annexation of Manchuria. At this inopportune moment, the Foreign Ministry was thrown into disarray by the sudden death of Murav'ev on 21 June. Meanwhile, the Boxers had no intention of sacrificing any part of China and concentrated their venom on the Russian presence in Manchuria by sending a large army north.

By mid-July the Boxers had interrupted traffic on the Amur River and laid

83. Zabriskie, *American-Russian Rivalry*, pp. 57–59.
84. To Murav'ev, 7 January 1899, f. 133, op. 470, d. 110, AVPR.
85. To Murav'ev, 15/28 March 1900, f. 133, op. 470, d. 109, pt. 2, AVPR.
86. Zabriskie, *American-Russian Rivalry*, pp. 56–64.

siege to Russia's biggest city in the region, Blagoveshchensk, effecting a state of war between Russia and China.[87] After three weeks and with the help of a large, steel-decked river barge borrowed from Enoch Emery, the Russian army relieved the city. The soldiers engaged in violent retribution against the sizable Chinese population, which was forcibly driven out and into the river. Few could swim, and many were apparently killed by both Chinese and Russian gunfire. Emery, who witnessed the aftermath and himself employed a number of Chinese, estimated 5,000 were killed at Blagoveshchensk and 7,000 in other towns along the border. "The men whose lives were sacrificed were not implicated or interested in the war, and had they been spared they would have continued their work and saved Christianity from a stain I shall never forget."[88]

In the meantime, a group of American and Swedish missionaries survived a harrowing escape through Mongolia and reached the Russian border at Kiakhta, where, after some initial hesitation, they were given refuge and the best Siberian hospitality. One of them, James Hudson Roberts, expressed his appreciation to be finally in "a land of law and order, a country thoroughly policed, under a strong and civilized government, which was both able and willing to protect us."[89] Obviously, views of autocratic, reactionary Russia depended on perspective—or place and conditions of entry. Roberts and his companions continued their homeward journey through Irkutsk and Moscow to St. Petersburg.

Siberia in the American Mind

Beginning with the travels of John Ledyard, John D'Wolf, and Peter Dobell in the late eighteenth and early nineteenth centuries, Americans developed a special fascination for Siberia, a land larger than their own country, the rest of Russia, or China. It was the ultimate westward or eastward destination and stood out on all Mercator projection world maps. Trading posts along the coast and whaling in the Sea of Okhotsk drew commercial ventures, and a continual American presence gradually moved inland to the

87. The United States received firsthand reports on the Amur situation from Emery; Tower to Hay, 18 July 1900, DUSM, Russia, vol. 56 (roll 56, M 35), RG 59, NA.

88. Undated Emery letter in Pierce to Hay, 22 September 1900, DUSM, Russia, vol. 57 (roll 57, M 35), RG 59, NA. The loss of life easily exceeded that of all the anti-Jewish pogroms in Russian history before 1917.

89. Roberts, *A Flight for Life and an Inside View of Mongolia* (Boston: Pilgrim Press, 1903), p. 281. He added (p. 285) in reference to Kennan, "Siberia has been called a prison, but we found it a land of freedom." For the other refugees, see Pierce to Hill, 19 September 1900, DUSM, Russia, vol. 57 (roll 57, M 35), RG 59, NA.

new cities and opportunities by the end of the century. Serving as guide-posts for a wave of true globe-trotters were Enoch Emery and his brother Charles in Blagoveshchensk, consul Greener and the Frederick Prays in Vladivostok, and J. C. Smith in Khabarovsk. Publicity about the building of the Trans-Siberian Railroad fired the American imagination, and the race was soon on to see and write about it, almost always in a positive light. Joseph Pangborn had been one of the first to catch the new Siberian fever: "Here in Siberia it is the exceptional naturalness, the rare simplicity and the perfect open heartedness of mankind from the very highest official down through all grades, which is the charm and one feels how good it is to live when life brings such a contact."[90]

And Roberts was not the only American clergyman to penetrate the region in 1900. On an educational mission for the Young People's Society of Christian Endeavor, Francis Clark set out with a group from Vladivostok by train and river steamer, taking snapshots with his Kodak.[91] With graphic description and illustrations, he emphasized a sense of Russia awakening from the East.[92] John Bookwalter in 1898 was even more pictorial and tended to make comparisons with the American West: no Indian corn, the potential for beef, the absence of blizzards, grain rotting along the track, buffet-style restaurants in stations. He believed that the United States should recognize the inevitability of Russian supremacy in East Asia and use Russian good-will to promote its China trade.[93] The new government settlement program impressed many Americans, evoking romantic memories of their own conquest and "civilizing" of the American West.[94] Providing technical details on the new railroad, an American engineer named Lodian noted the Russians' propensity to avoid tunnels by blasting huge portions of hills away, adding that they had adopted the American style of light, strong bridges. Con-

90. Pangborn (Krasnoiarsk) to Breckinridge, 20 January 1896, DPR, Russia, vol. 4451 (misc. received), RG 84, NA.
91. Clark, *A New Way Around an Old World* (New York and London: Harper and Bros., 1901), reprinted as *The Great Siberian Railway: What I Saw on My Journey* (London: S. W. Partridge, 1904).
92. Ibid., p. 183.
93. Bookwalter, *Siberia and Central Asia* (New York: Frederick A. Stokes, 1899); "Russia in the Far East," New York *Times*, 23 December 1898, p. 7; "Russia and the East," New York *Times*, 24 December 1898, p. 6.
94. Donald Treadgold astutely concluded, "With all its contrasts with the American movement, Siberian migration produced a society more like that of America than was the Russian society from which it stemmed." *The Great Siberian Migration: Government and Peasant in Resettlement from Emancipation to the First World War* (Princeton, N.J.: Princeton University Press, 1957), p. 7.

cerned about the frequency of accidents, he had little respect for the Russian-made locomotives except that many burned oil, thus reducing the need to carry bulky coal.[95]

One reporter on Siberia, making his way from Port Arthur north and east, found the people to be friendly, open, and easygoing: "no scowling, fur-clad Muscovite with handy knout, no lurking 'secret' police pouncing down at an inadvertant sneeze or a conjured flaw of passport. . . . These have all gone, perhaps into the limbo of that famous Tartar, who was said to appear when one scratched a Russian."[96] Others praised the unexpected comforts and industry in the vast space. "There is no one, be he rich or poor, who can find a country in the civilized world where he can see more that is new and strange and interesting and instructive and thoroughly enjoyable than he can in the great Slav Empire."[97]

Although many Americans described Siberia, the most complete, factual, and focused portrayals were written by George Frederick Wright and Michael Shoemaker.[98] While acknowledging the presence of prisoners, Wright took aim at Kennan by positing their good treatment: "The scattering of so many prisoners over Siberia is therefore not so much an evil inflicted upon them as upon the country."[99] In fact, the government was using the more remote and isolated Sakhalin Island as much as Siberia for criminal detention. Among other influential "American Siberiophiles" was the head of the National Geographic Society, Edwin Grosvenor, who wrote an article and devoted the annual address to the subject in 1901.[100]

Americans naturally viewed the Russian development of Siberia and the expansion toward China in American historical terms—manifest

95. L. Lodian, "Railway Notes from the Ural Range," *Cassier's Magazine* 18, 3 (July 1900): 188–94.

96. Clarence Cary, *The Trans-Siberian Route, or Notes of a Journey from Peking to New York in 1902* (New York: Evening Post, 1902), pp. 45–46.

97. Ewing Cockrell, "Travel in Russia: Three Thousand Miles for Fifteen Dollars," *Outing* 39, 5 (February 1902): 564, 568.

98. Wright, *Asiatic Russia*, 2 vols. (New York: McClure, Phillips, 1902); Shoemaker, *The Great Siberian Railway: From St. Petersburg to Pekin* (New York and London: G. P. Putnam's, 1903). Wright made excellent use of Russian data, for example, citing from the 1897 census, that of the 28,933 people in Vladivostok, 24,443 were males (2:406).

99. Wright, *Asiatic Russia* 2:337. Wright followed up the book with a series of articles: "Western Siberia and Turkestan," *Chautauquan* 37, 2 (May 1903): 144–59; and "Eastern Siberia and Manchuria," ibid. 37, 3 (June 1903): 245–62.

100. Edwin A. Grosvenor, "Siberia," *National Geographic Magazine* 12, 9 (September 1901): 317–24; see also Ebenezer Hill, "A Trip Through Siberia," *National Geographic Magazine* 13, 2 (February 1902): 36–54, with pictures.

destiny, the Monroe Doctrine, and "the white man's burden." As Grosvenor wrote, with a touch of social Darwinism,

> Russia, not so much pursuing a definite Eastern policy as fitting in to
> the exigencies of her Eastern situation, has acted and still acts in the
> old hemisphere exactly as the United States have acted and still act in
> the new. She has simply conformed to the law of her being and to the
> logic of events. The "rectification of frontiers" to the advantage of the
> more powerful has been the course which the greater states without ex-
> ception have followed from the beginning and will follow to the end of
> time.[101]

The parallel was even extended to create a twin image. "With its farms like
the wheat fields of Dakota, its mines like those of Colorado, its rivers like
the Mississippi, and its forests like those of Canada, Siberia is a country of
marvelous promise—an Eastern California."[102]

By 1900 Siberia seems to have replaced Tolstoy as the chief topic of conversation with visiting Russians. Vladimir Bogoraz, sailing to New York in
first-class dignity in 1899, recounted his experience in the ship's dining
room: "The moment I sat down in the midst of this group, conversations
about Salem and New York stopped and my American acquaintances, as
was their wont, began to ply me with questions about Russia, the Siberian
railroad, and Siberia in general. Such questions arose in inexhaustible variety day after day and touched on every aspect of human life and endeavor."[103] Encouraged by Russians in high places, such as Mikhail
Khilkov,[104] Americans saw Siberia as a rich land of economic opportunity
and Russian ascendancy there as in their interests. Indeed, it was forecasted
that the gold production of the region would exceed that of South Africa,[105]

101. Grosvenor, "Siberia," p. 323.
102. S. M. Williams, "The New California," *Munsey's Magazine* 26, 6 (March 1902):
755. The author poeticized his observations while betraying a common racial bias.
"The yellow races do the labor, the Americans plan the fortunes. From Lake Baikal to
the Pacific the mountains are filled with gold, with iron and coal. It is a new California,
and the Americans of the Pacific coast are not blind to its potentialities." Ibid., p. 761.
103. Bogoraz [V. A. Tan], "At the Entrance to the New World," in Olga Peters
Hasty and Susanne Fusso, eds. and trans., *America Through Russian Eyes, 1874–1926*
(New London, Conn., and London: Yale University Press, 1988), p. 102.
104. Though intending a low-profile visit to the United States in 1896, Khilkov
nonetheless received considerable American capitalist attention; New York *Times*, 18
and 21 October.
105. Chester Wells Purington, "The Gold Mines of Siberia," *Engineering Magazine*
21, 6 (September 1901): 903.

and Enoch Emery publicized himself as an example of the fortunes to be made.[106]

A Russian El Dorado?

Some American companies substantiated the sense of an unfolding Russian economic boom: Westinghouse and New York Air Brake established factories for equipping railcars and locomotives with air brakes; Singer built a plant near Moscow and a headquarters in St. Petersburg; Duluth-Smith, Macmillan and Company of Philadelphia set up a new plant to build locomotives; and McCormick made plans for expansion. All these ventures were directly or indirectly connected to Siberian development and the "Witte system" of industrial progress. International investor John Hays Hammond recalled: "As I told Witte in 1898, the vast opportunities grip the imagination of Americans, because the problems presented in the industrial development of Russia would not be new to the American captains of industry."[107]

The American trademarks covered the country, from the large lathes that bored the guns for battleships, to dredges on the Volga, steamers on the Amur, cotton gins in Central Asia, and locomotives on the Siberian railroad.[108] As the Moscow consul summed it up, "Russia is a very large importer of such articles from the United States and the American Machinery is preferred above all other nationalities."[109] Emery told Frank Vanderlip in 1901 that he had $26,000 worth of John Deere plows on order for Siberia.[110]

One observer believed that the best example of American technological transfer was in the oil industry, especially in the construction of a pipeline from Baku to Batum on the Black Sea. A complete pipe mill was imported through William E. Smith along with a number of Worthington pumps for

106. Interview with Emery "An American in Siberia," *World's Work* 5 (February 1903): 3139–40. Travelers regularly commented on the popularity of American products in Siberia. See, for example, William Bunker, "American Trade Helped by Siberian Railroad," New York *Times*, 19 November 1900, p. 5.

107. *The Autobiography of John Hays Hammond*, 2 vols. (New York: Farrar and Rinehart, 1935), 2:475.

108. "The American Commercial Invasion of Russia," *Harper's Weekly*, 22 March 1902, pp. 362–63; Alexander Hume Ford, "America's Agricultural Regeneration of Russia," *Century* 62 (August 1901): 501–7.

109. Thomas Smith to Hill, 23 September 1901, DUSC, Moscow, vol. 2 (roll 2, M 456), RG 59, NA.

110. Vanderlip diary, 17 April 1901, box D-4, Vanderlip Papers, Columbia University.

the pumping stations.[111] In fact, American machinery of various kinds was in great demand in Russia—cranes, scales, punches, shears, dies, grinders, drills, rollers, typewriters, etc. Little, however, was accounted for in the trade statistics. As Alexander Hume Ford, who toured Siberia in 1899, noted, "Direct American export to Russia will probably show a shrinkage, Germany and England acting as clearing houses and being credited with Yankee ingenuity." He estimated that the value of American machines sent into Russia in 1900 by these countries, mainly through Hull or Hamburg, was $20 million, more than double the "official" American exports to Russia.[112] The reason most often cited for this was the reluctance of Americans to grapple directly with Russian regulations and bureaucracy; instead they preferred to leave such details to those closer to the scene.

Optimistic views of commercial relations were balanced by incongruities and problems in the compatibility of American technology and Russian development, symbolized by a photograph of a McCormick reaper pulled by camels and a note that the heavy Baldwin locomotives were demolishing the lightly laid track across Manchuria.[113] Other perspectives rang the alarm about Russian economic interests inevitably clashing with American ones in East Asia. American trade or technical assistance would only hasten Russia's capture of the China market.[114] Or, placed in a general context, "Russia is organizing the machinery of her economic system in a manner to make her the early and dangerous rival of the great industrial nations."[115]

Proposals for direct loans to the Russian government fell through in 1898, revealing weaknesses in the presumed links between the two countries. One joint Anglo-American venture whose principals were Hammond and Leopold Hirsch was to be guaranteed by platinum concessions, which re-

111. Ernest H. Foster, "A Russian Petroleum Pipeline: Carrying Oil from Baku to Batoum," *Cassier's Magazine* 19, 1 (November 1900): 3–16; Smith to Charles R. Crane, 22 August/4 September 1901, box 2, Crane Papers, BA, Columbia University.

112. Ford, "Russia as a Market for Machinery and Machine Tools," *Engineering Magazine* 21, 4 (July 1901): 494. Not surprisingly, some Englishmen became anxious about the rising American presence in Russia; Edward Lunn, "The Progress of the Russian Empire," *Eclectic Magazine* 68, 6 (December 1898): 835–38; Charles Johnson, "The Americanizing of Russia," *Harper's Weekly*, 25 April 1903, pp. 680–81.

113. Ford, "America's Agricultural Regeneration," p. 62: 504; Ford, "Engineering Opportunities in the Russian Empire," *Engineering Magazine* 21, 1 (April 1901): 33.

114. Romney Wheelock, "Russia's Blow at American Commerce," *Gunton's Magazine* 20 (May 1901): 432–40.

115. Charles A. Conant, "Russia as a World Power," *North American Review* 507 (February 1899): 178.

quired a time-consuming and exhausting tour of the Urals region and Siberia. Hammond told Witte that the main problem encountered was bureaucratic obstruction, but the Russians were also wary of such a sweeping arrangement.[116] Another project involving a solely American loan of $80 million was proposed in 1898 by Charles Flint and William Ivins on behalf of a financial consortium that included J. P. Morgan and John D. Rockefeller.[117] To chargé d'affaires Herbert Pierce, Witte evinced surprise at this, because he thought that the United States was a borrower and not a creditor nation. Pierce believed that the offer had definitely made Witte more respectful of American economic power.[118] Indeed, the Russian minister immediately dispatched Ivan Vyshnegradskii and Vladimir Rutkovskii to the United States. According to one source, their mishandling of the negotiation was the reason that Morgan pulled out and the proposal was withdrawn.[119]

Yet a major problem was a fundamental difference in economic outlook. Minneapolis businessman Frank T. Heffelfinger visited St. Petersburg in February and March 1901 expressly to investigate the possibilities of building grain elevators along the new Siberian railroad. He had already been warned in Hamburg that "while they need badly just what I suggest, at the same time . . . it will take years to bring it about." He was told that Witte was the man to see.[120] In St Petersburg Tower advised him to see Khilkov first, who was supportive and encouraging, and through him Heffelfinger gained entry to Minister of State Domains Aleksei Ermolov, who also voiced interest but had no authority. Finally, with Freshville as interpreter, he spoke with Witte for ten to fifteen minutes. Although the minister ruled out Heffelfinger's plan for an Ob River rail-water transit system for Siberian grain, he would consider a written proposal on elevators.[121]

Heffelfinger, however, decided not to pursue the matter. Among the reasons he stated were the poor condition of the railroads, the loose manner of doing business "on the principle that if it is not done to-day you can do it

116. Hammond, *Autobiography* 2:455–65.

117. Viacheslav V. Lebedev, *Russko-amerikanskie ekonomicheskie otnosheniia (1900–1917 gg.)* (Moscow: Nauka, 1964), pp. 34–35.

118. To Hitchcock, 24 November 1898, box 37, Hitchcock Papers, RG 316, NA; Hitchcock to Hay, 28 and 31 December 1898, DUSM, Russia, vol. 53 (roll 53, M 35), RG 59, NA.

119. Lebedev, *Russko-amerikanskie otnosheniia*, pp. 35–36.

120. Journal, 2 February 1900, Heffelfinger Papers, MinnHS.

121. Ibid., 2 March 1900.

tomorrow," and no regularly established commodity markets or grading of grain. Finally, in reference to Siberia: "The Government feel like this, that it is all there to be developed and will not get away, so (unlike we Americans who want to do it all in a day) part of it can go on now and the balance can be done in the next century. We cannot understand why they are so slow and they in their turn say, why are we rushing so."[122] Large-scale construction of grain elevators, such as those dominating the prairie landscape, was never undertaken in Russia.[123]

To meet the need for equipment for the new railroads Russia had induced both Westinghouse and New York Air Brake to establish factories. Then, in another example of the risks of doing business in Russia, the government decided to save money and not to use modern air brakes on the Siberian freight cars. Westinghouse still had a contract for equipping locomotives, while New York Air Brake, with some success, switched to producing oil-burning engines. Expectations were in general not met, and the plant was eventually sold to McCormick-International Harvester. In 1901 Westinghouse reported losses of $200,000 to $300,000 a year in Russia, at least in part because of an old spinning mill still operating in St. Petersburg.[124]

While some Americans were tendering loans, building factories, and selling machinery, intense commercial rivalries between the two countries continued on two fronts: grain and oil. The new combination of Nobel and the French Rothschilds competed with Standard Oil (Rockefeller) for the rapidly growing world demand for kerosene, producing a scramble for markets, especially in East Asia, where it was feared that Russia would drive out the American product completely.[125] Consequently, the United States was kept well informed of Russian oil developments.[126] Competition was matched by attempts to reach an understanding on an equitable division of the market between the two giant concerns. Because of depletion of the Pennsylvania

122. Ibid.

123. In a conversation (September 1990) with the author, Sergei Khrushchev inquired about the circular metal buildings he saw on Kansas farms. When told they were for grain storage, he observed that his father had wanted to erect these on Soviet farms but never accomplished it.

124. Vanderlip diary, 15 April 1901, box D-4, Vanderlip Papers, Columbia University.

125. Edward Bedloe (Canton consul), "Russia in the Chinese Markets," CR 58, 218 (November 1898): 397–98.

126. For example, see Chambers's lengthy report from Batum of 7 March 1898, CR 47, 212 (May 1898): 37–50.

wells, in 1898 Standard Oil even tried to buy a substantial interest in the Baku fields, but Russian interests would not consider it.[127]

Prospects of cooperation persuaded National City Bank of New York, with strong Rockefeller support, to organize a St. Petersburg branch in 1899. Other direct attempts to acquire financing were spearheaded by Adolf Rothstein, director of the St. Petersburg International Bank. An able financier who was often referred to as "Witte's Jew," Rothstein visited the United States in quest of loans in 1900. He was lavishly entertained by leading American capitalists but to little avail. Factors affecting the negative outcome were the rivalry between the interests of Rockefeller (National City Bank) and Morgan (New York Life) and the failure of Rothstein's bank in 1901. Ultimately, most American financial projects for Russia came to nothing, with Russia's intransigence in Asia and oil competition bearing much of the blame.[128]

The American-Siberian connection had one more interesting dimension. In 1898 minister Khilkov sent a delegation to the United States "to learn what Americans do through the Young Men's Christian Association for the religious and philanthropic advantage of railway employees."[129] The YMCA's growing international mission thereafter focused on Russia. With the patronage of New York benefactors James Stokes and John D. Rockefeller, Jr., and the dedication of John R. Mott and Baron Pavel Nikolai, the YMCA was launched in Russia by 1900.[130] Initially directed toward isolated railroad workers, it was soon organized in major cities. Despite occasional Russian conservative reaction, the YMCA prospered and expanded through World War I, until it made a last stand—in Siberia—in 1920.

Globe-trotters

Siberian dreams, Eastern tensions, business opportunities, and diplomatic propaganda increased the traffic between the two countries considerably in

127. Alexander A. Fursenko, *The Battle for Oil: The Economics and Politics of International Corporate Conflict over Petroleum, 1860–1930*, trans. and ed. Gregory Freeze (Greenwich, Conn., and London: Jai Press, 1990), pp. 81–92.

128. Such is the conclusion of the leading Russian authority on the subject: Alexander A. Fursenko, "Iz istorii Russko-Amerikanskikh otnoshenii na rubezhe xix-xx vv.," in *Iz istorii imperializm v Rossii* (Moscow-Leningrad: Nauka, 1959), pp. 250–66; see also Lebedev, *Russko-amerikanskie otnosheniia*, pp. 55–64.

129. "Russian Railroad Y.M.C.A.," *Chautauquan* 32, 2 (November 1900): 121.

130. C. Howard Hopkins, *John R. Mott, 1865–1955: A Biography* (Grand Rapids, Mich.: William B. Eerdmans, 1979), pp. 250–53, 332–35.

On the Trans-Siberian Railroad, 1903. From Burton Holmes, Travelogues *(1908)*

the years just before the Russo-Japanese War. Although the blandishments of seasoned American officials inspired tourism,[131] some travelers may have thought of themselves as emulating the heroic and much-publicized feats of Teddy Roosevelt as they ventured into Siberia and Central Asia. Extended stays were also more common: a special count of Americans in Moscow during the 1905 revolution found over a hundred in permanent residence. Most short-term tourists were simply lost in the crowds, but there were a few notable American visitors who would attract attention wherever they went: Indiana Senator Albert Beveridge, Senator Henry Cabot Lodge, William Rainey Harper, Burton Holmes, George Kennan, Henry Adams, Chicago businessmen Horace Porter and Charles Crane, erstwhile presidential contender William Jennings Bryan, Clara Barton, and banker Frank Vanderlip, who, as assistant secretary of treasury, had won laurels for financing the Spanish-American War.

Beveridge leveraged his way in the summer of 1901 through several interviews—Khilkov, Witte, and Pobedonostsev. With Burton Holmes tagging along annoying everyone with his sixty-millimeter movie camera, the senator conferred with the laird of Yasnaya Polyana.[132] He then covered as much of the Trans-Siberian Railway as was possible en route to Manchuria and China. In his detailed observations of Russia for the *Saturday Evening*

131. For example, Pierce, "Russia," *Atlantic Monthly* 90, 540 (October 1902): 465–74.
132. George Kennan to his wife, 7 July 1901, box 15, Kennan Papers, LC. Jeremiah Curtin, who was also there at the time, grumbled that "for every ounce of flesh [Beveridge] has a pound of conceit." *Memoirs*, p. 848.

Post, later expanded into *The Russian Advance*, Beveridge was at once critical and sympathetic. For example, he was surprised at the decrepit condition of the Tolstoy estate and adjoining village but also at the number and variety of newspapers and journals available there.[133] He contrasted antiquated factories and slipshod management of railroads with visionary plans for development and resource potential. He saw a huge expanse of American opportunity waiting in the Russian Far East.

Already drifting into an anti-Russian stance politically, Lodge went to Russia in 1901 to find out "how soon they will reach the point of dangerous and destructive rivalry."[134] His companion was Bostonian Henry Adams, who was struck by Russian backwardness. Adams recalled a prescient conversation with his fellow traveler:

> The tourist-student . . . asked the Senator whether he should allow three generations, or more, to swing the Russian people into the Western movement. The Senator seemed disposed to ask for more. . . . Very likely, Russia would instantly become the most brilliant constellation of human progress through all the ordered stages of good; but meanwhile one might give a value as movement of inertia to the mass, and assume a slow acceleration that would, at the end of a generation, leave the gap between east and west relatively the same.[135]

Year one of the new century was indeed a busy time for Americans in Russia. George Kennan, having excused himself from Russian affairs to serve the Red Cross and journalistic enterprise in Cuba, melted into the crowd in St. Petersburg, but as soon as his presence was detected, he was politely escorted back over the Russian frontier. He had, however, renewed acquaintances, met more people, and gathered material during the four-week sojourn that would lend authenticity to another batch of critical articles.[136]

Drawn by business, culture, and curiosity, Crane and Porter made regular trips to Russia. Crane was already a convert to a better American under-

---

133. *The Russian Advance* (New York: Harper, 1904).

134. According to William C. Widenor, *Henry Cabot Lodge and the Search for an American Foreign Policy* (Berkeley and Los Angeles: University of California Press, 1980), p. 157. Caution must be used, especially for this period, in citing "contemporary" impressions that may have been molded by later events.

135. *The Education of Henry Adams: An Autobiography* (Boston: Houghton Mifflin, 1918), p. 410.

136. Frederick Travis, *George Kennan and the American-Russian Relationship, 1865-1924* (Athens: Ohio University Press, 1990), p. 254.

standing of the "good" Russia and devoted much time and money to it, while Porter, at least according to his daughter, was more circumspect and mystified by the dual nature of the country. Enjoying the luxuries of St. Petersburg, including a luncheon with Nicholas II in 1902, he was acutely aware of the conditions in the countryside. As his daughter related,

> A government that tolerated such extravagance among its upper classes and such misery among the people, my father kept saying, was bound to collapse, and with a pretty hard tumble. . . . Because the average intelligent Russian likes to write and to talk,—especially talk,—but does not like to work. . . .
>
> The Tsar had impressed my father as a ruler having little force of character or sound judgement. "They need a man like old Peter the Great, but I don't believe that even he could keep this country together."[137]

Vanderlip also experienced contrasts: an otherworldly Easter service at St. Isaac's Cathedral in St. Petersburg followed conversations on rapid economic progress with Witte in Moscow.[138] Bryan went to Russia in November 1903, conversed with Nicholas II about the virtues of free speech, and talked and walked in the snow with Tolstoy at Yasnaya Polyana. He concluded that Russia had a great future but that it would be a difficult and unpredictable passage.[139]

In general Russia received a good press in the United States into 1903. Painting a positive if naive portrait of the country were experienced Russophiles Isabel Hapgood and Edmund Noble, the latter writing for the *Chautauquan*.[140] And Pierce threw the weight of his official position as embassy secretary into his judgement that "accounts have greatly exaggerated the proportion of exiles deported into Siberia for political offenses. . . . There is

---

137. Elsie Porter Mende, *An American Soldier and Diplomat: Horace Porter* (New York: Frederick A. Stokes, 1927), p. 251.

138. Vanderlip, *From Farm Boy to Financier*, (New York and London: Appleton-Century, 1935), pp. 121–23.

139. *The Memoirs of William Jennings Bryan* (Philadelphia: United Publishers, 1925), p. 317.

140. As examples, Hapgood, "Russian Women," *Chautauquan* 32, 6 (March 1901): 589–94; 33, 7 (April 1901): 14–20; and "Up the Volga," 36, 4 (January 1903): 370–88; Noble, "Russia's Holy City," *Chautauquan* 36, 5 (February 1903): 475–90; and "The Capital of All the Russias," *Chautauquan* 37, 1 (April 1903): 26–42.

nothing cruel either in the national character or in that of the average Russian official."[141]

There were discordant voices, but most were ignored until later. During an unusually venturesome honeymoon in 1902, William Seymour Edwards recorded "a profound and monstrous discontent—a discontent so deep-rooted and so intense that when the inevitable hour strikes, as strike it must, the world will then behold in Russia a saturnalia of blood and tears, a squaring of ten centuries' accounts, more fraught with human anguish and human joy than ever dreamed a Marat and a Robespierre, more direful and more glad than yet mankind have known."[142] Subsequent events may have honed this insight before it was published in 1906.

With blatant social Darwinism, Edmund Noble predicted a major political revolution occurring in the wake of a military disaster. "They need a more advanced type of government; they need still more, the modern and progressive institutions which such a type would serve. In the realm of nature, the advent of the fit may be retarded, but it cannot be permanently delayed."[143] Others simply foresaw Russia following a predestined and geopolitically predetermined American path to freedom, democracy, and affluent capitalism.[144]

Once More the Grand Dukes

The Russian parade to the United States around the turn of the century was not quite as distinguished as earlier, but it did include the eccentric Vasily Vereshchagin, some minor composers, university lecturers, students, and a couple of grand dukes. In December 1899, Grand Duke Kirill, a naval officer, first cousin of Nicholas II, and father of one of the last generally recognized heads of the Romanov family,[145] came through San Francisco from Japan and, pestered by reporters at every stop across the country, quickly

141. Pierce, "Russia," 466.
142. Letter to his father, St. Petersburg, 18 September 1902, in *Through Scandinavia to Moscow* (Cincinnati, Ohio: Robert Clarke, 1906), p. 153.
143. Noble, "The Future of Russia," *Atlantic Monthly* 76, 517 (November 1900): 616.
144. For example, Charles Johnston, "The Americanizing of Russia," *Harper's Weekly*, 25 April 1903, pp. 680–81.
145. Grand Duke Vladimir Kirillovich died in 1991 soon after enjoying a nostalgic homecoming in St. Petersburg.

reached New York. He spent only a few days there visiting the Russian Orthodox church, a theater, and a Russian club. He recalled being impressed
by San Francisco harbor, Chicago, the comfort of Pullman sleepers, and
New York night life.[146]

Kirill's brother Boris followed the same route more leisurely and with con-
siderably more fanfare in 1902. After three days at Yosemite, he dallied in
Chicago, visiting the stockyards and the meat-packing plants of Swift and
Armour. His chief hosts were Charles and Richard Crane and William
Rainey Harper, who guided him around the university.[147] He also had a little
excitement after lunch at the Saddle and Cycle Club, when he insisted on
taking the wheel of an automobile, "leaving behind a group of apprehensive
Russian officials." He zigzagged down the street, climbed an embankment,
and slammed into a tree, but was luckily uninjured.[148]

In the East the grand duke and his party enjoyed a relaxed stay in a
twelve-room suite at the Waldorf-Astoria, attending a light opera at the
Knickerbocker, shopping at Tiffany's, and walking in Central Park. Despite
his Chicago mishap, he also visited an auto dealership. He was quoted as
saying, "What a wonderful country this is. It's nothing but electricity here,
there, and everywhere."[149] After a safe ride on the yacht of shipping magnate
Charles Flint, he reviewed the cadets at West Point and lodged with the
Vanderbilts at Newport.[150] Former secretary of legation Pierce and ambassador Cassini conducted him from there to Oyster Bay for lunch with President Roosevelt and his family.[151] Then he missed the boat for his scheduled
departure—because Cornelius Vanderbilt's yacht broke down—and had to
stay an additional week.[152]

146. Cassini to Murav'ev, 24 December 1899, f. 133, op. 470, d. 110, AVPR; Grand
Duke Kirill Vladimirovich, *My Life in Russia's Service—Then and Now* (London: Selwyn
and Blount, 1939), pp. 98–100. One of his companions on the American ship crossing
the Pacific was Alexander Graham Bell.

147. "Grand Duke Boris Here," Chicago *Tribune*, 16 August 1902, p. 3; "Czar's
Cousin Likes Chicago," Chicago *Tribune*, 17 August 1902.

148. "Duke Boris in Auto Runaway," Chicago *Tribune*, 18 August 1902, p. 1.

149. "Grand Duke Boris Here for a Visit," New York *Times*, 29 August 1902, p. 9.

150. Charles R. Flint, *Memories of an Active Life: Men, and Ships, and Sealing Wax*
(New York and London: G. P. Putnam's Sons, 1923), p. 196; "Grand Duke Boris Visits
West Point," New York *Times*, 31 August 1902, p. 7.

151. Pierce to Cassini, 3 September, 1902, f. 170, op. 512/1, d. 158, AVPR; "Grand
Duke Boris the President's Guest," New York *Times*, 5 September 1902, p. 8. The
United States took the visit seriously in another respect, assigning two secret service
men to the ducal party.

152. "Grand Duke Boris Missed His Steamer," New York *Times*, 10 September 1902,
p. 7.

Russians Educate America

A new form of contact was initiated by distinguished Russians on the lecture circuit, most notably Sergei Volkonskii, "anarchist-prince" Peter Kropotkin, historian and sociologist Maksim Kovalevskii, and historian and liberal politician Paul Miliukov. Volkonskii, descendant of a leading Decembrist and Siberian developer, followed up his Chicago fair visit with a series of talks on Russian history and literature. Speaking in fluent English, he lectured at Cornell and Stanford and then at the Lowell Institute in Boston, at Cornell again, and at the University of Chicago in 1896–1897.[153] He stressed the progression of Russian dissent from the Decembrists through Westerners and Slavophiles to the nihilists. He thought he achieved his greatest success at Chicago: "In no place in the country have I had the feeling of touching *all* social classes and the consciousness of not only 'lecturing,' not only offering an entertainment, but of doing a 'work.' "[154]

Kropotkin had spent five involuntary years helping to "develop" Siberia, and during his subsequent emigré life he visited America in 1897 and again in 1901 to expound his doctrine of "anarchist communism." He took a Canadian transcontinental journey on his first trip and then spoke mainly to working-class groups in Boston, New York, Philadelphia, and Chicago. In 1901 he was invited to present a series of lectures at the Lowell Institute on Russian literature and appeared on a number of college campuses—Harvard, Wellesley, Chicago, Wisconsin, Illinois.[155] Among the prominent Americans he met were Jane Addams, Booker T. Washington, Charles Eliot Norton, Andrew Carnegie, and Edward Everett Hale.

By this time William Rainey Harper, backed by Charles Crane and inspired by Volkonskii's success, was eager to organize a genuine Russian studies center at the University of Chicago. He toured Russia with Crane in

153. Albert Parry, "Charles R. Crane, Friend of Russia," *Russian Review* 6, 2 (Spring 1947): 25; White, *Autobiography* 2:45; William Rainey Harper to Volkonskii, 18 February 1896, box 2, file 22, W. R. Harper Papers, University of Chicago; Sergei Volkonskii, *Moi Vospominaniia* (Munich: Mednyi Vsadnik, 192?), pp. 258–69. For the published version of his lectures, see Prince Serge Wolkonsky, *Pictures of Russian History and Russian Literature* (Boston: Lamson, Wolffe, 1897).

154. Volkonskii (Chicago) to Charles Norton, 10 April 1896, file 7604, Norton Papers, Houghton Library, Harvard University.

155. Martin A. Miller, *Kropotkin* (Chicago and London: University of Chicago Press, 1976), p. 171; George Woodcock and Ivan Avakumovic, *The Anarchist Prince: A Biographical Study of Peter Kropotkin* (London: T. V. Boardman, 1949), pp. 274–85.

1900 and met Pobedonostsev and Witte as well as Tolstoy. In an interview with Nicholas II he related his plans to establish a chair of Russian and invite special lecturers. The emperor was apparently very pleased to hear this and was delighted with Crane's remark that they had really appreciated his "Oriental hospitality." "That is one thing we do not want to change," he observed.[156] Harper and Crane tried to induce Tolstoy to come to Chicago to inaugurate the series but with no success: "The old gentleman was much interested but is, I think, much too feeble."[157]

Then Kovalevskii and Miliukov, the liberal teacher and his most prominent student, were sought out for special university lectures in 1901 and 1903, respectively.[158] Both had large, attentive audiences for their presentations on Russian institutions, history, and culture. Kovalevskii, who had traveled in the United States in 1881 and published articles on American education, settlement policies, and immigration, seemed to enjoy himself in the aristocratic company of the Crane set in Chicago and of Henry Adams in Washington, D.C.[159] He was, however, disappointed to find the university "an educational institution rather than a place of higher learning and research."[160] As if to confirm that observation, Harper hired a Greco-Russian undergraduate, Xenophon Kalamatiano, to offer the first Russian class at the university in 1902.[161]

The more extensive lectures of Miliukov, delivered during the hot summer of 1903, helped him to crystallize his political thought on the eve of the rev-

156. As quoted by Crane to Cornelia Crane (wife), 28 May 1900, box 1, Crane Papers, BA, Columbia University.

157. Crane to Cornelia Crane, 1 May 1900, ibid. According to Curtin, who saw Tolstoy soon afterwards, the "old gentleman" was not impressed by Harper: "The man is unable to grasp any of the higher ideas of life." As quoted in Curtin, Memoirs, p. 784.

158. Miliukov to Crane, 25 April 1902, box 2, Crane Papers, BA, Columbia University, in which he offered to double the number of lectures (twelve) given by Kovalevskii and guaranteed fresh material—for the right money. Miliukov might have come earlier, except that the visiting position for 1902 was already promised to Thomas Masaryk, the liberal Czech historian.

159. Maksim M. Kovalevskii, "American Impressions," Russian Review 10, 1 (January 1951): 39–44.

160. Russian Review 10, 2 (April 1951): 107.

161. This colorful graduate (1898) of the Culver Military Academy in Indiana taught without salary in order to keep his eligibility as a long-distance runner for Alonzo Stagg's cross-country and track teams; Kalamatiano to W. R. Harper, 2 January 1902, and Harper to Kalamatiano, 4 January 1902 (c), box 6, file 4, W. R. Harper Papers, University of Chicago; Cap and Gown 8 (1902): 68, 172, 178. He is singled out here because of his mysterious future role (1917–1921) as a sort of American Sidney Reilly.

Paul Miliukov. From William English Walling, Russia's Message *(1910)*

olution of 1905. Specifically, he called for an alliance of liberals and moderate socialists to execute the revolution; either group alone would be too weak to constitute an effective democratic government.[162] He acknowledged his debt to Crane, who in turn was pleased with Miliukov's Chicago reception: "Mr. Milyukov had more success than the other lecturers and toward the end had as many as one hundred and fifty auditors."[163] At least a few Americans were being briefed on the approaching storm.

After intervals in Macedonia (with Crane), London, St. Petersburg, and Paris, Miliukov returned to the United States in the fall of 1904 to lecture at the Lowell Institute in Boston, again sponsored by Crane. At the same time

162. Thomas Riha, *A Russian European: Paul Miliukov in Russian Politics* (Notre Dame, Ind., and London: University of Notre Dame Press, 1969), pp. 49–52; Pavel Miliukov, *Vospominaniia 1859–1917*, 2 vols. (Moscow: Sovremennik, 1990), 1:218–24.

163. To Cornelia Crane, 18 June 1903, box 1, Crane Papers, BA, Columbia University.

a popular Russian radical and terrorist, Ekaterina Breshko-Breshkovskaia, whose hardships in Siberia had already been highlighted by Kennan, was speaking to less-dignified audiences in Boston.[164] So was Russian-Jewish anarchist Emma Goldman, who achieved notoriety for revolutionary activism and street-corner preaching. And the applause of American audiences seemed to move Russians toward even more radical stances.

Scientific inquiry was also fostered by Russian contacts. Vladimir Bogoraz of the Ethnographic Museum of the Academy of Sciences in St. Petersburg led a field team on behalf of the American Museum of Natural History to northeastern Siberia in 1900–1901.[165] His was part of a larger expedition funded by Morris Jessup to confirm the relationships between the peoples of northeastern Siberia with those of northwestern America. A poet and liberal supporter of the revolutionary cause, Bogoraz then worked at the museum in New York, publishing his findings in *American Anthropologist*, and later collecting them into a book.[166] Bogoraz and his associates complemented the comparative folklore investigations of Jeremiah Curtin.[167]

America for Russian Eyes

A few Russians continued to seek life experiences in the United States out of curiosity, for adventure, to find employment, and incidentally or primarily to publish for home consumption. Inspired by writings about America and in search of a career as an actor, a young Russian, writing under the name of Bostunov, described being down and out in Hoboken, Pittsburgh, and Chicago and working as a bellboy, waiter, seaman, doorman, babysitter, itinerant artist, and finally in a poorhouse and as a hobo, hopping freight trains and hosting parasites.[168] The depiction of the lower depths of American life was done, however, without bitterness and with a sense of humor.

164. Riha, *A Russian European*, pp. 66–68; Miliukov, *Vospominaniia* 1:226–28. Miliukov's memoirs are useful for impressions and character sketches but not reliable on dates.

165. Hasty and Fusso, *American Through Russian Eyes*, pp. 85–98.

166. Bogoraz, *The Folklore of Northeastern Asia as Compared with That of Northwestern America* (New York: G. P. Putnam's Sons, 1902). See also Stanley A. Freed, Ruth S. Freed, and Laila Williamson, "Scholars Amid Squalor," *Natural History* 97, 3 (March 1988): 60–68.

167. Curtin, *A Journey in Southern Siberia* (Boston: Little, Brown, 1909).

168. E. Bostunov, "Bez pulia i iakoria," *Istoricheskii Vestnik* 69, 11 (November 1897): 493–524; 70, 12 (December 1897): 821–52. British author Mayne Reid was his particular inspiration.

The journal *Istoricheskii Vestnik* (Historical herald) also published a series of articles by two other Russians in America, Evgenyi Pravdin and Evgenyi Matrosov. Although Pravdin concentrated on members of the fairer sex and how they advertised themselves for marriage,[169] Matrosov chose such traditional subjects as Russians in the United States and a description of the federal capital.[170] Most of these stories were written informally for a general audience to show the United States in a fairly positive light. Matrosov did publish an unflattering account of slum conditions in New York, Boston, and Chicago after resentment flared because of American support for Japan.[171] Bogoraz also described immigrant life, especially Jewish sweatshops, in grim tones, but he marveled at discovering while on a transcontinental train trip three black porters who were working their way through medical school. He felt embarrassed when one of them asked how the "emanicipated" serfs were doing in Russia.[172]

Demonstrating that not all Russian visitors were poor immigrants, grand dukes, or sensation seekers, Raphael Zon came to the United States to study forestry at Cornell University. A graduate of the University of Kazan, Zon was from a prominent Russianized Jewish family (Masinzon) of the Volga region. After Cornell, he worked in the Department of Agriculture in Washington, married a more traditional Jewish woman from Vilna, and quickly settled into American middle-class professional life.[173]

Witte and the United States

Although frequently bothered by a variety of American fortune hunters, Sergei Witte aspired to bolster the old American connection, mainly because of his fascination with the American "economic miracle." Witte, in fact, had caught at least a mild case of *Amerikanizm*—the belief in an American economic model for Russia. Carried away with the ideas of Friedrich List concerning the central government's role in shaping industrial progress, he saw their clearest successes in

169. Pravdin, "Zhenshchina v strane svobody," *Istoricheskii Vestnik* 90, 9 (October 1899): 289–324; 92, 12 (December 1899): 1177–1210.

170. Matrosov, "Zaokeonskaia Rus'," *Istoricheskii Vestnik* 67, 1 (January 1897): 131–60; "Vashington, stolitsa Soedinennykh shtatov (po povodu ego stoletiia)," *Istoricheskii Vestnik* 85, 9 (September 1901): 1042–89.

171. Matrosov, "Amerikanskiia trushchoby (sotsiologichesko-opisatel'ny: ocherk)," *Istoricheskii Vestnik* 96, 4 (April 1904): 171–88.

172. "The Black Student," in Hasty and Fusso, *America Through Russian Eyes*, pp. 120–21.

173. Various correspondence, Zon Papers, MinnHS.

American "experiments" (Homestead Act, railroad land grants), which accounts for his interest in the 1893 Chicago exposition. In 1897 when Emperor Wilhelm of Germany privately warned Witte about the American trade threat to Europe and the need for common protective tariffs, he politely refused to participate, pointing out that the United States was a traditional friend and that Britain was the greater menace.[174]

Some Americans who failed to win Russian concessions thought that Witte was steering a hard-line against the United States. In part, they were correct in that Witte's foremost objective was to foster Russian industrial development. On the other hand, Americans did obtain a considerable amount of Russian business—on the Siberian railroad, mining enterprises in Siberia, building a dry dock in Vladivostok, the Singer Company's expansion—and Witte even came to the rescue of life insurance companies under attack by Russian interests. In July 1901 he told ambassador Tower:

> We like Americans, and we want to keep good relations with them, because they are the people we have the most confidence in. They are the most honest and single minded. They declare that their interests are commercial and we believe them. When they come into our country for trade, we know that they are sincere in their representations; and that what they assert to be their purpose *is in fact their purpose*, not as in the case of certain other people we have to deal with. . . .
>
> America is a young and growing country, like our own; and there are no enmities or jealousies between us, because there are no conflicts of interest, and there cannot be any. I say to you frankly, . . . that we want you to direct your commerce and your trade into Russia, but we do *not* want the Germans and the English here! When I am told of an American enterprise that seeks to gain a foothold in the Empire, I give it all the encouragement I can; and I assure you I do not do that in the case of these other nations.[175]

Witte's hearty welcome to American trade may have been genuine, but his assertion of no conflict between the two countries could be considered "famous last words."

Trade did grow during this period, especially on the import side of the

174. *The Memoirs of Sergei Witte*, trans. and ed. Sidney Harcave (Armonk, N.Y.: M. E. Sharpe, 1990), p. 268.
175. As quoted by Tower to Hay, 3 July 1901, DUSM, Russia, vol. 58 (roll 58, M 35), RG 59, NA.

ledger. In 1904, according to Russian records, American imports held a respectable third place, $31.2 million, behind Germany ($112.6 million) and Britain ($51.2 million).[176] As has already been noted, a large quantity of American goods came through Germany and other European states and were counted in the statistics of those countries. One of the most knowledgeable experts on trade estimated that cotton alone, directly and indirectly imported from the United States, totaled $40 million annually.[177] In reality the United States probably held second place, not far behind Germany. Americans also generated considerable business within Russia. New York Life had emerged as by far the largest insurance company in the country with $10,469,005 in outstanding policies. The largest Russian company held $5,678,162, while Equitable was in fifth place with $3,750,000.[178] Singer, International Harvester, Westinghouse, and other companies, whose stock was held primarily by Americans, operated in Russia as Russian companies.

East Asia

As Kropotkin, Miliukov, Breshko-Breshkovskaia, and most other Russian liberals and radicals who lectured in the United States were basking in the hospitality and support for their cause, Russian conservative nationalists were becoming much less enamored of a nation that seemed to be posing a more serious foreign and domestic threat.[179] Pravdin, writing from Pennsylvania in 1898, warned Russians of American political and economic expansionism in the Pacific, of a new "American messianism."[180] Historians of both countries, such as William Appleman Williams and Lev Zubok, have

176. Watts to Loomis, 17 April 1905, DUSC, St. Petersburg, vol. 24 (roll 18, M 81), RG 59, NA. In fourth place was Russia's ally France—$13 million.

177. Herbert Pierce to Hay, 11 October 1899, DUSM, Russia, vol. 55 (roll 55, M 35), RG 59, NA. Much of it was coming from U.S. southern ports to Marseilles, then being transshipped to Black Sea ports; Thomas Smith to Day, 4 July 1898, DUSC, Moscow, vol. 4 (roll 2, M 456), RG 59, NA.

178. Watts to Loomis, 21 May 1904, DUSC, St. Petersburg, vol. 24 (roll 18, M 81), RG 59, NA.

179. A good example is a book by an old visitor to the United States, the conservative historian Konstantin Skal'kovskii, *Vneshnaia politika Rossii i polozhenie inostranikh gosudarstv* (St. Petersburg, 1901).

180. Pravdin, "Novorozhdennyi messianizm strany dollara i staryi svet," *Istoricheskii Vestnik* 74, 11 (November 1898): 704–21.

emphasized imperialist aggression and rivalry during this period.[181] And indeed the evidence exists—such as Theodore Roosevelt's often-cited plan to use Japan against Russia for American gain.

The official view of the Russian government at the turn of the century, however, still emphasized traditional friendship. For example, while recognizing the importance of Hawaii, the government considered it more in Russia's interest for the islands to be under American control than Japanese, that is, for the United States to be a barrier to rising Japanese influence.[182] What complicated the situation was the simultaneous expansion of interests of all three countries in East Asia: Russia in constructing the railroad across Manchuria, Japan in acquiring mainland hegemony in Korea, the United States in the search for the northern China market. And trade opportunities in Manchuria beckoned, certainly to Secretary of State John Hay as he formulated the open door policy, which was at least partly provoked by an increased Russian presence there.[183] Cassini at first believed that the new American initiative was not contrary to Russian interests, that Russia could even take advantage of it to expand its Far Eastern market with Central Asian cotton, Siberian grain, and Caucasus kerosene. But after the summer of 1899, he became more alarmed about a shift in public opinion against Russia that was reflected in sensationalist American newspapers.[184]

A negative view of Russia had always existed in the United States but had become increasingly apparent since 1880 because of the Jewish problem and Kennan's attacks on the "system." Ameliorated to some extent by the Tolstoy fever, business opportunities, and reminders of historic amity, the American tide was again turning against Russia at the beginning of the twentieth century. Developments in East Asia were one pressing cause. That this was the contemporary impression is illustrated by the appraisal of University of Wisconsin professor Paul Reinsch.

Though the expansion of Russian influence in Asia is undoubtedly a serious matter, and may entail very grave consequences on Western

181. Williams, *American-Russian Relations, 1781–1947* (New York: Rinehart, 1952), and Zubok, *Ekspansionistskaia politika SShA v nachale XX veka* (Moscow: Nauka, 1969).

182. Project of instructions to Cassini, 29 January 1898, f. 133, op. 470, d. 113, AVPR.

183. Tyler Dennett, *John Hay: From Poetry to Politics* (New York: Dodd, Mead, 1933), p. 291.

184. Cassini to Murav'ev, 25 October/6 November 1899, f. 133, op. 470, d. 113, AVPR.

Civilization, that gross misrepresentation of every act, motive, and impulse of the northern empire and its government, with which we are constantly meeting, tends to obscure the clear vision of actual political facts, and at the same time is likely to engender deep resentment among the Russian people.[185]

The Boxer Rebellion in 1900 produced some unity of action and purpose but also an expanded and extended Russian military presence in Manchuria. When Russia was slow to withdraw these forces as promised, it heightened the suspicion that this Eurasian power was taking advantage of unrest in the area. In Reinsch's judgement, "It is by combining strength of purpose, irresistable will, and the show of great force, with the milder methods of corruption and official blandishment, that Russia is so successful in the Orient."[186] And Russia was indeed doing what some Americans feared most: consolidating an exclusive trade zone, most obviously for the kerosene market.[187]

What John Hay saw happening in East Asia was a dangerous precedent that could lead to its division into economic zones. As he sought international support for his open door policy against perceived Russian intransigence, Cassini interpreted his actions to St. Petersburg as steering the United States toward Britain and Japan, a long-held Russian fear.[188] Complicating matters was the fact that the Foreign Ministry had little influence over Russian policy in the Far East; much of it was handled personally by Witte or by the tsar himself, who had nurtured a special interest in the region since his 1891 tour. Witte even controlled the substantial railroad "police" in Manchuria. The ministry under Lamzdorf was in a weakened condition, to Witte's advantage. As one official recalled, "A certain attitude of assumed nonchalance was typical of the entire department. To show excessive zeal was considered to be in bad taste."[189]

185. Reinsch, *World Politics at the End of the Nineteenth Century* (London: Macmillan, 1900), p. 26.
186. Ibid., p. 49.
187. Fursenko, *Battle for Oil*, pp. 92–98; "Our Trans-Pacific Interests," *World's Work* (August 1903): 3721–22.
188. Cassini to Murav'ev, 16 December 1899, 2/14 February 1900; to Lamzdorf, 9/22 September 1900, f. 133, op. 470, d. 109; to Lamzdorf, 6 June 1901, f. 133, op. 470, d. 105, AVPR.
189. Kalmykow, *Memoirs*, p. 139.

Approaching War

Following the Boxer eruption, Witte felt obliged to take control of Russian economic and foreign policy in the Far East. His goal was to strengthen the Russian position in Manchuria while avoiding conflict with other powers. The new Russian maneuvers, however, resulted in an Anglo-Japanese treaty in early 1902 that bolstered Japan diplomatically, more American cries of alarm about Russian violation of the "open door" amid reports that the United States might join that alliance,[190] Witte's resignation, and, ultimately, the Russo-Japanese War.[191]

Witte's high-handed ways and broadened powers also aroused the enmity of the Russian army and navy and even Nicholas II himself. A few friends of the tsar, led by Esper Ukhtomskii,[192] Grand Duke Alexander, Admiral Aleksei Abaza, and Aleksandr Bezobrazov, gained the upper hand during the winter and spring of 1903 and pushed for an even more aggressive policy in the Far East. Bezobrazov exercised the charm that won over Nicholas II to a project of timer concessions across the Yalu River in northern Korea, generally regarded as a Japanese sphere of interest.[193] This, coupled with an increased army presence in Manchuria, thwarted Witte's monopoly over policy in the area. Especially tense was the spring of 1903, when it appeared to many Americans, stuck in their half-opened door, that Russia was reneging

190. In March 1903, the German emperor told the resident ambassadors his view that Britain was striving for an Anglo-Japanese-American alliance "designed to paralyze the policy of the other Great Powers of Europe in the Far East" but that it would be defeated by a union of Germany, Russia, and France. Nikolai Osten-Saken to Lamzdorf, 17/30 March 1903, f. 138, op. 467, d. 212/213, AVPR. Not long after, Russia made a firmer commitment to the opening of Manchurian ports.

191. For a full account, see John Albert White, *The Diplomacy of the Russo-Japanese War* (Princeton, N.J.: Princeton University Press, 1964), pp. 50–131.

192. Ukhtomskii gained the favor of the tsar while accompanying and serving as reporter for the grand Asian tour. See his lavishly produced, six-volume *Puteshestvie na vostok ego Imperatorskago vysochestva gosudaria naslednika tsesarevicha, 1890–1891* (St. Petersburg and Leipzig: Brokgauz, 1893–1897).

193. David M. McDonald, *United Government and Foreign Policy in Russia, 1900–1914* (Cambridge: Harvard University Press, 1992), pp. 51–57; Vladimir Gurko, *Features and Figures of the Past: Government and Opinion in the Reign of Nicholas II,* Hoover Library Publication no. 14 (Stanford, Calif.: Stanford University Press, 1939), pp, 258–74. The granddaughter of Ulysses Grant was living in St. Petersburg and recalled, "The names of Abaza, Alexeef and Bezobrasoff were at the time constantly circulating and were anathema." Countess Speransky nee Grant Cantacuzene, *My Life Here and There* (New York: Charles Scribner's Sons, 1922), p. 260.

on the promise to withdraw military forces from Manchuria.[194] Witte was particularly vocal in warning of the futility of any plan to annex this territory. "Not America, not England, not Japan, not any of their open or secret allies, not China would ever have agreed to let us have Manchuria," he reflected.[195]

Hay remained cautious and circumspect. To Roosevelt he counseled:

> I am sure you will think it is out of the question that we should adopt any scheme of concerted action with England and Japan which could seem openly hostile to Russia. Public opinion in this country would not support such a course, nor do I think it would be to our permanent advantage. Russia is trying to impress us by the most fervent protestation that, whatever happens in Manchuria, our national interests will not suffer. This is an object which I have been striving for for four years, and if worst comes to the worst, I think we can gain it; but there is something due to self-respect also, and it is pretty hard to stand by and see an act of spoliation accomplished under our eyes.[196]

The secretary of state was especially apprehensive about the terms of a proposed Russo-Chinese convention, just leaked out of Peking, that would preserve exclusive Russian rights in Manchuria and northern China. He privately cabled McCormick to ascertain Russia's intentions.[197] Lamzdorf assured the American ambassador that Russian military presence was required to protect the railway and that "American commerce and American capital were of all other countries, the ones Russia most desired to attract for the benefit of her Eastern Chinese railway, which would be rendered more profitable by the opening up of the . . . territory."[198] Cassini, also on instructions from Lamzdorf, took up three hours of Hay's Sunday arguing that the American copy of the convention was garbled and that Russia had no desire to exclude American business from Manchuria.[199]

194. A State Department official wrote privately, "Thanks to our Russian friends and their inconquerable love of indirection and equivocation in diplomacy, . . . I have not found time to write you." Rockhill to Jeremiah Curtin, 21 May 1903, box 8, Curtin Papers, MCHS.

195. Witte, *Memoirs*, p. 366.

196. Hay to Roosevelt, 25 April 1903 (c), vol. 4 (roll 4), Hay Papers, LC.

197. Hay to McCormick, 25 April 1903 (c), ibid.

198. As quoted in McCormick to Hay, 29 April 1903, DUSM, Russia, vol. 60 (roll 60, M 35), RG 59, NA.

199. Hay to Roosevelt, 28 April 1903 (c), two letters same date, vol. 4 (roll 4), Hay Papers, LC.

When conflicting reports multiplied, Hay's frustration grew. "Dealing with this government with whom mendacity is a science is an extremely difficult and delicate matter."[200] He was certain that Russia was making demands on China that they denied making, but neither he nor anyone else knew what was going on at the highest levels of the Russian government. With the outrage over the Kishinev pogrom adding pressure, Cassini presented Hay with a new memorandum that appeared to be a surrender. Hay was still suspicious: "They are a strange race, and you may expect anything of them except straight-forwardness."[201] He thought they were only trying to head off the presentation of a Jewish petition.

As a sign of Russia's concern about American feelings, Vladimir Vonliarliarskii obtained a concession for exploring the mineral wealth on Chukotsk Peninsula and then sublet it to the American-managed North East Siberia Company with permission to bring 300 American prospectors to the region.[202] By this time a number of Americans, led by John Hays Hammond, were investigating the potential of Siberia's resources, leaving Amerian business interests divided and confused over which lines of opportunity to pursue. Another critical juncture was the establishment of an extraministerial authority in the Russian Far East by the appointment in August 1903 of another expansionist, Admiral Evgenyi Alekseev, as viceroy of the Amur with responsibility only to the tsar. Bezobrazov had masterminded this move, and not even Minister of War Kuropatkin, who wanted to concentrate Russia's military forces in Europe, had much control over a situation that was propelling Russia toward war in the East.[203] He feared a Japanese reprisal, while Alekseev naturally discounted it.

By September 1903 Washington and the American press viewed war between Japan and Russia as likely.[204] Regarding the Russians, Hay confided to his assistant, "They are a nasty lot to deal with. Sometimes I think it will be a valuable lesson to them if Japan does fly at their throat."[205] In the area itself, opinion was mixed; consul Henry Miller in Neuchang noted, "Russia must now give up Manchuria or go to war. . . . One day it looks like war and

200. To Roosevelt, 12 May 1903, ibid.

201. To Roosevelt, 14 July 1903 (c), ibid.

202. Riddle to Hay, 5 June 1903, ibid.

203. Zabriskie, *American-Russian Rivalry*, pp. 85–98; "Russia's Latest Move," New York *Times*, 18 August 1903, p. 6.

204. "Japan and Russia and the Control of the Orient," *World's Work* (September 1903): 3834.

205. To Adee, 18 September 1903 (c), vol. 4 (roll 4), Hay Papers, LC.

the next like peace."[206] And American sentiment was veering toward Japan because of Russia's aggressive actions and the expectation of a Russian advantage in the conflict. As Hay wrote in January 1904, on the eve of the war, "They think—that is Alexieff and Bezobrazoff, who seem to have complete control of affairs—that now is the time to strike, to crush Japan and to eliminate her from her position of influence in the Far East. They evidently think there is nothing to be feared from us—and they have of course secured pledges from Germany and France, which make them feel secure in Europe."[207] There was widespread belief in this scenario, and the resultant change in American attitude seemed to encourage Japan to take the initiative and secure the leverage of surprise. Cassini reported first detecting a significant shift in American opinion around 20 December and thought that it prompted Japan to act.[208]

The Russian ambassador himself inflamed matters and provoked the secretary of state's growing nervousness with his haughty and overbearing demeanor and his insistence on belaboring Hay with long diatribes. After one such appointment on 8 February, Hay noted, "He spent most of the time accusing Japan of lightness and vanity; he seemed little affected by the imminence of war, expecting a speedy victory, but admitting that the war, however it resulted, would profit nobody."[209] So when Japan attacked Port Arthur that very day, it had the benign support of the United States government and American public opinion.

To his credit, Cassini warned St. Petersburg of the changed climate and quoted to Lamzdorf a speech he gave to Francis Loomis, Hay's assistant: "You pretend to do everything to maintain peace but you are doing everything to push Japan to war. You say your only aim in the Far East is to safeguard your commerce and open the two ports. . . . You do everything to arouse the suspicion that you are on the side of our adversaries.[210] The acuteness of the situation apparently began to register with the obstinate Nicholas II if not with his clique of advisers. In mid-January he assured McCor-

206. Miller to son Kenneth, 27 January 1904, Miller Papers, University of Oregon.

207. Diary, 5 January 1904, in William Roscoe Thayer, ed., *The Life and Letters of John Hay*, 2 vols. (Boston: Houghton Mifflin, 1915), 2:370.

208. Cassini to Lamzdorf, 17/30 December 1903 and 31 December 1903/13 January 1904, f. 133, op. 470, d. 129, pt. 1, AVPR.

209. Thayer, *Life of John Hay* 2:371. In a follow-up on 10 February, Cassini was impressed with Hay's "correct but stiff" reception; to Lamzdorf, 28 January/10 February 1904, f. 133, op. 470, d. 129, pt. 1, AVPR.

210. Cassini to Lamzdorf (private), 14/27 January 1804, f. 133, op. 470, d. 129, pt. 2, AVPR.

mick privately that Russia did not want war and promised to recognize the commercial rights of Americans in Manchuria.[211]

Cecil Spring Rice, the British ambassador to Russia (and Roosevelt's confidential agent), observed, "What a dreadful business this is! It is a real case of drifting into war. Both ships gradually drawing together until the collision comes." If so, the bump was barely felt in St. Petersburg, since he reported that the city was surprisingly quiet as he escorted the Japanese ambassador to the train station.[212] The usually staid secretary of war, Elihu Root, was ecstatic: "Was not the way the Japs began to fight bully? Some people in the United States might well learn the lesson that mere beginning does not take the place of perfect preparation and readiness for instant action."[213]

Kishinev

Russian belligerence in the Far East was not the only factor that swayed American opinion against Russia and toward Japan. On Easter Sunday/Passover, 19 April 1903, the Jewish quarter of the Bessarabian provincial capital found itself suddenly under attack from the Orthodox Moldavan and Russian residents. Ransacking and carnage continued two more days with token intervention by authorities. The result of the Kishinev "massacre" was an almost complete devastation of Jewish property in the town, the killing of forty-seven, and the wounding of hundreds more, by far the worst such incident in Russia since 1881.[214]

In the background were a series of smaller outbreaks in neighboring Rumania, worsening land hunger and poverty in the Russian countryside, the

211. McCormick to Hay (confidential), 15 January 1904, DUSM, Russia, vol. 60 (roll 60, M 35), RG 59, NA.

212. Spring Rice to Roosevelt, 11 February 1904, roll 41, Roosevelt Papers, LC.

213. Root to Roosevelt, 15 February 1904, ibid.

214. For a detailed account of the Kishinev pogrom, see Edward H. Judge, *Easter in Kishinev: Anatomy of a Pogrom* (New York and London: New York University Press, 1992). The population of Kishinev was about 150,000—one-third Jewish, one-third Moldavan, and one-third others, including 8,000 Russians. Shlomo Lambroza, "The Pogroms of 1903–1906," in John D. Klier and Shlomo Lambroza, eds., *Pogroms: Anti-Jewish Violence in Modern Russian History* (Cambridge: Cambridge University Press, 1992), pp. 195–205. The American consul in Odessa listed the dead by name and estimated 700 houses gutted and 600 stores looted; Heenan to Hill, 19 May 1903, DUSC, Odessa, vol. 13 (roll 7, M 459), RG 59, NA. He also reported, "The educated classes are more affected by this Kishenev disaster, and more deeply deplore it, than can well be expressed in words."

alleged ritual murder of a Christian a few months earlier, and a rabble-rousing, anti-Semitic local newspaper. More than anything, the reactionary Russification program made it acceptable to blame all of Russia's many ills on non-Russians, particularly on the Jewish population at the bottom rung. The disease had spread across Russia; for example, the brother of Raphael Zon wrote from Orenburg, "It's almost an Asiatic city populated with Bash-kirs, Tartars—They chase Jews like in some Russian city."[215] And *Harper's Weekly* noted that the perpetrators in Kishinev were mostly non-Russian.[216]

Although scholarly studies have shown that the central authorities did not directly instigate the riot, the world reaction, especially from the United States, was immediate and gained strength when the Russian government mishandled the situation by first denying that a pogrom had occurred and then trying to justify it.[217] This time, in contrast to 1881, the American Jew-ish community was organized, financially secure, and already seething about visa discrimination. Massive immigration to the United States had also sta-bilized since the avalanche of 1891–1892.

Urged on by mass protest meetings in Brooklyn, at Carnegie Hall, and in Chicago and backed by newspaper editorials, Jacob Schiff, Simon Wolf, and Oscar Straus led a campaign for government action and met with Hay and Roosevelt.[218] B'nai B'rith and its president Leo Levi joined the assault and held a conference in mid-June to draw up a sharply worded petition to present to Russia through Hay and Roosevelt. In an important missive to the president, Schiff argued that the United States should revive the pass-

215. G. Zon to R. Zon, 1 January 1902, box 1, Zon Papers, MinnHS. A contempo-rary observer contended that pogroms had the effect of diverting the attention of the common people from the real causes of their discontent; Alexander Rovinsky, "Russia and the Jews," *Arena* 30, 2 (August 1903): 133.

216. Editorial, *Harper's Weekly*, 30 May 1903, p. 910. An American consul empha-sized as a new factor that many of the Jews, who had spread throughout Russia had been driven back into the Pale, where they increased the Jewish ghetto populations, competed economically, and were resented by local non-Russian peoples; the latter fur-ther suspected that these Russianized Jews were part of the government's Russification policies. Hernandez DeSoto (Warsaw), "Conditions Prevailing Among Jews in Poland," 25 November 1914, DPR, Russia, vol. 184, RG 84, NA.

217. A typical reaction: "The plain fact is this, that life for the Jew in Russia . . . has passed beyond the enduring point." Richard Gottheil, "Kishineff," *Forum* 35, 1 (July 1903): 160.

218. Gary Dean Best, *To Free a People: American Jewish Leaders and the Jewish Prob-lem in Eastern Europe, 1890–1914* (Westport, Conn.: Greenwood Press, 1982), pp. 70–74; "Denunciation of Russia," *New York Times*, 11 May 1903, p. 3; Philip Ernst Schoen-berg, "The American Reaction to the Kishinev Pogrom of 1903," *American Jewish His-torical Quarterly* 58, 3 (March 1974): 262–83.

port issue and couple its protest with bolder opposition to Russia in East Asia. Under such mounting pressures and intrigued by potential political gains, Roosevelt agreed in July to cable the petition to Russia, even though the foreign minister had stated in advance that he would not receive it.[219] More significant, the document was released to the press and received wide publicity, thus magnifying the image of international friction.

While not underrating the American response to the Kishinev pogrom in reports to St. Petersburg, Cassini emphasized Roosevelt's political position vis-à-vis the next election, Irish support for Russia, and the short lifespan of such American tempests.[220] In interviews with Hay and Roosevelt, he dismissed the protest rallies by mentioning the lynchings of blacks and beatings of Italians and Chinese.[221] The impression he gave was that the Kishinev reaction was probably ephemeral and should not be taken seriously. Unfortunately, Cassini left Washington in early July and did not return until mid-November, disrupting the line of communications.[222]

Roosevelt saw in Kishinev an opportunity to wave his "big stick," as Hay recounted to Elihu Root:

> To tell you the honest truth, there was not much in what we did in the Kisheneff matter, except good intentions. We did succeed, in spite of the refusal of the Russian Government to consider the prayer for the American Jews, in getting that prayer before the world. What the President said . . . was reprinted all over the world, and had a certain influence and effect.

219. Best, *To Free a People*, pp. 75–82; Taylor Stults, "Roosevelt, Russian Persecution of Jews, and American Public Opinion," *Jewish Social Studies* 33, 1 (January 1971): 13–22; Riddle to Hay (confidential), 16 July 1903, DUSM, Russia, vol. 60 (roll 60, M 35), RG 59, NA. Hay congratulated Roosevelt for embarrassing Russia and appeasing the Jewish committee: "What inept asses they are, these Kalmucks! They could have scored by receiving the petition and pigeon-holeing it. I think you have scored, as it is. You have done the right thing in the right way. . . . As to our 'good relations' with Russia—they have more interest in them than we have, and they will soon come around, and lie to us as volubly as ever." To Roosevelt, 22 July 1903 (c), vol. 4 (roll 4), Hay Papers, LC.

220. Cassini to Lamzdorf, 7/20 May, 21 May/3 June, 4/17 June 1903, f. 133, op. 470, d. 113 (1903), AVPR. Some contemporary opinion supported the ambassador's view: "In spite of alarmist talk and imprudent official utterances, the traditional relations between the United States and Russia will undergo no unfavorable change." "The United States and Russia," *Chautauquan* 38, 1 (September 1903): 4.

221. Cassini to Lamzdorf (private), 30 June 1903, f. 133, op. 470, d. 113 (1903), AVPR. The ambassador claimed that 3,060 blacks had been lynched over a period of twenty years, far more than the number of victims of Russian pogroms.

222. Cassini to Lamzdorf, 18 June/1 July and 5/13 November 1903, ibid.

The passport matter is another affair. We have been hammering at Russia for years about it. We have absolutely refused to accept their action as satisfactory, have protested against it time and again, and it has been the subject of more than a dozen interviews between Cassini and me. Short of war or a dissolution of diplomatic relations, we cannot do more than we have done and are doing, and yet it is not enough to alleviate the sense of wrong under which our Jewish friends in this country labor.[223]

Discrimination in issuing visas thus became a permanent thorn in the side of Russian-American relations until the revolution of 1917.

The clamor against Russia did not diminish but was actually heightened by Russian inaction, other violent attacks against Jews, such as one at Gomel in September, and rumors of more to come. Sympathy came from many non-Jewish sources and attested to the fact that the United States at the beginning of the century was cutting its moralistic as well as imperialistic teeth. George Kennan resumed his attack in a series of unsigned editorials for *Outlook* on Russian anti-Semitic, anti-Finnish, and antirevolutionary actions.[224] As another commentator put it a few months later, "America is no longer an outsider, and the attempt to treat her as one does but turn valuable friendship into bitterness."[225]

The other side of that coin was Russian resentment of outside interference in internal affairs. Although Minister of Interior Viacheslav Plehve was trying to moderate Russian anti-Semitic policies and to treat with Jewish leaders, it seemed from afar that Russia was doing little to change discriminatory laws against Jews and nothing on the passport issue. For various reasons each side did not take the professed intentions of the other very seriously. The revival of the Jewish Question in a politically militant form combined with Russian aggressive policies in East Asia to tarnish Russian-American relations on the eve of the Russo-Japanese War.

The War and American Opinion

Japan achieved a military and psychological advantage by the surprise attack on Port Arthur in February 1904, and American approval continued through the first year of the war. Anyone with an anti-Russian grudge

223. Hay to Root, 6 June 1904, box 39, Root Papers, LC.
224. Travis, *George Kennan*, pp. 256, 303 n. 22.
225. "Russia and America," *Living Age* 242 (July 1904): 252.

quickly entered the fray in support of Japan. With encouragement from President Roosevelt, George Kennan rushed to Japan to write an extensive series of articles on the war from the Japanese perspective, provide anti-Russian material for the Japan *Times*, propagandize among Russian prisoners of war, and serve as an informant for the White House.[226] He predicted social and political revolution resulting from Russian defeat. Former minister Andrew White veered sharply against Russia as he was completing his autobiography, and Poultney Bigelow cataloged past grievances.[227]

But some respected voices advised caution, at least privately. On learning of the opening salvo, Charles Eliot Norton wrote to a Japanese friend: "Even should Russia be worsted in the struggle, I dread the consequences of war for you. Its best issue cannot but bring many evils in its train. . . . It would be an immense triumph for civilization could the question in dispute between Russia and Japan be referred, even at this last moment, to the Hague Tribunal."[228] And William Dean Howells counseled publicly, "There is probably no valuable possession that a man is so lavish of as his sympathies, and yet there is nothing he so much hates to have wasted on an unworthy object. . . . We must think more than twice whether we side with Japan or with Russia in the actual contest; our sympathies may have a consequence which we shall always regret unless we apply them with the greatest possible caution."[229] He viewed the Russians as the initial aggressors but also as "our ancient and faithful allies." Even Oscar Straus urged Roosevelt to invoke the mediation articles of the Hague convention.[230]

American public opinion was pummeled by the reporters rushing to cover the war scene. Most at first followed the easy route over the Pacific to Japan, with the result that Americans were initially exposed mostly to the Japanese side. Some of these correspondents, notably Stanley Washburn for the Chi-

226. Travis, *George Kennan*, pp. 257–60; Roosevelt to Kennan, 18 February 1904, box 2, Kennan Papers, LC.

227. Poultney Bigelow, *Seventy Summers*, 2 vols. (New York: Longmans, Green, 1925), 1:325; White, "A Diplomat's Recollections of Russia (1892–1894), *Century* 69, 1 (November 1904): 127–38.

228. To Nariaki Kozaki, 10 February 1904, in *Letters of Charles Eliot Norton*, ed. Sara Norton and M. A. DeWolfe Howe, 2 vols. (Boston: Houghton Mifflin, 1913), 2:337.

229. "What Shall We Do With Our Sympathies," *Harper's Weekly*, 27 February 1904, p. 321.

230. Straus to Roosevelt, 8 February 1904 (t), roll 41, Roosevelt Papers, LC. In response, the president advised Straus that Japan had made it clear no mediation would be considered; to Straus, 9 February 1904, vol. 45 (roll 333), ibid. Straus immediately responded: "Japan is certainly battling on the side of civilization—may wisdom and victory be on her side." To Roosevelt, 11 February 1904, roll 41, ibid.

cago *Daily News* and the *Times* of London and George Kennan for *Outlook*, rapidly made names for themselves, not only for detailing military progress but also for their colorful depictions of Japanese society.[231] The taking of Port Arthur received the most intense early scrutiny, especially from the pens of Frederick McCormick of *Collier's* and Richard Barry, giving the Russian and Japanese viewpoints, respectively.[232] Most of the American reporters, however, were disappointed by the limited access to the scenes of action.

News of the war was soon balanced by the reporting of David Macgowan (*Century*), Howard Thompson (Associated Press), and novelist Francis Warrington Dawson (Associated Press) from European Russia. Luckily, Melville Stone had visited St. Petersburg at the beginning of 1904 on behalf of Associated Press and managed to secure from Lamzdorf—and again from the tsar in an interview just a week before the war began—authority for uncensored cables at low rates and special access to information.[233] He argued persuasively that Americans should see Russia directly and not through British eyes, and he hired a prominent New York journalist, John Callan O'Laughlin, to oversee with Thompson the initial operations. Sympathetic to the Russian side, his appearance in Washington was not welcomed by Hay: "Melville Stone . . . is deeply grieved at our treatment of Russia. He seems to have been lubricated and swallowed up by the Russian officials in St. Petersburg. I understand he is to be here soon to tell us what we ought to do."[234] Soon a whole string of correspondents arrived in Russia, led by James Whigham and Richard Harding Davis of *Collier's*, Thomas Millard of the New York *Herald*, Hector Fuller of the Indianapolis *News*, and Maynard of *Harper's Weekly*. But because of scant knowledge of Russian, the climate, bureaucratic frustrations, and illness, few stayed more than a couple of weeks.[235]

231. For Washburn, clippings and pictures are in scrapbook 2, box 1, Washburn Papers, MinnHS.

232. Their contemporary reports were collected in books: McCormick, *The Tragedy of Russia in Pacific Asia*, 2 vols. (New York: Outing, 1907), and Barry, *Port Arthur: A Monster Heroism* (New York: Moffat, Yard, 1905).

233. Melville E. Stone, "M.E.S." *His Book: A Tribute and a Souvenir of the Twenty-Five Years 1893–1918 of the Service of Melville E. Stone as General Manager of the Associated Press* (New York and London: Harper and Bros., 1918), pp. 140–46. He maintained (p. 142) that "the restrictions put upon foreign correspondents had been so great that they had virtually abandoned Russia; and when I arrived there, with the exception of our man who had preceded me, no foreign correspondent was sending daily telegrams from St. Petersburg."

234. Hay to Roosevelt, 12 March 1904 (c), vol. 5 (roll 4), Hay Papers, LC.

235. For an example of one experience, see Francis Dawson to his wife, 11 April 1904, and Mrs. Dawson to Emmie, 17 May 1904, Dawson Papers, Duke University.

Russia still had political friends in the United States, though they were often ignored, retreated to moderate statements, or remained silent. Charles Emory Smith, a former minister to Russia, challenged Bigelow directly and called for a historical outlook: "Russia just now is at best a tempting but perilous theme. Half a century hence it will be possible to look back through the clear perspective of years and measure the true relations of the events of today to a new career of progress and greatness. But in the present hour we see the portents without the promise, and Russia is shadowed by the gloom of the clouds without the gleam."[236] Melville Stone added a cautious defense of Russia in an article for *Harper's Weekly.*[237] William Rainey Harper was obviously depressed by events and wrote in June 1905, a few months before his death, "I am of course greatly broken up over the Russian situation. I think that this gives me more trouble than my own physical condition."[238]

The American Betrayal

Just before the war began, Harper's son Samuel arrived in Russia for the first time to live with a family in Moscow in order to improve his knowledge of Russian. He found everything in turmoil and anti-American sentiment growing rapidly. Russians were perplexed, he wrote, by "our taking such a lively interest in the war and our siding with the Japs."[239] Even a thoroughly Americanized Russian, Zenaida Ragozin, could not understand "the incomprehensible attitude Americans generally have chosen to assume in their idolatrous worship of their yellow pets."[240] Some reporters, such as Dawson, were shocked by the Russian coolness and retreated from the territory.[241]

Matters certainly were not helped by stories circulating in Russia about the *Variag*, which had the distinction of being the first casualty of the war. This modern cruiser, recently launched in the United States, left the Korean port of Chemulpo on 7 February, when an advance Japanese squadron on

236. Smith, "Russia," *National Geographic Magazine* 16, 2 (February 1905): 55.
237. Stone, "The Russian View of the War," *Harper's Weekly*, 26 March 1904, pp. 465, 479.
238. To Samuel (his son), 5 June 1905, box 8, W. R. Harper Papers, University of Chicago.
239. To his father, 22 February/6 March 1904, box 1, S. Harper Papers, University of Chicago.
240. Zeraida Ragozin to Margaret Reynolds, 25 September/9 October 1904, box 9, Norman Hapgood/Reynolds Family Papers, LC.
241. Dawson to his wife, 11 April 1904, Dawson Papers, Duke University.

its way to Port Arthur fired on it. Heavily damaged, it limped back to the harbor where it was scuttled to avoid capture. Ambassador McCormick in St. Petersburg denied Russian charges that the vessel was intentionally badly designed by the American builder and that a nearby American ship, the *Vicksburg*, had refused to receive wounded crew members who then fell into the hands of the Japanese. A number of Americans thought that American companies lost large contracts because of this incident.[242]

John Hay expressed his frustration to a protégé, Spencer Eddy, in St. Petersburg: "Every time the Russians get a kick from the Japanese, they turn and swear at us. If they would devote their energies to their real enemies and stop nagging and quarreling with their friends it would be better for them. I have never in my life seen anything so destitute of common sense as this rage against the United States in Russia." He then summed up the American policy for 1904: "We can do nothing but stand by, and wait till the storm plays itself out."[243] Actually, the United States was very concerned about the impact of the war on China and kept a close watch on events.

A host of American military attachés and observers was dispatched to report on the war. Colonel T. Bentley Mott was the first to reach Russia and to find that American sympathy for Japan "made us very unpopular in St. Petersburg. . . . The Russians were genuinely surprised and hurt." Evaluating his assignment, he later recalled that "this decision turned out to be a useless waste of the government's money and my time, for few people in the capital seemed to feel the smallest interest in the war, and those few had to wait for the arrival of the London papers to get much information as to how it was being conducted."[244] Other early military observers on the Russian side included Captain William Judson of the army and Lieutenant Newton McCully of the navy, both of whom would apply in later years the knowledge gained about Russia during this period.

At least some of the Russian resentment toward the attachés was the fault of the Americans: too many inexperienced, low-ranking officers sent, and none of general rank; improper or little preparation; summary recalls with-

242. McCormick to Lamzdorf, 16/29 February 1904, f. 133, op. 470, d. 69, AVPR; A. McK. Griggs, "An Interview with the Russian Ambassador," *Harper's Weekly*, 5 March 1904, p. 363; W. D. Childs (St. Petersburg) to Watts, 24 February 1904, DPR, vol. 4462 (misc. received), RG 84, NA; Watts to Loomis, 26 February 1904, DUSC, St. Petersburg, vol. 23 (roll 18, M 81), RG 59, NA.

243. To Eddy, 7 June 1904 (c), vol. 5 (roll 4), Hay Papers, LC.

244. Mott, *Twenty Years as Military Attaché* (New York and London: Oxford University Press, 1937), p. 124.

out explanation; and inadequate communications. Besides McCully, the most successful agent was probably Colonel Valery Havard, who, as a medical officer, was able to penetrate military and Red Cross medical operations in St. Petersburg and on the battlefields.[245] The experienced and knowledgeable Walter Schuyler was disgusted with the infighting and jealousy among the observers and about his sudden recall. "I left the [Russian] Army when I had just arrived at the point where having gained the confidence and made the personal acquaintance of the Russian officers with whom I was associated, I was prepared to work to advantage."[246]

Trying to make the best of a bad situation, Cassini reported that some newspapers, notably the Hearst chain, had become less anti-Russian after the start of the war and that one important one, the New York *Herald*, was trying to be neutral, thanks to his intervention.[247] Lamzdorf congratulated Cassini for his success and for beginning a deliberate effort to cultivate American public opinion. He advised that Melville Stone might be useful and that Esper Ukhtomskii was being sent as a special publicity agent.[248]

Stone indeed played an important role in getting the Russian perspective before the American public. After obtaining guarantees against censorship, precedence for news dispatches, a discount on telegraphic rates, and access to government departments, he hired knowledgeable Russians to provide stories for Associated Press and Reuters wire services. Soon a number of foreign correspondents were fanning out over Russia and clamoring for permission to get to the front lines. Although some reporting was naturally critical of Russia, the main result by the end of 1904 was less distortion and reliance on the rumor mill and a full and fairly objective coverage of the Russian side of the war.[249]

Ukhtomskii was another story. He came to the United States in May ostensibly to represent Russia at a "world's press congress" in connection with the St. Louis world's fair that summer but in reality on a mission to counter the unfavorable press Russia had been getting. He argued that Russia was saving Asia from "rapacious and violent Japan" and that with right on her

245. John Thomas Greenwood, "The American Observers of the Russo-Japanese War (1904–1905)" (Ph.D. diss., Kansas State University, 1971), pp. 183–212.

246. "Report of Service with the Russian Army in Manchuria, 1904," p. 6, Walter Schuyler Papers, Huntington Library, Calif.

247. Cassini to Lamzdorf, 25 February/9 March and 24 March/6 April 1904, f. 133, op. 470, d. 129, pt. 1, AVPR.

248. Lamzdorf to Cassini, 13/26 May 1904 (c), f. 138, op. 467, d. 231/232, AVPR.

249. Stone, *"M.E.S." His Book,* pp. 140–54.

side, "Western" Russia would crush the infidels.[250] According to Cassini, this disturbed American listeners who thought it meant that Russia was planning to dominate Asia.[251] More successful was Peter Demens, the prosperous California citrus grower and real estate promoter. He wrote a number of articles in 1904 simultaneously trying to explain Russia to Americans and the United States to Russians.[252] But when Demens wrote directly to high Russian officials such as Pobedonostsev, Cassini snubbed him as an unwelcome intruder.[253] The Russian ambassador's tactlessness was further demonstrated when he openly favored Roosevelt's opponent in the 1904 election.[254]

The war disrupted Russian plans for displays at the 1904 Louisiana Purchase Exposition in St. Louis. Special emissaries to Europe overcame initial Russian resistance to participation, and a commission, headed by Sergei Aleksandrovskii and Sergei Korff, arrived in St. Louis in the summer of 1903 to inspect the site. With the help of a $150,000 grant from Plehve and the assistance of private businessmen such as Thomas Smith of Moscow and Edward Grunwaldt of St. Petersburg, a large, ostentatiously Russian pavilion, complete with onion domes, was disassembled and shipped to St. Louis. It arrived in January 1904 and was in process of being set up in the middle of what is now the Washington University campus when the war began, and the pavilion was dismantled and scrapped.[255]

Plans for an extensive art display were allowed to continue on a private basis before Russia reversed itself again. The two railcars of exhibits that finally arrived at the end of July consisted primarily of paintings, from icons to likenesses of the royal family. The largest-ever Russian art exhibit in the United States, it featured the Russian school known as "the Wanderers" and included some prominent works of Repin, the Makovskii brothers, and Vereshchagin.[256] In a hostile incident, several of the Romanov portraits were

250. Prince Esper Oukhtomsky, "A Russian View of American Sympathy," *Harper's Weekly*, 28 May 1904, p. 826.

251. Cassini to Lamzdorf, 29 June/12 July 1904, f. 133, op. 470, d. 129, pt. 2, AVPR.

252. For example, "Why Japan Was Eager for War," Los Angeles *Times*, 5 April 1904, and "Pis'ma iz Ameriki," *Novoe Vremia*, 19 March 1904, clippings in box 6, Demens Papers, LC.

253. Cassini to Lamzdorf, 20 April/3 May 1904, f. 133, op. 470, d. 129, pt. 2, AVPR.

254. He thought a Democratic administration would be more supportive of Russia; Hay to Roosevelt, 14 September 1904 (c), vol. 5 (roll 4), Hay Papers, LC.

255. Robert C. Williams, *Russian Art and American Money, 1900–1940* (Cambridge: Harvard University Press, 1980), pp. 44–49.

256. "Russia's Exhibits Reach St. Louis," clipping in Schlippenbach to Cassini, 16/29 July 1904, f. 170, op. 512/1, d. 585, AVPR.

defaced in early October, but only the protective glass was damaged.[257] Other exhibits included a Trans-Siberian Railway car, a decorative replica of a log house, and some furs. Few Russians made an appearance, and the fair, in contrast to the one in Chicago, had little if any impact on Russia.

American Intervention in the Russo-Japanese War

Although the American government was formally neutral and had no intention of military involvement, the universal perception was that it favored Japan. Some officials, especially those with Far Eastern experience such as William Rockhill, were openly anti-Russian;[258] Ambassador McCormick in St. Petersburg was frequently criticized for being pro-Russian, whereas others were rarely assailed for being pro-Japanese. Nevertheless, the United States was the most trusted nonpartisan, since Britain and France were tightly bound by alliances to opposite sides. Consequently, Americans were called upon to inspect conditions of prisoners of war and to handle various charges of misconduct, such as the possibly deliberate shelling of Vladivostok hospitals by the Japanese. In particular, Thomas Smith, consul in Moscow, performed yeoman service on behalf of Japanese war prisoners and civilian detainees.[259] And the several official military observers, no matter what their individual bias, were models of restraint and impartiality.

Private individuals and institutions, however, became more directly committed to one side or the other with the advantage going to Japan in the form of money. American Jewish leaders, led by Jacob Schiff, sought out opportunities to back Japan's war effort financially with the result that the Japanese were actually surprised at how easy it was to obtain loans. The first in May 1904 was for $50 million and was divided equally between American and British institutions. Adding in three larger loans that followed, Americans contributed $180 million to Japan. All were considerably oversubscribed. If Japan had chosen to go further into debt, it could have financed the entire war with American money. On the other side, American institutions not only rebuffed any Russian but also worked actively to sabotage

257. David Francis to Cassini, 6 October 1904, ibid.
258. Paul A. Varg, *Open Door Diplomat: The Life of W. W. Rockhill*; Illinois Studies in the Social Sciences vol. 33, no. 4 (Urbana: University of Illinois Press, 1952), p. 57.
259. Approximately 10,000 Japanese civilians were caught in Russian territory when the war began and evacuated from the war zone.

Russian borrowing efforts in France and Germany.[260] Since Russia's poor fiscal condition certainly contributed to military defeat and revolution, Americans could take some responsibility for both. No wonder the Russian press continued to be sharply anti-American.

Unfortunately, a compelling reason for continued American hostility was a wave of pogroms, as many as forty-three in Russia in 1904, with many killed and wounded and much property damage. Some of these incidents were more like civil wars than earlier attacks, since the Jewish communities were better armed and organized. Most of them occurred in long-settled areas in Poland and Ukraine, but a few were also in distant cities such as Samara. The majority were related to the war, that is, provoked by discouraging news from the fronts and by reports that Jews were undermining the Russian war effort and supporting Japan.[261] There was some truth to this, at least as far as American Jews were concerned. When the Russian government, preoccupied with the war, failed to prevent the pogroms or punish the instigators, mutual hostility escalated. Reports about American Jewish bankers arranging loans for Japan spread widely in Russia, thus contributing to the anti-Semitic violence and perpetuating a vicious circle.

A few Americans with motives of business and past friendship tried to assist Russia. Prominent entrepreneur Charles Flint, who had hosted Grand Duke Boris in 1902, directed and paid for Pinkerton surveillance of Japanese military purchasing missions in San Francisco and at the John Holland submarine yard in Quincy, Massachusetts, and provided intelligence to the Russian embassy.[262] And a Russian agent, Grigori Vilenkin, was reportedly working with American opportunists in an unlikely attempt to lure leading Jewish bankers to Russia to consummate a loan.[263] A more realistic plan for substantial investment in a St. Petersburg factory, the Nevsky Machine and Shipbuilding Plant, by John O'Laughlin also came to nothing.[264]

Wharton Barker offered his services directly to Lamzdorf and Witte: "I am in a position to understand political conditions here and in position to learn from the inside what goes on at Washington in the highest official quarters."[265] He denied that American public opinion was instinctively anti-

260. Best, *To Free a People*, pp. 94–97. Since all of these bonds were traded internationally, it is likely that some Americans subscribed to Russian war bonds.

261. Klier and Lambroza, eds., *Pogroms*, pp. 213–19.

262. Cassini to Lamzdorf, 10/23 August 1904, f. 133, op. 470, d. 129, pt. 2, AVPR.

263. Cassini to Lamzdorf, 6/19 October 1904, ibid.

264. O'Laughlin to Khilkov, 17 January 1905, box 1, O'Laughlin Papers, LC.

265. To Lamzdorf, 9 February 1905 (c), box 10, Barker Papers, LC.

Vladimir Lamzdorf, Russian foreign minister. From Munsey's Magazine, *February 1902*

Russian but contended that it was being manipulated by Roosevelt and Hay. He promised Cassini he could change it—for $300,000.[266] Isaac Rice, president of the Holland Boat Company, which was already building submarines for Japan, sought business in St. Petersburg. Displaying extraordinary impartiality and opportunism, Rice offered to sell vessels to Russia for a high price and indicated that if Russia did not buy, Japan would. An agent of the Cramp shipyards at Hampton Roads was also said to be on the scene.[267]

Flint was the most energetic pursuer of Russian military business, making at least four trips to Russia during the war, mostly surreptitiously. In his first

266. Cassini to Lamzdorf, 12 May 1905 (c), and Barker to Cassini, 22 May 1905, box 10, Barker Papers, LC.

267. T. Jefferson Coolidge (Boston banker) to Meyer, 11 April 1905; Meyer to Coolidge, 10/23 April 1905; and Meyer to Roosevelt, 22 April/5 May 1905, box 3, Meyer Papers, MassHS. Coolidge had prior connections with Russia through his nephew and protégé, Archibald Coolidge.

scheme, he offered to buy Argentine cruisers for the Russian navy, if only to prevent them from becoming Japanese. During an April–May 1905 visit to St. Petersburg, his main contacts for negotiating battleship and submarine sales were Grand Duke Alexander, Grand Duke Alexis, and top-level naval officials.[268] Enlisting the help of industrialist Charles Schwab of Bethlehem Steel, Flint arranged the purchase of six submarines from the Simon Lake shipyards in Bridgeport. One was secretly loaded at night aboard a Russia-bound ship anchored off Staten Island, while the others were shipped in parts to St. Petersburg and thence by train to Vladivostok. Ten torpedo boats were also constructed by Lake for the Black Sea fleet, with payments routed through French banks totaling 150 million francs.[269] Although none of these ships could be deployed before the war had ended, they were an important contribution to the rebuilding of the navy after Tsushima. The war clearly promoted some American business.

A few Americans chose neutral ground out of principle. James Wilson wrote to his friend John Foster, former minister to Russia, about a lecture he was to give in Cincinnati:

> I shall always hope to treat Russia as she deserves, philosophically and sensibly, ignoring her internal policies entirely and leaving her as the rest of mankind have been left, to work out her own destinies in her own way. Most nations have had to work their way from semi-barbarism to civilization, from arbitrary government to constitutional government, and they have had to do it on their own lines. I think it is fair to Russia to let her settle her race questions, her religious questions, her provincial questions and her questions of internal government, according to her own lights and this I shall leave her to do.[270]

Others raised concerns about the influence of Jewish activism on foreign policy or the unfair advantage wielded by Japan.

268. Flint, *Memories of an Active Life*, pp. 197–202; Meyer to Coolidge, 10/23 April 1905, and to Roosevelt, 22 April/5 May 1905, box 3, Meyer Papers, MassHS. In the latter Meyer concluded, "Nothing was absolutely settled and Flint has staid [sic] on in the hope of consummating a deal." Grand Duke Alexander, code-named "Bottle," handled the business on the Russian end.

269. Flint, *Memories of an Active Life*, pp. 199–210.

270. Wilson to Foster, 9 April 1904, Foster Papers, LC. Wilson added, "I have suspected from the outgivings from Washington that having become a world power, we are drifting away from our earlier policy of 'friendly relations with all, entangling alliances with none.' "

The Revolution of 1905

Not all Russian resentment was directed against the Jewish population. The revolutionary movement, now three generations old, continued to build and become better organized in spite of or perhaps as a result of repression. Assassination was still a goal of many of the radical revolutionaries, and a chief target was reactionary Minister of Interior Plehve. Boris Savinkov of the Socialist Revolutionary Battle Organization finally engineered a successful plot on 15 July 1904, with the connivance of notorious police agent Evno Azef. Despite the protection of a special armored carriage, Plehve was blown apart by a bomb thrown by Egor Sazonov.[271] This was the "first shot" of the revolution of 1905.

Since it was widely but mistakenly believed that Plehve had directed the wave of pogroms that began with Kishinev, his death was joyously celebrated by Jews, liberals, radicals, and even a number of conservatives and government officials in Russia, the United States, and elsewhere. Although the Russian government suddenly seemed vulnerable, it also appeared to be headed for important reforms, for the new minister of interior, Petr Sviatopolk-Mirskii, was a moderate who planned to introduce an elected, national legislative body. In fact, he had apparently secured the tsar's approval in December 1904, before the project was overthrown through the influence of Pobedonostsev.[272] As meaningful reforms failed to materialize and as the war proved that Russia was ill-prepared logistically to fight either a land or naval war in the Far East, resentment mounted in the larger Russian cities, especially after the loss of Port Arthur.

That dissatisfaction could find an outlet was due to two major changes in Russian society around the turn of the century, one primarily in the countryside, the other in the cities. The 1864 reform of Alexander II establishing local representative bodies (the land assemblies, or zemstvos) survived the years of reaction and matured, especially in the northern and central (non-pogrom) areas. This created two new "elements" (or tiers) of government, the first being the central bureaucracy: the elected representatives themselves, who pressed for a responsible "national zemstvo," and the state employees—doctors, teachers, veterinarians, agronomists, etc.—known as the "third element." To some, such as the British reporters Donald MacKen-

271. See Edward H. Judge, *Plehve: Repression and Reform in Imperial Russia, 1902–1904* (Syracuse, N.Y.: Syracuse University Press, 1983), pp. 225–37.
272. Andrew Verner, *The Crisis of Russian Autocracy: Nicholas II and the 1905 Revolution* (Princeton, N.J.: Princeton University Press, 1990), pp. 129–40.

zie Wallace and E. J. Dillon, Russia seemed to be on the verge of making the jump into Western parliamentary liberalism. One of Sviatopolk-Mirskii's few accomplishments was allowing a national congress of zemstvo leaders to meet in November 1904.

The other significant change was occurring in the cities as a result of the industrial development championed by Witte—a substantial increase in factory wage-workers. And this in turn promoted the dissemination of Marxist socialism, which attracted the talents of several of the current generation of the Russian radical intelligentsia. The Russian Social Democratic Labor Party, founded in 1898, held its second congress abroad in 1903, where a Simbirsk/St. Petersburg attorney (Lenin) and an Odessa Jew (Leon Trotsky) emerged as prominent and rival leaders. The first had already made some claim to theoretical prestige through a wordy program of action, *What Is To Be Done?* blatantly capitalizing on the fame and martyrdom of Chernyshevsky. The party's cause had a ready audience among the seasoned and most skilled workers in the industrial and port cities, where the war had come to mean longer hours, depressed conditions, conscription, and incessant news of defeat. In an effort to head off problems, the government responded to the demand for trade unions and sponsored worker's assemblies such as the St. Petersburg League of Factory Workers. One of the league's leaders was an Orthodox priest, Georgi Gapon, who soon became committed to the interests of the workers.[273]

A sense of changing times and an awareness of long-standing grievances of various kinds among the most oppressed of the urban population stirred up radical students and led to partially organized protests in the capital and in Moscow. Samuel Harper in Moscow described the growing excitement surrounding the sentencing of the assassin of Plehve in December.[274] More strikes and unrest followed, culminating in a large demonstration in St. Petersburg on 22 January 1905 ("Bloody Sunday") that was brutally suppressed by the army and the police; as many as a thousand were killed, many of them innocent bystanders. Gapon, the popular writer Maxim

273. For background, see especially W. Bruce Lincoln, *In War's Dark Shadow: The Russians Before the Great War* (New York: Dial Press, 1983), and Walter Sablinsky, *The Road to Bloody Sunday: Father Gapon and the St. Petersburg Massacre of 1905* (Princeton, N.J.: Princeton University Press, 1976).

274. Samuel Harper (Moscow) to Paul Harper (brother), 4/17 December 1904, folder 6, box 1, S. Harper Papers, University of Chicago. To his father he wrote, "I seem to understand the situation less every day. The Russians themselves seem to be 'in the air' too. Can't get used to the freedom (comparat. of course) they are enjoying these days. . . . Even the cabmen are waking up and taking some interest in the situation." 10 December 1904, ibid.

Gorky, university students, and numerous others decried the brutality and insensitivity of the government. Few outside the imperial family would mourn the retaliatory assassination in February of Grand Duke Sergei Aleksandrovich, military commander of the Moscow district.

Joining the protest were a number of bright, young American liberals and socialists that included Jack London, Lincoln Steffens, Arthur Bullard, William English Walling, and Ernest Poole, and some older critics such as Mark Twain, George Kennan, and Jane Addams. Most of them believed in the cause of "Russian freedom" but also saw in the civil strife in Russia a boon to their own social goals. Thus was forged the Russian revolutionary connection to the American Left that would persist for a generation or more.

The foundation had been laid for a sympathetic American response to Russian dissidents by the violence against Jews and the hard-hitting attacks of Kennan. More positively, the philanthropy of Charles Crane had provided a forum for the influential lectures in the United States of Ekaterina Breshko-Breshkovskaia and Paul Miliukov on the eve of the revolution. American feelings ranged from deep hatred to simple disgust with the tsar and his bureaucracy, and sentiments were bolstered by an increasing confidence in a worldwide triumph of the "American way." Mark Twain, for example, delivered a take-off on "the emperor's clothes"; Bloody Sunday had revealed a tsar who had no power naked: "Clothes and titles are the most potent thing, the most formidable influence in the earth."[275] And a long defender of Russia was moved to admit that

> Russia is a country of *extraordinary contrasts:* of imperial splendor and of widespread poverty; of the magnificence of the court and of the squalor of the moujik; of the stately grandeur of St. Petersburg and of the dreary, dead level of dull and endless plains; of the highest culture and the broadest ignorance; of the boundless treasures of the unequaled Winter Palace . . . and of the boundless destitution of almost uncounted millions.[276]

Even some official representatives in Russia condemned the government's action. Consul Heenan, for instance, volunteered his insightful opinion from distant Odessa: "History is being made very rapidly in this country and we are on the eve of stirring events. . . . The brutality displayed by the authorities in St. Petersburg last Sunday, has brought to the front a move-

275. "The Czar's Soliloquy," *North American Review* 580 (March 1905): 322.
276. Charles Emory Smith, "Russia," *New England Magazine* 32 (March 1905): 115.

ment which, with care, might have been held in abeyance for fifty years to come. I allude to a revolutionary movement among the peasantry and working classes combined."[277] Ambassador McCormick, however, thought the whole affair of January 1905 had been greatly exaggerated by the press.[278]

In a new development, a modern generation of American social reformers centered primarily in Lower East Side New York and at Hull House in Chicago rallied behind Russian revolutionary aspirations. A typical example was Ernest Poole, who grew up amid the wealth of bustling Chicago and spent summers on the shore at Lake Forest—except for 1893 when he roamed the world's fair. He went to Princeton in 1898, read Turgenev and Tolstoy, discovered a social conscience, and graduated in 1902 to the University Settlement on the Lower East Side, where he met others of the same ilk—Bullard, Walling, Leroy Scott, Howard Brubaker, Fred King. Drawn into the group were a few Russian Jewish radicals such as Abraham Cahan, who believed that pogroms fueled the extremism of the revolutionary movement.[279] "Quickly he became my friend and opened up a Russian world of revolution, books and plays, that stirred me deep, as Tolstoy and Turgeniev had in my last year of college," Poole reminisced.[280] With occasional relief in visits home, he worked in sweatshops, tenements, labor halls, and immigrant taverns, wrote sporadic articles for *Outlook* or *McClure's*, and received inspiration from conversations with Steffens, Sinclair, and Breshko-Breshkovskaia.

After the news of Bloody Sunday, Poole obtained a letter of credit from the *Outlook* and sailed for Russia. Befriended in St. Petersburg by Harold Williams, correspondent of the Manchester *Guardian*, he succeeded in penetrating the elusive enclaves of urban revolutionaries, the "third element" in the northern countryside, and the southern peasant villages. Then he posed as the American ambassador (fellow Chicagoan Robert McCormick) for officials in the Caucasus and came across a Georgian rebel who spoke colloquial midwestern English, having spent four years pretending to be a Cossack for Buffalo Bill's Wild West show. Poole considered Moscow, where radical sprites seemed to lurk in every shadow, most exciting and returned

277. Heenan to Hay, 28 January 1905, DUSC, Odessa, vol. 13 (roll 7, M 459), RG 59, NA.

278. To Hay (confidential), 18/31 January 1905, DUSM, Russia, vol. 62 (roll 62, M 35), RG 59, NA.

279. Cahan, "Jewish Massacres and the Revolutionary Movement in Russia," *North American Review* 560 (July 1903): 49–62.

280. Poole, *The Bridge: My Own Story* (New York: Macmillan, 1940), p. 74.

home in the summer thoroughly infected with the contagion of Russian revolution, a revolution that was still far from over.[281]

Roosevelt and Russia

The American "president by accident" had spent much of 1904 campaigning for the office. With that accomplished, Theodore Roosevelt proceeded to chart a more active foreign policy as his own secretary of state. The illness and prolonged absences of John Hay eased the shift in that direction, and the Russo-Japanese War offered an opportunity. Besides personal ambition, Roosevelt's initial motive was to protect Chinese neutrality and prevent that country from becoming the spoils of an unregulated peace. The president, however, could not stand the arrogant and pompous Cassini, nor the charming and cultivated McCormick. The ambassadorial problem he partly solved in December 1904 by asking George von Lengerke Meyer, an old friend and fellow Harvard man, to move from his post in Rome to St. Petersburg.[282] This could be achieved only after the proper amenities were shown to those concerned.

In the meantime the president sounded out both Japan and Russia for a mediated peace using various channels and employing trusted friends: Speck von Sternberg, the German ambassador in Washington; Cecil Spring Rice, who was then attached to the British embassy in St. Petersburg; and George Kennan. Sternberg visited St. Petersburg and conferred with Nicholas II in January 1905, apparently after Bloody Sunday and the news of the fall of Port Arthur had been received. He found the emperor open to concluding "a peace with honor" but adamantly opposed to a "congress," because the one at Berlin had treated Russia so badly after its last war. He wanted Roosevelt to "give a warning to Japan in time" that a long war of at-

---

281. Ibid., pp. 113–69.

282. Henry F. Pringle, *Theodore Roosevelt: A Biography* (New York: Harcourt, Brace, 1931), p. 381. Unlike most of his recent predecessors, Roosevelt had some prior knowledge of the countries he was dealing with. For example, in the summer of 1901 he conferred at length with Frederick Holls just after his return from Russia and sought the advice of Secretary of Interior Ethan Allen Hitchcock, former ambassador to Russia. Roosevelt (Oyster Bay) to Hitchcock, 21 August 1901, box 1, Hitchcock Papers, RG 316, NA. For a barely adequate biography of Meyer, see M. A. DeWolfe Howe, *George von Lengerke Meyer: His Life and Public Services* (New York: Dodd, Mead, 1920).

trition was at hand.[283] Roosevelt "summoned" Spring Rice from St. Petersburg for a conference at the White House to obtain his expert advice on Russian conditions; the consultation was brief, for the British diplomat returned to his post by the same steamer.[284] Regardless, the president learned through the Japanese envoy that Japan was not yet interested in compromise.

Roosevelt tried another direct but informal approach to Japan. He asked Japan-bound journalist Richard Barry to relay his views to Kennan in Tokyo, who in turn would meet with leading Japanese officials in Tokyo. In Kennan's words, the president's stance as conveyed by Barry was: "I have, from the beginning, favored Japan and have done all I could do, consistent with international law, to advance her interests. I thoroughly admire and believe in the Japanese. They have always told the truth and the Russians have not."[285] Kennan was asked through Barry to use this candid statement to convince the Japanese not to make exorbitant demands. He did so in a two-hour interview with the foreign minister but with no clear result. Kennan's own views—that Japan should have Vladivostok and that Russia should not be allowed a single naval station in the Pacific—made him a less than satisfactory envoy.[286]

International pressure for peace increased as revolutionary disorders spread in Russia and after the Russian army suffered a crucial defeat in Manchuria in March. A potentially major balance-of-power shift in East Asia now energized the American impetus for a negotiated peace. Meyer consulted with Wilhelm II and the former ambassador to Russia, Charlemagne Tower, in Berlin in February, while the French foreign minister, Theophile Delcasse, wanting to save his ally from further humiliation, used his influence to advise Japan against insistence on an indemnity and cession of territory. Feeling the international heat, Japan turned to Roosevelt to arrange a settlement that would include both territorial and monetary gains. Nicholas II was now stalling, hoping for favorable results from the Baltic armada that was approaching Chinese waters. Roosevelt, who had departed in early

283. Sternberg to Roosevelt, 24 March 1905, series 4A, roll 320, Taft Papers, LC. This original was found in the Taft Papers rather than Roosevelt's apparently because it arrived when Roosevelt was touring in the West and Taft was in charge in Washington, D.C.

284. Roman Rosen, *Forty Years of Diplomacy*, 2 vols. (New York: Alfred A. Knopf, 1922), 1:256–57.

285. Kennan quoting Barry quoting Roosevelt, to Roosevelt, 30 March 1905, roll 53, Roosevelt Papers, LC.

286. Ibid.; Raymond A. Esthus, *Double Eagle and Rising Sun: The Russians and Japanese at Portsmouth in 1905* (Durham, N.C.: Duke University Press, 1988), pp. 21–22.

April for a western tour and a reunion with the Rough Riders in San Antonio, was exasperated:

> As for the Japanese demands, I have been expecting that they would be materially increased after the smashing overthrow of Kuropatkin at Mukden. My own view is that the Russians would do well to close with them even now; but the Czar knows neither how to make war nor to make peace. If he had an ounce of sense he would have acted on my suggestion last January and have made peace then. There is nothing for us to do now but to sit and wait events.[287]

But he also feared that Russia might join a new Franco-German accord, leaving the United States isolated or forced to join with Britain and Japan.

Secretary of War Taft, following Roosevelt's instructions in his absence, conversed regularly with the Japanese minister in Washington, stressing that peace negotiations should proceed directly between the two parties without the intervention of other powers and without preconditions regarding terms. The Japanese, however, volunteered their demands: Port Arthur (now captured), control of Korea, restoration of Manchuria to China, the return of Sakhalin Island (relinquished to Russia in 1875), and a sizable indemnity. Roosevelt thought all were reasonable except the last two and returned early to Washington to devote more attention to peacemaking.[288]

In the meantime, Meyer dallied in Rome and Paris, among other things arranging for a new Mercedes to be shipped ahead to St. Petersburg, where he himself finally arrived on 7 April. He immediately instructed all consuls to send in weekly reports on conditions in their districts, and the response was enthusiastic. Soon valuable information—perhaps better than the government's own sources—was flowing into the American embassy.[289]

At his first audience with Nicholas II on 12 April, the new envoy firmly tendered the president's good offices in securing peace but felt the response

287. To Taft, 8 April 1905, series 4A, roll 320, Taft Papers, LC.

288. To Taft (Glenwood Springs), 18, 20, 27 April 1905, ibid.; Cassini to Lamzdorf, 4/17 May 1905, f. 133, op. 470, d. 121, pt. 1, AVPR. Cassini reported that there was even a suggestion in Congress that the United States solve one problem by buying Sakhalin from Russia; Cassini to Lamzdorf, 6/19 April 1905, ibid. For the full story of the American involvement in the peace negotiations, see the excellent study by Esthus, *Double Eagle and Rising Sun.*

289. A neglected source for what was happening during 1905 in major Russian cities, the originals are preserved in DPR, Russia, vols. 4558 and 4559 (consular reports), RG 84, NA.

was restrained by the presence of the empress. "The Empress watched him [Meyer] like a cat—She is for continuing the war."[290] Meyer was disappointed by the formal nature of the occasion and that Nicholas II seemed disconcerted when the matter of arbitration was raised.[291] Meyer conscientiously made the rounds of the grand dukes and officials and took the pulse of St. Petersburg society. He found the war sentiment still high and listened to claims that internal troubles had been exaggerated by the press. Minister of Navy Grand Duke Alexis, fiddling while Rome burned, reminisced about shooting buffalo on the American prairie.[292] But Meyer detected an air of foreboding as well: "The Czar does not seem to realize the importance of doing something to relieve his people."[293] From the consular reports, he described to Washington peasant riots, railroad strikes, and other disturbances in the spring of 1905, concluding that "the whole country is in a state of subdued political ferment and disaffection. . . . The prisons are full to overflowing, but the authorities do not seem to be able to get at the roots, and snipping off the branches only intensifies and exasperates those who are at the bottom of the movement."[294] Similar accounts came from other sources, creating the impression in Washington that Russia was becoming more and more unstable, "drifting without a pilot," in Meyer's words.[295] One bright spot for diplomatic affairs was the appointment in mid-May of "Baron" Roman Rosen, a former Russian minister to Japan and veteran of several years' service in the United States, to replace Cassini.[296]

At that time everyone seemed to be awaiting the outcome of the dispatch of the Russian Baltic fleet to the Pacific. Meyer rode his new polo ponies at the Beloselskii grounds, went on several hunting expeditions, and aired out the Kleinmichel Palace for his wife's arrival on 20 May—with two maids, two birds, three turtles, twenty-five bags, and twenty-five trunks.[297]

290. Diary, 12 April 1905, box 2, Meyer Papers, LC; Meyer to Hay, 13 April 1905, DUSM, Russia, vol. 62 (roll 62, M 35), RG 59, NA.
291. Meyer to Alice (his wife), and to Roosevelt (c), 31 March/13 April, box 3, Meyer Papers, MassHS.
292. Diary, 20 April 1905, box 2, Meyer Papers, LC.
293. Ibid., 16 April 1905.
294. To Hay, 1 May 1905, DUSM, Russia, vol. 63 (roll 63, M 35), RG 59, NA.
295. To Hay, 10/23 May 1905 (c), box 3, Meyer Papers, MassHS.
296. Rosen had cultivated Americans, including the Berdan family, at his various diplomatic posts even before his first assignment to the United States in 1871; Sarah Hagar to Kate, 18 March 1871, Hagar Papers, University of Vermont. In fact, Rosen was expected to replace Kantakuzen in 1893; Webb to White, 11 July 1893, roll 60, White Papers, Cornell University.
297. Alice Meyer journal of trip, box 3, Meyer Papers, MassHS.

Roosevelt thought privately that the odds favored Japan and that the chances were one in three that the Russian fleet would meet disaster—"so I guess there is nothing to do but watch them fight it out."[298]

The battle in Tsushima Strait between Japan and Korea at the end of May produced a stunned shock in the Russian capital. As Meyer reported, "Everyone is in the dark as to the Emperor's future policy. Procrastination, lack of decision, no plan of action appears to be the order of the day."[299] Even Roosevelt was surprised, as he wrote to "Springy":

> Well, it seems to me that the Russian bubble has been pretty thoroughly pricked. I thought the Japanese would defeat Rojestvensky; but I had no conception, and no one else had any conception . . . that there would be a slaughter rather than a fight, and that the Russians would really make no adequate resistance whatever. I have never been able to persuade myself that Russia was going to conquer the world at any time . . . and I suppose this particular fear is now at an end everywhere.[300]

As the president predicted, however, the diplomatic deadlock was indeed broken by the Russian naval debacle. Not only was this a severe blow to the tsar's pride, it also produced an unusually bitter and public criticism of the government. In his detailed observations on the war, Lieutenant McCully also blamed not just the incompetence of a few leaders for Russia's defeat but the whole autocratic system.[301] Meyer cabled, "Indignation and wrath is poured out freely upon Bureaucracy, which is alone held responsible for all misfortunes of war."[302] According to Sternberg, Cassini had turned contrite: "He came of [*sic*] his horse and confessed that the position of Russia was hopeless."[303] Roosevelt personally urged Cassini to call for peace negotia-

298. To Meyer (personal), 24 May 1905, ibid.

299. To Roosevelt, 23 May/5 June 1905 (c), box 4, Meyer Papers, MassHS.

300. To Spring Rice, 16 June 1905 (confidential) (c), vol. 56 (roll 338), Roosevelt Papers, LC.

301. Charles J. Weeks, Jr., *An American Naval Diplomat in Revolutionary Russia: The Life and Times of Vice Admiral Newton A. McCully* (Annapolis, Md.: Naval Institute Press, 1993), pp. 70–71. Being an official report, it remained buried in military files until 1977: Newton A. McCully, *The McCully Report: The Russo-Japanese War, 1904–1905*, ed. Richard A. von Doenhoff (Annapolis, Md.: Naval Institute Press, 1977).

302. To Hay, 2 June 1905, DUSM, Russia, vol. 63 (roll 63, M 35), RG 59, NA. An American officer advised Roosevelt that Russian battleships had been equipped with fake armor; Lt. Comdr. William Sims to Roosevelt, 25 July 1905 (c), box 4, Sims Papers, LC.

303. Sternberg to Roosevelt, 31 May 1905, roll 54, Roosevelt Papers, LC.

tions.[304] Across the Atlantic, Wilhelm II wrote ambassador Tower on 4 June, "strictly confidential," that he feared for the life of his cousin "Nicky" and that he was pressing the tsar to accept mediation without delay.[305]

Roosevelt cabled Meyer on 6 June to seek an audience with Nicholas II at once. The ambassador immediately approached Lamzdorf, who informed him that the emperor was booked up, especially busy with his wife's birthday the following day. Soon afterwards he informed Meyer that Nicholas would see him at 2:00 P.M. on the seventh.[306] The historic meeting between the two occurred at the Tsarskoe Selo summer palace in Nicholas's private study. The emperor agreed to negotiations without intermediaries, to be arranged by Roosevelt in strict secrecy and to be held in Europe at Paris or The Hague. The vulnerability of Sakhalin after Tsushima and its threatened loss was a key factor in the emperor's readiness. He also expressed the hope that by his consent the old friendship with the United States would return. A formal confirmation was delivered by Lamzdorf on 12 June,[307] but a problem soon arose over the location, since Japan's acceptance had been premised on Washington as the conference site. To the Russians this city was not only hot and uncomfortable in summer but also saturated with pro-Japanese sentiment, but they reluctantly agreed to this *fait accompli*.

With Russia's objections in mind but also with an eye to their own comfort, Roosevelt's staff sought a more hospitable environment, considering Atlantic City, Newport, Bar Harbor, and Portland, Maine. They finally decided on the naval yard in the Portsmouth, New Hampshire, harbor (actually in Kittery, Maine) as a cool and relatively isolated site, yet possessing excellent communication links. A new storehouse could be quickly converted for the formal meeting rooms.[308] Not far along the coast was the Wentworth Hotel, which could house the visiting delegations with appropriate charm and scenery (notwithstanding the mosquitoes).

In the meantime, both parties had difficulty naming a head of delegation who would command respect and could be trusted with plenipotentiary powers. At first senior diplomat and ambassador to France Aleksandr Neli-

304. Cassini to Lamzdorf, 31 May/13 June 1905, f. 133, op. 470, d. 121, pt. 1, AVPR.

305. "William" to Tower, 4 June 1905 (c), cabled with Tower to Roosevelt, 4 June 1905, roll 54, Roosevelt Papers, LC.

306. Diary, 6 and 7 June 1905, box 2, Meyer Papers, MassHS.

307. Meyer to Hay, 12 June (t) and 16 June (letter) 1905, DUSM, Russia, vol. 63 (roll 63, M 35), RG 59, NA.

308. Correspondence relating to preparations is in General Records of the Navy Department, box 732, RG 80, NA.

dov was named by Nicholas II, but his age, health, and bare knowledge of English forced his withdrawal. Alexander Izvolsky in Denmark also declined. Then Nikolai Murav'ev, the ambassador in Rome, was the next choice, but after interviews with Witte and Nicholas II, he also withdrew.[309] Reluctantly, but with Lamzdorf's urging, Nicholas II in mid-July turned to his former economic strategist, Sergei Witte, who had opposed the war from the beginning. He would be preceded by Rosen, taking up his new post in Washington, and accompanied by Fedor Martens, an expert on international law. Among others on the staff, Ivan Korostovets would be an able secretary and record keeper.

Japan's equivalent of Witte was elder statesman Hirobumi Ito, who had also championed a peace policy, but he declined the offer to head the delegation. Foreign Minister Jutaro Komura was then designated. Most Japanese expected not only the removal of Russian influence from Korea and Manchuria, including Port Arthur, but also the acquisition of a considerable part of the Russian Far East and a substantial indemnity with which to pay the foreign debt. With leverage in mind, Japan refused the Russian request for an armistice, so the war technically continued until the treaty was signed. To encourage compromise, Russia, though thoroughly beaten militarily, was patently boosting its new forces and supplies in the Far East during the summer of 1905. Both countries, however, shared financial exhaustion.

Revolution Continues

Meanwhile, another sensational revolutionary event occurred, but this one raised ominous questions about the reliability of the Russian armed forces. At the end of June while on a training cruise in the Black Sea, the crew of a battleship mutinied and seized the ship. The revolt was provoked by poor conditions, low morale, radical agitation, and rumors that the Black Sea fleet was next to be dispatched to the Pacific to face the Japanese. Steaming into Odessa harbor flying red and black flags, the mutiny inspired riots in the city that were cruelly repressed with considerable loss of life.[310] The American consul, Thomas Heenan, watched the *Potemkin*'s dramatic entry.

309. Vladimir N. Kokovtsov, *Iz moego proshlago: Vospominaniia 1903–1919 gg.* (1933; reprint, The Hague: Mouton, 1969), pp. 72–73. According to Witte, Murav'ev was upset over the small expense account and Lamzdorf's opposition; *Memoirs*, pp. 422–23.

310. Heenan to Hay, 28 June (t) and 6 July (letter) 1905, DUSC, Odessa, vol. 13 (roll 7, M 459), RG 59, NA.

On Tuesday about 6:30 P.M. I could see from my office window a battle-ship and a torpedo boat slowly approaching, and there was something in the appearance of the boats which excited my curiosity; they moved in a slovenly manner and in unusual order, the torpedo boat following the battleship in a direct line astern. . . . On Wednesday the startling intelligence was brought to the office that the battleship and torpedo boat were in the hands of the crews and that the officers had been mur-dered at sea, between Sevastopol and Odessa and their bodies thrown overboard. . . . The battleship was the *Kniaz Potemkin Tavricheski*.[311]

He also observed the American steamer *Garonne*, carrying part of the gar-rison of Port Arthur captured by the Japanese, come into the port under the bow of the *Potemkin*. Because of the confusion ashore, it was forced to seek a quieter haven at Feodosia.[312] Heenan was duly impressed at the restraint of the sailors and critical of the local authorities. "I should like to . . . speak a good word for the crew of the *Potemkin* who had strong provocation to de-stroy Odessa and kill thousands of its inhabitants, and yet refrained from doing so."[313] After creating more alarm along the Black Sea coast, the rebel sailors sought asylum in Rumania.

Had it been an isolated incident, the mutiny on the battleship *Potemkin* might have had less significance, but it stimulated a new wave of riots, strikes, and pogroms over Russia in late June and July that alarmed both Russian and American peacemakers. From Kronstadt to Rostov-on-Don and the Caucasus came reports to the American embassy of serious disor-ders.[314] Moreover, the Russian revolution was now hitting home, as the Singer and New York Air Brake factories in the vicinity of Moscow became particular targets of major strikes.[315] In frequent personal letters to the presi-dent Meyer stressed all of this and the importance of retaining the Russian autocracy for stability.

Thus on the eve of the peace conference, Roosevelt became more con-

311. Heenan to Meyer, 29 June 1905, DPR, Russia, vol. 4559 (consular reports), RG 84, NA.
312. Heenan to Hay, 6 July 1905, DUSC, Odessa, vol. 13 (roll 7, M 459), RG 59, NA.
313. Heenan to Meyer, 4 July 1905, DPR, Russia, vol. 4558 (consular reports), RG 84, NA.
314. Wigius (Kronstadt), 30 June; Stuart (Batum), 1 and 15 July; and Martin (Ros-tov), 23 July 1905, to Meyer, ibid.
315. Samuel Smith (Moscow) to Meyer, 1 July 1905, ibid.; Thomas Purdy (Lubertzy) to Meyer, 2/15 December 1905, DPR, Russia, vol. 4465 (misc. received), RG 84, NA.

vinced that the preservation of the Russian Empire was in the vital interests of the United States. In a private letter he indicated his disgust with Cassini, whom he had consulted about the *Potemkin* affair and who would have fired into it and destroyed the vessel. Roosevelt thought Russia should certainly make peace now with concessions in order to have a free hand at home. Sergei Witte, he added, was the only one who could accomplish it.[316] Although a number of sources regard the Tsushima fiasco as decisive in shifting official American opinion away from Japan and toward Russia,[317] the *Potemkin* affair had the effect of "strike two." To Americans it was one thing for downtrodden workers to be shot on Russian streets, another for uniformed sailors and soldiers to revolt. Jolted simultaneously by the rise of a new power in the East and by the mean and unpredictable turn in the revolution of 1905, American public opinion scurried behind Russia during the summer.[318]

The Meeting at Portsmouth

Preparations for the peace negotiations proceeded at a slow pace after the naming of the delegations. Witte consulted a number of leading officials, especially Lamzdorf and Minister of Finance Vladimir Kokovtsov, who had once been his assistant. He listened as the navy asserted the impossibility of giving up Sakhalin and as the tsar declared that dignity would not allow the payment of an indemnity. Within the government there was a consensus about relinquishing positions in Korea, the Liaotung Peninsula, and Manchuria and using the Chinese Eastern Railway as a bargaining chip.[319] Witte also cleverly manipulated public opinion in advance with a candid and friendly interview for the Associated Press. On 19 July he left St. Petersburg for Paris and the transatlantic crossing.

Anxious to prepare Russia for acceding to more Japanese demands in the interests of peace and stability, Roosevelt applied pressure through various diplomatic channels, again using Sternberg and Spring Rice, among others. He counted especially on the influence of Wilhelm II, the tsar's cousin and

316. To John O'Laughlin, 29 June 1905, box 1, O'Laughlin Papers, LC.

317. For example, A. Bonch-Osmolovskii, *Soedenennye Shtaty i probelma Tikhogo Okeana* (Moscow-Leningrad: Gosizdat, 1930), p. 40.

318. For a thorough discussion of this, see Arthur Thompson and Robert Hart, *The Uncertain Crusade: America and the Russian Revolution of 1905* (Amherst: University of Massachusetts Press, 1970).

319. Eugene P. Trani, *The Treaty of Portsmouth: An Adventure in American Diplomacy* (Lexington: University of Kentucky Press, 1969), pp. 100–105.

friend, but this nearly backfired.[320] At a meeting between the two emperors in early July, Wilhelm coaxed Nicholas into agreeing to an alliance that would have undermined Russia's connection with France. Although details of this "treaty" did not become known, even to Lamzdorf, until after Portsmouth, it had the contrary effect of stiffening the tsar's resolve to stand firm against concessions and to resume the war.[321]

Meanwhile, Rosen presented his credentials in Washington on 5 July, bade farewell to the departing Cassini, and established a preconference base near Roosevelt's summer home, Sagamore Hill, on Long Island. Herbert Pierce, temporarily in charge of the State Department after Hay's death, chaperoned Rosen to a family lunch with the president on 14 July. The Russian envoy was pleased to hear that "not Russia but Japan is now the real opponent of the United States in trade-industrial relations. . . . The complete removal of Russia from the Pacific Ocean was most undesirable in general and especially undesirable for America in consideration of the necessity of a political balance in the Far East." Roosevelt stressed the precarious position of Russia in the Far East and the urgency of accepting a peace that included harsh conditions. He further warned of Britain's interest in a Japanese victory and cited Peter the Great's 1711 Pruth peace with the Ottoman Empire as a precedent for bowing to military reality.[322] The president was still pessimistic about success, annoyed with the Russians for not taking matters more seriously, and irritated with the Japanese for being so belligerent and for not sending a plenipotentiary delegation.[323]

A few days later the president followed up his private chat with a request to see Rosen and possibly Witte before the formal presentations.[324] Obviously, Roosevelt expected to assume a key role in bringing the two sides to-

320. Ibid., p. 107.

321. Lamzdorf found Nicholas very pleased with his meeting and inclined to continue the war; to Witte, 16 July 1905, f. 138, op. 467, d. 691/733, AVPR. The foreign minister did not accompany Nicholas, since the German foreign minister was not to be there; Lamzdorf to Witte, 8 July 1905, ibid.

322. Rosen to Lamzdorf, 1/14 July 1905, ibid. John Hay was often accused of being the architect of an anti-Russian policy, but he privately denied this in a letter to Meyer in which he stressed instead the traditional American friendship "for Russia, in America, and the President and the State Department share it." Hay (Paris) to Meyer, 1 June 1905, box 4, Meyer Papers, MassHS. The appointment of Herbert Pierce, certainly a friend of Russia's, as his assistant supports this.

323. Zabriskie, *American-Russian Rivalry*, pp. 120–21.

324. "Do you come to see me before Mr. Witte comes, or shall I wait and get you to bring him out informally before the regular presentation?" Roosevelt to Rosen, 18 July 1905, f. 128, op. 467, d. 689/731, AVPR.

*President Roosevelt and the peace envoys before the Portsmouth
Conference; Witte and Rosen are on the left. Harper's Weekly,
19 August 1905, courtesy of the Kansas Collection, University of
Kansas Libraries*

gether. In the meantime, the two delegations took leisurely passages across
their respective oceans, the Japanese arriving first and having an informal
meeting with Roosevelt at Sagamore Hill on 28 July. Rosen's next interview
on 31 July was a two-hour session in which the president revealed that Japan
had to seek an indemnity because their bankers insisted on it.[325]

Sailing on the *Kaiser Wilhelm der Grosse* that arrived at Hoboken on 2
August, the Russian delegation was met by a happy crowd of well-wishers,
mainly Slavic residents of the New York area. On Friday, 4 August, Witte
and Rosen lunched with the president before the official introduction to the

325. Rosen to Lamzdorf, 19 July/1 August 1905 (t), f. 138, op. 467, d. 690/732,
AVPR. Rosen recalled this meeting occurring on his initiative—to protest the Japanese
occupation of Sakhalin; Rosen, *Forty Years*, pp. 260–61.

Japanese the next day. Rosen thought that Witte made a very good impression on the president.[326] After these preliminaries, they traveled northward along the coast for more formalities and festivities in the navy yard and at the Portsmouth courthouse on 8 August. The delegates settled into the Wentworth Hotel, which quickly became a beehive of journalists and curiosity seekers. Although the talks finally began on 10 August, it was only to decide on negotiating rules—such as holding closed sessions, despite Russian objections, and not mentioning the origins of the war. Witte nevertheless played to a larger audience from the beginning, openly discussing the negotiations and intentionally courting American public opinion with the assistance of British journalist E. Joseph Dillon and the elderly friends of Russia, Wharton Barker and Jeremiah Curtin. Witte's imposing, towering figure—beside the diminutive Komura—provided visual reinforcement. Perceiving this positive impact from other sources, Lamzdorf even suggested that Witte go on a tour of the United States "to make use of favorable inclination of public opinion regarding relations with Russia."[327]

At the negotiating table, progress was slow through several sessions, finally coming to the expected impasse over Japanese demands for Sakhalin and an indemnity. Russia remained firm about not surrendering any of its real territory or paying compensation. Roosevelt was exasperated that his cajoling and arm-twisting behind the scenes failed to produce a compromise. During these days of August, American sentiment, at least on the East Coast, tilted even more toward Russia, for which Witte later claimed credit.[328] However, many Americans felt the Japanese were being unreasonable and had cheated by invading Sakhalin on the eve of the peace negotiations in order to hold it for ransom to help pay for the war.

Russia at last broke the deadlock. Minister of Finance Kokovtsov kept up separate, regular communications with his former mentor, in which he underscored Russia's deteriorating financial position and internal upheaval. He even obtained the tsar's request for Witte to travel the country and lay the sympathetic groundwork for negotiating a loan.[329] Witte's response was

326. To Lamzdorf, 23 July/6 August 1905 (t), f. 138, op. 467, d. 690/732, AVPR.

327. Lamzdorf to Witte (secret telegram), 28 July/10 August 1905, f. 138, op. 467, d. 694/737, AVPR. But Lamzdorf dropped the request a few days later; to Witte, 31 July/13 August 1905, ibid.

328. Witte, *Memoirs*, p. 433.

329. Kokovtsov to Witte (t), 3/16 August, 4/17 August, and 5/18 August 1905, f. 138, op. 467, d. 691/733, AVPR. Kokovtsov and Witte castigated each other bitterly in their respective memoirs, with the latter blaming Kokovtsov, "hampered by a narrow, bureaucratic mind," for Russia's financial woes; Witte, *Memoirs*, p. 424.

that "the situation in America is inclining to our side, but [for this to be sustained] it is necessary for [the Russian] Government to continue to seek peace."[330] He sent a strongly worded telegram stressing that "Petersburg must decide the question of war or peace." Deliberately circumventing Lamzdorf, he asked Kokovtsov to mobilize government leaders, especially Pobedonostsev and Dmitri Sol'skii, chairman of the State Council, to convince the emperor of the necessity of compromise, concluding, "I trust in your energy and silence."[331]

Kokovtsov moved cautiously, admitting difficulty in the face of a popular slogan, "not an inch of ground, not a kopeck of compensation." Nevertheless, he cabled Witte on 21 August that he had written what he thought was a strong statement to Nicholas II opposing the payment of an indemnity but advocating the sacrifice of half of Sakhalin. The tsar had to accept "the ruin of our finances by a continuation of the war." Yet he and Lamzdorf each reported on 21 August that the tsar was still disposed against such a compromise by reports from the commander in chief of the army.[332] Oddly, Witte contended that the military advisers assigned to him from the army favored peace at virtually any cost.[333]

Fearing a collapse of negotiations and resumption of war as very likely and probably with Witte's prompting, Roosevelt returned to a previously successful strategy by instructing Meyer on 22 August to seek an immediate interview with Nicholas II. The ambassador again managed the tsar beautifully in a long meeting the next day at the imperial summer cottage. Meyer argued persuasively that the southern half of Sakhalin had been Japanese before 1875 and that even the United States had modified its territorial claims (over Oregon) to avoid war. Facing renewed pressure from several sides, Nicholas finally agreed to divide the island but remained adamant about not paying an indemnity—though he said he would liberally fund the care of prisoners. No doubt he was simply tired of the whole business. Meyer wrote in his diary, "He impressed me today as a man of no force and who was swayed by his conscience without using his mind to reason in order to

330. To Kokovtsov, 5/18 August 1905, f. 138, op. 467, d. 691/733, AVPR.
331. To Kokovtsov, 6/19 August 1905, ibid.
332. Kokovstov to Witte, 8/21 August 1905 (t), and Lamzdorf to Witte, 8/21 August 1905 (c), ibid. Although Kokovtsov should receive credit for having suggested the final solution, in his memoirs he goes to some length to give Nicholas II—and especially to not give Witte or Roosevelt—the honor of developing these terms; *Iz moego proshlago,* pp. 77–79.
333. Witte, *Memoirs,* p. 426. For a detailed analysis of the negotiations at Portsmouth, see Esthus, *Double Eagle and Rising Sun,* pp. 101–51.

ascertain if it was influencing in the right way and for the best interests of his country."[334]

Again transoceanic cables were busy as Roosevelt battled both sides over the compensation issue. After several days of waiting for a reply from Tokyo, the Japanese finally agreed to split Sakhalin without receiving an indemnity for the surrender of the northern half. Roosevelt reflected privately, "My own view is that the Russians could well have afforded to go further in the way of concessions than they did in order to gain peace, but if they would not do so it was Japan's interest to make peace anyhow."[335]

Subordinate staff worked out the remaining details. The war thus drew to a close, but no one was very happy: the Japanese had the sense that they had won the war but lost the peace; the Russians had given up territory and felt aggrieved that enemies had capitalized on their domestic strife; the delegates on both sides were vilified at home for their compromises, and even Witte, who had saved Russia from much grief, was labeled "Count Half-Sakhalin"; all felt betrayed by their "friends."

Witte at least was able to celebrate in New York society—while courting a loan. He visited General Fred Grant, son of the president, whose daughter was married to a Russian prince, and toured Columbia University. On a side trip to Washington, by his own special request he was given a ride down the Potomac on a naval vessel and a private tour of Mount Vernon. Similarly, J. P. Morgan escorted him up the Hudson to the usual military show at West Point. And the busy staff of Sagamore Hill once more served dinner to the Russian delegation. Roosevelt took advantage of this less-pressing occasion to bring up the Jewish visa problem, and Witte agreed to carry home a letter to Nicholas II, which would quickly be relegated to a bureaucratic niche in the Ministry of Interior.[336] Witte then canceled his proposed tour of

334. Diary, 23 August 1905, box 2, Meyer Papers, LC. In a private letter Meyer summed up the crux of the negotiations at Portsmouth: "It depends now entirely on whether Japan continues to insist on a war indemnity, which Russia will not pay, as she claims that Japan is getting all she went to war for and a great deal more than she ever expected under any circumstances to obtain." To Julia, 12/25 August 1905, file of letters, Meyer Papers, LC.

335. To John O'Laughlin (strictly personal), 31 August 1905, box 1, O'Laughlin Papers, LC.

336. Witte, *Memoirs*, pp. 446–49. Roosevelt pressed the point in writing: "In furtherance of our conversation of last evening I beg you to consider the question granting passports to reputable American citizens of Jewish faith. I feel that if this could be done it would remove the last cause of irritation between the two nations whose historic friendship for one another I wish to do my best to maintain." To Witte, 10 September 1905, f. 138, op. 467, d. 694/737, AVPR.

the United States, hinting in his memoirs that he had grown tired of plain American food and accommodations, had already exceeded his expense account, and was not feeling well. He had also taken to heart Morgan's advice to negotiate a new loan from a consortium of international banks in Paris or St. Petersburg rather than in New York.[337]

Peace, despite the expectations of American officials, did not rescue Russia from more serious revolutionary disturbances. Meyer confidently left St. Petersburg on 9 September for a leisurely tour of Europe and home rest. Immediately after reaching the United States, he dined at the White House on 4 October and discussed the possibility of a cabinet appointment. The news of further unrest in Russia and the general strike in October convinced Roosevelt that Meyer should return at once, despite the illness of his wife. He arrived in St. Petersburg on 8 December to report that things had settled down in the capital but were still at a critical stage in Moscow.[338]

Indeed, strikes and turmoil jeopardized the existence of the Russian government from October through December 1905. Normal life in much of the country ground to a halt because of revolutionary agitation and the dissatisfaction acted out by a large portion of students, workers, and peasants. Ideologically committed parties, led by bright, young talents such as Leon Trotsky, were fomenting sharp attacks against existing authorities and owners and managers of businesses at the local and national levels. Persons and property were now threatened as never before in modern Russian history. And this included a sizable number of Americans resident in Russia.

Both official and private accounts were soon sounding the klaxon. Prolonged violence and bloody confrontations in Moscow and other urban and industrial centers in late 1905 were especially worrisome. A new American consul in Batum, William Stuart, was the first casualty, receiving a superficial gunshot wound in the arm. No wonder he declared, "The whole country is simply permeated with sedition and reeking with revolution, racial hatred and warfare, murder, incendiarism, brigandage, robbery and crime of every kind."[339] He also reported that as a result of "horrible and almost incredible outbursts of the most savage and cruel passions of which man in his

337. Witte, Memoirs, pp. 446, 450.
338. Diary, 9 September, 4 October, 8 November, and 8 December 1905, box 2, Meyer Papers, LC.
339. Stuart to Meyer, 13 October 1905, enclosed in Eddy to Root, 19 October 1905, DUSM, Russia, vol. 64 (roll 64, M 35), RG 59, NA.

uncultured state is capable," damage to the oil fields in the Caucasus exceeded $13 million.[340]

Another new appointee, Roger Greene, arrived at Vladivostok in the midst of a riot in November and calculated that Americans alone had lost $250,000 in property.[341] There was greater fear, however, for Moscow, the second largest city in the empire but perhaps the most important for its central location and tradition of representing the real Russia. The outbreak of violence there was intense from its beginning in October, but Henry Hiller, who was on his annual buying trip for Tiffany's, was relieved that at first it was not directed against private property.[342] Severe destruction occurred later in December when heavy artillery suppressed the revolution with a loss of over a thousand lives. To add to the climate of hysteria, communications in the area had been severely interrupted by the use of telegraph poles for barricades.[343]

The violence seemed to be spreading to the Baltic provinces, and there were discouraging incidents of mutiny and insubordination in the emperor's pride and glory, the Baltic fleet.[344] The news was no better from Odessa: "A most serious aspect of the situation is that many factories have been obliged to close down through lack of funds, and thousands of people have been thrown out of employment, which in the excited state of the workpeople may lead to serious trouble."[345]

Nicholas II had reason to be glum at the annual New Year's diplomatic reception in 1906. When Captain Roy Smith, incoming American naval attaché, was introduced, "The Tsar questioned him about our fleet coming to the Mediterranean and added: 'I suppose you are sending it into warmer waters during the winter, as we do,'—then correcting himself: 'as we used to do, when we had a fleet.'"[346] A leaking ship was sailing into uncharted waters with a dispirited, indecisive pilot at the helm.

340. Stuart to Loomis, 7 October 1905, DUSC, Batum, vol 1 (roll 1, M 482), RG 59, NA.

341. Greene to Bacon, 11 December 1905, DUSC, Vladivostok, vol. 1 (roll 1, M 486), RG 59, NA.

342. Hiller to wife, 16/29 October and 25 October/7 November 1905, box 2, vol. 7, Hiller Papers, Mystic Seaport Library.

343. Meyer to Root, 26, 28, and 31 December 1905 and 5 January 1906 (t), DUSM, Russia, vol. 65 (roll 65, M 35), RG 59, NA.

344. Meyer to Root, 3 January 1906, ibid.

345. Heenan to Bacon, 23 December 1905, DUSC, Odessa, vol. 13 (roll 7, M 459), RG 59, NA.

346. Meyer to Root, 15 January 1906, ibid.

7

Hopes and Fears, 1905–1914

When Russians and Americans came together during the period after the American Civil War, they often referred to the traditional friendship that existed between the two countries. The event that would frequently be cited as proof was the 1863–1864 visit of Russian naval squadrons to the United States in the middle of a very difficult period in American history. The idea permeated into articles, books, and public lectures that the Russian ships were not only a sign of friendship toward the Union but were also intended to ward off a more active British or French intervention on the side of the Confederacy and would have been made available to the United States in the event of war with another European power.

From the 1880s new problems and a resulting coolness in relations shook the earlier rapport and caused Russian spokesmen to become more hyperbolic in references to past favors and the idea of natural accord. As an example, Vladimir Holstrem wrote in 1899 in the influential *North American Review*: "Our destinies, following their special lines, are developing in such harmony, are so mysteriously interwoven, that our mere existence is mutually beneficial."[1] However, American hostility cast a shadow over the idea of an enduring amity. In 1900 Evgenyi Matrosov was still defending the "friendship fleet" and Russian benevolence toward the United States, but

1. Holstrem, "Ex Oriente Lux!: A Plea for a Russo-American Understanding," *North American Review* 512 (July 1899): 28. Among those responding to Holstrem was A. Maurice Low, "Russia, England, and the United States," *Forum* 28 (September 1899): 172–77, emphasizing America's more natural affinity with Britain.

after 1904 this theme was frequently combined with public outcry over American "ingratitude" in taking Japan's side.[2]

American opponents of the perpetual friendship theory centered their rebuttal on the fleet visit, contending that the ships were sent by Russia purely for self-serving reasons—to avoid their being bottled up in the Baltic in the event of a conflict with Britain and France over Russian suppression of a revolt in Poland in 1863. They argued that the ships were never intended to assist the Union, and it was the United States that had shown generous hospitality by providing neutral harbors. This position gained more adherents after Kishinev[3] and Russian expansion in the Far East and was employed to justify or excuse support for Japan. Both perspectives—one detecting motives of friendship, the other, of self-interest—tended to solidify as time passed.

In the Russian-American reflections over the fleet visits, little hard evidence was produced one way or the other, and arguments were weakened by obvious errors. Ralph McKenzie claimed that the real mission of the fleet was to take the imperial jewels to safety, that it was commanded by Grand Duke Alexis, and that it came to the United States because Russia had nowhere else to send it.[4] The debate extended to the sale of Alaska, with Americans denying that friendly relations had anything to do with the transaction[5] and conservative Russians maintaining that Alexander II had rashly sold Alaska to buy American friendship, which was not worth the price, in the context of 1904.

At the turn of the century, Thomas Willing Balch collected private correspondence while researching the Alaskan boundary dispute between the United States and Canada and investigating any connection between the fleet visit and the purchase of Alaska.[6] George Pierce related to Balch his father's claim that Andrew Curtin had seen (circa 1870) Admiral Stepan Lesovskii's sealed orders placing the Russian fleet at the disposal of President

2. Matrosov, "Chrezvychainoe Amerikanskoe posol'stvo v Rossii, v 1866 godu," *Istoricheskii Vestnik* 93, 1 (January 1900): 265–66; McCormick to Lambert Tree, 18/31 August 1904, Tree Papers, Newberry Library.

3. An editorial on Kishinev in *Harper's Weekly* (30 May 1903) specifically discounted 1863 friendship.

4. McKenzie, *Jew Baiting in Russia and Her Alleged Friendship for the United States* (Washington, D.C.: By author, 1903), pp. 18–25.

5. For example, in Oscar S. Straus, "The United States and Russia: Their Historical Relations," *North American Review* 585 (August 1905): 248.

6. Balch to Frederick Seward, 6 December 1901, vol. 1, Alaskan Boundary, Balch Papers, HSP.

Lincoln in the case of war.[7] Wharton Barker also informed Balch that in a casual conversation with Alexander II in 1879, the emperor remarked that a British or French recognition of the Confederacy was to be considered a casus belli for Russia and that the fleet was sent expressly to prevent that. In his 1904 article on the subject, Barker recalled the tsar saying: "I acted because I understood that Russia would have a more serious task to perform if the American Republic with advanced industrial development was broken up and Great Britain left in control of most branches of modern industrial development."[8]

Harper's Weekly revived the theme in the wake of the Portsmouth treaty, noting past favors received from Russia and the importance of friendship in effectively promoting improvements in Russia: "Let . . . the St. Petersburg government be convinced that Americans, while ardent friends of the Russian people, are also gratefully mindful of their debts to the House of Romanoff, and, therefore, desire to reconcile the progress of political reform with the stability of the dynasty."[9] The reputation of the fleet visit would continue to wane and wax according to the political climate—hopes and promises, fears and hostility—and on the basis of individual images of the Russian present and future.[10]

Revolutionary Changes

In general, a wave of optimism greeted the signing of the Portsmouth treaty in September 1905. The invitation by the tsar to a new Hague international

7. Pierce to Balch, 3 February 1899, ibid. The same story had surfaced after the assassination of Alexander II, with M. A. Dane claiming that he had confirmed it directly with Curtin and that Curtin had said he had discussed it with State Department officials upon his return. Letter to editor, *New York Herald*, 22 March 1881, p. 3.

8. To Balch, 1 January 1901, vol. 1, Alaskan Boundary, Balch Papers, HSP; repeated publicly in Barker, "The Secret of Russia's Friendship," *Independent* 56, 2886 (24 March 1904): 648. More convincing was the observation of Secretary of State Seward's son, also his private secretary: "Of course, we knew that we might count on its aid, if needed, but fortunately we did not need it." Frederick W. Seward to Balch, 10 December 1901, vol. 1, Alaskan Boundary, Balch Papers, HSP.

9. "The United States and Russia," *Harper's Weekly*, 23 September 1905, 1368.

10. Frank Golder gained access to Russian naval archives in 1915 and found no direct evidence of a Russian plan to help the United States—although he acknowledged that the appearance of the fleet did foster the belief; Golder, "The Russian Fleet and the Civil War," *American Historical Review* 20, 4 (July 1915): 801–12. Nonetheless, the debate periodically resumes, especially in such times of tension as the Cold War. See N. N. Bolkhovitinov's discussion in *Russko-Amerikanskie otnosheniia i prodazha Aliaski, 1834–1867* (Moscow: Nauka, 1990), pp. 167–70.

peace conference, the August decree calling for a national legislature, and the watershed October Manifesto promising basic rights of speech and assembly signaled to many Americans a fundamental new direction for Russian government and society. These were given prominence in the United States because of the involvement of Sergei Witte, who had successfully captured public opinion during the peace negotiations.[11]

Witte's ulterior motive was to obtain a substantial American loan for the Russian government. The primary source of Russian credit, France, was presently unsettled because of the death of Baron Alphonse de Rothschild of Paris and the passage of leadership to the London branch. With this in mind, Witte visited with J. Pierpont Morgan, Jr., on his yacht in early September and convinced him and George W. Perkins to meet with European bankers in St. Petersburg for further negotiations.[12] Although they were prepared to offer 100 million francs as the American contribution to a large loan, the transaction was caught up in the October turmoil of labor strife and rural rebellion.

A surge of urban strikes and provincial violence, the latter directed especially against Jews, began in late September and gained momentum in October, virtually paralyzing the country. Transport Minister Khilkov even reprised his role as an American engineer by taking the controls of a Russian locomotive, but he could not curb a railroad workers' walkout that plunged the country into a general strike, and he subsequently resigned. Radical parties seized the opportunity to establish a "strike council," the St. Petersburg Soviet of Workers Deputies, in which Trotsky was a key figure. In a government reorganization Witte emerged in a new post as chairman of the Council of Ministers, roughly equivalent to prime minister.

American chargé d'affaires Spencer Eddy, in Meyer's absence, reported in detail on events in St. Petersburg and that Morgan and Perkins were at a loss as to how to proceed. He hinted that Witte was using their presence and the loan negotiations to pressure the tsar to issue the October Manifesto and reestablish order.[13] Nevertheless, rebellious Russia in late October 1905 did

11. For example, Charles Johnston, "The Dawn of Liberty in Russia," *Harper's Weekly*, 11 November 1905. For Witte's role in Russian governmental affairs after Portsmouth, see Howard D. Mehlinger and John M. Thompson, *Count Witte and the Tsarist Government in the 1905 Revolution* (Bloomington and London: Indiana University Press, 1972).

12. Rosen to Lamzdorf, 20 September/3 October 1905, f. 133, op. 470, d. 1121, pt. 2; and Lamzdorf to Rosen, 22 September/5 October 1905 (c), f. 170, op. 512/2, d. 174, AVPR.

13. Eddy to Root (confidential), 27 October 1905, DUSM, Russia, vol. 64 (roll 64, M 35), RG 59, NA.

not seem to be a good financial risk, and the emissaries left on 1 November. Morgan cabled home that "it would be impossible to float a Russian loan in the United States at this time,"[14] though his father wired assurances to Witte that they still hoped to underwrite Russian bonds in the future. As Eddy noted, "They kept in close touch with this Embassy during their entire stay, and although the project for the loan has, for the moment, fallen through, . . . they expect to return to Russia at a later day, when such negotiations can be carried on with more security."[15]

Visiting St. Petersburg on business, Moscow consul Thomas Smith, in a letter to Ambassador Meyer, voiced optimism about American postwar prospects in Russia: "The Russians do not keep up resentment for long, and speedily forget anything which may have given offense. . . . Now is really the time for Americans to go in for Russian business, and I trust you will be back ere long to assist in promoting good relations and commercial enter-prise between the two countries."[16] Front-page reports of continuing revolu-tionary violence, however, discouraged potential investors.

Contrary to its purpose, the October Manifesto was greeted by the out-break of virtual civil war in many parts of Russia. In some places the vio-lence was clearly ethnic in nature, and the Jewish population was particu-larly vulnerable. Not only was anti-Semitism rising among the Slavic population, and with it the tendency to blame the Jews for all problems, but Jews had kept a high profile in radical activity. In Odessa, with a Jewish pop-ulation reaching one-third (nearly 150,000) of the total, Jews were at the helm of many businesses, including grain exports, and were prominent among radical workers and university students. As soon as the October Manifesto was announced and martial law lifted, students organized a mass demonstration that displayed strident antigovernment slogans. The next day the Orthodox population countered with a show of loyalty to the tsar and anti-Semitic vitriol. The lines being drawn, what followed was a general assault on Jewish people, homes, and businesses, especially in poorer sub-urbs, clearly abetted by police and soldiers.[17] Judeophobic rage spread

14. As quoted in John Douglas Forbes, *J. P. Morgan, Jr., 1867–1943* (Charlottesville: University Press of Virginia, 1981), p. 57. Forbes contends that Morgan was actually meeting with Witte on 17/30 October when the manifesto was announced.

15. Eddy to Root, 6 November 1905, DUSM, Russia, vol. 64 (roll 64, M 35), RG 59, NA.

16. T. Smith to Meyer, 20 October/2 November 1905, DPR, Russia, vol. 4464 (misc. received), RG 84, NA.

17. Heenan to Root, 8 November 1905, DUSC, Odessa, vol. 13 (roll 7, M 459), RG 59, NA.

through the Pale and was especially pronounced in new industrial areas, where frustrated miners and workers vented their anger on the Jews.[18] Although these attacks were not pogroms in the strict sense, their overall toll was by far the greatest in Russian history—800 Jews killed and 5,000 wounded in Odessa alone and a total of 3,100 deaths over the whole country (compared to 93 Jewish lives lost during all of 1903 and 1904).[19] Increased emigration to the United States would be one result, though it was a response that would encounter concern and opposition from Americans.

Theodore Roosevelt, alarmed by the continuing unrest in Russia, prevailed on his ambassador to return to his post promptly.[20] Meyer left New York on 21 November, stopping over in Berlin, where he listened to Russian diplomats complain that the emperor lacked resolve, the empress was an evil influence, and no one had confidence in Witte except a few close followers.[21] In St. Petersburg the impression was no better. Meyer cabled: "Russian nation appears to have gone temporarily insane; government practically helpless to restore law and order throughout the country; departments at sixes and sevens; also crippled by postal and telegraph strike. Only the socialists appear to be well organized to establish strikes when and wherever they like."[22] Conditions, he thought, had severely deteriorated since his departure in August.

Meyer's pessimism grew as reports came in of turmoil in other cities, especially Moscow. He took a preliminary step to safeguard Americans and their property by ordering consuls to conduct a census, thereby creating a valuable registry of Americans and their occupations in Russia.[23] Of particular concern was the Lubertzy brake works, about fifteen miles south of Moscow,

18. See Charters Wynn, *Workers, Strikes, and Pogroms: The Donbass-Dnepr Bend in Late Imperial Russia, 1870–1905* (Princeton, N.J.: Princeton University Press, 1992).

19. Shlomo Lambroza, "The Pogroms of 1903–1906," and Robert Weinberg, "The Pogrom of 1905 in Odessa: A Case Study," in John D. Klier and Shlomo Lambroza, eds., *Pogroms: Anti-Jewish Violence in Modern Russian History* (Cambridge: Cambridge University Press, 1992), pp. 195–290.

20. Diary, 8 November 1905, box 2, Meyer Papers, LC.

21. Ibid., 1 December 1905; Meyer (Berlin) to Root, 5 December 1905, DUSM, Russia, vol. 64 (roll 64, M 35), RG 59, NA.

22. To Root (t), 11 December 1905, DUSM, Russia, vol. 64 (roll 64, M 35), RG 59, NA.

23. The totals for European Russia were 283, probably shy a few: Moscow 107, St. Petersburg 84, Riga 33, Odessa 32, Warsaw 22, Viborg 2, and Rostov, Helsingfors, and Novorossisk 1 each. Only 129 had currently valid passports, indicating that most were "permanent" residents. To Root, 14 March 1906, DUSM, Russia, vol. 65 (roll 65, M 35), RG 59, NA.

which had shifted production to munitions and gasoline engines during the war. Plagued by strikes and violence through 1905, the plant was again facing a crisis in mid-December. Owner-manager Thomas Purdy reported that the 450 workers were armed and led by about 16 socialist agitators. Their demands included construction of houses, libraries, schools, and baths—"all of which are social and not industrial questions and I have no capital for that purpose."[24] They even briefly seized the factory, but Meyer sought and obtained liberation of the area by loyal troops.[25]

The major uprising in Moscow in December was reported to Meyer in detail by consul Smith by telegraph and telephone, despite general disruption of communications, and in a day-by-day journal.[26] After a bloody and brutal suppression by the army, the ambassador cabled Washington: "I am glad to state that as yet I have heard of no injuries occurring to American citizens in Moscow; in fact in all these disturbances that have taken place in the various cities the revolutionists and strikers have refrained in all instance from attacking foreign consulates, and I believe this also applies to the property of foreign individuals."[27] An exception was Vladivostok, where the consul estimated $250,000 in American property destroyed by fire in November riots that leveled seventy-five buildings, but he did not indicate that Americans were being singled out for attack.[28]

Reports from the south of Russia and the Caucasus, where law and order seemed to have broken down completely, provided more reasons for gloom. From Rostov-on-Don the ambassador learned, "No real attempts to check the disorders seem to have been made by the authorities, although by acting energetically at once they might have been greatly minimized."[29] Unrest in

24. Purdy to Meyer, 2/15 December 1905, DPR, Russia, vol. 4464 (misc. received), RG 84, NA. See also, George S. Queen, "An American Employer and Russian Labor in 1905," *Journal of Modern History* 15, 2 (June 1943): 120–26.

25. Purdy to Meyer, 19 December 1905/1 January 1906, DPR, Russia, vol. 247, RG 84, NA; Meyer to Root, 5 January 1906, DUSM, Russia, vol. 65 (roll 65, M 35), RG 59, NA.

26. Smith to Meyer, 2 January 1906, DPR, Russia, vol. 4560, RG 84, NA.

27. To Root, 5 January 1906, DUSM, Russia, vol. 65 (roll 65, M 35), RG 59, NA.

28. Greene to Bacon, 11 December 1905, DUSC, Vladivostok, vol. 1 (roll 1, M 486), RG 59, NA. In contrast, during a January outburst, "there was no burning or pillaging of either public or private property." To Root, 29 January 1906, ibid.

29. Martin to Meyer, 31 October/13 November 1905, DPR, Russia, vol. 4558 (consular reports) (111), RG 84, NA. One American newspaperman raced dramatically back and forth across the Black Sea to send reports back home via safe transmission lines; Stanley Washburn, *The Cable Game: The Adventures of an American Press-Boat in Turkish Waters During the Russian Revolution* (Boston: Sherman, French, 1912).

the more western Baltic region manifested an overt anti-German bias.[30] "Business is absolutely demoralized and the destruction and burning of the estates goes on as yet unhindered, especially in the Baltic provinces."[31] Meyer also believed that the revolutionaries had severely damaged the prospects for progressive reforms in Russia. "By the attempted capture of Moscow, by their riots and rebellions in other parts of the country, followed by destruction of life and property, they have forced the Government into repression and reactionary methods in order to restore law and order."[32]

But the capital itself retained a pretense of normalcy. The court New Year's reception was held as usual. Meyer was pleased to find that he had moved up considerably in diplomatic precedence and that Nicholas II confided to him personally—and repeated it with feeling—that he would never forget all that President Roosevelt had done to help Russia.[33] As were many other Americans, Meyer was hopeful about the approaching elections for the new national legislature, the State Duma. With Charles Flint he even discussed the idea of getting Congress to appropriate $1 million to be divided among the Russian political parties to support campaigning.[34]

In all of these Russian clouds, some Americans found silver linings. Flint, for one, expected a constitutional government to devote more energy to economic development and education, and he advocated joint-venture-style partnerships with foreign companies to the new minister of commerce and industry.[35] William English Walling envisioned the breaking down of autocracy as leading to Europeanization—that authority rather than tradition had been the chief roadblock. "Scratch a Russian and you will find not a Tartar but a new European."[36] His bride-to-be, Anna Strunsky, wrote to her friend Jack London, "You need Russia. Why Jack, it is the only live place in the world! It is melodrama, farce and tragedy, heaven and hell, despair and its every antithesis. It is the revolution of revolutions."[37] Arthur Bullard thought that internal violence had regenerated Russia and

30. Bornholdt (Riga) to Meyer, 3 January and 19 March 1906, DPR, Russia, vol. 4560, RG 84, NA.

31. Meyer to Root, 3 January 1906, DUSM, Russia, vol. 65 (roll 65, M 35), RG 59, NA.

32. To Root, 29 January 1906, ibid.

33. Diary, 14 January 1906, box 2, Meyer Papers, LC.

34. Ibid., 1 March 1906.

35. Flint to Timiarazev, 16 November 1905 (c), DPR, Russia, vol. 247, RG 84, NA.

36. Walling, *Russia's Message: The True World Import of the Revolution* (New York: Doubleday, Page, 1908), p. 4.

37. Anna Strunsky (St. Petersburg) to Jack London, 24 March 1906, box 5, Anna Strunsky Walling Papers, Huntington Library, Calif.

would produce a new society. "The Moscow barricades, then, have brought great Russia, as well as the outlying provinces, not only to a guerilla civil war but also to a social revolution."[38] The winners would be the intellectual liberals and the middle class. So much for the keen American grasp of Russian revolution.

In the meantime, Russia's financial position continued to decline without foreign support. In January, Emile Noetzlin, director of the Bank of Paris, visited St. Petersburg to begin negotiations with Witte for a substantial loan by an international syndicate that would include financial interests in France, Britain, and the United States (Morgan). Partly because of strained relations with Russia over the Moroccan crisis, Germany refused to join. By April, J. P. Morgan, Jr., was back in St. Petersburg, but American participation again fell through; Witte thought it was due to German pressure, but the senior Morgan's concern about rumors of Witte's removal and local Jewish opposition were also factors.[39] Regardless, British, French, and Dutch banks completed the arrangements, thus planting the seeds of the Triple Entente of World War I. Confirmed in mid-April, it was the largest single foreign loan ever floated to that time—2.25 billion francs, though that was 500 million less than Witte had expected with American participation.[40]

Although finally achieving a primary goal, at the end of April Witte submitted his resignation, which was promptly accepted by the tsar. Public hostility, poor health, and constant dissension within the cabinet, especially from conservative Minister of Interior Petr Durnovo, over the "fundamental laws" (the ground rules for the new parliament) contributed to his decision. His aversion to the new regime of constitutionalism was another reason. Behind the scenes, enemies such as Dmitri Trepov, governor general of St. Petersburg and palace

38. "Moscow," *Independent* 60, 2989 (15 March 1906): 600.
39. *The Memoirs of Sergei Witte*, trans. and ed. Sidney Harcave (Armonk, N.Y.: M. E. Sharpe, 1990), p. 569; Gart Dean Best, *To Free a People: American Jewish Leaders and the Jewish Problem in Eastern Europe, 1890-1914* (Westport, Conn.: Greenwood Press, 1982), p. 127; Forbes, *Morgan*, p. 61; Viacheslav V. Lebedev, *Russko-amerikanskie ekonomicheskie otnosheniia (1900-1917 gg.)* (Moscow: Nauka, 1964), pp. 86–89. Witte expressed his disappointment to Meyer; diary, 12 April 1906, box 2, Meyer Papers, LC. The Moroccan crisis involved a German show of diplomatic and military force against an Anglo-French agreement to set up a French protectorate over Morocco. With Russia supporting Germany, Britain and France agreed to an international conference at Algeciras in early 1906—at which Russia abandoned Germany, and the French got their way.
40. For the loan negotiations, see Mehlinger and Thompson, *Count Witte*, pp. 209–40, and Vladimir N. Kokovtsov, *Iz moego proshlago: Vospominaniia 1903-1919 gg.* (1933; reprint, The Hague: Mouton, 1969), pp. 60–98.

commandant, and Ivan Goremykin, elderly bureaucrat and former minister of interior, won the consent of the tsar for Witte's removal.[41]

Goremykin was appointed to Witte's position as chairman of the Council of Ministers with authority to name an entirely new cabinet. Thus, Lamzdorf also resigned and was replaced by Alexander Izvolsky, a veteran diplomat with little experience or knowledge of the Foreign Ministry but with a reputation for being a liberal supporter of Western parliamentarism.[42] Izvolsky had served briefly in Washington and as ambassador to Japan, but most of his time had been spent at quiet European capitals. His lack of court experience and careless demeanor meant that foreign affairs took a backseat in the new government—or rather was determined by the cabinet. Vladimir Gurko described the new minister's attendance at meetings:

> Izvolsky . . . was late almost every day as he came from dinner at some foreign embassy, wearing a dress coat. . . . For some unknown reason he preferred to sit astride his chair, facing its back, a position not altogether in harmony with the tone of the gathering and the seriousness of the discussion. His face reminded one of a pug dog, and he wore a monocle. He was anxious to pass as an authority on parliamentary practice and procedure; but his influence was negligible.[43]

This helps explain why an able ambassador such as Roman Rosen would accomplish so little in the United States.

The First Duma and Belostok

Although ambassador Meyer had resumed the usual rounds of dinners, opera, ice-skating, and hunts and attended another Easter mass at St. Isaac's

41. Dillon reported to Meyer as early as 9 April that Witte wanted to retire; diary, box 2, Meyer Papers, LC. For background and colorful description of the Russian political personalities of this period, see Vladimir Gurko, *Features and Figures of the Past: Government and Opinion in the Reign of Nicholas II*, Hoover Library Publication no. 14 (Stanford, Calif.: Stanford University Press, 1939), and Dominic Lieven, *Russia's Rulers Under the Old Regime* (New Haven, Conn., and London: Yale University Press, 1989).

42. David M. McDonald, *United Government and Foreign Policy in Russia, 1900–1914* (Cambridge: Harvard University Press, 1992), pp. 93–97. Witte asserts (*Memoirs*, p. 650) that Izvolsky owed his appointment to service in Denmark, the dowager empress's homeland. For a general assessment of immediate post-1905 Russian foreign policy, see Anatolii Ignat'ev, *Vneshniaia Politika Rossii v 1905–1907 gg.* (Moscow: Nauka, 1986); on the domestic scene, see Abraham Ascher, *The Revolution of 1905: Authority Restored* (Stanford, Calif.: Stanford University Press, 1992).

43. Gurko, *Features and Figures*, p. 471.

Cathedral, he warned his wife to await the outcome of the first Duma session before returning to Russia. Meanwhile, he continued to send his meditations on the new Russia to his friend Teddy. On 26 April he attended a party for Grand Duke Vladimir Alexandrovich, president of the Academy of Arts, where, he noted, there were ten tables of bridge. "Lots of bridge parties are going on, and quite a number of dinners, and St. Petersburg is really waking up and recovering, although they are again beginning to get nervous over the Duma. An unknown quantity is always mysterious."[44] On 28 April he dined with the Wittes at their apartment in the Winter Palace, perhaps the last such official occasion for the Russian statesman.[45]

Two weeks later, Meyer and several American reporters, including Samuel Harper, gathered in a makeshift gallery of the hastily remodeled ballroom of the Tauride Palace to watch the subdued opening of the first State Duma.[46] Initial reactions were sanguine but reserved. Dominated by the liberal Constitutional Democrats (Kadets) and an assortment of peasant representatives, the Duma's subsequent sessions became increasingly tumultuous. After William Jennings Bryan witnessed an especially riotous meeting, he opined that it was at least a good thing they had an opportunity to let off steam. He considered Izvolsky pessimistically frank about the government's inability to work with the new parliament.[47] Vance Thompson provided a typical journalistic assessment of the first month of parliamentary Russia: "The Duma is a ferment of men and ambitions. . . . One and all demand a freedom greater than the world has known. And this poor little Duma has been thrown to them as one throws a worm into an ant-heap. It is the beginning, not the end. Surely never any nation was so charged with the elements of hate, of fearful hope, of lawless idealism.[48] Meyer was even less enthusiastic about government leaders. "[Goremykin] did not impress me as a man of force or equal in any way to the present situation." The chairman did not understand the Duma or representative government in general.[49]

44. To his wife, 13/26 April 1906, letter file, Meyer Papers, LC.

45. Diary, 28 April 1906, box 2, Meyer Papers, LC.

46. Meyer to Root, 10 May 1906, DUSM, Russia, vol. 66 (roll 66, M 35), RG 59, NA. The following representatives of the American press were certified to attend: Howard Thompson (AP), Seymour Hay (New York *Herald*), Robert Crozier Long (Hearst chain), Guy Scull (*McClure's*), Samuel Harper (Chicago *Tribune*), Madam Dobkiewicz (Scripp's), and Henry La Marc (Chicago *Daily News*). Ivan Obolensky to Eddy, 24 April/4 May 1906, DPR, Russia, vol. 157 (notes received), RG 84, NA.

47. Meyer to Root, 15 June 1906, DUSM, Russia, vol. 66 (roll 66, M 35), NA; diary, 14 June 1906, box 2, Meyer Papers, LC.

48. "The Dawn of Russian Liberty," *Everybody's Magazine* 15, 1 (July 1906): 32.

49. Diary, 20 June 1906, box 2, Meyer Papers, LC.

Predictably, his tenure would be short. Meyer also had nothing good to say about Izvolsky, who was distracted from foreign affairs by the Duma debates, except that he liked to be entertained and had an attractive wife.[50] Still, many looked for hope in the birthing pains.

Just as Russia seemed to be settling into a political transition, in May 1906 the American vice-consul in Batum was murdered. Although a British citizen, William Stuart was connected with an American copper-mining concern in the Caucasus and was best known for representing American interests in this important but volatile region.[51] His death was probably not intended as a direct attack on the United States but was symptomatic of continuing disorder and random violence in the country.[52]

During the winter and spring of 1905–1906 the incidence of Jewish pogroms sharply diminished, despite the increased activity and organization of conservative, anti-Semitic groups loosely forming the "Black Hundreds," or Union of the Russian People. Expected Easter raids failed to materialize. Suddenly, however, in June a serious clash occurred at Belostok in Russian Poland, leaving 200 dead and 700 injured. What made this pogrom especially notable was evidence of complicity by both central (Ministry of Interior) and local officials and the publicity given to it in subsequent Duma debates.[53] On one hand, the attack aroused American Jewish organizations to action and provoked another round of anti-Russian rhetoric in the American press, which in turn produced a congressional resolution extending sympathy for Russia's Jewish victims.[54] On the other, the Duma charges broadened the gap between it and the government, which led Nicholas II to dissolve the Duma and call for new elections, delivering a blow to the infant constitutional arrangement that merely exacerbated American reaction.[55]

Liberal members reassembled in Finland at the end of July to appeal to

50. Ibid., 26 June and 22 November 1906.

51. Chambers to Loomis, 25 March 1904, DUSC, Batum, vol. 1 (roll 1, M 482), RG 59, NA. In recommending his replacement, Chambers reported that Stuart was an accomplished linguist, a man of broad education, and "the most influential foreigner in this country [region] with the Russian officials."

52. For a vivid description of unrest, particularly in this region of Russia, in 1906, see Kellogg Durland, *The Red Reign: The True Story of an Adventurous Year in Russia* (New York: Century, 1908), pp. 78–89.

53. Meyer to Root, 27 June 1906, DUSM, Russia, vol. 66 (roll 66, M 35), RG 59, NA.

54. See, for example, New York *Times*, 17–23 June 1906.

55. Some knowledgeable Americans, however, saw no other recourse: "They were certainly drifting into a condition which must have brought nothing but anarchy and chaos." Melville Stone to Rosen, 26 July 1906, enclosed in Rosen to Lamzdorf, 20 July/2 August 1906, f. 133, op. 470, d. 143, pt. 1, AVPR.

the country over the government in the Vyborg Manifesto, only to be denied the opportunity of reelection. Then on 1 August a prominent economics professor and outspoken Jewish Kadet member of the First Duma, Mikhail Gerzenstein (Hertzenstein), was assassinated while strolling on a Finnish beach, producing another American outcry about officially directed anti-Semitism. At the same time a series of mutinies shook the Baltic fleet. In mid-August the bombing of the summer home and attempted murder of the new chairman of the Council of Ministers, Peter Stolypin, engendered a negative American reaction to the liberal-radical cause in Russia.[56] A bloody pogrom at Sedlits in Russian Poland in September was clearly sponsored by the conservative Monarchist League, but after this, there was a gradual and surprising reduction of such lamentable events. The credit went to iron-handed Stolypin, who led a concerted government effort to curb radical violence from both the left and right.

Meyer was soon no longer available to supply reports on Russian affairs, having been rewarded in early 1907 with the post of secretary of navy. His replacement, John Wallace Riddle, was a true exception to the ambassadorial procession—a career diplomat. A Harvard-educated bachelor from St. Paul, Riddle maintained a low profile in Russia, though sympathizing with both its people and their government. He at least knew some Russian and had an able first secretary, Montgomery Schuyler.

The Second Hague Peace Conference

Although in 1904 Theodore Roosevelt had suggested a second attempt toward establishing a system of peaceful arbitration and limiting the weapons of war, he deferred to Nicholas II, who had initiated the first one, to issue the invitation. This was done without much enthusiasm in early 1906, but the turmoil in Russia and an already scheduled Pan American conference necessitated a postponement until the following year.[57] Although delegations to the Hague were larger and more numerous than in 1899, with forty-four nations sending representatives, members were less distinguished on the whole. The aging and ailing Aleksandr Nelidov, Russian ambassador to France, served as the presiding officer. Fedor Martens headed an important commission that dealt with issues of neutrality, contraband, and blockade.

56. "Russia's Only Hope," editorial, New York *Times*, 28 August 1906, p. 8.
57. Lamzdorf to Rosen, 27 March 1906, f. 133, op. 470, d. 143, pt. 2, AVPR.

His high-handed conduct of meetings and vocal opposition to the American proposal for the immunity of private property at sea earned him the hostility of the American and several other delegations.[58]

Surprisingly, considering Roosevelt's presumed interest, the American party was especially weak. It was headed by popular New York Republican Joseph Choate, who delivered long, impassioned speeches in English despite the fact that the official language of the conference was French. General George Davis and Admiral Charles Sperry represented the army and navy, respectively. One veteran American statesman, John Foster, who had been both minister to Russia and secretary of state, attended but as a representative of China. The American agenda included an effort to expand the scope of arbitration, strengthening the principles of the Geneva Convention, and establishing a permanent world court. The best-known American legacy to the 1907 meeting, however, was the independent endowment by Andrew Carnegie for a "peace palace"; in a typical American embellishment, the Russian idea of peace conferences materialized as a building. Public opinion was disdainful of the lavish entertainments and peace-posturing that attended the conference, and one source noted that "scarcely a pretence of cherishing the former purpose had been made by Russia and the majority of the great Powers."[59]

Limitations on weapons were, as expected, opposed by Germany and others and relegated to the sidelines, yet a vague sense of forward movement prevailed at The Hague during the summer of 1907. From the discussion of maritime rights, which was continued at a London conference in 1909, the Russians secured provisions easing the fueling of belligerent ships.[60] In fact, two unresolved situations from the Russo-Japanese War were embroiled in this issue. An American ship, *Arabia*, marooned in Vladivostok at the beginning of the war, suffered considerable damage, and a British ship, *Oldhamia*, carrying a cargo of Standard Oil kerosene, was confiscated off Formosa by the Russian fleet on the grounds that it was taking fuel to Japan.[61] Complicated claims for damage regarding these two vessels persisted into World

58. John Watson Foster, *Diplomatic Memoirs*, 2 vols. (Boston: Houghton Mifflin, 1909), 2:221.

59. "The United States at the Hague," *Harper's Weekly*, 17 August 1907, p. 1191.

60. Nikolai Charykov [Tcharykow], *Glimpses of High Politics: Through War and Peace, 1855–1929* (London: George Allen and Unwin, 1931), pp. 157–61.

61. The Russian Foreign Ministry argued that the kerosene was headed for Japan and was contraband because it could be used for military purposes, citing the use of fire ships at Port Arthur; Wheeler to Izvolsky, 10/23 July 1910, DPR, Russia, vol. 4548 (130), and Sazonov to Rockhill, 6/19 October 1910, DPR, Russia, vol. 4528 (162), RG 84, NA.

War I, although they would have been good trial cases for a court of arbitration. Despite minimal gains and public apathy about international peace, a third conference was planned for 1915.

Jews and Passports

Another Russian-American dialogue achieved no constructive results whatsoever. Russian treatment of the Jewish population at home and the discriminatory issuance of visas to American Jews, whether of Russian background or not, continued to be hotly pursued topics in certain quarters. The rise of conservative, anti-Semitic views within the Russian government after 1905 precluded a favorable resolution, though some easing of tensions occurred from fewer American Jews desiring to visit Russia. However, a number of new Russian-Jewish immigrants who had been participants in the 1905 revolution now resumed their antigovernment crusade from more friendly foreign shores—a source of concern for Russian officials as well as many Americans.

The new wave of Jewish refugees after 1905 also conflicted with a growing American sentiment to restrict immigration. Russian Jews were rivaled only by Italians and Poles as the most numerous ethnic group arriving in the United States during this period, but legal obstacles to their return tended to make emigration more permanent for the Jews.[62] Their political leverage increased in conjunction with their numbers and business and cultural achievements, but like other immigrant groups, they faced considerable social discrimination and tended, even more than before, to congregate in "little Odessa" urban ghettos.

Back in Russia, general civil chaos obscured the severe pogroms of late 1905. Such violence, unusual for that time of year, raised fears about what might happen during the Russian Easter week of 1906. Prompted by the Russo-Jewish Committee in London, the American Jewish Committee called on President Roosevelt to intervene. Oscar Straus even discussed with him on 7 April at the State Department a direct appeal to Russia,[63] and a telegram was immediately sent to Meyer. The president summoned Rosen, and

62. Although many more Italians and almost as many Poles as Jews entered the United States during these years, about half returned to the home country, whereas less than 5 percent of the Jews went back; Mark Wyman, *Round Trip to America: The Immigrants Return to Europe, 1880–1930* (Ithaca, N.Y., and London: Cornell University Press, 1993), pp. 10–12.

63. Best, *To Free a People*, p. 125.

the Russian ambassador, expecting a conversation about The Hague peace conference, was taken aback by the vehemence of Roosevelt's admonition. He warned the president that American Jewish agitation did more harm than good, because it led Russians "to perceive their own Jews as solidly anti-Russian."[64] Witte, meanwhile, assured Meyer that measures had been instituted and nothing would happen over Easter, which proved to be the case. Perhaps the voice of America did, in fact prevent serious trouble for Jews in the empire, or at least induced local authorities to step up their vigilance.

But then came Belostok in June and more protests, mass meetings, telegrams to the president, and finally a congressional resolution, all conscientiously reported in detail by Rosen to St. Petersburg.[65] Taking advantage of a lull at the end of the year and, significantly, after Straus had been named secretary of commerce, the Russian ambassador pressed the importance of the passport question on Izvolsky—that it was a key factor in American support of Japan in 1904, that it continued to fester—and asked whether Russian obstinancy was worth the diplomatic cost.[66] Still the Russian government did nothing.

The United States was reluctant to hammer the issue, sensitive to charges of interference in the internal affairs of another country, especially one whose condition was so fragile. Besides, as the chief of the passport office pointed out, removing the religious question from the visa process would leave in force the Russian law that denied the naturalization of former citizens, Jew and Gentile alike. In other words, Russian-born Jews upon return would still be subject to arrest for violating nondiscriminatory Russian laws against naturalization in another country without permission.[67] The United States then proceeded to seek a solution through a separate naturalization treaty, but negotiations, entrusted to subordinates, foundered. One draft would have extended protection to all American naturalized citizens for a stay of up to two years in Russia. As embassy secretary Montgomery Schuyler tried to explain to Izvolsky's assistant:

The friendly feeling of our nation towards other nations is . . . influenced by the treatment which American citizens of foreign birth receive when they return to visit the land from which they came. . . . It

64. Rosen to Lamzdorf, 31 March/13 April 1906, f. 133, op. 470, d. 143/1, AVPR.
65. For example, Rosen to Izvolsky, 10/23 June 1906, ibid.
66. To Izvolsky (confidential), 12/25 December 1906, ibid.
67. Hunt memorandum, 2 April 1907, NMF, file 2608 (roll 263, M 862), RG 59, NA.

was never designed to confer American citizenship upon those who intended to use that citizenship merely as a cloak to protect them from performing the duties of citizenship to any country, and the policy of the Government of the United States is opposed to enabling them to effect that purpose.[68]

Russia's concern was that emigré revolutionaries would return to Russia protected by American citizenship. To the State Department under Elihu Root, this seemed reasonable, and Root went so far as to issue a circular denying passports for Russia to former Russian subjects or to any Jews unless the applicants could verify that they had permission to enter. To the American Jewish Committee, this appeared to be enforcing Russian discrimination. Root asserted that the department was only trying to save Jews from visa troubles but, under pressure from Roosevelt, quickly rescinded the directive.[69] In February 1908 New York Congressman Henry Goldfogel formally raised the passport question in Congress for the first time. Soon after this, Russia withdrew from negotiations for a naturalization treaty.[70] The passport battle had reached a new stage.

Led by Mayer Sulzberger, the American Jewish Committee now centered on the 1832 commercial treaty, which, according to its interpretation, guaranteed equal treatment to all Americans. Elevating it to a national campaign issue, the committee declared that the treaty should be honored or abrogated.[71] The State Department was slow to react and then, in October, found Izvolsky preoccupied with a Balkan fiasco of his own making, the Bosnian annexation crisis.[72] Ambassador Riddle cautiously explained to Root why the issue remained potent: "As many American citizens wishing to visit

68. To Konstantin Gubastov, 27 September/10 October 1907, DPR, Russia, vol. 4545 (notes sent), RG 84, NA.

69. Root to Lauterbach and Marshall, 1 February 1908, and Hunt (Passport Office) to Root, 18 February 1908, ibid.; Best, *To Free a People*, pp. 168–69.

70. Rosen to Izvolsky, 6/19 February 1908, f. 133, op. 470, d. 139, AVPR.

71. Naomi W. Cohen, "The Abrogation of the Russo-American Treaty of 1832," *Jewish Social Studies* 35 (January 1963): 3–10.

72. Rosen to Izvolsky, 15/28 October 1908, f. 133, op. 470, d. 139, AVPR; Root to Riddle, 6 October 1908, NMF, file 15994 (roll 942, M 862), RG 59, NA. During a tour of European capitals, Izvolsky thought he had gained an understanding with Austria-Hungary to support its annexation of the Ottoman province of Bosnia (occupied since 1878) in return for Austria-Hungary's support for Russian control of the Bosphorus and Dardanelles straits in the future. Austria went ahead and declared Bosnia annexed, leaving Russia empty-handed and Izvolsky embarrassed.

Russia on business or on account of family ties belong to the excluded class, this prohibition is particularly obnoxious to us."[73] No other action was forthcoming from the American government.

In reviving the subject in early 1909, Schuyler argued that the old treaty's "provisions have not kept pace with the march of modern times toward freer association and more complete association between sovereign nations," but that an ongoing negotiation for a new treaty would suspend any threat of abrogation.[74] Izvolsky did not sense any emergency and waited five months before signaling his readiness to enter into talks. In his simplistic understanding, "the existing treaty now in force between Russia and the United States should remain in force until such time as the new proposed treaty shall come into existence."[75]

Ambushed by yet-another Jewish delegation, President Taft made a somewhat casual request of Secretary of State Philander Knox in September:

> One of the matters referred to much in the last national campaign was this matter of passports in Russia for the Jews. I wish you would look into the matter and see the status that exists, and find out whether we can not in some way bring pressure to bear as strong as possible to better the condition that exists in this regard. Set one of your secretaries to work in making a resume of the correspondence and negotiations on the subject, so that we can talk about it intelligently when we next meet.[76]

In due course, two months later, Knox's assistant vaguely summarized the situation: "It is a case where Russian inertia is hard to overcome from without, but there are indications of forces from within tending to start the mass in a direction favorable to our contention."[77]

One reason for the stalemate was divisions within the Jewish community. Some feared the effects of increased immigration and did not want to inflame matters in Russia, producing more departures. Jewish settlements in New York and other cities were growing rapidly and becoming more resis-

73. Riddle to Root, 6 November 1908, NMF, file 15994 (roll 942, M 862), RG 59, NA.

74. Schuyler to Izvolsky, 19 January/1 February 1909, DPR, Russia, vol. 4547 (notes sent), RG 84, NA.

75. Izvolsky to Riddle, 26 May/8 June 1909, DPR, Russia, vol. 4527 (notes received), RG 84, NA.

76. Taft (Beverly) to Knox (Valley Forge), 11 September 1909, entire text, NMF, file 2608 (roll 263, M 862), RG 59, NA.

77. Alvey Adee to Knox, 30 November 1909, ibid.

tant to assimilation. Some of the immigrants, for the sake of relatives and continued contact with them, adopted a more conservative or apolitical stance. More than a few returned or, dismayed by their new circumstances, looked back fondly on aspects of their Russian existence. There were also ways around the passport problem: bribing officials, obtaining false papers, or, more commonly, joining a nondenominational church, such as "the People's Church," and listing that as one's religious affiliation.

The wife of Raphael Zon, who was now a forestry expert in the Department of Agriculture, chose the latter method in order to visit her family in Simbirsk in 1908. She wrote to her husband, "In general in Russia it is so much easier to live a more interesting life. They take everything so much easier." "I like living here better than in Washington and in America in general. It's somehow a different atmosphere. . . . As I see it, you and I [as Americans] are becoming the most mercenary of all the people I meet."[78] The Zons considered leaving materialistic American society and returning to Russia, but his wife finally ruled it out: "It's very difficult for people who have seen America to live in Russia. . . . True, life comes much easier without such effort, but it is subject to conditions."[79] This typifies the Russian Jewish immigrant dilemma.

Also not so easy were the lives of Russian revolutionaries after 1905. Attracted by expressions of concern for the plight of Russia's disadvantaged masses, some radicals gravitated to the United States to find a sympathetic audience but more practically to obtain money and arms. Famous dissidents, such as Nikolai Chaikovskii, Maxim Gorky, Aleksei Aladin, and Ivan Narodnyi, came to make headlines and gain support for renewing their recently lost cause. Most, however, preferred the more congenial, traditional, and cheaper hide-outs in Zurich, Paris, or London.

From East to West

William Howard Taft was the first president since James Buchanan to have prior direct knowledge of Russia. In 1907, in preparation for the upcoming election campaign, Secretary of War Taft set off on a round-the-world tour. Focusing on the new American imperial destiny, he journeyed westward to Hawaii, the Philippines, Japan, and China, before reaching Vladivostok,

78. Anna (Simbirsk) to Raphael Zon, 5/18 and 12/25 June 1908, box 1, Zon Papers, MinnHS.

79. Anna to her husband, 4 September 1908, ibid. She also wrote, 20 August/8 September, "I think we could get richer in Russia but not as Jews."

which was under martial law after a series of revolts and riots. There he was introduced to vodka and *zakuskis*, traditional appetizers. Accompanied by Mrs. Taft, their son Charles, General Clarence Edwards, secretary Fred Carpenter, and a few reporters, Taft boarded a special imperial armored car on 19 November for the long journey on the Trans-Siberian Railway, which served grand fare, including a fine Thanksgiving Day dinner.[80] At every stop he attracted crowds as the American "minister of war" and for "his stalwart proportions, which were given additional impressiveness by a magnificent fur-lined topcoat, which he had tailored for him in Shanghai."[81]

At Harbin a Chinese band played "Yankee Doodle" in his honor,[82] and at stations in Siberia Taft would listen to tedious welcoming speeches and their translations, to which he was then obliged to respond. According to William Allen White, to speed the procedure at one place Taft outlined in general what he wanted to say to an interpreter, who then fashioned an appropriately flowery oration. An attentive greeter spoke up in excellent English that he understood perfectly what Taft said but could not make heads or tails of what followed in Russian.[83] The party toured Irkutsk, lodged at the National Hotel in Moscow, and devoted a day to the Kremlin and evenings to opera, ballet, and the circus. Resident American businessmen Henry Lehrs and Alexander Bary hosted a reception, followed by a command performance of the imperial ballet.[84]

During the brief visit to St. Petersburg, the schedule was more formal and ceremonial. Arriving on the morning of 3 December, Taft called at the Foreign Ministry, where Izvolsky chided him for being pro-Japanese during the recent war. He was later entertained by the city's American colony. Taft had wanted to avoid a formal interview with Nicholas II but felt obliged to acknowledge the lavish Russian hospitality and spent the morning of the fifth in audience, reviewing troops and lunching with the tsar. The chief topics of conversation were the Philippines, the Trans-Siberian, and the Duma.[85] That evening the Foreign Ministry gave a dinner in Taft's honor attended by a number of ministers, including Izvolsky and Stolypin, the latter making a

80. Scrapbooks, vol. 12, series 17, roll 624, Taft Papers, LC.

81. Robert H. Murray, *Around the World with Taft: A Book of Travel, Description, History* (Detroit, Mich.: F. B. Dickerson, 1909), p. 257.

82. Ibid., p. 286.

83. White, "Taft, a Hewer of Wood," *American Magazine* 66, 1 (May 1908): 19.

84. Murray, *Around the World*, pp. 310–15.

85. Taft to Roosevelt, 17 November 1907, and Schuyler to Root, 7 December 1907, NMF, file 8422 (roll 609, M 862), RG 59, NA; Murray, *Around the World*, pp. 353–58; Ralph E. Minger, "William Howard Taft's Forgotten Visit to Russia," *Russian Review* 22, 2 (April 1963): 151–52.

very favorable impression.[86] The visit naturally elicited the scrutiny of the press. Veteran journalist-publisher Aleksei Suvorin even compared it with that of Gustavus Fox in 1866, which he had also covered.[87]

The Tafts seem to have enjoyed their long trek through Russia. Mrs. Taft remembered that Russia was not as sad a place as she expected. She observed naively, "We met trainload after trainload of happy colonists on their way to the new settlements, and at all the well-built stations along the way we saw a great number of sturdy peasant farmers and their families who looked thoroughly comfortable and contented."[88] Upon his return Taft wrote to a friend planning a similar journey on the Trans-Siberian: "We found the trip very comfortable. While it is rather long, it is very interesting to see the country and we much enjoyed it."[89] To the American residents in St. Petersburg, Taft repeated the familiar manifest destiny refrain: "The country [Siberia] is like the Dakotas or Nebraska and will support a population of millions. The opportunities for development, therefore, of Russia toward the Pacific on one hand are quite like the actual development in the United States towards the Pacific on the other."[90]

From Merchants to Manufacturers

While the Tafts' tour renewed American interest in Siberia, the foremost American contributor to its development, Enoch Emery, was fading rapidly from the scene. He had apparently exhibited strange behavior on several occasions, especially during a 1903–1904 visit to Boston, but he suddenly had a complete mental breakdown in January 1908 and was confined to the

86. "He seemed a man most patriotic and earnest in his work." Taft, "Some Impressions of 150,000 Miles of Travel," *National Geographic Magazine* 57, 5 (May 1930): 587.

87. Translation of article from *Novoe Vremia* in Schuyler to Root, 12 December 1907, NMF, file 8422 (roll 609, M 862), RG 59, NA.

88. Mrs. William Howard Taft, *Recollections of Full Years* (New York: Dodd, Mead, 1915), pp. 317–18.

89. Taft to William Lobdell, 9 January 1908, vol.1, Lobdell Papers, ChicagoHS.

90. As quoted in Minger, "Taft's Forgotten Visit," p. 153. To a reporter, Taft said that "Siberia . . . impressed him as being similar to the Canadian Northwest. The first and most difficult step, that of a transcontinental railroad, already had been taken, and when the world began to help Russia in the development of Siberia as it had helped the United States with money, immigrants, and trained engineers for exploiting the territorial West, Siberia would become one of the most productive lands in the world." New York *Times*, 8 December 1907, sec. 3, p. 3.

Krasnoselsk Psychological Hospital in Moscow.[91] Although Emery became less violent during the summer, physicians ruled out a suggestion that he be transferred to the United States.[92] Consul Samuel Smith and V. E. Marsden looked after his affairs, which were complicated by a recent divorce, estrangement from his brother in Boston, and his secretive business methods. They soon located an account containing 75,000 rubles in the Volga-Kama Bank, along with 300 shares of the Kalashnikov Brewery and 1,500 shares of the large Putilov enterprise in St. Petersburg, the latter alone worth 150,000 rubles ($75,000).[93] This was a small part of a vast estate that gradually came under the management of Horace Kilborn of New York National City Bank with the American consul general in Moscow serving as Emery's guardian.[94]

Settling the estate after Emery's death in June 1911 was a messy process because of a challenged will that left everything to nieces and nephews and because of the scattered nature of the property, some of which had been held illegally or without proper title.[95] For example, Kilborn discovered to his surprise a cash account of over $62,000 and 500 shares each of a number of American railroads in the central branch of his own bank.[96] Similar holdings came to light in several Russian financial institutions.

Emery's mercantile empire in Siberia may have ended, but other long-established Americans—Henry Lehrs, whose father had worked for Winans in Russia in the 1840s, and Thomas and Samuel Smith—expanded their lucrative operations as wholesale importers of primarily American goods. In manufacturing, Alexander Bary continued to supply the Russian oil industry with tankers, storage tanks, pipes, and boilers from several factories; the

91. Samuel Smith to Charles Emery (Boston), 29 January 1908 (c), and to Dr. Frederick Peterson (New York), 12 February 1908 (c), DPR, Russia, vol. 4246 (Moscow, letters sent), RG 84, NA.

92. Harry Suslow to Smith, 25 September/5 October 1908, DPR, Russia, vol. 4260 (Moscow, letters received), RG 84, NA.

93. Volga Kama Bank to Moscow Orphan's Court, 5 July 1908, DPR, Russia, vol. 4259 (Moscow, misc. received), RG 84, NA.

94. Snodgrass to Knox, 29 May 1912 (c), DPR, Russia, vol. 4227, RG 84, NA. The consul general reported that Emery had been diagnosed as paranoid, was irrational, and could recognize none of his friends. "However, he appears quite contented, enjoys good health, eats and sleeps well, and takes exercise with an attendant every day. . . . He has confounded the English and Russian languages and speaks with little intelligence." To Mrs. Herbert Linnell, 23 December 1910 (c), DPR, Russia, vol. 4250, RG 84, NA.

95. Snodgrass to Guild, 1 August 1912 (c), DPR, Russia, vol. 4589 (274), RG 84, NA.

96. Kilborn report, 21 July 1911, DPR, Russia, vol. 4477 (misc. received), RG 84, NA.

main plant was located near the Simonov Monastery in Moscow.[97] After his death in 1913, his son Victor managed the operations. William Ropes and Company of St. Petersburg, now under third-generation manager Ernest Ropes, had turned chiefly to specialized oil refining—mineral oil, vaseline, and machine and spindle oil.

One impediment to selling American goods in Russia was that the largest distribution items—sewing machines and agricultural implements—were handled by company-managed networks of agents who were not allowed to handle other products. In the case of Singer, many were recruited in Russia, trained in Hamburg, and assigned to districts. The "Kompaniia Zinger" trademark, with the shrewd addition of a black eagle logo acquired from the imperial family for 20,000 rubles, was becoming one of the most familiar on any manufactured item in the country. Sales boomed with shipments from the Podolsk plant near Moscow actually increasing through the war and revolution: 1904—113,735; 1905—120,386; 1906—155,745; 1907—189,434.[98] Gross sales, including imports, reached 484,683 in 1908, steadily rising to over 675,000 in 1913; around 500,000 of these were made in Russia.[99] Regardless, production and imports could not keep up with demand, which included calls for new, more expensive models. This was clearly one of the biggest transnational corporate success stories of the period.

A key to Singer success was self-sufficiency, pushed by Albert Flohr, general manager until he was crippled by a stroke in 1905. The plant director, Walter Dixon, bragged in 1908 that only oil cans and screwdrivers were not made at Podolsk, although in early years parts had been shipped in and consumable items such as needles would continue to be.[100] In order to ensure a reliable supply of thread, Singer contracted with a St. Petersburg factory for its entire output. When adequate supplies of high-quality cabinet wood became a problem, the company purchased over 100,000 acres of timberland in Kostroma province in 1913 and operated its own sawmill. Russian Singer also adopted the American advertising gimmick of distributing free knives, scissors, and pencils with its logo prominently displayed.

Singer's growth came not without difficulties. The Russian-made ma-

97. For a description, see Kennedy to Funk, 24 January/6 February 1910, BB 4-03, box 1, file 1237, IH Papers, SHSW.

98. Balance sheets, file 2, box 106, Singer Sewing Machine Company Papers, SHSW.

99. Final reports, file 1, box 106, and file 2, box 157, ibid. Figures apparently include a few machines distributed beyond the Russian borders in Manchuria and Persia.

100. Dixon to Douglas Alexander, 27 November/10 December 1908, file 2, box 106, ibid.

Podolsk, with the Singer Factory in the background, 1910. From Singer Papers, State Historical Society of Wisconsin, WHi(x3)48638

chines were sometimes rejected by field agents as inferior to imports, not because they did not work as well but because of an ingrained belief in the inferiority of Russian manufactures that was substantiated by careless plating, painting, packing, shipping, and warehousing.[101] Dixon explained to the New York office in 1908 that "Russia is essentially a farming and not a manufacturing country and ever since the writer has been over here, he has noticed the feeling among the people that Russian made machinery cannot in the very nature of things be as good as that made in foreign countries where the children are born and brought up in, as it were, a mechanical atmosphere."[102] Continued complaints prompted an inspection tour of "centrals" (distribution warehouses), agencies, and the factory by the European operations manager the following year, but his report generally confirmed Dixon's.[103]

There were also disputes over operations between the plant and the central office of the "Russian company" in St. Petersburg and between Dixon and Flohr at Podolsk.[104] Labor troubles and the expense of training were bal-

101. Dixon to Alexander, 27 October/9 November 1908, and 24 January/6 February 1909, ibid.

102. To Alexander, 27 October/9 November 1908, ibid.

103. Franklin Park (Kharkov) to Alexander, 2 October 1909, ibid.

104. Dixon to Alexander, 5 September 1809, and Alexander to Park, 17 September 1909, ibid.

anced by cheaper operating costs. Given distances and transportation inefficiency, adequate supplies of thread, needles, and parts were always a problem. Securing skilled repairmen in the provinces was another obstacle,
especially with several million machines in service by 1914. By that time
Singer was one of the largest private employers in Russia: around 30,000
were on the payroll, with some 3,000 workers and staff at Podolsk and the
remainder in sales and service throughout the country.

The Singer headquarters building on Nevsky Prospect in St. Petersburg
had become an albatross plagued with seepage and plumbing problems. Its
distinctive tower was still not finished during the 1905 troubles, and other,
original tenants—New York Life and Westinghouse—moved out because of
high rents. Although Flohr urged the transfer of the central offices to Moscow to be near production and distribution operations, the building would
continue to be owned by and associated with Singer for many years.[105]
Singer flourished in Russia, with sales reaching over $30 million (61.5 mil-
lion rubles) in 1913. The shares of outstanding stock of Kompaniia Zinger,
owned entirely by British and Americans, rose in value from 13,725,391 rubles in 1904 to 91,881,314 rubles at the beginning of 1914, paying in January
of that year 2,242,767 rubles in dividends.[106] The war, however, would inflict
immense difficulties on the company.

International Harvester in Russia

Besides Singer, at least six other American-owned factories were operating
in Russia by 1908: Westinghouse Air Brake in St. Petersburg and a separate
electricity generating plant in Moscow; the American "Trigolnik" Rubber
Company;[107] the Ropes oil refinery, also in the capital; the Bary family metal
works in Moscow,[108] and New York Air Brake in nearby Lubertzy. All of

105. Alexander memorandum, 1906 tour, file 8, box 155, ibid. Nationalized in the
1920s, the building housed the main bookstore for Leningrad/St. Petersburg.

106. Dixon, Singer deposition, 9/22 September 1915, DPR, Russia, vol. 290, RG 84,
NA; Lebedev, *Russko-amerikanskie otnosheniia,* p. 140.

107. Although little information is available on this operation, it was generally referred to as "American." One source indicated that the plant employed 6,000 and produced 52,000 galoshes a day, in addition to bicycle and carriage tires and rubber
sponges. It was unique in that a substantial amount of what was produced was exported
to other European countries; Vanderlip diary, 17 April 1901, Vanderlip Papers, Columbia University.

108. The American consul general in Moscow considered Alexander Bary "the lead-
ing American citizen" in Russia in 1910. His daughter Lydia earned a diploma from the
University of Moscow that year. Snodgrass to Rockhill, 1 September 1910 (c), DPR,
Russia, vol. 4562 (106), RG 84, NA.

The Singer Building (on right), Nevsky Prospect, St. Petersburg, ca. 1910. From Singer Papers, State Historical Society of Wisconsin, WHi(x3)48637

these were in a relatively prosperous condition, having carved out comfortable, secure niches in the Russian market. None, however, sought or expected to expand; some were even for sale.

International Harvester had come into being in 1902 when several midwestern implement companies (including Deering and Plano) consolidated under the initiative and direction of McCormick. Now boasting a large foreign market and over twenty-five years of operation in Russia, International Harvester decided in 1908 to consider establishing a factory in Russia as part of a general European expansion. Flourishing branch houses of the company were already operating in Odessa, Kharkov, Rostov, Riga, Moscow, Samara, Omsk, and Vladivostok, thanks to the close supervision of a former McCormick dealer from Iowa, William Couchman.

European sales of this American conglomerate grew rapidly at the beginning of the twentieth century but most of all in Russia, easily outstripping the capacity of its one European plant at Norkopping in Sweden. Additional production in Europe would give the company the advantage by reducing shipping costs and making it more competitive in sales, parts, and repairs. Basic designs could also be adapted to local European customs. A survey was thus made of the three likely sites—Germany, France, or Russia—by the "auditor of manufacturing." To emphasize the rapid growth of sales in Russia after 1905, he listed 1907 sales as follows: 5,097 binders, 27,868 reapers, 23,836 mowers, 27,868 rakes, and 5,071 other mower units, or a total of close to 100,000 implements sold in one year. By comparison, 73,000 units were sold in France and 48,000 in Germany. He anticipated that the Russian market had more potential growth, especially in Siberia.[109] But the primary arguments for production in Russia were, first, indications that the Russian government would revoke tariff exemptions on imported, complex agricultural machinery and, second, to realize an opportunity to compete in the sale of the *lobogreika,* the simplified Russian reaper.[110]

Cyrus Hall McCormick, Jr., the president of the company and main proponent of expansion as against his more cautious Deering partners, went to Europe in 1909 to investigate the Russian project firsthand. He met with Russian financial agent Aleksandr Rutkovskii in London, stressed the need for the "approval and the cooperation of the Russian Government in every reasonable way," and asked about concessions on duties on parts and tax waivers.[111] Rutkovskii responded that treaties with other countries could not be violated but that special priveleges were possible if they were negotiated unofficially with ministers in St. Petersburg.

Arriving in the capital in early July, McCormick, assisted by Montgomery Schuyler of the embassy staff, called on Minister of Agriculture Aleksandr Krivoshein, who supported the plan and suggested Ekaterinburg in the Urals as an ideal site. Next came Minister of Commerce and Industry Vasily Timiriazev, who spoke English and was even more encouraging. He advised that the easiest path was to form, like Singer, a separate Russian company, and he also offered special services in finding a location. The most crucial conversation, that with Finance Minister Vladimir Kokovtsov, dealt with another bonus factor for situating in Russia. Kokovtsov was an ardent supporter of high tariffs to protect Russian industry, though duties were not yet feasible on reaper and binder imports because none were made in Russia and they were badly needed. But if International Harvester made these machines in Russia, the government could impose import duties, giving the company a protected, monopolistic market and Russia some revenue, as well

109. "Foreign Requirements—Germany, Russia and France," W. B. Brinton to W. M. Reay, 5 June 1908, BB 4-03, box 1, file 1228, IH Papers, SHSW.

110. Elizabeth Pickering, "The International Harvester Company in Russia: A Case Study of a Foreign Corporation in Russia from the 1860s to the 1930s" (Ph.D. diss., Princeton University, 1967), pp. 70–78.

111. "C. H. McCormick's Interviews Regarding Russian Factory," McCormick's notes, June–July 1909, BB 4-03, box 1, file 1228, IH Papers, SHSW.

as advancing a more consistent tariff policy.[112] However, this redoubled Mc-Cormick's concern about obtaining a waiver or reduction of tariffs on the more complex parts during a start-up period, ideally for six years, until a Russian plant could achieve sufficient production levels. Such a dispensation would not be easy to secure, since writing this into a tariff law under the new political circumstances would incur the scrutiny of the Duma, and consequently of the media.

The next question involved finding a site for the factory. To that end, B. A. Kennedy, director of manufacturing for the company, followed McCormick's trip with an extensive tour of the country in July and August 1909. The initial preference was to purchase a plant already producing the *lobogreika*, so that International Harvester could begin at once competing in this market, and then enlarge the facility to make American-style binders and reapers. The problem, as Kennedy discovered, was that most of the Russian producers were little more than oversize blacksmith shops with poor organization and no room for expansion, meaning that the process would still involve building a new plant and training workers. The best *lobogreika* factories were foreign-owned (British and German) and not for sale. At a special meeting in Cologne after his trip, Kennedy also warned that most of them were located in large cities, "where you are more liable to be affected by labour troubles. I consider it better to get a little on the outside of the big cities, as have the Singer Company."[113]

Kennedy had the ideal site in mind—the New York Air Brake plant at Lubertzy, consisting of six modern brick buildings about twenty miles southwest of Moscow along the Kazan railroad, which provided a direct link to Siberia. The big advantage over acquiring an existing *lobogreika* factory or constructing an entirely new plant was that "the educational work has been done and the organization perfected. The workmen there are educated to use the same machines that we would use in many of our operations, in other words they are already trained in our line." The main roadblock was cost, since owner-director Thomas Purdy claimed a value of over $2.5 mil-

112. Notes of 5–7 July 1909, ibid. To Schuyler McCormick confided, "Personally I have favored this plan [a plant in Russia] for a long time, but my associates in Chicago hesitate because they feel that foreign capital might not receive the protection and encouragement which is accorded in other countries where they welcome foreign capital." Schuyler memorandum, July 1909, DPR, Russia, vol. 4474 (misc. received), RG 84, NA.

113. "Meeting Held at Dom Hotel Coeln on the Question of a Plant in Russia," 21 August 1909, BB 4-03, box 1, file 1238, IH Papers, SHSW.

lion for the Lubertzy property, much of it representing his own investments. McCormick estimated an additional $200,000 would be required for "services."[114]

Another consideration in favor of this enterprise was that the plant was already manufacturing an oil-burning engine for the Russian market at a good profit, and International Harvester increasingly needed engines for its machinery but only made gasoline models. After dismissing for the time being the idea of establishing two plants in Russia in order to guard against the effects of strikes, the meeting adjourned with an agreement to investigate further the acquisition of the Lubertzy factory.

An important consideration at Cologne was predicting future growth of implement sales in Russia. Although exact figures for 1908 were not yet available, the members accepted the following estimates:[115]

	Binders	Mowers	Reapers	Rakes	Lobogreika
IH Siberia	1,900	18,000	10,000	18,000	
Competition	850	8,500	2,000	7,500	10,000
Total Siberia	2,750	12,000	12,000	25,500	10,000
IH Eur. Russia	2,000	10,500	15,000	13,500	
Competition	1,000	3,500	5,000	5,000	50,000
Total Eur. Russia	3,000	14,000	20,000	18,500	50,000
Grand total 1908	5,750	40,500	32,000	44,000	60,000
Forecast of IH sales in five years	10,000	45,000	35,000	45,000	20,000

As can be seen, International Harvester was already supplying through imports roughly three-quarters of Russia's needs in binders, reapers, mowers, and rakes, but it would be impossible for imports to meet a potential three-fold increase in demand within five years.

At a subsequent meeting in Chicago on 1 November, the company proposed a $2 million offer for Lubertzy; employing the skilled labor there and investing $1.5 million for reaper and binder production would result in a

114. Thomas Purdy was a large shareholder in New York Air Brake, perhaps even representing ownership of the factory, but the parent company held the title. Kennedy inspection report, 23 July and 5 August 1909, BB 4-03, box 1, file 1238, IH Papers, SHSW.

115. Ibid.

net savings of about $900,000 over building an entire factory from scratch.[116] In the meantime profits could accrue from sales of engines and air brakes. The company also added $500,000 for "goodwill and organization." It was pointed out that the air brake inventory and equipment might be sold to Westinghouse for an estimated $270,000.[117] By the end of December, New York Air Brake agreed to a price of $2.25 million, including all inventory and equipment, and the International Harvester board ratified the deal on 10 January 1910.[118]

The next stage, another round of negotiations in Russia, was conducted by Kennedy in January–February 1910. He met with ministers to secure the necessary clearances and discuss tariff waivers and contracted with the present manager of the factory, Alfred Bray, to continue for another year at a considerably larger salary. In trying to obtain the American embassy's support for Russian favors, Kennedy underscored the cost of training Russian workers and the overall increased production expenses in comparison with Chicago.[119] He was disappointed: "The ambassador [Rockhill] and his entire office seemed to be helpless or afraid to approach the ministers and seemed to be entirely without any information on any of the matters that we are interested in."[120] Rockhill's reluctance was, in fact, based on the belief that Harvester production in Russia would exclude other American companies from competition.[121] In Moscow, however, consul general Snodgrass furnished useful information and introduced Kennedy to other businessmen

116. "Conference on Russian Situation," 1 November 1909, BB 4-03, box 1, file 1225, ibid. The meeting also produced new estimates for 1909 sales—4,335 binders, 18,425 reapers, 17,772 mowers, and 20,637 rakes—and projections for 1914—10,000 binders, 28,000 reapers, 32,000 mowers, and 36,000 rakes. Another source placed the value of 1909 sales in Russia and Siberia at $6.4 million; Funk to Knox, 22 April 1910 (c), file 1235, ibid.

117. "Conference on Russian Situation," file 1225, ibid. James Deering felt the price was still too high.

118. C. A. Starbuck (New York Air Brake) to Philip Post, 23 December 1909, ibid.; Fred V. Carstensen, *American Enterprise in Foreign Markets: Studies of Singer and International Harvester in Russia* (Chapel Hill and London: University of North Carolina Press, 1984), pp. 172–73.

119. To Rockhill, 29 January 1910, DPR, Russia, vol. 4475 (misc. received), RG 84, NA.

120. Kennedy (St. Petersburg) to Funk, 17/30 January 1910, BB 4-03, box 1, file 1225, IH Papers, SHSW. He also had a low opinion of the consular section: "The Consul at St. Petersburg is also a man with very little if any knowledge of things that are worth knowing and it is questionable if he would ever be of any great service to Americans who wished for information." To Funk, 24 January/6 February 1910, ibid.

121. Carstensen, *American Enterprise*, pp. 182–83.

such as Bary, who advised Harvester not to push for concessions, especially with government ministers as unreliable as the current ones, because "they would obligate us in such a way that we would be in trouble forever afterwards."[122]

Based on Kennedy's reports, a preliminary decision was made on what to do with the new Russian plant—to manufacture engines, air brakes, *lobogreikas,* and the simpler parts of binders and reapers while operating "a kindergarten for training and educating workmen for the binder and mower manufacture. . . . The oil engines and air brakes and lobogreikas are merely introductory to the main purpose of the Russian plant, which is a complete factory for binders, mowers, and rakes."[123] Finally, in mid-March the official transfer of ownership occurred in New York.[124] After the plan became public, this diversion of American manufacturing to foreign soil caused some concern in the United States. In an explanation to the State Department, Harvester general manager Clarence Funk declared that the company was doing this only to preserve a business already established and that it would result in greater exports to Russia.[125] Yet at the same time, the company was promising Russia self-sufficiency in homemade agricultural machines.

During the summer of 1910 a delegation headed by Harold F. McCormick, the company president's younger brother, toured Russia. Beginning in Odessa, it visited branch houses in Kiev, Kharkov, and Rostov. From Kharkov, McCormick remarked, "This place is pretty nearly off the map. It has a touch of barbarism and much that is uncouth. Flashy women abound—and musk scent is in the air."[126] Everywhere they found supplies short and people crying to buy machines. McCormick concluded: "We have all been much impressed and it seems to me we cannot afford to do things on a small scale when it comes to manufacturing. It will be hard to keep pace with the growth even if we get ready *now* to care for our existing tonnage." He also

122. Kennedy to Funk, 24 January/6 February 1910, BB 4-03, box 1, file 1225, IH Papers, SHSW.

123. Memorandum of conference, 24 February 1910, ibid.

124. Funk commented, "This has been a long, tedious, complicated matter as it has had to be handled by everyone at long range but I think unless something unforeseen occurs that the transfer will be made Monday, the 14th." To Cyrus McCormick, 11 March 1910, BA 1-01, box 1, file 1356, ibid.

125. To Knox, 22 April 1910 (c), BB 4-03, box 1, file 1235, ibid.

126. Harold (Rostov) to Cyrus McCormick, 17 June 1910 (c), file 1355, ibid. Kharkov would later be the site of the largest (Harvester-built) tractor factory in Soviet Russia.

recommended that salespeople in the provinces be paid more, after seeing the conditions in which they lived.[127]

McCormick went on to St. Petersburg to confer again with officials about tariffs. After interviews with the ministries of commerce, agriculture, and finance, he advised that the company should modify its requests to win the necessary Duma approval and should agree to minor tariff reductions on a smaller number of parts and machines. He thought that serious outside competition—mentioning Massey Harris and John Deere—was unlikely and that the company had overestimated the difficulties of manufacture in Russia.[128]

Meanwhile, Bray came to Chicago for orientation and to meet with management. He strongly urged that the company resume air brake production and, by buying out or undercutting Westinghouse, take over the Russian market.[129] McCormick had little interest in this, or in Bray, especially when it was learned that engine production was operating at a loss and the transition to agricultural implements was going slow. Instead, after prolonged dickering, Harvester sold the air brake business to Westinghouse,[130] dismissed Bray, and sent Christopher Borg and August Halverson, the manager at Norkopping, to Russia to coordinate the conversion, with Kennedy himself supervising the retooling and expansion of the plant.[131] Under their direction starting in 1911 Lubertzy moved steadily into implement production, first the *lobogreika* and mowers, then, in December 1911, the first Deering reapers.[132] Belatedly, the Orthodox church dedicated and blessed the plant on 30 September 1911.

Still, progress was slow, and most of the Russian demand in 1912 was met by imports. A forecast for 1913 called for the following shipments from American factories: Deering—6,000 binders, 10,000 reapers; Plano—600

127. Ibid. He especially noted the dangers of cholera, having escaped Rostov just before a quarantine was imposed. Another American observer noted the flourishing implement sales in Rostov in 1910: "The Cossacks buy a great deal of machinery and implements." William Eleroy Curtis, *Around the Black Sea: Asia Minor, Armenia, Caucasus, Circassia, Daghestan, the Crimea, Roumania* (New York: Hodder and Stoughton, 1911), p. 259.

128. Harold to Cyrus McCormick, 1 July 1910, BA 1-01, box 1, file 1335, IH Papers, SHSW; Conner report, "Tariff on Agricultural Machines," 19 May 1910, DPR, Russia, vol. 4255 (Moscow cons.), RG 84, NA.

129. "Air Brake Business in Russia," statement of Bray, 19 July 1910, BA 3-01, box 1, file 1399, IH Papers, SHSW.

130. Westinghouse to Funk, 18 November 1911, and Borg to Funk, 8/21 February 1912, BB 5-02, box 2, file 1319, ibid.

131. Kennedy to Funk, 17/30 September 1910, BB 4-03, box 1, file 1237, ibid.

132. Carstensen, *American Enterprise*, pp. 192–93.

binders, 3,500 reapers; McCormick—6,300 binders, 11,000 reapers; Milwaukee—1,500 binders, 2,100 reapers.[133] In that year Lubertzy assembled 11,266 reapers; in 1914, the number was 19,840, a significant increase. At the same time *lobogreika* output rose even higher than planned, to 21,708, one-third of the total Russian market.[134]

The Russian plant operated independently as International Company of Harvesting Machines in Russia, personally chartered by the tsar in August 1910, with rights to parent company patents. However, it sold its output to International Harvesting Machine Company of America, which continued to control the entire sales organization in Russia. Then, in 1913, as part of a trust-splitting maneuver, the Russian company purchased the sales network and warehouse inventory from the American company. This greater autonomy facilitated equipment adaptation, credit extensions to sales agents, and expansion to full-service dealerships by offering for sale imported hay tedders, balers, drills, and thousands of Moline plows.[135]

Production costs remained higher at Lubertzy than in the United States, but Harvester succeeded in obtaining special government subsidies and won the favor of many local zemstvos and the powerful Siberian Settlement Office (Sklad). Its sales organization soon matched that of Singer and employed almost as many people, though problems remained in obtaining enough machines and, after the company practically gave up on training Russians, enough qualified and willing American and German supervisors and mechanics.[136] The oldest and largest dealership was in Odessa and represented a major factor in the economy of the city, according to the American consul; as such, it became the target of rivals and the pride of local chauvinists: "The International Harvester Company's branch in this city is one of the largest taxpayers here, being, besides, one of the largest distributors in the matter of payment of wages and duties upon imports."[137]

To a much lesser degree other American implement companies profited from Russian business. John Deere sold many carloads of plows, making inroads on the turf of established German companies. Xenophon Kalama-

133. T. H. Loberg to Kennedy, 11 May 1912, BB 5-02, box 1, file 1309, IH Papers, SHSW.

134. Carstensen, *American Enterprise*, pp. 200–202.

135. Pickering, "International Harvester," pp. 159–67.

136. Ibid., pp. 227–29. Nevertheless, besides Borg and Halverson, at least twenty other Americans were employed in 1912 at Lubertzy in managerial and engineering positions; list of American citizens in Moscow, 19 March 1912, DPR, Russia, vol. 4277 (Moscow cons.), RG 84, NA.

137. Grout to Wheeler, 9 August 1911, DPR, Russia, vol. 4564, RG 84, NA.

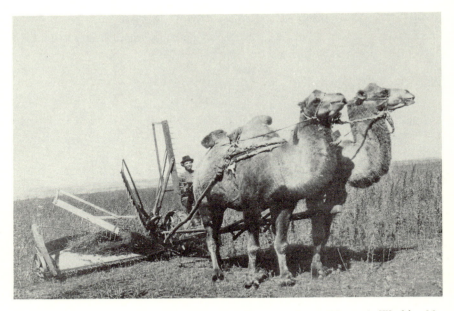

East meets West: an American harvesting machine in Siberia. Harper's Weekly, 22
March 1902, courtesy of the Kansas Collection, University of Kansas Libraries

tiano, a graduate of the University of Chicago, was recruited in 1905 by the
local I. M. Case Company to develop sales of various implements abroad,
first in France and from 1907 in Odessa. He switched to Deere in 1909 and
then back to Case in 1911.[138] A large number of independent dealers in Russia could—and did—place orders with a variety of foreign manufacturers,
with those of Britain and Germany dominating the threshing business. It is
estimated, however, that the United States, chiefly International Harvester,
supplied over half the value of Russia's foreign agricultural machinery imports from 1905 through 1914. Certainly, American products blanketed the
Russian countryside, as Stolypin's plan for reorganizing Russian agriculture
into American-type farms served as an added boon to Harvester business.[139]

138. Statement by Arnold Friend, box 2, file 7, S. Harper Papers, University of Chicago; Kalamatiano (Odessa) to Marye, 15/28 December 1914, DPR, Russia, vol. 286,
RG 84, NA.
139. Using decree power, the prime minister in 1907 provided for the breakup of the
traditional Russian communal village in three stages. A gigantic project, less than 10
percent of villages had reached stage three by 1914; the revolution in 1917 dismantled
the program.

Other American Business in Russia

Under the direction of William E. Smith, Westinghouse continued to manufacture air brakes in its converted cotton mill in St. Petersburg, but at a slow pace. The government preferred cheaper hand brakes which were adequate for slow-speed freight trains. The primary business was then in replacements and parts for passenger trains and locomotives. In 1909 the work force had dropped to 300, supervised by engineers trained in the United States. Low productivity and efficiency appalled International Harvester inspectors. Westinghouse also operated, with no better success, an electricity plant in Moscow that employed 600.[140]

During the "interwar" years the United States was minimally involved in one of the biggest markets in Russia—sales of weaponry. The Simon Lake shipyards of Bridgeport, Connecticut, had supplied a number of vessels and submarines by the close of the Russo-Japanese War.[141] Four much-larger submarines were ordered from Lake as part of the postwar naval reconstruction on condition that they be built at Libau under Lake's supervision. This required the dispatch of forty engineers and workmen under the direction of Lewis Nixon.[142] The revolutionary disorders of 1905–1906, technological problems, accidents, manufacture of major sections in St. Petersburg, and general mismanagement caused delays and escalating costs. The result was the financial embarrassment of the company by 1909 with the ships as yet incomplete. Lake was still trying to collect money owed by Russia in 1912 and was on the verge of filing for bankruptcy.[143]

A large variety of smaller American products entered the Russian market by diverse channels: independent dealers, branch houses of American and German companies, and direct agents. As examples, Western Electric established an office in St. Petersburg to supply and service telephones and switchboards; and Gillette Safety Razor sold 10,000 razors and 100,000 blades in Russia annually through Richard Harder of Hamburg.[144] A Berlin

140. Kennedy to Funk, 21 July 1909, BB 4-03, box 1, file 1238, IH Papers, SHSW. He dismissed it with: "Details of no interest, as the whole plant was only an evidence of how not to do it."

141. Thomas Smith to Meyer, 2/15 May 1906, DPR, Russia, vol. 248, RG 84, NA.

142. Charles R. Flint, *Memories of an Active Life: Men, and Ships, and Sealing Wax* (New York and London: G. P. Putnam's Sons, 1923), pp. 199–201.

143. Guild memorandum, 5 November 1912, DPR, Russia, vol. 178, RG 84, NA; E. H. Hill (Connecticut congressman) to Knox, 30 October 1912, DPR, Russia, vol. 275, RG 84, NA.

144. F. H. Leggett (Western Electric) to consul, Batum, 8 June 1910, and Gillette Co. to Thomas Pelham, 7 November 1914, DPR, Russia (Batum cons.), RG 84, NA.

concern that handled only American goods was even appropriately named "Best USA." The consul in Odessa reported that a branch of a New York house there did a million dollars' worth of business in 1910 in tools, typewriters, cash registers, shoes, pianos, processed food, and carpet sweepers.[145] Russia joined the first "word processing" revolution at the turn of the century, as sales of typewriters soared. The value of imports in 1908 was listed as follows: from Germany, $206,000; United States, $94,000; and Great Britain, $11,000. However, many of those from Germany were reshipments of American models. The consul general counted twenty-two different American makes at twenty-three Moscow dealers in 1910 with Remington, Underwood, J. C. Smith, Royal, Monarch, and Hammond leading the list. Several companies sent their own American-trained agents, and Underwood set up a typing school. Hammond, with the advantage of interchangeable type (Cyrillic and Latin), sold 1,200 to 1,500 annually at $115 apiece.[146]

Another item of the new industrial century, the automobile, was gaining in market importance despite the dearth of suitable roads.[147] Russia naturally relied heavily on imports, but few of them were American. Snodgrass wrote the Ford Paris office that their car was considered "too fragile" for Russian conditions: "The Oldsmobile gave American cars a bad reputation in Russia, as you may know, and they take advantage of any gossip of dealers that may tend to injure the extension of our trade here. . . . Russia offers the last field in Europe for the introduction of American cars but they must be strongly built and reasonable credits offered."[148] Although American cars gradually increased in sales in Russia, and a Ford even won the Odessa Auto

---

145. Grout, Odessa report 1910, DPR, Russia, vol. 4255 (Moscow cons.), RG 84, NA. He later noted that American cash registers were seen everywhere but not adding machines, "it being difficult to induce Russian business men to break away from the old-fashioned abacus." Odessa report 1913, DPR, Russia, vol. 283, RG 84, NA. Root beer also did not sell, because kvas dominated the market; Snodgrass to Charles Hires, 28 May 1912, DPR, Russia, vol. 4280, RG 84, NA.

146. Snodgrass, "Growth of Sales of Typewriters," 26 October 1910, DPR, Russia, vol. 4562 (106), RG 84, NA. William Curtis was surprised to find an advertisement for Remington typewriters in Samarkand; *Turkestan: "The Heart of Asia"* (New York: Hodder and Stoughton, 1911), p. 230.

147. One American found a way to beat the bad Russian roads—by flying over them, in a much-publicized feat; John Henry Mears, *Racing the Moon (and Winning)* (New York: Rae D. Hinkle, 1928), pp. 268–72.

148. To Ford office (Paris), 12 March 1910 (c), DPR, Russia, vol. 4248 (Moscow cons.), RG 84, NA.

Club's endurance test in 1912, European models, especially Benz, would continue to dominate the market.[149]

In the air, Russia, or rather Igor Sikorsky, won acclaim and American attention for setting records in transportation. His 1914 airbus could carry seventeen passengers in comfort, offering light and heat, a washroom, and even an observation platform.[150] Since this civilian achievement was of little interest to the army, the first Russian military planes would be French and American.

Trade Growth

American consuls, such as Grout in Odessa, saw many opportunities for expansion of machinery sales in Russia, if only Americans would take advantage of them: "There is much to be done here by such of our manufacturers as may be willing to go to the expense of sending over representatives to personally canvas the field, ascertain demands and conditions of the market, and select reliable agents, but for the others it must in the end result in either disappointment, or, at the most, a maximum amount of trade which could have been much more had the work of introduction been pursued upon a more solid basis."[151] Yet some did just that and were stymied by red tape. In exploring the possibility of selling American pharmaceutical products, the local representative of Parke, Davis complained that a request for permits had to be submitted to the Duma. "In view of the fact, however, that our Duma, since its existence, has not brought to life one single important law, it is quite clear that the Government is using the Duma as an excuse."[152] But other items, such as canned goods, apparently had no problem

149. Wilson to Knox, 4 September 1912, DPR, Russia, vol. 276, RG 84, NA. Wilson estimated that there were about 6,000 cars in service in Russia in 1912, 1,500 of them in St. Petersburg. For the same year, however, the Odessa consul counted 3,455 imports, 321 of them American: 75 Ford, 65 Case, 25 Overland, 12 Hubmobile, 10 Paige, 10 Studebaker. Grout, "Development of Automobilism in Russia," 20 August 1913, DPR, Russia, vol. 280, RG 84, NA.

150. "A Russian 'Airbus,'" *World's Work* 28 (July 1914): 360.

151. Grout, Odessa report 1912, DPR, Russia, vol. 4257, RG 84, NA.

152. Ruffmann (Parke, Davis) to Rockhill, 7/20 January 1911, DPR, Russia, vol. 4476, RG 84, NA. Then he was told that a drug marketed in Russia would have to list exact contents so any local druggist could make it! To Rockhill, 28 April/11 May 1911, ibid.

in finding a Russian market through middlemen and in probable disregard of such regulations.[153]

Official figures on direct Russian-American trade continued to show a relatively low level of activity: for the years 1906–1913 products from the United States averaged 8 percent of total Russian imports, while only one percent of the American imports came from Russia.[154] However, according to the American consul general's report, by 1911 imports from the United States, counting indirect channels, were second only to Germany's, having doubled between 1909 and 1911. Cotton still dominated the list, estimated at $80 million to $90 million in value.[155] The increased American presence in Russian trade was part of the growing outreach of American capital in the early twentieth century.[156]

Russian exports to the United States also rose during these years but still remained at only about 15 percent of what Russia imported from the United States, or around $20 million annually. Leading the list in approximate order were wool, manganese and copper, furs, hides, bristles, caviar, licorice, alcohol, potash, sheepskins, tobacco, sausage casings, and walnut logs; the items came mainly from the Caucasus and south Russia. Most of these goods, as in the case of American exports to Russia, were handled by western European middlemen, and much less was credited to Russia on official records than was actually imported.[157] Because of the lower volume and undistinguished nature of the items (except for caviar), Americans would have been less aware of Russian trade than Russians were of American.

Growth and a sense of untapped opportunity inspired efforts to coordinate American trade with Russia, to form more direct contacts, and to combat political sensitivities. In Moscow, Feliks Zimmer, a Russian subject, founded in October 1909 the "Russian American Trade and Industry Agency" to act as a clearinghouse for orders and a distribution center for

153. For example, eight St. Petersburg grocers sold fifty-seven varieties of Heinz products; H. J. Heinz (Pittsburgh) to Guild, 23 July 1912, DPR, Russia, vol. 4589 (274), RG 84, NA.

154. Lebedev, *Russko-amerikanskie otnosheniia*, p. 123.

155. Snodgrass, "Increasing Trade with Russia," 12 March 1912, DPR, Russia, 1912, vol. 4227 (Moscow cons.), and Snodgrass to Knox, 30 December 1911, DPR, Russia, vol. 4276, RG 84, NA.

156. Alexander A. Fursenko, "Proekt Amerikanskogo banka v Moskve," *Istoriia SSSR* 3 (1986): 142–43.

157. Snodgrass, "Increasing Trade with Russia," 12 March 1912, DPR, Russia, vol. 4227 (Moscow cons.); Conner, St. Petersburg report, 1 October 1912, DPR, Russia, vol. 274, RG 84, NA.

catalogs.[158] He won the support of the consul general—"Mr. Zimmer has been proving his worth to this office, and I have found him to be honest and faithful"—but somehow incurred the wrath of American financier Frank Stillman.[159] In any event Zimmer soon transferred the agency to a naturalized American, Bruno Wunderlich, but retained a relationship with it until June 1912.[160]

About the same time, in St. Petersburg an informal Russian-American Chamber of Commerce was set up by Harry Vezey and S. G. Weinberg with the goal of restoring "the warm feeling of friendship, which was felt in Russia towards America prior to the war."[161] An active Russian promoter and publicist named Imchanitskii took up its banner. The American consul, however, was pessimistic about its prospects: "I had it pretty straight from Russian businessmen, that no such scheme could succeed, if backed by Jews."[162] Despite this, and because of the initiative of Franklin Gaylord of the YMCA, interested parties met at the ambassador's residence to organize and elect Frank Corse of New York Life as president.[163] With imperial blessing, the chamber sponsored Imchanitskii's visit to America in July 1913.[164]

Emulating this idea in Moscow in early 1914, consul general Snodgrass quietly spurred prominent Russian and American businessmen there to establish a more ambitious "Russian-American Chamber of Commerce" with Nikolai Guchkov, recent mayor of the city and brother of a Duma leader, as president. The first meeting was held at the Guchkov residence, where Ivan Ozerov, economics professor and American specialist, was chosen vice-

158. Zimmer to Conner, 6/19 October 1909, DPR, Russia, vol. 4261, RG 84, NA. "The principal activity of the agency consists in arranging *direct* business connections between American and Russian firms, as to avoid, as much as possible, the middlemanship of other countries, especially of Great Britain and Germany, causing immense losses to America and this country."

159. Snodgrass to Victor Electric Co., and to E. J. Gibson (Bureau of Manufacturing), both dated 11 January 1910, DPR, Russia, vol. 4248, RG 84, NA. In the correspondence with Gibson, Snodgrass mentioned an insulting letter sent by Stillman to Zimmer: "Such communications go to strengthen the opinion of the majority of foreigners that the average American businessman is a vulgar product of a nation not overburdened with aestheticism and good breeding."

160. Snodgrass to S. O. Ochs (Boston), 14 February 1910, ibid.; and Snodgrass to Zimmer, 27 June 1912, DPR, Russia, vol. 4281, RG 84, NA.

161. Weinberg memorandum, 9/22 July 1909, NMF, file 21083 (roll 1080, M 862), RG 59, NA.

162. Conner to Knox, 7 December 1909, ibid.

163. Minutes of meetings of 21 November and 4 December 1909, DPR, Russia, vol. 4474 (misc. received), RG 84, NA.

164. "Russia Reaches Out; Invites Our Trade," New York *Times*, 13 July 1913, sec. 2, p. 9.

president, Vasily Bary second vice-president, and Henry Lehrs treasurer. By
May it had forty-one dues-paying members. Its main goal was to stimulate
direct trade between the two countries while avoiding Germany.[165] Snodgrass plugged the organization at every opportunity.

American Investment in Russia

One of the most successful American operations in Russia in terms of sales
and capital obligations remained insurance, with the New York Life Russian
subsidiary, under the direction of Corse, as by far the largest insurance company in Russia. As in the case of Singer and International Harvester, a network of salesmen and agencies was the key to success. In 1916 New York Life
was reported to be "the largest individual holder of Russian securities in the
world," mostly in government and railroad bonds.[166] Already by 1912 its investments totaled over 45 million rubles.[167] Its primary competitor in the insurance business, the Russia Company, also expanded internationally after
1905, especially into maritime insurance; that branch was managed by an
American, and much of its sales was underwritten in the United States by
other companies, including New York Life.[168]

A partial list of direct American business investments in Russia was compiled by International Harvester in 1911.[169]

New York Life Insurance (capital and reserve)	$22,500,000
International Harvester Company of America (sales org.)	20,000,000
Singer Sewing Machine Company	12,000,000
Standard Oil (Russia Oil Company)	7,500,000
Equitable Life Assurance Society (capital and reserve)	5,000,000
Westinghouse Electric Company (Moscow)	5,000,000

165. Snodgrass to Bryan, 25 February 1914, and to Lehrs, 20 June 1914, DPR, Russia, vol. 4, RG 84, NA. Samuel Harper even planned to write an article about it;
Harper to Snodgrass, 4 March 1914, ibid.

166. Marye to Sazonov, 12/25 April 1916 (c), DPR, Russia, vol. 297, RG 84, NA.

167. Lebedev, *Russko-amerikanskie otnosheniia*, p. 142. P. V. Ol', cited by Lebedev,
placed American ownership of Russian bonds and stocks in 1914 at 113,900,000 rubles.

168. Edwin Grenville Seibels, "The Great Experiment, 1933," 18 February 1933,
Kosmos Club, Columbia, South Carolina, USC. This is the typescript memoir of an
American agent of the Russia Company.

169. List enclosed in Funk to McCormick, 17 June 1911, BB 5-02, box 3, file 1343,
IH Papers, SHSW. Some figures may be exaggerated because a new corporate tax, based
on profits as a percentage of capital outlay, encouraged manipulative inflation.

International Harvester in Russia	$3,500,000
Westinghouse Air Brake Company (St. Petersburg)	2,500,000
Vacuum Oil Company (Riga)	500,000
Worthington Pump Company	500,000
International Taxicab Co.	100,000
J. C. Lencke	100,000
Total	$79,200,000

Because this was based on a hurried survey made by International Harvester preliminary to the purchase of the Lubertzy factory, the compilation is obviously incomplete. It did not include many commercial and mining enterprises or independent merchant houses—for example, the Ropes, Lehrs, and Bary operations.[170]

Resource Extraction

The multinational character of business and investment blurs exact accounting because details fall between the cracks of national consular reports. This is especially true of the exploitation of Russian mineral resources. For example, M. Guggenheim of New York was part of the Morgan-Guggenheim syndicate that invested $423,000 in the Northeastern Siberian Company of St. Petersburg, which was in turn absorbed into the Anadyrsky Gold Mining Company.[171] The much-larger Perm Corporation of London was involved in copper, gold, quartz, and iron mining, primarily in the Urals region, as well as oil exploration in the Caucasus. Perm was backed by the Hirsch syndicate, and it is best known for its association with an Iowa-born and California-educated engineer, Herbert Hoover.[172]

One operation of this London-based company in Russia was the use of steam shovels in the Orsk gold fields near the mouth of the Amur River, not far from Nikolaevsk. Work there was supervised by a California-Alaska

170. St. Petersburg consul Conner at about the same time estimated American total investment in Russia at $156,731,660, crediting Ropes and Company with $750,000; to Rockhill, 30 March 1911, DPR, Russia, vol. 4563, RG 84, NA. Snodgrass (to Rockhill, 4 February 1911, ibid.) was not certain whether to count Singer as American since it was registered in Russia and the operating management was primarily Russian, German, and British, but American Singer owned the controlling portion of stock. It had become a true transnational enterprise.

171. Guggenheim to Guild, 8 May 1912, DPR, Russia, vol. 259, RG 84, NA.

172. John H. Allen report, 14 September 1908, box 52, Pre-Commerce, Hoover Papers, Hoover Library.

group under the direction of Chester Purington and Jerome Landfield, beginning in 1907 and continuing through 1911.[173] They first employed Chinese and Korean laborers but found they were unreliable. Russians were little better—six were needed to do the work of two Californians. "His servile, whining disposition, protected as he is by excessive government paternalism, combined with deep-rooted adherence to the custom of a priest-ridden country, make him a dangerous member of a mining community," Purington wrote.[174] He moved on to other companies, for example, the Lenskoi Gold Mining Company in 1914 in the vicinity of Irkutsk.[175]

Hoover was directly involved in a more profitable development effort on the large Kyshtim estate, located in Orenburg province not far from Ekaterinburg in the southern Urals. Copper and iron mines were expanded (a new one was named "Amerikantsy"), and a large, modern smelter was built, producing 5,000 tons of finished copper in 1911. Although Hoover was involved mainly with arranging (and manipulating) the financing, he did become a director of the company and visited the site twice, in 1911 and in 1913.[176] After the latter visit, Hoover cautioned against further expansion but advocated remodeling for greater efficiency.[177] An unsuccessful gamble was the attempt by subsidiary Maikop and General Petroleum Trust to develop a newly discovered oilfield in the Caucasus near the Black Sea for British consumption, beginning in 1909. Hoover, his brother Theodore, Lindon Bates, and other British and American investors were engaged in this disappointing project.[178]

Farther out beyond the Urals in northern Central Asia, at Akmolinsk, E. Nelson Fell, an American, managed the Spasskii Copper Mines, another primarily British enterprise. The largest, mainly American mining investment in Russia was apparently in the Caucasus Copper Company at

173. E. C. Bloomfield (Nikolaevsk) to Hoover, 11 August 1910, box 48, ibid.

174. Purington, *Sluicing at the Kolchan Mines, East Siberia* (San Francisco, Calif.: Mining and Scientific Press, 1911), p. 22.

175. Purington to Guild, 10 June 1914, DPR, Russia, vol. 281, RG 84, NA.

176. Annual reports for 1912 and 1913, box 52, Pre-Commerce, Hoover Papers, Hoover Library. As in Russia generally, the Kyshtim enterprises suffered from worker hostility; in late 1912, an American manager, Horace Emerick, was murdered. *Russkoe Slovo*, 5 January 1913, in DPR, Russia, vol. 4554 (277), RG 84, NA.

177. Hoover (St. Petersburg) memorandum for Kyshtim Corporation, October 1913, mining folder, box 49, Pre-Commerce, Hoover Papers, Hoover Library.

178. George H. Nash, *The Life of Herbert Hoover: The Engineer, 1874–1914* (New York and London: W. W. Norton, 1983), pp. 429–51. As his biographer acknowledges, Hoover's role in these Russian enterprises is obscured by little surviving evidence and conflicting memoir versions.

Aleksandrovsk in Armenia near the Turkish border. British and American capital were both ventured, but in 1914 it employed at least twenty American engineers, including manager Robeson White.[179] Similarly, a census taken at the beginning of the war found a number of American technical experts working in the oilfields around Baku and Grozny. New American drilling technology was especially critical for this sagging Russian industry. Leading the United States at the beginning of the century, Russian production had actually dropped, owing primarily to civil disruptions; meanwhile, new fields in Texas, Oklahoma, and Kansas tripled American oil output.[180]

A substantial number of other American technicians and engineers were employed in various capacities around the country, providing an indeterminate amount of specialized and administrative know-how for Russia's resource development. Among them were: at Akmolinsk, Andrew Barton (mine manager), Thomas McCorley (mining engineer), Herman Shrefer (drilling engineer); at Tomsk, Arnold Willis (Russian Gold Mining Company), Nicolas Batmani (Siberian Printing Company), Arthur Dill (Petropavlovsk Gold Mines); in Moscow, David Hough (subway and rail construction); in Central Asia, Arthur Davis (hydrographer), Lindon Bates (dredging); in Siberia, Washington Vanderlip (mining engineer).

Agricultural Exchanges

Although industry and resources were becoming increasingly important for the United States and Russia, both countries were still predominantly agricultural and depended on farm exports to balance trade with the rest of the world. Each turned to the other for improvements that would enhance variety and productivity. Because of the most famous of these borrowings, by 1914 vast areas of the North American Great Plains had been planted with

179. Cauldwell (Batum) to Guild, 22 February 1912, DPR, Russia, vol. 4565, and Smith (Batum) to Guild, 13 August 1914, DPR, Russia, vol. 281, RG 84, NA. Producing 3,276 tons in 1913, the Caucasus Copper Company was second only to a French company in terms of size in the region; Leslie Davis, Batum report 1913, DPR, Russia, vol. 283, RG 84, NA.

180. According to the Batum consul's report, Russian production had dropped from 10,984,000 tons in 1901 to 9,016,000 in 1913; America's grew from 8,951,000 tons to 31,984,000 during the same period. Davis, "Annual Report on Commerce and Industries in the Caucasus During 1913," DPR, Batum, 1914, pt. 3, RG 84, NA.

hard-red and durum winter wheat that originated in Russia and that supported a huge economic complex of farming, milling, and shipping.[181] Mennonite and Russian-German immigrants from Russia to the United States
certainly contributed to this agricultural transformation.

Other efforts were less spectacular or profitable. One involved Charles C.
Young, who was born Karl Jungk in the Bessarabian-German colony of
Akkermann. Emigrating as a boy with his family to the Dakotas, he was a
prime example of immigrant success, becoming by 1904 a prominent eye surgeon in Chicago. Remembering his agricultural roots, Young invested in
land in South Dakota, near Fort Worth and El Paso, Texas, and across the
border in Mexico. Armed with an letter of introduction from Theodore
Roosevelt, he returned to Russia early in 1908 ostensibly as an agent of a
Texas railroad to organize emigration from Bessarabia.[182]

Young soon initiated a scheme to ship out of Russia prized karakul (black
wool) sheep from Central Asia for breeding stock on his Texas ranches and
made additional trips to Russia for that purpose.[183] He even conferred with
President Taft in September 1912 in order to obtain the support of the embassy for the project.[184] With the ambassador's reluctant assistance, Young
obtained the necessary permits and traveled extensively throughout Russia
to find the best sheep; at the same time he collected material for a book and
chautauqua lectures.[185] The sheep experiment was apparently a failure, prob-

---

181. For background, see K. S. Quisenberry and L. P. Reitz, "Turkey Wheat: The
Cornerstone of Empire," *Agricultural History* 48, 1 (January 1974): 98–110; Mark A.
Carleton, "Hard Wheats Winning Their Way," in *Yearbook of the United States Department of Agriculture 1914* (Washington, D.C.: Government Printing Office, 1915), pp.
391–420; Homer E. Socolofsky, "History of Wheat," in *Wheat-Field to Market: The Story
of the Golden Crop*, 2d ed. (Hutchinson: Kansas Wheat Commission, 1969), pp. 7–24;
Norman E. Saul, "Myth and History: Turkey Red Wheat and the 'Kansas Miracle,' "
Heritage of the Great Plains 22, 3 (Summer 1989): 1–13.
    182. Riddle to General Schaufuss (minister of transportation), 29 January/11 Febru-
ary 1908, DPR, Russia, vol. 4546 (notes sent), RG 84, NA; Charles C. Young, *Abused
Russia* (New York: Devin-Adair, 1915), p. 11.
    183. Young to Rockhill, 28 November 1910, DPR, Russia, vol. 4475 (misc. received),
RG 84, NA. A similar breed of sheep, perhaps originally from Central Asia, was raised
in Bessarabia; Louis Guy Michael, *More Corn for Bessarabia: Russian Experience,
1910–1917* (East Lansing: Michigan State University Press, 1983), p. 39.
    184. Young to Rudolph Forster (Taft's secretary), 17 September 1912, and Taft mem-
orandum, 16 September 1912, cf. 3796 (reel 446), Taft Papers, LC; Driscoll to Taft, 9
September 1912, Young to Forster, 16 September 1912, Forster to Guild, 17 September
1912, and Young to Guild, 27 October 1912, DPR, Russia, vol. 273, RG 84, NA.
    185. Young to Guild, 16 November 1912 (St. Petersburg), 2 December 1912 (Sa-
mara), and 12 January 1913 (Bokhara), DPR, Russia, vol. 273, RG 84, NA.

ably because of climate differences. Nor did Young's effort to transplant American buffalo, cattalo, and elk to Russia come to anything.[186]

Bessarabia, where corn production had begun many years earlier under Turkish administration, was the site of another interesting Russian-American agricultural exchange. The provincial zemstvo in 1909 sought through the International Harvester agent in Odessa a corn expert from the United States and in particular one who had been involved in a successful Iowa campaign to improve yields.[187] The program had received international publicity, and Professor Perry Holden of Iowa State College, its initiator, recommended his assistant, Louis Michael, for the Russian venture. Arriving in Kishinev in February 1910, Michael learned to his chagrin that he was expected to confine his activities to the estate of the political leader of the zemstvo.[188] After overcoming this and other restrictions, Michael expanded his project, dubbed "More Corn for Bessarabia," which consisted mainly of better seed selection and testing. Both peasants and provincial officials had expected the American to have a magic solution or a new miracle variety to increase production, and at first they refused to believe that much could be gained by more routine work and improved techniques in seed selection and cultivation.[189] He was dismayed by the peasants' cry for more land while they misused what they had. He gallantly stayed on several years and ultimately introduced some American strains of corn.[190]

More professional were the expeditions of the Office of Foreign Seed and Plant Introduction of the Bureau of Plant Industry in the Department of Agriculture. The experts there, led by David Fairchild, were especially drawn to Russia because of their interest in finding new varieties adaptable to the expanses of the Great Plains currently being settled. Although samples of seeds and plants had been obtained from Russia since the middle of the nineteenth century, cereologist Mark Carleton led the first systematic

186. F. Armstrong (Young's secretary; Goodnight, Texas) to B. N. Krondesberg (Russian embassy secretary), 27 January 1911, file 170, op. 512/1, d. 276, AVPR.

187. The request first came to the attention of the Department of Agriculture in January 1909; James Burke to James Wilson, 21 January 1909, Records of the Office of Secretary of Agriculture, letters sent, vol. 128, RG 16, NA.

188. Michael, *Corn for Bessarabia*, pp. 19–40.

189. Ibid., pp. 19–99; Grout, Odessa report 1910, DPR, Russia, vol. 4255 (Moscow cons.), RG 84, NA.

190. Michael to Grout, 9 December 1911, DPR, Russia, vol. 4255 (Moscow cons.), RG 84, NA.

searches for steppe grains beginning in the 1890s. By 1906, he was supervising the collecting and testing of a large variety of wheat, rye, barley, buckwheat, flax, and oat seeds from Russia. In one instance, H. L. Bolley brought back 268 lots of flax seeds in 1905 for testing at the North Dakota Agricultural College and Experiment Station.[191]

Field explorer Niels Hansen made several trips to Russia in search of other hardy grasses. In 1908 he endured over a thousand miles of rough riding across Central Asia and Siberia in a *tarantas* (springless carriage) in search of forage plants that might be suited for the northern plains—alfalfa, vetch, wild peas, and clover. After two weeks of arranging passes and government cooperation, Hansen hired three Moscow botany students as helpers and set off to the east. Near Samara he located a superior, drought-resistant vetch "to help conquer the great 'American desert' " and bought several bushels of seed.[192] More promising, in Omsk province he discovered a western Siberian alfalfa being grown in village common fields. "All stock eat it greedily and bees work on it industriously," he reported.[193] Taproots over three feet long made it quite drought resistant. Since it was a perennial, he could not find any seed available, so he purchased a large haystack and hired local peasants to pick out the seeds. On the border south of Irkutsk, he recruited a combination of Mongolian nomads, Chinese coolies, and Russian soldiers to gather alfalfa seeds from the desert, "an interesting experience I assure you."[194] By November he had collected 1,100 pounds of seeds to be dispatched to Washington from Riga.[195]

Another intrepid rummager of Russia was Frank Meyer, though his quest was for the more exotic fruits, nuts, berries, and shrubs. He was first intrigued by the promise of new varieties of herbs and plants during a cross-country trip in 1906 on his way to Manchuria.[196] Following another lengthy excursion to China and India, in 1909 he began an expedition through Russia, starting at the Imperial Botanical Gardens in St. Petersburg. After exasperating holdups—"Why the Russian Government should feel obliged to be so particular about this journey is as yet a puzzle to

191. Papers of BPI, 1904–1908 Closed Projects, vol. 142 (roll 37, M 840), RG 54, NA.
192. Hansen to Wilson, 15 July 1908, Hansen reports, BPI Expedition Reports, vol. 91 (roll 25, M 840), RG 54, NA.
193. To Wilson, 12 August 1908, ibid.
194. Hansen report (Manchuria), 22 September 1908, ibid.
195. Hansen to Wilson, 5 November 1908, ibid.
196. Meyer (Mukden) to Fairchild, 21 January 1907, BPI Expedition Reports, vol. 105 (roll 28, M 840), RG 54, NA.

me"[197]—Meyer headed southward through Moscow to the Crimea. Keeping the embassy informed of his progress, by March he was in Tiflis, May in Baku, June in Samarkand, and July in Tashkent, running several months behind schedule because of delays in obtaining permission, problems with interpreters, and cumbersome shipment of seeds and specimens through the Batum consulate.[198] This was not an easy journey; as he wrote from Tiflis, "This is a difficult land and I wonder not any longer why travellers shun it like the plague. The people themselves are ignorant, but good natured on the whole, but conditions are downright bad."[199] Spending the winter in Central Asia, Meyer crossed into Mongolia the following year and returned through Siberia in the summer.

Agricultural explorers probably covered more of Russia than any other Americans and certainly saw more of the countryside and native peoples. Their focus was scientific, however, with only the occasional social or economic observation penetrating their reports. Their work no doubt had an impact, as many seeds and plants from Russia were successfully propagated in the United States or were used to produce new, hardy hybrids. Yet along with beneficial yields for human consumption came, by accident, undesirable weeds, such as Russian thistles. These foreign intrusions had ecological and visual repercussions for the American landscape.

Russia in turn sent agricultural missions to the United States. Evgenyi Skorniakov spent two years, 1908–1910, investigating irrigation projects in the western United States, primarily in Colorado and Idaho, and published an extensive, well-illustrated report describing what he had seen.[200] In 1910 Sergei Syromiatnikov visited the Department of Agriculture in Washington and was given "all proper facilities within our power" to study irrigation.[201] John Hays Hammond, venture capitalist and friend of Taft's, also saw irrigation as a special opportunity for American enterprise and conversed in 1910

197. Meyer to Fairchild, 21 December 1909, BPI Expedition Reports, vol. 106 (roll 29, M 840), RG 54, NA. It would not have helped that he was taking a Russian Jew, Chaim Moses Newman, with him; Schuyler to Izvolsky, 27 November/10 December 1909, DPR, Russia, vol. 4547 (notes sent) (129), RG 84, NA.

198. Planned itinerary in Meyer to Riddle, 24 November/7 December 1919, DPR, Russia, vol. 4474 (misc. received); and various letters from Meyer, Batum consulate (misc. received 1910 and 1911), RG 84, NA.

199. Meyer to Fairchild, 4 March 1910, BPI Expedition, vol. 106 (roll 29, M 840), RG 54, NA.

200. Skorniakov, *Orashenie i kolonizatsiia pustyn' v Severnoi Amerike*, 2 vols. (St. Petersburg: Golike and Vil'borg, 1911).

201. Wilson to Knox, 19 May 1910, Records of the Office of the Secretary of Agriculture, letters sent, vol. 140, RG 16, NA; Maksimov to Schuyler, 27 January 1910, DPR, Russia, vol. 4475 (misc. received), RG 84, NA.

with Nicholas II and Stolypin on that subject and on building grain elevators.[202] "My visit resulted in confirming in detail what I knew about Russia as a country offering fine opportunities for the investment of American capital. . . . There is not only room for capital there, but for American initiative, machinery, and American genius. There is a large area of land that could be reclaimed by irrigation."[203]

Hammond was especially interested in the mass production of grain elevators, the shortage of which was a continuing Russian weakness, and, during his visit, the progressive *Novoe Vremia* took up the cause. "If we had a system of elevators we should not have been obliged to hurry in the disposal of our wheat at low prices lest it rot at the railway stations." Their construction, the editor argued, would benefit the United States: "She will receive a double advantage; she will make money on equipping us with elevators, but [realize] still greater benefits thanks to the regulation of the wheat market, which is now spoiled by the fact that Russia is at times forced to dispose of its wheat at any price."[204]

With so many agricultural developments sprouting in the United States, the Russian government decided in 1909 to establish an agency in St. Louis and designated as its head Fedor Khristopovich, a trained agronomist and farmer who had lived for some time in California.[205] As Rockhill reported, "The Agency proposed to facilitate the sale in Russia of plants whose cultivation in America has been most successful and to introduce distinctively Russian products into America."[206] Russian agricultural experts had great respect for the work of the U.S. Department of Agriculture, and noted plant physiologist Kliment Timiriazev testified to their admiration in the preface to a Russian translation of William Harwood's romanticized account of American agricultural progress, *The New Earth.*

202. New York *Times*, 23 December 1910, p. 4; William C. Askew, "Efforts to Improve Russo-American Relations Before the First World War: The John Hays Hammond Mission," *Slavonic and East European Studies* 31, 76 (December 1952): 180–81. Hammond's advice had been solicited by Russian financial agent Grigori Vilenkin; New York *Times*, 13 December 1910, p. 5; Hammond, *Autobiography of John Hays Hammond*, 2 vols. (New York: Farrar and Rinehart, 1935), 2:468–72.

203. As quoted in "Business Opportunities in Russia," New York *Times*, 4 February 1911, p. 3.

204. *Novoe Vremia*, 27 November/10 December 1910, translation in Rockhill to Knox, 24 December 1910, series 6, cf. 204 (reel 374), Taft Papers, LC.

205. Riddle to Knox, 24 July 1909, NMF, file 10165 (roll 1080, M 862), RG 59, NA. Khristopovich had apparently gone to Russia in 1909 to seek the job.

206. Rockhill to Knox, 25 March 1910, ibid. William Anderson replaced Khristopovich at the St. Louis agency in 1913; Bakhmetev to Bryan, 17 October 1913, DFIA, Russia, 861.607 (roll 132, M 316), RG 59, NA.

In another energetic initiative, about 1908 the Kharkov Agricultural Society and the Ekaterinoslav zemstvo in Ukraine hired Joseph Rosen, a Russian immigrant to the United States and graduate of Michigan Agricultural College. His task was to set up an office in Minneapolis and collect seeds and information on American agriculture. Rosen's employers published thirteen of his reports in Russian, including a 326-page study of the American agricultural extension service. Rosen also organized displays on American farming at the South Russian Exposition in 1910.[207]

Although much of this Russian outreach was promoted by the conservative but reform-minded Stolypin and by zemstvo progressivism, Russian backwardness and perverse logic were hard to overcome. An article in a leading newspaper again called attention to the need for grain elevators in Russia, for two reasons: because "America has managed to ruin us with its competition in the cereal trade," and because the absence of government elevators allowed Jews to control the grain trade.[208] More creditably, freelance writer Evgenyi Matrosov, who claimed American citizenship, wrote astute articles on agriculture for both Russian and American periodicals, while Russian-American Vasily Vil'iams became the first director of the new Moscow Agricultural Institute. Vil'iams was an advocate of planting grasses everywhere and was deemed politically safe, then and later under Stalin.[209]

Cultural Exchanges

Direct exchanges of high culture in the performing arts continued through and after 1905, but mostly from the Russian side. Vasily Safonov, director of the Moscow Conservatory, made a number of appearances as a guest conductor of American orchestras, and one performance in 1906 that featured Tchaikovsky's Fifth Symphony earned special acclaim.[210] In February 1907 the Russian Symphony Society opened its fourth consecutive (and last) sea-

207. Dana Dalrymple, "Joseph A. Rosen and Early Russian Studies of American Agriculture," *Agricultural History* 38, 3 (July 1964): 157–60.

208. *Novoe Vremia*, 10/23 April 1912.

209. Matrosov to Rockhill, 7 January 1910, DPR, Russia, vol. 4475 (misc. received), RG 84, NA. Vil'iams was the son of Robert O. Williams, originally connected with the Winans locomotive and car manufacture in the 1850s; Vasily would become prominent, even infamous, as a "Lysenko-type" soil scientist in the 1930s. See David Joravsky, *The Lysenko Affair* (Cambridge: Harvard University Press, 1970), pp. 24–25.

210. *Harper's Weekly*, 1 December 1906, p. 1719.

son at Carnegie Hall with a concert entirely of Russian music.[211] The following year the same hall witnessed the first performance of a Tchaikovsky opera, *Eugene Onegin*, by the New York Symphony.

As a rare example of transfer in the other direction, concert pianist Joseph Hofmann began annual tours of Russia in 1907. An American citizen, he was Polish-born and had studied under Anton Rubenstein, so his repertoire was primarily Russian. He indefatigably beat the bushes through the Russian provinces—Tula, Kiev, Kharkov, Voronezh, Tambov, Saratov, Samara, Rostov, etc.—noting that he always played faster in the provinces, otherwise the audience would go to sleep.[212]

The Russian ballet, in its golden years, naturally won American attention, though not quite as much as in avant-garde Europe. Frequent European and even American tours furnished ample opportunities to see the company and prompted much discussion in high society about the productions of Sergei Diaghilev, the choreography of Mikhail Fokin and George Balanchine, and the relative merits of dancers such as Anna Pavlova, Alexandra Danilova, and Vaslav Nijinsky.[213] Few visitors to Russia—business, political, or tourist—could escape exposure to this Russian national treasure. Ambassador Curtis Guild, for one, became something of an addict, reveling in performances of "The Nutcracker" and "Sleeping Beauty": "The theatre here continues to be a perpetual delight and the Russian ballet is really the most wonderful thing in the world of its kind."[214] Talent and staging likewise drew Americans to the opera. After seeing Fedor Chaliapin perform *Boris Godunov* at the Marinsky Theater, Guild observed, "The plot is dull, the music of the modern kind without one single melody, but the man sings and acts magnificently and the stage settings, costumes, etc. are simply gorgeous."[215]

By happenstance about 600 of the best Russian works of art of the period were disbursed throughout the United States as a result of the bankruptcy of an exhibit promoter at the St. Louis world's fair in 1904. After complicated legal and financial bickering, the federal government auctioned off the bulk of the artwork in San Francisco to settle customs storage charges of $20,000. The net was only $39,000, though the collection was conserva-

211. Lawrence Gilman, "Music from Russia," *Harper's Weekly*, 23 February 1907, p. 278.

212. Journal of his wife, Maria, 19 February 1907, Hofmann Papers, USC.

213. For example, Ellen Terry, "The Wonderful Russian Ballet," *McClure's Magazine* 41, 5 (September 1913): 33–44.

214. To Lulu (sister), 21 November 1911, Guild Papers, BPL.

215. To Lulu, 10 November 1912, ibid.

tively appraised at $300,000. Most of the paintings by Nicholas Roerich were later recovered for the Roerich Museum in New York, but many others remain scattered in American galleries and private collections or have disappeared.[216] None of the paintings ever returned to Russia, and the artists received little or no compensation. Aside from this accidental infusion of Russian art, critic and buyer Christian Brinton,[217] as well as individual travelers, purchased other pieces for their own and public enjoyment.

American tourists, visiting Russia in ever-increasing numbers and often in groups, focused on Russian art and music. Seeing the largely non-Russian collections of the Hermitage was obligatory, but many Americans sought out things Russian in the Tretiakov Gallery in Moscow and at the opera houses. Eugene Simpson reported for *Musical Courier* on his trip to Klin to see Tchaikovsky's home and talk with his brother Modest, on the many Russian operas and concerts he attended, and about his recording of boatmen songs along the Volga.[218] On another visit he traveled through Ukraine and the Crimea with Alexander Glazunov, director of the St. Petersburg Conservatory.[219]

A more typical tourist, Margaret Rogers of Denver, came in the wintertime with a guided group of twenty and saw a state funeral at the Alexander Nevsky Cathedral, the graves of Rubenstein and Tchaikovsky, the newly opened Alexander III museum of Russian art, and Chaliapin singing at the opera house. In Moscow she was impressed by the puppet theater, the Tretiakov Gallery, and the Christmas service at the Church of Our Savior: "I never in my life heard such music, it just seemed impossible that it was real."[220]

Exchanges of literary and scientific materials continued apace, and immigrant requests encouraged the collection of publications. The New York Public Library was subscribing to over seventy Russian newspapers and periodicals and desperately searching for ephemeral literature, because "the large Russian population in this city puts upon us unusual demands."[221] One

216. Robert C. Williams, *Russian Art and American Money, 1900–1940* (Cambridge: Harvard University Press, 1980), pp. 76–82; Snodgrass to Knox, 13 June 1912, DPR, Russia, vol. 4227, RG 84, NA.
217. Brinton's interests were eclectic; he wrote knowledgeably about the Russian theater, discussing the contributions of Konstantin Stanislavsky and Maxim Gorky. "Idols of the Russian Masses," *Cosmopolitan* 40, 6 (April 1906): 613–20.
218. Eugene E. Simpson, *Travels in Russia 1910 and 1912* (Taylorville, Ill.: By author, 1916), pp. 1–47.
219. Ibid., pp. 69–126.
220. Rogers diary, 1909–1910, item 3588, SHSM.
221. Bellings to Meyer, 22 June 1906, DPR, Russia, vol. 248, RG 84, NA.

transplanted Russian, Alexis Babine, made a significant contribution while serving as director of the Slavic Division of the Library of Congress. In 1905 he purchased the large private library of Siberian merchant Gennady Yudin of Krasnoiarsk. Crated and shipped in 1907, these 80,000 volumes (fifty tons), combined with the acquisition of the Hattala collection from Prague, made the Library of Congress one of the premier sites for Slavic materials in the world.[222] With annual additions of four or five shipments, the library's Slavic collection would only be fully appreciated many years later.

Russia was also the target of field investigations by academicians and scientists during this period. These included Theodore Lyman, physicist of Harvard, in the Altai Mountains, 1912; George Mixter, zoologist of the Smithsonian, in Lake Baikal region, 1912; George Blakeslee, historian of Clark University, peasant villages, 1907; Robert H. Lord, historian of Harvard, St. Petersburg archives, 1909; William Warfield of Princeton, Caucasus, 1913; Worthington C. Ford, historian of the Massachusetts Historical Society, St. Petersburg archives, 1909; A. V. William Jackson, linguist from Columbia University, Central Asia, 1911; Dexter Perkins, historian of Harvard, St. Petersburg archives, 1912; Frank Golder of Washington State College on behalf of the Carnegie Institute, archival survey, 1914; Ralph Catterall, immigration historian from Cornell, 1907; Copley Amory, Jr., ethnologist of the Smithsonian, in northeast Siberia, 1914; W. W. Campbell, astronomer of the Lick Observatory, 1914; Robert Nabours of Kansas State Agricultural College, sheep breeding in Central Asia, 1914; and Hoffman Nickerson of New York Zoological Society, preserving the walrus, 1914. Ivan Ozerov, an economist at the University of Moscow, even proposed in 1911 a regular exchange of professors between the United States and Russia, an idea that would finally come to fruition in 1958.[223]

American experts also attended international meetings in Russia. For example, Samuel June Barrows was a delegate to a congress on prison reform in St. Petersburg in 1907. He was impressed by Russian progress, at least on paper, and, with the help of prison director Aleksandr Maksimovich, se-

222. Alexis V. Babine, *The Yudin Library, Krasnoiarsk* (Washington, D.C.: By author, 1905); Marcus Lorenzo Taft, *Strange Siberia Along the Trans-Siberian Railway* (New York: Eaton and Mains, 1911), p. 180; Babine (Krasnoiarsk) to Meyer, 7 December 1906, DPR, Russia, vol. 249, RG 84, NA. The collection was fairly well-known—at least among such exiles as Lenin, who used it in 1897; *Lenin, Krupskaia and Libraries*, ed. S. Simsova Fla (London: Clive Bingley, n.d.), pp. 59–60. Unfortunately, it languished for some time uncataloged, because Babine was busy caring for his ill parents in Russia through World War I; vita, February 1924, and Herbert Putnam to Babine, 1 December 1910, box 1, Babine Papers, LC.

223. Askew, "Efforts to Improve Relations," p. 185.

cured building plans that would be used at Sing Sing. "Every opportunity was given me to see the penal institutions of Russia, and especially to acquaint myself with progressive Russian ideas of prison structure."[224]

Although few of these knowledgeable travelers had time to record their observations, Ralph Catterall was an exception. With the help of Samuel Harper, he managed to interview Paul Miliukov, other Duma leaders, and several resident Americans. Miliukov he found to be suddenly gray, too tyrannical for his party, and losing ground because of it.[225] A New York Life agent told him that insurance rates were higher in Russia because Russians were bad risks, and a local businessman griped that "there are plenty of practical Russians, but there is no field for them to exert their activity in."[226] Catterall observed that "people here who know the Russians well are in a state of despair over them. Some say the hope of the future is with the peasantry. Others declare that the peasants never can be brought out, that they cannot be taught. Everyone says that the Russians are dishonest, liars, thieves, and extremely immoral."[227] He thought that the Duma was a mess, that Russians did not really know what they wanted, and that, overall, Russia did not present a very hopeful picture.

Popular Culture

The greatest American cultural imprint on Russia was the least studied, because its domain was the daytime race track and the nighttime music halls. A substantial contingent of jockeys, drivers, and horse trainers and breeders (and possibly bookmakers) nearly controlled the rapidly growing business of the Russian track. Leading the way were Frank Caton and his two sons, William and Samuel. As manager of the stables for General Illarion Vorontsov-Dashkov, the elder Caton imported American stock for crossbreeding with Russian horses, operated a stud farm in Tula province, and published a turf magazine. The top two horses of 1911, "General H" and "Bob Douglass," were American.[228] At least nine other American horsemen, mostly from

224. Barrows to Riddle, 25 July 1907, DPR, Russia, vol. 4470 (251), RG 84, NA.
225. Catterall diary, 1 July 1907, Cornell University.
226. Ibid., 12–13 July 1907.
227. Ibid., 5 July 1907.
228. Thomas Smith to Meyer, 22 December 1905, DPR, Russia, vol. 4558 (consular reports) (111), and Watts to Meyer, 7 February 1906, DPR, Russia, vol. 247, RG 84, NA; Ruth Kedzie Wood, *The Tourist's Russia* (New York: Dodd, Mead, 1912), pp. 40–41.

Tennessee and Kentucky, were associated with race horses in the Moscow area, including Winfield Scott Smith, who also worked as a tourist guide.[229]

American equine expertise was sought for other than entertainment purposes. An officer, when buying American horses for the Russian army, solicited the services of Montana horseman Fred Barton in the breaking and training of horses on a Mongolian ranch under contract to the Russian army. Barton traveled as far as St. Petersburg gathering breeding stock.[230]

African-Americans held a firm niche in light entertainment. Foremost was Frederic Thomas, the owner-manager of Moscow's largest and most popular restaurant, the Aquarium. The commodious stage in the middle of this glass-covered pavilion featured vaudeville acts and American minstrel-style music. Thomas was originally from Chicago, where he waited tables at the Auditorium Hotel during the Columbian Exposition; he moved to Europe and married a German woman. According to one American visitor, they had three children who attended the best schools. "Thomas is rich and has other enterprises. When the real cold weather comes along he operates an enormous skating rink in connection with the restaurant."[231]

Russians still apparently enjoyed American minstrel and ragtime music. "The Louisiana Amazon Guards," a vaudeville troupe of seven African-American women, performed in Moscow and St. Petersburg in 1904 and 1905. The group, which included Ollie Burgoyne, Emma Harris, Virginia Shepherd, Fannie Smith, and Coretta Alfred, disbanded during the revolution, but two members stayed behind in Russia. Harris contined to sing in concert, married a Russian, but left the country during World War I; Alfred studied at the St. Petersburg Conservatory and became a well-known Soviet opera singer in the 1920s and 1930s under the name of Arle-Tilz.[232]

In Vladivostok in 1907 the Taft party was entertained with a ragtime concert by "a grinning darkey" from Baltimore who had served in a black regiment in the Philippines.[233] Also in Siberia, Lindon Bates found a performer named Johnson, originally from Charleston, singing "Suwannee River" in Russian. "He is thinking in frozen Irkutsk, of the old Carolina homestead,

229. Register of U.S. citizens in Moscow, 1905, DUSM, Russia, vol. 65 (roll 65, M 35), RG 59, NA.

230. Ralph Miracle, "Asian Adventures of a Cowboy from Montana," *Montana: The Magazine of Western History* 27, 2 (April 1977): 44–47.

231. Undated clipping [c. 1908], vol. 1, Lobdell Papers, ChicagoHS. Margaret Rogers noted with disdain that only American music was played in cafés; diary, 8 January 1911, SHSM.

232. Eileen Southern, *Biographical Dictionary of Afro-American and African Musicians* (Westport, Conn.: Greenwood Press, 1982), p. 17.

233. Murray, *Around the World with Taft*, p. 258.

and is singing and dancing his way back."[234] In 1909, George and Wesley Carr toured south Russia as "The Creole Twins: Monarchs of Song and Dance," featuring soft shoes and canes.[235] Jacob Hines of Wilmington, North Carolina, was billed in Baku as "The Jolly Coon in His Laughing Song."[236] An "Indian" named Arthur Collins, performing in Kharkov, turned out also to be African-American, but the genuine Mohawk family of James Deer did appear in shows in the Odessa area.[237]

American influence was instrumental in the rapid expansion of cinemas in Russia. Snodgrass reported that in 1910 there were already 1,200 movie houses, many of which showed mediocre American films:

> The Russians as well as other nations are tired of Wild West shows and demonstrations of the rougher side of American life. They are also surfeited with the dramatic or comic feature in which the American millionairess is looking for an opportunity to exchange her dollars for a European title; these subjects have been worn threadbare in Russia, and no longer prove interesting or entertaining.[238]

But Russian film companies used Kodak film to imitate many of the same primitive themes as a means to discovering real talent.

Another interesting transfer of culture concerned the collection and sale of folk art. Vera Blumenthal of Pasadena, California, organized regular channels through the Golitsyn family, Paul Miliukov, and the Riazan zemstvo for obtaining peasant crafts, especially needlework, with most of the proceeds going directly back to the villages. The Russian Peasant Handicraft Center in Pasadena opened its doors about 1902 and grew steadily. Blumenthal even sponsored an exhibit at the Art Institute of Chicago.[239] And

234. Lindon Bates, Jr., *The Russian Road to China* (Boston: Houghton Mifflin, 1910), p. 85. This may be the Charles Johnson who was performing at the Aquarium in 1914; Snodgrass to Wilson, 31 October 1914, DPR, Russia, vol. 283, RG 84, NA.

235. George Carr (Kiev) to Riddle, 12/25 February 1909, DPR, Russia, vol. 4473 (254), RG 84, NA.

236. Hines to Guild, 24 June 1912, DPR, Russia, vol. 259; Davis (Batum) to Wilson, 24 July 1912, DPR, Russia, vol. 273, RG 84, NA. Other African-Americans are mentioned as serving in the imperial household and on various noble estates; they usually enter the consular files only when deaths are recorded.

237. Grout to Rockhill, 18 November 1910, DPR, Russia, vol. 4562 (106), and to Wheeler, 21 August 1910, vol. 4564 (108), RG 84, NA.

238. Snodgrass, "Cinematography in Russia," 16 November 1910, DPR, Russia, vol. 4562 (106), RG 84, NA.

239. Snodgrass to Knox, 2 July 1912, DPR, Russia, vol. 4227, RG 84, NA; Blumenthal to Snodgrass, 23 May 1914, and Snodgrass to Bryan, 13 July 1914, DPR, Russia, vol. 5 (Moscow cons.), RG 84, NA.

in Boston, S. O. and Vera Ochs conducted a profitable business dealing in such Russian items as enamelware, jewelry, nested dolls (*matryoshkas*), and samovars.[240] At the connoisseur level, Henry Hiller continued to buy for Tiffany's—precious stones, bronzes, enamelware, fine silverware and china, and linens—into World War I, enduring strikes, revolutions, tariff and customs changes, and embargos.[241]

Among miscellaneous cultural contacts, Post Wheeler, an embassy secretary, collected and translated a number of *skazki*, or popular folk tales, including careful reproductions of unique illustrations by Ivan Bilibin.[242] Jeremiah Curtin concluded his long career of studying Russian history, culture, and antecedents with *The Mongols and Russia* and *A Journey in Southern Siberia*, published posthumously in 1908 and 1909, respectively. To serve another American interest, Charles Crane arranged a tour by a Russian Orthodox choir in 1910 at his own expense. And the Andreev balalaika orchestra toured the United States in 1910–1911 to mostly favorable receptions.[243]

The masterpieces of Russian literature continued to appear in new American translations, with Tolstoy, Turgenev, Dostoevsky, Gogol, and Pushkin the most popular. Newcomers on the scene were Maxim Gorky and Anton Chekhov, whose works at first had a limited circulation.[244] Gorky's visit to the United States in 1906, however, created a scandal—and increased demand for his publications—when the press revealed that he was not married to his female companion. The host group in New York included Mark Twain, William Dean Howells, and Jane Addams, and notoriety followed him to Boston where he was a guest of New England literati. On his part, the Russian writer did not conceal his contempt for tepid American radicalism. Even Addams was hard-pressed to defend his behavior.[245] Twain finally

240. Ochs to Rockhill, 27 January 1910, DPR, Russia, vol. 4262; Vera Ochs to Guild, 3 September 1912, DPR, Russia, vol. 273, RG 84, NA.

241. Hiller Papers, Mystic Seaport Library; Wood, *Tourist's Russia*, p. 144, credits Hiller as the father of the Russian enamel industry.

242. Wheeler, *Russian Wonder Tales* (New York: Century, 1912).

243. The Russian ambassador sent a personal invitation to President Taft to attend their concert in Washington, D.C., but since the performance in New York drew a Jewish anti-Russian demonstration, the president declined. Rosen to Taft, 27 November 1910, series 6, cf. 205 (roll 374), Taft Papers, LC; Egert to Guild, 21 February/5 March 1912, DPR, Russia, vol. 259, RG 84, NA.

244. The first of Gorky's major works published in an American translation was *Foma Gordeev* in 1901, but the Appleton edition of *Mother* in 1907 won a broader acceptance.

245. Jane Addams, *Twenty Years at Hull House with Autobiographical Notes* (New York: Macmillan, 1914), p. 421.

Maxim Gorky in New York. Harper's Weekly, *28 April
1906, courtesy of the Kansas Collection, University of
Kansas Libraries*

protested Gorky's insulting and condescending demeanor: "He hits the
public in the face with his hat and then holds it out for contributions."[246]
Gorky responded in kind with critical essays and letters about America, especially about New York, "The City of the Yellow Devil." He spent a productive summer, however, at a writer's retreat in the Adirondacks. From
there he wrote to a friend, "I'm working on my novel. I am also observing
American culture with the avid curiosity of a savage. On the whole it makes
me sick, but sometimes I laugh like mad. I already feel able to write a certain
something about America for which I'll be kicked out of here."[247] Nonethe-

246. As quoted in Dan Levin, *Stormy Petrel: The Life and Work of Maxim Gorky* (New
York: D. Appleton-Century, 1965), p. 129.
247. To A. V. Amfiteatrov, late August 1906, in Gorky, *The City of the Yellow Devil:
Pamphlets, Articles and Letters About America* (Moscow: Progress Publishers, 1972), p.
134.

less, the American edition of *Mother* in 1907 was a success, as was *The Lower Depths*, which followed in 1912.

Similarly, American literature in Russian translation was mainly restricted to the older "classics": Cooper, Hawthorne, Irving, Stowe, Longfellow, Emerson, Whitman, Twain. Writings on American history left much to be desired, though a few solid, if polemical, works by Russians who had lived for some time in the United States circulated.[248] The American consul in Batum could still justly complain, "I find on the whole a lamentable ignorance of America and American affairs even among the best people who have a knowledge of the English language. Outside of New York and its tall buildings, and a half dozen other big cities, little is known."[249]

Russian studies in the United States, after a promising beginning around the turn of the century, suffered growing pains in the 1905–1914 period. Having subsidized Samuel Harper's instructorship in Russian studies at the University of Chicago for three successive years, Charles Crane was discouraged by the small enrollments and persuaded by an unenthusiastic new president, H. N. Judson, to not renew his support.[250] After a year as a research fellow at Columbia University, Harper joined Bernard Pares's new Russian Center at the University of Liverpool in 1910.[251] It too had difficulties, and the program and its ground-breaking *Russian Review* were on the verge of collapse in 1914, owing to Pares's mismanagement and marital problems.[252] At the University of California, George Noyes also encountered resistance to learning Russian, though in the 1912–1913 academic year enrollment rose to fifteen.[253] More successful was a new program developed by Max Mandell at Yale that emphasized Russian theater. He reported that his translation and direction of *The Cherry Orchard* in 1908 drew enthusiastic audi-

248. For example, Pavel Mizhuev, *Istoriia Velikoi Amerikanskoi Demokratii* (St. Petersburg: Brokgauz-Efron, 1906); Grigorii De-Vollan, *V strane miliardov i demokratii: Ocherki i zametiki* (St. Petersburg-Moscow: M. O. Vol'f, 1907); Alexis Babine, *Istoriia Severo-Amerikanskikh Soedinennykh Shtatov*, 2 vols. (St. Petersburg: Bashmakov, 1912).

249. Cauldwell to Guild, 18 January 1912, DPR, Russia, vol. 4565 (109), RG 84, NA.

250. Albert Parry, *America Learns Russian: A History of the Teaching of the Russian Language in the United States* (Syracuse, N.Y.: Syracuse University Press, 1967), pp. 60–61.

251. Pares to Harper, 18 March and 9 October 1910, box 1, file 10, S. Harper Papers, University of Chicago.

252. "People don't ask for much, but there is a want of co-ordination between B's public aims and private life which it is hard to swallow when accompanied by such high sounding doctrines." Margaret Pares (Liverpool) to Samuel Harper, 10 May 1914, box 2, S. Harper Papers, University of Chicago.

253. Parry, *America Learns Russian*, pp. 55–56.

ences.[254] At least a network of Russianist scholars, students, and library resources now existed.

A few Russian lecturers plied the American circuit but not to the same extent as before. Most notable was Paul Miliukov's much-publicized visit of early 1908; he spent three intensive days in the country, highlighted by a lecture at Carnegie Hall analyzing the current situation in Russia. Following this was a quick trip, at the invitation of Congressman Herbert Parsons, to Washington.[255] After conferring with Rosen, Roosevelt agreed not to receive Miliukov unless the ambassador requested it, though the Russian liberal dined with a small group that included Secretary of War Taft, Secretary of Interior Garfield, and Secretary of Commerce Straus on 15 January. "My dear Baron," Roosevelt told Rosen the next day, "I must tell you all the fun I had this morning keeping that Mr. Miliukoff out of my office."[256] As this episode illustrates, Americans were increasingly caught between sympathy for Russian democratic causes and a desire for stability in that part of the world.

The Passport Question

The tactic of seeking redress for discriminatory treatment of Jews in Russia through pressure from the American government centered on the Russian policy of denying visas to Jewish-American citizens. William Howard Taft had made a vague campaign commitment to negotiate a new treaty with Russia, which ambassador Rosen felt was solely for electoral purposes—to win the Jewish vote.[257] Taft also touched on the matter in his 1909 inaugural address in reference to protecting the rights of American citizens abroad regardless of creed or race, also duly noted by the Russian ambassador.[258] In a

254. Mandell to Harper, 1908, box 1, file 10, S. Harper Papers, University of Chicago.

255. Paul Miliukov, *Political Memoirs, 1905–1917*, ed. Arthur Mendel (Ann Arbor: University of Michigan Press, 1967), pp. 172–74.

256. As quoted by Rosen to Izvolsky, 6/19 February 1908, file 133, op. 470, d. 139, AVPR.

257. Rosen to Izvolsky, 15/28 October 1908, ibid. The "promise" was also contained in a public letter from Root to Schiff in October 1908. The literature on the passport question is considerable, and the following is based, in addition to document and memoir citations, on the studies of Naomi Cohen, Ann Healy, Jeannette Tuve, and Gary Dean Best, as well as A. Yodfat, "The Jewish Question in American-Russian Relations (1875–1917)" (Ph.D. diss., American University, 1963); and V. V. Engel', "Amerikanskii pasport i russko-evreiskii vopros v kontse XIX-nachale XX veka," in *Amerikanskii Ezhegodnik 1991* (Moscow: Nauka, 1992), pp. 104–20.

258. Rosen to Izvolsky, 20 February/5 March 1909, file 133, op. 470, d. 138, AVPR.

conversation with the new secretary of state, Philander Knox, Rosen explained the Russian position and argued that it was similar to the American exclusion of Chinese. Knox countered that the Russian denial gave American Jews a weapon for anti-Russian agitation, so that it was in Russia's interest to remove this pretext.[259]

Izvolsky had indicated that Russia was ready to negotiate a new treaty of commerce and that recent agreements with Germany, France, and Italy could be used as models.[260] But the change in the Foreign Ministry—from Izvolsky to Sergei Sazonov—and in ambassadors in St. Petersburg extended the usual Russian procrastination. With nothing happening, the American Jewish Society strengthened its opposition to the 1832 treaty in early 1910. The campaign was led by Jacob Schiff, whom Rosen considered an "extraordinarily clever man." According to the ambassador, Schiff was carrying out a vendetta against Russia that had begun with his financing of Japan's war effort in 1904, but his true purpose was to stem the tide of poor Russian refugees to the United States.[261]

The issue was soon caught up in a vicious circle of Russian anti-Semitism and American Jewish anti-Russianism. In June 1910, in reaction to new Russian restrictions on Jews living in Kiev, the society worked through Congressman Parsons and the House Committee on Foreign Affairs to demand that the treaty be abrogated according to its terms—a one-year notice effected by a resolution of Congress. But few as yet took this matter very seriously. In early 1911, Louis Marshall addressed the Council of the Union of American Hebrew Congregations on "Russia and the American Passport" and called for immediate annulment of the treaty.[262] Shortly thereafter, on 10 February, Parsons introduced a joint resolution to repudiate the treaty, and Congressman William Sulzer of New York followed with an even more strongly worded alternative.[263] Many civic and religious organizations, especially in the East, publicly supported abrogation.

259. Rosen to Izvolsky, 13/26 March 1909, ibid.

260. Izvolsky to Riddle, 26 May/8 June 1909, DPR, Russia, vol. 4527 (notes received) (161), RG 84, NA.

261. Rosen to Sazonov, 3/16 February 1910, f. 133, op. 470, d. 132, AVPR.

262. Ann E. Healy, "Tsarist Anti-Semitism and Russian-American Relations," *Slavic Review* 42, 3 (Fall 1983): 419.

263. Ibid.; Kudashev to Sazonov, 1/14 February 1911, f. 133, op. 470, d. 133, AVPR. The New York *Times* quoted Parsons: "No longer will this country be a party to a treaty which is construed by the other side to entitle it to discriminate between American citizens on the grounds of their religious belief." "Protection of Jews Comes Up in House," 11 February 1911, p. 3.

Dollar imperialism, however, countered Jewish influence. At a luncheon conference with Jewish leaders on 15 February, arranged by Simon Wolf, President Taft denied that he had pledged to secure a treaty revision and lectured them on moderation and restraint.[264] Outraged, Schiff donated $25,000 to the Jewish society for a lobbying campaign, and a war of words was on. An anonymous pamphlet, "The Russian Treaty of 1832 and Its Interpretation," asserted that the treaty only allowed Russia the discrimination that America openly practiced. Otherwise, Britain, for example, could demand that its black citizens, such as Jamaicans, be given the same rights everywhere in the United States as other British citizens, and the right to exclude Chinese would be imperiled.[265] In July Taft told Russian chargé Nikolai Kudashev, "I shall do my best to stop that movement for the denunciation of the treaty with Russia, but I wish Mr. Stolypine would help us!"[266] That statesman, however, could not even help himself, for he was soon to be assassinated.

American Fleet Visit

In the late spring of 1911 a squadron of American battleships was sent to Europe to impress people with the advancing naval capability of the United States. Secretary of Navy Meyer, a former ambassador to Russia, saw to it that Russia was included in the courtesy calls. Although only a brief stay at Reval was initially planned, a special invitation from the tsar brought the squadron on to Kronstadt.[267] The fleet visit was an opportunity to rekindle memories of friendship and hospitality in the middle of the passport controversy.

The *Louisiana*, *Kansas*, and *New Hampshire*, commanded by Rear Admiral Charles Badger, arrived at Kronstadt in the late afternoon of 11 June for a week-long visit. In typically generous style, the Russians welcomed the fleet with dinners, luncheons, and receptions. Escorted by Captain Aleksandr Butakov, Badger and his staff lunched with Nicholas II at his summer cot-

264. Simon Wolf, *The Presidents I Have Known from 1860 to 1918*, 2d ed. (Washington, D.C.: Byron Adams, 1918), pp. 293-313.
265. Undated, it is included in diplomatic materials of July 1911; DPR, Russia, vol. 4477 (misc. received) (258), RG 84, NA.
266. Quoted in English, Kudashev to Anatoly Neratov, 4/17 July 1911, f. 133, op. 470, d. 133, AVPR.
267. Kudashev to Neratov, 13/26 April 1911, and Neratov to Kudashev, 2 May 1911, ibid.

tage and were received by Stolypin and the new naval minister, Admiral Ivan Grigorovich. They in turn hosted the emperor on board, as well as a separate Duma delegation, and held lavish receptions on the *Louisiana* and *Kansas*. A highlight of the tour was a baseball game on 16 June, no doubt the first in Russia, played between the crews of the *Kansas* and the *New Hampshire* on the St. Petersburg polo grounds.[268] A Russian challenge to a football match was declined, however, because of lack of knowledge of the European game. The climax came on 18 June in a formal review, as Nicholas II accepted deafening thirty-one-gun salutes from all ships and "six cheers, four ruffles, and the Russian national air" as he passed.[269]

The American press virtually ignored the entire affair,[270] but a Russian newspaper reported evidence of discord and resentment by attributing to Admiral Badger an insulting speech about the importance of democratic feelings. He denied the charge: "I thought that the reception was warm and sincere—it surely was among all those with whom I came in contact, from the Emperor down."[271] The timing and distinctive honor of such a courteous visit probably softened the Russian reaction to the approaching abrogation.

Abrogation Resolution

Diplomatic change further delayed treaty progress: Georgi Bakhmetev formally replaced Rosen, while Curtis Guild filled the fumbling William Rockhill's shoes.[272] Although Bakhmetev was a typical middle-level Russian diplomat, he had experience in the United States and had married an American socialite, whose sister and influential brother-in-law had lobbied Taft to re-

268. Captain Henry Hough (naval attaché) to Meyer, 4 July 1911, "Visit of the Second Division, U.S. Atlantic Fleet to Cronstadt," C-9-b, file 1175, Office of Naval Operations, RG 38, NA; Rockhill diary, 15 and 17 June 1911, 646M-386E, Rockhill Papers, Houghton Library, Harvard University; Logbook, *Kansas*, May 1911–Jan. 1912, RG 24, NA.

269. Rockhill to [St. Petersburg] Sports Society, 31 May/13 June 1911, DPR, Russia, vol. 4497 (189), RG 84, NA; Logbook, 18 June, *New Hampshire*, March 1911–Nov. 1911, RG 24, NA.

270. Kudashev to Neratov, 8/21 June 1911, f. 133, op. 470, d. 133, AVPR.

271. Badger (Kiel) to Wheeler, 25 June 1911, DPR, Russia, vol. 4476 (misc. received) (257), RG 84, NA.

272. Taft welcomed the Bakhmetevs, while noting that Rosen "was particularly *persona grata* here." Taft to Guild (confidential), DPR, Russia, vol. 4477 (misc. received) (258), RG 84, NA.

quest the transfer.[273] As a favor to the president, Russia complied. Curtis Guild, on the other hand, was a well-known Boston publisher, former governor, and friend of Taft's and had even written a book about Russia, a rarity indeed among American diplomats.

Bakhmetev began his mission by helping Guild get settled in St. Petersburg. The two new envoys also discussed the top item on their agenda, a new commercial treaty, agreeing that it would be better negotiated in Washington to avoid bureaucratic battles and anti-Semitic sentiments in St. Petersburg. Both thought that a mountain was being made out of a molehill in the United States and that in fact only a very small number of Jews were denied visas. Guild suggested that the consular question be changed from "What is your religion?" to "Do you belong to any of the classes of persons excluded from Russia by Russian law?" Since the United States excluded the Chinese by law, the government should have difficulty objecting.

Taft and the State Department still sought a new treaty. As late as August 1911 the president wrote Guild, "I am very hopeful that if we can get Russia into the attitude of approval of such a treaty, we might induce her to take a reasonable view of the Jewish passport question."[274] Guild cautioned Taft that, as in the United States, Russian public opinion was becoming vehemently opposed to any concessions, citing especially *Novoe Vremia*. "Far from favoring them, it comes out defying the United States to abrogate treaties and shows that the United States, not Russia, would be the sufferer thereby."[275] He then noted, "The same force seeking to influence American public opinion against Russia on one pretext is seeking to influence Russian opinion against America on another." Whatever moderation and accommodation that the governments might try to achieve, both were caught in a maelstrom of public rancor. Taft saw the predicament: "The passport question is still a very heated one, and I am afraid it is going to figure very prominently in the transactions [of Congress]. I wish Russia could understand that we wish that she could make some concessions in that regard. We could afford to do a good deal for her."[276]

273. George Horton, *Recollections Grave and Gay: The Story of a Mediterranean Consul* (Indianapolis: Bobbs-Merrill, 1927), p. 79; Taft to Rockhill, 24 December 1910 (confidential) and Rockhill to Taft, 28 January and 14 February 1911 (personal), Rockhill letters, 46M-646, Rockhill Papers, Houghton Library, Harvard University. John R. McLean, Bakhmetev's brother-in-law, was the publisher of the Washington *Post*.

274. 10 August 1911 (confidential), DPR, Russia, vol. 4477 (misc. received) (258), RG 84, NA.

275. Guild to Taft (confidential), 28 August 1911, roll 369, Taft Papers, LC.

276. To Guild, 14 September 1911, ibid.

Unfortunately, the Russian government was in no condition to act expeditiously. Foreign Minister Sazonov was incapacitated by a serious respiratory illness through most of the year, leaving foreign affairs in the hands of Anatoly Neratov, whom one historian has described as "a long-time 'inventory item' in the ministry's chancellery . . . who had 'neither the breadth nor the authority' to direct Russian diplomacy."[277] And bureaucratic confusion and turmoil descended on St. Petersburg in September with the assassination of Stolypin. Having delayed his departure for Washington, where any treaty talks were expected to occur, Bakhmetev strongly appealed to the new cabinet head, Vladimir Kokovtsov, that it was in Russia's real interest "to swallow the American pill."[278] Arriving in the United States finally at the end of November, Bakhmetev was met by another piece of bad news— charges of Russian implication in the ouster of Americans from Persia.[279]

In 1911, complicated infighting over supremacy in Teheran nearly derailed the Anglo-Russian convention of 1907, as Persian leaders attempted to become independent of both Russian and British controls. A new factor was the appearance of W. Morgan Shuster, American businessman-adventurer, as treasurer general in the government, and Russian resentment increased proportionate to his growing popularity. Neratov, as if confusing two issues, accused Shuster of being anti-Russian because he was Jewish and launched an aggressive attack on his presence in Persia. After much diplomatic maneuvering in late 1911, separate Russian and British pressures forced Shuster's dismissal, much to the annoyance of Washington.[280] Neratov's personal involvement may have contributed to the generally anti-

277. McDonald, *United Government*, p. 172.

278. Bakhmetev to Neratov, 22 November/5 December 1911, f. 133, op. 470, d. 134, AVPR.

279. Ibid., 20 November/3 December 1911. The Russian minister to Persia is quoted by an American businessman on the scene as saying, "It was a monumental error to bring Americans to this country—I know them—I know for what they stand—the condition under which they live—freedom, liberty, equality and democracy and you can't make them 'fit' in this country." Turin Bradford Boone, "Persian Diary," 13 January 1912, Duke University.

280. For the details of this intriguing episode, see Robert A. McDaniel, *The Shuster Mission and the Persian Constitutional Revolution* (Minneapolis: Bibliotheca Islamica, 1974); Firuz Kazemzadeh, *Russia and Britain in Persia, 1864–1914: A Study in Imperialism* (New Haven, Conn., and London: Yale University Press, 1968); Rose Louise Coughlin (Greaves), "British Policy in Persia, 1888–1914" (Ph.D. diss., University of Kansas, 1952); Shuster's own account, *The Strangling of Persia: A Personal Narrative* (New York: Century, 1912); and a Russian review, "Persia's American Dictator," trans. from *Rossiia*, 23 November/5 December 1912, in Guild to Knox, 17 December 1912, DPR, Russia, vol. 275, RG 84, NA.

American resolution. On the other side, George Kennan perceived a linkage between the Shuster affair and the passport question: "It's curious to see what our government will do to protect Shuster if the Russian Government attempts to put him out by force. Our State Department is bound to protect the rights of an American citizen, even if he is in the employ of the Persians; but, as everybody knows, it hasn't much back-bone, or much ability."[281]

Partly because of the Persian problem, Bakhmetev was not able to see Secretary of State Knox until 5 December. He was then asked to provide some evidence of Russia's willingness to renegotiate the treaty, since the president was about to make a statement to that effect in his message to Congress to be delivered on 7 December: "I believe the Russian Government is addressing itself seriously to the need of changing the present practice under the treaty."[282] Bakhmetev immediately cabled St. Petersburg but received no response. Actually, Kokovtsov, who retained his post as minister of finance, was busy trying to institute a collegial management of foreign policy, and Nicholas II had relapsed into his usual passivity.[283] Both awaited the recovery of Sazonov.

Business Reactions

American business concerns in Russia were naturally worried about the consequences of an abrogation but were unlikely to take the offensive against Jewish interests. Wharton Barker continued to pursue his long-standing efforts to initiate Russian-American schemes but was frustrated by Russian bureaucrats who failed to follow his advice. He retreated in 1911 into eccentric political projects, such as the left-wing Men and Religion Forward Movement.[284] Barker even sent Nicholas II a copy of its political program.[285]

At this juncture, Taft may have had an opportunity to make use of his friend John Hays Hammond, whom some considered to be the power behind the throne, certainly one of a few influential confidants of the president. Hammond had visited Russia in late 1910 on behalf of projects that

281. To his wife, 4 December 1911, box 15, Kennan Papers, LC.

282. Knox to Bakhmetev, 6 December 1911, file 170, op. 512/2, d. 115 (1913), and Bakhmetev to Neratov, 23 November/6 December 1911 (t), file 133, op. 470, d. 134, AVPR.

283. McDonald, *United Government*, pp. 175–77.

284. "Wharton Barker for New Party; Only Hope, He Says," Philadephia *North American*, 15 August 1910, in box 10, Barker Papers, LC.

285. Barker to Nicholas II, 31 December 1911 (c), ibid.

President and Mrs. Taft with John Hays Hammond (in the middle). Harper's Weekly, *16 January 1909, courtesy of the Kansas Collection, University of Kansas Libraries*

would use American capital to build grain elevators, erect irrigation systems, and foster various municipal improvements. As a prominent and wealthy developer (especially of gold mines in South Africa) and "an old and sincere partisan of rapprochement between United States and Russia," he received favorable attention in the Russian press and official quarters, all of which was reported in detail to the president.[286] In December 1910, Nicholas II gave a private audience to Hammond who apparently made quite an impression on the tsar. Hammond even brought up the sensitive Jewish question, in response to the complaint about American sympathy for Japan during the war. Nicholas noted, "I can understand the American point of view. . . . But there are six million Jews in Russia—more than half the number in the entire world." Hammond answered, "Couldn't the administrative regulations which restrict Jews to certain congested localities be modified? Wouldn't a policy of dispersion eliminate the sore spots?" Nicholas responded that the idea had already occurred to him.[287] According to Hammond, Stolypin, Sazonov, Kokovtsov, Rosen, and others were all stunned by the emperor's receptivity.

286. Rockhill to Knox, 24 December 1910, series 6, cf. 204 (roll 374), Taft Papers, LC, enclosing excerpt from *Golos Moskvy*, 26 November/9 December 1910.

287. As quoted in Hammond, *Autobiography* 2:471.

The question arises, then, why Hammond was not sent as a special envoy in 1911 to negotiate a settlement. As the president's trusted adviser, he could have wielded real clout and knew it. Taft did indeed name him special ambassador—but to the coronation of George V in London that summer. It seems that Hammond, as an ambitious investor, simply did not want to risk alienating powerful American Jews. In fact, Jacob Schiff had already accused him of working against abrogation on behalf of the Russian government. Hammond wrote Vilenkin, denying this: "I have many friends among Jews, and no one is more desirous than I to see the condition of Jews in Russia improved." Although he added, "I shall take up the subject myself with Schiff and give him some talk straight from the shoulder," neither Schiff nor Hammond mention the episode in their memoirs.[288]

Hammond backed away from his Russian plans, leaving Russian leaders mystified. In a conversation with Curtis Guild shortly before his assassination, Stolypin denied any hostility toward the United States, declared his desire to cultivate good relations, but wondered what had become of Hammond and his elevator and irrigation projects. Guild related again the good impression Hammond had made on Russian leaders.

> The absence of any substantial results of his visit is provoking a sort of restlessness here that is likely to result in a most unfavorable revulsion of feeling against the United States if nothing should come of it after such great hopes have been excited. . . . Of course, if Mr. Hammond does secure this most desirable investment of American capital in Russia, he will have performed a tremendous and most patriotic service to his country.[289]

Guild's report of a Russian understanding that Hammond's Russian ventures had the support of the American government drew a quick denial from Taft.[290] Hammond also fell in line: "The President does not know whether or not I have any interests in Russia. As a matter of fact I have none there, although I may acquire some in the future. . . . I have had my

288. Hammond to Vilenkin, 9 April 1911 (personal copy), series 6, cf. 204 (roll 374), Taft Papers, LC.
289. Guild to Knox, 22 August 1911, forwarded to Taft in Huntington Wilson to Hilles (Taft's secretary), 12 September 1911, series 6, cf. 204 (roll 374), Taft Papers, LC.
290. Taft to Wilson, 13 September 1911, ibid. "I should be very glad to have American capital invested in Russia, but I do not want it thought that Mr. Hammond visited Russia as an agent of mine or even at the suggestion, for I did not know he was going until he had gone, and I do not know whom he represented."

hands full with enterprises in other parts of the world."[291] The caution displayed by both Taft and Hammond was partly motivated by the approaching election, since the latter was considered a vice-presidential prospect. Regardless, it nullified Hammond's political and economic usefulness in the resolution of Russian conflicts.

Cyrus McCormick, Jr., hoped to discuss the visa problem with Stolypin and the emperor himself during his September 1911 visit, but the former's murder and the latter's absence left only the minister of agriculture, Sergei Timashev. Although he liked McCormick's idea of having the State Department issue passes to "business" Jews, he had no authority to negotiate. In a long letter to the president, McCormick warned: "In conclusion I may refer to the fact that the citizens of the United States are having a rapidly increasing interest in manufacturing in Russia. The International Harvester Company in Russia is already a large manufacturer and has favorable prospects of extending its activities. All these interests would be seriously harmed if the treaty of 1832 should be abrogated."[292]

Both sides were admittedly handicapped by circumstances, but neither made much of an attempt to resolve issues, which gave the antitreaty forces the advantage. In addition to the original passport matter, impatience and general disgust with apparent Russian stonewalling angered the American people. George Kennan, who maintained a low profile during the debate, thought in early December that the tide had definitely turned for abrogation. "[The State Department] never would attempt to enforce the rights of our Jewish citizens in Russia if it were not compelled to do so, but public opinion on the Russian passport question is now becoming so overwhelming that Taft and Knox will have to yield."[293] A forum promoting renunciation of the treaty was held in a packed Carnegie Hall on 6 December. Although former minister Andrew White argued for referring the matter to The Hague tribunal, sentiment clearly favored immediate government action. The next week the House of Representatives approved the stronger Sulzer resolution by a landslide vote of 300 to 1.

Bakhmetev and Taft thought there was still time to head off Senate

291. Hammond to Hilles, 20 November 1911, series 6, cf. 204 (roll 374), Taft Papers, LC. Taft went out of his way later to clear Hammond of any implication that he supported the Russian position; Taft to Wolf, 26 November 1917, in Wolf, *Presidents I Have Known*, p. 321.

292. McCormick (Chicago) to Taft, 11 December 1911, series 6, cf. 89 (roll 365), Taft Papers, LC.

293. To his wife, 4 December 1911, box 15, Kennan Papers, LC.

action.[294] Although that body passed a more moderate version sponsored by Henry Cabot Lodge, it was unanimously adopted by the House. A Taft veto would obviously have been in vain. Instead, he offered Russia a face-saving joint abrogation, which was firmly rejected by Sazonov, who had finally returned to office and who informed Guild that the United States simply did not understand the Russian situation—that free admission of foreigners, given the threat to the Russian state from emigré revolutionaries, was impossible.[295]

The foreign minister finally replied to Bakhmetev's many telegrams in January by observing that the action of Congress was "decidedly negative towards Russia." He belatedly advised the ambassador to work with Taft and Knox to prevent abrogation and indicated a willingness to negotiate a new treaty. In response to a specific question, Sazonov wrote that what would happen after the expiration of the yearlong grace period would depend on actions of the United States and the decision of a conference committee of the Council of Ministers.[296] In a separate statement to *Collier's*, Kokovtsov candidly reemphasized the unfairness of giving foreign Jews special privileges that Russian Jews did not have.[297] The passport treaty abrogation debacle demonstrated on both sides how moralistic and ethnic passion was gaining over inept and lackadaisical government actions—a clear sign of approaching disaster.

Impact of Abrogation Resolution

Given its swiftness and decisiveness after years of discussion, the congressional action and subsequent diplomatic notification came as a shock to many Russians and Americans. Even Schiff was surprised; no one was certain what would happen next. Some feared an immediate Russian protest in the form of a boycott of American goods, but *Russkoe Slovo* (Russian word), a progressive newspaper, was bold enough to state: "The true national feeling has always been offended by the fact that we do not possess the elementary foundation of equal rights of citizenship. This is indeed a disgrace to the na-

294. Bakhmetev to Neratov, 2/15 and 3/16 December 1911 (t), file 133, op. 470, d. 134, AVPR.
295. Healy, "Tsarist Anti-Semitism," p. 422.
296. Sazonov to Bakhmetev, 29 December 1911/10 January 1912 (c), file 170, op. 512/2, d. 115 (1913), AVPR. Although the draft is clearly dated 1911, it is filed with papers of 1913.
297. Kokovtsov, "Russia's Attitude on the Abrogated Treaty," *Collier's* 47 (27 January 1912): 10.

tion."[298] A corollary impression in the United States was that the American position was right, and right would prevail. As the *Chautauquan* editorialized, "In the end, it cannot be doubted, Russia will surrender and meet our demands. It is her position, not ours, that is untenable and indefensible."[299] Snodgrass reported from Moscow the popular feeling that the governments would work things out in the near future.[300]

Another prevalent view was that the controversy was wholly the result of American political maneuvering in anticipation of the election of 1912. Elihu Root, now a senator, reflected:

> The fact is that a lot of fellows here saw an opportunity to get some political advantage at home through voicing the bitter feelings of their constituents and they did not appreciate at all the necessity of courtesy in international affairs. . . . I am in hopes that whatever feeling there is in Russia will die away as the matter cools off and that we may sometime be able to restore the friendly feeling which formerly existed between Americans and Russians and which has received so many severe blows in recent years.[301]

Eventually the storm would die down, he thought.

This was also the tenor of the discussion at an assembly held at the House of Nobility in St. Petersburg on 22 February 1912, at which economic progressives Aleksandr Protopopov, Vladimir Bobrinskii, and V. P. von Egert spoke for the Russian position on the passport question. The latter also wrote a fifty-three-page statement urging moderation and understanding that was translated into English and circulated in the United States with the assistance of the American embassy.[302]

In assessing the new situation for International Harvester, William Couchman betrayed his annoyance with Washington: "There is no reason why a new official treaty cannot be negociated [*sic*] providing America is willing to leave internal matters to Russia. If the government in America is

298. Cited in Snodgrass to Knox, 5 January 1912, DPR, Russia, vol. 4276, RG 84, NA.
299. "Russia, American Passports and Treaty Rights," *Chautauquan* 5, 3 (February 1912): 295.
300. Snodgrass to Knox, 30 December 1911, DPR, Russia, vol. 4276, RG 84, NA.
301. Root to Guild, 5 February 1912, DPR, Russia, vol. 259, RG 84, NA.
302. Egert, "Obshchee sobranie 9 fevralia 1912 goda v S.-Peterburg," and Egert to Guild, 22 March/4 April 1912, DPR, Russia, vol. 259, RG 84, NA; Egert, "The Conflict Between the United States and Russia" (St. Petersburg, 1912), in f. 170, op. 512/2, d. 115, AVPR.

simply going to do nothing and let the year go by without negotiating a new treaty, it is impossible for anyone to judge what the result will be." He consoled himself, however, with the evidence that Russia was willing to parley and would not react rashly. After all, he asked, where else could Russia find the 10,000 binders, 30,000 reapers, 28,000 mowers, and 33,000 rakes that his company annually supplied?[303]

In St. Petersburg, International Harvester director Theodore Kosters received reassurances from Guild that Washington was maintaining "a tacit dignified receptive silent attitude":

Mr. and Mrs. Guild are being treated with marked consideration by official Russian society. This is sufficiently marked to force the conclusion that Russia wishes to make it easy for Washington to climb down. The Ambassador seems to fear that nothing will be done until political matters are out of the way. Russia does not want trouble. It needs American cotton, as well as machinery. How far public opinion will force the Russian Government to abandon its present passive attitude and become aggressive, is a question.[304]

This was a good statement of the Russian position from a local business expert.

A leading opponent of the congressional action in the United States was free-trade advocate James Davenport Whelpley, who saw the abrogation as a direct and malicious interference with commerce.

One nation's honor or dignity cannot be compromised for the sake of continuing favorable commercial relations with another; but it is a serious matter for one government, at the dictation of whatever interest it may be, or whatever may be the result to be gained at home, to destroy the long existing friendship and profitable commercial exchanges of two peoples without a full understanding of the consequences of such action. The United States cannot impose its views upon Russia, for the

---

303. To Legge, 5 March 1912, BB 4-02, box 1, file 1237, IH Papers, SHSW. Legge was equally disgusted and thought the whole business was the result of "just a mob of politicians who are paying attention to practically nothing but politics." As quoted by Pickering, "International Harvester Company," p. 132.

304. Kosters to Legge, 3/16 March 1912, BB 4-02, box 1, file 1237, IH Papers, SHSW.

good and sufficient reason that such views do not coincide with the ne-
cessities of Russian interior government. The United States has no
power to punish her old friend for not agreeing with her; in fact, quite
the reverse, hence an *impasse*.[305]

The State Department did indeed anticipate higher tariffs on American
goods; Case agent Kalamatiano complained about tighter Customs regulations in Odessa; and Snodgrass in Moscow detected a flurry of interest in ir-
rigating more of Central Asia to avoid dependency on American cotton.[306]
Yet the passport affair was soon swept away by a particularly absorbing
three-way election race (Taft, Wilson, Roosevelt) in 1912. There were also serious concerns about Mexican and Chinese revolutions on one side and
about destabilizing Balkan eruptions on the other.[307]

In June some zemstvos tried to boycott American machinery, but in general Russians were still friendly toward Americans and business remained
undisturbed. As Snodgrass observed, "I am convinced that Russia (not the
existing Government but the thinking people) is the best friend the United
States have in Europe. Though the Government may suspect every move on
our part, the people have faith in American institutions and the American
Government, and the jealousy, that is so evident in Germany and England,
does not appear here."[308] More alarming was ambassador Guild's belief that
other nations, particularly Germany, were taking advantage of the treaty
abrogation to foment discord between Russia and the United States. "There
has been no unpleasant conflict between the two embassies [American and
German], but the diplomatic hostility of the present German Ambassador
has been supplemented by his apparent personal dislike of everything and
everybody connected with the United States."[309]

Guild held preliminary talks about treaty revision with officials of the
Foreign Ministry in July but made no progress. In August he reported whis-
pers about a proposed law that would double duties on American goods and
forbid operations of American companies in Russia. But St. Petersburg was

305. Whelpley, *The Trade of the World* (New York: Century, 1913), pp. 338–39.

306. Kalamatiano to Guild, 27 March/9 April 1913, DPR, Russia, vol. 4555 (178);
Huntington Wilson (State Department) to Hitchcock, 13 March 1912 (c), DPR, Russia,
vol. 4276; and Snodgrass to Knox, 21 March 1912, DPR, Russia, vol. 4227, RG 84, NA;
Wilson to Taft, 27 March 1912, series 6, cf. 89 (roll 365), Taft Papers, LC.

307. For a good overview, see Lloyd Gardner, *Safe for Democracy: The Anglo-
American Response to Revolution, 1913–1923* (New York and Oxford: Oxford University
Press, 1987), pp. 45–80.

308. To Knox, 6 June 1912, DPR, Russia, vol. 4227, RG 84, NA.

309. To Knox, 5 July 1912 (c), DPR, Russia, vol. 4588 (275), RG 84, NA.

in more than the usual doldrums during the summer of 1912, diverted by the Stockholm Olympic Games in July and by a severe heat spell in August.[310] With time running out in the fall Guild wrote a political friend of the president-elect that the "misunderstanding in the United States of problems here is so serious and the condition here so delicate that I have . . . twice crossed the ocean within a year because, *in strict confidence,* these were matters that could not be trusted to the mails. . . . This office is filled daily with American businessmen or their representatives protesting against what has been done."[311]

In Washington, Bakhmetev was reduced to recording the unfolding political scene before and after the November election. Knox, he reported, thought it was a waste of time to negotiate if the passport question would not be considered.[312] And Taft's election defeat placed the matter in limbo. Since the treaty would expire before the new administration took office, Knox and Bakhmetev reached an understanding, first referred to as a *modus vivendi* and later as *status quo,* to continue the existing tariffs.[313]

When rumors of this circulated, Jewish leaders became alarmed. Louis Marshall wrote to Taft, "Such a *modus vivendi* would renew the rejected treaty, so far as it would be advantageous to Russia." And Simon Wolf thought it was "practically abrogating the abrogation, and modifying the wish of the American people."[314] However, he was appeased by Taft's denial of such an agreement.[315] Nevertheless, just before the end of the year—and the expiration of the treaty—letters changed hands confirming the principle of adhering to minimum tariffs on imports.[316] Another exchange followed formal approval by the Russian Council of Ministers in April 1913.[317] The Jewish lobby reluctantly but quietly respected the arrangement.

Russia continued to deny visas to American Jews but no more than be-

310. Guild to Lulu, 14 July (Stockholm) and 10 August 1912 (St. Petersburg), Guild Papers, BPL.

311. To Josiah Quincy, 8 November 1912, Guild misc., MassHS.

312. Bakhmetev to Sazonov, 25 April/8 May 1912, file 133, op. 470, d. 126, AVPR.

313. Bakhmetev to Sazonov, 3/18 November and 21 November/8 December 1912, ibid.

314. Marshall to Taft, 15 November 1912, and Wolf to Taft, 22 November 1912, series 6, cf. 89 (roll 365), Taft Papers, LC.

315. Taft to Wolf, 26 November 1912 and Wolf to Taft, 30 November 1912, ibid.

316. Bakhmetev to Sazonov, 18/31 December 1912, and Sazonov to Bakhmetev, 14 December 1912, file 133, op. 470, d. 126, AVPR; H. Wilson to Guild, 24 December 1912 (t), DPR, Russia, vol. 275, RG 84, NA.

317. Osobyi Zhurnal Soveta Ministerov, 28 February 1913, and John B. Moore to Bakhmetev, 10 June 1913, file 170, op. 512/2, d. 115, AVPR; Moore to Wilson, 10 June 1913, DPR, Russia, vol. 4555 (178), RG 84, NA.

fore. Many were able to enter the country by bribing officials, by staging phony religious conversions, or with forged papers. The port of Libau was a notoriously easy access point; as Guild confessed to the consular agent there, "It is . . . most embarrassing to be told that there is one port in Russia where American Jews, for example, can enter freely and without any visa, while all the others require special permits."[318] An influential Jewish community apparently made the difference. Thus, the travel of American Jews to Russia still represented a substantial international tourist business.

In practical terms, then, the nagging passport question created only minimal obstacles to Jewish mobility between the two countries. It was the Russian government's unwillingness to compromise on the issue and the continuation of the pogroms that transformed a minor problem into a serious rift. Ill feelings on both sides intensified to the point that the commercial treaty was abrogated—which again had little practical effect but damaged official diplomatic relations because of the insult entailed in annulling a treaty. There matters stood on the eve of the Great War.

Russian Anti-Semitism

Whether the abrogation had any effect on Russian government policy toward the Jewish population in Russia is open to question. It certainly did not appear to improve matters, and Guild was even convinced that the American action caused a deterioration in the position of Jews.

> Instead of encouraging a more lenient treatment of Jews it would appear that the abrogation of the treaty, by causing stricter enforcement of all those repressive laws, has actually if anything made the condition of the Jews in Russia distinctly worse than it was before, which naturally was the exact opposite effect which the prime movers of the bill for the abrogation of the treaty expected would be the case.[319]

He repeated this on several occasions but denied that American Jews among the foreign residents were being singled out for attack.[320]

His interim replacement, Charles Wilson, in early 1914 found the situation worsening.

318. To Alfred Seligman, 16 November 1911, DPR, Russia, vol. 4255 (Moscow cons.), RG 84, NA.
319. To Knox, 28 January 1913 (c), DPR, Russia, vol. 4555 (178), RG 84, NA.
320. To Bryan, 11 April 1913 (c), ibid.

It is not only my personal opinion, but that of the majority of the foreign diplomats, that the efforts of the United States in behalf of American Jews visiting Russia, which led to the abrogation of the Commercial Treaty of 1832, has, instead of helping the position of American Jews, had the contrary effect, and spurred on the Russian Government to enforce existing regulations against all Jews, both foreign and native, and even to put into force new and more severe ones.[321]

But independently increasing Russian anti-Semitism may have been the real impulse. In response, the more affluent Russian Jews made compromises, bowing to circumstances by accepting Russification and/or conversion for the sake of economic and social gains.

In Russia most of the newspapers voiced anti-Semitic sentiments under pressure from the Union of the Russian People. Other conservative groups drowned out the few pleas for understanding and reform that arose from such organs as *Rech* (Speech), which was funded by the American Jewish Society. In the United States the opposite situation prevailed, with the bulk of the press, led by the New York *Times*, denouncing Russian anti-Semitism, The rhetoric was definitely more moderate, however, after 1912. Russian-language newspapers in New York, such as *Golos Truda* (Voice of labor) and *Novyi Mir* (New world), continued their previous Jewish focus but increasingly appealed to a broader cross-section of Slavic immigrants with populist and socialist themes. Meanwhile, the Russian government provided an annual subsidy of $1,500 to the conservative and Orthodox *Russkii Emigrant* in an effort to promulgate a divergent point of view.[322]

During the abrogation process, another sensational event in Russia exposed latent anti-Semitism. In March 1911 the mangled body of a thirteen-year-old Ukrainian boy was found near Kiev. Despite evidence of the involvement of a criminal gang, the family accused Mendel Beilis, the thirty-nine-year-old father of five children, of having perpetrated the murder of a Christian youth for blood to be used in a ritual, according to a rampant anti-Semitic legend. Both local and central authorities, especially Minister of Justice Ivan Shcheglovitov, expedited the arrest, imprisonment, and prosecution of Beilis.

This time the prominent Jewish community rushed to the rescue in declaring his innocence and the ridiculousness of the charge. After prolonged

321. Wilson to Bryan, 14 March 1914, DPR, Russia, vol. 284, RG 84, NA.
322. Bakhmetev to Sazonov, 4/17 August 1914, file 133, op. 470, d. 312, AVPR; Robert A. Karlowich, *We Fall and Rise: Russian-Language Newspapers in New York City, 1889–1914* (Metuchen, N.J., and London: Scarecrow Press, 1991), pp. 189–97.

preliminaries, a public trial was held in Kiev in October 1913, and surprisingly Beilis was acquitted.[323] Although government influence on the side of the prosecution was obvious and conservative officials claimed a victory because the existence of Jewish ritualistic murder was not disproved, the result seemed to indicate progress for civil rights and the Russian legal system.

Although the Beilis case did not directly involve Americans, the episode was carefully watched in the United States, bringing public scrutiny again to bear on Russian anti-Semitism. Bakhmetev expressed his concern to the foreign minister about the anti-Russian publicity that accompanied the affair. More unfortunate, the trial aroused anti-Semitic tendencies in the United States with charges that Jewish money had "bought" the verdict. Henry Fulford of Chicago wrote Bakhmetev, "You should find some means of reprinting and publishing (in America and England) the evidence in the Beilis trial in Kiev. Americans only hear the Jews side of the story. Why dont you give us the other side?"[324]

Other manifestations of blatant and officially condoned Russian anti-Semitism occurred in the army. The American attaché, Captain Nathan Averill, while observing maneuvers in the Volga region, noted a regimental commander beating a Jewish soldier, "not in any particular anger for he was a benevolent looking old chap, but because this particular laggard belonged to that race against which there is strong feeling throughout the country and throughout the army."[325] On another occasion he reported a standard routine in a regimental barracks:

"Who are our enemies?"
"Our enemies are divided into two classes, first the external enemies,
    second, the internal enemies."
"Who are our external enemies?"
"The Germans and the Gentlemen English."
"Who are our internal enemies?"
"First the Jews, second the Poles, third the students."[326]

---

323. The jurors were actually divided, six to six, which according to Russian law meant acquittal. For details of the case and trial, see Maurice Samuel, *Blood Accusation—The Strange History of the Beilis Case* (Philadelphia: Jewish Publication Society, 1966), and Ezekiel Leikin, *The Beilis Transcripts: The Anti-Semitic Trial That Shook the World* (North Vale, N.J.: Jason Aronson, 1993).

324. Undated original, Beilis file, f. 170, op. 512/2, d. 109, AVPR.

325. "A Day's Journey on the Volga with a Line Regiment of Russian Infantry," 13 October 1911, War College Division General Correspondence, 6566-8, box 127, RG 165, NA.

326. "Russian Soldiers Barracks Life," 15 April 1911, 6566-1, ibid.

Diplomatic Hiatus

Back in St. Petersburg, Curtis Guild weathered another Russian winter with the help of ballet, opera, and bridge parties. In March 1913 four days were given over to celebrating the anniversary of Romanov rule, and Guild boasted that only the United States had full delegations for all the formal occasions. Although the new president had paid him the compliment of wanting his advice "before he does anything about Russia," Guild complained more and more frequently about Russian life, American policies, and his health.[327] To his sister he wrote, "The new administration is starting out to break down all foreign relations with all nations. God help the United States!"[328] Under doctor's orders he retired from Russia in April 1913.

Charles Crane was at first rumored to be Woodrow Wilson's choice as Guild's replacement, but Crane faced opposition (for supporting both Roosevelt and Wilson) and had unfinished private business. At the beginning of 1914 Henry Pindell of Illinois was confirmed by the Senate, but he had to resign when it was disclosed that he planned to stay only a few months. William Sharp of Ohio was then suggested—until Bakhmetev reminded Secretary of State William Jennings Bryan that he had been a leading voice of the abrogation movement.[329] Sharp went to France instead. At last, in June 1914, California banker George Marye, without any diplomatic or Russian experience, was assigned to the Russian court. Over a year and a half had passed without a full-fledged American representative in Russia. The Wilson administration's Russian policy was not off to an auspicious start.

In most other respects it was business as usual in Russian-American relations. American meddling in Russian religious affairs seemed to have few if any repercussions. The influential New York Baptist minister Robert Mac-Arthur came and went with only a grumble from Guild: "As usual the entire body of worshippers in all countries leave all other Embassies alone in order to make trouble for this one."[330] The Congregational Anglo-American

327. To his sister, 22 December 1912 and 11 March 1913, and to his brother Courtney, 15 March 1913, Guild Papers, BPL.

328. To his sister, 22 March 1913, Guild Papers, BPL.

329. Bakhmetev to Sazonov, 22 January/4 February 1914, f. 133, op. 470, d. 308; and 19 June/2 July 1914 enclosing copy of Bryan to Bakhmetev, 22 June 1914, f. 133, op. 470, d. 312, AVPR.

330. Guild to his sister, 3 January 1912, Guild Papers, BPL.

church under the venerable Alexander Francis quietly continued its missionary outreach activities. American Methodist pastor George Simonds expanded from his bridgehead in Finland to St. Petersburg in 1913.[331] Furthermore, the Russian government and Orthodox church were grateful for the American assistance in removing troublesome religious sects such as the Dukhobors and Molokans from Russia.

The American YMCA in Russia continued to build from its base in St. Petersburg. Inaugurated in 1900 by Franklin Gaylord and Clarence Hicks as the "Society for Cooperating with St. Petersburg Young Men in the Attainment of Moral and Physical Development," the organization proudly hosted rounds of American and Russian associates.[332] With the patronage of James Stokes and the support of Francis and Westinghouse director William E. Smith, the periodical *Mayak* was published and a building was purchased in 1905. The association had at first accepted Jews, but now ejected them; similarly, a number of radicals were forced to leave the membership after 1905.[333] Still, the organization flourished and expanded with the backing of influential Russian clergymen, such as Father John of Kronstadt. During 1909–1913, there were even large evangelistic meetings conducted by John R. Mott, Sherwood Eddy, and others in St. Petersburg and Moscow.[334]

Military relations remained cordial for the most part. Although a visit to the United States by the Russian navy to reciprocate the American one of 1911 was postponed indefinitely, the armored cruiser *Rossiia* arrived at Newport News for repairs during the 1913–1914 winter. Bakhmetev considered that the desertion of 8 sailors of the 868-man crew "due to Jewish propaganda" was relatively minor and less than the average for visiting foreign naval ships.[335]

Attaché Averill continued to enjoy access to offices and information,

331. Leslie Marshall, *The Romance of a Tract and Its Sequel: The Story of an American Pioneer in Russia and the Baltic States* (Riga: Latvian Farmers' Union, 1928), pp. 18–22.

332. William Lyon Phelps, *Autobiography with Letters* (New York and London: Oxford University Press, 1939), pp. 522–28.

333. Ethan T. Colton, *Forty Years with Russians* (New York: Association Press, 1940), pp. 14–16.

334. Ibid., pp. 17–20; C. Howard Hopkins, *John R. Mott, 1865–1955: A Biography* (Grand Rapids, Mich.: William B. Eerdmans, 1979), pp. 332–35. In the United States, ironically, the Russian Orthodox church was accused of preventing Americanization as well as the forced conversion of non-Orthodox Slavs. "Russia's Conspiracy Against Americanizing Aliens," *New York Times*, 16 March 1913, sec. 6, p. 14.

335. To Sazonov, 22 January/4 February 1914, f. 133, op. 470, d. 308, AVPR.

which he employed in his many detailed reports.[336] The number and intensity of Russian military missions to the United States still enticed American business, despite some second thoughts about revealing military secrets.[337] The Russian army, for example, was interested in the invention of Edward Acheson, a former associate of Thomas Edison, who produced a form of graphite called "Oildag" that could lubricate rifles and other weapons. Vladimir Kovalevskii invited him to address the Imperial Russian Technological Society in early 1913.[338] Feted by what he referred to as an "Arabian Night Fairy Tale," he was won over to the manufacture of graphite in Russia for military and naval use. "Little does the outside world at large appreciate Russia, at least so far as it is represented in St. Petersburg, and as I now know it to be."[339] Although "Oildag" was widely distributed in Russia, Acheson did not establish a subsidiary there because of apparent misunderstandings over financing and a falling-out with his European agent.[340]

Russian-American business, trade, and manufacturing, in general, advanced in volume and variety in the last years before the Great War, spearheaded by the new factory of International Harvester. More than compensating for the economic effects of abrogation were rapidly increasing American international market penetration and simultaneous strains in relations between Russia and its chief trading partner, Germany. Among others, the Russian-American Chamber of Commerce not only effectively promoted such a shift but through the Guchkov connection managed to moderate considerably the anti-American rhetoric in the Duma.[341]

In early 1914 Secretary of State Bryan, with Russian blessings, issued a call for a third international peace conference to meet in 1915. Charles Wilson, chargé in St. Petersburg, thought the time was propitious to propose a new treaty, "chiefly due to the very unsatisfactory relations, both commer-

336. For example, "The Real Condition of the Russian Army," 20 August 1913, War College Division General Correspondence, 6566-24, box 127, RG 165, NA. This was fourteen pages of general observation, but other reports were more detailed and some over fifty pages in length. For listing, see War College Division Record Cards, box 7 and 13, RG 165, NA.

337. Major Crawford to Colonel Golejewski, 31 December 1913, War College Division General Correspondence, 7636-19, box 128, RG 165, NA.

338. Acheson to Vladimir Kovalevskii, 8 January 1913, box 26, Acheson Papers, LC.

339. Acheson to Kovalevskii, February 1913, box 27, ibid.

340. James Vickery (European agent) to Acheson, 16 and 23 May 1913, and enclosed copy of Vickery to Colonel Bianchi, 23 May 1913, box 27; Acheson to Kovalevskii, 3 February 1914, box 28, Acheson Papers, LC.

341. Snodgrass to Bryan, 25 February 1914, DPR, Russia, vol. 4, (Moscow cons.), RG 84, NA.

cial and political, now existing between Germany and Russia."[342] The State Department responded that a new commercial treaty was in fact under consideration.[343] Both countries, however, became engrossed in other affairs—Mexico, the Balkans, the visit of the French president to Russia—and nothing was done before the series of events leading to world war began in June and July.

342. Wilson to Bryan, 17 April 1914, DPR, Russia, vol. 284, RG 84, NA.
343. Lansing to Charles Wilson, 15 May 1914, ibid.

Conclusion:
Concord or Conflict

During the fifty-year period before World War I, the Russian-American relationship had grown and matured. Until the 1880s harmony and friendship prevailed, swept along by a sense of mutual interest and common destiny. The progressive reform era of Alexander II corresponded to Reconstruction and economic expansion in the United States. The peopling of the plains introduced yet another reflective image, and the identification with steppeland Russia was highlighted by direct transfer of people and seeds from one to the other. At the same time, advocates of more rapid social and political change from a new class of radical intelligentsia in Russia took America as a model, and a few even traveled to the United States to experiment or see for themselves.

After the assassination of Alexander II, the resulting conservative reaction, and the wave of pogroms in Jewish settlements, a more critical American view of Russia emerged, reinforced by the Jewish emigration and by the exposure of the harsh conditions of political exile in Siberia. George Kennan quickly won a number of converts to his morally correct crusade for civil rights in Russia, and together they called for the overthrow of the existing regime, the creation of a "New Russia." In like manner, the Russian revolutionary movement was nurtured and strengthened by American sympathy and support.

At the same time Russian literature, music, and art became popular in the United States, attracting the admiration of many for the creative genius of Russians of various political and social views. The impression of rapid industrialization and development, symbolized by the beginning of construction on the Trans-Siberian Railroad, revived the sense of a common geopolitical destiny. Countering this perception was the conflict and competition that arose over East Asia at the turn of the century. When aggressive Russian actions resulted in war—and then revolution—in 1905, many Americans sided with Japan and the revolutionaries.

Russians and Americans were mutually impressed with the size and scale of their sister country; the problems and the potential of each seemed to dwarf those of other nations. Like the tale of the blind men groping an elephant and coming to drastically different conclusions, Russian and America perspectives varied considerably. A common American view saw Russia being Americanized, especially through the East: "For Siberia, somewhat relieved from the deadening bonds of autocratic officialdom, is teaching individual resourcefulness and independence through its vast plains, dense forests, lofty mountains, and great rivers. Slowly but surely the fuller, freer life of Asiatic Russia is bringing into higher and harmonious relations with its environment the godlike soul of man."[1]

Others saw new market opportunities for American manufactured goods such as sewing machines and agricultural implements, which in turn prompted some Russian officials to extol the American economic model. The Russian policy of denying visas to many American Jews who wanted to go to Russia, no matter how legally defensible, led to anti-Russian agitation and the embarrassing process of abrogating the commercial treaty of 1832. Many Russians, in and out of the government, felt betrayed by their old friends. The familial ties between Russia and the United States, having become closer, were now in danger of breaking up. Yet continuing common interests in business and culture resulted more in wounded alienation than active feuding.

The most serious American observers considered Russia a mystery, one that held them in a certain fascination and awe but also produced frustration. As a student of Russian explained to Samuel Harper, "Do you not realize that even a chance acquaintance with Russia means an indissoluble bond, for Russia is magnetic, one has to return to her."[2] But Russia often seemed annoyingly unpredictable. Harper himself commented, "There is something in Russia that seems to operate against sustained effort—that is why the Russians are always just doing and never pulling off."[3] Or perhaps the closer the examination, the more blurred the image became.

One reason for the perplexity is that most Americans encountering Rus-

1. A. W. Greely, "The Land of Promise," *National Geographic Magazine* 23, 11 (November 1912): 1090.

2. Esther Smith (St. Petersburg) to Harper, 23 January 1907, box 1, file 7, S. Harper Papers, University of Chicago.

3. Harper to his mother, 24 January 1914, box 2, file 1, ibid. Or, as a lady friend wrote, "In Russia I feel as though I were on an entirely different planet. . . . seichas demain, zavtra jamais [now is tomorrow, tomorrow is never]." Elizabeth Reynolds (Rapallo) to Harper, 8/21 February 1914, ibid.

sians were from the broad middle-class, while few Russians were cut from the same mold. One visitor emphasized this:

> The non-existence of the so-called bourgeois class is very noticeable in Moscow. There are the well-to-do, who ride in droschkies and dine and wine at luxurious restaurants. And there are the proletarians, who work and walk, and who gather by the hundreds in the smoke-filled cafes to eat bread and sausages and to drink kvass, beer and vodka. But the great gulf between these two is not bridged, as in other countries, by the middle class, who live comfortably on moderate incomes and by their thrift and industry become owners of a little property.[4]

Others remarked about the irony of autocracy coupled with much less prudish censorship than in the United States, a laxity repellent to Americans ranging from socialists to Christian missionaries.[5]

The American answers to the old question "Whither Russia?" were thus divided into three views: that Russia was on the road to reform and development along the American model, toward a United States of Russia; that Russia was hopelessly mired in reactionary policies and practices for which the only solution was revolution; that Russia somehow was different socially and culturally and would find its separate and unique destiny and could be appreciated for its distinctness. On the latter Ambassador Guild wrote, "I have grown very fond of Russia and of its people. They are utterly different. Their methods of life are not the same, but the *plain people* are *kind* and, after all, that is the principal thing."[6]

Similarly, Russian views of America had separated into three basic categories: that the United States was the most appropriate model for liberal political reform and/or economic development—*Amerikanizm*—and that American practices and policies could be used, selectively or wholesale, in overcoming backwardness; that American sympathy and direct and indirect support could help spark and sustain a *Russian* revolution, which might or might not fulfill American expectations; that close relationships with or influences from the United States, as the most extreme of the West, were a dangerous threat to Russia, in terms of its culture and its political and social

---

4. Jared Waterbury Scudder, *Russia in the Summer of 1914: With Discussions of Her Pressing Problems* (Boston: Richard G. Badger, 1920), p. 145.

5. For example, Nevin O. Winter, *The Russian Empire of To-Day and Yesterday* (London: Simpkin, Marshall, Hamilton, Kent, 1914), p. 262.

6. To his sister, 10 August 1912, Guild Papers, BPL.

aspirations. And finally, among non-Russians rose the dream that American democratic ideals and ethnic consciousness could assist the realization of territorial independence and the breakup of the empire.

Americans seemed genuinely confused about how to react to these mutually exclusive perceptions; drawn to the American people, Russians did not know exactly how to take America as a nation. As Joseph Goodrich observed, "Russians love the Americans, but they are too apt to hate America. . . . As individuals, they find us companionable, liberal, sympathetic, and appreciative; as representatives of a government so diametrically opposed to their own ideals, they cannot bring themselves to approve of us whole-heartedly."[7] These perspectives, so contradictory in many respects, left the way open for disparate responses and for an even more complex relationship through the approaching turmoil of war and revolution.

7. Goodrich, *Russia in Europe and Asia* (Chicago: A. C. McClurg, 1912), p. 2.

Appendix A

American Ministers and Ambassadors in Russia

Name	Tenure	Former Position	Later Position
Cassius Clay 1810–1903 (Kentucky)	1861–1862, 1863–1869	None	None
Andrew Curtin 1817–1894 (Pennsylvania)	1869–1872	Governor	Congressman
James Orr 1822–1873 (South Carolina)	1872–1873	Governor	None
Marshall Jewell 1825–1883 (Connecticut)	1873–1874	Governor	None
George Henry Boker 1823–1890 (Pennsylvania)	1875–1878	Minister, Ottoman Empire	None
Edwin Wallace Stoughton 1818–1882 (New York)	1878–1879	Businessman	None
John Watson Foster 1836–1917 (Indiana)	1880–1881	Minister, Mexico	Secretary of State
William Henry Hunt 1823–1884 (Louisiana)	1882–1884	Cabinet	None
Alphonso Taft 1810–1891 (Ohio)	1884–1885	Minister, Austria	None
George Van Ness Lothrop 1817–1897 (Michigan)	1885–1887	Publisher	Publisher
Lambert Tree 1832–1910 (Illinois)	1889	Judge	Judge
Charles Emory Smith 1842–1908 (Pennsylvania)	1890–1892	Publisher	Publisher
Andrew Dickson White 1832–1918 (New York)	1892–1894	College president	Ambassador, Germany
Clifton Rodes Breckinridge 1846–1932 (Arkansas)	1894–1897	Congressman	None
Ethan Allen Hitchcock 1854–1914 (Missouri)	1897–1898	Business	Cabinet
Charlemagne Tower 1848–1923 (Pennsylvania)	1899–1902	Ambassador, Austria-Hungary	Ambassador, Germany
Robert S. McCormick 1849–1919 (Illinois)	1903–1905	Ambassador, Austria-Hungary	Ambassador, France
George von Lengerke Meyer 1858–1918 (Massachusetts)	1905–1907	Ambassador, Italy	Cabinet
John Wallace Riddle 1864–1941 (Minnesota)	1907–1909	Secretary, Russia	Army

William W. Rockhill 1854–1914 (Pennsylvania)	1909–1911	Minister, China	Ambassador, Turkey
Curtis Guild 1860–1915 (Massachusetts)	1911–1913	Governor	None

Appendix B

Russian Ministers and Ambassadors to the United States

Name	Tenure	Former Position	Later Position
Eduard Stoeckl	1854–1868	Secretary	None
Konstantin Katakazi 1830–1890	1869–1871	Foreign Ministry	None
Heinrich Offenberg 1821–1888	1872–1875	Minister, Rumania	None
Nikolai Shishkin 1830–1912	1875–1880	Minister, Serbia	Minister, Greece
Mikhail Bartolomai 1836–1895	1880–1882	Minister, Greece	Minister, Japan
Karl Struve 1835–1907	1882–1892	Minister, Japan	Ambassador, Netherlands
Grigori Kantakuzen 1843–1902	1892–1895	None	Minister, Württemburg
Ernst Kotzebue 1838–1914	1895–1897	Minister, Württemburg	None
Arthur Cassini 1835–?	1897–1905	Minister, China	Ambassador, Spain
Roman Rosen 1847–1921	1905–1911	Minister, Japan	State Council
Georgi Bakhmetev 1848–1928	1911–1917	Minister, Japan	None

Appendix C

Foreign Ministers/U.S. Secretaries of State, 1867–1914

Foreign Ministers of Russia

Alexander Gorchakov	1856–1882
Nikolai Giers	1882–1895
Aleksei Lobanov-Rostovsky	1895–1896
Mikhail Murav'ev	1896–1900
Vladimir Lamzdorf	1900–1906
Alexander Izvolsky	1906–1910
Sergei Sazonov	1910–1916

U.S. Secretaries of State

William H. Seward	1861–1869
Elihu Washburne	1869
Hamilton Fish	1869–1877
William M. Evarts	1877–1881
James G. Blaine	1881
Frederick Frelinghuysen	1881–1885
Thomas F. Bayard	1885–1889
James G. Blaine	1889–1892
John W. Foster	1892–1893
Walter Q. Gresham	1893–1895
Richard Olney	1895–1897
John Sherman	1897–1898
William R. Day	1898
John Hay	1898–1905
Elihu Root	1905–1909
Robert Bacon	1909
Philander C. Knox	1909–1913
William J. Bryan	1913–1915

Appendix D

Secretaries of Legation and Consuls in Russia

Secretaries of Legation

Name	Date	Official Residence
Jeremiah Curtin	1865–1869	Wisconsin
Titian Coffey	1869–1870	Pennsylvania
Eugene Schuyler	1870–1876	New York
Hoffman Atkinson	1876–1877	West Virginia
Wickham Hoffman	1877–1884	New York
George Wurts	1884–1893	Pennsylvania
Creighton Webb	1893–1896	New York
Herbert H. D. Pierce	1895–1898	Massachusetts
Herbert Hagerman	1898–1901	Massachusetts
John Riddle	1901–1903	Minnesota
Spencer Eddy	1903–1906	Illinois
Montgomery Schuyler, Jr.	1907–1909	New York
Post Wheeler	1909–1912	Washington
Charles S. Wilson	1912–1914	Maine

American Consuls

Name	Date	Official Residence
St. Petersburg, Consuls General		
George Pomutz	1865–1878	Iowa
George Henry Prince (interim)	1875–1877	St. Petersburg
William Henry Edwards	1878–1880	Ohio
Gaun M. Hutton (interim)	1879–1883	St. Petersburg
Edgar Stanton	1881–1885	Illinois
George Dobson (interim)	1883–1885	St. Petersburg
Pierce M. B. Young	1885–1887	Georgia
James V. R. Swann (interim)	1885–1886	St. Petersburg
George Osgood Prince (interim)	1886–1887	St. Petersburg
William Henry Dunster (interim)	1887–1897	St. Petersburg
Charlton H. Way	1887–1889	Georgia
John M. Crawford	1889–1894	Ohio
Charles Jonas	1894	

John Karel	1894–1897	Illinois
William R. Holloway	1897–1903	Indiana
Ethelbert Watts	1903–1907	
John Mueller (interim)	1902–1906	St. Petersburg
Jacob Conner (consul)	1908–1914	

Moscow

John P. Hatterscheidt	1861–1867	Kansas
Riker Fitzgerald	1865	Pennsylvania
James Wentworth	1866	Missouri
Samuel P. Young	1867	New York
Eugene Schuyler	1867–1869	New York
George T. Allen	1869–1870	Illinois
Samuel P. Young	1870–1878	Moscow
Robert P. Wilson	1879–1880	Pennsylvania
August Weber	1880–1882	Moscow
Eccles J. Van Riper	1882–1886	Moscow
N. W. Hornstedt	1887–1888	England
Nicholas Wertheim	1889–1891	Moscow
N. W. Hornstedt	1892–1893	Moscow
Adolph Billhardt	1894–1897	Ohio
Thomas and Samuel Smith	1897–1906	New Jersey and Moscow
John Snodgrass, consul general	1906–1914	

Odessa

Timothy C. Smith	1866–1874	Vermont
Leander Dyer	1875–1881	Tennessee
Fulton Paul	1882–1884	New York
George Scott	1884	Nebraska
Thomas E. Heenan	1885–1906	Minnesota
Alfred W. Smith	1906–1908	Odessa
John H. Grout	1908–1914	

Riga

Alexander Schwartz	1824–1872	Riga
Nils Peter Bornholdt	1890–1906	Riga
Herman Schoenfeld	1895	New York
Charles Schulin (interim)	1900–1906	Riga
Alexander Heingarten	1906–1910	Riga
Hernando de Soto	1910	Warsaw
William F. Doty	1910–1913	St. Petersburg
Douglas Jenkins	1913–1914	

Reval

Henry Stacey	1867–1869	Vermont
Waldemar Mayer	1868	Reval
Samuel D. Jones	1869	New York
Eugene Schuyler	1869–1870	New York
Christian Rotermann	1910–1914	Reval

Warsaw

Joseph Rawicz	1875–1901	Warsaw
Boleslaw Horodynski	1901–1902	Warsaw
Hernando de Soto	1902–1904	
Clarence R. Slocum	1903–1905	
Albert Leffinwell	1905–1906	
Thomas E. Heenan	1906–1910	Odessa
Hernando de Soto	1910–1914	Warsaw

Helsingfors

Reynold Frenckell	1850–1878	Helsingfors
Herman Donner	1879–1897	Helsingfors
Victor Ek	1898–1914	Helsingfors

Batum

James C. Chambers	1890–1904	New York
William H. Stuart	1904–1906	England
Frederick Cauldwell	1907–1911	Pennsylvania
Leslie Davis	1911–1913	
F. Willoughby Smith	1913–1914	Odessa

Amur, Commercial Agency and Petropavlovsk, commecial agents

Henry W. Hiller	1867–1868	Massachusetts
O. S. Smith	1869–1870	
H. G. O. Chase	1871–1872	Massachusetts
Enoch Emery	1873	Massachusetts
Henry W. Hiller	1873	Massachusetts

Vladivostock, commercial agents

Richard Greener	1898–1905	Pennsylvania
Roger S. Greene	1905–1908	
Harold F. New Hard	1909–1911	
? Maynard	1911–1914	

Bibliography

Manuscripts and Unpublished Sources

Arkhiv Vneshnoi Politiki Rossii [AVPR], Moscow
    fond 133, kantselariia
    fond 138, sekretnyi
    fond 170, posol'stvo v Vashingtone
Boston Public Library [BPL]
    Curtis Guild Papers
    Eugene Schuyler letter
California Historical Society [CHS], San Francisco
    Alaska Commercial Company Minutes
    William H. Ennis Papers
Chicago, University of, Regenstein Library, Manuscript Department
    Samuel Harper Papers
    William Rainey Harper Papers
Chicago Historical Society [ChicagoHS]
    Ralph Isham Papers
    Edwin Lobdell Papers
Columbia University Library, Manuscript Division
    Moncure Conway Correspondence
    Charles R. Crane Papers, Bakhmetev Archive [BA]
    William Eleroy Curtis Papers
    Frederick Holls Papers
    George W. Perkins Papers
    Montgomery Schuyler Papers
    Frank Vanderlip Papers
    Sergei Witte Papers
Cornell University Library
    George Burr Papers
    Ralph Catterall Diary
    Andrew Dickson White Papers
Duke University Library, Manuscript Department
    Anonymous Diary, 1878
    Nathan Appleton Papers
    Turin Bradford Boone Diary
    G. Hope Chamberlain Papers
    Francis Warrington Dawson Papers
    Garwood Papers
    Ramsay Papers
Gosudarstvennoi Arkhiv Rossiskoi Federatsii [GARF; TsGAOR], Moscow
    fond 641, Empress Mariia Aleksandrovna Papers
    fond 678, Alexander II Papers

fond 828, Gorchakov Papers
Harvard University
  Baker Library, Manuscript Department
    Augustus Heard Company Papers
  Houghton Library
    Autograph File—George Boker letter
    Curtis Guild Papers
    Charles Norton Papers
    William Rockhill Papers
    William Stedman Collection
  Radcliffe College, Women's Archive
    Louise Stoughton Diary
Hoover Presidential Library, West Branch, Iowa
  Herbert Hoover Papers, Pre-Commerce
Howard University Library, Washington, D.C.
  Richard Greener Papers
Huntington Library, San Marino, Calif.
  Walter Schuyler Papers
  Anna Strunsky Walling Papers
Iowa State Historical Society [ISHS], Des Moines
  Iowa State Famine Relief Committee
  Benjamin Tillinghast Papers
Jackson County Historical Society, Independence, Mo.
  Simon Few Papers
Library of Congress [LC], Manuscript Division
  Edward Acheson Papers
  Henry T. Allen, Jr., Papers
  George L. Anderson Papers
  Alexis Babine Papers
  Wharton Barker Papers
  Clara Barton Papers
  Anson Burlingame Papers
  Peter Demens Papers
  Hamilton Fish Papers
  John W. Foster Papers
  William Dudley Foulke Papers
  Harry A. Garfield Papers
  Elijah Halford Papers
  Norman Hapgood / Reynolds Family Papers
  Burton Harrison Papers
  John Hay Papers
  William Hunt Papers
  George Kennan Papers
  George Kunz Papers
  McCook Family Papers
  Alfred von Lengerke Meyer Papers
  John Callan O'Laughlin Papers
  Theodore Roosevelt Papers
  Elihu Root Papers
  Eugene Schuyler Letterbook
  Philip Sheridan Papers

William T. Sherman Papers
William S. Sims Papers
William Howard Taft Papers
Talmage Papers
William Allen White Papers
James Wilson Papers
Lincoln Memorial University, Harrogate, Tenn.
Cassius Clay Papers
Massachusetts Historical Society [MassHS], Boston
R. L. Dabney Diaries
Theodore Dwight Autograph Collection
Curtis Guild misc.
George von Lengerke Meyer Papers
William Washburn Papers, Cassius Clay letter
Milwaukee County Historical Center Library [MCHC], Milwaukee
Jeremiah and Alma Curtin Papers
Minnesota Historical Society [MinnHS], St. Paul
Hascal Russell Brill Papers
William C. Edgar Papers
Hamilton Fish file
Frank T. Heffelfinger Papers
William Lochren Family Papers
Alexander Ramsay Papers
Stanley Washburn Papers
William Windom Papers
Raphael Zon Papers
Missouri, State Historical Society of [SHSM], Columbia
Margaret Rogers Diary
Edward Rollins Papers
Missouri, State Historical Society of, Kansas City
Mary Dwight Eamon Bright Journal
Mystic Seaport Library, Mystic, Conn.
Henry Hiller Papers
National Archives [NA], Washington, D.C.
Record Group 16, Department of Agriculture
Records of the Office of Secretary of Agriculture
Record Group 24, Records of the Bureau of Naval Personnel
Ship Logbooks
Record Group 38, Navy Department
Office of Naval Operations, Office of Naval Intelligence (attaché reports)
Record Group 54, Department of Agriculture
Expedition Reports, Bureau of Plant Industry [BPI] (M 840)
Record Group 59, Department of State
Decimal Files, 1910–1929, Records Relating to the Internal Affairs of Russia and the Soviet Union [DFIA] (M 316)
Decimal Files, 1910–1929, Records Relating to the Political Relations with Russia and the Soviet Union [DFPR] (M 333)
Despatches from United States Consuls [DUSC]: St. Petersburg (M 81); Moscow (M 456); Odessa (M 459); Warsaw (M 467); Batum (M 482); Reval (M 484); Riga (M 485); Vladivostok (M 486); Petropavlovsk (T 104); Amur (T 111)
Despatches from United States Ministers [DUSM], Russia (M 35)

Diplomatic Instructions [DI] (M 77)
Notes from Foreign Legations, Russia [NRL] (M 39)
Notes to Foreign Legations [NFL] (M 99)
Numerical and Minor Files, 1906–1910 [NMF] (M 862)
Record Group 80, Department of the Navy
    General Records of Navy Department
Record Group 84, Department of State
    Diplomatic Post Records [DPR], Russia, American Legation, Embassy and Consulates, 1867–1914
Record Group 165, War Department
    War College Division General Correspondence and Record Cards
Record Group 200, Gifts
    American Red Cross Papers
Record Group 261, State Department
    Records of Russian Consulates in the United States (M 1486)
Record Group 316, Special Gifts
    Ethan Allen Hitchcock Papers
New-York Historical Society [NYHS]
    Hoyt and Meacham Papers
New York Public Library [NYPL], Manuscript Division
    Robert Bonner Papers
    William Frey Papers
    Francis Greene Papers
    Isabel Hapgood Papers
    George Kennan Papers
    Frederic Remington Papers
    Mary Stoughton Diary
Newberry Library, Chicago
    Carter Harrison Papers
    William V. Judson Papers
    Lambert Tree Papers
North Carolina, University of [UNC], Southern Collection, Chapel Hill
    James Orr Papers
    Phillips-Meyers Papers (George Kennan)
Oregon, University of, Eugene
    Henry B. Miller Papers
Pennsylvania, Historical Society of [HSP], Philadelphia
    Thomas Willing Balch Papers
    Society Misc.—Blankenburg Papers
Princeton Theological Seminary, Speer Library
    Samuel Prime Diary
Rochester, University of, Rush-Rhees Library
    George Kennan Papers
    William H. Seward Papers
    Henry Augustus Ward Papers
Russian National Library, Moscow
    Mikhail Katkov Papers
Smithsonian Institution Archives [SA]
    William H. Dall Papers
    Record Group 26, Secretary's Correspondence, 1853–1889, Incoming
    Record Group 31, Records of the Office of Secretary, 1866–1927

Record Group 33, Secretary's Correspondence, 1889–1930, Outgoing
    Western Union Telegraph Expedition Collection
South Carolina, University of [USC], South Caroliniana Library, Columbia
    Joseph Hofmann Papers
    Seibels typescript memoir
Vermont, University of, Burlington
    Sarah Hagar Papers
Virginia, University of, Barrett Library, Charlottesville
    Barrett Collection—Walt Whitman draft
    Richard Harding Davis Papers
Wisconsin, State Historical Society of [SHSW], Madison
    George L. Anderson Papers
    Jeremiah Curtin Papers
    DeWitt Clinton Poole Papers
    McCormick Company Papers [McC]
    International Harvester Company Papers [IH]
    Singer Sewing Machine Company Papers

Published Documents and Reference Sources

Ahlborn, Richard Eighme, and Vera Beaver-Bricken Espinola, eds. *Russian Copper Icons and Crosses from the Kunz Collection: Castings of Faith.* Smithsonian Studies in History and Technology, no. 51. Washington, D.C.: Smithsonian Institution Press, 1991.
Alaska Boundary Tribunal: The Case of the United States. Washington, D.C.: Government Printing Office, 1903.
Amburger, Erik. *Geschichte der Behördenorganisation Russlands von Peter dem Grossen bis 1917.* Leiden: E. J. Brill, 1966.
Annuaire diplomatique de l'empire de Russia. Vols. 6–20. St. Petersburg: Journal de St.-Petersbourg, 1867–1885.
Aziatskaia Rossiia. 2 vols. St. Petersburg: Resettlement Directorate, 1914.
Babey, Anna. *Americans in Russia, 1776–1917: A Study of the American Travelers in Russia from the American Revolution to the Russian Revolution.* New York: Comet Press, 1938.
Baedeker, Karl. *Russland: Handbuch fur Reisende.* Leipzig: Baedeker, 1888, 1892.
[Barker, Wharton, comp.] *Reports and Correspondence Relating to Projected Coal and Iron Industries in Southern Russia.* Philadelphia: By author, c. 1880.
Bograd, V. E. *Zhurnal "Otechestvennye zapiski," 1868–1884: Ukazatel' soderzhaniia.* Moscow: Kniga, 1971.
Bolkhovitinov, N. N., ed. *Russia and the United States: An Analytical Survey of Archival Documents and Historical Studies.* Trans. and ed. J. Dane Hartgrove. Armonk, N.Y.: M. E. Sharpe, 1986.
Bolkhovitinov, N. N., et al., eds. *Istoriia vneshnei politiki i diplomatii SShA, 1775–1877.* Moscow: Mezhdunarodnye otnosheniia, 1994.
Bradley, Claudia, et al., comps. *List of Logbooks of U.S. Navy Ships, Stations, and Miscellaneous Units, 1801–1947.* Washington, D.C.: National Archives and Records Service, 1978.
British Documents on Foreign Affairs, Reports and Papers from the Foreign Office Confidential Print. Series A, part I: *Russia, 1859–1914.* Bethesda, Md.: University Publications of America, 1990.

Commercial Relations of the United States: Reports from the Consuls of the United States on the Commerce, Manufacturing, etc. of Their Consular Districts. Washington, D.C.: Government Printing Office, 1870–1914 [CR].

DeArmond, R. N., ed. *Lady Franklin Visits Sitka, Alaska 1870.* Anchorage: Alaska Historical Society, 1981.

Fetridge, W. Pembroke. *Harper's Hand-Book for Travellers in Europe and the East . . . in Three Volumes.* 17th ed. New York: Harper and Bros., 1878.

Fla, S. Simsova, ed. *Lenin, Krupskaia and Libraries.* London: Clive Bingley, n.d.

Gaylord, Franklin. *The Builders of the Atoll and Other Poems.* New Haven, Conn.: Tuttle, Morehouse and Taylor, 1934.

Giliarovskii, Vladimir Alekseevich. *Sochineniia.* 4 vols. Moscow: Pravda, 1968.

Golder, Frank A. *Guide to Materials for American History in Russian Archives.* 2 vols. Washington, D.C.: Carnegie Institution, 1917, 1937.

Grant, Steven A., comp. *Scholar's Guide to Washington, D.C., for Russian/Soviet Studies.* 2d ed., rev. Bradford Johnson and Mark Teeter. Washington, D.C.: Smithsonian Institution Press, 1983.

Grant, Steven A., and John H. Brown, comps. *Russian Empire and Soviet Union: A Guide to Manuscripts and Archival Materials in the United States.* Kennan Institute for Advanced Russian Studies, Wilson Center Publication. Boston: G. K. Hall, 1981.

Hamersly, Lewis R. The Records of Living Officers of the U.S. Navy and Marine Corps. Rev. ed. Philadelphia: J. B. Lippincott, 1870.

Hapgood, Isabel. *The Epic Songs of Russia.* New York: Scribner's, 1886.

Honcharenko, Agapius. *Russian and English Phrase Book.* San Francisco, Calif.: A. Roman, 1868.

Karlowich, Robert A., comp. Guide to Scholarly Resources on the Russian Empire and the Soviet Union in the New York Metropolitan Area. Social Science Research Council Publication. Armonk, N.Y., and London: M. E. Sharpe, 1990.

Kirillov, Aleksandr. *Geografichesko-statisticheskii slovar' Amurskoi i primorksoi oblastei.* Blagoveshchensk: D. O. Moken, 1894.

"K istorii pervoi Gaagskoi konferentsii 1899 g." *Krasnyi Arkhiv* 50–51 (1932): 36–40.

Klaus, A. A. *Nashi kolonii: Opyty i materialy po istorii i statistike inostrannoi kolonizatsii v Rossii.* St. Petersburg: Nusvalt, 1869.

Libman, Valentina Abramovna. *Amerikanskaia literatura v Russkikh perevodakh i kritike bibliografiia 1776–1975.* Moscow: Nauka, 1977.

———, comp. *Russian Studies of American Literature: A Bibliography.* Trans. Robert V. Allen. Chapel Hill: University of North Carolina Press, 1969.

McCully, Newton A. *The McCully Report: The Russo-Japanese War, 1904–1905.* Ed. Richard von Doenhoff. Annapolis, Md.: Naval Institute Press, 1977.

McGraw-Hill Encyclopedia of Russia and the Soviet Union. Ed. Michael T. Florinsky. New York: McGraw-Hill, 1961.

Making Things Work: Russian-American Economic Relations, 1900–1930. Stanford, Calif.: Hoover Institution Press, 1992

Mironenko, S. V., comp. *Dekabristy: Biograficheskii spravochnik.* Moscow: Nauka, 1988.

Modern Encyclopedia of Russian and Soviet History. Ed. Joseph L. Wiecynski. 56 vols. Gulf Breeze, Fla.: Academic International Press, 1976–.

Nerhood, Harry W., comp. *To Russia and Return: An Annotated Bibliography of Travelers' English-Language Accounts of Russia from the Ninth Century to the Present.* Columbus: Ohio State University Press, 1968.

Papers Relating to the Foreign Relations of the United States. Washington, D.C.: Government Printing Office, 1867–1914 [PRFRUS].

Reinsch, Paul Samuel. *World Politics at the End of the Nineteenth Century.* London: Macmillan, 1900.

Russia in the Twentieth Century: The Catalogue of the Bakhmeteff Archive of Russian and East European History and Culture. Columbia University Library Publication. Boston: G. K. Hall, 1987.

Russkii biograficheskii slovar'. 25 vols. St. Petersburg: Lissner i Sovko, 1896–1914.

Sbornik glavneishikh offitsial'nykh dokumentov po upravleniiu Vostochnoiu Siber'iu. 4 vols. Irkutsk: I. P. Sinitsyn, 1882.

Schroeder, William, and Helmut T. Huebert. *Mennonite Historical Atlas.* Winnepeg, Manitoba: Springfield Publishers, 1990.

Scott, Leroy. *The Shears of Destiny* [novel]. New York: Doubleday, Page, 1910.

Semevskii, M. I. *Znakomye: Al'bom M. I. Semevskago, 1867–1888.* St. Petersburg: Russkaia Starina, 1888.

"Severno-Amerikanskie Soedinennye Shtaty i tsarskaia Rossiia v 90–kh gg. XIX v." *Krasnyi Arkhiv* 52 (1932): 125–42.

Shavit, David. *United States Relations with Russia and the Soviet Union: A Historical Dictionary.* Westport, Conn.: Greenwood Press, 1993.

"S. Iu. Vitte, frantsuzskaia presa i russkie zaimy." *Krasnyi Arkhiv* 10 (1925): 36–40.

Skal'kovskii, Konstantin. *Russkaia torgovlia v Tikhom Okeane.* St. Petersburg: Suvorin, 1883.

Southern, Eileen. *Biographical Dictionary of Afro-American and African Musicians.* Westport, Conn.: Greenwood Press, 1982.

Stoddard, John Lawson. *John L. Stoddard Lectures.* 10 vols. Boston: Balch Bros., 1898.

Tauer, Sharlemain [Charlemagne Tower]. *Katalog russkikh knig prinesennyi v dar universitetu v Pennsil'vanii.* St. Petersburg: N.p., 1902.

Ukhtomskii, Esper. *Puteshestvie na vostok ego Imperatorskago vysochestva gosudaria naslednika tsesarevicha, 1890–1891.* 6 vols. St. Petersburg and Leipzig: Brokgauz, 1893–1897.

Voeikov, Aleksandr Ivanovich. *Izbrannye sochineniia.* Vol. 1. Ed. A. A. Grigor'ev. Moscow-Leningrad: Nauka, 1948.

Wheeler, Post. *Russian Wonder Tales.* New York: Century, 1912.

Zhuravlev, V. I., ed. " 'Eto vopros ne politiki, eto vopros gumannosti': dokumenty o pomoshchi amerikanskogo naroda vo vremia goloda v Rossii 1891–1892 gg." *Istoricheskii Arkhiv: Nauchno-Publikatorskii Zhurnal* 1 (1993): 194–209.

Published Memoirs, Diaries, and Other Primary and Contemporary Materials

Abbott, Lyman. *Impressions of a Careless Traveller.* New York: Outlook, 1909.

Adams, Henry. *The Education of Henry Adams: An Autobiography.* Boston: Houghton Mifflin, 1918.

Addams, Jane. "Recent Picture of Tolstoy in Peasant Dress." *Craftsman* 10, 1 (April 1906): 88.

———. *Twenty Years at Hull House with Autobiographical Notes.* New York: Macmillan, 1914.

Aldrich, Herbert L. *Arctic Alaska and Siberia, or Eight Months with the Arctic Whalemen.* Chicago: Rand, McNally, 1889.

Alexsander Mikhailovich, Grand Duke. *Once a Grand Duke.* New York: Farrar and Rinehart, 1932.

Allen, Thomas G., "The Khodinsky Disaster." *Bachelor of Arts* 3, 4 (October 1896): 490–96.

Allen, Thomas G., and William Lewis Sachtleben. *Across Asia on a Bicycle: The Journey of Two American Students from Constantinople to Peking.* New York: Century, 1897.

"Amerikanki razlichnykh sloev (lichnyia nabliudeniia russkoi)." *Ustoi* 1 (December 1881): 1–39.

Armstrong, W. J. *Siberia and the Nihilists: Why Kennan Went to Siberia.* Oakland, Calif.: Pacific Press, 1890.

Babine, Alexis V. *The Yudin Library, Krasnoiarsk.* Washington, D.C.: By author, 1905.

Ballou, Maturin M. *Due North, or Glimpses of Scandinavia and Russia.* Boston: Ticknor, 1887.

Barker, Rear Admiral Albert S. *Everyday Life in the Navy.* Boston: Richard G. Badger, 1928.

Barker, Wharton. "The Secret of Russia's Friendship." *Independent* 56, 2886 (24 March 1904): 645–49.

Barrows, Isabel C. *A Sunny Life: The Biography of Samuel June Barrows.* Boston: Little, Brown, 1913.

Barry, Herbert. *Ivan at Home, or Pictures from Russian Life.* London: Publishing Company, 1872.

———. *Russia in 1870.* London: Publishing Company, 1871.

Barton, Clara. *The Red Cross: A History of This Remarkable International Movement in the Interest of Humanity.* Washington, D.C.: American National Red Cross, 1898.

Bates, Lindon, Jr. *The Russian Road to China.* Boston: Houghton Mifflin, 1910.

Bayne, Samuel Gamble. *Derricks of Destiny: An Autobiography.* New York: Brentano's, 1924.

Bell, Lilian. "Lilian Bell on the Russian Frontier." *Ladies Home Journal* 15, 7 (June 1898).

Beveridge, Albert. *The Russian Advance.* New York: Harper, 1904.

Bigelow, John. *Reflections of an Active Life.* 5 vols., New York: Baker and Taylor, 1909–1913.

Bigelow, Poultney. *The Borderland of Czar and Kaiser: Notes from Both Sides of the Russian Frontier.* New York: Harper and Bros., 1895.

———. *Seventy Summers.* 2 vols. New York: Longmans, Green, 1925.

Blum, Emil. "Russia of To-Day." *Arena* 3, 17 (May 1891): 658–73.

Boardman, Mabel T. *Under the Red Cross Flag at Home and Abroad.* Philadelphia and London: J. B. Lippincott, 1915.

Bobrinskoi, Andrei. "Amerikanskaia pomoshch' v 1892 i 1893 godakh." *Russkii Vestnik* 39, 2 (February 1894): 252–54.

Bogoraz, Vladimir Germanovich. *The Folklore of Northeastern Asia as Compared with That of Northwestern America.* New York: G. P. Putnam's Sons, 1902.

Bookwalter, John Wesley. *Siberia and Central Asia.* New York: Frederick A. Stokes, 1899.

Botkine, Pierre [Petr Botkin]. "A Voice for Russia." *Century* 45, 4 (February 1893): 611–15.

Bouton, John Bell. *Roundabout to Moscow: An Epicurean Journey.* New York: D. Appleton, 1887.

Brodhead, Jane M. N. *Slav and Moslem: Historical Sketches.* Aiken, S.C.: Aiken Publishing Company, 1894.

Brown, Arthur Judson. *Russia in Transformation.* New York.: Fleming H. Revell, 1917.

Browne, J. Ross. *The Land of Thor.* New York: Harper and Bros., 1870.

Bryan, William Jennings. *The Memoirs of William Jennings Bryan.* Philadelphia: United Publishers, 1925.

Buckley, James Monroe. *The Midnight Sun, the Tsar and the Nihilist: Adventures and Observations in Norway, Sweden and Russia.* Boston: D. Lothrop, 1886.

Buel, James W. *A Nemesis of Misgovernment*. Philadelphia: Historical Publishing Co., 1900.

_____. *Russian Nihilism and Exile Life in Siberia*. St. Louis: Historical Publishing Company, 1883.

Buell, Augustus C. *The Memoirs of Charles H. Cramp*. Philadelphia and London: J. B. Lippincott, 1906.

Bullard, Arthur. "The Social Revolution in Russia." *Independent* 60, 2982 (25 January 1906): 192–95.

Butin, Mikhail D. *Pis'ma iz Ameriki*. St. Petersburg: Demakov, 1872.

Butterfield, Julia, ed. *A Biographical Memorial of General Daniel Butterfield Including Many Addresses and Military Writings*. New York: Grafton Press, 1904.

Cahan, Abraham. "Jewish Massacres and the Revolutionary Movement in Russia." *North American Review* 560 (July 1903): 49–62.

Cantacuzene, Countess Speransky nee Grant. *My Life Here and There*. New York: Charles Scribner's Sons, 1922.

Cary, Clarence. *The Trans-Siberian Route, or Notes of a Journey from Peking to New York in 1902*. New York: Evening Post, 1902.

Catacazy, M. de [Konstantin Katakazi]. *Un incident diplomatique: Lettre au Chief Justice S. Chase*. Paris: Arnyot, 1872.

Charykov [Tcharykow], Nikolai V. *Glimpses of High Politics: Through War and Peace, 1855–1929*. London: George Allen and Unwin, 1931.

Cherevkova, A. A. "Chikago (iz puteshestvia po Amerike)." *Russkaia Mysl'* 23, 11 (November 1902): pt. 2, 35–55; "Niagra-Niu-Iork." *Russkaia Mysl'* 23, 12 (December 1902): pt. 2, 133–56.

Child, Theodore. *The Tsar and His People, or Social Life in Russia*. New York: Harper and Bros., 1891.

Christian, R. F., ed. *Tolstoy's Letters*. New York: Charles Scriber's Sons, 1978.

Clark, Rev. Francis E. *A New Way Around an Old World*. New York and London: Harper and Bros., 1901. Reprinted as *The Great Siberian Railway: What I Saw on My Journey*. London: S. W. Partridge, 1904.

Clark, John Spencer, ed. *The Life and Letters of John Fiske*. 2 vols. Boston: Houghton Mifflin, 1917.

Clay, Cassius Marcellus. *The Life of Cassius Marcellus Clay: Memoirs, Writings, and Speeches*. Cincinnati: J. Fletcher Brennan, 1886.

Cockrell, Ewing. "Travel in Russia: Three Thousand Miles for Fifteen Dollars." *Outing* 39, 5 (February 1902): 564–69.

Colton, Ethan T. *Forty Years with Russians*. New York: Association Press, 1940.

Conway, Moncure Daniel. *Autobiography: Memories and Experiences*. 2 vols. Boston: Houghton Mifflin, 1904.

Coolidge, Archibald Cary. "A Plea for the Study of the History of Northern Europe." *American Historical Review* 2, 1 (October 1896): 34–39.

Cox, Samuel Sullivan. *Arctic Sunbeams: or From Broadway to the Bosphorus by Way of the North Cape*. New York: Putnam's, 1882.

_____. *Diversions of a Diplomat in Turkey*. New York: Charles L. Webster, 1893.

Crawford, Laura MacPherson. *Dear Family: The Travel Letters and Reminiscences of Laura MacPherson Crawford*. Ed. Ruth Saunders. Claremont, Calif.: Privately Published, 1946.

Cruger, Mary Van Rensselaer [Julienne Gordon]. *Diplomat's Diary*. Philadelphia: Lippincott's, 1890.

Curtin, Jeremiah. *A Journey in Southern Siberia*. Boston: Little, Brown, 1909.

_____. *Memoirs of Jeremiah Curtin.* Ed. Joseph Schafer. Wisconsin Biography Series no. 2. Madison: State Historical Society of Wisconsin, 1940.

Curtis, William Eleroy. *Around the Black Sea: Asia Minor, Armenia, Caucasus, Circassia, Daghestan, the Crimea, Roumania.* New York: Hodder and Stoughton, 1911.

_____. *Turkestan: "The Heart of Asia."* New York: Hodder and Stoughton, 1911.

Cushman, Mary Ames. *She Wrote It All Down.* New York: Charles Scribners' Sons, 1936.

Cutting, Charles F. *Glimpses of Scandinavia and Russia.* Boston: Thomas Groom, 1887.

Cyon, Elie de. *Histoire de l'entente Franco-Russe, 1886–1894: Documents et souvenirs.* Paris: A. Charles, 1895.

Dall, William H. *Alaska and Its Resources.* Boston: Lee and Shepard, 1870.

Dana, Charles A. *Eastern Journeys: Some Notes of Travel in Russia, in the Caucasus and to Jerusalem.* New York: D. Appleton, 1898.

Davis, Richard Harding. *Adventures and Letters of Richard Harding Davis.* Ed. Charles Belmont Davis. New York: Charles Scribner's Sons, 1918.

Debogorii-Mokrievich, Vladimir. *Vospominaniia.* Paris: J. Allemane, 1894.

De Long, Emma. *Explorer's Wife.* New York: Dodd, Mead, 1938.

De Long, George Washington. *The Voyage of the Jeannette: The Ship and Ice Journals.* Ed. by Emma De Long. Boston: Houghton Mifflin, 1883.

Demens, Peter. *See* Tverskoi, Petr.

De-Vollan, Grigorii. *V strane miliardov i demokratii: Ocherki i zametiki.* St. Petersburg-Moscow: M. O. Vol'f, 1907.

De Windt, Harry. *Siberia As It Is.* London: Chapman and Hall, 1892.

Dixon, William Hepworth. *Free Russia.* New York: Harper and Bros., 1870.

Dole, Nathan Haskell. "A Plea for the Study of Russian." *Harvard Graduate's Magazine* 3, 10 (December 1894): 180–85.

Durland, Kellogg. "The Kronstadt Fiasco." *Independent* 61, 3019 (11 October 1906): 864–67.

_____. *The Red Reign: The True Story of an Adventurous Year in Russia.* New York: Century, 1908.

Edgar, William C. *The Russian Famine of 1891 and 1892.* Minneapolis: Millers and Manufacturers Insurance, 1893.

Fell, E. Nelson. *Russian and Nomad: Tales of the Kirghiz Steppe.* New York: Duffield, 1916.

Feoktistov, Evgenii M. *Vospominaniia E. M. Feoktistova: Za kulisami politiki i literatury, 1848–1896.* Ed. Iu G. Oksman. Leningrad: Priboi, 1929. Reprint. Newtonville, Mass.: Oriental Research Partners, 1975.

Fischer, Henry W. *Abroad with Mark Twain and Eugene Field: Tales They Told to a Fellow Correspondent.* New York: Nicholas Brown, 1922.

Fisk, Ethel F., comp. *The Letters of John Fiske.* New York: Macmillan, 1940.

Flint, Charles R. *Memories of an Active Life: Men, and Ships, and Sealing Wax.* New York and London: G. P. Putnam's Sons, 1923.

Ford, Alexander Hume. "America's Agricultural Regeneration of Russia." *Century* 62 (August 1901): 501–7.

_____. "Engineering Opportunities in the Russian Empire." *Engineering Magazine* 21, 1 (April 1901): 29–42.

_____. "Russia as a Market for Machinery and Machine Tools." *Engineering Magazine* 21, 4 (July 1901): 493–507.

_____. "Russia's Field for Anglo-Saxon Enterprise in Asia." *Engineering Magazine* 19, 3 (June 1900): 354–72.

Foster, John Watson. *Diplomatic Memoirs.* 2 vols. Boston: Houghton Mifflin, 1909.

Foulke, William Dudley. *A Hoosier Autobiography.* New York: Oxford, 1922.

Francis, Alexander. *Americans: An Impression.* London: Andrew Melrose, 1909.

Franklin, S. R. *Memoirs of a Rear-Admiral.* New York and London: Harper and Bros., 1898.

Geins, V. K. "Prezidentskaia kampaniia v Amerike: Poiavlenie tret'ei partii." *Otechestven-nyia Zapiski* 230, 2 (February 1877): 415–53.

Gilder, William H. *Ice-Pack and Tundra: An Account of the Search for the Jeannette and a Sledge Journey Through Siberia.* London: Sampson Low, Marston, Searle, and Rivington, 1883.

Gillin, Arnold. *Otgoloski novago sveta: Razskazy i ocherky iz Amerikanskoi zhizni.* St. Petersburg: Slavianskoi pechetnaia, 1879.

Gillis, Charles J. *A Summer Vacation in Iceland, Norway, Sweden and Russia.* New York: J. J. Little, 1898.

Gleaves, Rear Admiral Albert, ed. *The Life of an American Sailor: William Helmsley Emory, from His Letters and Memoirs.* New York: George H. Doran, 1923.

Gore, Alain. "Six Months in a Country House in Russia." *Lippincott's Magazine* 27 (March 1881): 252–60.

Gorky, Maxim. *The City of the Yellow Devil: Pamphlets, Articles and Letters About America.* Moscow: Progress Publishers, 1972.

Gowing, Lionel F. *Five Thousand Miles in a Sledge.* New York: D. Appleton, 1890.

Grant, Julia Dent. *The Personal Memoirs of Julia Dent Grant.* Ed. John Y. Simon. New York: G. P. Putnam's Sons, 1975.

Gray, Alice. "My Russian Friends." *Galaxy* 13, 2 (February 1872): 229–37.

Greene, Francis V. *Report on the Russian Army and Its Campaigns in Turkey in 1877–1878.* 2 vols. New York: D. Appleton, 1879.

———. *Sketches of Army Life in Russia.* New York: Charles Scribner's Sons, 1880.

Grosvenor, Edwin A. "Siberia." *National Geographic Magazine* 12, 9 (September 1901): 317–24.

Guild, Curtis. *Britons and Muscovites, or Traits of Two Empires.* Boston: Lee and Shepard, 1888.

Gurko, Vladimir. *Features and Figures of the Past: Government and Opinion in the Reign of Nicholas II.* Hoover Library Publication no. 14. Stanford, Calif.: Stanford University Press, 1939.

Hadley, James Albert. "A Royal Buffalo Hunt." *Transactions of the Kansas State Historical Society, 1907–1908* 10 (1908): 569–80.

Hagerman, Herbert J. *Letters of a Young Diplomat.* Santa Fe, N.Mex.: Rydal Press, 1937.

Hammond, John Hays. *The Autobiography of John Hays Hammond.* 2 vols. New York: Farrar and Rinehart, 1935.

Hapgood, Isabel. "Harvest-Tide on the Volga." *Atlantic Monthly* 69, 413 (March 1892): 314–27.

———. "A Journey on the Volga." *Atlantic Monthly* 69, 412 (February 1892): 231–40.

———. "My Experience with the Russian Censor." *The Nation* 51, 1321 (23 October 1890): 318–21.

———. "Passports, Police, and Post Office in Russia," *Atlantic Monthly* 72, 420 (July 1893): 42–49.

———. "A Russian Professorship." *Nation* 54, 1407 (16 June 1892): 447.

———. *Russian Rambles.* Boston: Houghton Mifflin, 1895.

———. "Up the Volga." *Chautauquan* 36, 4 (January 1903): 370–88.

Harper, Samuel Northrop. *The Russia I Believe In: The Memoirs of Samuel Northrop Harper.* Ed. Paul V. Harper. Chicago: University of Chicago Press, 1945.

Harrison, H. Carter. *A Race with the Sun.* New York: Putnam's, 1889.

Heath, Perry S. *A Hoosier in Russia: The Only White Tsar—His Imperialism, Country and People.* New York: Lorborn Publishing, 1888.

Hill, Ebenezer. "A Trip Through Siberia." *National Geographic Magazine* 13, 2 (February 1902): 36–54.

Hoffman, Wickham. *Leisure Hours in Russia*. London: George Bell and Sons, 1883.

Holls, Frederick W. *The Peace Conference at The Hague*. New York: Macmillan, 1900.

Holmes, Burton. *Travelogues*. Vol. 8. New York: McClure, 1910.

Honeyman, A. V. D., ed. *From America to Russia in the Summer of 1897*. Plainfield, N.J.: Honeyman, 1897.

Hoover, Herbert. *The Memoirs of Herbert Hoover*. Vol. 1, *The Years of Adventure, 1877–1920*. New York: Macmillan, 1951.

Horton, George. *Recollections Grave and Gay: The Story of a Mediterranean Consul*. Indianapolis: Bobbs-Merrill, 1927.

Hovey, Esther Lancraft. "The Old Post-Road from Tiflis to Erevan." *National Geographic Magazine* 12, 8 (August 1901): 300–309.

Howe, M. A. DeWolfe. *George von Lengerke Meyer: His Life and Public Services*. New York: Dodd, Mead, 1920.

Hume, George. *Thirty-Five Years in Russia*. London: Simpkin, Marshall, Hamilton, Kent, 1914.

Huntington, Ellsworth. *The Pulse of Asia: A Journey in Central Asia Illustrating the Geographic Basis of History*. Boston: Houghton Mifflin, 1907.

Ianzhul, Ivan. *Vospominaniia I. I. Ianzhula o perezhitom i vidennom v 1864–1909 gg*. 2 vols. St. Petersburg: Stoikovyi, 1910–1911.

Iswolsky [Izvolsky], Alexander. *Recollections of a Foreign Minister*. Garden City, N.Y.: Doubleday, Page, 1921.

[Ivaniukov, Ivan] "Iz Ameriki, pis'mo pervoe." *Otechestvennyia Zapiski* 179, 8 (August 1868): 180–86.

Jackson, Sheldon. *Alaska and Missions on the North Pacific Coast*. New York: Dodd, Mead, 1880.

———. *Tenth Annual Report on Introduction of Reindeer into Alaska . . . 1900*. Washington, D.C.: Government Printing Office, 1901.

Kalmykow, Andrew D. *Memoirs of a Russian Diplomat: Outposts of the Empire, 1893–1917*. New Haven, Conn.: Yale University Press, 1971.

Kellogg, Clara Louise. *Memoirs of an American Prima Donna*. New York and London: G. P. Putnam's Sons, 1913.

Kennan, George. "The Mountains and Mountaineers of the Eastern Caucasus." *Journal of the American Geographical Society of New York* 5 (1874): 169–93.

———. *Siberia and the Exile System*. Reprint. New York and London: Praeger, 1970.

———. "Siberia—The Exiles' Abode." *Journal of the American Geographical Society of New York* 14 (1882): 13–68.

———. *Stepnaia zhizn v Sibiri: Stranstviia mezhdu koriakami i drugami plemenami Kamchatki i Severnoi Azii*. St. Petersburg: M. Khana, 1871.

———. *Tent Life in Siberia and Adventures Among the Koraks and Other Tribes in Kamchatka and Eastern Siberia*. New York: G. P. Putnam's Sons, 1870.

———. "A Voice for the People of Russia: A Reply to 'A Voice for Russia'." *Century* 46, 3 (July 1893): 461–72.

Ker, David. *Cossack and Czar*. New York: Tait, 1893.

———. *From the Hudson to the Neva*. Boston: D. Lothrop, 1883.

———. *On the Road to Khiva*. London: Henry S. King, 1874.

Kirill Vladimirovich, Grand Duke. *My Life in Russia's Service—Then and Now*. London: Selwin and Blount, 1939.

Knox, Thomas W. *The Boy Travellers in the Russian Empire.* New York: Harper and Bros., 1886.

———. *Overland Through Asia: Pictures of Siberian, Chinese, and Tartar Life.* Chicago: F. S. Gilman, 1870.

———. "Siberian Exiles." *Atlantic Monthly* 22, 131 (September 1868): 273–85.

———. *The Siberian Exiles.* New York: R. Bonner's Sons, 1893.

Kokovtsov, Vladimir N. *Iz moego proshlago: Vospominaniia 1903–1919.* 1933. Reprint. The Hague: Mouton, 1969.

———. *Out of My Past: The Memoirs of Count Kokovtsov.* Trans. Laura Matveev. Hoover War Library Publication no. 6. Stanford, Calif.: Stanford and Oxford University Press, 1935.

Kovalevskii, Maksim M. "American Impressions." *Russian Review* 10, 1–3 (January, April, July 1951): 37–45, 106–17, 176–84.

Kravchinskii, Sergei [Stepniak]. *The Russian Storm-Cloud.* New York: Harper and Bros., 1886.

———. *Russia Under the Tzars.* New York: Charles Scribner's Sons, 1885.

Kurbskii, A. S. *Russkii rabochii u Amerikanskago planatatora.* St. Petersburg: A. Khomikovskii, 1875. Serialized in *Vestnik Evropy,* 1873.

Lamzdorf, Vladimir. *Dnevnik, 1891–1892.* Ed. F. A. Rotshtein. Moscow-Leningrad: Academia, 1934.

Lansdell, Henry. *Through Siberia.* 3d ed. Boston: Houghton Mifflin, 1882.

Lee, Helen C. [Mrs. John Clarence]. *Across Siberia Alone: An American Woman's Adventures.* New York: John Lane, 1914.

Leland, Charles G. *Memoirs.* New York: D. Appleton, 1893.

Leland, Lilian. *Traveling Alone: A Woman's Journey Around the World.* New York: American News, 1890.

Letters from Theodore Roosevelt to Anne Roosevelt Cowles, 1879–1918. New York and London: Charles Scribner's Sons, 1924.

Life and Letters of Edward Everett Hale. 2 vols. Boston: Little, Brown, 1917.

Linden, Lieutenant. "Zametki o Kalifornii i Sandvichevykh ostrovakh." *Morskoi Sbornik* 118, 1 (January 1872): 75–95.

Lineva, Evgeniia. *Russian Folk-Songs as Sung by the People.* Chicago: C. F. Summy, c. 1893.

Lodian, L. "Railway Notes from the Ural Range." *Cassier's Magazine* 18, 3 (July 1900): 188–94.

Logan, John A., Jr. *In Joyful Russia.* New York: D. Appleton, 1897.

Lopukhin, Aleksandr. *Religii v Amerike.* St. Petersburg: Dobrodeev, 1882.

———. *Zhizn' za okeanom.* St. Petersburg: Dobrodeev, 1881.

Lothrop, Almira. *The Court of Alexander III: Letters of Mrs. Lothrop.* Ed. William Prall. Philadelphia: John C. Winston, 1910.

Low, A. Maurice. "Russia, England, and the United States." *Forum* 28 (September 1899): 172–77.

Lukanina, Adelaida N. "God v Amerike: Iz vospominanii zhenshchiny-medika." *Vestnik Evropy* 16, 8 (August 1881): 621–66; 16, 9 (September 1881): 31–78; 17, 4 (April 1882): 495–538.

McCagg, Ezra Butler. *Six Weeks of Vacation in 1883.* Chicago: McDonnell Bros., 1884.

McClure, Alexander K. *Recollections of Half a Century.* Salem, Mass.: Salem Press, 1902.

McClure, Alfred J. P. "The Siberian Exile Petition Movement of Philadelphia." *Century* 40, 4 (August 1890): 636–37.

McCormick, Frederick. *The Tragedy of Russia in Pacific Asia.* 2 vols. New York: Outing, 1907.

MacGahan, Barbara. *Xenia Repnina: A Story of Russia To-day* [novel]. New York and London: George Routledge and Sons, 1890.

MacGahan, Januarius. *Campaigning on the Oxus, and the Fall of Khiva.* New York: Harper and Bros., 1874.

Maclay, Edgar Stanton. *Reminiscences of the Old Navy: From the Journals and Private Papers of Captain Edward Trenchard, and Rear Admiral Stephen Decatur Trenchard.* New York and London: G. P. Putnam's, 1898.

Mahan, Alfred Thayer. *Letters and Papers of Alfred Thayer Mahan.* Ed. Robert Seager II and Doris D. Maguire. 4 vols. Annapolis, Md.: Naval Institute Press, 1975.

Meakin, Annette M. B. *Russia: Travels and Studies.* Philadelphia: J. B. Lippincott, 1906.

Mears, John Henry. *Racing the Moon (and Winning).* New York: Rae D. Hinkle, 1928.

Melville, George W. *In the Lena Delta: A Narrative of the Search for Lieut.-Commander De Long and His Companions.* Boston: Houghton Mifflin, 1885.

Mendeleev, Dmitri. "Neftanaia promyshlennost' v Severo-Amerikanskom shtate Pensil'vanii i na Kavkaze." In *Sochineniia*, vol. 10. Leningrad-Moscow: Nauka, 1949.

Meriwether, Lee. *A Tramp Trip: How to See Europe on Fifty Cents a Day.* New York: Harper and Bros., 1887.

Michael, Louis Guy. *More Corn for Bessarabia: Russian Experience 1910-1917.* East Lansing: Michigan State University Press, 1983.

Michie, Peter S. *The Life and Letters of Emory Upton.* New York: D. Appleton, 1885.

Miles, Nelson A. *Military Europe: A Narrative of Observations and Personal Experience.* New York: Doubleday and McClure, 1898.

——. *Serving the Republic: Memoirs of the Civil and Military Life of Nelson A. Miles.* Reprint. Freeport, N.Y.: Books for Libraries Press, 1971.

Miliukov, Pavel [Paul]. *Vospominaniia, 1859-1917.* 2 vols. Moscow: Sovremennik, 1990.

——. *Political Memoirs, 1905-1917.* Ed. Arthur Mendel. Ann Arbor: University of Michigan Press, 1967.

Moore, Benjamin Burgess. *From Moscow to the Persian Gulf: Being the Journal of a Disenchanted Traveller in Turkestan and Russia.* New York and London: Putnam's, 1915.

Morley, Henry, ed. *Sketches of Russian Life Before and During the Emancipation of the Serfs.* London: Chapman and Hall, 1866.

Mott, T. Bentley. *Twenty Years as Military Attaché.* New York and London: Oxford University Press, 1937.

Murray, Robert H. *Around the World with Taft: A Book of Travel, Description, History.* Detroit, Mich.: F. B. Dickerson, 1909.

Nekliudov, A. V. *Diplomatic Reminiscences Before and During the War, 1911-1917.* London: John Murray, 1920.

Newcomb, Simon. *The Reminiscences of an Astronomer.* Boston: Houghton Mifflin, 1903.

Newton, William Wilberforce. *A Run Through Russia: The Story of a Visit to Count Tolstoi.* Hartford, Conn.: Student Publishing, 1894.

Noble, Edmund. "The Future of Russia." *Atlantic Monthly* 76, 517 (November 1900): 606-16.

——. *Russia and the Russians.* Boston: Houghton Mifflin, 1900.

——. "Russia's Holy City." *Chautauquan* 36, 5 (February 1903): 475-90.

Noble, Lydia Pimenov. *Before the Dawn: A Story of Russian Life.* Boston: Houghton Mifflin, 1901.

Norman, Henry. *All the Russias: Travels and Studies in Contemporary European Russia, Finland, Siberia, the Caucasus, and Central Asia.* New York: Scribner's, 1903.

Norton, Charles Eliot. *Letters of Charles Eliot Norton.* Ed. Sara Norton and M. A. DeWolfe Howe. 2 vols. Boston: Houghton Mifflin, 1913.

Ogg, Frederic Austin. "The Rise of the Russian Nation." *Chautauquan* 36, 3 (December 1902): 239–52.

Ogorodnikov, Pavel. *Ot N'iu Iorka do San' Frantsisko i obratno v Rossiiu.* St. Petersburg: Kolesov and Mikhin, 1872.

_____. *V Strane svobody.* 2 vols. 2d ed. St. Petersburg: Rossiiskoi bib., 1882.

Orbinskii, Robert. *Iz otcheta R. V. Orbinskogo o nastoiashchem polozhenii khlebnogo vyvoza iz Odessy.* Odessa: N.p., 1881.

_____. *Ot Khlebnoi torgovlie Soedinennykh Shtatov Severnoi Ameriki.* St. Petersburg: Trenke i Fusno, 1880.

Panafidine, Emma Cochrane. *Russia—My Home: An Intimate Record of Personal Experiences Before, During and After the Bolshevist Revolution.* Indianapolis: Bobbs-Merrill, 1931.

Pangbourne [Pangborn], Major [Joseph Gladding]. *Side Lights on Management World Systems Railways.* 2d ed. Baltimore, Md.: By author, 1901.

Pennell, Joseph. *The Jew at Home: Impressions of a Summer and Autumn Spent with Him.* New York: D. Appleton, 1892.

Phelps, William Lyon. *Autobiography with Letters.* New York and London: Oxford University Press, 1939.

Pierce, Herbert H. D. "The Mujik and the New Regime in Russia." *Atlantic Monthly* 97 (January 1906): 101–9.

_____. "Russia." *Atlantic Monthly* 90, 540 (October 1902): 465–74.

Poole, Ernest. *The Bridge: My Own Story.* New York: Macmillan, 1940.

_____. " 'Peasant Cattle': What the Cossacks Think of the Peasants." *Everybody's Magazine* 13, 4 (October 1905): 494–504.

Popov, P. I. *V Amerike: Ocherki Amerikanskoi zhizne, po lichnym nabliudeniiam avtora, prozhivshago v Amerike bezvyezdno dvadtsat'-tri goda (1872–1895).* St. Petersburg: Feniks, 1906.

Praisa, G. M. [George Moses]. *Russkie Evrei v Amerike: Ocherki iz istorii zhizni i byta russko-evreiskikh emigrantov v Soedinennykh Shtatakh Sev. Ameriki s 1881 g. po 1891 g.* St. Petersburg: Landau, 1893.

Pravdin, Evgenyi. "Novorozhdennyi messianizm strany dollara i staryi svet (sotsiologicheskii ocherk)." *Istoricheskii Vestnik,* 74, 11 (November 1898): 704–21.

_____. "Ocherki Amerikanskoi deiatel'nosti: Pravosudie v strane svobody." *Istoricheskii Vestnik* 20, 2 (February 1899): 656–78.

Preston, Harriet Waters. "The Spell of Russian Writers." *Atlantic Monthly* 60, 358 (August 1887): 199–213.

Prime, Samuel Irenaeus. *The Alhambra and the Kremlin: The South and the North of Europe.* New York: Anson D. F. Randolph, 1873.

Prime, Wendell, ed. *Samuel Irenaeus Prime: Autobiography and Memorials.* New York: Anson D. F. Randolph, 1888.

Proctor, Edna Dean. "Moscow and Southern Russia." *Scribner's Monthly* 5, 6 (April 1873): 669–84.

_____. *A Russian Journey.* Boston: James R. Osgood, 1872.

Purington, Chester Wells. "The Gold Mines of Siberia." *Engineering Magazine* 21, 6 (September 1901): 891–903.

_____. *Sluicing at the Kolchan Mines, East Siberia.* San Francisco, Calif.: Mining and Scientific Press, 1911.

Reeves, Francis B. *Russia Then and Now, 1892–1917: My Mission to Russia During the Famine of 1891–1892 with Data Bearing upon Russia To-Day.* New York and London: Putnam's, 1917.

Roberts, James Hudson. *A Flight for Life and an Inside View of Mongolia.* Boston: Pilgrim Press, 1903.

Rogers, Mrs. William Barton, ed. *Life and Letters of William Barton Rogers.* Vol. 2. Boston: Houghton Mifflin, 1896.

Rosen, Baron Roman. *Forty Years of Diplomacy.* 2 vols. New York: Alfred A. Knopf, 1922.

Sands, William Franklin. *Undiplomatic Memories: The Far East, 1896–1904.* London: John Hamilton, n.d.

Savage, Richard Henry. *My Official Wife: A Novel.* New York: Home Publishing, 1891.

Sazonov, Sergei. *Fateful Years, 1909–1916: The Reminiscences of Sergei Sazanov.* London: J. Cape, 1928.

_____. *Vospominaniia.* Moscow: Mezh. ot., 1991.

Schaeffer, Evelyn Schuyler. "A Ship-Load of Iowa Corn." *New Peterson Magazine* 1, 5 (May 1893): 472–77.

Schuyler, Eugene. *Selected Essays.* New York: Scribner's, 1901.

_____. *Turkistan: Notes of a Journey in Russian Turkistan, Khokan, Bukhara, and Kuldja.* 2 vols. New York: Scribner, Armstrong, 1877.

Scudder, Jared Waterbury. *Russia in the Summer of 1914: With Discussions of Her Pressing Problems.* Boston: Richard G. Badger, 1920.

Selfridge, Thomas O., Jr. *Memoirs of Thomas O. Selfridge, Jr.* New York and London: G. P. Putnam's, 1924.

Senn, Nicholas. *Around the World via Siberia.* Chicago: W. B. Conkey, 1902.

Sessions, Francis. *From the Land of the Midnight Sun to the Volga.* New York: Welch, Fracker, 1890.

Sherman, William T. "Extracts from the Diary of General W. T. Sherman." *Century* 57, 6 (April 1899): 866–75.

Shoemaker, Michael. *The Great Siberian Railway: From St. Petersburg to Pekin.* New York and London: G. P. Putnam's, 1903.

Simonin, Louis Laurent. *The Rocky Mountain West in 1867.* Trans. and annotated by Wilson O. Clough. Lincoln: University of Nebraska Press, 1966.

Simpson, Eugene E. *Travels in Russia 1910 and 1912.* Taylorville, Ill.: By author, 1916.

Skal'kovskii, Konstantin. *V strane iga i svoboda: Putevyia vpechatleniia.* St. Petersburg: Obshchestvennaia pol'za, 1878.

Slavinskii, Nikolai. *Pis'ma ob Amerike i Russkikh pereselentsakh.* St. Petersburg: P. P. Merkulev, 1873.

Smith, Charles Emory. "The Famine in Russia." *North American Review* 154, 426 (May 1892): 541–51.

_____. "Russia." *National Geographic Magazine* 16, 2 (February 1905): 55–63.

_____. "The Young Czar and His Advisers." *North American Review* 458 (January 1895): 21–28.

Solov'ev, Iurii. *Dvadtsat' piat' let moei diplomaticheskoi sluzhby (1893–1918).* Moscow-Leningrad: Gosizdat, 1928.

Spalding, Henry C. "The Black Sea and the Caspian." *Van Nostrand's Eclectic Engineering Magazine* 15, 92 (August 1876): 122–27.

Start, Edwin A. "Nicholas II of Russia." *Chautauquan* 37, 4 (July 1903): 361–66.

Stead, William T. *Truth About Russia.* London: Cassell, 1888.

Steiner, Edward A. *Tolstoy the Man.* New York: Outlook, 1904.

Stepniak. *See* Kravchinskii, Sergei.

Stoddard, Charles Augustus. *Across Russia: From the Baltic to the Danube.* New York: Charles Scribner's Sons, 1892.

Stone, Melville E. *"M.E.S." His Book: A Tribute and a Souvenir of the Twenty-Five Years*

1893–1918 of the Service of Melville E. Stone as General Manager of the Associated Press. New York and London: Harper and Bros., 1918.

Stoughton, Edwin W. "Popular Fallacies about Russia." *North American Review* 283 (June 1880): 523–46.

Strong, George Templeton. *Diary of George Templeton Strong.* 4 vols. New York: Macmillan, 1952.

Suvorin, A. S. *Dnevnik A. S. Suvorina.* Ed. Mikhail Krichevskii. Moscow-Petrograd: L. D. Frankel', 1923.

Sviatlovskii, Vladimir. "Pis'ma iz Ameriki." *Russkoe Obozrenie* 21, 6 (June 1893): 784–817; 22, 8 (August 1893): 831–42; 23, 4 (September 1893: 327–38; 23, 5 (October 1893): 887–909; 24, 6 (November 1893): 317–45.

Taft, Marcus Lorenzo. *Strange Siberia Along the Trans-Siberian Railway.* New York: Eaton and Mains, 1911.

Taft, William Howard. "Some Impressions of 150,000 Miles of Travel." *National Geographic Magazine* 57, 5 (May 1930): 523–98.

Taft, Mrs. William Howard. *Recollections of Full Years.* New York: Dodd, Mead, 1915.

Talmage, T. De Witt. *T. De Witt Talmage: His Life and Work.* Ed. Louis A. Banks. London: O. W. Binkerd, 1902.

Taube, M. A. *La politique russe d'avant-guerre et la fin de l'empire des tsars, 1904–1917.* Paris: Librairie Ernest Leroux, 1928.

Thayer, William Roscoe. *The Life and Letters of John Hay.* 2 vols. Boston: Houghton Mifflin, 1915.

Thompson, Vance. *Diplomatic Mysteries.* Philadelphia and London: Lippincott, 1905.

Thorndike, Rachel Sherman. *The Sherman Letters: Correspondence between General and Senator Sherman from 1837 to 1891.* New York: Charles Scribner's Sons, 1894.

Tsaknii, Nikolai. "Kartiny polozheniia truda v Soedinennykh Shtatakh." *Slovo* 3, 2–3 (February-March 1880): 23–38.

_____. "Pis'ma ob Amerike." *Slovo* 3, 10 (October 1880): 37–49; 4, 1 (January 1881): 116–30.

Tsimmerman, Eduard R. "Osnovye novykh shtatov v Amerike." *Otechestvennyia Zapiski* 199, 12 (December 1871): 369–402.

_____. *Puteshestvie po Amerike v 1869–1870 g.* Moscow: Grachev, 1871.

_____. *Soedinennye Shtaty Severnoi Ameriki: Iz puteshestvii 1857-58; 1869-70 godov.* Moscow: K. T. Soldatenkov, 1873.

_____. "Stoletniaia godovshchina v S. Amerike: Ocherki iz istorii Soedinennykh shtatov." *Otechestvennyia Zapiski* 225, 4 (May 1876): 667–89; 226, 6 (June 1876): 421–52; 228, 9 (September 1876): 91–120; 228, 10 (October 1876): 549–66; 229, 12 (December 1876): 349–84.

Tucker, William W. *His Imperial Highness the Grand Duke Alexis in the United States of America During the Winter of 1871–1872.* Cambridge, Mass.: Riverside Press, 1872. Reprint. New York: Interland, 1972.

Tverskoi, Petr A. [Peter Demens]. *Ocherki Severo-Amerikanskikh Soedinennykh Shtatov.* St. Petersburg: I. N. Skorokhodov, 1895.

Twain, Mark [Samuel Clemens]. "The Czar's Soliloquy." *North American Review* 580 (March 1905): 321–25.

Vanderlip, Frank A. *From Farm Boy to Financier.* New York and London: Appleton-Century, 1935.

Vanderlip, Washington B. *In Search of a Siberian Klondike.* New York: Century, 1903.

Vatson, Ernst K. *Etiudy i ocherki po obshchestvennym voprosam (s portretom i biografiei avtora).* St. Petersburg: Skorokhodov, 1892.

Verestchagin, Alexander. *At Home and in War, 1853-1881*. New York: Thomas Y. Crowell, 1888.

Vladimirov, M. M. *Russkii sredi Amerikanstsev: Moi lichnyia vpechatleniia kak tokari, chernorabochago, plotnika i puteshestvennika, 1872-1876*. St. Petersburg: Obshchestvennaia pol'za, 1877.

Volkonskii [Wolkonsky], Sergei. *Addresses*. Chicago: J. C. Winship, 1893.

———. *Moi Vospominaniia*. Munich: Mednyi Vsadnik, 192?.

———. *Pictures of Russian History and Russian Literature*. Boston: Lamson, Wolffe, 1897.

Waddington, Mary King. *Letters of a Diplomat's Wife, 1883–1900*. London: Smith, Elder, 1905.

Walling, William English. *Russia's Message: The True World Import of the Revolution*. New York: Doubleday, Page, 1908.

Washburn, Stanley. *The Cable Game: The Adventures of an American Press-Boat in Turkish Waters during the Russian Revolution*. Boston: Sherman, French, 1912.

Weber, John B. *Autobiography of John B. Weber*. New York: J. W. Clement, 1924.

Wellesley, Frederick A. *With the Russians in Peace and War: Recollections of a Military Attaché*. London: Eveleigh Nash, 1905.

Wheeler, William Webb. *The Other Side of the Earth*. St. Joseph, Mo.: Combe Printing, 1913.

Wheelock, Romney. "Russia's Blow at American Commerce." *Gunton's Magazine* 20 (May 1901): 432–40.

White, Andrew Dickson. *Autobiography of Andrew Dickson White*. 2 vols. New York: N.p., 1905.

———. "A Day with Andrew D. White at his Home in Ithaca." *Craftsman* 8, 6 (September 1905): 715–34.

———. *The Diaries of Andrew Dickson White*. Ed. Robert Morris Ogden. Ithaca, N.Y.: Cornell University Library, 1959.

———. "A Statesman of Russia: Constantine Pobedonostzeff." *Century* 56 (1898): 114–16.

Whymper, Frederick. *Travel and Adventures in the Territory of Alaska*. New York: Harper and Bros., 1869.

Williams, Charles Richard, ed. *Diary and Letters of Rutherford Birchard Hayes*. 5 vols. Columbus: Ohio State Archeological and Historical Society, 1926. Reprint. New York: Kraus, 1971.

Witte, Sergei. *The Memoirs of Sergei Witte*. Trans. and ed. Sidney Harcave. Armonk, N.Y.: M. E. Sharpe, 1990.

Wolf, Simon. *The Presidents I Have Known from 1860 to 1918*. 2d ed. Washington, D.C.: Byron Adams, 1918.

Wood, Ruth Kedzie. *The Tourist's Russia*. New York: Dodd, Mead, 1912.

Woodman, Abby Johnson. *Picturesque Alaska*. Boston: Houghton Mifflin, 1889.

Wright, George Frederick. *Asiatic Russia*. 2 vols. New York: McClure, Phillips, 1902.

Wright, Richardson, and Bassett Digby. *Through Siberia: An Empire in the Making*. New York: McBride, Nast, 1913.

Young, Charles C. *Abused Russia*. New York: Devin-Adair, 1915.

Young, John Russell. *Around the World with General Grant: A Narrative of the Visit of General U. S. Grant, ex-President of the United States, to Various Countries in Europe, Asia, and Africa, in 1877, 1878, 1879*. New York: Subscription Book Dept., 1880.

Newspapers and Journals

Abilene *Chronicle*
Amerikanska Rus [American Russia], Allegheny, Pa.

Arena
Army and Navy Journal
Athenaeum: Journal of Literature, Science, the Fine Arts, Music, and the Drama, Boston
Atlantic Monthly
Birzhevnaia Gazeta [Exchange gazette]
Boston *Daily Advertiser*
Boston *Daily Evening Transcript*
Boston *Globe*
Boston *Herald*
Cassier's Magazine
Century
Charleston *Daily Courier*
Chicago *Tribune*
Cleveland *Plain Dealer*
Commonwealth, Boston
Cosmopolitan
Critic
Daily Alta California, San Francisco
Delo [Affair]
Dial
Dwight's Journal of Music
Eclectic Magazine
Engineering Magazine
Everybody's Magazine
Figaro, Paris
Fortnightly Review
Forum
Frank Leslie's Illustrated Newspaper
Golos [Voice], St. Petersburg
Harper's Monthly
Harper's New Monthly Magazine
Harper's Weekly
Hours at Home
Howard County Ledger, Elk Falls, Kansas
Independent
Istoricheskii Vestnik [Historical herald]
Kansas City *Star*
Kansas State Record, Topeka
Krasnyi Arkhiv [Red archive]
Lawrence *Daily Kansas Tribune*
Leavenworth *Times*
Lippincott's Magazine
Living Age
Memphis *Daily Appeal*
Milwaukee *Daily Journal*
Milwaukee *Daily News*
Mobile *Daily Register*
Morskoi Sbornik [Naval journal], St. Petersburg
Moskovskiia Vedomosti [Moscow record]
Munsey's Magazine
Musical Courier

National Geographic Magazine
Nedelia [Week], St. Petersburg
New York *Herald*
New York *Times*
New Orleans *Daily Picayune*
Niva, [Field], St. Petersburg
Norfolk *Virginian*
North American Review
Northwestern Miller, Minneapolis
Novoe Vremia [New Times]
Omaha *Daily Herald*
Osage Chronicle, Burlingame, Kans.
Otechestvennyia Zapiski [Fatherland notes], St. Petersburg
Outing
Outlook
Overland Monthly
Peabody *Gazette*, Kans.
Philadelphia *Inquirer*
Progressive Communist, Cedar Vale, Kans.
Russkie Vedomosti [Russian record]
Russkii Mir [Russian world],St. Petersburg
Russkii Vestnik [Russian herald], St. Petersburg
Russkoe Bogatstvo [Russian wealth]
Russkoe obozrenie [Russian review]
St. Louis *Missouri Republican*
St. Peterburgskiia Vedomosti [St. Petersburg record], St. Petersburg
Scribner's Magazine,
Severnyi Vestnik [Northern herald], St. Petersburg
Slovo [Word], Moscow
Topeka Daily Commonwealth
Ustoi [Foundation], St. Petersburg
Vestnik Evropy [Herald of Europe], St. Petersburg
Washington *Chronicle*
Washington *Evening Post*
Washington *National Republican*
World's Work

Secondary Sources: Background Studies

Altschuler, Glenn C. *Andrew D. White—Educator, Historian, Diplomat.* Ithaca and London: Cornell University Press, 1979.

Ambrose, Stephen E. *Crazy Horse and Custer: The Parallel Lives of Two American Warriors.* Garden City, N.Y.: Doubleday, 1975.

Ananich, Bors. *Bankirskie doma v Rossii 1860–1914 gg.: Ocherki istorii chastnogo predprinimatel'stva.* Leningrad: Nauka, 1991.

Aronson, I. Michael. *Troubled Waters: The Origins of the 1881 Anti-Jewish Pogroms in Russia.* Pittsburgh: University of Pittsburgh Press, 1990.

Babin, Aleksei. *Istoriia Severo-Amerikanskikh Soedinennykh Shtatov.* 2 vols. St. Petersburg: Bashmakov, 1912.

Baltzell, E. Digby. *Philadelphia Gentlemen: The Making of a National Upper Class.* Glencoe, Ill.: Free Press, 1958.

Baron, Salo W. *The Russian Jew Under Tsars and Soviets.* 2d ed. New York: Macmillan, 1964.

Barooshian, Vahan D. *V. V. Vereshchagin: Artist at War.* Gainesville: University of Florida Press, 1993.

Barratt, Glynn. *Russian Shadows on the British Northwest Coast of North America, 1810–1890: A Study of Rejection of Defence Responsibilities.* Vancouver: University of British Columbia Press, 1983.

Batueva, T. M. "Prokhozhdenie dogovora o pokupke Aliaski v kongresse SShA v 1867–1868 gg." *Novaia i Noveishaia Istoriia* 4 (July-August 1971): 120–24.

Becker, William H. "American Manufacturers and Foreign Markets, 1870–1900: Business Historians and the 'New Economic Determinists.'" *Business History Review* 47, 4 (Winter 1973): 466–81.

Beliaev, Nikolai Ivanovich. *Russko-turetskaia voina, 1877–1878 gg.* Moscow: Voenizdat, 1956.

Bennett, Charles Alpheus. *History of Manual and Industrial Education 1870 to 1917.* Peoria, Ill.: By author, 1937.

Beskrovnyi, Liubomir Grigor'evich. *Russkaia armiia i flot v XIX veke.: Voenno-ekonomicheskii potentsial Rossii.* Moscow: Nauka, 1973.

Bestuzhev, I. V. *Bor'ba po voprosam vneshnei politiki v Rossii, 1906–1910.* Moscow: Nauka, 1961.

Billington, James H. *Fire in the Minds of Men: Origins of the Revolutioanry Faith.* New York: Basic Books, 1980.

Blakely, Allison. *Russia and the Negro: Blacks in Russian History and Thought.* Washington, D.C.: Howard University Press, 1986.

Blankenburg, Lucretia Longshore. *The Blankenburgs of Philadelphia, by One of Them.* Philadelphia: John C. Winston, 1929.

Bradley, Edward Sculley. *George Henry Boker, Poet and Patriot.* Philadelphia: University of Pennsylvania Press, 1927.

Bogdanov, S. M. *Zemledelie na Parizhskoi vsemirnoi vystavke 1889 goda.* St. Petersburg: Demakov, 1889.

Bolkhovitinov, N. N. "Obshchestvennost' SShA i ratifikatsiia dogovora 1867 g." *Amerikanskii Ezhegodnik 1987.* Moscow: Nauka, 1987.

Bovykin, V. I. *Formirovanie finansovogo kapital v Rossii konets XIX v-1908 g.* Moscow: Nauka, 1984.

Bowen, Catherine Drinker. *"Free Artist": The Story of Anton and Nicholas Rubenstein.* New York: Random House, 1939.

Bowers, Claude B. *Beveridge and the Progressive Era.* New York: Literary Guild, 1932.

Braisted, William Reynolds. *The United States Navy in the Pacific, 1897–1909.* Austin: University of Texas Press, 1958.

Brewster, Dorothy. *East-West Passage: A Study in Literary Relationships.* London: George Allen and Unwin, 1954.

Brooks, Jeffrey. *When Russia Learned to Read: Literacy and Popular Literature, 1861–1917.* Princeton, N.J.: Princeton University Press, 1985.

Brooks, Van Wyck. *New England: Indian Summer, 1865–1915.* New York: E. P. Dutton, 1940.

Budd, Louis J. "Twain, Howells, and the Boston Nihilists." *New England Quarterly* 32, 3 (September 1959): 351–71.

Buley, R. Carlyle. *The Equitable Life Assurance Society of the United States, 1859–1964.* 2 vols. New York: Appleton-Century-Crofts, 1967.

Burtis, Mary Elizabeth. *Moncure Conway, 1832–1907.* New Brunswick, N.J.: Rutgers University Press, 1952.

Byrnes, Robert F. *Awakening American Education to the World: The Role of Archibald Cary Coolidge, 1866–1928.* Notre Dame, Ind.: University of Notre Dame Press, 1982.

―――. *Pobedonostsev: His Life and Thought.* Bloomington and London: Indiana University Press, 1986.

Caldwell, Genoa, ed. *The Man Who Photographed the World: Burton Holmes Travelogues, 1886–1913.* New York: Harry N. Abrams, 1977.

Campbell, Charles S., Jr. "The Anglo-American Crisis in the Bering Sea." *Mississippi Valley Historical Review* 48, 3 (December 1961): 393–414.

―――. "The Bering Sea Settlements of 1892." *Pacific Historical Reveiw.* 32, 4 (November 1963): 347–67.

―――. *The Transformation of American Foreign Relations, 1865–1900.* New York: Harper and Row, 1976.

Carleton, Mark A. "Hard Wheats Winning Their Way." In *Yearbook of the United States Department of Agriculture 1914,* pp. 391–420. Washington, D.C.: Government Printing Office, 1915.

Carlson, Maria. *No Religion Higher Than Truth: A History of the Theosophical Movement in Russia, 1875–1922.* Princeton: Princeton University Press, 1993.

Coletta, Paolo E. *The Presidency of William Howard Taft.* Lawrence: University Press of Kansas, 1973.

―――. *William Jennings Bryan: Political Evangelist, 1860–1908.* Lincoln: University of Nebraska Press, 1964.

Coolidge, Harold Jefferson, and Robert Howard Lord. *Archibald Cary Coolidge: Life and Letters.* Boston: Houghton, Mifflin, 1932.

Coopersmith, Jonathon. *The Electrification of Russia, 1880–1926.* Ithaca and London: Cornell University Press, 1992.

Crisp, Olga. *Studies in the Russian Economy Before 1914.* New York: Barnes and Noble, 1976.

Crouthamer, James L. *Bennett's New York Herald and the Rise of the Popular Press.* Syracuse, N.Y.: Syracuse University Press, 1989.

Curti, Merle. *American Philanthropy Abroad: A History.* New Brunswick, N.J.: Rutgers University Press, 1963.

Curtis, William Eleroy. *The United States and Foreign Powers.* Meadville, Pa.: Flood and Vincent, 1892.

Davies, Robert Bruce. "The International Operations of the Singer Manufacturing Company, 1854–1895." Ph.D. diss. University of Wisconsin, 1967.

Dennett, Tyler. *John Hay: From Poetry to Politics.* New York: Dodd, Mead, 1933.

―――. *Roosevelt and the Russo-Japanese War: A Critical Study of American Policy in Eastern Asia in 1902–1905.* Garden City, N.Y.: Doubleday, Page, 1925.

Dobson, John M. *American Ascent: The United States Becomes a Great Power, 1880–1914.* DeKalb: Northern Illinois University Press, 1978.

Dubnov, S. M. *The History of the Jews in Russia and Poland.* 3 vols. Philadelphia: Jewish Publishing Society, 1916–1920.

Durman, Karel. *The Time of the Thunderer: Mikhail Katkov, Russian Nationalist Extremism and the Failure of the Bismarckian System, 1871–1887.* Boulder, Colo.: East European Monographs, 1988.

Eggert, Gerald G. *Richard Olney: Evolution of a Statesman.* University Park and London: Pennsylvania State University Press, 1974.

Egle, William H., ed. *Life and Times of Andrew Gregg Curtin.* Philadelphia: Thompson Publishing, 1896.

Evans, Oliver H. *George Henry Boker.* Boston: Twayne, 1984.

Forbes, John Douglas. *J. P. Morgan, Jr., 1867–1943.* Charlottesville: University Press of Virginia, 1981.

Fursenko, Alexander A. *The Battle for Oil: The Economics and Politics of International Corporate Conflict over Petroleum, 1860–1930.* Trans. and ed. by Gregory Freeze. Greenwich, Conn., and London: Jai Press, 1990.

Ganelin, Rafail Sholomovich. *Rossiiskoe samoderzhavie v 1905 godu: reformy i revoliutsiia.* St. Petersburg: Nauka, 1991.

Ganzel, Dewey. *Mark Twain Abroad: The Cruise of the "Quaker City."* Chicago and London: University of Chicago Press, 1968.

Gatrell, Peter. *The Tsarist Economy, 1850–1917.* New York: St. Martin's Press, 1986.

Gay, James T. "Harrison, Blaine, and Cronyism." *Alaska Journal* 3, 1 (Winter 1973): 12–19.

Geyer, Dietrich. *Russian Imperialism: The Interaction of Domestic and Foreign Policy, 1860–1914.* New Haven, Conn., and London: Yale University Press, 1987.

Giesinger, Adam. *The Story of Russia's Germans from Catherine to Khrushchev.* Battleford, Saskatchewan: Marian Press, 1974.

Good, Jane E., and David R. Jones. *Babushka: The Life of the Russian Revolutionary Ekaterina K. Breshko-Breshkovskaia (1844–1934).* Newtonville, Mass.: Oriental Research Partners, 1991.

Greaves, Rose Louise. "Some Aspects of the Anglo-Russian Convention and Its Working in Persia, 1907–1914." *Bulletin of the School of Oriental and African Studies* 31, 2 (1968): 290–308.

Gresham, Matilda. *The Life of Walter Quintin Gresham, 1832–1895.* 2 vols. Chicago: Rand McNally, 1919.

Hamburg, G. M. *Politics of the Russian Nobility, 1881–1905.* New Brunswick, N.J.: Rutgers University Press, 1984.

Hardy, Deborah. *Land and Freedom: The Origins of Russian Terrorism, 1876–1879.* Westport, Conn.: Greenwood Press, 1987.

Harlow, Virginia. *Thomas Sergeant Perry: A Biography.* Durham, N.C.: Duke University Press, 1950.

Harrington, Fred Harvey. *Fighting Politician: Major General N. P. Banks.* Philadelphia: University of Pennsylvania Press, 1948.

Herlihy, Patricia. *Odessa: A History, 1794–1914.* Cambridge: Harvard University Press, 1986.

Hinkley, Ted C. *The Americanization of Alaska, 1867–1897.* Palo Alto, Calif.: Pacific Books, 1967.

———. "William Henry Seward and His Sitka Address of August 12, 1869." In *Alaska and Japan: Perspectives of Past and Present,* ed. Tsuguo Arai, pp. 49–61. Anchorage: Alaska Methodist University Press, 1972.

Hobart, F. W. A. *History of the Machine Gun.* New York: Drake, 1972.

Hohenberg, John. *Foreign Correspondence: The Great Reporters and Their Times.* New York and London: Columbia University Press, 1964.

Holbo, Paul S. *Tarnished Expansion: The Alaska Scandal, the Press, and Congress, 1867–1871.* Knoxville: University of Tennessee Press, 1983.

Holzman, Robert S. *Stormy Ben Butler.* New York: Octagon Books, 1978.

Hunt, William R. *Arctic Passage: The Turbulent History of the Land and People of the Bering Sea, 1697–1975.* New York: Charles Scribner's Sons, 1975.

Hutton, Paul Andrew. *Phil Sheridan and His Army.* Lincoln and London: University of Nebraska Press, 1985.

Jelavich, Barbara. *A Century of Russian Foreign Policy, 1814–1914.* Philadelphia: Lippincott's, 1964.

———. *Russia's Balkan Entanglements, 1806–1914.* Cambridge: Cambridge University Press, 1991.

Jelavich, Barbara, and Charles Jelavich. *The Education of a Russian Statesman: The Memoirs of Nicholas Karlovich Giers.* Berkeley and Los Angeles: University of California Press, 1962.

Jelavich, Charles. *Tsarist Russia and Balkan Nationalism: Russian Influence in the Internal Affairs of Bulgaria and Serbia, 1879–1886.* Berkeley and Los Angeles: University of California Press, 1958.

Jones, James Pickett. *John A. Logan: Stalwart Republican from Illinois.* Tallahassee: University Presses of Florida, 1982.

Joseph, Samuel. *History of the Baron de Hirsch Fund: The Americanization of the Jewish Immigrant.* Philadelphia: Jewish Publication Society of America, 1935.

Judge, Edward H. *Easter in Kishinev: Anatomy of a Pogrom.* New York and London: New York University Press, 1992.

———. *Plehve: Repression and Reform in Imperial Russia, 1902–1904.* Syracuse, N.Y.: Syracuse University Press, 1983.

Kahk, Juhan. "The Spread of Agricultural Machines in Estonia from 1860 to 1880." *Agricultural History* 62, 3 (Summer 1988): 33–44.

Kaun, Alexander, and Ernest J. Simmons. *Slavic Studies.* Ithaca, N.Y.: Cornell University Press, 1943.

Kazemzadeh, Firuz. *Russia and Britain in Persia, 1864–1914: A Study in Imperialism.* New Haven, Conn., and London: Yale University Press, 1968.

Keller, Werner. *East Minus West = Zero: Russia's Debt to the Western World, 1862–1962.* New York: G. P. Putnam's Sons, 1962.

Kennan, George F. *The Decline of Bismarck's European Order: Franco-Russian Relations, 1875–1890.* Princeton, N.J.: Princeton University Press, 1979.

———. *The Fateful Alliance: France, Russia, and the Coming of the First World War.* New York: Pantheon Books, 1984.

Khitrovo, A. *Dmitrii Aleksandrovich Slavianskii i ego deiatel'nost'.* Tver: F. S. Murav'ev, 1887.

Klier, John. "The Russian Press and the Anti-Jewish Pogroms of 1881." *Canadian-American Slavic Studies* 17, 2 (Summer 1983): 199–221.

Klier, John D., and Shlomo Lambroza, eds. *Pogroms: Anti-Jewish Violence in Modern Russian History.* Cambridge: Cambridge University Press, 1992.

Koenig, Louis W. *Bryan: A Political Biography of William Jennings Bryan.* New York: G. P. Putnam's Sons, 1971.

Krahn, Cornelius. "Abraham Thiessen: A Mennonite Revolutionary?" *Mennonite Life* (April 1969): 73–75.

LaFeber, Walter. *The American Age: U.S. Foreign Policy at Home and Abroad.* 2d ed. New York and London: W. W. Norton, 1994.

———. *The New Empire: An Interpretation of American Expansion, 1860–1898.* Ithaca, N.Y.: Cornell University Press, 1963.

Lasch, Christopher. *The American Liberals and the Russian Revolution.* New York: McGraw-Hill, 1972.

Laverychev, Vladimir Iakovlevich. *Gosudarstvo i monopolii v dorevoliutsionnoi Rossii.* Moscow: Mysl', 1982.

Lederer, Ivo, ed. *Russian Foreign Policy: Essays in Historical Perspective.* New Haven, Conn., and London: Yale University Press, 1962.

Leikin, Ezekiel. *The Beilis Transcripts: The Anti-Semitic Trial That Shook the World*. North Vale, N.J.: Jason Aronson, 1993.

Lensen, George Alexander. *The Russian Push Toward Japan: Russo-Japanese Relations, 1697–1875*. Princeton, N.J.: Princeton University Press, 1959.

Leonard, Lewis Alexander. *Life of Alphonso Taft*. New York: Hawke Publishing, 1920.

Lieven, Dominic. *Nicholas II: Twilight of Empire*. New York: St. Martin's Press, 1994.

_____. *Russia and the Origins of the First World War*. New York: St. Martin's Press, 1983.

_____. *Russia's Rulers Under the Old Regime*. New Haven, Conn., and London: Yale University Press, 1989.

Lincoln, W. Bruce. *The Conquest of a Continent: Siberia and the Russians*. New York: Random House, 1994.

_____. *The Great Reforms: Autocracy, Bureaucracy and the Politics of Change in Imperial Russia*. DeKalb: Northern Illinois University Press, 1990.

_____. *In War's Dark Shadow: The Russians Before the Great War*. New York: Dial Press, 1983.

Long, James W. *From Privileged to Dispossessed: The Volga Germans, 1860-1917*. Lincoln: University of Nebraska Press, 1988.

Loughborough, John Norton. *The Great Second Advent Movement: Its Rise and Progress*. Washington, D.C.: Review and Herald Publishing Company, 1909. Reprint. New York: Arno Press, 1972.

McDaniel, Robert A. *The Shuster Mission and the Persian Constitutional Revolution*. Minneapolis: Bibliotheca Islamica, 1974.

McDonald, David M. *United Government and Foreign Policy in Russia, 1900–1914*. Cambridge: Harvard University Press, 1992.

McFeely, William S. *Grant: A Biography*. New York and London: W. W. Norton, 1981.

McGrew, Roderick E. *Russia and the Cholera, 1823–1832*. Madison: University of Wisconsin Press, 1965.

McKay, John P. *Pioneers for Profit: Foreign Entrepreneurship and Russian Industrialization, 1885–1913*. Chicago and London: University of Chicago Press, 1970.

MacKenzie, David. *The Lion of Tashkent: The Career of General M. G. Cherniaev*. Athens: University of Georgia Press, 1974.

Mahan, Alfred T. *Admiral Farragut*. Reprint. New York: Haskell House, 1968.

Malozemoff, Andrew. *Russian Far Eastern Policy, 1881–1904: With Special Emphasis on the Causes of the Russo-Japanese War*. Berkeley and Los Angeles: University of California Press, 1958.

Marks, Steven G. *Road to Power: The Trans-Siberian Railroad and the Colonization of Asian Russia, 1850–1917*. Ithaca, N.Y.: Cornell University Press, 1991.

Mehlinger, Howard D., and John M. Thompson. *Count Witte and the Tsarist Government in the 1905 Revolution*. Bloomington and London: Indiana University Press, 1972.

Mende, Elsie Porter. *An American Soldier and Diplomat: Horace Porter*. New York: Frederick A. Stokes, 1927.

Miller, Martin A. *Kropotkin*. Chicago and London: University of Chicago Press, 1976.

Mizhuev, Pavel. *Istoriia Velikoi Amerikanskoi Demokratii*. St. Petersburg: Brokgauz-Efron, 1906.

Morris, Roy, Jr. *Sheridan: The Life and Wars of General Phil Sheridan*. New York: Crown, 1992.

Morrison, Elting E. *Admiral Sims and the Modern American Navy*. New York: Russell and Russell, 1942.

Morse, John T., Jr. *Thomas Sergeant Perry: A Memoir*. Boston; Houghton Mifflin, 1929.

Naimark, Norman. *Terrorists and Social Democrats: The Russian Revolutionary Movement Under Alexander III*. Cambridge: Harvard University Press, 1983.

Nardova, V. A. *Nachalo monopolizatsii neftianoi promyshlennosti Rossii: 1880–1890-e gody.* Leningrad: Nauka, 1974.

Narochnitskii, A. L. *Kolonial'naia politika kapitalisticheskikh derzhav na Dal'nem Vostoke, 1860–1895.* Moscow: Nauka, 1956.

Nash, George H. *The Life of Herbert Hoover: The Engineer, 1874–1914.* New York and London: W. W. Norton, 1983.

Nevins, Allan. *Hamilton Fish: The Inner History of the Grant Administration.* 2 vols. New York: Dodd, Mead, 1936.

Nifontov, Aleksandr S. *Zernovoe proizvodstvo Rossii vo vtoroi Polovine XIX veka: po materialam ezhegodnoi statistiki urozhaev Evropeiskoi Rossii.* Moscow: Nauka, 1947.

Noble, Valerie. *Hawaiian Prophet: Alexander Hume Ford.* Smithtown, N.Y.: Exposition Press, 1980.

Nordhoff, Charles. *The Communistic Societies of the United States.* New York: Harper and Bros., 1875.

Nugent, Walter. *Crossings: The Great Transatlantic Migration, 1870–1914.* Bloomington: Indiana University Press, 1992.

O'Connor, Richard. *The Scandalous Mr. Bennett.* Garden City, N.Y.: Doubleday, 1962.

Owen, Thomas C. *Capitalism and Politics in Russia: A Social History of the Moscow Merchants, 1855–1905.* Cambridge: Cambridge University Press, 1981.

Ozerov, Ivan. *Amerika idet na Evropu.* St. Petersburg: V. Kirschbaum, 1903.

Pokshishevskii, Vadim Viacheslavovich. *Povest' o znamenitom russkom geografe Aleksandre Ivanoviche Voeikove.* Moscow: Gosizdetslit, 1955.

Pringle, Henry F. *Theodore Roosevelt: A Biography.* New York: Harcourt, Brace, 1931.

Pryor, Elizabeth Brown. *Clara Barton: Professional Angel.* Philadelphia: University of Pennsylvania Press, 1987.

Rambaud, Alfred Nicholas. *History of Russia from the Earliest Times.* Trans. Leonna Lang. 3 vols. Boston: Estes and Lauriat, 1879–1882.

Rempel, David G. "The Mennonite Colonies in New Russia: A Study of Their Settlement and Economic Development from 1789 to 1914." Ph.D. diss., Stanford University, 1933.

Richardson, H. Edward. *Cassius Marcellus Clay: Firebrand of Freedom.* Lexington: University of Kentucky Press, 1976.

Rieber, Alfred J. *Merchants and Entrepreneurs in Imperial Russia.* Chapel Hill: University of North Carolina Press, 1982.

Riha, Thomas. *A Russian European: Paul Miliukov in Russian Politics.* Notre Dame, Ind., and London: University of Notre Dame Press, 1969.

Robbins, Richard G. *Famine in Russia, 1891–1892: The Imperial Government Responds to a Crisis.* New York and London: Columbia University Press, 1975.

Robinson, Judith. *The Hearsts: An American Dynasty.* Newark: University of Delaware Press, 1991.

Rogger, Hans. *Jewish Policies and Right-Wing Politics in Imperial Russia.* Berkeley and Los Angeles: University of California Press, 1986.

Rosenberg, Emily S. *Spreading the American Dream: American Economic and Cultural Expansion, 1890–1945.* New York: Hill and Wang, 1982.

Ross, Isabel. *An American Family: The Tafts—1678 to 1964.* Westport, Conn.: Greenwood Press, 1964.

Russell, Don. *The Lives and Legends of Buffalo Bill.* Norman: University of Oklahoma Press, 1960.

———. *The Wild West, or A History of the Wild West Shows.* Austin and Dallas: Steck-Warlick, 1970.

Sablinsky, Walter. *The Road to Bloody Sunday: Father Gapon and the St. Petersburg Massacre of 1905.* Princeton, N.J.: Princeton University Press, 1976.

Samedov, V. A. *Neft' i ekonomika Rossii (80-90-e gody XIX veka).* Baku: Elm, 1988.

Samuel, Maurice. *Blood Accusation—The Strange History of the Beilis Case.* Philadelphia: Jewish Publication Society, 1966.

Samuels, Peggy, and Harold Samuels. *Frederic Remington: A Biography.* Garden City, N.Y.: Doubleday, 1982.

Saul, Norman E. "Myth and History: Turkey Red Wheat and the 'Kansas Miracle.'" *Heritage of the Great Plains* 22, 3 (Summer 1989): 1–13.

Scholes, Walter, and Marie V. Scholes. *The Foreign Policies of the Taft Administration.* Columbia: University of Missouri Press, 1970.

Shatsillo, Konstantin F. *Russkii imperializm i razvitie flota: Nakanune pervoi mirovoi voiny (1906–1914 gg.).* Moscow: Nauka, 1968.

Shepelev, Leonid Efimovich. *Aktsionernye kompanii v Rossii.* Leningrad: Nauka, 1973.

_____. *Tsarizm i burzhuaziia v 1904–1914 gg.* Leningrad: Nauka, 1987.

_____. *Tsarizm i burzhuaziia vo vtoroi polovine XIX veka.* Leningrad: Nauka, 1981.

Skorniakov, Evgeny E. *Orashenie i kolonizatsiia pustyn' v Servernoi Amerike.* 2 vols. St. Petersburg: Golike and Vil'borg, 1911.

Smoluchowski, Louise. *Lev and Sonya: The Story of the Tolstoy Marriage.* New York: Paragon, 1987.

Socolofsky, Homer E., and Allan B. Spetter. *The Presidency of Benjamin Harrison.* Lawrence: University Press of Kansas, 1987.

Solov'eva, Aida M. *Zheleznodoroshnyi transport Rossii vo vtoroi polovine XIX v.* Moscow: Nauka, 1975.

Sopov, Petar. "Eugene Schuyler—Distinguished Politician, Statesman, Diplomat and Scientist." *Bulgarian Historical Review* 11, 2 (1983): 66–73.

Starnes, William DeMarcus. "The Diplomacy and European Foreign Policies of Prince Alexander Gorchakov." Ph.D. diss., University of Pennsylvania, 1951.

Stephan, John J. *The Russian Far East: A History.* Stanford, Calif.: Stanford University Press, 1994.

Stewart, Robert Laird. *Sheldon Jackson.* New York: Fleming H. Revell, 1908.

Still, William N., Jr. *American Seapower in the Old World: The United States Navy in European and Near Eastern Waters, 1865–1917.* Westport, Conn.: Greenwood Press, 1980.

Strakhovsky, Leonid I. "Russia's Privateering Projects of 1878." *Journal of Modern History* 7, 1 (March 1935): 22–40.

Sumner, B. H. *Russia and the Balkans, 1870–1880.* Oxford: Clarendon Press, 1937.

Taylor, A. J. P. *The Struggle for Mastery in Europe, 1848–1918.* Oxford: Clarendon Press, 1954.

Thompson, A. Beeby. *The Oil Fields of Russia and the Russian Petroleum Industry.* New York: D. Van Nostrand, 1904.

Tolf, Robert W. *The Russian Rockefellers: The Saga of the Nobel Family and the Russian Oil Industry.* Stanford, Calif.: Hoover Institution Press, 1976.

Treadgold, Donald W. *The Great Siberian Migration: Government and Peasant in Resettlement from Emancipation to the First World War.* Princeton, N.J.: Princeton University Press, 1957.

Tuve, Jeannette. *The First Russian Women Physicians.* Newtonville, Mass.: Oriental Research Partners, 1984.

Twichell, Heath, Jr. *Allen: The Biography of an Army Officer, 1859–1930.* New Brunswick, N.J.: Rutgers University Press, 1974.

Ulam, Adam B. *In the Name of the People: Prophets and Conspirators in Prerevolutionary Russia.* New York: Viking Press, 1977.

Uzzell, Thomas H. "Learning to Speak Russian in Six Months." *Independent* 75, 3376 (14 August 1913): 379–82.

Varg, Paul A. *Open Door Diplomat: The Life of W. W. Rockhill.* Illinois Studies in the Social Sciences vol. 33, no. 4. Urbana: University of Illinois Press, 1952.

Venturi, Franco. *Roots of Revolution: A History of the Populist and Socialist Movements in Nineteenth-Century Russia.* New York: Grosset and Dunlap, 1966.

Vinogradov, Kirill Borisovich. *Mirovaia politika 60–80–kh godov XIX veka: Sobytiia i liudi.* Leningrad: Leningrad University, 1991.

Verner, Andrew. *The Crisis of Russian Autocracy: Nicholas II and the 1905 Revolution.* Princeton, N.J.: Princeton University Press, 1990.

Von Laue, Theodore H. *Sergei Witte and the Industrialization of Russia.* New York: Atheneum, 1974.

Voronin, Mikhail, and Margarita Voronina. *Pavel Petrovich Mel'nikov, 1804–1880.* Leningrad: Nauka, 1977.

Vorpahl, Ben Merchant. *Frederic Remington and the West: With the Eye of the Mind.* Austin and London: University of Texas Press, 1972.

Vucinich, Alexander. *Science in Russian Culture, 1861–1917.* Stanford, Calif.: Stanford University Press, 1970.

Wahl, Paul, and Donald R. Toppel. *The Gatling Gun.* London: Herbert Jenkins, 1966.

Walker, Dale L. *Januarius MacGahan: The Life and Campaigns of an American War Correspondent.* Athens: Ohio University Press, 1988.

Wallace, Donald McKenzie. *Russia.* 2 vols. New York: Holt, 1877.

Whelan, Heide W. *Alexander III and the State Council: Bureaucracy and Counter-Reform in Late Imperial Russia.* New Brunswick, N.J.: Rutgers University Press, 1982.

Whelpley, James Davenport. *The Trade of the World.* New York: Century, 1913.

White, John Albert. *The Diplomacy of the Russo-Japanese War.* Princeton, N.J.: Princeton University Press, 1964.

White, William Allen. "Taft, a Hewer of Wood." *The American Magazine* 66, 1 (May 1908): 19–32.

Widenor, William C. *Henry Cabot Lodge and the Search for an American Foreign Policy.* Berkeley and Los Angeles: University of California Press, 1980.

Williams, Hattie Plum. *The Czar's Germans with Particular Reference to the Volga Germans.* Reprint. Lincoln, Nebr.: American Historical Society of Germans from Russia, 1975.

Winter, Nevin O. *The Russian Empire of To-Day and Yesterday.* London: Simpkin, Marshall, Hamilton, Kent, 1914.

Woodcock, George, and Ivan Avakumovic. *The Anarchist Prince: A Biographical Study of Peter Kropotkin.* London: T. V. Boardman, 1949.

Wyman, Mark. *Round Trip to America: The Immigrants Return to Europe, 1880–1930.* Ithaca, N.Y., and London: Cornell University Press, 1993.

Wynn, Charters. *Workers, Strikes, and Pogroms: The Donbass-Dnepr Bend in Late Imperial Russia, 1870–1905.* Princeton, N.J.: Princeton University Press, 1992.

Yost, Nellie Snyder. *Buffalo Bill: His Family, Friends, Fame, Failures, and Fortunes.* Chicago: Swallow Press, 1979.

Younger, Edward. *John A. Kasson: Politics and Diplomacy from Lincoln to McKinley.* Iowa City: Iowa State Historical Society, 1955.

Zaionchkovskii, Petr A. *Krizis samoderzhaviia na rubezhe 1870–1880 godov.* Moscow: Nauka, 1964.

———. "Perevsoruzhenie russkoi armii v 60–70–kh godakh XIX v." *Istoricheskie Zapiski* 36 (1951): 64–100.

———. *Samoderzhavie i russkaia armiia na rubezhe XIX-XX stoletii, 1881–1903.* Moscow: Mysl', 1973.

Secondary Sources: Russian-American Relations

Allen, Robert V. *Russia Looks at America: The View to 1917.* Washington, D.C.: Library of Congress, 1988.

Askew, William C. "Efforts to Improve Russo-American Relations Before the First World War: The John Hays Hammond Mission." *Slavonic and East European Studies* 31, 76 (December 1952): 179–85.

Bailey, Thomas A. *America Faces Russia: Russian-American Relations from Early Times to Our Day.* Ithaca, N.Y.: Cornell University Press, 1950.

Bensen, Basil. *Russian Orthodox Church in Alaska, 1794–1967.* Sitka, Alaska: Russian Orthodox Church, 1967.

Best, Gary Dean. *To Free a People: American Jewish Leaders and the Jewish Problem in Eastern Europe, 1890–1914.* Westport, Conn.: Greenwood Press, 1982.

Blakely, Allison. "Richard Greener and the 'Talented Tenth's' Dilemma." *Journal of Negro History* 59, 4 (October 1974): 305–21.

Boden, Dieter. *Dan Amerikabild im russischen Schrifttum bis zum Ende des 19. Jahrhunderts.* Hamburg: 1968.

Bolkhovitinov, N. N. *Russko-Amerikanskie otnosheniia i prodazha Aliaski, 1834–1867.* Moscow: Nauka, 1990.

Bonch-Osmolovskii, A. *Soedenennye Shtaty i problema Tikhogo Okeana.* Moscow-Leningrad: Gosizdat, 1930.

Bradley, Joseph. *Guns for the Tsar: American Technology and the Small Arms Industry in Nineteenth-Century Russia.* DeKalb: Northern Illinois University Press, 1990.

Brodskii, Roman Mikhailovich. "K voprosu o pozitsii SShA v Russko-iaponskoi voine i portsmutskikh peregovorakh." *Voprosy Istorii* 2 (February 1959): 144–55.

Brown, James Seay, Jr. "Eugene Schuyler, Observer of Russia: His Years as a Diplomat in Russia, 1867–1875." Ph.D diss., Vanderbilt, 1971.

Carrol, E. J. "The Foreign Relations of the United States with Tzarist Russia, 1867–1900." Ph.D. diss., Georgetown, 1953.

Carstensen, Fred V. *American Enterprise in Foreign Markets: Studies of Singer and International Harvester in Russia.* Chapel Hill and London: University of North Carolina Press, 1984.

Carstensen, Fred V., and Richard Hume Werking. "International Harvester in Russia: The Washington–St. Petersburg Connection?" *Business History Review* 57, 3 (Autumn 1983): 347–66.

Cassedy, Steven. "Chernyshevskii Goes West: How Jewish Immigration Helped Bring Russian Radicalism to America." *Russian History* 21, 1 (Spring 1994): 1–22.

Cohen, Naomi W. "The Abrogation of the Russo-American Treaty of 1832." *Jewish Social Studies* 35 (January 1963): 3–10.

Coleman, Marion Moore. "Eugene Schuyler: Diplomat Extraordinary from the United States to Russia, 1867–1876." *Russian Review* 7, 1 (Autumn 1947): 33–48.

Dalrymple, Dana. "Joseph A. Rosen and Early Russian Studies of American Agriculture." *Agricultural History* 38, 3 (July 1964): 157–60.

Dement'ev, Igor Petrovich. "L. N. Tolstoi i sotsial'nye kritiki v SShA na rubezhe XIX–XX vv." *Novaia i Noveishaia Istoriia* 6 (November 1978): 33–50.

Dubie, Alain. *Frank A. Golder: An Adventure of a Historian in Quest of Russian History.* Boulder, Colo.: East European Monographs, 1989.

Dvoichenko-Markova, E. M. "Uchenye Rossii na mezhdunarodnoi vystavke v Filadelfii v 1876 g." *Novaia i Noveishaia Istoriia* 4 (July 1975): 151–53.

Egan, Clifford L. "Pressure Groups, the Department of State, and the Abrogation of the Russian-American Treaty of 1832." *Proceedings of the American Philosophical Society* 115 (20 August 1971): 328–34.

Engel', V. V. "Amerikanskii pasport i russko-evreiskii vopros v kontse XIX-nachale XX veka." In *Amerikanskii Ezhegodnik 1991*, pp. 104–20. Moscow: Nauka, 1992.

Esthus, Raymond A. *Double Eagle and Rising Sun: The Russians and Japanese at Portsmouth in 1905.* Durham, N.C.: Duke University Press, 1988.

Evseeva, M. "Russkie muzykanty i russkie muzykal'nye traditsii v ispolnitel'skoi kul'ture SShA." In *Vzaimodeistveie kul'tur SSSR i SShA: XVIII–XX vv*, pp. 213–19. Moscow: Nauka, 1987.

Freed, Stanley A., Ruth S. Freed, and Laila Williamson. "Scholars Amid Squalor." *Natural History* 97, 3 (March 1988): 60–68.

Fursenko, Alexsander A. "Iz istorii Russko-Amerikanskikh otnoshenii na rubezhe XIX–XX vv." In *Iz istorii imperializm v Rossii*, pp. 219–69. Moscow-Leningrad: Nauka, 1959.

———. "Proekt Amerikanskogo banka v Moskve." *Istoriia SSSR* 3 (1986): 142–43.

Gaddis, John Lewis. *Russia, the Soviet Union, and the United States: An Interpretive History.* 2d ed. New York: McGraw-Hill, 1990.

Gettman, Royal. *Turgenev in England and America.* Illinois Studies in Language and Literature vol. 17, no. 2. Urbana: University of Illinois Press, 1941.

Goble, Paul A. "Samuel N. Harper and the Study of Russia: His Career and Collection." *Cahiers du monde Russe et Sovietique* 14, 4 (October–December 1973): 608–20.

Golder, Frank. "The Russian Fleet and the Civil War." *American Historical Review* 20, 4 (July 1915): 801–12.

Good, Jane E. "America and the Russian Revolutionary Movement, 1888–1905." *Russian Review* 41, 3 (July 1982): 173–87.

———. " 'I'd Rather Live in Siberia': V. G. Korolenko's Critique of America." *Historian* 44, 2 (February 1982): 190–206.

Gregory, Bishop (Afonsky). *A History of the Russian Orthodox Church in Alaska, 1794–1917.* Kodiak, Alaska: St. Herman's Seminary Press, 1977.

Greenwood, John Thomas. "The American Observers of the Russo-Japanese War (1904–1905)." Ph.D. diss., Kansas State University, 1971.

Grossman, Joan Delanay. *Edgar Allan Poe in Russia: A Study in Legend and Literary Influence.* Würzburg: Jal-verlag, 1973.

Hasty, Olga Peters, and Susanne Fusso, eds. and trans. *America Through Russian Eyes, 1874–1926.* New London, Conn., and London: Yale University Press, 1988.

Healy, Ann E. "Tsarist Anti-Semitism and Russian-American Relations." *Slavic Review* 42, 3 (Fall 1983): 408–25.

Hecht, David. *Russian Radicals Look to America, 1825–1894.* Cambridge: Harvard University Press, 1947.

Holmstrem, Vladimir. "Ex Oriente Lux!: A Plea for a Russo-American Understanding." *North American Review* 512 (July 1899): 6–32.

Holzle, Erwin. *Amerika und Russland: Entstehung ihres Weltgegensatzes.* Gottingen: Muster-Schmidt Verlag, 1980.

Hopkins, C. Howard. *John R. Mott, 1865–1955: A Biography.* Grand Rapids, Mich.: William B. Eerdmans, 1979.

Jensen, Oliver, ed. *America and Russia: A Century and a Half of Dramatic Encounters.* New York: Simon and Schuster, 1962.

Jensen, Ronald J. *The Alaska Purchase and Russian-American Relations.* Seattle and London: University of Washington Press, 1975.

———. "The Politics of Discrimination: America, Russia and the Jewish Question, 1869–1872." *American Jewish History* 75 (March 1986): 280–95.

Joseph, Samuel. *Jewish Immigration to the United States: From 1881 to 1910.* New York: Columbia University Press, 1914.

Karlowich, Robert A. *We Fall and Rise: Russian-Language Newspapers in New York City, 1889–1914.* Metuchen, N.J., and London: Scarecrow Press, 1991.

Kelly, Georgianna. "Adelaide Lukanina's 'A Year in America': A Critical View of Nineteenth Century America." Master's thesis, University of Kansas, 1995.

Kuropiatnik, G. P. *Rossiia i SShA: Ekonomicheskie, kul'turnye i diplomaticheskie sviazi, 1867–1881.* Moscow: Nauka, 1981.

Laserson, Max M. *The American Impact on Russia, 1784–1917.* New York: Collier Paperback, 1962.

Lebedev, Viacheslav V. *Russko-amerikanskie ekonomicheskie otnosheniia (1900–1917 gg.).* Moscow: Nauka, 1964.

Leicester, Henry M. "Mendeleev's Visit to America." *Journal of Chemical Education* 34, 7 (July 1957): 331–33.

McCormick, Thomas. "The Wilson-McCook Scheme of 1896–1897." *Pacific Historical Review* 36, 1 (February 1967): 47–58.

McKenzie, Ralph. *Jew Baiting in Russia and Her Alleged Friendship for the United States.* Washington, D.C.: By author, 1903.

Malkova, Irina. "Istoriia i politika SShA na stranitsakh russkikh demokraticheskikh zhurnalov *Delo i Slovo.*" In *Amerikanskii Ezhegodnik 1971,* pp. 273–94. Moscow: Nauka, 1971.

Marshall, Carlyse. "Famine in Russia and American Charity, 1891–1893." Master's thesis, University of Kansas, 1994.

Marshall, Leslie. *The Romance of a Tract and Its Sequel: The Story of an American Pioneer in Russia and the Baltic States.* Riga: Latvian Farmers' Union, 1928.

Matrosov, Evgenyi. "Chrezvychainoe Amerikanskoe posol'stvo v Rossii, v 1866 godu." *Istoricheskii Vestnik* 93, 1 (January 1900): 229–66.

Melamed, E. I. *Dzhordzh Kennan protiv tsarisma.* Moscow: Nauka, 1981.

Minger, Ralph E. "William Howard Taft's Forgotten Visit to Russia." *Russian Review* 22, 2 (April 1963): 149–56.

Miracle, Ralph. "Asian Adventures of a Cowboy from Montana." *Montana: The Magazine of Western History* 27, 2 (April 1977): 44–47.

Neunherz, Richard Emerson. "The Purchase of Russian America: Reasons and Reactions." Ph.D. diss., University of Washington, 1975.

Nikoliukin, Aleksandr. "Chekhov i Amerika." In *Vzaimodeistvie kul'tur SSSR i SShA: XVIII–XX vv.,* pp. 143–53. Moscow: Nauka, 1987.

––––––. *Vzaimosviazi literatur Rossii i SShA: Turgenev, Tolstoi, Dostoevskii i Amerika.* Moscow: Nauka, 1987.

––––––, ed. *A Russian Discovery of America.* Moscow: Progress Publishers, 1986.

Parry, Albert. *America Learns Russian: A History of the Teaching of the Russian Language in the United States.* Syracuse, N.Y.: Syracuse University Press, 1967.

––––––. "Charles R. Crane, Friend of Russia." *Russian Review* 6, 2 (Spring 1947): 20–36.

Patkanov, S. *Itogi statiskiki immigratsii v Soedinennye Shataty Sev. Ameriki iz Rossii za desiatiletie 1900–1909 gg.* St. Petersburg: Nyrkin, 1911.

Pattock, Florence Baggert. "American Russian Relations, 1861–1869: A Period of Calculated Coexistence." Ph.D. diss., University of Minnesota, 1973.

Pickering, Elizabeth. "The International Harvester Company in Russia: A Case Study of a Foreign Corporation in Russia from the 1860s to the 1930s." Ph.D. diss., Princeton University, 1967.

Pierce, Richard A. "Prince D. P. Maksutov: Last Governor of Russian America." *Journal of the West* 6, 3 (July 1967): 395–416.

Poster, John B. "A Warmth of Soul: Samuel Northrup Harper and the Russians, 1904–1943." *Journal of Contemporary History* 14, 2 (April 1979): 235–52.

Queen, George S. "An American Employer and Russian Labor in 1905." *Journal of Modern History* 15, 2 (June 1943): 120–26.

———. "The McCormick Harvesting Machine Company in Russia." *Russian Review* 23, 2 (April 1964): 164–81.

———. "The United States and the Material Advance in Russia, 1881–1905." Ph.D. diss., University of Illinois, 1941.

———. "Wharton Barker and Concessions in Imperial Russia, 1878–1892." *Journal of Modern History* 17, 3 (September 1945): 202–14.

Quisenberry, K. S., and L. P. Reitz. "Turkey Wheat: The Cornerstone of Empire." *Agricultural History* 48, 1 (January 1974): 98–110.

Rabinovich, I. M. "Proniknovenie amerikanskogo kapitala v ekonomiku dorevoliutsionnoi Rossii." *Trudy Leningradskogo korablestroitel'nogo Instituta* 16 (1957).

Reimer, Gustav E., and G. R. Gaeddert. *Exiled by the Czar: Cornelius Jansen and the Great Mennonite Migration, 1874.* Newton, Kans.: Mennonite Publication Office, 1956.

Robertson, James Rood. *A Kentuckian at the Court of the Tsars: The Ministry of Cassius Marcellus Clay to Russia, 1861–1862 and 1863–1869.* Berea, Ky.: Berea College Press, 1935.

Rogger, Hans. "America Enters the Twentieth Century: In *Felder und Vorfelder russischer Geschichte: Studien zu Ehren von Peter Scheibert,* ed. Inge Auerbach, Andreas Hillgruber, and Gottfried Schramm. Freiburg: Rombach Verlag, 1985.

———. "America in the Russian Mind—or Russian Discoveries of America." *Pacific Historical Review* 47, 1 (February 1978): 27–51.

———. "*Amerikanizm* and the Economic Development of Russia." *Comparative Studies in Soviet History* 23, 3 (July 1981): 382–420.

Romanov, B. A. *Ocherki diplomaticheskoi istorii Russko-iaponskoi voiny, 1895–1907.* Moscow-Leningrad: Nauka, 1947.

Salov, V. V. *Zemledelie—glavnaia osnova blagosostoianiia Rossii: Sravnitel'nyi ocherk sostoianiia zemledeliia v Soedinennykh Shtatakh Severnoi Ameriki i v Rossii po noveishim dannym.* St. Petersburg: Tip. Min. Putei Soobshchenia, 1909.

Saul, Norman E. *Distant Friends: The United States and Russia, 1763–1867.* Lawrence: University Press of Kansas, 1991.

———. "The Migration of the Russian-Germans to Kansas." *Kansas Historical Quarterly* 40, 1 (Spring 1974): 38–62.

———. "Through Curious and Foreign Eyes: Grigori Machtet Chronicles the Kansas Frontier, 1872–1873." *Kansas History* 17, 2 (Summer 1994): 76–90.

Schoenberg, Philip Ernst. "The American Reaction to the Kishinev Pogrom of 1903." *American Jewish Historical Quarterly* 58, 3 (March 1974): 262–83.

Seyersted, Per E. "Turgenev's Interest in America, As Seen in His Contacts with H. H. Boyesen, W. D. Howells and Other American Authors." *Scando-Slavica* (Copenhagen) 11 (1965): 25–39.

Smith, C. Henry. *The Coming of the Russian Mennonites: An Episode in the Settling of the Last Frontier, 1874–1884.* Berne, Ind.: Mennonite Book Concern, 1927.

Smith, Harold F. "Bread for the Russians: William C. Edgar and the Relief Campaign of 1892." *Minnesota History* 42, 2 (Summer 1970): 54–62.

Sokolov, A. S. "Rossiia na vsemirnoi vystavke v Chikago v 1893 g." *Amerikanskii Ezhegodnik 1984,* pp. 152–64. Moscow: Nauka, 1984.

———. "Rossiiskaia trudovaia immigratsiia v Ameriku v poslednei cherverti XIX v." *Sovetskaia Etnografiia* 2 (March-April 1986): 98–99.

Spetter, Allan. "The United States, the Russian Jews and the Russian Famine of 1891–1892." *American Jewish Historical Quarterly* 64, 3 (March 1975): 236–44.

Starr, S. Frederick. "Why Did Russia Let Seward's Folly Go on the Cheap?" *Smithsonian* 10, 9 (1979): 144–45.

Straus, Oscar S. "The United States and Russia: Their Historical Relations." *North American Review* 585 (August 1905): 237–50.

Stults, Taylor. "Imperial Russia Through American Eyes, 1894–1904: A Study in Public Opinion." Ph.D. diss., University of Missouri, 1970.

_____. "Roosevelt, Russian Persecution of Jews, and American Public Opinion." *Jewish Social Studies* 33, 1 (January 1971): 13–22.

Sverdlov, N. V. "K istorii russko-amerikanskikh otnoshenikh na Tikhom Okeane i Dal'nem Vostoke v xix-nachale xx v." In *Sbornik statei po istorii Dal'nego Vostoka*, pp. 309–15. Moscow: Nauka, 1958.

Szajkowski, Zosa. "The European Aspect of the American-Russian Passport Question." *Publications of the American Jewish Historical Society* 46, 2 (December 1956): 86–100.

Tarasar, Constance J., ed. *Orthodox America, 1794–1976: Development of the Orthodox Church in America*. Syosset, N.Y.: Orthodox Church in America, 1975.

Tarsaidze, Alexandre. " 'Berdanka.' " *Russian Review* 9, 1 (January 1950): 30–36.

_____. *Czars and Presidents: The Story of a Forgotten Friendship*. New York: McDowell, Obolensky, 1958.

Thompkins, Pauline. *American-Russian Relations in the Far East*. New York: Macmillan, 1949.

Thompson, Arthur, and Robert Hart. *The Uncertain Crusade: America and the Russian Revolution of 1905*. Amherst: University of Massachusetts Press, 1970.

Trani, Eugene P. "Russia in 1905: The View from the American Embassy." *Review of Politics* 31 (January 1969): 440–61.

_____. *The Treaty of Portsmouth: An Adventure in American Diplomacy*. Lexington: University of Kentucky Press, 1969.

Travis, Frederick F. *George Kennan and the American-Russian Relationship, 1865–1924*. Athens: Ohio University Press, 1990.

Tsverava, Grant Konstantinovich. "Iz istorii russko-amerikanskikh nauchnykh sviazei v XIX v.: Dzhozef Genri i Aleksandr Ivanovich Voeikov." *Priroda* 7 (July 1979): 79–85.

Tsvirkun, A. F. "Nekotorye voprsy vneshnei politiki SShA v 1898–1914 gg. v osveshchenii russkoi Burzhuazno-liberal'noi pechati." In *Amerikanskii Ezhegodnik 1986*, pp. 169–82. Moscow: Nauka, 1986.

Tudorianu, N. L. "Sotsial'no-ekonomicheskoe polozhenie Rossiiskikh emigrantov v SShA v kontse XIX-nachala XX veka." *Istoriia SSSR* 3 (March 1986): 146–55.

Tuve, Jeannette. "Changing Directions in Russian-American Economic Relations, 1912–1917." *Slavic Review* 31, 1 (March 1972): 52–70.

Wallace, William S. "A Montanan in Russo-American Relations: The Case of John Ginzberg." *Pacific Northwest Quarterly* 40, 1 (January 1949): 35–43.

Weeks, Charles J., Jr. *An American Naval Diplomat in Revolutionary Russia: The Life and Times of Vice Admiral Newton A. McCully*. Annapolis, Md.: Naval Institute Press, 1993.

White, John I. "Red Carpet for a Romanoff: 1872 Hunting Party in Honor of the Grand Duke of Russia." *America West* 9, 1 (January 1972): 4–10.

Wiebe, David V. *They Seek a Country: A Survey of Mennonite Migrations With Special Reference to Kansas and Gnadenau*. Hillsboro, Kans.: Mennonite Brethren Publishing House, 1959.

Williams, Robert C. *Russian Art and American Money, 1900–1940*. Cambridge: Harvard University Press, 1980.

Williams, William A. *American-Russian Relations, 1781–1947*. New York: Rinehart, 1952.

Willis, James F. "An Arkansan in St. Petersburg: Clifton Rodes Breckinridge, Minister to Russia, 1894–1897." *Arkansas Historical Quarterly* 38, 1 (Spring 1979): 3–31.

Yarmolinsky, Avrahm. *A Russian's American Dream: A Memoir on William Frey*. Lawrence: University Press of Kansas, 1965.

Yoffe, Elkhonon. *Tchaikovsky in America: The Composer's Visit in 1891*. New York and Oxford: Oxford University Press, 1986.

Zabriskie, Edward H. *American-Russian Rivalry in the Far East: A Study in Diplomacy and Power Politics, 1895–1914*. Westport, Conn.: Greenwood Press, 1973.

Zornow, William F. "When the Tsar and Grant Were Friends." *Mid-America* 43, 3 (July 1961): 164–81.

Zubok, Lev I. *Ekspansionistskaia politika SShA v nachale XX veka*. Moscow: Nauka, 1969.

Index